THE **M&F** SOL

Print
+
Online

M&F⁴ delivers all the key terms and core concepts for the **Marriage and Family** course.

M&F Online provides the complete narrative from the printed text with additional interactive media and the unique functionality of **StudyBits**—all available on nearly any device!

What is a StudyBit™? Created through a deep investigation of students' challenges and workflows, the StudyBit™ functionality of **M&F Online** enables students of different generations and learning styles to study more effectively by allowing them to learn their way. Here's how they work:

COLLECT WHAT'S IMPORTANT
Create StudyBits as you highlight text, images or take notes!

WEAK

FAIR

STRONG

UNASSIGNED

RATE AND ORGANIZE STUDYBITS
Rate your understanding and use the color-coding to quickly organize your study time and personalize your flashcards and quizzes.

StudyBit™

TRACK/MONITOR PROGRESS
Use Concept Tracker to decide how you'll spend study time and study YOUR way!

85%

PERSONALIZE QUIZZES
Filter by your StudyBits to personalize quizzes or just take chapter quizzes off-the-shelf.

○ CORRECT

○ INCORRECT

○ INCORRECT

○ INCORRECT

M&F4

David Knox

Vice President, General Manager:
 Lauren Murphy

Product Manager: Clinton Kernen

Content/Media Developer: Sarah Keeling

Product Assistant: Lauren Dame

Marketing Manager: James Finlay

Marketing Coordinator: Quynton Johnson

Sr. Content Project Manager: Kim Kusnerak

Manufacturing Planner: Ron Montgomery

Production Service: MPS Limited

Sr. Art Director: Bethany Casey

Internal Design: Joe Devine/
 Red Hangar Design

Cover Design: Lisa Kuhn: Curio Press,
 LLC/Trish & Ted Knapke: Ke Design

Cover Image: Hero Images/Getty Images

Title Page, Back Cover, and In Book Ad
 Images: Computer/tablet illustration:
 iStockphoto.com/furtaev; Smart Phone
 illustration: iStockphoto.com/dashadima;
 Students: Rawpixel.com/Shutterstock.com

Background screens: iStockphoto.com/Alex
 Belomlinsky

Intellectual Property Analyst: Alexandra
 Ricciardi

Intellectual Property Project Manager:
 Carly Belcher

For product information and technology assistance, contact us at
Cengage Learning Customer & Sales Support, 1-800-354-9706

For permission to use material from this text or product,
submit all requests online at **www.cengage.com/permissions**

Further permissions questions can be emailed to
permissionrequest@cengage.com

Unless otherwise noted, all items © Cengage Learning

Library of Congress Control Number: 2016955678

Student Edition ISBN: 978-1-337-11697-8

Student Edition with Online ISBN: 978-1-337-11696-1

Cengage Learning
20 Channel Center Street
Boston, MA 02210
USA

Cengage Learning is a leading provider of customized learning solutions with employees residing in nearly 40 different countries and sales in more than 125 countries around the world. Find your local representative at **www.cengage.com**.

Cengage Learning products are represented in Canada by Nelson Education, Ltd.

To learn more about Cengage Learning Solutions, visit **www.cengage.com**.

Purchase any of our products at your local college store or at our preferred online store **www.cengagebrain.com**.

Printed in the United States of America
Print Number: 04   Print Year: 2020

DAVID KNOX
M&F⁴

BRIEF CONTENTS

Hero Images/Getty Images

CONTENTS

6 Enhancing Sexuality in Relationships 114

7 Examining GLBTQIA Relationships 132

8 Exploring Diversity in Marriage Relationships 152

9 Integrating Work and Relationships 176

10 Reacting to Abuse in Relationships 190

Bobby Davis

11 Deciding about Children 208

1 Exploring Marriages and Families Today

SECTIONS

After finishing this chapter go to **PAGE 23** for **STUDY TOOLS**

<h2 align="center">Marriage is a covered dish.</h2>

—SWISS PROVERB

Diversity and change—these two words reveal the state of marriage and family today. Same-sex marriages, single-parent families, and interracial marriages are examples of diversity. Delay in getting married, fewer marriages, and fewer children are examples of change. And this is just the beginning. The forecast for marriage and family is increased diversity and change.

This text is focused on the human connection and relationship choices. Nothing is more important. It is something we all have in common—the search for meaningful love connections which result from deliberate, thoughtful, considered choices in one's relationships. Many of these intense and sustained love relationships end up in marriage and having a family—the bedrock of society. All individuals were born into a family (however one defines this concept), and most will end up in a family of their own.

The top values of 9,949 undergraduates (in order) are "having a happy marriage," "having a career I love," and "financial security" (Hall & Knox, 2016). While popular media spin tales of doom about marriage and the family, the data show otherwise. In this chapter, we define marriage and family, the various ways of studying these phenomena, how marriage and family are changing , and trends.

1-1 MARRIAGE

While young adults think of marriage in terms of love and a committed life together, the federal government regards **marriage** as a legal relationship that binds a couple together for the reproduction, physical care, and socialization of children. Each society works out its own details of what marriage is. In the United States, marriage is a legal contract between two people of any sexual orientation and the state in which they reside, that specifies the economic relationship between the couple (they become joint owners of their income and debt) and encourages sexual fidelity.

Self-Assessment: Attitudes toward Marriage Scale

Take the "Attitudes toward Marriage Scale" in the self-assessment section at the end of this chapter to assess your view of marriage.

National Data

Of adult women and men in the United States over the age of 65, 96% have married at least once (*Proquest Statistical Abstract of the United States, 2016,* Table 32).

Various elements implicit in the marriage relationship in the United States are as follows.

1-1a Elements of Marriage

No one definition of marriage can adequately capture its meaning. Rather, marriage might best be understood in terms of its various elements.

LEGAL CONTRACT Marriage in U.S. society is a legal contract into which two individuals (heterosexual or homosexual) who are of legal age may enter when they are not already married to someone else. The age required to marry varies by state and is usually from 16 to 18 (most states set 17 or 18 as the requirement). In some states (e.g., Alabama) individuals can marry at age 14 with parental or judicial consent. In California, individuals can marry at any age with parental consent. The marriage license certifies that a legally empowered representative of the state perform the ceremony, often with two witnesses present. The marriage contract gives power to the state over the couple—should they decide to divorce, the state can dictate the terms—in child custody, division of property, and child support. One of the reasons some individuals cite for not marrying is to "keep the government out of my business."

Under the laws of the state, the marriage license means that spouses will jointly own all future property acquired and that each will share in the estate of the other. In most states, whatever the deceased spouse owns is legally transferred to the surviving spouse at the time of death. In the event of divorce and unless the couple has a prenuptial agreement, the property is usually divided equally regardless of the contribution of each partner. The license also implies the expectation of sexual fidelity

> **marriage** a legal relationship that binds a couple together for the reproduction, physical care, and socialization of children.

in the marriage. Though less frequent because of no-fault divorce, infidelity is a legal ground for both divorce and alimony in some states.

The marriage license is also an economic authorization that entitles a spouse to receive payment from a health insurance company for medical bills if the partner is insured and to collect Social Security benefits at the death of one's spouse. Spouses are also responsible for each other's debts. One mother warned her son, "If you marry her, you are taking on her $80,000 in student loan debt."

Though the courts are reconsidering the definition of what constitutes a "family," the law is currently designed to protect spouses, not lovers or cohabitants. An exception is **common-law marriage**, in which a heterosexual couple who cohabit and present themselves as married will be regarded as legally married in those states that recognize such marriages. Common-law marriages exist in 14 states (Alabama, Colorado, Georgia, Idaho, Iowa, Kansas, Montana, New Hampshire, Ohio, Oklahoma, Pennsylvania, Rhode Island, South Carolina, and Texas) and the District of Columbia. Even in these states, not all persons can marry by common law—they must be of sound mind, be unmarried, and must have lived together for a certain period of time (e.g., three years). Persons married by common law who move to a non-common-law state are recognized as being married in the new state to which they move.

> Marriage equality is not a choice. It is a legal right.
>
> —CORY BOOKER, SENATOR FROM NEW JERSEY

EMOTIONAL RELATIONSHIP Ninety-three percent of married adults in the United States point to love as their top reason for getting married. Other reasons include making a lifelong commitment (87%), companionship (81%), and having children (59%) (Cohn, 2013). American emphasis on love as a reason to marry is not shared throughout the world. Individuals in other cultures (e.g., India) do not require feelings of love to marry—love is expected to follow, not precede, marriage. In these countries, parental approval and similarity of religion, culture, education, and family background are considered more important criteria for marriage than love. While love is an important motivation for marriage, it

common-law marriage a heterosexual cohabiting couple presenting themselves as married.

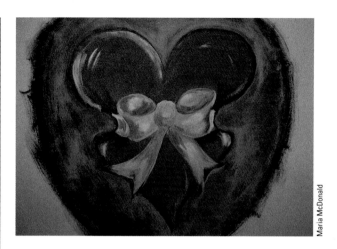

is companionship in the United States which promotes a couple in courtship to remain committed and move toward marriage (Ogolsky et al., 2016).

SEXUAL MONOGAMY Marital partners expect sexual fidelity. Almost two-thirds (66%) of 9,661 undergraduates agreed with the statement, "I would divorce a spouse who had an affair" (Hall & Knox, 2016). There is also a stigma associated with couples who are nonmonogamous (Cohen, 2016).

LEGAL RESPONSIBILITY FOR CHILDREN Although individuals marry for love and companionship, one of the most important reasons for the existence of marriage from the viewpoint of society is to legally bind a male and a female for the nurture and support of any children they may have. In our society, child rearing is the primary responsibility of the family, not the state.

Marriage is a relatively stable relationship that helps to ensure that children will have adequate care and protection, will be socialized for productive roles in society, and will not become the burden of those who did not conceive them. Even at divorce, the legal obligation of the noncustodial parent to the child is maintained through child-support payments.

PUBLIC ANNOUNCEMENT The legal binding of a couple in a public ceremony is often preceded by an engagement announcement. Following the ceremony there is a wedding announcement in the newspaper. Public knowledge of the event helps to solidify the commitment of the partners to each other and helps to marshal social and economic support to launch the couple into married life.

1-1b Benefits of Marriage

When married people are compared with singles, the differences are strikingly in favor of the married

TABLE 1.1 BENEFITS OF MARRIAGE AND THE LIABILITIES OF SINGLEHOOD

	Benefits of Marriage	Liabilities of Singlehood
Health	Spouses have fewer hospital admissions, see a physician more regularly, and are sick less often. They recover from illness/surgery more quickly.	Single people are hospitalized more often, have fewer medical checkups, and are sick more often.
Longevity	Spouses live longer than single people.	Single people die sooner than married people.
Happiness	Spouses report being happier than single people.	Single people report less happiness than married people.
Sexual satisfaction	Spouses report being more satisfied with their sex lives, both physically and emotionally.	Single people report being less satisfied with their sex lives, both physically and emotionally.
Money	Spouses have more economic resources than single people.	Single people have fewer economic resources than married people.
Lower expenses	Two can live more cheaply together than separately.	Costs (e.g., housing) are greater for two singles than one couple.
Drug use	Spouses have lower rates of drug use and abuse.	Single people have higher rates of drug use and abuse.
Connected	Spouses are connected to more individuals who provide a support system—partner, in-laws, etc.	Single people have fewer individuals upon whom they can rely for help.
Children	Rates of high school dropouts, teen pregnancies, and poverty are lower among children reared in two-parent homes.	Rates of high school dropouts, teen pregnancies, and poverty are higher among children reared by single parents.
History	Spouses develop a shared history across time with significant others.	Single people may lack continuity and commitment across time with significant others.
Crime	Spouses are less likely to commit a crime.	Single people are more likely to commit a crime.
Loneliness	Spouses are less likely to report loneliness.	Single people are more likely to report being lonely.

(see Table 1.1). The advantages of marriage over single-hood have been referred to as the **marriage benefit** and are true for first as well as subsequent marriages. Explanations for the marriage benefit include economic resources (e.g., higher income/wealth/can afford health care), social control (e.g., spouses ensure partner moderates alcohol/drug use, does not ride a motorcycle), and social/emotional/psychosocial support (e.g., in-resident counselor, loving and caring partner).

1-1c Types of Marriage

Although we think of marriage in the United States as involving two spouses, other societies view marriage differently. **Polygamy** is a generic term for marriage involving more than two spouses. There are three forms of polygamy: polygyny, polyandry, and pantagamy.

POLYGYNY IN THE UNITED STATES Polygyny involves one husband and two or more wives and is practiced illegally in the United States by some religious fundamentalist groups. These groups are primarily in Arizona, New Mexico, and Utah (as well as Canada), and have splintered off from the Church of Jesus Christ of Latter-day Saints (commonly known as the Mormon Church). To be clear, the Mormon Church does not practice or condone polygyny (the church outlawed it in 1890). Those that split off from the Mormon Church represent only about 5% of Mormons in Utah. The largest offshoot is called the Fundamentalist Church of Jesus Christ of the Latter-day Saints (FLDS). Members of the group feel that the practice of polygyny is God's will. Joe Jessop, an elder of the FLDS in his late 80s, had 5 wives, 46 children, and 239 grandchildren. Although the practice is illegal, polygynous individuals are rarely prosecuted because a husband will have only one

Courtesy of E Fred Johnson, Jr.

marriage benefit when compared to being single, married persons are healthier, happier, live longer, have less drug use, etc.

polygamy a generic term for marriage involving more than two spouses.

polygyny type of marriage involving one husband and two or more wives.

legal wife while the others will be married in a civil ceremony. Women are socialized to bear as many children as possible to build up the "celestial family" that will remain together for eternity.

It is often assumed that polygyny in FLDS marriages exists to satisfy the sexual desires of the man, that the women are treated like slaves, and that jealousy among the wives is common. In most polygynous societies, however, polygyny has a political and economic rather than a sexual function. Polygyny, for members of the FLDS, is a means of having many children to produce a celestial family. In other societies, a man with many wives can produce a greater number of children for domestic or farm labor. Wives are not treated like slaves (although women have less status than men in general); all household work is evenly distributed among the wives; and each wife is given her own house or private sleeping quarters. In FLDS households, jealousy is minimal because the female is socialized to accept that her husband is not hers alone but is to be shared with other wives "according to God's plan." The spouses work out a rotational system for conjugal visits, which ensures that each wife has equal access to sexual encounters, while the other wives take care of the children.

POLYANDRY Tibetan Buddhists foster yet another brand of polygamy, referred to as **polyandry**, in which one wife has two or more (up to five) husbands. These husbands, who may be brothers, pool their resources to support one wife. Polyandry is a much less common form of polygamy than polygyny. The major reason for polyandry is economic. A family that cannot afford wives or marriages for each of its sons may find a wife for the eldest son only. Polyandry allows the younger brothers to also have sexual access to the one wife that the family is able to afford.

PANTAGAMY Pantagamy describes a group marriage in which each member of the group is "married" to the others. Pantagamy is a formal arrangement that was practiced in communes (e.g., Oneida) in the

polyandry type of marriage in which one wife has two or more husbands.

pantagamy a group marriage in which each member of the group is "married" to the others.

19th and 20th centuries. Pantagamy is, of course, illegal in the United States. Some polyamorous individuals see themselves in a group marriage.

Our culture emphasizes monogamous marriage and values stable marriages. One cultural expression of this value is the existence of family policies in the form of laws and services designed to support the family (see the Family Policy section for marriage education, which is designed to improve mate selection and strengthen marriage relationships).

1-1d Is Marriage Obsolete?

News media regularly suggest that marriage is done for, that it is no longer relevant to the needs of individuals, and that it will slowly cease to exist. Nonsense. Only 12% of a national sample agreed that "marriage is old fashioned and out of date" (Karpowitz & Pope, 2015). While there is a decline in the percentage of individuals choosing to marry, "this group is primarily those without college degrees who are struggling economically" notes Paul Amato (2015b), past president of the National Council on Family Relations. He notes that among the college educated who have degrees and salaries, marriage remains a popular choice. It is only with the loss of well-paying jobs (and the availability of alternatives such as cohabitation) that marriage rates have dropped. As the number of individuals who have both

kuleczka/Shutterstock.com

Family Policy: Marriage Preparation/Relationship Education

While the terms (e.g., marriage preparation, premarital counseling, marriage education, couple and relationship education) and content (e.g., conflict resolution, communication skills) differ, the federal government has a vested interest in premarriage, marriage, and relationship education programs. One motivation is economic since divorce sometimes plunges ex-spouses into poverty and results in their dependency on public resources. The philosophy behind marriage preparation education is that building a fence at the top of a cliff is preferable to putting an ambulance at the bottom. Hence, to the degree that people select a mate wisely and have the skills to manage conflict/communicate/ stay married, there is greater economic stability for the family and less drain on social services in the United States for single-parent mothers and the needs of their children (Schramm et al., 2013).

African American clergy have been particularly involved in marriage preparation. In a study comparing 141 members of seven primarily African American denominations with 793 clergy from the 15 largest, predominantly White, congregations, African American clergy were significantly more likely than clergy in the comparison group to address premarital content, to use a skills-based approach, to require a longer waiting period/more sessions/more homework assignments, and to consider marriage preparation an important part of their ministry (Wilmoth & Blaney, 2016).

Over 2,000 public schools nationwide offer a marriage preparation course. In Florida, all public high school seniors are required to take a marriage and relationship skills course. Researchers Toews and Yazedjian (2013) emphasized that these programs provide the tools necessary for building and maintaining healthy relationships. They noted that the most positive effects occur when both partners attend the programs and when the programs are integrated into the existing educational curriculum. Significant positive increases in attitudes, knowledge, communication skills, and relationship characteristics result when undergraduates/ emerging adults experience these programs (Cottle et al., 2014, 2015). Similarly, Ma et al. (2013) found in a study of 1,604 students that those exposed to relationship material had fewer faulty relationship views (e.g., one true love, love conquers all) and more realistic views about cohabitation (e.g., cohabitation does not ensure marital success). Couple and relationship education (CRE) programs are also effective for lower income couples (Hawkins & Erickson, 2015) and individuals, particularly females (Spuhler et al., 2014). Regardless of the source—school, child welfare, communication, or clergy—marriage education supplies positive outcomes at any time in a couple's relationship, and in either the first or subsequent marriage (Lucier-Greer et al., 2012).

In spite of the benefits, there is opposition to marriage preparation education in the public school system. Opponents question using school time for relationship courses. Teachers report that they are overworked, and an additional course on marriage can be a burden. In addition, some teachers lack the training to provide relationship courses (however, many schools already have programs in family and consumer sciences, and teachers in these programs are trained in teaching about marriage and the family). A related concern with teaching about marriage and the family in high school is the fear on the part of some parents that the course content may be too liberal. Some parents who oppose teaching sex education in the public schools fear that such courses lead to increased sexual activity.

college degrees and good jobs increases, the marriage rate increases. "Marriage is not passé or irrelevant to most Americans" (p. 3). Lee (2015) also noted that it is the loss of good-paying jobs for American men who cannot afford to marry/support a family that contributes to lower marriage rates.

1-2 FAMILY

Most couples who marry want to have children. However, the definition of what constitutes a family is sometimes unclear. This section examines how families are defined, the various types, and how marriages and families have changed in the past 50 years.

1-2a Definitions of Family

The U.S. Census Bureau defines **family** as a group of two or more people related by blood, marriage, or adoption. This definition has been challenged because it does not include foster families or long-term couples who live together. In a survey of 105 faculty members from 19 PhD marriage and family therapy programs, the researcher found no universal agreement on the definition of the family (Marshall, 2013). Same-gender couples, children of same-gender couples, and children with nonresidential parents were sometimes excluded from the definition of the family (this study was conducted before same-sex marriage became legal).

The answer to the question "Who is family?" is important because access to resources such as health care, Social Security, and retirement benefits is involved. Unless cohabitants are recognized by the state in which they reside as in a "domestic partnership," cohabitants are typically not viewed as "family" and are not accorded health benefits, Social Security, and retirement benefits of the partner. Indeed, the "live-in partner" may not be allowed to see the beloved in the hospital, which may limit visitation to "family only."

The definition of who counts as family is being challenged. In some cases, families are being defined by function rather than by structure—for example, what is the level of emotional and financial commitment and interdependence between the partners? How long have they lived together? Do the partners view themselves as a family?

Friends sometimes become family. Due to

family a group of two or more people related by blood, marriage, or adoption.

transnational family family in which the mother and child live in another country from the father.

civil union a pair-bonded relationship given legal significance in terms of rights and privileges.

domestic partnerships relationships in which cohabiting individuals are given some kind of official recognition by a city or corporation so as to receive partner benefits (e.g., health insurance).

Diversity in Family Relationships

Dragojlovic (2016) interviewed 24 women from Europe, Australia, or the United States who had vacationed in Bali, fell in love with a Balinese man, and had one or more children. While there were variations in the various patterns of commitment and relationships, a common theme was that the women were "playing family" by living/rearing their children in their native land while maintaining a relationship with the father of the children. Even though he may be married to and have other children with a Balinese woman, the woman would visit annually to maintain the relationship with the partner/father of the child. These nonconventional **transnational families** challenge the nuclear family norm.

mobility, spouses may live several states away from their respective families. Although they may visit their families for holidays, they often develop close friendships with others on whom they rely locally for emotional and physical support. Persons in the military who are separated from their parents and siblings (or deployed spouse) often form close "family" relationships with other military individuals, couples, and families.

Sociologically, a family is defined as a kinship system of all relatives living together or recognized as a social unit, including adopted people. The family is regarded as the basic social institution of society because of its important functions of procreation and socialization; the family is found in some form in all societies.

Same-sex couples (e.g., Ellen DeGeneres and her partner Portia de Rossi) certainly define themselves as family. Short of marriage, in some countries committed gay relationships may be recognized as **civil unions** (pair-bonded relationship given legal significance in terms of rights and privileges).

Over 24 cities, 11 states, and numerous countries (including Canada) recognize some form of domestic partnership. **Domestic partnerships** are relationships in which cohabiting individuals are given some kind of official recognition by a city or corporation so as to receive partner benefits (e.g., health insurance). The Walt Disney Company recognizes domestic partnerships. Domestic partnerships do not confer any federal recognition or benefits.

Pets are regarded as family members with over $58 billion spent on their care annually (Kanat-Maymon et al., 2016). Examples of treating pets like children include requiring a fenced in backyard for where one rents or buys an apartment/house, staying only in pet friendly motels, feeding the pet a special diet, hanging a stocking and/or buying presents for the pet at Christmas, buying "clothes" for the pet, and leaving money in one's will for the care of one's pet. Some cohabitants get a puppy which symbolizes their commitment to "family." Some pet owners buy accident insurance—Progressive insurance covers pets. And pets are often identified in divorce papers the custody and visitation rights being assigned.

In addition to meeting one's psychological need for connectedness/well-being beyond the human connection (Kanat-Maymon et al., 2016), positive outcomes in terms of decreased behavioral outbursts and increased social interactions have been observed for autistic children interacting with animals (Zemanek, 2014).

Pets are regarded as family members and sources of enormous companionship and enjoyment.

1-2b Types of Families

There are various types of families.

FAMILY OF ORIGIN Also referred to as the **family of orientation**, this is the family into which you were born or the family in which you were reared. It involves you, your parents, and your siblings. When you go to your parents' home for the holidays, you return to your *family of origin*. Your parents remaining married (Amato, 2015b) and their high marital satisfaction is related to your remaining married and being happy in your own marriage (Kopystynska et al., 2015).

Siblings in one's family of origin also provide a profound influence on one another's behavior, emotional development, adjustment, and happiness (Incerti et al., 2015; McHale et al., 2012). The relationship with one's siblings, particularly the sister-sister relationship, often represents the most enduring relationship in a person's lifetime.

FAMILY OF PROCREATION The **family of procreation** represents the family that you will begin should you marry and have children. Of U.S. citizens living in the United States 65 years old and over, 96% have married with most establishing their own family of procreation (*Proquest Statistical Abstract of the United States, 2016*, Table 32). Across the life cycle, individuals move from their family of orientation to their family of procreation.

NUCLEAR FAMILY The **nuclear family** refers to either a family of origin or a family of procreation. In practice, this means that your nuclear family consists either of you, your parents, and your siblings or of you, your spouse, and your children. Generally, one-parent households are not referred to as nuclear families. They are binuclear families if both parents are involved in the child's life, or single-parent families if only one parent is involved in the child's life.

TRADITIONAL, MODERN, AND POSTMODERN FAMILY Sociologists have identified three central concepts of the family (Silverstein & Auerbach, 2005). The **traditional family** is the two-parent nuclear family, with the husband as breadwinner and the wife as homemaker. The **modern family** is the dual-earner family, in which

These siblings have forged a close relationship and are likely to remain in each other's lives.

family of orientation also known as the family of origin, the family into which a person is born.

family of procreation the family a person begins typically by getting married and having children.

nuclear family consists of you, your parents, and your siblings or you, your spouse, and your children.

traditional family the two-parent nuclear family, with the husband as breadwinner and the wife as homemaker.

modern family the dual-earner family, in which both spouses work outside the home.

TABLE 1.2 DIFFERENCES BETWEEN MARRIAGE AND THE FAMILY IN THE UNITED STATES

Marriage	Family
Usually initiated by a formal ceremony	Formal ceremony not essential
Involves two people	Usually involves more than two people
Ages of the individuals tend to be similar	Individuals represent more than one generation
Individuals usually choose each other	Members are born or adopted into the family
Ends when spouse dies or is divorced	Continues beyond the life of the individual
Sex between spouses is expected and approved	Sex between near kin is neither expected nor approved
Requires a license	No license needed to become a parent
Procreation expected	Consequence of procreation
Spouses are focused on each other	Focus changes with addition of children
Spouses can voluntarily withdraw from marriage	Parents cannot divorce themselves from obligations via divorce to children
Money in unit is spent on the couple	Money is used for the needs of children
Recreation revolves around adults	Recreation revolves around children

Reprinted by permission of the estate of Lee Axelson.

both spouses work outside the home. **Postmodern families** include lesbian or gay couples and their children as well as mothers who are single by choice.

BINUCLEAR FAMILY A **binuclear family** is a family in which the members live in two separate households. This family type is created when the parents of the children divorce and live separately, setting up two separate units, with the children remaining a part of each unit. Each of these units may also change again when the parents remarry and bring additional children into the respective units (**blended family**). Hence, the children may go from a nuclear family with both parents, to a binuclear unit with parents living in separate homes, to a blended family when parents remarry and bring additional children into the respective units.

EXTENDED FAMILY The **extended family** includes not only the nuclear family (or parts of it) but other relatives as well. These relatives include grandparents, aunts, uncles, and cousins. An example of an extended family living together would be a husband and wife, their children, and grandparents. The extended family is particularly important for African American married couples.

postmodern family lesbian or gay couples and mothers who are single by choice, which emphasizes that a healthy family need not be the traditional heterosexual, two-parent family.

binuclear family a family in which the members live in two households.

blended family a family created when two individuals marry and at least one of them brings a child or children from a previous relationship or marriage. Also referred to as a stepfamily.

extended family the nuclear family or parts of it plus other relatives such as grandparents, aunts, uncles, and cousins.

1-3 DIFFERENCES BETWEEN MARRIAGE AND THE FAMILY

Marriage can be thought of as a social relationship that sometimes leads to the establishment of a family (e.g., children). Indeed, most societies or cultures have mechanisms (from "free" dating to arranged marriages) for guiding their youth into permanent emotional, legal, or social relationships (marriage) that are designed to have and rear offspring (an exception is Iceland that does not promote marriage as a major life goal for everyone). Although the concepts of marriage and the family are sometimes used synonymously, they are distinct. The late sociologist Lee Axelson identified some of these differences in Table 1.2.

A family is a risky venture, because the greater the love, the greater the loss.... That's the trade-off. But I'll take it all.

—BRAD PITT, ACTOR

1-4 CHANGES IN MARRIAGE AND THE FAMILY

Whatever families we experience today, they were different previously and will change yet again. A look back at some changes in marriage and the family follow.

1-4a The Industrial Revolution and Family Change

The Industrial Revolution refers to the social and economic changes that occurred when machines and factories, rather than human labor, became the dominant mode for the production of goods. Industrialization occurred in the United States during the early- and mid-1800s and represents one of the most profound influences on the family.

Before industrialization, families functioned as an economic unit that produced goods and services for its own consumption. Parents and children worked together in or near the home to meet the survival needs of the family. As the United States became industrialized, more men and women left the home to sell their labor for wages. The family was no longer a self-sufficient unit that determined its work hours. Rather, employers determined where and when family members would work. Whereas children in preindustrialized America worked on farms and contributed to the economic survival of the family, children in industrialized America became economic liabilities rather than assets. Child labor laws and mandatory education removed children from the labor force and lengthened their dependence on parental support. Eventually, both parents had to work away from the home to support their children. The dual-income family had begun.

During the Industrial Revolution, urbanization occurred as cities were built around factories and families moved to the city to work in the factories. Living space in cities was crowded and expensive, which contributed to a decline in the birthrate and thus smaller families. The development of transportation systems during the Industrial Revolution made it possible for family members to travel to work sites away from the home and to move away from extended kin. With increased mobility, many extended families became separated into smaller nuclear family units consisting of parents and their children. As a result of parents leaving the home to earn wages and the absence of extended kin in or near the family household, children had less adult supervision and moral guidance. Unsupervised children roamed the streets, increasing the potential for crime and delinquency.

Industrialization also affected the role of the father in the family. Employment outside the home removed men from playing a primary role in child care and in other domestic activities. The contribution men made to the household became primarily that of economic provider.

Finally, the advent of industrialization, urbanization, and mobility was associated with the demise of **familism**

Families from familistic cultures such as Taiwan who immigrate to the United States soon discover that their norms, roles, and values are challenged.

(focus on what is important for the family) and the rise of **individualism** (focus on what it important for the individual). When family members functioned together as an economic unit, they were dependent on one another for survival and were concerned about what was good for the family. This familistic focus on the needs of the family has since shifted to a focus on self-fulfillment—individualism. Families from familistic cultures who immigrate to the United States soon discover that their norms, roles, and values begin to alter in reference to the industrialized, urbanized, individualistic patterns and thinking. Individualism and the quest for personal fulfillment are thought to have contributed to high divorce rates, absent fathers, and parents spending less time with their children.

Hence, although the family is sometimes blamed for delinquency, violence, and divorce, it is more accurate to emphasize changing social norms and conditions of which the family is a part. When industrialization took parents out of the home so that they could no longer be constant nurturers and supervisors, the likelihood of aberrant acts by their children/adolescents increased. One explanation for school violence is that absent, career-focused parents have failed to provide close supervision for their children.

Various researchers including Coontz (2016) have noted the enormous changes that have occurred in marriage and the family since the 1950s. Table 1.3 reflects

familism philosophy in which decisions are made in reference to what is best for the family as a collective unit.

individualism philosophy in which decisions are made on the basis of what is best for the individual.

TABLE 1.3 CHANGES IN MARRIAGES AND FAMILIES, 1950 AND 2020

	1950	2020
Family relationship values	Strong values for marriage and the family. Individuals who wanted to remain single or childfree were considered deviant, even pathological. Husband and wife should not be separated by jobs or careers.	Individuals who remain single or childfree experience social understanding and sometimes encouragement. Single and childfree people are no longer considered deviant or pathological but are seen as self-actuating individuals with strong job or career commitments. Husbands and wives can be separated for reasons of job or career and live in a commuter marriage. Married women in large numbers have left the role of full-time mother and housewife to join the labor market.
Gender roles	Rigid gender roles, with men dominant and earning income while wives stay home, taking care of children.	Egalitarian gender roles with both spouses earning income and involved in parenting children.
Sexual values	Marriage was regarded as the only appropriate lifestyle in middle-class America. Living together was unacceptable, and children born out of wedlock were stigmatized. Virginity was expected or exchanged for marital commitment.	Focus on having safe sex has taken precedence over the marital context for sex. Virginity before marriage is rare. Cohabitation has become a stage in a couple's relationship that may or may not lead to marriage. Having children outside of marriage is acceptable. Hooking up is normative among singles.
Homogamous mating	Strong social pressure existed to date and marry within one's own racial, ethnic, religious, and social class group. Emotional and legal attachments were heavily influenced by approval of parents and kin.	Dating and mating reflect more freedom of the individual to select a partner outside his or her own racial, ethnic, religious, and social class group. Pairings are less often influenced by parental approval.
Cultural silence on intimate relationships	Intimate relationships were not an appropriate subject to discuss in the media.	Interviews on television and features in magazines reveal intimate details of the lives of individuals. Survey results in magazines are open about sexuality/relationships.
Divorce	Society strongly disapproved of divorce. Familistic values encouraged spouses to stay married for the children. Strong legal constraints keep couples together. Marriage was forever.	Divorce has replaced death as the endpoint of marriage. Less stigma is associated with divorce. Individualistic values lead spouses to seek personal happiness. No-fault divorce allows for easy severance. Increasing numbers of children are being reared in single-parent homes.
Familism versus individualism	Families were focused on the needs of children. Mothers stayed home to ensure that the needs of their children were met. Adult concerns were less important.	Adult agenda of work and recreation has taken on increased importance, with less attention given to children. Children are being reared in day care centers due to dual career parents. Some parents are helicopter parents.
Homosexuality	Same-sex emotional and sexual relationships were culturally hidden phenomenon. Gay relationships were invisible/stigmatized.	Gay individuals are more open about their identity and relationships. Same-sex marriage legal in U.S. culture embraces diversity of relationships including gay relationships.
Scientific scrutiny	Aside from Kinsey's, few studies were conducted on intimate relationships.	Acceptance of scientific study of marriage and intimate relationships.
Family housing	Husbands and wives lived in same house.	Husbands and wives may "live apart together" (LAT), which means that, although they are emotionally and economically connected, they (by choice) maintain two households, houses, condos, or apartments.
Communication technology	Nonexistent except land line phone.	Smartphones, texting, sexting, social media.

some of these changes. A basic change has been in the reasons for marriage. The most basic purpose for marriage in history has been to acquire the advantages of having in-laws and to expand the family labor source (Coontz, 2016). Marriage not only connects an individual to a larger set of resources (in-laws = people with resources) but provides the context for

having children who are an unpaid labor source and who become heirs.

 1-5 WAYS OF VIEWING MARRIAGE AND THE FAMILY

Ways of viewing marriage and the family, also known as **theoretical frameworks** (a set of interrelated principles designed to explain a particular phenomenon and

> **theoretical frameworks**
> a set of interrelated principles designed to explain a particular phenomenon.

provide a point of view) help us to understand marriage and family. These various ways follow:

1-5a Social Exchange Framework

The **social exchange framework** is one of the most commonly used theoretical perspectives in marriage and the family. The framework views interaction and choices in terms of cost and profit.

The social exchange framework also operates from a premise of **utilitarianism**—the theory that individuals rationally weigh the rewards and costs associated with behavioral choices.

A social exchange view of marital roles emphasizes that spouses negotiate the division of labor on the basis of exchange. For example, a man participates in child care in exchange for his wife earning an income, which relieves him of the total financial responsibility. Social exchange theorists also emphasize that power in relationships is the ability to influence, and avoid being influenced by, the partner. Over half (63%) of 9,410 undergraduates from two universities reported that they had the same amount of power in the relationship as their partner. Sixteen percent felt that they had less power; 21% more power (men reported that they had more power than women in 24% of cases versus 21%) (Hall & Knox, 2017).

1-5b Family Life Course Development Framework

The **family life course development** framework emphasizes the important role transitions of individuals that occur in different periods of life and in different social contexts. For example, young unmarried lovers may become cohabitants, then parents, grandparents, retirees, and widows. While the family life course development framework identifies a traditional set of stages through which most individuals pass, not all do so (e.g., the childfree).

The family life course developmental framework has its basis in sociology (e.g., role transitions), whereas the **family life cycle** has its basis in psychology, which emphasizes the various developmental tasks family members face across time (e.g., marriage, childbearing, preschool, school-age children, teenagers). If developmental tasks at one stage are not accomplished, functioning in subsequent stages will be impaired. For example, one of the developmental tasks of early American marriage is to emotionally and financially separate from one's family of origin. If such separation from parents does not take place, independence as individuals and as a couple may be impaired. The value for independence in American society is not shared in all cultures. In Spain, for example, offspring may be unmarried and living at home in their forties with no stigma or pressure from their parents to move out.

1-5c Structure-Function Framework

The **structure-function framework** emphasizes how marriage and family contribute to society. Just as the human body is made up of different parts that work together for the good of the individual, society is made up of different institutions (e.g., family, religion, education, economics) that work together for the good of society. Functionalists view the family as an institution with values, norms, and activities meant to provide stability for the larger society. Such stability depends on families performing various functions for society.

First, families serve to replenish society with socialized members. Because our society cannot continue to exist without new members, we must have some way of ensuring a continuing supply. However, just having new members is not enough. We need socialized members—those who can speak our language and know the norms and roles of our society.

Second, marriage and the family promote the emotional stability of the respective spouses. Society cannot provide enough counselors to help us whenever we have emotional issues/problems. Marriage ideally provides in-residence counselors who are loving and caring partners with whom people share (and receive help for) their most difficult experiences.

Children also need people to love them and to give them a sense of belonging. This need can be fulfilled in a variety of family contexts (two-parent families, single-parent families, extended families). The affective function of the family is one of its major benefits. No other institution focuses so completely on meeting the emotional needs of its members as marriage and the family.

Third, families provide economic support for their members. Although modern families are no

social exchange framework views interaction and choices in terms of cost and profit.

utilitarianism individuals rationally weigh the rewards and costs associated with behavioral choices.

family life course development the stages and process of how families change over time.

family life cycle stages that identify the various developmental tasks family members face across time.

structure-function framework emphasizes how marriage and family contribute to society.

longer self-sufficient economic units, they provide food, shelter, and clothing for their members. One need only consider the homeless in our society to be reminded of this important function of the family.

In addition to the primary functions of replacement, emotional stability, and economic support, other functions of the family include the following:

▶ **Physical care.** Families provide the primary care for their infants, children, and aging parents. Other agencies (neonatal units, day care centers, assisted-living residences, shelters) may help, but the family remains the primary and recurring caretaker. Spouses also show concern about the physical health of each other by encouraging each other to take medications and to see a doctor.

▶ **Regulation of sexual behavior.** Spouses are expected to confine their sexual behavior to each other, which reduces the risk of having children who do not have socially and legally bonded parents, and of contracting or spreading sexually transmitted infections.

▶ **Status placement.** Being born into a family provides social placement of the individual in society. One's family of origin largely determines one's social class, religious affiliation, and future occupation. Babies Prince George Alexander Louis and Princess Charlotte Elizabeth Diana of Kate Middleton and Prince William of the royal family of Great Britain were born into the upper class and were destined to be in politics by virtue of being born into a political family.

▶ **Social control.** Spouses in high-quality, durable marriages provide social control for each other that results in less criminal behavior. Parole boards often note that the best guarantee against recidivism is a nonconvicted spouse who expects the partner to get a job and avoid criminal behavior and who reinforces these behaviors (Andersen et al., 2015).

1-5d Conflict Framework

Conflict framework views individuals in relationships as competing for valuable resources (time, money, power). Conflict theorists recognize that family members have different goals and values that produce conflict. Adolescents want freedom (e.g., stay out late with new love interest) while parents want their child to get a

conflict framework the view that individuals in relationships compete for valuable resources.

symbolic interaction framework views marriages and families as symbolic worlds in which the various members give meaning to each other's behavior.

Justin Sullivan/Getty Images

good night's sleep, not get pregnant, and stay on track in school.

Conflict theorists also view conflict not as good or bad but as a natural and normal part of relationships. They regard conflict as necessary for the change and growth of individuals, marriages, and families. Cohabitation relationships, marriages, and families all have the potential for conflict. Cohabitants are in conflict about commitment to marry, spouses are in conflict about the division of labor, and parents are in conflict with their children over rules such as curfew, chores, and schools their children are to attend. These three units may also be in conflict with other systems. For example, cohabitants are in conflict with the economic institution for health benefits for their partners. Similarly, employed parents are in conflict with their employers for flexible work hours, maternity or paternity benefits, and day care facilities.

1-5e Symbolic Interaction Framework

The **symbolic interaction framework** views marriages and families as symbolic worlds in which the various members give meaning to one another's behavior. The term *symbolic interaction* refers to the process of interpersonal interaction and involves the concepts of the definition of the situation, the looking-glass self, and the self-fulfilling prophecy.

DEFINITION OF THE SITUATION Two people who have just spotted each other at a party are constantly

> Language, after all, is only the use of symbols.
>
> —GEORGE HENRY LEWES, ENGLISH PHILOSOPHER

defining the situation and responding to those definitions. Is the glance from the other person (1) an invitation to approach, (2) an approach, or (3) a misinterpretation—was he or she looking at someone else? Or just gazing into space thinking of someone else? The definition each partner has will affect his or her interaction.

LOOKING-GLASS SELF The image people have of themselves is a reflection of what other people tell them about themselves. People develop an idea of who they are by the way others act toward them. If no one looks at or speaks to them, they will begin to feel unsettled. Similarly, family members constantly hold up social mirrors for one another into which the respective members look for definitions of self. Parents are particularly intent on holding up positive social mirrors for their children (e.g., "you are a good student and we are proud of you").

SELF-FULFILLING PROPHECY Once people define situations and the behaviors in which they are expected to engage, they are able to behave toward one another in predictable ways. Such predictability of behavior affects subsequent behavior. If you feel that your partner expects you to be faithful, your behavior is likely to conform to these expectations. The expectations thus create a self-fulfilling prophecy.

1-5f Family Systems Framework

The **family systems framework** views each member of the family as part of a system and the family as a unit that develops norms of interacting, which may be explicit (e.g., parents specify when their children must stop texting for the evening and complete homework) or implicit (e.g., spouses expect fidelity from each other). These rules serve various functions, such as the allocation of keeping the education of offspring on track and solidifying the emotional bond of the spouses.

Rules are most efficient if they are flexible (e.g., they should be adjusted over time in response to a child's growing competence). A rule about not leaving the yard when playing may be appropriate for a 4-year-old but inappropriate for a 14-year-old.

Family members also develop boundaries that define the individual and the group and separate one system or subsystem from another. A boundary may be physical, such as a closed bedroom door, or social, such as expectations that family problems will not be aired in public. Boundaries may also be emotional, such as communication, which maintains closeness or distance in a

"Because one believes in oneself, one doesn't try to convince others. Because one is content with oneself, one doesn't need others' approval. Because one accepts oneself, the whole world accepts him or her."

— LAO-TZU, PHILOSOPHER

relationship. Some family systems are cold and abusive; others are warm and nurturing.

In addition to rules and boundaries, family systems have roles (leader, follower, scapegoat) for the respective family members. These roles may be shared by more than one person or may shift from person to person during an interaction or across time. In healthy families, individuals are allowed to alternate roles rather than being locked into one role. In problem families, one family member is often allocated the role of scapegoat, or the cause of all the family's problems (e.g., an alcoholic spouse).

Family systems may be open, in that they are receptive to information and interaction with the outside world, or closed, in that they feel threatened by such contact. The Amish have a closed family system and minimize contact with the outside world.

1-5g Human Ecology Framework

The **human ecology framework** (also known as the ecological perspective) (Shelton, 2015) looks at family as an ecosystem which interacts with the environment. Humans are biological organisms and social beings that interact with their environment. Individuals, couples, and families are dependent on the environment for survival and on other human beings for social interaction. The well-being of individuals and families cannot be considered apart from the well-being of the environment. For example, nutrition and housing are important to the functioning of families. If a family does not have enough to eat or have adequate housing, it will not be able to function at an optimal level.

family systems framework views each member of the family as part of a system and the family as a unit that develops norms of interaction.

human ecology framework views the family and the environment as an ecosystem.

1-5h Feminist Framework

Although a **feminist framework** views marriage and family as contexts of inequality and oppression for women, there are 11 feminist perspectives, including lesbian feminism (emphasizing oppressive heterosexuality), psychoanalytic feminism (focusing on cultural domination of men's phallic-oriented ideas and repressed emotions), and standpoint feminism (stressing the neglect of women's perspective and experiences in the production of knowledge) (Lorber, 1998). Regardless of which feminist framework is being discussed, all feminist frameworks have the themes of inequality and oppression. According to feminist theory, gender structures our experiences (e.g., women and men will experience life differently because there are different expectations for the respective genders). Feminists seek equality in their relationships with their partners. In addition, this framework has been adapted to examine other inequalities and oppressions such as sexism, lookism, and heterosexualism.

1-5i Couple and Family Technology Framework

In response to the increased use of technology, the couple and family technology framework focuses on the roles, rules, and boundaries in the respective contexts (Cravens, 2015; Hertlein & Blumer, 2013). For example, what roles are partners/spouses to play in regard to each others' texts, emails, blogs, and Facebook/Twitter accounts? What are the rules about the use of technology in regard to adult sites (e.g., pornography, webcam)? And what are the boundaries in regard to interacting with others (e.g., former romantic partners)? The CFT framework emerged since the existing frameworks did not address the new issues brought on by new technology in communication.

The major theoretical frameworks for viewing marriage and the family are summarized in Table 1.4.

1-6 CHOICES IN RELATIONSHIPS: VIEW OF THIS TEXT

Another view of marriage and family is that of choices in relationships. Whatever your relationship goal, you can take a proactive approach of taking charge of your life and making wise relationship choices. Making the right choices in your relationships, including

feminist framework views marriage and family as contexts of inequality and oppression for women.

> Feminism isn't about making women stronger. Women are already strong. It is about changing the way the world perceives that strength.
>
> —G. D. ANDERSON, POET

marriage and family, is critical to your health, happiness, and sense of well-being. Your times of greatest elation and sadness will be in reference to the choices you make in your relationships.

The central theme of this text is choices in relationships. Although we will make many choices, among the most important are whether to marry, whom to marry, when to marry, whether to have children, whether to remain emotionally/sexually faithful to one's partner, and whether to protect oneself from sexually transmitted infections and unwanted pregnancy. Though structural and cultural influences are operative, a choices framework emphasizes that individuals have some control over their relationship destiny by making deliberate choices to initiate, nurture, or terminate intimate relationships.

1-6a Facts about Choices in Relationships

The facts to keep in mind when making relationship choices include the following.

NOT TO DECIDE IS TO DECIDE Not making a decision is a decision by default. If you are sexually active and decide not to use a condom or to be indiscriminate in the choice of a sexual partner, you have made a decision to increase your risk for contracting a sexually transmissible infection, including HIV. If you don't make a deliberate choice to end a relationship that is unfulfilling, abusive, or going nowhere, you have made a choice to continue that relationship and eliminate the possibility of getting into a more positive and flourishing relationship. If you don't make a decision to be faithful

> Nobody can go back and start a new beginning, but anyone can start today and make a new ending.
>
> —MARIA ROBINSON, AUTHOR

TABLE 1.4 THEORETICAL FRAMEWORKS FOR MARRIAGE AND THE FAMILY

Theory	Description	Concepts	Level of Analysis	Strengths	Weaknesses
Social exchange framework	In their relationships, individuals seek to maximize their benefits and minimize their costs.	Benefits Costs Profit Loss	Individual Couple Family	Provides explanations of human behavior based on outcome.	Assumes that people always act rationally and all behavior is calculated.
Family life course development framework	All families have a life course that is composed of all the stages and events that have occurred within the family.	Stages Transitions Timing	Institution Individual Couple Family	Families are seen as dynamic rather than static. Useful in working with families who are facing transitions in their life courses.	Difficult to adequately test the theory through research.
Structure-function framework	The family has several important functions within society; within the family, individual members have certain functions.	Structure-function	Institution	Emphasizes the relation of family to society, noting how families affect and are affected by the larger society.	Families with nontraditional structures (single-parent, same-sex couples) are seen as dysfunctional.
Conflict framework	Conflict in relationships is inevitable, due to competition over resources and power.	Conflict Resources Power	Institution	Views conflict as a normal part of relationships and as necessary for change and growth.	Sees all relationships as conflictual, and does not acknowledge cooperation.
Symbolic interaction framework	People communicate through symbols and interpret the words and actions of others.	Definition of the situation Looking-glass self Self-fulfilling prophecy	Couple	Emphasizes the perceptions of individuals, not just objective reality or the viewpoint of outsiders.	Ignores the larger social interaction context and minimizes the influence of external forces.
Family systems framework	The family is a system of interrelated parts that function together to maintain the unit.	Subsystem Roles Rules Boundaries Open system Closed system	Couple Family	Very useful in working with families who are having serious problems (violence, alcoholism). Describes the effect family members have on each other.	Based on work with systems, troubled families, and may not apply to nonproblem families.
Human ecology framework	Family as ecosystem which interacts with the environment.	Ecosystem, interaction	Individual, couple, environment	Emphasizes interaction of humans and environment.	Linkages sometimes seem contrived.
Feminist framework	Women's experience is central and different from man's experience of social reality.	Inequality Power Oppression	Institution Individual Couple Family	Exposes inequality and oppression as explanations for frustrations women experience.	Multiple branches of feminism may inhibit central accomplishment of increased equality.
Couple and family technology framework	Impact of use of technology on couple and family.	Roles, rules, boundaries	Individual, couple, family	Emphasizes need for communication related to technology use.	Limited research to suggest optimum guidelines.

to your partner, you have made a decision to be vulnerable to cheating.

ACTION MUST FOLLOW A CHOICE Making a decision but not acting on it is no decision at all. You must pull the trigger. If you decide to only have safe sex, you must buy condoms, have them available, and use them. The What's New? section emphasizes that taking action on one's choices sometimes means taking a chance.

Being overweight and out-of-shape is hard. Being lean and in-shape is hard. Choose your hard.

—MOLLY GALBRAITH, FITNESS GURU

Taking Relationship and Sexual Chances

Individuals differ in the degree to which they are willing to take risks (Yang, 2015). Making choices sometimes includes taking chances—moving in together after knowing each other for a short time, changing schools to be together, and forgoing condom usage thinking "this time won't end in a pregnancy." To assess the degree to which undergraduates take chances in their relationships, 381 students completed a 64-item questionnaire posted on the Internet. The majority of respondents were female (over 80%) and White (approximately 74%). Over half of the respondents (53%) described their relationship status as emotionally involved with one person, with 4% engaged or married.

Findings

Of the various risk-taking behaviors identified on the questionnaire, eight were identified by 25% or more of the respondents as behaviors they had participated in. These eight are identified below.

Almost three-fourths (72%) of the sample self-identified as being a "person willing to take chances in my love relationship." However, only slightly over one-third of the respondents indicated that they considered themselves as risk takers in general. This suggests that college students may be more likely to engage in risk-taking behavior in love relationships than in other areas

Individuals often take chances in both their relationship and sexual decision making.

of their lives. Both love and alcohol were identified as contexts for increasing one's vulnerability for taking chances in romantic relationships—60% and 66%, respectively. Both being in love and drinking alcohol (both love and alcohol may be viewed as drugs) give one a sense of immunity from danger or allow one to deny danger.

Source: Adapted and abridged from Elliott, L., B. Easterling, & D. Knox. (2016). Taking chances in romantic relationships. *College Student Journal, 50:* 241–245.

MOST FREQUENT RELATIONSHIP AND SEXUAL CHANCES N = 381	
Risk-Taking Behavior	**Percent**
Unprotected sex	70
Being involved in a "friends with benefits" relationship	63
Broke up with a partner to explore alternatives	46
Had sex before feeling ready	41
Disconnected with friends because of partner	34
Maintained long-distance relationship (one year)	32
Cheated on partner	30
Lied to partner about being in love	28

Interracial couples enjoy their love relationship but sometimes experience the trade-offs of prejudice and discrimination.

CHOICES INVOLVE TRADE-OFFS By making one choice, you relinquish others. Every relationship choice you make will have a downside and an upside.

If you decide to hook up with someone, you may enjoy the sexual excitement but you may feel regretful in the morning and decrease the chance that the night will transition into a relationship. If you decide to marry, you will give up your freedom to pursue other emotional and/or sexual relationships. However, your marriage may result in a stable lifetime of shared positive memories.

Any partner that you select will also have characteristics that must be viewed as a trade-off. One woman noted of her man, "he doesn't do text messaging or email…he doesn't even know how to turn on a computer. But he knows how to build a house, plant a garden, and fix a car…and he loves me…trade-offs I'm willing to make."

SOME CHOICES REQUIRE CORRECTION Some of our choices, although appearing correct at the time that we make them, turn out to be disasters. Once we realize that a choice has consistently negative consequences, it is important to stop defending it, make new choices, and move forward. Otherwise, we remain consistently locked into continued negative outcomes for a "bad" choice. The analogy is that no matter how far you have gone down the wrong road, you can always turn back.

> One's philosophy is not best expressed in words; it is expressed in the choices one makes…and the choices we make are ultimately our responsibility.
>
> —ELEANOR ROOSEVELT, FIRST LADY

CHOICES INCLUDE SELECTING A POSITIVE OR A NEGATIVE VIEW As Thomas Edison progressed toward inventing the light bulb, he said, "I have not failed. I have found ten thousand ways that won't work."

In spite of an unfortunate event in your life, you can choose to see the bright side. Regardless of your circumstances, you can opt for viewing a situation in positive terms. A partner who breaks up with you can be viewed as providing an opportunity to become involved in a new, mutual, love relationship. The discovery of your partner cheating on you can be viewed as an opportunity to open up communication channels with your partner, and to develop a stronger connection, or to motivate you to end the relationship and to find a faithful partner. Discovering that you have a sexually transmitted infection can be viewed as a challenge to face adversity with your partner. It is not the event but your view of it that determines its effect on you.

MOST CHOICES ARE REVOCABLE; SOME ARE NOT Most choices can be changed. For example, a person who has chosen to be sexually active with multiple partners can decide to be monogamous or to abstain from sexual relations in new relationships. People who have been unfaithful in the past can elect to be emotionally and sexually committed to a new partner.

Other choices are less revocable. For example, backing out of the role of parent is very difficult. Social pressure keeps most parents engaged, but the law (e.g., forced child support) is the backup legal incentive. Hence, the decision to have a child is usually irrevocable. Choosing to have unprotected sex may also result in a

TABLE 1.5 FIVE GENERATIONS IN RECENT HISTORY

Great Generation: Years of the Great Depression, World War II (veterans and civilians). Culture steeped in traditional values.

Baby boomers: Children of World War II's Great Generation, born between 1946 and 1964. Questioning of traditional values.

Gen X (Generation X): Children born between 1975 and 1985. Generation of change, MTV, AIDS, diversity.

Gen Y (Generation Y): Known as Millennial Generation, persons born from early 1980s to early 2000s. Change jobs frequently; no loyalty to corporations.

Gen Z (Generation Z): New, Silent Generation, born between 1995 and 2007. They were born in the information age, digital age, digital globalization.

Each player must accept the cards life deals him or her. But once they are in hand, he or she alone must decide how to play the cards in order to win the game.

—VOLTAIRE (1694–1778), HISTORIAN AND WRITER

lifetime of coping with a sexually transmitted infection (e.g., genital herpes).

CHOICES OF GENERATION Y Generations vary (see Table 1.5). Those in Generation Y (typically born between early 1980s and early 2000s) are the children of the baby boomers (Generation X). Numbering about 80 million, these Generation Yers (also known as the Millennial or Homeland Generation) have been the focus of their parents' attention. They have been nurtured, coddled, and scheduled into day care to help them get ahead. The result is a generation of high self-esteem, self-absorbed individuals who believe they are "the best." Unlike their parents, who believe in paying one's dues, getting credentials, and sacrificing through hard work to achieve economic stability, Generation Yers focus on fun, enjoyment, and flexibility. They might choose a summer job at the beach if it buys a burger and an apartment with six friends over an internship at IBM that smacks of the corporate America sellout. Other generations are shown in Table 1.5.

CHOICES ARE INFLUENCED BY THE STAGE IN THE FAMILY LIFE CYCLE The choices a person makes tend to be individualistic or familistic, depending on the stage of the family life cycle that the person is in. Before marriage, individualism characterizes the thinking and choices of most individuals. Individuals are concerned only with their own needs. Once married, and particularly after having children, the person's familistic values ensue as the needs of a spouse and children begin to influence behavioral choices. For example, evidence of familistic values and choices is reflected in the fact that spouses with children are less likely to divorce than spouses without children.

While some go to a palm reader to make decisions about their love life, others want to know what research has to say about love/relationship issues.

1-7 RESEARCH IN MARRIAGE AND FAMILY

Research is valuable since it helps to provide evidence for or against a hypothesis. For example, it is assumed that hookups do not become monogamous love relationships. But almost a fourth of couples (23%) in one study who reported having hooked up also noted that these transitioned into a long-term romantic relationship (Erichsen et al., 2016).

> The measure of greatness in a scientific idea is the extent to which it stimulates thought and opens up new lines of research.
>
> —PAUL A.M. DIRAC, PHYSICIST

Researchers follow a standard sequence when conducting a research project, and there are certain caveats to be aware of when reading any research finding.

1-7a Steps in the Research Process

Several steps are used in conducting research.

1. **Identify the topic or focus of research.** Select a subject about which you are passionate. For example, are you interested in studying cohabitation of college students? Give your project a title in the form of a question—"Do People Who Cohabit Before Marriage Have Happier Marriages than Those Who Do Not Cohabit?"

2. **Review the literature.** Go online to the various databases of your college or university and read research that has already been published on cohabitation. Not only will this prevent you from "reinventing the wheel" (you might find that a research study has already been conducted on exactly what you want to study), but it will also give you ideas for your study.

3. **Develop hypotheses.** A **hypothesis** is a suggested explanation for a phenomenon. For example, you might hypothesize that cohabitation results in greater marital happiness and less divorce because the partners have a chance to "test-drive" each other and their relationship.

4. **Decide on type of study and method of data collection.** The type of study may be **cross-sectional**, which means studying the whole population at one time—in this case, finding out from persons now living together about their experience—or **longitudinal**, which means studying the same group across time—in this case, collecting data from the same couple each of their four years of living together during college. The method of data collection could be archival (secondary sources such as journals), survey (questionnaire), interview (one or both partners), or case study (focus on one couple). A basic differentiation in method is quantitative (surveys, archival) or qualitative (interviews/case study).

5. **Get IRB approval.** To ensure the protection of people who agree to be interviewed or who complete questionnaires, researchers must obtain IRB approval by submitting a summary of their proposed research to the Institutional Review Board (IRB) of their institution. The IRB reviews the research plan to ensure that the project is consistent with research ethics and poses no undue harm to participants. When collecting data from individuals, it is important that they are told that their participation is completely voluntary, that the study maintains their anonymity, and that the results are confidential. Respondents under age 18 need the consent of their parents.

6. **Collect and analyze data.** Various statistical packages are available to analyze data to discover if your hypotheses are true or false.

hypothesis a suggested explanation for a phenomenon.

cross-sectional research studying the whole population at one time (e.g., finding out from all persons now living together at your university about their experience).

longitudinal research studying the same subjects across time (e.g., collecting data from the same couple during each of their four years of living together during college).

7. **Write up and publish results.** Writing up and submitting your findings for publication are important so that your study becomes part of the academic literature.

1-7b Caveats to Consider in Evaluating Research Quality

"New Research Study" is a frequent headline in popular magazines such as *Cosmopolitan*, *Glamour*, and *Redbook* promising accurate information about "hooking up," "what women want," "what men want," or other relationship, marriage, and family issues. As you read such articles, as well as the research in texts such as these, be alert to their potential flaws. *Nature* has an 18-point checklist for authors to ensure that research results can be replicated (Amato, 2015a). Many of the various issues to keep in mind when evaluating research are identified in Table 1.6. An additional concern is that those who do not respond to Internet surveys are different from those who do. In a study of 2,049 individuals where extensive information was known, Busby and Yoshida (2015) found virtually no differences (of 18 factors such as personality,

family of origin measures, etc.) between those who had valid email addresses and those who did not.

 ## 1-8 TRENDS

Marriage will continue to be the dominant lifestyle choice for about 85% of adults in the United States. About 15% will not just put off marriage, but do so for good, making older never-married individuals a growing segment of the U.S. population (Asadi, 2015). Diversity in marriage

TABLE 1.6	POTENTIAL RESEARCH PROBLEMS IN MARRIAGE AND FAMILY	
Weakness	**Consequences**	**Example**
Sample not random	Cannot generalize findings	Opinions of college students do not reflect opinions of other adults.
No control group	Inaccurate conclusions	Study on the effect of divorce on children needs control group of children whose parents are still together.
Age differences between groups of respondents	Inaccurate conclusions	Effect may be due to passage of time or to cohort differences.
Unclear terminology	Inability to measure what is not clearly defined	What is definition of cohabitation, marital happiness, sexual fulfillment, good communication, and quality time?
Researcher bias	Slanted conclusions	A researcher studying the value of a product (e.g., the latest diet program) should not be funded by the organization being studied.
Time lag	Outdated conclusions	Often-quoted Kinsey sex research is over 70 years old.
Distortion	Invalid conclusions	Research subjects exaggerate, omit information, and/or recall facts or events inaccurately. Respondents may remember what they wish had happened.
Deception	Public misled	Dr. Anil Potti (Duke University) changed data on research reports and provided fraudulent results (Darnton, 2012).

and family life will also continue as evidenced by same-sex marriages/families, single-parent families, childfree families, and poly families. The latter reflects several adults who are pair bonded with each other and who decide to live together/rear their children together.

Finnish students were asked to predict the future of the family in their country (Forsberg & Natkin, 2016). They noted three potential outcomes: that their families would strengthen, would weaken, or a catastrophe would threaten to destroy their families. The major agents of change were identified as the economy, values, and religion as well as family policies and ecological factors. All of these factors are operative in the United States and impact our families.

Finally, the future will involve knowledge of behavior based on the interaction of genes and the environment from the new field of Gene × Environment interaction (cGxE). While controversial, the field is now looking at specific genes and how they interact with the environment to produce what outcome (Salvatore & Dick, 2015).

STUDY TOOLS 1

READY TO STUDY? IN THE BOOK, YOU CAN:

☐ Rip out the chapter review card at the back of the book for a handy summary of the chapter and key terms.

☐ Assess yourself with the following self-assessment.

ONLINE AT CENGAGEBRAIN.COM YOU CAN:

☐ Collect StudyBits while you read and study the chapter.

☐ Quiz yourself on key concepts.

☐ Prepare for tests with M&F4 Flash Cards as well as those you create.

SELF-ASSESSMENT

Attitudes toward Marriage Scale

The purpose of this survey is to assess the degree to which you view marriage positively. Read each item carefully and consider what you believe. There are no right or wrong answers. After reading each statement, select the number that best reflects your level of agreement, using the following scale:

1	2	3	4	5	6	7
Strongly disagree						*Strongly agree*

_____ **1.** I am married or plan to get married.

_____ **2.** Being single and free is not as good as people think it is.

_____ **3.** Marriage is NOT another word for being trapped.

_____ **4.** Single people are more lonely than married people.

_____ **5.** Married people are happier than single people.

_____ **6.** Most of the married people I know are happy.

_____ **7.** Most of the single people I know think marriage is better than singlehood.

_____ **8.** The statement that singles are more lonely and less happy than spouses is mostly true.

_____ **9.** It is better to be married than to be single.

_____ **10.** Spouses enjoy their lifestyle more than single people.

_____ **11.** Spouses have a more intimate relationship than singles do in their relationships.

_____ **12.** Spouses have a greater sense of joy than singles.

_____ **13.** Being married is a more satisfying lifestyle than being single.

_____ **14.** People who think that married people are happier than single people are correct.

_____ **15.** Single people struggle with avoiding loneliness.

_____ **16.** Married people are not as lonely as single people.

_____ **17.** The companionship of marriage is a major advantage of the lifestyle.

_____ **18.** Married people have better sex than singles.

_____ **19.** The idea that singlehood is a happier lifestyle than being married is nonsense.

_____ **20.** Singlehood as a lifestyle is overrated.

Scoring

After assigning a number from 1 (strongly disagree) to 7 (strongly agree), add the numbers. The higher your score (140 is the highest possible score), the more positive your view of marriage. The lower your score (20 is the lowest possible score), the more negatively you view marriage. The midpoint is 60 (scores lower than 60 suggest a more negative view of marriage; scores higher than 60 suggest a more positive view of marriage).

Norms

The norming sample of this self-assessment was based on 37 males and 174 females at East Carolina University. The average score of the males was 93 and the average score of the females was 96, suggesting a predominantly positive view of marriage (with females more positive than males).

Source: "Attitudes toward Marriage Scale" was developed for this text by David Knox. Norms were updated in 2015. It is to be used for general assessment and is not designed to be a clinical diagnostic tool or as a research instrument.

M&F
ONLINE
STUDY YOUR WAY
WITH STUDYBITS!

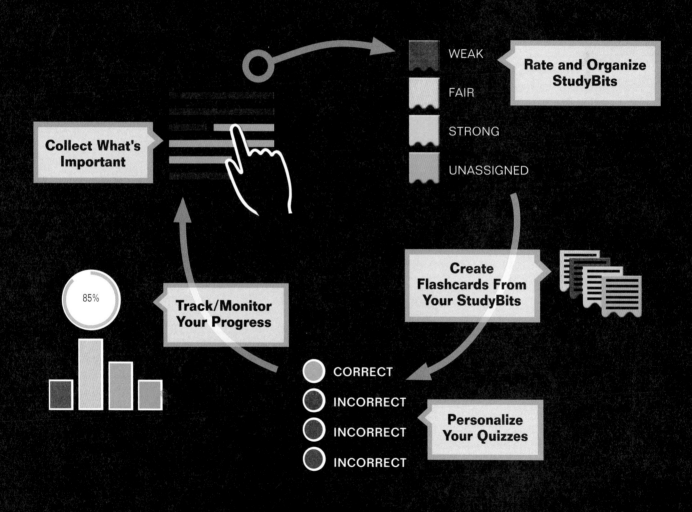

WEAK

FAIR

STRONG

UNASSIGNED

Rate and Organize StudyBits

Collect What's Important

Create Flashcards From Your StudyBits

85%

Track/Monitor Your Progress

CORRECT

INCORRECT

INCORRECT

INCORRECT

Personalize Your Quizzes

4LTR
PRESS

Access M&F ONLINE at www.cengagebrain.com

2 | Making Choices about Singlehood, Hooking Up, Cohabitation, and Living Apart Together

Madelyn Coates

SECTIONS

2-1 Singlehood

2-2 Ways of Finding a Partner

2-3 Long-Distance Relationships

2-4 Cohabitation

2-5 Living Apart Together

2-6 Trends in Singlehood

After finishing this chapter go to **PAGE 43** for **STUDY TOOLS**

> It's not just OK to be single for both men and women—it's wonderful to be single, and society needs to embrace singlehood in all its splendiferous, solitary glory.
>
> —CHELSEA HANDLER, HOST OF CHELSEA ON NETFLIX

The quote above reflects the thought, feeling, and value of an increasing number of young adults. While, previously, getting married was the only lifestyle option for adults (Trost, 2016), individuals today are in no hurry to get married and regard society's disapproval as nonsense. They enjoy the freedom of singlehood and put off marriage until their late twenties and beyond (the same is true of youth in France, Germany, and Italy). In the meantime, the process of courtship includes hanging out (small groups of individuals interacting), hooking up (the new term for "one-night stand"), and "being in a relationship" (seeing each other exclusively and announcing one's relationship status on Facebook), which may include cohabitation and rearing children as a prelude to marriage. We begin with an examination of singlehood.

2-1 SINGLEHOOD

In this section, we discuss the reasons for remaining single, how social movements have increased the acceptance of singlehood, the various categories of single people, and the choice to be permanently unmarried.

2-1a Reasons for Remaining Single

A number of reasons have been identified for remaining single (Muraco & Curran, 2012). These reasons include financial stability, ability to pay for a wedding, doubts about self as a potential spouse, doubts about partner as spouse, quality of relationship, doubts about self as parent, doubts about partner as parent, capability of being economic provider, partner capability of being economic provider, fear of divorce, infidelity, in-laws, and bringing children from own and partner's previous relationships together.

Table 2.1 lists some other standard reasons people give for remaining single. The primary advantage of remaining single is freedom and control over one's life. Others do not set out to be single but drift into singlehood longer than they anticipated, discover that they like it, and remain single.

Still other individuals remain single out of fear. Their parents, siblings, and friends are divorced so they feel their chances for happiness are better remaining single. " I know I can be happy single," said one of our students. "It's marriage that scares me."

 Self-Assessment: Attitudes toward Singlehood Scale
Take the Attitudes toward Singlehood Scale self-assessment at the end of this chapter to assess your suitability for singlehood.

Related to the reason for remaining single is the reason for delaying marriage. Birger (2015) suggested that one of the motivations for delaying marriage is an oversupply of educated women—four college graduate women for every three college graduate men aged 22 to 29. There is a reluctance to marry someone with a different educational level. "Classism is bigger than racism in dating," says Evan Marc Katz (Birger, 2015). Hence, with men less inclined to marry women who are more

TABLE 2.1 REASONS TO REMAIN SINGLE	
Benefits of Singlehood	**Limitations of Marriage**
Freedom to do as one wishes	Restricted by spouse or children
Variety of lovers	One sexual partner
Spontaneous lifestyle	Routine, predictable lifestyle
Close friends of both sexes	Pressure to avoid close other-sex friendships
Responsible for one person only	Responsible for spouse and children
Spend money as one wishes	Expenditures influenced by needs of spouse and children
Freedom to move as career dictates	Restrictions on career mobility
Avoid being controlled by spouse	Potential to be controlled by spouse
Avoid emotional and financial stress of divorce	Possibility of divorce

DEPARTURES

Kansas City Airport Visual Paging

Royals!   MAR 25   7:07

Welcome

Joyce Chang

and permitted intercourse outside the context of marriage. No longer did people feel compelled to wait until marriage for involvement in a sexual relationship. Hence, the sequence changed from dating, love, maybe intercourse with a future spouse, and then marriage and parenthood to "hanging out," "hooking up" with numerous partners, maybe living together (in one or more relationships), marriage, and children. (For some, living together is a required relationship stage.)

The women's movement emphasized equality in education, employment, and income for women. As a result, rather than get married and depend on a husband for income, women earned higher degrees, sought career opportunities, and earned their own income. This economic independence brought with it independence of choice. Women could afford to remain single or to leave an unfulfilling or abusive relationship. Commanding respect and an egalitarian relationship have become normative to today's relationships.

The gay liberation movement, has increased the visibility of gay individuals and relationships. The Supreme Court ruling for gay marriage, openly gay politicians (e.g., Steve Gallardo), NFL athletes (e.g., Michael Sam), and celebrities (e.g., Ellen DeGeneres) infuse new norms into our society. Though some gay people still marry heterosexuals to provide a traditional social front, the gay liberation movement has provided support for a lifestyle consistent with one's sexual orientation.

In effect, there is a new wave of youth who feel that their commitment is to themselves in early adulthood and to marriage in their late twenties and thirties, if at all. The increased acceptance of singlehood translates into staying in school or getting a job, establishing oneself in a career, and becoming economically and emotionally independent from one's parents. The old pattern was to leap from

educated, the result is that there are more women who want to marry than men. So men can have their pick, take their time, and enjoy singlehood in the meantime. Birger suggests that the hookup culture is a by-product of the oversupply of women.

Will those who are delaying marriage eventually marry? Probably. We need to wait till the current cohort of youth reach age 75 and beyond to see if as high a percentage (96%) eventually marry as is true of the current percentage of those age 75 and older (*Proquest Statistical Abstract of the United States, 2016*, Table 57).

Regardless of the reason, will those who delay getting married eventually marry? Ninety-five percent of 9,716 undergraduates (slightly higher percent of females than males) at two universities agreed that "Someday, I want to marry" (Hall & Knox, 2016). About 85% of young adults today actually marry (Coontz, 2016). In the meantime, the existence and enjoyment of singlehood is facilitated by three social movements.

2-1b Social Movements and the Acceptance of Singlehood

The acceptance of singlehood as a lifestyle can be attributed to social movements—the sexual revolution, the women's movement, and the gay liberation movement. The sexual revolution involved openness about sexuality

Gay relationships have become more normative. This couple has been together over 25 years and host an annual Christmas party of over 200 guests. Gay marriage is now legal in every state.

Stacy Huff

high school into marriage. The new pattern is to wait until after college, become established in a career, and enjoy themselves.

2-1c Unmarried Equality Organization

According to the mission statement identified on the website of the Unmarried Equality (http://www.unmarried .org), the emphasis of the organization is to advocate

> …for equality and fairness for unmarried people, including people who are single, choose not to marry, cannot marry, or live together before marriage. We provide support and information for this fast-growing constituency, fight discrimination on the basis of marital status, and educate the public and policymakers about relevant social and economic issues. We believe that marriage is only one of many acceptable family forms, and that society should recognize and support healthy relationships in all their diversity.

The Unmarried Equality organization exists, in part, because a stigma toward remaining single and never marrying remains. See the Personal View section which reveals the stereotypes, positives, and negatives of singlehood by one of the speakers in the author's marriage and family class.

2-1d Legal Blurring of the Married and Unmarried

The legal distinction between married and unmarried couples is blurring. Whether it is called the deregulation of marriage or the deinstitutionalization of marriage, the result is the same—more of the privileges previously

reserved for the married are now available to unmarried and/or same-sex couples. Domestic partnerships, recognized in some cities and by some corporations, convey rights and privileges (e.g., health benefits for a partner) previously available only to married people.

> Single is no longer a lack of options—but a choice. A choice to refuse to let your life be defined by your relationship status but to live every day Happily and let your Ever After work itself out.
>
> —MANDY HALE, *THE SINGLE WOMAN: LIFE, LOVE, AND A DASH OF SASS*

2-1e Categories of Singles

The term **singlehood** is most often associated with young unmarried individuals. However, there are three categories of single people: the never married, the divorced, and the widowed. Combined, there are 121 million single people in the United States (*Proquest Statistical Abstract of the United States, 2016*, Table 57).

NEVER-MARRIED SINGLES There are 81 million never-married adults aged 15 and over in the United States. What are the characteristics of those who never marry? Single men are likely to be less educated (Murray, 2012) and to have lower incomes (Ashwin & Isupova, 2014) than married men. Those who are never married (both women and men) also tend to be obese (Sobal & Hanson, 2011), to be at greater risk for a heart attack (Kilpi et al., 2015), and to have been reared in single-parent families (Valle & Tillma, 2014).

singlehood state of being unmarried.

> Many alternatives to marriage have emerged.
>
> —STEPHANIE COONTZ, AUTHOR/HISTORIAN

A Never-Married Single Woman's View of Singlehood

A never-married woman, 40 years of age, revealed her experience of being a single woman. The following is from the outline she used in making this presentation to the author's marriage and family class.

Stereotypes about Never-Married Women

Various assumptions are made about the never-married woman and why she is single. These include the following:

Unattractive. *She's either overweight or homely, or else she would have a man.*

Lesbian. *She has no real interest in men and marriage because she is homosexual.*

Workaholic. *She's career-driven and doesn't make time for relationships.*

Poor interpersonal skills. *She has no social skills, and she embarrasses men.*

History of abuse. *She has been turned off to men by the sexual abuse of, for example, her father, a relative, or a date.*

Negative previous relationships. *She's been rejected again and again and can't hold a man.*

Man-hater. *Deep down, she hates men.*

Frigid. *She hates sex and avoids men and intimacy.*

Promiscuous. *She is indiscriminate in her sexuality so that no man respects or wants her.*

Too picky. *She always finds something wrong with each partner and is never satisfied.*

Too weird. *She would win the Miss Weird contest, and no man wants her.*

Positive Aspects of Being Single

1. Freedom to define self in reference to own accomplishments, not in terms of attachments (e.g., spouse).

2. Freedom to pursue own personal and career goals and advance without the time restrictions posed by a spouse and children.

3. Freedom to come and go as you please and to do what you want, when you want.

4. Freedom to establish relationships with members of both sexes at desired level of intensity.

5. Freedom to travel and explore new cultures, ideas, and values.

Negative Aspects of Being Single

1. **Increased extended-family responsibilities.** The unmarried sibling is assumed to have the time to care for elderly parents.

2. **Increased job expectations.** The single employee does not have marital or family obligations and consequently can be expected to work at night, on weekends, and holidays.

3. **Isolation.** Too much time alone does not allow others to give feedback such as "Are you drinking too much?" "Have you had a checkup lately?" or "Are you working too much?"

4. **Decreased privacy.** Others assume the single person is always at home and always available. They may call late at night or drop in whenever they feel like it. They tend to ask personal questions freely.

5. **Less safety.** A single woman living alone is more vulnerable than a married woman with a man in the house.

Munsch (2015) emphasized that not all singles are stigmatized equally. Never-married singles are more stigmatized than divorced singles. And while singles in the workplace are assumed to be more competent and committed, the rewards to them compared to marrieds is not forthcoming. That there is still some stigma associated with being older and not being married, Jerry Seinfeld said when he was in his early forties: "I'm forty-two years old. I'm not married. That's not real mature. That's nothing to be proud of. You know, I should settle down by now" (Oppenheimer, 2002, p. 295). Seinfeld married two years later and now has three daughters.

The pressure is worse for single women. Even amid today's cultural approval of diverse lifestyles and

6. **Feeling different.** Many work-related events are for couples, husbands, and wives. A single woman sticks out.

7. **Lower income.** Single women have much lower incomes than married couples.

8. **Less psychological intimacy.** The single woman does not have an emotionally intimate partner at the end of the day.

9. **Negotiation skills lie dormant.** Because single people do not negotiate issues with someone on a regular basis, they may become deficient in compromise and negotiation skills.

10. **Patterns become entrenched.** Because no other person is around to express preferences, the single person may establish a very repetitive lifestyle.

Maximizing One's Life as a Single Person

1. **Frank discussion.** Talk with parents about your commitment to and enjoyment of the single lifestyle and request that they drop marriage references. Talk with siblings about joint responsibility for aging parents and your willingness to do your part. Talk with employers about spreading workload among all workers, not just those who are unmarried and childfree.

2. **Relationships.** Develop and nurture close relationships with parents, siblings, extended family, and friends to have a strong and continuing support system.

3. **Participate in social activities.** Go to social events with or without a friend. Avoid becoming a social isolate.

4. **Be cautious.** Be selective in sharing personal information such as your name, address, and phone number.

Oprah Winfrey is an example of a never-married woman who has maximized her life as a single person.

5. **Money.** Pursue education to maximize income; set up a retirement plan.

6. **Health.** Exercise, have regular checkups, and eat healthy food. Take care of yourself.

a woman's individual choice for singlehood, Budgeon (2016) notes that while women are free to enjoy whatever sexual relationships they want, they must "undertake whatever remedial measures necessary to make a 'good' relationship with a man work" (p. 414).

Stereotypes of singles abound. One is that singles are social isolates. Research by Sarkisian and Gerstel

(2016) demonstrates that singles have more contact with family and friends than spouses.

Are singles less happy than spouses? Yes. While over three-quarters of 5,500 single individuals reported that they were happy with their personal life (Walsh, 2013), when compared to those who are married, they are less happy. Rauer (2013) also compared the unmarried (she included divorced and widowed) with the married and found that the latter were happier, healthier, etc., and that these benefits were particularly pronounced in the elderly—that "the negative effects of being unmarried are disproportionately felt by older adults."

Increasingly, individuals are choosing to live alone: 28% of all households were single households in 2011 compared to 9% in 1950. And "why not?" asks sociologist Klinenberg (2012), "living alone helps to pursue sacred modern values such as individual freedom, personal control and self-realization." His book *Going Solo* reflects interviews with 300 who live alone and, for the most part, enjoy doing so. Eck (2013) interviewed single individuals and found most content in being unmarried.

DIVORCED SINGLES Another category of those who are single is the divorced. There were 15 million divorced females and 11 million divorced males in the United States in 2015 (*Proquest Statistical Abstract of the United States, 2016*, Table 56). While some divorced singles may have ended the marriage, others were terminated by their spouse. Hence, some are voluntarily single again while others are forced into being single again.

The divorced have a higher suicide risk. Denney (2010) examined the living arrangements of over 800,000 adults and found that being married or living with children decreases one's risk of suicide. Spouses are more likely to be "connected" to intimates; this "connection" seems to insulate a person from suicide. Of course, intimate connections can occur outside of marriage but marriage tends to ensure these connections over time.

Spouses look out for the health of each other. Spouses often prod each other to "go to the doctor," "have that rash on your skin looked at," and "remember to take your pills." Single people often have no one in their life to nudge them toward regular health maintenance.

WIDOWED SINGLES Although divorced people often choose to leave their spouses and be single again, the widowed are forced into singlehood. There are over 15 million widowed singles in the United States—11.3 million widowed females and 3.3 widowed males in the United States (*Proquest Statistical Abstract of the United States, 2016*, Table 56). Approximates a 10:1 ratio of females to males. The stereotype of the widow and widower is utter loneliness, even though there are compensations (e.g., escape from an unhappy marriage, social security). Kamiya et al. (2013) found that widowhood for men was associated with depressive symptoms. But this association was mitigated by income.

2-2 WAYS OF FINDING A PARTNER

Being connected to someone is a goal for many singles. In a sample of undergraduates at two universities, 47% of 7,582 women and 40% of 2,367 men reported that finding a partner with whom to have a happy marriage was a top value (Hall & Knox, 2016). In this section, we review the various ways of finding a partner to hang out with or to marry.

2-2a Hanging Out

Hanging out, also referred to as getting together, refers to going out in groups where the agenda is to meet others and have fun. The individuals may watch television, rent a DVD, go to a club or party, and/or eat out. Of 9,855 undergraduates, 91% reported that "hanging out for me is basically about meeting people and having fun" (Hall & Knox, 2016). Hanging out may occur in group settings such as at a bar, a sorority or fraternity party, or a small gathering of friends that keeps expanding. Friends may introduce individuals, or they may meet someone "cold," as in initiating a conversation. Hanging out is basically about screening and interviewing a number of potential partners in one setting. At a party, one can drift over to a potential who "looks good" and start talking. If there is chemistry in the banter and perceived interest from the person, the interaction will continue and can include the exchange of phone numbers for subsequent texting. If there is no chemistry, the individual can move on to the next person without having invested any significant time. Both partners are in the process of assessing the other.

hanging out going out in groups where the agenda is to meet others and have fun.

Bait and Switch in Online Dating Profiles?

Internet dating is rapidly becoming the most common way of meeting a partner. One posts a profile, identifies what he or she is looking for, and waits for interested persons to surface and express an interest. Researchers Jankowiak and Escasa-Dorne (2016) conducted a content analysis of profiles posted on a "large, casual sex dating website." The site is worldwide (e.g., United States, Europe, Asia, and Africa) and describes itself as an "adult personal website" where individuals can advertise themselves and seek like-minded individuals. A sample of 1,223 profiles was analyzed, most of whom were Caucasian, college educated, heterosexual, and age 30 or above.

Three types of profiles were identified in terms of what the individuals were looking for:

1. **Romance.** Preference for a continuous relationship (i.e., no one-night stands) or dating.
2. **Casual relationship.** Preference for meeting numerous partners and for sexual encounters.
3. **Mixed message.** Preference for a friends with benefits (FWB) relationship. Women wanted a partner who would be available for a weekend of walks, talks, dinner, movies, and sex; men wanted a sex partner who would meet at an appointed place for an allotted amount of time.

Of heterosexual women, over half reported preferring a romantic partner; 12% reported preferring casual sex or FWB. Those expressing an openness to casual sex reported that they had recently come out of a sexless marriage and wanted to feel sexually desirous again. Hence, they were looking for sexual validation rather than physiological pleasure.

The researchers emphasized that "the majority of heterosexual women's profiles, regardless of sexual explicitness, overwhelmingly noted a preference for sex within some type of ongoing or sought relationship. In this way, evidence of preference for sex with no strings attached or sexual variety for its own sake continues to be absent." That these profiles were posted on "an adult website" specific to sex suggests a "bait" and "switch" tactic, for example, I love sex but want this in the context of a relationship going somewhere.

These women were also specific about what they wanted. For example, one 24-year-old heterosexual woman wrote:

> I'm on the prowl for athletic guys that take very good care of their bodies and have a great style. Finally ended a bad relationship and am ready for something totally new and different. I'm fun, athletic blond and brown with crazy night and a very active day life. If you are fat or gross don't bother, yes you know who you are. My age limit is 26, if over that don't bother.

Maria McDonald

There is usually no agenda beyond meeting and having fun. Of the respondents noted above, only 6% said that hanging out was about beginning a relationship that may lead to marriage (Hall & Knox, 2016).

2-2b Hooking Up

Hooking up is a sexual encounter that occurs between individuals who have no relationship commitment.

Lewis et al. (2013) defined hooking up in their survey as: "event where you were physically intimate (any of the following: kissing, touching, oral sex, vaginal sex, anal sex) with someone whom you were not dating or in a romantic relationship with at the time and in which you understood there was no mutual expectation of a

> **hooking up** having a one-time sexual encounter in which there are generally no expectations of seeing one another again.

romantic commitment." Their sample of 1,468 revealed that, while definitions vary, most define hooking up as involving some type of sex (vaginal, oral, anal), not just kissing.

For those who hook up there is generally no expectation of seeing one another again and alcohol is often involved. Chang et al. (2012) identified the unspoken rules of hooking up—hooking up is not dating, hooking up is not a romantic relationship, hooking up is physical, hooking up is secret, one who hooks up is to expect no subsequent phone calls from their hooking up partner, and condom/protection should always occur (though only 57% of their sample reported condom use on hookups). Aubrey and Smith (2013) also noted that there is a set of cultural beliefs about hooking up. These beliefs include that hooking up is shameless/fun, will enhance one's status in one's peer group, and reflects one's sexual freedom/control over one's sexuality.

LaBrie et al. (2014) noted the effect of drinking alcohol on hooking up. Of 828 college students, over half (55%) reported hooking up in the last year. Of those who hooked up 31% of the females and 28% of the males reported that they would not have hooked up had they not been drinking. A similar percent reported they would not have gone as far physically had they not been drinking. Females who had been drinking and hooked up were more likely to feel discontent with their hookup decisions.

Hooking up is becoming the norm on college and university campuses. Not only do female students outnumber men students (60 to 40) (which means women are less able to bargain sex for commitment since men have a lot of options), individuals want to remain free for summer internships, study abroad, and marriage later

(Uecker & Regnerus, 2011). Allison (2016) reported that 13% of college students hook up 6 to 15 times compared to 31% of male athletes.

The hooking up experience is also variable. Bradshaw et al. (2010) compared the experiences of women and men who hooked up. Men benefited more since they were able to have casual sex with a willing partner and no commitment. Women were more at risk for feeling regret/guilt, becoming depressed, and defining the experience negatively. About a quarter of hookup experiences transition into a romantic relationship (Erichsen & Dignan, 2016).

2-2c The Internet: Meeting Online

Increasingly, individuals are using the Internet (and attendant technology) to find partners for fun, companionship, and marriage. Based on a sample of 2,252 adults, almost 40% (38%) of Americans who are currently single and actively looking for a partner have used online dating. Of these almost two-thirds (66%) have been out on a date with someone they met through a dating site or app. Almost a quarter have met their spouse or a long-term partner through these sites (Smith & Duggan, 2013).

Sociologist Rosenfeld of Stanford University followed 926 unmarried couples over a three-year period—those who met online were twice as likely to marry as those offline, 13% to 6%. Twenty percent of all new relationships begin online (Jayson, 2013).

INTERNET PARTNERS: THE UPSIDE In regard to advantages, a primary attraction of meeting someone

This couple met on Tinder. They were not hookups but quickly became a stable long-term couple who moved in together.

Finding Tinderella Tonight

The global positioning system, or GPS, is a satellite-based navigation system originally intended for military use. Civilian use of GPS became available in the 1980s, and adaptations have included finding a partner to hook up with. Geosocial dating apps such as Grindr and Tinder have altered the landscape of finding a partner/hooking up. Tinder is the largest U.S. dating app, available worldwide in many languages, and estimated to be worth $1.6 billion (Cook, 2015). Every day, more than 26 million "matches" are made (Holden, 2015), and 1.6 billion profiles are viewed on Tinder (Trenholm, 2015).

After selecting age group, proximity, and gender, Tinder users have access to a large pool of potential partners immediately. Swiping to the right ("liking the picture") and swiping to the left ("not liking the picture") in real time is a quick and easy way to find a potential partner. If the attraction is mutual, Tinder notifies the two users of a "new match" and the users may start communicating. Since one's photo determines which way one is "swiped," posting a high-quality/attractive solo picture is the first step in online dating (Holden, 2015). The first text message will also need to break the ice, convey a positive self-image, and lead to more conversation (Chang & Kennedy, 2001).

Swiping (Tinder), liking (Facebook), or winking (Match) reflect that there are hundreds of dating sites and apps. The term *attention deficit daters* has been used to describe current singles who are flooded with dating options, yet have very low attention spans (Ruiz, 2014).

There are downsides from Tinder use. Using a photo as the sole foundation of a potential date and getting a "match" may give the users a false sense of compatibility (Finkel, 2015). Although hooking up has been prevalent among young adults years before Tinder was launched, Tinder has been accused of causing a "dating apocalypse," where users bypass romance and courtship and dive directly into hooking up (Sales, 2015). Traditional dating has become antiquated. Calling up someone several days ahead of time to ask for a "date," going out to eat/seeing a movie, making out in the car, and saying goodnight underneath the parents' porch light have vanished as the dating script of today's youth. "Hooking up," said one of our students, "and then getting to know each other is the new norm." Finding a partner begins with swiping for Mr. Tinder or Tinderella.

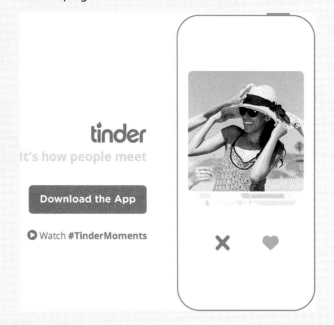

online is efficiency. It takes time and effort to meet someone at a coffee shop for an hour, only to discover that the person has habits (e.g., does or does not smoke) or values (e.g., religious or agnostic) that would eliminate them as a potential partner. On the Internet, one can spend a short period of time and literally scan hundreds of profiles of potential partners. For noncollege people who are busy in their job or career, the Internet offers the chance to meet someone outside their immediate social circle. "There are only six guys in my office," noted one female Internet user. "Four are married and the other two are alcoholics. I don't go to church and don't like bars so the Internet has become my guy store."

Another advantage of looking for a partner online is that it removes emotion/chemistry/first meeting magic from the mating equation so that individuals can focus on finding someone with common interests, background, values, and goals. Some websites exist to target persons with specific interests such as Black singles (BlackPlanet.com), Jewish singles (Jdate.com), and gay people (Gay.com).

Pros:
- Highly efficient
- Develop a relationship without visual distraction
- Avoid crowded, uncomfortable locations, like bars
- Can disappear quickly if want to

Online Meeting

Cons:
- Deceptive
- Fall in love too quickly
- Can't assess "chemistry" through computer screen
- Can't assess nonverbal behavior

INTERNET PARTNERS: THE DOWNSIDE There are also downsides to meeting on the Internet. Lying occurs in Internet dating (as it does in non-Internet dating). Hall et al. (2010) analyzed data from 5,020 individuals who posted profiles on the Internet in search of a date who revealed seven categories of misrepresentation. These included personal assets ("I own a house at the beach"), relationship goals ("I want to get married'), personal interests ("I love to exercise"), personal attributes ("I am religious"), past relationships ("I have only been married once"), weight, and age. Men were most likely to misrepresent personal assets, relationship goals, and personal interests whereas women were more likely to misrepresent weight. Lo et al. (2013) noted that deception is motivated by the level of attractiveness of the target person—higher deception if the target person is particularly attractive. In addition, women were more deceptive than men.

Some online users also lie about being single. They are married, older, and divorced more times than they reveal. But to suggest that the Internet is the only place where deceivers lurk is to turn a blind eye to those people met through traditional channels. Be suspicious of everyone until you know otherwise.

It is important to be cautious of meeting someone online. Although the Internet is a good place to meet new people, it also allows someone you rejected or an old lover to monitor your online behavior. Most sites note when you have been online last, so if you reject someone online by saying, "I'm really not ready for a relationship," that same person can log on and see that you are still looking. Some individuals become obsessed with a person they meet online and turn into a cyber stalker when rejected. A quarter of the respondents in the Pew Research Center study said they were harassed or made to feel uncomfortable by someone they had met online (Smith & Duggan, 2013). Some people also use the Internet to try on new identities. For example, a person who feels he or she is attracted to same-sex individuals may present a gay identity online.

Other disadvantages of online meeting include the potential to fall in love too quickly as a result of intense mutual disclosure; not being able to assess "chemistry" or how a person interacts with your friends or family; the tendency to move too quickly (from texting to phone to meeting to first date) to marriage, without spending much time to get to know each other and not being able to observe nonverbal behavior. In regard to the nonverbal issue, Kotlyar and Ariely (2013) emphasized the importance of using Skype (which allows one to see the partner/assess nonverbal cues) as soon as possible and as a prelude to meeting in person to provide more information about the person behind the profile.

Another disadvantage of using the Internet to find a partner is that having an unlimited number of options sometimes results in not looking carefully at the options one has. Wu and Chiou (2009) studied undergraduates looking for romantic partners on the Internet who had 30, 60, and 90 people to review and found that the more options the person had, the less time the undergraduate spent carefully considering each profile. The researchers concluded that it was better to examine a small number of potential online partners carefully than to be distracted by a large pool of applicants, which does not permit the time for close scrutiny.

It is also important to use Internet dating sites safely, including not giving out home or business phone numbers or addresses, always meeting the person in one's own town with a friend, and not posting photos that are "too revealing," as these can be copied and posted elsewhere. Take it slow—after connecting in an email through the dating site, move to instant messages, texting, phone calls, Skyping, then meet in a public place with friends near. Also, be clear about what you want (e.g., "If you are looking for a hookup, keep moving. If you are looking for a lifetime partner, 'I'm your gal'").

APPS Online dating is moving from websites to apps on mobile devices. Seven percent of smartphone users say they have used a dating app on their phone (Smith & Duggan, 2013). Tinder.com (on the basis of a photo) allows one to identify and connect with someone (who also selected their photo) in the area. Some users of Tinder.com refer to it as "the newest hookup device."

2-2d Speed-Dating: The Eight-Minute Date

Dating innovations that involve the concept of speed include the eight-minute date. The website http://www.8minutedating.com/ these "Eight-Minute Dating Events" throughout the country, where a person has eight one-on-one "dates" at a bar that last eight minutes each. If both parties are interested in seeing each other again, the organizer provides contact information so that the individuals can set up another date. Speed-dating saves time because it allows daters to meet face to face without burning up a whole evening.

Rangizzz/Shutterstock.com

2-2e International Dating

Go to Google.com and type in "international brides," and you will see an array of sites dedicated to finding foreign women for Americans. American males often seek women from Asian countries who are thought to be more traditional. Women from other countries seek American males as a conduit for entry into U.S. citizenship.

> She affected me, even when she was absent.
>
> —SHANNON A. THOMPSON,
> *SECONDS BEFORE SUNRISE*

SIX FUNCTIONS OF INVOLVEMENT WITH A PARTNER

1. Confirmation of a social self
2. Recreation
3. Companionship, intimacy, and sex
4. Anticipatory socialization
5. Status achievement
6. Mate selection

2-3 LONG-DISTANCE RELATIONSHIPS

About 4.5 million college students (33% of all college relationships) are in nonmarital long-distance relationships (Miss Your Mate, 2015). These relationships may have begun online or resulted in partners needing to pursue education or career opportunities apart from each other. Regardless of the reason for being in a long-distance relationship, the partners are "regretfully apart"—they would choose to be physically together (Jurkane-Hobein, 2015). Hence, they are not like the living apart together (discussed later) who deliberately choose to live in separate households.

There is considerable reluctance to become involved in a long-distance relationship. In a sample of 5,500 never-married undergraduates, about half (51% of the men and 47% of the women) reported that a long-distance relationship was "out of the question" (Walsh, 2013).

This couple met on the Internet, married, and were in a long-distance relationship due to their respective jobs for three years before retirement when they were able to live together full-time.

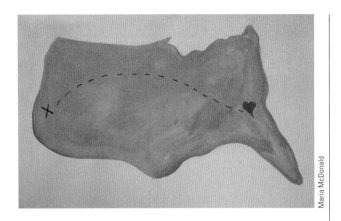

Maria McDonald

The primary advantages of **long-distance dating relationships (LDDRs)** (defined here as being separated from a romantic partner by 500 or more miles, which precludes regular weekly face-to-face contact) include: positive labeling ("even though we are separated, we care about each other enough to maintain our relationship"), keeping the relationship "high" since constant togetherness may result in the partners being less attentive to each other, having time to devote to school or a career, and having a lot of one's own personal time and space. A comparison of 474 women and 243 men in long-distance dating relationships and 314 women and 111 men in geographically close relationships revealed few differences in the respective type of relationships. The researchers concluded that individuals in long-distance dating relationships are not at a disadvantage and that relationship and individual characteristics predict relationship quality (Dargie et al., 2015).

People suited for such relationships have developed their own autonomy or independence for the times they are apart, have a focus for their time such as school or a job, have developed open communication with their partner to talk about the difficulty of being separated, and have learned to trust each other because they spend a lot of time away from each other. Another advantage is that the partner may actually look better from afar than up close. One respondent noted that he and his partner could not wait to live together after they had been separated—but "when we did, I found out I liked her better when she wasn't there." The primary disadvantages of long-distance relationships include being frustrated over not being able to be with the partner and loneliness. Du Bois et al. (2016) found greater relationship stress. Other disadvantages of involvement in a long-distance relationship are missing out on other activities and relationships, less physical intimacy, spending a lot of money on phone calls/ travel, and not discussing important relationship topics.

For couples who have the goal of maintaining their LDDRs and reducing the chance that the distance will result in their breaking up, some specific behaviors to engage in include:

1. **Maintain daily contact via text messaging.** Texting allows individuals to stay in touch throughout the day.

2. **Enjoy/use the time when apart.** While separated, it is important to remain busy with study, friends, work, sports, and personal projects.

3. **Avoid arguing during phone conversations.** Talking on the phone should involve the typical sharing of events. When the need to discuss a difficult topic arises (e.g., trust), the phone is not the best place for such a discussion. Rather, it may be wiser to wait and have the discussion face to face.

4. **Stay monogamous.** Agreeing not to be open to other relationships is crucial to maintaining a long-distance relationship (LDR). Individuals who say, "Let's date others to see if we are really meant to be together," often discover that they are capable of being attracted to and becoming involved with numerous "others."

5. **Skype.** Skyping allows the partners to see and hear each other. Frequent Skype encounters allow the partners to "date" even though they cannot touch each other. Some partners also become sexual by stripping for each other, which is a way of being intimate with each other while physically separated.

6. **Be creative.** Some partners in long-distance relationships watch Netflix's movies together—they each pull up the movie on their computer and talk on the phone while they watch it. Others send video links, photos, etc., throughout the day.

2-4 COHABITATION

Cohabitation, also known as living together, involves two adults, unrelated by blood or by law, involved in an emotional and sexual relationship who sleep in the same

long-distance dating relationship (LDDR) lovers are separated by a distance, usually 500 miles, which prevents weekly face-to-face contact.

cohabitation (living together) two unrelated adults (by blood or by law) involved in an emotional and sexual relationship who sleep in the same residence at least four nights a week for three months.

This couple represent the "engaged and planning to marry" category of cohabitation. While not formally engaged, they are planning their lives together.

residence at least four nights a week for three months. Seven million other-sex couples and 727,000 same-sex couples cohabit. Not all cohabitants are college students. Indeed, only 12% of other-sex cohabitants and 4% of same-sex cohabitants are under the age of 25. The largest percentage are between the ages of 25 and 34—35% of other sex and 16.5% of same sex. Most cohabitants are White (76%) or Black (11%) (*Proquest Statistical Abstract of the United States, 2016*, Table 75). The average duration of a cohabitation relationship among young individuals is two years (Manning & Brown, 2015). Cohabitation has become a stage through which couples pass on their way to marriage (Sassler et al., 2016). Based on a national sample of 2,774 individuals aged 18–39 who had begun a sexual relationship, 27% reported cohabiting within 12 months (Sassler et al., 2016). Being older, having stepparents, and being White were associated with an increased chance of cohabitation.

Reasons for the increase in cohabitation include career or educational commitments; increased tolerance of society, parents, and peers; improved birth control technology; desire for a stable emotional and sexual relationship without legal ties; avoiding loneliness; and greater disregard for convention. Two-thirds of 122 cohabiters reported concerns about divorce (Miller et al., 2011).

2-4a Nine Types of Cohabitation Relationships

There are various types of cohabitation:

1. **Here and now.** These new partners have a fun relationship and are focused on the here and now, not the future of the relationship.

2. **Testers.** These couples are involved in a relationship and want to assess whether they have a future together.

3. **Engaged.** These cohabiting couples are in love and are planning to marry. Engaged cohabitant couples who have an agreed upon future report the highest level of satisfaction, the lowest level of conflict, and, in general, have a higher quality relationship than other types of cohabitants (Willoughby et al., 2012). After three years, 40% of first premarital cohabitants end up getting married, 32% are still cohabiting, and 27% have broken up.

4. **Money savers.** These couples live together primarily out of economic convenience. They are open to the possibility of a future together but regard such a possibility as unlikely.

5. **Pension partners.** These cohabitation partners are older, have been married before, still derive benefits from their previous relationships, and are living with someone new. Getting married would mean giving up their pension benefits from the previous marriage.

6. **Alimony maintenance.** Related to widows who cohabit are the divorced who are collecting alimony which they would forfeit should they remarry.

7. **Security blanket cohabiters.** Some of the individuals in these cohabitation relationships are drawn to each other out of a need for security rather than mutual attraction. Being alone is not an option. They want somebody, anybody, in the house.

8. **Rebellious cohabiters.** Some couples use cohabitation as a way of making a statement to their parents that they are independent and can make their own choices. Their cohabitation is more about rebelling from parents than being drawn to each other.

9. **Marriage never (cohabitants forever).** Ten percent of cohabitants view their living together not as a prelude to marriage but as a way of life (Sommers et al., 2013). The respective cohabitant partners in a relationship may differ in terms of whether they want to marry. In a sample of 1,837 couples who were cohabitating, those relationships in which only one partner wanted to delay getting married and placed a lower importance on marriage were associated with less stability, poorer

communication, and lower relationship satisfaction (Willoughby & Belt, 2016).

Some couples who view their living together as "permanent" seek to have it defined as a **domestic partnership**, a relationship involving two adults who have chosen to share each other's lives in an intimate and committed relationship of mutual caring

2-4b Does Cohabitation Result in Marriages That Last?

Individuals who live together before getting married assume that doing so will increase their chances of having a happy and durable marriage relationship. But will it? Researchers disagree and some research suggests that "It depends." For individuals (particularly women, Manning & Cohen, 2012) who have only one cohabitation experience with the person they eventually marry, there is no increased risk of divorce (Jose et al., 2010). In contrast, Coontz (2016) says that cohabitation no longer raises the risk of divorce.

Cohabitation may be disadvantageous to the couple who marry if they do so in reference to structure and restraints. Rhoades et al. (2012) studied 120 cohabiting couples and found that restraints often keep a couple together. These include signing a lease, having a joint bank account, and having a pet. In some cases couples may move forward toward marriage for reasons of constraint rather than emotional desire. Whatever the reason, cohabitants should not assume that cohabitation will make them happier spouses or insulate them from divorce.

Kuperberg (2014) provided data to confirm that previous research linking cohabitation with divorce did not account for the age at which coresidence began. She suggested that it is the age at which individuals begin their lives together (coresidence) which impacts divorce, not cohabitation per se. She suggested that individuals delay their marriage into their mid-twenties "when they are older and more established in the lives, goals and careers, whether married or not at the time of co-residence rather than avoiding premarital cohabitation altogether" (p. 368). It is also important to keep in mind that marriage does not always result from cohabitation. In Iceland, living together and having children is normative. Marriage is not the social context of adulthood (Roberts, 2016).

domestic partnership
a relationship in which individuals who live together are emotionally and financially interdependent and are given some kind of official recognition by a city or corporation so as to receive partner benefits.

living apart together (LAT)
a long-term committed couple who does not live in the same dwelling.

LIVING APART TOGETHER

The definition of **living apart together (LAT)** is a long-term committed couple who does not live in the same dwelling. Some couples (including spouses) find that living apart together is preferable to their living in the same place (Hess, 2012). In a study of 68 adults (93% married), 7% reported that they preferred a LAT arrangement with their spouse. Forty-six percent said that living apart from your spouse enhances your relationship (Jacinto & Ahrend, 2012). The Census Bureau estimates that 1.7 million married couples are living in this arrangement (Gottman, 2013).

Three criteria must be met for a couple to be defined as a living apart together couple: (1) they must define themselves as a committed couple; (2) others must define the partners as a couple; and (3) they must live in separate domiciles. The lifestyle of living apart together involves partners in loving and committed relationships (married or unmarried) identifying their independent needs in terms of the degree to which they want time and space away from each other. People living apart together exist on a continuum from partners who have separate bedrooms and baths in the same house to those who live in a separate place (apartment, condo, house) in the same or different cities. LAT couples are not those couples who are forced by their career or military assignment to live separately. Rather, LAT partners choose to live in separate domiciles and feel that their relationship benefits from the LAT structure.

2-5a LAT Structure

LAT is the end point for couples who enjoy this lifestyle—they are unlikely to cohabit or to marry (Brown et al., 2016). The primary reason for LAT participants to maintain separate domiciles is to preserve their autonomy, not because they are less committed to each other (Brown et al., 2016).

LAT may also become more frequent among the elderly. Benson and Coleman (2016) interviewed a sample of elderly individuals in regard to their feelings about LAT. While they ranged from rejection to ambivalence to advocacy, it is clear that age was involved. One of the respondents said:

I reasoned it out that if we were young people going to start a family, I would not do this. I would never have done this before marriage and neither would he, as a young person. But it's different because, you are not, it's not affecting the family whatsoever. You're not

The author and his partner lived in this two-unit condominium structure for 12 years. The author owned the unit upstairs; his partner owned the unit downstairs. Each had children from a former marriage so it was easier to provide a living space for the respective families, yet they could all live close to each other. After the children left home, the couple sold the units and moved into a house together. They married about half way through their living apart together arrangement.

gonna have children, but you need this, you need this loving, and I had not had much [in my marriage].

The living apart together lifestyle or family form is not unique to couples in the United States (e.g., the phenomenon is more prevalent in European countries such as France, Sweden, and Norway). Couples choose to maintain separate domiciles primarily to preserve their autonomy, not because they are less committed to each other. Sixty-one percent of a national sample of 578 living apart individuals report that they are "very happy"; their level of commitment is 4.2 out 5 (Brown et al., 2016).

Upton-Davis (2015) interviewed 20 women over the age of 45 who had chosen the living apart together arrangement (over cohabitation). Here is a excerpt from one of the interviews:

"So I'm curious Celia, is your LAT relationship something you sat down and talked about or did it just evolve into a LAT?"

"It definitely just evolved. Larry and I have been together 10 years now and I think at the start we were both thinking we would move in together—he was thinking that more than I was I think. But as time went by and the relationship was working out so well the way it was I thought why change it?

Larry is gorgeous, generous, my family adores him, and he gets on socially with everyone. But honestly I don't think we would last five minutes if we lived together."

"Why's that?"

"I like my space. Besides, Larry and I are very different, we like different things. He has a very nice house just a couple of suburbs away, it's very nice—but it's not my cup of tea if you know what I mean," she adds quietly.

I look around her apartment, at the carefully placed, internationally acquired object d'art and can imagine what she means. (Upton-Davis, 2015, p. 8)

2-5b Advantages of LAT

The benefits of LAT relationships include the following:

1. **Space and privacy.** Having two places enables each partner to have a separate space to read, watch TV, talk on the phone, or whatever. This not only provides a measure of privacy for the individuals, but also as a couple. When the couple has overnight guests, the guests can stay in one place while the partners stay in the other place. This arrangement gives guests ample space and the couple private space and time apart from the guests.

2. **Career or work space.** Some individuals work at home and need a controlled quiet space to work on projects, talk on the phone, and focus on their work without the presence of someone else. The LAT arrangement is particularly appealing to musicians for practicing, artists to spread out their materials, and authors for quiet (Hemingway built a separate building where he would do his writing in Key West).

3. **Variable sleep needs.** Although some partners enjoy going to bed at the same time and sleeping in the same bed, others like to go to bed at radically different times and to sleep in separate beds or rooms.

4. **Allergies.** Individuals who have cat or dog allergies may need to live in a separate antiseptic environment from their partner who loves animals and would not live without them. "He likes his dog on the bed," said one woman.

5. **Variable social needs.** Partners differ in terms of their need for social contact with friends, siblings,

and parents. The LAT arrangement allows for the partner who enjoys frequent time with others to satisfy that need without subjecting the other to the presence of a lot of people in one's life space. One wife from a family of seven children enjoyed frequent contact with both her siblings and parents. The LAT arrangement allowed her to continue to enjoy her family at no expense to her husband who was upstairs in a separate condo.

6. **Blended family needs.** LAT works particularly well with a blended family in which remarried spouses live in separate places with their children from previous relationships.

7. **Keeping the relationship exciting.** The term **satiation** is a well-established psychological principle. The term means that a stimulus loses its value with repeated exposure. Just as we tire of eating the same food, listening to the same music, or watching the same movie, so satiation is relevant to relationships. Indeed, couples who are in a long-distance dating relationship know the joy of "missing" each other and the excitement of being with each other again. Similarly, individuals in a LAT relationship help ensure that they will not "satiate" on each other but maintain some of the excitement in seeing or being with each other.

8. **Self-expression and comfort.** Partners often have very different tastes in furniture, home décor, music, and temperature. With two separate places, each can arrange and furnish their respective homes according to their individual preferences. The respective partners can also set the heat or air conditioning according to their own preferences, and play whatever music they like.

9. **Cleanliness or orderliness.** Separate residences allow each partner to maintain the desired level of cleanliness and orderliness without arguing about it. Some individuals like their living space to be as ordered as a cockpit. Others simply do not care.

10. **Elder care.** One partner may be taking care of an elderly parent in his or her own house. The partner may prefer not to live with an elderly parent. A LAT relationship allows for the partner taking care of the elderly parent to do so and a place for the couple to be alone.

> **satiation** a stimulus loses its value with repeated exposure or people get tired of each other if they spend relentless amounts of time with each other.

11. **Maintaining one's lifetime residence.** Some retirees, widows, and widowers meet, fall in love, and want to enjoy each other's companionship. However, they don't want to move out of their own home. The LAT arrangement does not require that the partners move.

12. **Leaving inheritances to children from previous marriages.** Having separate residences allows the respective partners to leave their family home or residential property to their biological children from an earlier relationship without displacing their surviving spouse.

2-5c Disadvantages of LAT

There are also disadvantages of the LAT lifestyle.

1. **Stigma or disapproval.** Because the norm that married couples move in together is firmly entrenched, couples who do not do so are suspect. "People who love each other should want to live in their own house together . . . those who live apart aren't really committed" is the traditional perception of people in a committed relationship.

2. **Cost.** The cost of two separate living places can be more expensive than two people living in one domicile. But there are ways LAT couples afford their lifestyle. Some live in two condominiums that are cheaper than owning one larger house. Others buy housing out of high-priced real estate areas. One partner said, "We bought a duplex 10 miles out of town where the price of housing is 50% cheaper than in town. We have our LAT context and it didn't cost us a fortune."

3. **Inconvenience.** Unless the partners live in a duplex or two units in the same condominium, going between the two places to share meals or be together can be inconvenient.

4. **Lack of shared history.** Because the adults are living in separate quarters, a lot of what goes on in each house does not become a part of the life history of the couple.

 Self-Assessment: Living Apart Together (LAT) Scale
Take the Living Apart Together (LAT) Scale at the end of the chapter to assess your suitability for this lifestyle.

5. **No legal protection.** The legal nature of the LAT relationship is ambiguous. Currently there are no legal protections in the United States for LAT partners as there are for spouses.

2-6 TRENDS IN SINGLEHOOD

Singlehood will (in the cultural spirit of diversity) lose some of its stigma; more young adults will choose this option; and those who remain single will, increasingly, find satisfaction in this lifestyle.

Individuals will continue to be in no hurry to get married. Completing their education, becoming established in their career, and enjoying hanging out and hooking up will continue to delay serious consideration of marriage. The median age for women getting married is 27; for men, 29. This trend will continue as individuals keep their options open in America's individualistic society.

Cohabitation will become the typical first union for young adults (Guzzo, 2014). The percent of cohabitants will increase not just for those who live together before marriage (now about two-thirds) but also in the prevalence of serial cohabitation (Vespa, 2014). Previously, only those rebelling against the institution of marriage lived together (Trost, 2016). Today, cohabitation has become normative and fewer will transition to marriage, even among the engaged (Guzzo, 2014). Living apart together will also increase, particularly among middle and older adults who have less to gain from cohabitation or marriage (Brown et al., 2016).

STUDY TOOLS 2

READY TO STUDY? IN THE BOOK, YOU CAN:

☐ Rip out the chapter review card at the back of the book for a handy summary of the chapter and key terms.

☐ Assess yourself with the following self-assessments.

ONLINE AT CENGAGEBRAIN.COM YOU CAN:

☐ Collect StudyBits while you read and study the chapter.

☐ Quiz yourself on key concepts.

☐ Prepare for tests with M&F4 Flash Cards as well as those you create.

SELF-ASSESSMENT

Attitudes toward Singlehood Scale

The purpose of this survey is to assess the degree to which students view remaining single (never getting married) positively. Read each item carefully and consider what you believe. There are no right or wrong answers, so please give your honest reaction and opinion. After reading each statement, select the number that best reflects your level of agreement, using the following scale:

1	2	3	4	5	6	7
Strongly disagree						*Strongly agree*

_____ **1.** I plan to remain single.

_____ **2.** Getting married is not as advantageous as it used to be.

_____ **3.** Marriage is another word for being trapped.

_____ **4.** Singlehood is another word for being free.

_____ **5.** Single people are happier than married people.

_____ **6.** Most of the married people I know are unhappy.

_____ **7.** Most of the single people I know enjoy their lifestyle.

_____ **8.** The statement that singles are lonely and unhappy is not true.

_____ **9.** It is better to be single than to be married.

_____ **10.** Of the two lifestyle choices, single or married, single is better.

_____ **11.** Singles have more friendships/social connections than spouses.

_____ **12.** Singles have a greater sense of independence than spouses.

_____ **13.** Being single is a more satisfying lifestyle than being married.

_____ **14.** People who think you must be married to be happy are wrong.

_____ **15.** You can be alone and not be lonely.

_____ **16.** The freedom of singlehood outweighs any advantage of marriage.

_____ **17.** The companionship of marriage is overrated.

_____ **18.** Singles have better sex than spouses.

_____ **19.** The idea that only spouses are fulfilled is nonsense.

_____ **20.** Marriage as a lifestyle is overrated.

_____ **21.** Most people who are married have envy for those who are single.

_____ **22.** Spouses lose control of their lives while singles maintain control.

_____ **23.** There is entirely too much social pressure to get married.

_____ **24.** People are finding out that being single is a better deal than being married.

_____ **25.** The singles I know are happier than the spouses I know.

Scoring

After assigning a number from 1 (strongly disagree) to 7 (strongly agree), add the numbers. The higher your score (175 is the highest possible score), the more positively you view remaining single. The lower your score (25 is the lowest possible score), the more negatively you view singlehood. A score of 75 is the midpoint. Scores below 75 tend to reflect a negative view of singlehood while scores above 75 reflect a positive view of singlehood.

Norms

A score of 75 is the midpoint. Scores below 75 tend to reflect a negative view of singlehood while scores above 75 reflect a positive view of singlehood. The norming sample of this self-assessment was based on the responses of 187 undergraduates (24 men and 163 women) at a large southeastern university. The mean score for the total sample was 86. The mean for the men was 95; for the women, 85. Hence, the total sample tended to regard singlehood positively with men having more positive attitudes toward singlehood than women.

Source: "Attitudes toward Singlehood Scale," 2014, by Mark Whatley, Ph.D., Department of Psychology, Valdosta State University, Valdosta, GA 31698-0100. Used by permission. Other uses of this scale only by written permission of Dr. Whatley (mwhatley@valdosta.edu). This scale is intended to provide basic feedback about one's view of singlehood. It is not designed to be a sophisticated research instrument.

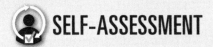 **SELF-ASSESSMENT**

Living Apart Together (LAT) Scale

This scale will help you assess the degree to which you might benefit from living in a separate residence from your spouse or partner with whom you have a lifetime commitment. There are no right or wrong answers.

Directions

After reading each sentence carefully, circle the number that best represents the degree to which you agree or disagree with the sentence.

1	2	3	4	5
Strongly agree	*Mildly agree*	*Undecided*	*Mildly disagree*	*Strongly disagree*

		SA	MA	U	MD	SD
1.	I prefer to have my own place (apart from my partner) to live.	1	2	3	4	5
2.	Living apart from my partner feels "right" to me.	1	2	3	4	5
3.	Too much togetherness can kill a relationship.	1	2	3	4	5
4.	Living apart can enhance your relationship.	1	2	3	4	5
5.	By living apart you can love your partner more.	1	2	3	4	5
6.	Living apart protects your relationship from staleness.	1	2	3	4	5
7.	Couples who live apart are just as happy as those who don't.	1	2	3	4	5
8.	Couples who LAT are just as much in love as those who live together in the same place.	1	2	3	4	5
9.	People who LAT probably have less relationship stress than couples who live together in the same place.	1	2	3	4	5
10.	LAT couples are just as committed as couples who live together in the same residence.	1	2	3	4	5

Scoring

Add the numbers you circled. The lower your total score (10 is the lowest possible score), the more suited you are to the living apart together lifestyle. The higher your total score (50 is the highest possible score), the least suited you are to the living apart together lifestyle. A score of 25 places you at the midpoint between being the extremes. One hundred and thirty undergraduates completed the LAT scale with an average score of 28.92, which suggests that both sexes view themselves as less rather than more suited (30 is the midpoint between the lowest score of 10 and the highest score of 50) for a LAT arrangement with females registering greater disinterest than males.

3 | Revealing Gender in Relationships

After finishing this chapter go to **PAGE 61** for **STUDY TOOLS**

Girls can be athletic. Guys can have feelings. Girls can be smart. Guys can be creative. And vice versa. Gender is specific only to your reproductive organs (and sometimes not even to those), not your interests, likes, dislikes, goals, and ambitions.

— CONNOR FRANTA, *A WORK IN PROGRESS*

Issues related to gender continue to be visible. Caitlyn Jenner remains a force in her transition, Jeffrey Tambor won an Emmy for outstanding lead actor in a comedy series-Transparent, and the workplace/politics has an embarrassing absence of female CEOs and senators.

Sociologists note that one of the defining moments in an individual's life is when the sex of a fetus (in the case of an ultrasound) or an infant (in the case of a birth) is announced. "It's a boy" or "It's a girl" immediately summons an onslaught of cultural programming affecting the color of the nursery (blue for a boy and pink for a girl), name of the baby (there are few gender-free names such as Chris), and sport participation alternatives (e.g., volleyball but not golf). The social script for women and men is radically different so that being identified as either is to put one's life on a path quite different than if the person had been reared as the other gender. In this chapter, we examine variations in gender roles and how they impact relationships. We begin by looking at the terms used to discuss gender issues.

3-1 TERMINOLOGY OF GENDER ROLES

In common usage, the terms *sex* and *gender* are often interchangeable, but sociologists, family or consumer science educators, human development specialists, and health educators do not find these terms synonymous. After clarifying the distinction between *sex* and *gender*, we discuss other relevant terminology, including *gender identity*, *gender role*, and *gender role ideology*.

3-1a Sex

Sex refers to the biological distinction between females and males. Hence, to be assigned as a female or male, several factors are used to determine the biological sex of an individual:

▶ **Chromosomes.** XX for females; XY for males

▶ **Gonads.** Ovaries for females; testes for males

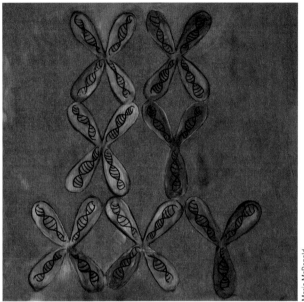

Maria McDonald

▶ **Hormones.** Greater proportion of estrogen and progesterone than testosterone in females; greater proportion of testosterone than estrogen and progesterone in males

▶ **Internal sex organs.** Fallopian tubes, uterus, and vagina for females; epididymis, vas deferens, and seminal vesicles for males

▶ **External genitals.** Vulva for females; penis and scrotum for males

Even though we commonly think of biological sex as consisting of two dichotomous categories (female and male), biological sex exists on a continuum. Sometimes not all of the five bulleted items just listed are found neatly in one person (who would be labeled as a female or a male). Rather, items typically associated with females or males might be found together in one person, resulting in mixed or ambiguous genitals; such persons are called **intersexed individuals**.

sex the biological distinction between being female and being male.

intersexed individuals people with mixed or ambiguous genitals.

Indeed, the genitals in these intersexed (or middlesexed) individuals (about 2% of all births) are not clearly male or female. **Intersex development** refers to congenital variations in the reproductive system, sometimes resulting in ambiguous genitals. The self-concept of these individuals is variable. Some may view themselves as one sex or the other or as a mix. Since our culture does not know how to relate to mixed sex individuals, the individual is typically reared as a woman or as a man. However, an intersexed person who is reared as and presents as a woman may have no ovaries and will not be able to have children.

3-1b Gender

The term **gender** is a social construct and refers to the social and psychological characteristics associated with being female or male. Women are often thought of as soft, passive, and cooperative; men as rough, aggressive, and forceful (Clemans & Graber, 2016). In popular usage, gender is dichotomized as an either-or concept (feminine or masculine). Each gender has some characteristics of the other. However, gender may also be viewed as existing along a continuum of femininity and masculinity.

Gender differences are a consequence of biological (e.g., chromosomes and hormones) and social factors (e.g., male/female models such as parents, siblings, peers). The biological provides a profound foundation for gender role development. Evidence for this biological influence is the experience of the late John Money, psychologist and former director of the now-defunct Gender Identity Clinic at Johns Hopkins University School of Medicine, who encouraged the parents of a boy (Bruce Reimer) to rear him as a girl (Brenda) because of a botched circumcision that left the infant without a penis. Money

argued that social mirrors dictate one's gender identity, and thus, if the parents treated the child as a girl (e.g., name, clothing, toys), the child would adopt the role of a girl and later that of a woman. The child was castrated and sex reassignment began.

However, the experiment failed miserably; the child as an adult (now calling himself David) reported that he never felt comfortable in the role of a girl and had always viewed himself as a boy. He later married and adopted his wife's three children.

In the past, David's situation was used as a textbook example of how nurture is the more important influence in gender identity, if a reassignment is done early enough. Today, his case makes the point that one's biological wiring dictates gender outcome. Indeed, David Reimer noted in a television interview, "I was scammed," referring to the absurdity of trying to rear him as a girl. Distraught with the ordeal of his upbringing and beset with financial difficulties, he committed suicide in 2004 via a gunshot to the head.

> I believe gender is a spectrum, and I fall somewhere between Channing Tatum and Winnie the Pooh.
>
> —STEPHEN COLBERT

The story of David Reimer emphasizes the power of biology in determining gender identity. Other research supports the critical role of biology. Nevertheless, **socialization** (the process through which we learn attitudes, values, beliefs, and behaviors appropriate to the social positions we occupy) does impact gender role behaviors, and social scientists tend to emphasize the role of social influences in gender differences.

3-1c Gender Identity

Gender identity is the psychological state of viewing oneself as a girl or a boy, and later as a woman or a man. Such identity is largely learned and is a reflection of society's conceptions of femininity and masculinity. Some individuals experience **gender dysphoria**,

intersex development refers to congenital variations in the reproductive system, sometimes resulting in ambiguous genitals.

gender the social and psychological behaviors associated with being female or male.

socialization the process through which we learn attitudes, values, beliefs, and behaviors appropriate to the social positions we occupy.

gender identity the psychological state of viewing oneself as a girl or a boy and, later, as a woman or a man.

gender dysphoria the condition in which one's gender identity does not match one's biological sex.

Diversity in Gender Role Socialization

Although her research is controversial, Margaret Mead (1935) focused on the role of social learning in the development of gender roles in her study of three cultures. She visited three New Guinea tribes in the early 1930s, and observed that the Arapesh socialized both men and women to be feminine, by Western standards. The Arapesh people were taught to be cooperative and responsive to the needs of others. In contrast, the Tchambuli were known for dominant women and submissive men—just the opposite of our society. Both of these societies were unlike the Mundugumor, which socialized only ruthless, aggressive, "masculine" personalities. The inescapable conclusion of this cross-cultural study is that human beings are products of their social and cultural environments and that gender roles are learned.

a condition in which one's gender identity does not match one's biological sex. An example of gender dysphoria is transgender or transsexualism.

The word **transgender** is a generic term for a person of one biological sex who displays characteristics of the other sex. Caitlyn Jenner brought nationwide visibility to the issue of transgender individuals in her *20/20* interview in 2015 with the announcement, "I have always thought of myself as more of a woman." A **crossdresser** is a person of one biological sex who enjoys dressing in the clothes of the other sex—for example, a biological man who enjoys dressing up as a woman. **Transsexuals** are individuals with the biological and anatomical sex of one gender (e.g., female) but the self-concept of the other sex (e.g., male). "I am a female trapped in a man's body" reflects the feelings of the male-to-female transsexual (MtF), who may take hormones to develop breasts and reduce facial hair and may have surgery to artificially construct a vagina. Such a person lives full-time as a woman.

The female-to-male transsexual (FtM) is a biological and anatomical female who feels "I am a man trapped in a female's body." This person may take male hormones to grow facial hair and deepen her voice and may have

surgery to create an artificial penis. This person lives full-time as a man. Individuals need not take hormones or have surgery to be regarded as transsexuals. The distinguishing variable is living full-time in the role of the gender opposite one's biological sex. A man or woman who presents full-time as the opposite gender is a transsexual by definition.

> Cinderella,
> I want to wear your shoes
> Dress in pastel pink, not blues
> Wear red lipstick and rouge
> Maybe this year on Halloween
> I'll dress up just like you
> And the world will finally see me
> From my own point of view
>
> —CAROLINE SCHACHT, SOCIOLOGIST

3-1d Gender Roles

 Self-Assessment: Gender Role Attitudes: Family Life Index
Take the self-assessment on gender role attitudes at the end of the chapter to assess your view of the roles of respective family members.

Gender roles are social norms which specify the socially appropriate behavior for females and males in a society. All societies have expectations of how boys and girls, men and women "should" behave. And these "shoulds" have consequences. (See "He Works, She Works.")

Gender impacts one's life experiences. The What's New? section provides data on how sexual and relationship experiences are different for women and for men.

transgender a generic term for a person of one biological sex who displays characteristics of the opposite sex.

cross-dresser a generic term for individuals who may dress or present themselves in the gender of the opposite sex.

transsexual an individual who has the anatomical and genetic characteristics of one sex but the self-concept of the other.

gender roles behaviors assigned to women and men in a society.

HE WORKS, SHE WORKS

But What Different Impressions They Make

Family picture on his desk: Ah, a solid, responsible family man.

Family picture on her desk: Hmm, family will come before career.

His desk is cluttered: He's obviously a hard worker and busy man.

Her desk is cluttered: She's obviously disorganized and scatterbrained.

He's talking with co-workers: He must be discussing the latest deal.

She's talking with co-workers: She must be gossiping.

He's not at his desk: He must be at a meeting.

She's not at her desk: She must be out shopping.

He has lunch with the boss: He's on his way up.

She has lunch with the boss: They must be having an affair.

The boss criticized HIM: He'll improve his performance.
The boss criticized HER: She'll be very upset.

He got an unfair deal: Did he get angry?
She got an unfair deal: Did she cry?

He's getting married: He'll get more settled.
She's getting married: She'll get pregnant and leave.

He's having a baby: He'll need a raise.
She's having a baby: She'll cost the company money in maternity benefits.

He's going on a business trip: It's good for his career.
She's going on a business trip: What does her husband say?

He's leaving for a better job: He recognizes a good opportunity.
She's leaving for a better job: Women are undependable.

Source: From *Paths to Power* by Natasha Josefowitz Ph.D. Copyright 1980.

The term *sex roles* is often confused with and used interchangeably with the term *gender roles*. However, whereas gender roles are socially defined and can be enacted by either women or men, **sex roles** are defined by biological constraints and can be enacted by members of one biological sex only—for example, wet nurse, sperm donor, child bearer.

3-1e Gender Role Ideology

Gender role ideology refers to beliefs about the proper role relationships between women and men in a society. Traditionally, men initiated relationships, called women for dates, and were expected to be the ones who proposed. New norms include that women may be first to initiate an interaction, text men for time together, and ask men if they want to get married. Indeed, with the power shift toward women at work and at home, Myers (2016) has suggested that the traditional male is dying out. He asserts that men will "be increasingly defined, dominated, and

This female-to-male transgender person (right) reports that his sex is fluid. "Sometimes I wake up as a woman and sometimes as a man—I can't control it." His lesbian girlfriend says, "I love the person . . . the fact that he/she changes is part of the fun we have in our relationship. We want to marry and have children."

controlled by women." As evidence he notes that women earn 60% of the college degrees and that jobs are increasingly going to the college educated. Men today are also more likely to have grown up in a single-parent

sex roles behaviors defined by biological constraints.

gender role ideology the proper role relationships between women and men in a society.

Different Gender Worlds on Sex, Betrayal, and Love

In spite of egalitarian changes in our society, women and men report significantly different experiences. The table below reflects some of these differences in a large non-random sample of 9,732 undergraduates.

PERCENT AGREEMENT ON SEX, BETRAYAL, AND LOVE*

Item	Women N = 7,420	Men N = 2,312	Sig.
Sexual experiences			
I have masturbated.	68.9%	96.7%	.000
I could hook up and have sex with someone I liked.	24.3%	58.3%	.000
I have hooked up/had sex with a person I just met.	22.7%	34.1%	.000
I regret my choice for sexual intercourse the first time.	25.9%	16.5%	.000
Betrayed			
I have been involved with someone who cheated on me.	58.3%	52.2%	.000
Love at first sight			
I have experienced love at first sight.	24.0%	34.3%	.000

*Based on original data from Hall, S., & D. Knox. (2016). Relationship and sexual behaviors of a sample of 9,732 university students. Department of Family and Consumer Sciences, Ball State University and Department of Sociology, East Carolina University.

Some females lift weights with the same focus/dedication as some males.

home headed by a female or to have seen a higher earning income mother in the home with his father. The result is men with less power in relationships, while greater power of women is increasing.

The language of our culture is changing. The words *man* and *mankind* have now been replaced by *individuals* and *humankind*.

3-2 THEORIES OF GENDER ROLE DEVELOPMENT

Various theories attempt to explain why women and men exhibit different characteristics and behaviors.

3-2a Biosocial/Biopsychosocial

Biosocial theory emphasizes that social behaviors (e.g., gender roles) are biologically based and have an evolutionary survival function. For example, women tend to select and mate

biosocial theory (sociobiology)
emphasizes the interaction of one's biological or genetic inheritance with one's social environment to explain and predict human behavior.

with men whom they deem will provide the maximum parental investment in their offspring. The term **parental investment** refers to any venture by a parent that increases the offspring's chance of surviving and thus increases reproductive success of the adult. Parental investments require time and energy. Women have a great deal of parental investment in their offspring (including nine months of gestation), and they tend to mate with men who have high status, economic resources, and a willingness to share those economic resources. As we will see in Chapter 12 on parenting, economic resources are not inconsequential as the average cost today of rearing a child from birth to age 18 (does not include college) is almost $250,000.

The biosocial explanation (also referred to as **sociobiology**) for mate selection is extremely controversial. Critics argue that women may show concern for the earning capacity of a potential mate because they have been systematically denied access to similar economic resources, and selecting a mate with these resources is one of their remaining options. In addition, it is argued that both women and men, when selecting a mate, think more about

parental investment any investment by a parent that increases the chance that the offspring will survive and thrive.

sociobiology emphasizes the interaction of one's biological or genetic inheritance with one's social environment to explain and predict human behavior.

their partners as companions to have fun with than as future parents of their offspring.

3-2b Bioecological Model

The bioecological model, proposed by Urie Bronfenbrenner, emphasizes the importance of understanding bidirectional influences between an individual's development and his or her surrounding environmental contexts. The focus is on the combined interactive influences so that the predispositions of the individual interact with the environment/culture/society, resulting in various gender expressions. For example, the individual will read what gender role behavior his or her society will tolerate and adapt accordingly.

3-2c Social Learning

Derived from the school of behavioral psychology, the social learning theory emphasizes the roles of reward and punishment in explaining how a child learns gender role behavior. This is in contrast to the biological explanation for gender roles. For example, consider

Increasingly, women are entering professions previously held only by men.

the real-life example of two young brothers who enjoyed playing "lady"; each of them put on a dress, wore high-heeled shoes, and carried a pocketbook. Their father came home early one day and angrily demanded, "Take those clothes off and never put them on again. Those things are for women." The boys were punished for "playing lady" but rewarded with their father's approval for boxing and playing football (both of which involved hurting others).

3-2d Identification

Although researchers do not agree on the merits of Freud's theories (and students question its relevance), Freud was one of the first theorists to study gender role acquisition. He suggested that children acquire the characteristics and behaviors of their same-sex parent through a process of identification. Boys identify with their fathers, and girls identify with their mothers.

3-2e Cognitive-Developmental Theory

The cognitive-developmental theory of gender role development reflects a blend of the biological and social learning views. According to this theory, the biological readiness of the child, in terms of cognitive development, influences how the child responds to gender cues in the environment (Kohlberg, 1966). For example, gender discrimination (the ability to identify social and psychological characteristics associated with being female or male) begins at about age 30 months. However, at this age, children do not view gender as a permanent characteristic. Thus, even though young children may define people who wear long hair as girls and those who never wear dresses as boys, they also believe they can change their gender by altering their hair or changing clothes.

Not until age 6 or 7 do children view gender as permanent (Kohlberg, 1966, 1969). In Kohlberg's view, this cognitive understanding involves the development of a specific mental ability to grasp the idea that certain basic characteristics of people do not change.

3-3 AGENTS OF SOCIALIZATION

Three of the four theories discussed in the preceding section emphasize that gender roles are learned through interaction with the environment. Indeed,

though biology may provide a basis for one's gender identity, cultural influences in the form of various socialization agents (parents, peers, religion, and the media) shape the individual toward various gender roles. These powerful influences, in large part, dictate what people think, feel, and do in their roles as men or women. In the next section, we look at the different sources influencing gender socialization.

3-3a Family

An early scene in *American Sniper* (the movie) featured a father in the woods with his son who was being socialized how to shoot his first deer. Later in the movie, this child, as an adult, gave his son instruction in shooting his first deer. In both cases, males were socializing males. The family is a gendered institution in that female and male roles are highly structured by gender. The names parents assign to their children, the clothes they dress them in, the toys they buy them, and the games they direct (e.g., hunting for boys) all reflect gender roles.

In regard to sex, daughters are more likely than sons to be encouraged to be discriminating in allocating sexual access and to be abstinent (Kuhle et al., 2015). Parents (particularly African American mothers) may also be stricter on female children—determining the age they are allowed to leave the house at night, the time of curfew, and using directives such as "text me when you get to the party." Female children are also assigned more chores (Mandara et al., 2010).

> We've begun to raise daughters more like sons ... but few have the courage to raise our sons more like our daughters.
>
> —GLORIA STEINEM, JOURNALIST AND FEMINIST

Parents who expose their daughters to Barbie dolls may inadvertently be socializing them to a more limited set of career possibilities. Sherman and Zurbriggen (2014) created a context where 37 girls aged 4–7 played with

Individuals learn from their peers appropriate gender behavior.

in the U.S. dioceses. In addition, the Mormon Church is dominated by men and does not provide positions of leadership for women. Maltby et al. (2010) also observed that the stronger the religiosity for men, the more traditional and sexist their view of women. This association was not found for women.

Barbie dolls for five minutes and were then asked how many of 10 different occupations they themselves could do in the future and how many of those occupations a boy could do. Girls reported that boys could do significantly more occupations than they could themselves, especially when considering male-dominated careers.

Siblings also influence gender role learning. Growing up in a family of all sisters or all brothers intensifies social learning experiences toward femininity or masculinity. A male reared with five sisters and a single-parent mother is likely to reflect more feminine characteristics than a male reared in a home with six brothers and a stay-at-home dad.

3-3b Peers

Though parents are usually the first socializing agents that influence a child's gender role development, peers become increasingly important during the school years (particularly in regard to the use of alcohol and engaging in sexual behavior).

3-3c Religion

Americans affiliated with an organized religion are 77.2% (Pew Research Center, 2015). An example of how religion impacts gender roles involves the Roman Catholic Church, which does not have female clergy. Men dominate the 19 top positions

Fa'afafine in Samoan society, these are effeminate males socialized and reared as females due to the lack of women to perform domestic chores.

Cultural Diversity in Gender Roles

Samoan society/culture provides a unique example of gender role socialization via the family. The **Fa'afafine** (commonly called Fafa) are males reared as females. There are about 3,000 Fa'afafine in Samoa. The practice arose when there was a lack of women to perform domestic chores and the family had no female children. Thus, effeminate boys were identified and socialized/reared as females. Fa'afafine represent a third gender, neither female nor male; they are unique and valued, not stigmatized. Most Samoan families have at least one Fa'afafine child who takes on the role of a woman, including having sex with men (Abboud, 2013).

3-3d Education

The educational institution is another socialization agent for gender role ideology. However, such an effect must be considered in the context of the society or culture in which the "school" exists and of the school itself. Schools are basic cultures of transmission in that they make deliberate efforts to reproduce the culture from one generation to the next.

3-3e Economy

The economy of the society influences the roles of the individuals in the society. The economic institution is a very gendered institution. **Occupational sex segregation** is the concentration of men and women in different occupations which has grown out of traditional gender roles. Men dominate in construction (e.g., brickmasons), mining, and firefighting; women dominate in secretarial/administrative work, teaching, and nursing. Only recently have women become NASCAR drivers (e.g., Danica Patrick).

3-3f Mass Media

Mass media, such as the Internet, movies, television, magazines, newspapers, books, music, computer games, and music television videos, both reflect and shape gender roles. Media images of women and men typically conform to traditional gender stereotypes, and media portrayals depicting the exploitation, victimization, and sexual objectification of women are common. In regard to television for young children, Krisch and Murnen (2015) examined the "heterosexual script" operative in seven popular American children's TV programs and found that the most common theme was boys objectifying and valuing girls solely for their appearance and girls engaging in self-objectification and ego stroking of boys. As for TV programming for tweens, Gerding and Signorielli (2014) analyzed content of gender role portrayals in 49 episodes of 40 U.S. tween television programs of two genres: teen scene (geared toward girls) and action adventure (geared toward boys). Results

revealed that females were underrepresented in the action-adventure genre. Also, compared to males, females were more attractive, more concerned about their appearance, and received comments about their "looks." Brook (2015) discussed "bromance" movies as similar to a heterosexual "chick flick" except the emotional bonding is between two males (without a homosexual-suggested relationship). Kronz (2016) found 36 of 1,000 films produced between 2001 and 2011 featuring gender in a trangressive way. Cross-dresser was the most usual representation and comedy was the genre.

As for gender role influence of music, a qualitative analysis of lyrics of 30 popular songs by Jasper (2015) revealed women as being childlike, as a possession of men, and as valuable for their physical characteristics. Flynn et al. (2016) conducted a content analysis of rap and R&B hip-hop and found frequent references to female body objectification.

News media perpetuate male bias. In an analysis of 400,000 Reuters' news messages, the use of *he* pronouns was nine times more frequent than the use of *she* pronouns. The researchers concluded that the data confirm prevalent gender stereotypes which contribute to gender inequities (Senden et al., 2015).

The cumulative effects of family, peers, religion, education, the economic institution, and mass media perpetuate gender stereotypes. Each agent of socialization reinforces gender roles that are learned from other agents of socialization, thereby creating a gender role system that is deeply embedded in our culture. All of these influences affect relationship choices (see Table 3.1).

 ## 3-4 CONSEQUENCES OF TRADITIONAL GENDER ROLE SOCIALIZATION

This section discusses positive and negative consequences of traditional female and male socialization in the United States.

3-4a Traditional Female Role Socialization

In this section, we summarize some of the negative and positive consequences of being socialized as a woman in U.S. society.

occupational sex segregation the concentration of women in certain occupations and men in other occupations.

TABLE 3.1 EFFECTS OF GENDER ROLE SOCIALIZATION ON RELATIONSHIP CHOICES

Women	Men
1. A woman who is not socialized to pursue advanced education (which often translates into less income) may feel pressure to stay in an unhappy relationship with someone on whom she is economically dependent. Increasingly women are pursuing education.	1. Men who are socialized to define themselves in terms of their occupational success and income may find their self-esteem and masculinity vulnerable if they become unemployed, retired, or work in a low-income job.
2. Women who are socialized to play a passive role and not initiate relationships are limiting interactions that might develop into valued relationships.	2. Men who are socialized to restrict their experience and expression of emotions are denied the opportunity to discover the rewards of emotional interpersonal involvement.
3. Women who are socialized to accept that they are less valuable and less important than men are less likely to seek, achieve, or require egalitarian relationships with men.	3. Men who are socialized to believe it is not their role to participate in domestic activities (child rearing, food preparation, house cleaning) will not develop competencies in these life skills. Potential partners often view domestic skills as desirable.
4. Women who internalize society's standards of beauty and view their worth in terms of their age and appearance are likely to feel bad about themselves as they age. Their negative self-concept, more than their age or appearance, may interfere with their relationships.	4. Heterosexual men who focus on cultural definitions of female beauty overlook potential partners who might not fit the cultural beauty ideal but who would be wonderful life companions.
5. Women who are socialized to accept that they are solely responsible for taking care of their parents, children, and husband are likely to experience role overload. In this regard, some women may feel angry and resentful, which may have a negative impact on their relationships.	5. Men who are socialized to have a negative view of women who initiate relationships will be restricted in their relationship opportunities.
6. Women who are socialized to emphasize the importance of relationships in their lives will continue to seek relationships that are emotionally satisfying.	6. Men who are socialized to be in control of relationship encounters may alienate their partners, who may desire equality.

Each consequence may or may not be true for a specific woman. For example, although women in general have less education and income, a particular woman may have more education and a higher income than a particular man.

NEGATIVE CONSEQUENCES OF TRADITIONAL FEMALE ROLE SOCIALIZATION There are several negative consequences of being socialized as a woman in our society.

1. **Less income.** Although women earn more college degrees than men and earn 46% of PhDs (National Science Foundation, 2015), they have lower academic rank and earn less money. The lower academic rank is because women give priority to the care of their children and family over their advancement in the workplace. Women still earn about three-fourths of what men earn, even when their level of educational achievement is identical (see Table 3.2). Women are still more likely than men to be more family than career oriented (Fernandez-Cornejo et al., 2016) and their visibility in the ranks of high corporate America is also still low. While 5% of the CEOs at Fortune 500 companies are women (Swanson,

2015), there are exceptions such as Virginia Rometty, CEO of IBM—the first female head of the company in 100 years.

However, the value women place on a high-income career job is changing. The Pew Research Center (2012) reports a reversal of traditional gender roles with young women surpassing young men in saying that achieving success in a high-paying career or profession is important in their lives.

2. **Feminization of poverty.** Another reason many women are relegated to a lower income status is the **feminization of poverty**. This term refers to the disproportionate

dcwcreations/Shutterstock.com

feminization of poverty
the idea that women disproportionately experience poverty.

TABLE 3.2 WOMEN'S AND MEN'S MEDIAN INCOME WITH SIMILAR EDUCATION

	Bachelor's	Master's	Doctoral Degree
Men	$58,170	$75,407	$93,712
Women	$39,201	$50,507	$64,001

Source: *Proquest Statistical Abstract of the United States, 2016*, online ed., Table 724. Washington, DC: U.S. Bureau of the Census.

percentage of poverty experienced by women living alone or with their children. Single mothers are particularly associated with poverty.

When head-of-household women are compared with married-couple households, the median income is $36,154 versus $76,509 (*Proquest Statistical Abstract of the United States*, 2016, Table 714). The process is cyclical—poverty contributes to teenage pregnancy because teens have limited supervision and few alternatives to parenthood (the median income for head-of-household men is $50,625). Such early childbearing interferes with educational advancement and restricts women's earning capacity, which keeps them in poverty. Their offspring are born into poverty, and the cycle begins anew.

Low pay for women is also related to the fact that they tend to work in occupations that pay relatively low incomes. Indeed, women's lack of economic power stems from the relative dispensability (it is easy to replace) of women's labor and how work is organized (men occupy and control positions of power). Women also live longer than men, and poverty is associated with being elderly.

When women move into certain occupations, such as teaching, there is a tendency in the marketplace to segregate these occupations from men's, and the result is a concentration of women in lower-paid occupations. The salaries of women in these occupational roles increase at slower rates. For example, salaries in the elementary and secondary teaching profession, which is predominately female, have not kept pace with inflation.

Conflict theorists assert that men are in more powerful roles than women and use this power to dictate incomes and salaries of women and "female professions." Functionalists also note that keeping salaries low for women keeps women dependent and in child-care roles so as to keep equilibrium in the family. Hence, for both conflict and structural reasons, poverty is primarily a feminine issue. One of the consequences of being a woman is to have an increased probability of feeling economic strain throughout life.

3. **Higher risk for sexually transmitted infections.** Due to the female anatomy, women are more vulnerable to sexually transmitted infections and HIV (they receive more bodily fluids from men). Some women also feel limited in their ability to influence their partners to wear condoms (East et al., 2011).

4. **Negative body image.** Compared to males, females have a lower positive self-concept (75.0% versus 78.3%) (Hall & Knox, 2016).

American women also live in a society that devalues them in a larger sense. Their lives and experiences are not taken as seriously as men's. **Sexism** is an attitude, action, or institutional structure that subordinates or discriminates against individuals or groups because of their sex. Sexism against women reflects the tradition of male dominance and presumed male superiority in U.S. society.

Benevolent sexism (reviewed by Maltby et al., 2010) is a related term and reflects the belief that women are innocent creatures who should be protected and supported. While such a view has positive aspects, it assumes that women are best suited for domestic roles and need to be taken care of by a man since they are not capable of taking care of themselves.

5. **Less marital satisfaction.** Demaris et al. (2012) analyzed data on 707 marriages and found that couples characterized by more traditional attitudes toward gender roles were significantly less satisfied than others. Wives in traditional marriages are particularly likely to report lower marital satisfaction (Bulanda, 2011). Such lower marital satisfaction of wives is attributed to power differentials in the marriage. Traditional husbands expect to be dominant and expect their wives to take care of the house and children. Women have been socialized to believe that they can have both a family and a career—that they can have it all. In reality, they have discovered that they "can have two things half way" and that men are not much help (Haag, 2011, p. 47). In large nonclinical samples comparing wives and husbands on marital satisfaction (which include egalitarian marriages), wives do not report lower marital satisfaction. In regard to personal depression, femininity is associated with less depression (Gibson et al. 2016).

6. **Fearful of Talking about Sex/Taught to Live in Fear.** Women are also more uncomfortable talking about sex than men. Based on interviews with 95 women ages 20–68, the researchers noted

sexism an attitude, action, or institutional structure that subordinates or discriminates against an individual or group because of their sex.

benevolent sexism the belief that women are innocent creatures who should be protected and supported.

Young girls tend to feel more negatively about their bodies than boys due to the cultural emphasis on being thin and trim.

that the respondents, in general, feared being disapproved of for communicating sexual desire or talking about sexual behavior (Montemurro et al., 2015).

Women are also taught to live in fear. Bedera and Nordmeyer (2015) noted four themes in rape prevention literature: there are no safe places for women, women can't trust anyone, women should never be alone, and women are vulnerable. Findings imply that the burden of college sexual assault prevention still falls primarily on female students.

POSITIVE CONSEQUENCES OF TRADITIONAL FEMALE ROLE SOCIALIZATION We have discussed the negative consequences of being born and socialized as a woman. However, there are also decided benefits.

1. **Longer life expectancy.** Women have a longer life expectancy than men. It is not clear if their greater longevity is related to biological or to social factors. Females born in the year 2015 are expected to live to the age of 81.7, in contrast to men, who are expected to live to the age of 77.1 (*Proquest Statistical Abstract of the United States, 2016*, Table 115).

2. **Stronger relationship focus.** Women prioritize family over work and do more child care than men (Craig & Mullan, 2010). Mothers provide more "emotion work," helping children with whatever they are struggling with (Minnottea et al., 2010).

> Relationships are made of talk—and talk is for girls and women.
>
> —DEBORAH TANNEN, COMMUNICATION SPECIALIST

3. **Keeps relationships on track.** Women are more likely to initiate "the relationship talk" to ensure that the relationship is moving forward (Nelms et al., 2012). In addition, when there is a problem in the relationship, it is the woman who moves the couple toward help (Eubanks Fleming & Córdova, 2012).

4. **Bonding with children.** Another advantage of being socialized as a woman is the potential to have a closer bond with children. In general, women (whether in heterosexual or same-sex relationships) tend to spend more time with children than men (Prickett et al., 2015). Although the new cultural image of the father is of one who engages emotionally with his children (and gay men excel) (Prickett et al., 2015), many fathers continue to be content for their wives to take care of their children, with the result that mothers, not fathers, become more emotionally bonded with their children. Table 3.3 summarizes the consequences of traditional female role socialization.

TABLE 3.3	CONSEQUENCES OF TRADITIONAL FEMALE ROLE SOCIALIZATION	
Negative Consequences	**Positive Consequences**
Less income (more dependent)	Longer life
Feminization of poverty	Stronger relationship focus
Higher STD/HIV infection risk	Keep relationships on track
Negative body image	Bonding with children
Less personal/marital satisfaction	Identity not tied to job

3-4b Consequences of Traditional Male Role Socialization

Male socialization in U.S. society is associated with its own set of consequences. As with women, each consequence may or may not be true for a specific man.

NEGATIVE CONSEQUENCES OF TRADITIONAL MALE ROLE SOCIALIZATION There are several negative consequences associated with being socialized as a man in U.S. society.

1. **Identity synonymous with occupation.** Ask men who they are, and many will tell you what they do. Society tends to equate a man's identity with his occupational role. Michniewicz et al. (2014) analyzed the perceived effect of threatened unemployment on men and found that men estimated a lower appraisal of themselves following an imagined job loss. That men are focused on their work role may also translate into fewer friendships and relationships. While friendships are important to both men and women (Meliksah et al., 2013), men have fewer sustained friendships than women across time. This is due not only to their work focus but also to the cultural values of independence which support men being the loner (Way, 2013).

Courtesy of Michelle North

> When men cry, women are caring/ nurturing and ask, "How can I help? When women cry, men say, 'I'm going to have a beer . . . let me know when you snap out of it.'"
>
> —JAY LENO, COMEDIAN

2. **Limited expression of emotions.** Most men not only cry less (Barnes et al., 2012) but are also pressured to disavow any expression that could be interpreted as feminine (e.g., emotional).

3. **Fear of intimacy.** Garfield (2010) reviewed men's difficulty with emotional intimacy and noted that their emotional detachment stems from the provider role which requires them to stay in control. Being emotional is seen by men as a sign of weakness.

4. **Custody disadvantages.** Courts are sometimes biased against divorced men who want custody of their children. Because divorced fathers are typically regarded as career focused and uninvolved in child care, some are relegated to seeing their children on a limited basis, such as every other weekend or four evenings a month.

5. **Shorter life expectancy.** Men typically die five years sooner (at age 77) than women. One explanation is that the traditional male role emphasizes achievement, competition, and suppression of feelings, all of which may produce stress. Not only is stress itself harmful to physical health, but it may also lead to compensatory behaviors such as smoking, alcohol, or other drug abuse, and dangerous risk-taking behavior (e.g., driving fast, binge drinking).

BENEFITS OF TRADITIONAL MALE SOCIALIZATION There are numerous benefits for being a male. As a result of higher status and power in society, men tend to have a more positive self-concept and greater confidence in themselves. In a sample of 2,379 undergraduate men, 78% "strongly agreed" with the statement, "I have a very positive self-concept." In contrast, 75% of 7,577 undergraduate women strongly agreed with the statement (Hall &

> When I'm talking to groups that are all men, we talk about how the masculine role limits them. They often want to talk about how they missed having real fathers, real loving, present fathers, because of the way that they tried to fit the picture of masculinity.
>
> —GLORIA STEINEM

TABLE 3.4	CONSEQUENCES OF TRADITIONAL MALE ROLE SOCIALIZATION
Negative Consequences	**Positive Consequences**
Identity tied to work role	Higher income and occupational status
Limited emotionality	More positive self-concept
Fear of intimacy; more lonely	Less job discrimination
Disadvantaged in getting custody	Freedom of movement; more partners to select from; more normative to initiate relationships
Shorter life	Happier marriage

Knox, 2016). Men also enjoy higher incomes and an easier climb up the good-old-boy corporate ladder. Other benefits are the following:

1. **Freedom of movement.** Unlike women (who are taught to fear rape, be aware of their surroundings, walk in well-lit places, and not walk alone after dark) men are oblivious to these fears and perceptions. They can go anywhere alone and are fearless about someone harming them.

2. **Greater available pool of potential partners.** Because of the mating gradient (men marry "down" in age and education whereas women marry "up"), men tend to marry younger women so that a 35-year-old man may view women from 20 to 40 years of age as possible mates. However, a woman of age 35 is more likely to view men her same age or older as potential mates. As she ages, fewer men are available.

3. **Norm of initiating a relationship.** Men are advantaged because traditional norms allow them to be aggressive in initiating relationships with women. Table 3.4 summarizes the consequences of being socialized as a male.

3-5 CHANGING GENDER ROLES

Androgyny, gender role transcendence, and gender postmodernism emphasize that gender roles are changing.

3-5a Androgyny

Androgyny is a blend of traits that are stereotypically associated with masculinity and femininity. Androgynous celebrities include Lady Gaga, Boy George, Patti Smith, and Annie Lennox. Two forms of androgyny are:

androgyny a blend of traits that are stereotypically associated with masculinity and femininity.

1. Physiological androgyny refers to intersexed individuals, discussed earlier in the chapter. The genitals are neither clearly male nor female, and there is a mixing of "female" and "male" chromosomes and hormones.

2. Behavioral androgyny refers to the blending or reversal of traditional male and female behavior, so that a biological male may be very passive, gentle, and nurturing and a biological female may be very assertive, rough, and selfish.

Androgyny may also imply flexibility of traits; for example, an androgynous individual may be emotional in one situation, logical in another, and assertive in another. Androgyny has been associated with positive mental health adjustment (Martin et al., 2016).

3-5b Gender Role Transcendence

Beyond the concept of androgyny is that of gender role transcendence. We associate many aspects of our world, including colors, foods, social, or occupational roles, and personality traits, with either masculinity or femininity.

The concept of **gender role transcendence** means abandoning gender frameworks and looking at phenomena independent of traditional gender categories.

Transcendence is not equal for women and men. Although females are becoming more masculine, in part because our society values whatever is masculine, men are not becoming more feminine. Indeed, adolescent boys may be described as very gender entrenched. Beyond gender role transcendence is gender postmodernism.

3-5c Gender Postmodernism

Gender postmodernism abandons the notion of gender as natural and emphasizes that gender is socially constructed. Almost 20 years ago, Monro (2000) noted that people in the postmodern society would no longer be categorized as male or female but be recognized as capable of many identities—"a third sex" (p. 37). A new conceptualization of "trans" people calls for new social structures, "based on the principles of equality, diversity and the right to self-determination" (p. 42). No longer would our society telegraph transphobia but would instead embrace pluralization "as an indication of social evolution, allowing greater choice and means of self-expression concerning gender" (p. 42).

Our society is being increasingly exposed to variations in gender expression. Caitlyn Jenner's transition from Bruce had the effect of confirming that one's gender is not necessarily fixed.

3-6 TRENDS IN GENDER ROLES

Imagine a society in which women and men each develop characteristics, lifestyles, and values that are independent of gender role stereotypes. Characteristics such as strength, independence, logical thinking, and aggressiveness are no longer associated with maleness, just as passivity, dependence, emotions, intuitiveness, and nurturance are no longer associated with femaleness. Both sexes are considered equal, and women and men may pursue the same occupational, political, and domestic roles. These changes are occurring…slowly.

Another change in gender roles is the independence and ascendency of women. Women will less often require marriage for fulfillment, will increasingly take care of themselves economically, and will opt for having children via adoption or donor sperm rather than foregoing motherhood. That women are slowly outstretching men in terms of education will provide the impetus for these changes.

gender role transcendence abandoning gender frameworks and looking at phenomena independent of traditional gender categories.

STUDY TOOLS 3

READY TO STUDY? IN THE BOOK, YOU CAN:

☐ Rip out the chapter review card at the back of the book for a handy summary of the chapter and key terms.

☐ Assess yourself with the following self-assessment.

ONLINE AT CENGAGEBRAIN.COM YOU CAN:

☐ Collect StudyBits while you read and study the chapter.

☐ Quiz yourself on key concepts.

☐ Prepare for tests with M&F4 Flash Cards as well as those you create.

 **SELF-ASSESSMENT**

Gender Role Attitudes: Family Life Index

Read each item and select the number that reflects your belief/attitude.

1	2	3	4
Strongly agree	*Agree*	*Disagree*	*Strongly disagree*

_____ **1.** The husband should be the head of the family.

_____ **2.** Babies and young children need to have their mothers around most of the day.

_____ **3.** It is much better for everyone involved if the man is the achiever outside the home and the woman takes care of the home and family.

_____ **4.** A woman's most important task in life is being a mother.

_____ **5.** By nature, women are better than men at making a home and caring for children.

_____ **6.** A preschool child is likely to suffer if his or her mother works outside the home.

_____ **7.** A husband should earn a larger salary than his wife.

_____ **8.** A woman should not be employed if her husband can support her.

_____ **9.** All in all, family life suffers when the wife has a full-time job.

Scoring

Add the numbers you selected for each item. 1 (strongly agree) is the most traditional response and 4 (strongly disagree) is the most egalitarian response. The lower your total score (9 is the lowest possible score), the more traditional your gender role attitudes. The higher your total score (36 is the highest possible score), the more egalitarian your gender role attitudes. A score of 22.5 places you at the midpoint between being very traditional and very egalitarian.

Norms

The norming sample of this self-assessment was based on 37 males and 172 females. The average score of the males was 23 and the average score of the females was 25, suggesting a lean toward being egalitarian by both males and females with females being more egalitarian.

Source: Adapted from Erarslan, A. B. & B. Rankin. (2013). Gender role attitudes of female students in single-sex and coeducational high schools in Istanbul. *Sex Roles, 69*: 455–469. Used by permission of A. B. Erarslan.

ONLINE

PREPARE FOR TESTS ON THE STUDYBOARD!

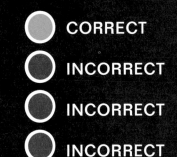

CORRECT

INCORRECT

INCORRECT

INCORRECT

Personalize Quizzes from Your StudyBits

Take Practice Quizzes by Chapter

CHAPTER QUIZZES

Chapter 1

Chapter 2

Chapter 3

Chapter 4

4LTR
PRESS

4 | Examining Love and Relationship Development

After finishing this chapter go to **PAGE 88** for **STUDY TOOLS**

> Love is the only thing I know that hurts so good.
>
> — DENNIS ROGERS, JOURNALIST

ove is the most powerful, engaging, wonderful feeling a person ever experiences. Abundant research documents the positive effects of love promoting one's mental (Stanton & Campbell, 2014), physical (Rauer et al., 2014), and marital well-being (Reis et al., 2014).

When love ends, it is the most devastating, gut wrenching, depressing feeling imaginable. Between the beginning and the end, individuals are reminded that love is forever changing and that it is the only game in town worth being involved in. In this chapter, we review the various views and origins of love, how it develops, and the various factors involved in finding and maintaining love with a specific person.

4-1 WAYS OF VIEWING LOVE

A common class exercise among professors who teach marriage and the family is to randomly ask class members to identify one word they most closely associate with love. Combining these terms often results in three categories: emotion (e.g., love is a feeling), social (e.g.. love involves approval of family/peers), and physical (e.g., touch/physical intimacy).

Love is often confused with lust and infatuation. Love (and attachment) is about deep, abiding feelings with a focus on the long term (Langeslag et al., 2013); **lust** is about sexual desire and the present. The word **infatuation** comes from the same root word as *fatuous*, meaning "silly" or "foolish," and refers to a state of passion or attraction that is not based on reason. Infatuation is characterized by euphoria (Langeslag et al., 2013) and by the tendency to idealize the love partner. People who are infatuated magnify their lovers' positive qualities ("My partner is always happy") and overlook or minimize their negative qualities ("My partner doesn't have a problem with alcohol; he just likes to have a good time").

In the following section, we look at the various ways of conceptualizing love.

> Say "Yes" to dreams of love and freedom. It is the password to utopia.
>
> —BROOKS ATKINSON, *ONCE AROUND THE SUN*

4-1a Romantic versus Realistic Love

Love may also be described as being on a continuum from romanticism to realism. For some people, love is romantic; for others, it is realistic. **Romantic love** is characterized in modern America by such beliefs as "love at first sight," "one true love," and "love conquers all."

Regarding love at first sight, 34% of 2,290 undergraduate males and 24% of 7,387 undergraduate females reported that they had experienced love at first sight (Hall & Knox, 2016). One explanation for men falling in love more quickly than women is that (from a biological/evolutionary perspective) men must be visually attracted to young, healthy females to inseminate them. This biologically based reproductive attraction is interpreted as a love attraction so that the male feels immediately drawn to the female, but what he may actually see is an egg needing fertilization.

 Self-Assessment: Love Attitudes Scale
You can assess the degree to which you are romantic or conjugal (realistic) in your attitude toward love by completing the Love Attitudes Scale self-assessment at the end of this chapter.

In contrast to romantic love is realistic love. Realistic love is also known as conjugal love. **Conjugal love** is the love between married people characterized by companionship, calmness, comfort, and security. Conjugal love is in contrast to romantic love, which is characterized by excitement and passion. Stanik et al. (2013) interviewed 146 African American couples who had been married from 3 to 25 years and confirmed a decrease in the intensity of love feelings across time.

4-1b Love Styles

Theorist John Lee (1973, 1988) identified various styles of love that describe the way individuals view love and relate to each other.

lust sexual desire.

infatuation emotional feelings based on little actual exposure to the love object.

romantic love an intense love whereby the lover believes in love at first sight, only one true love, and love conquers all.

conjugal (married) love the love between married people characterized by companionship, calmness, comfort, and security.

1. **Ludic.** The **ludic love style** views love as a game in which the player has no intention of getting seriously involved. The ludic lover refuses to become dependent on any one person and does not encourage another's intimacy. Two essential skills of the ludic lover are to juggle several partners at the same time and to manage each relationship so that no one partner is seen too often.

   These strategies help ensure that the relationship does not deepen into an all-consuming love. Don Juan represented the classic ludic lover, embodying the motto of "Love 'em and leave 'em." Tzeng et al. (2003) found that whereas men were more likely than women to be ludic lovers, ludic love characterized the love style of college students the least.

2. **Pragma.** The **pragma love style** is the love of the pragmatic—that which is logical and rational. Pragma lovers assess their partners on the basis of assets and liabilities. An undergraduate male dated his partner because she had an apartment and would cook for him. Pragma lovers do not become involved in interracial, long-distance, or age-discrepant relationships because logic argues against doing so. The Personal View section emphasizes using one's heart or head in making decisions.

> My mind would rule my heart. I didn't pay attention to the light in the dark.
>
> —DISCLOSURE WITH SAM SMITH, *OMEN REFLECTIONS*

Diversity in Love throughout the World

The theme of U.S. culture is individualism, which translates into personal fulfillment, emotional intimacy, and love as the reason for marriage. In Asian cultures (e.g., China) the theme is collectivism, which focuses on "family, comradeship, obligations to others, and altruism" with love as secondary (Riela et al., 2010). While arranged marriages are and have been the norm in Eastern societies, love marriages are becoming more frequent (Allendorf, 2013).

teolin/Shutterstock.com

ludic love style
love style that views love as a game in which the love interest is one of several partners, is never seen too often, and is kept at an emotional distance.

pragma love style love style that is logical and rational; the love partner is evaluated in terms of assets and liabilities.

eros love style love style characterized by passion and romance.

mania love style an out-of-control love whereby the person "must have" the love object; obsessive jealousy and controlling behavior are symptoms of manic love.

3. **Eros.** Just the opposite of the pragmatic love style, the **eros love style** (also known as romantic love) is imbued with passion and sexual desire. Eros is the most common love style of college women and men (Tzeng et al., 2003) and has been associated with higher relationship satisfaction (Vedes et al., 2016).

4. **Mania.** The **mania love style** is the out-of-control love whereby the person "must have" the love object. Jealousy, possessiveness, dependency, and controlling are symptoms of manic love.

> If I can't have you, no one else will.
>
> —MOTTO OF THE LOVE OF MANIA

5. **Storge.** The **storge love style**, also known as companionate love, is a calm, soothing, nonsexual love devoid of intense passion. Respect, friendship, commitment, and familiarity are characteristics that help define the storge (pronounced STOR-jay) love relationship. The partners care deeply about each

Love Dream Comes True

(Below is a note written by a husband on the 19th anniversary of his marriage to his wife.)

Dear Dianne,

I thought I would write this note instead of buying an anniversary card that someone else wrote that may or may not express my feelings:

I want you to know that I fell in love with the outside of you on our first date a little over nineteen years ago. I knew after we made love that first time that I had found someone extraordinary.

Dianne, it took me several weeks to find out that I also found someone extraordinary inside. I knew that you had that rare quality of unconditional love that people speak about but rarely find. I can tell you that if I could turn the clock back nineteen years I would not hesitate one second to marry you again.

I had a list of things I wanted in a woman before I met you, but frankly I did not think I could ever find someone who would have them all. Dianne, here is the list!

I wanted someone:

Who was beautiful both inside and out!

I wanted someone who was smart!

I wanted someone I could trust!

I wanted someone I could take anywhere and be proud of!

I wanted someone who would love my kid's like her own!

I wanted someone who would eventually be a wonderful grandmother!

I wanted someone I wanted to be with all the time!

I wanted someone who liked doing the things I like to do!

I wanted someone who I could spend the rest of my life with!

I wanted my wife to be my best friend!

I wanted a special lover!

I found all of these things and more in you. I thank God I found you nineteen years ago!!!!!!!!!

Thanks for being the best partner a man could have.

Love Always,

Ray

other but not in a romantic or lustful sense. One's grandparents who have been married 50 years are likely to have a storge type of love. Neto (2012) compared love perceptions by age group and found that the older the individual, the more important love became and the less important sex became.

6. **Agape.** **Agape love style** is characterized by a focus on the well-being of the person who is loved, with little regard for reciprocation. Key qualities of agape love are not responding to a partner's negativity and not expecting an exchange for positives but believing that the other means well and will respond kindly in time. Like the love style of eros, agape has been associated with relationship satisfaction (Vedes et al., 2016). The love parents have for their children is often described as agape love.

7. **Compassionate love.** While not one of the six love styles identified by John Lee, **compassionate love** (emotional feelings toward another that generate behaviors to promote the partner's well-being) is a unique and important style of love (Fehr et al., 2014). Specific behaviors associated with compassionate love include: concern for the other's well-being (doing things to help the partner achieve his or

> **storge love style** a love consisting of friendship that is calm and nonsexual.
>
> **agape love style** love style characterized by a focus on the well-being of the love object, with little regard for reciprocation; the love of parents for their children is agape love.
>
> **compassionate love** emotional feelings toward another that generate behaviors to promote the partner's well-being.

"Using One's Heart or Head to Make Relationship Decisions?"

Lovers are frequently confronted with the need to make decisions about their relationships, but they are divided on whether to let their heart or their head rule in such decisions. We asked students in our classes to fill in the details about deciding with their heart or their head. Some of their answers follow.

Heart

Those who relied on their hearts for making decisions felt that emotions were more important than logic and that listening to their heart made them happier. One woman said:

> In deciding on a mate, my heart would rule because my heart has reasons to cry and my head doesn't. My heart knows what I want, what would make me most happy. My head tells me what is best for me. But I would rather have something that makes me happy than something that is good for me.

Some men also agreed that the heart should rule. One said:

> I went with my heart in a situation, and I'm glad I did. I had been hanging out with a girl for two years when I decided she was not the one I wanted

and that my present girlfriend was. My heart was saying to go for the one I loved, but my head was telling me not to because if I broke up with the first girl, it would hurt her, her parents, and my parents. But I decided I had to make myself happy and went with the feelings in my heart and started dating the girl who is now my fiancée.

Relying on one's emotions does not always have a positive outcome, as the following experience illustrates:

> Last semester, I was dating a guy I felt more for than he did for me. Despite that, I wanted to spend any opportunity I could with him when he asked me to go somewhere with him. One day he had no classes, and he asked me to go to the park by the river for a picnic. I had four classes that day and exams in two of them. I let my heart rule and went with him. He ended up breaking up with me on the picnic.

Head

Some undergraduates make relationship choices based on their head as some of the following comments show:

> In deciding on a mate, I feel my head should rule because you have to choose someone that you

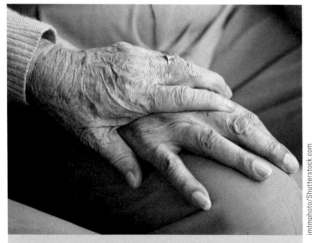

Older couples married many years are likely to have a storge type of love.

imtmphoto/Shutterstock.com

her goals/experience satisfaction), understanding/acceptance (adopting the other person's point of view), respect and admiration (value the person), and openness (being receptive to the other's preferences and opinions) (Reis et al., 2014).

While eros/romantic love style is hormonally driven, compassionate love involves self-sacrifice and support for the partner over time. The genders do not differ in their capacity for compassionate love (which is associated with relationship quality in terms of closeness, satisfaction, commitment) (Fehr et al., 2014).

4-1c Triangular View of Love

Sternberg (1986) developed the "triangular" view of love, which consists of three basic elements: intimacy, can get along with after the new wears off. If you follow your heart solely, you may not look deep enough into a person to see what it is that you really like. Is it just a pretty face or a nice body? Or is it deeper than that, such as common interests and values? The "heart" sometimes can fog up this picture of the true person and distort reality into a fairy tale.

Another student said:

Love is blind and can play tricks on you. Two years ago, I fell in love with a man whom I later found out was married. Although my heart had learned to love this man, my mind knew the consequences and told me to stop seeing him. My heart said, "Maybe he'll leave her for me," but my mind said, "If he cheated on her, he'll cheat on you." I broke up with him and am glad that I listened to my head.

Some individuals feel that both the head and the heart should rule when making relationship decisions.

When you really love someone, your heart rules in most of the situations. But if you don't keep your head in some matters, then you risk losing the love that you feel in your heart. I think that we should find a way to let our heads and hearts work together.

Madelyn Coates

Data suggest that women are more emotional/relational in their thinking than men, but that men may be more romantic. The result is that there may be few gender differences in whether the head or heart rules.

There is an adage, "Don't wait until you find the person you can live with; wait and find the person that you can't live without!" In your own decisions you might consider the relative merits of listening to your heart or head and moving forward recognizing there is not one "right" answer for all individuals on all issues.

passion, and commitment. The presence or absence of these three elements creates various types of love experienced between individuals, regardless of their sexual orientation. These various types include the following:

1. **Nonlove.** The absence of intimacy, passion, and commitment. Two strangers looking at each other from afar are experiencing nonlove.

2. **Liking.** Intimacy without passion or commitment. A new friendship may be described in these terms of the partners liking each other.

3. **Infatuation.** Passion without intimacy or commitment. Two people flirting with each other in a bar may be infatuated with each other.

4. **Romantic love.** Intimacy and passion without commitment. Love at first sight reflects this type of love.

5. **Conjugal love** (also known as married love). Intimacy and commitment without passion. A couple married for 50 years are said to illustrate conjugal love.

6. **Fatuous love.** Passion and commitment without intimacy. Couples who are passionately wild about each other and talk of the future but do not have an intimate connection with each other have a fatuous love.

7. **Empty love.** Commitment without passion or intimacy. A couple who stay together for social (e.g., children) and legal reasons but who have no spark or emotional sharing between them have an empty love.

8. **Consummate love.** Combination of intimacy, passion, and commitment; Sternberg's view of the ultimate, all-consuming love.

Individuals bring different combinations of the elements of intimacy, passion, and commitment (the triangle) to the table of love. One lover may bring a predominance of passion, with some intimacy but no commitment (romantic love), whereas the other person brings commitment but no passion or intimacy (empty love). The triangular theory of love allows lovers to see the degree to which they are matched in terms of passion, intimacy, and commitment in their relationship.

4-1d Love Languages

Gary Chapman's (2010) **five love languages** have become part of U.S. love culture. These five languages are gifts, quality time, words of affirmation, acts of service, and physical touch. Chapman encourages individuals to use the language of love most desired by the partner rather than the one preferred by the individual providing the love. Chapman has published nine books (e.g., for couples, singles, men, military) to illustrate the application of five love languages in different contexts. No empirical studies have been conducted on the five languages.

A new language of love is digital where relationships are begun and nurtured via texting. While texting allows one the freedom in response time, the norm is to reply within 24 hours. Using a variety of text options (e.g., photos, audio, and visual messages) enhances couple communication. Suggestions offered to potential romantic couples include (Milne, 2015): (1) Text on noteworthy occasions (e.g., "I had a great time yesterday" and "good luck on your interview today"). (2) Call if talking would be better. (3) Flirt

five love languages
identified by Gary Chapman and now part of American love culture, these are gifts, quality time, words of affirmation, acts of service, and physical touch.

Some partners define washing dishes as one of the languages of love.

with caution. Before diving into racy confessions, begin with general flirting, such as referring to holding hands or kissing. Increase flirting based on the other person's reaction. (4) Don't text at odd hours. Be respectful and thoughtful of others' schedules. Even if the cell is off, texting at 3 A.M. conveys lack of consideration. (5) Don't say anything you wouldn't say in person. If you anticipate the message will cause intense positive or negative emotional reactions, say it in person. The first "I love you" and difficult subjects should be talking with the person. (6) Don't text if you have been drinking. The "drunk text" is a turnoff.

Facebook is a pervasive event in the lives of many individuals and couples. Northrup and Smith (2016) studied how Facebook time affects a couple's romantic relationship. They found that "couples who engage in more Facebook maintenance tend to experience less love towards each other, and couples who feel more love towards each other engage in less relationship maintenance via Facebook" (p. 249). The researchers suggested that "healthy couples who engage in face-to-face relationship maintenance find that relationship maintenance via Facebook is not needed" (p. 249). "Why would couples who engage in more Facebook maintenance seem to experience less love?

The answer here may be that couples who feel less love for each other may feel the need to present to friends and family online as if everything is fine, and therefore engage in more relationship maintenance via Facebook" (p. 249).

4-1e Polyamory

Poly (many) and amory (love) make up the word **polyamory**—open emotional and sexual involvement with three or more people (honesty and respect are norms common upon polyamorists). An online survey of 34 self-identified polyamorists revealed that they tended to be Democratic, liberal, nonreligious but "spiritual," and accepting of abortion and gay marriage (Jenks, 2014). Being in their thirties and forties is common with as few as 1.2 million practicing polyamory (Scheff, 2014). Polyamorists are different from **swinging** (persons who exchange partners for the purpose of sex) in that the latter are more focused on sex. Swingers also tend to be older, more educated, and have higher incomes.

4-2 SOCIAL CONTROL OF LOVE

Though we think of love as an individual experience, the society in which we live exercises considerable control over our love object or choice. The ultimate social control of love is **arranged marriage**—mate selection pattern whereby parents select the spouse of their offspring. Parents arrange 80% of marriages in China, India, and Indonesia (three countries representing 40% of the world's population). In most Eastern countries marriage is regarded as the linking of two families; the love feelings of the respective partners are irrelevant. Love is expected to follow marriage, not precede it. Arranged marriages not only help guarantee that cultural traditions will be carried on and passed to the new generation, but they also link two family systems together for mutual support of the couple.

Parents may know a family who has a son or daughter whom they would regard as a suitable partner for their offspring. If not, they may put an advertisement in a newspaper identifying the qualities they are seeking. The prospective mate is then interviewed by the family to confirm his or her suitability. Or a third person—a matchmaker—may be hired to do the screening and introducing.

Selecting a spouse for a daughter may begin early in the child's life. In some countries (e.g., Nepal and Afghanistan), child marriage occurs whereby young females (ages 8 to 12) are required to marry an older man selected by their parents. Suicide is the only alternative "choice" for these children.

While parents in Eastern societies may exercise direct control by selecting the partner for their son or daughter, American parents influence mate choice by moving to certain neighborhoods, joining certain churches, and enrolling their children in certain schools. Doing so increases the chance that their offspring will "hang out" with, fall in love with, and marry people who are similar in race, religion, education, and social class. Parents want their offspring to meet someone who will "fit in" and with whom they will feel comfortable.

Diamond (2003) emphasized that individuals are biologically wired and capable of falling in love and establishing intense emotional bonds with members of their own or opposite sex. Discovering that one's offspring is in love with and wants to marry someone of the same sex is a challenge for many parents.

> There isn't anything in this world but mad love. Not in this world. No tame love, calm love, mild love, not so-so love. And, of course, no reasonable love. Also there are a hundred paths through the world which are easier than loving. But, who wants easier?
>
> —MARY OLIVER, POET

4-3 LOVE THEORIES: ORIGINS OF LOVE

Various theories have been suggested with regard to the origins of love.

4-3a Evolutionary Theory

The **evolutionary theory of love** is that individuals are motivated to emotionally bond with a partner to ensure a stable relationship for producing and rearing children. In effect, love is a bonding mechanism

polyamory open emotional and sexual involvement with three or more people.

swinging persons who exchange partners for the purpose of sex.

arranged marriage mate selection pattern whereby parents select the spouse of their offspring.

evolutionary theory of love theory that individuals are motivated to emotionally bond with a partner to ensure a stable relationship for producing and rearing children.

between the parents during the time their offspring are dependent infants. Love's strongest bonding lasts about four years after birth, the time when children are most dependent and when two parents are most beneficial to the developing infant. "If a woman was carrying the equivalent of a twelve-pound bowling ball in one arm and a pile of sticks in the other, it was ecologically critical to pair up with a mate to rear the young," observed anthropologist Helen Fisher (Toufexis, 1993). The "four-year itch" is Fisher's term for the time at which parents with one child are most likely to divorce—the time when the woman can more easily survive without parenting help from the male. If the couple has a second child, doing so resets the clock, and the "seven-year itch" is the next most vulnerable time.

4-3b Learning Theory

Unlike evolutionary theory, which views the experience of love as innate, learning theory emphasizes that love feelings develop in response to certain behaviors engaged in by the partner. Individuals in a new relationship who look at each other, smile at each other, compliment each other, touch each other endearingly, do things for each other, and do enjoyable things together are engaging in behaviors that encourage the development of love feelings. In effect, love can be viewed as a feeling that results from a high frequency of positive behavior and a low frequency of negative behavior. People who "fall out of love" may note the high frequency of negatives on the part of their partner and the low frequency of positives. People who say, "this is not the person I married," are saying the ratio of positives to negatives has changed dramatically.

4-3c Sociological Theory

Sixty years ago, Ira Reiss (1960) suggested the wheel model as an explanation for how love develops. Basically, the wheel has four stages—rapport, self-revelation, mutual dependency, and fulfillment of personality needs. In the rapport stage, each partner has the feeling of having known the partner before, feels comfortable with the partner, and wants to deepen the relationship.

Such desire leads to self-revelation or self-disclosure, whereby each reveals intimate thoughts to the other about oneself, the partner, and the relationship. Such revelations deepen the relationship because it is assumed that the confidences are shared only with special people, and each partner feels special when listening to the revelations of the other.

4-3d Psychosexual Theory

According to psychosexual theory, love results from blocked biological sexual desires. In the sexually repressive mood of his time, Sigmund Freud (1905/1938) referred to love as "aim-inhibited sex." Love was viewed as a function of the sexual desire a person was not allowed to express because of social restraints. In Freud's era, people would meet, fall in love, get married, and have sex. Freud felt that the socially required delay from first meeting to having sex resulted in the development of "love feelings." By extrapolation, Freud's theory of love suggests that love dies with marriage (access to one's sexual partner).

4-3e Biochemical Theory

"Love is deeply biological" wrote Carter and Porges (2013), who reviewed the biochemistry involved in the development and maintenance of love. They noted that oxytocin and vasopressin are hormones involved in the development and maintenance of social bonding. The hormones are active in forging emotional connections between adults and infants and between adults. They are also necessary for our social and physiological survival.

Oxytocin is released from the pituitary gland during the expulsive stage of labor that has been associated with the onset of maternal behavior in lower animals (but oxytocin may be manufactured in both women and men when an infant or another person

oxytocin a hormone released from the pituitary gland during the expulsive stage of labor that has been associated with the onset of maternal behavior in lower animals.

Love begins by the reciprocal sharing of words and feelings.

TABLE 4.1   LOVE THEORIES AND CRITICISMS

Theory	Criticism
Evolutionary. Love is the social glue that bonds parents with dependent children and spouses with each other to care for offspring.	The assumption that women and children need men for economic/emotional survival is not true today. Women can have and rear children without male partners.
Learning. Positive experiences create love feelings.	The theory does not account for (1) why some people share positive experiences but do not fall in love, and (2) why some people stay in love despite negative behavior by their partner.
Psychosexual. Love results from blocked biological drive.	The theory does not account for couples who report intense love feelings and have sex regularly.
Sociological. The wheel theory whereby love develops from rapport, self-revelation, mutual dependency, and personality need fulfillment.	Not all people are capable of rapport, revealing oneself, and so on.
Biochemical. Love is chemical. Oxytocin is an amphetamine-like chemical that bonds mother to child and produces a giddy high in young lovers.	The theory does not specify how much of what chemicals result in the feeling of love. Chemicals alone cannot create the state of love; cognitions are also important.
Attachment. Primary motivation in life is to be connected to others. Children bond with parents and spouses to each other.	Not all people feel the need to be emotionally attached to others. Some prefer to be detached.

is present—hence it is not dependent on the birth process) (Carter & Porges, 2013). Oxytocin has been referred to as the "cuddle chemical" because of its significance in bonding. Later in life, oxytocin seems operative in the development of love feelings between lovers during sexual arousal. Oxytocin may be responsible for the fact that more women than men prefer to continue cuddling after intercourse.

Phenylethylamine (PEA) is a natural, amphetamine-like substance that makes lovers feel euphoric and energized. The high that they report feeling just by being with each other is from PEA that the brain releases into their bloodstream. The natural chemical high associated with love may explain why the intensity of passionate love decreases over time. As with any amphetamine, the body builds up a tolerance to PEA, and it takes more and more to produce the special kick. Hence, lovers develop a tolerance for each other. "Love junkies" are those who go from one love affair to the next to maintain the high. Alternatively, some lovers break up and get back together frequently as a way of making the relationship new again and keeping the high going.

4-3f Attachment Theory

The attachment theory of love emphasizes that a primary motivation in life is to be emotionally connected with other people. Children abandoned by their parents and placed in foster care (400,000 are in foster care in the United States) are vulnerable to having their early emotional attachment to their parents disrupted and developing "reactive attachment disorder" (Stinehart et al., 2012). This disorder involves a child who is anxious and insecure since he or she does not feel to be in a safe and

protected environment. Such children find it difficult to connect emotionally, and this deficit continues into adulthood. Conversely, a secure emotional attachment with loving adults as a child is associated with the capacity for later involvement in satisfying, loving, communicative adult relationships.

Each of the theories of love presented in this section has critics (see Table 4.1).

4-4   LOVE AS A CONTEXT FOR PROBLEMS

> If love be good, from whennes comth my wo?
>
> —GEOFFREY CHAUCER, ENGLISH POET

For all of its joy, love involves heartache and problems. Six such problems follow.

4-4a Unrequited/Unreciprocated Love

Unrequited love is a one-sided love where one's love is not returned. In the 16th century, it was called "lovesickness"; today it is known as erotomania or erotic melancholy (Kem, 2010). An example is from the short story "Winter Dreams" by F. Scott Fitzgerald. Dexter Green is in love with Judy

unrequited love a one-sided love where one's love is not returned.

Jones. "He loved her, and he would love her until the day he was too old for loving—but he could not have her."

Blomquist and Giuliano (2012) assessed the reactions of a sample of adults and college students to a partner telling them "I love you." The predominant response by both men and women was "I'm just not there yet." Both genders acknowledged that while this response was honest, it would hurt the individual who was in love.

4-4b Making Risky, Dangerous Choices

Some research suggests that individuals in love make risky, dangerous, or questionable decisions. Nonsmokers who become romantically involved with a smoker are more likely to begin smoking (Kennedy et al., 2011). Similarly, couples in love and in a stable relationship are less likely to use a condom (doing so is not very romantic) (Warren et al., 2012). Of 381 undergraduates, 70% reported that they had engaged in unprotected sex with their romantic partner (Elliott et al., 2012).

4-4c Ending the Relationship with One's Parents

Some parents disapprove of the partner their son or daughter is involved with (e.g., race, religion, age) to the point that their offspring will end the relationship with their parents. "They told me I couldn't come home if I kept dating this guy, so I stopped going home" said one of our students who was involved with a partner of a different race. Choosing to end a relationship with one's parents is a definite downside of love.

4-4d Simultaneous Loves

While most individuals who are dating expect fidelity in their partners (Watkins & Boon, 2016), sometimes an individual is in love with two or

Valua Vitaly/Shutterstock.com

more people at the same time. While this is acceptable in polyamorous relationships where the partners agree on multiple relationships, simultaneous loves become a serious problem.

4-4e Abusive Relationships

Twenty-three percent of 2,375 undergraduate males and 37% of 7,573 undergraduate females reported that they had been involved in an emotionally abusive relationship with a partner. As for physical abuse, 5% of the males and 11% of the females reported such previous involvement (Hall & Knox, 2016). The primary reason individuals report that they remain in an abusive relationship is love for the partner.

> The hottest love has the coldest end.
>
> —SOCRATES, PHILOSOPHER

4-4f Profound Sadness/Depression When a Love Relationship Ends

Just as love (love defined as emotion, behavior, and commitment) is associated with relationship happiness (Harris et al., 2016), its end is the cause of profound sadness/depression. Fisher et al. (2010) noted that "romantic rejection causes a profound sense of loss and negative affect. It can induce clinical depression and in extreme cases lead to suicide and/or homicide." The researchers studied brain changes via magnetic resonance imaging of 10 women and five men who had recently been rejected by a partner but reported they were still intensely "in love." Participants alternately viewed a photograph of their rejecting beloved and a photograph of a familiar individual interspersed with a distraction-attention task. Their responses while looking at the photo of the person who rejected them included feelings of love, despair, good, and bad memories, and wondering about why this happened. Brain image reactions to being rejected by a lover are similar to withdrawal from cocaine.

While there is no recognized definition or diagnostic criteria for "love addiction," some similarities to substance dependence include: euphoria and unrestrained desire in the presence of the love object or associated stimuli (drug intoxication); negative mood and sleep disturbance when separated from the love object (drug withdrawal); intrusive thoughts about the love object; and problems associated with love which may lead to clinically significant impairment or distress (Reynaud et al., 2011).

Problems associated with love begin early. Starr et al. (2012) conducted a study of 83 seventh and eighth grade girls (mean age 13.8) and found an association between those who reported involvement in romantic activities (e.g., flirting, dating, kissing) and depression, anxiety, and eating disorders. The researchers pointed out that it was unclear if romance led to these outcomes or if the girls who were depressed, anxious, etc., sought romance to help cope with their depressive symptoms.

It is important to feel good about oneself if one is to fall in love.

4-5 HOW LOVE DEVELOPS IN A NEW RELATIONSHIP

Various social, physical, psychological, physiological, and cognitive conditions affect the development of love relationships.

4-5a Social Conditions for Love

Our society promotes love through popular music, movies, and novels. These media convey the message that love is an experience to pursue, enjoy, and maintain. People who fall out of love are encouraged to try again: "Love is lovelier the second time you fall." Unlike people reared in Eastern cultures, Americans grow up in a cultural context which encourages them to turn on their radar for love.

4-5b Psychological Conditions for Love

Various psychological conditions associated with falling in love include perception of reciprocal liking, personality, high self-esteem, and self-disclosure.

PERCEPTION OF RECIPROCAL LIKING Riela et al. (2010) conducted two studies on falling in love using both American and Chinese samples. The researchers found that one of the most important psychological factors associated with falling in love was the perception of reciprocal liking. When one perceives that he or she is desired by someone else, this perception has the effect of increasing the attraction toward that person. Such an increase is particularly strong if the person is very physically attractive (Greitemeyer, 2010).

PERSONALITY QUALITIES The personality of the love object has an important effect on falling in love (Riela et al., 2010). Viewing the partner as intelligent or having a sense of humor is an example of a quality that makes the lover want to be with the beloved.

SELF-ESTEEM High self-esteem is important for falling in love because it enables individuals to feel worthy of being loved. Feeling good about yourself allows you to believe that others are capable of loving you. Individuals with low self-esteem doubt that someone else can love and accept them.

SELF-DISCLOSURE Disclosing oneself is necessary if one is to fall in love—to feel invested in another. Ross (2006) identified eight dimensions of self-disclosure: (1) background and history, (2) feelings toward the partner, (3) feelings toward self, (4) feelings about one's body, (5) attitudes toward social issues, (6) tastes and interests, (7) money and work, and (8) feelings about friends. Disclosed feelings about the partner included "how much I like the partner," "my feelings about our sexual relationship," "how much I trust my partner," "things I dislike about my partner," and "my thoughts about the future of our relationship"—all of which are associated with relationship satisfaction. Of interest in Ross's findings is that disclosing one's tastes and interests was negatively associated with relationship satisfaction. By telling a partner too much detail about what he or she liked, partners discovered something that turned them off and lowered their relationship satisfaction.

It is not easy for some people to let others know who they are, what they feel, or what they think. **Alexithymia** is a personality trait which describes a person with little affect. The term means "lack of

> **alexithymia** a personality trait which describes a person with little affect.

From a Hookup to a Committed Love Relationship

Hooking up is defined as an initial sexual encounter between individuals who have no future relationship commitment. Outcomes include no subsequent hookups, hookups but the relationship remains sexual/casual, and hookups that transition to a committed relationship. The typical outcome is that the partners do not see each other again. If they do the relationship does not transition to a committed relationship. But some hookups transition to a committed relationship. The goal of this study was to identify how often a hookup transitions into a love relationship, what occurs, and what strategies are involved.

The sample consisted of 206 undergraduates at a large southeastern university who completed a 50-item Internet questionnaire. Seventy-one percent of the respondents reported that that they had hooked up before. Almost a quarter (22%) reported that they were currently in a relationship that began as a hookup. The time it took for most relationships to transition was between one and three months.

Sixty-two percent of the sample reported that they believed that hookups can lead to stable relationships. Those most likely to transition to a committed relationship reported various strategies, repeated hookups, discussion of their relationship/defined it as more than sexual, and spending time in nonsexual contexts enjoying each other and their relationship. A common scenario was:

We were "hooking up" every other day. The time we began to spend together evolved into emotion for one another. After we established this emotion for one another, it was evident that we had to pursue a long-term relationship.

An analysis of the written qualitative responses on the questionnaire revealed various ways in which hooking up facilitated transition to a committed relationship. Respondents identified sexual and romantic chemistry (54.4%) as the strongest facilitator of transition. The second-most frequently mentioned facilitator was out-of-bed time spent together (26.6%). Only a small percentage (3%) threatened to cut off the sex until the partner committed.

In terms of who initiated commitment, men were most likely to initiate relationship commitment (53.1%); women were the least likely (18.7%). Almost 30% (28.1%) indicated that the commitment process was mutual. Women were significantly more likely than men to report interest in transitioning a hookup if the partner's future aligned with his or her own.

In summary, over one in five hookups transitioned into committed relationships. Doing so involved strategies such as continuing to hook up, having a conversation that defined the relationship, spending time together doing things of mutual interest, and telling the partner that "I want a relationship, not just a sexual relationship."

Source: Adapted from Erichsen, K. & P. Dignam. (2016, April 2016). From hookup to husband: Transitioning a casual to a committed relationship. Paper, Southern Sociological Society Annual Meeting, Atlanta, GA.

words for emotions," which suggests that the person does not experience or convey emotion. Persons with alexithymia are not capable of experiencing psychological intimacy. Frye-Cox (2012) studied 155 couples who had been married an average of 18.6 years and found that an alexithymic spouse reported lower marital quality, as did his or her spouse. Alexithymia also tends to repel individuals in mate selection in that persons who seek an emotional relationship are not reinforced by alexithymics.

4-5c What Makes Love Last

Caryl Rusbult's investment model of commitment has been used to identify why relationships last. While love is important, there are other factors involved:

People become dependent on their relationships because they (a) are satisfied with the relationship—it gratifies important needs, including companionship, intimacy, and sexuality; (b) believe their alternatives are poor—their most important needs could not be

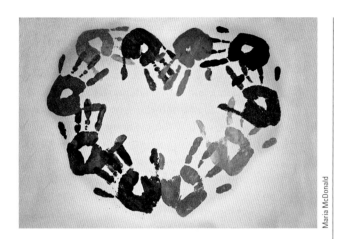

Maria McDonald

gratified independent of the particular relationship (e.g., in an alternative relationship, by friends and kin); and (c) have invested many important resources in the relationship (e.g., time, effort, shared friendship network, and material possessions). *(Finkenauer, 2010, p. 162)*

Hence, people stay in a relationship because their needs are being met, they have no place to go, and they have made considerable investment in getting where they are and do not want to give it all up. Lambert et al. (2012) also identified a behavior associated with weakening one's love/commitment to a partner—pornography. In a study of 240 undergraduates, higher use of pornography was associated with more flirting and infidelity in the form of hooking up. "Our research suggests that there is a relationship cost associated with pornography" (p. 432).

4-5d Loves That Don't Last

Ogolsky et al. (2016) analyzed how 232 couple relationships changed over a nine-month period. They interviewed the respective partners and categorized their relationships in terms of different types of commitment: dramatic commitment (34%), conflict commitment (12%), socially involved (19%), and partner focused (30%). The first two categories (46%) were characterized by negative attributions and behaviors. The second two categories (49%) were characterized by more positive feelings, attributions, and behaviors. Twenty percent of the couples broke up by the ninth month of the study. Partners most likely to break up were "passionately in love," suggesting great volatility. Those most likely to stay together were partner focused; they spent their time together and derived their satisfactions from each other, not the social context of courtship/other couples.

4-6 CULTURAL FACTORS IN RELATIONSHIP DEVELOPMENT

Individuals are not free to become involved with/marry whomever they want. Rather, their culture and society radically restrict and influence their choice. The best example of mate choice being culturally and socially controlled is the fact that *less than* 1% of the over 63 million marriages in the United States consist of a Black spouse and a White spouse (*Proquest Statistical Abstract of the United States, 2016*, Table 60). Indeed, up until the late sixties, such marriages in most states were a felony and mixed spouses were put in jail. In 1967, the Supreme Court ruled that mixed marriages (e.g., between Whites and Blacks) were legal. Only since June of 2015 have homosexuals had the legal right to marry.

Endogamy and exogamy are also two forms of cultural pressure operative in mate selection.

4-6a Endogamy

Endogamy is the cultural expectation to select a marriage partner within one's own social group, such as in the same race, religion, and social class. Endogamous pressures involve social approval from parents for selecting a partner within one's own group and disapproval for selecting someone outside one's own group. As noted above, the pressure toward an endogamous mate choice is especially strong when race is involved. Love may be blind, but it knows the color of one's partner as the overwhelming majority of individuals end up selecting someone of the same race to marry.

4-6b Exogamy

Exogamy is the cultural pressure to marry outside the family group (e.g., you cannot marry your siblings). Woody Allen experienced enormous social disapproval because he fell in love with and married in 1997 his long-time partner's adopted daughter Soon-Yi Previn. (They remain married.)

Incest taboos are universal; in addition, children are not permitted to marry the parent of the other sex in any society. In the United States, siblings and (in some states) first cousins are also prohibited from marrying each other. The reason for such restrictions is fear of genetic defects in children whose parents are too closely related.

endogamy the cultural expectation to select a marriage partner within one's social group.

exogamy the cultural expectation that one will marry outside the family group.

Once cultural factors have determined the general **pool of eligibles** (the population from which a person may select a mate), individual mate choice becomes more operative. However, even when individuals feel that they are making their own choices, social influences are still operative (e.g., approval from one's peers).

4-6c Continuum for Arranged Marriages

Pande (2016) revealed the continuum of arranged marriages in British–Indian London society. These include the "traditional arranged marriage," whereby the parents set up the meeting between the partners, they are not allowed to be alone, and they have little input into partner choice.

"Semi-arranged marriages" are those in which the parents and their offspring consult with each other, a viable candidate is identified, and the offspring would spend time with the person in the presence of the family with the goal of falling in love. Hence, the partner is preapproved and need only the love and agreement of the offspring.

"Love with arranged marriage" involves the partners meeting on their own, dating, falling in love, and then asking for their parents' permission. Since the partner chosen to fall in love with had characteristics (e.g., religion, education, age, family values) the parents would like, in most cases the parents would sign off and the wedding plans would go forward.

"Arranged weddings" are very similar to what happens in America: the couple alert the parents that they are getting married and the parents take over and arrange all the wedding plans. There is an understood agreement for mate choice by the parents since they are investing time and money.

4-6d The Digital Language of Love ("lylc < 3" love you like crazy, heart)

With the advent of smartphones, texting has become pervasive. According to the Pew Research Center (2015), 85% of young adults own smartphones, and text messaging is one of the most frequently used features. The median number of texts sent by teen users is 60 texts per day (Lenhart, 2012). Women college students spend an average of 10 hours a day on smartphones, men almost 8 hours (Robert & Williams, 2012).

Texting has become an integral part of our culture. Texting is convenient, immediate, discreet, and facilitates multitasking. Text messages are saved and individuals can respond when they choose. The versatility and creativity in texting are unique. Individuals can send multimedia messages with one swipe of a finger, and many are fluent in using symbols such as emojis (☺ smile), emoticons (☹ tears), and abbreviations (b4 before).

While texting allows one the freedom in response time, the norm is to reply within 24 hours. Using a variety of text options (e.g., photos, audio, and visual messages) enhances couple communication. Suggestions offered to potential romantic couples include (Milne, 2015): (1) Text on noteworthy occasions (e.g., "I had a great time yesterday" and "good luck on your interview today"). (2) Call if talking would be better. (3) Flirt with caution. Before diving into racy confessions, begin with general flirting, such as referring to holding hands or kissing. Increase flirting based on the other person's reaction. (4) Don't text at odd hours. Be respectful and thoughtful of others' schedules. Even if the cell is off, texting at 3 A.M. conveys lack of consideration. (5) Don't say anything you wouldn't say in person. If you anticipate the message will cause intense positive or negative emotional reactions, say it in person. The first "I love you" and difficult subjects should be talking with the person. (6) Don't text if you have been drinking. The "drunk text" is a turnoff.

Texting is involved in relationship formation and development. In order to minimize the pitfalls of texting, make expectations (e.g., how often) and boundaries (e.g., previous romantic partners) clear (Przybylski & Weinstein, 2012; Turkle, 2011). While texting cannot replace in-person communication, it provides a way for couples to stay connected throughout the day, exchange affection, and share information. Texting is the digital language of love.

4-7 SOCIOLOGICAL FACTORS IN RELATIONSHIP DEVELOPMENT

Numerous sociological factors are at work in bringing two people together who eventually marry.

4-7a Homogamy

Although endogamy refers to cultural pressure to select within one's own group, **homogamy** ("like selects like") refers to the tendency for the individual to seek a mate with similar characteristics (e.g., age, race, education). In general, the more couples have in common, the higher the reported relationship satisfaction and the more durable the relationship.

pool of eligibles the population from which a person selects an appropriate mate.

homogamy tendency to select someone with similar characteristics.

RACE Race refers to physical characteristics that are given social significance. Racism may be both blatant and subtle (Yoo et al., 2010). Blatant racism involves outright name calling and discrimination. Tiger Woods was once denied the right to play golf on a Georgia golf course because he is Black. Subtle racism involves omissions, inactions, or failure to help, rather than a conscious desire to hurt. Not sitting at a table where persons of another race are sitting or failing to stop to help a person because of his or her race is subtle racism.

Race is relevant to relationships in that some data suggested that there are power differentials. Hall and Knox (2017) examined power in 1,098 undergraduate heterosexual relationships reported by one of the partners at a Midwest and Southeastern university. There was considerable variation by race with White respondents more likely than non-White respondents to report having equal power with their partner (70.9% and 61.9%, respectively), and non-White respondents more likely than White respondents to report having more power in their relationship (26.5% and 18.3%, respectively). Hispanics were particularly likely to report having more power in the relationship (34.5%). Respondent gender, age, and religiosity were not related to reports of relationship power differences. Equality of power in relationships has been associated with relationship satisfaction.

Increasingly, American married couples involve someone whose partner is of a different race/ethnicity. Blacks, younger individuals, and the politically liberal are more willing to cross racial lines for dating and for marriage than are Whites, older individuals, and conservatives (Tsunokai & McGrath, 2011). These findings emerged from a study of 1,335 respondents on Match.com.

In general, as one moves from dating to living together to marriage, the willingness to marry interracially decreases. Of 2,295 undergraduate males, 34% reported that they had dated interracially; 39% of 7,380 undergraduate females had done so (Hall & Knox, 2016). But only about 15% actually marry interracially. Some individuals prefer and seek interracial/interethnic relationships (Yodanis et al., 2012). But these are often not Black–White mergers. Black–White marriages, like that of Kim Kardashian and Kanye West, are less than 1% of all marriages.

We have been discussing undergraduate attitudes toward interracial dating. But what about their parents? Ozay et al. (2012) analyzed data on 251 parents of undergraduates and found that that over a third (35%) disapproved of their child's involvement in an interracial relationship. Parental disapproval (which did not vary by gender of the parent) increased with the seriousness of relationship involvement (e.g., dating or marriage), and parents were more disapproving of their daughters' than of their sons' interracial involvement.

In regard to parental approval of their son's or daughter's interracial involvement, Black mothers and White fathers have different roles in their respective Black and White communities, in terms of setting the norms of interracial relationships. Hence, the Black mother who approves of her son's or daughter's interracial relationship may be less likely to be overruled by the father than the White mother. The White husband may be more disapproving and have more power over his White wife than the Black father/husband over his partner.

AGE Most individuals select a partner who is relatively close in age. Men tend to select women three to five years younger than themselves. The result is the **marriage squeeze**, which is the imbalance of the ratio of marriageable-aged men to marriageable-aged women. In effect, women have fewer partners to select from because men choose from not only their same age group but also from those younger than themselves. One 40-year-old recently divorced woman said, "What chance do I have with all these guys looking at all these younger women?"

INTELLIGENCE Dijkstra et al. (2012) studied the mate selection preferences of the intellectually gifted and found that intelligence was one of the primary qualities sought in a potential partner. While both genders valued an intelligent partner, women gave intelligence a higher priority.

EDUCATION Educational homogamy also operates in mate selection. Not only does college provide an opportunity to meet, hang out with and cohabit with potential partners, but it also increases one's chance that only a college-educated partner becomes acceptable as a potential cohabitant or spouse. Education becomes an important criterion to find in a partner.

OPEN-MINDEDNESS People vary in the degree to which they are **open-minded** (receptive to understanding alternative points of view, values, and behaviors). Homogamous pairings in regard to open-mindedness reflect that partners seek like-minded individuals. Such open-mindedness translates into tolerance of various religions, political philosophies, and lifestyles.

marriage squeeze
the imbalance of the ratio of marriageable-age men to marriageable-age women.

open-minded being open to understanding alternative points of view, values, and behaviors.

SOCIAL CLASS Social class reflects your parents' occupations, incomes, and educations as well as your residence, language, and values. If you were brought up by parents who were physicians, you probably lived in a large house in a nice residential area—summer vacations and a college education were given. Alternatively, if your parents dropped out of high school and worked blue-collar jobs, your home was likely smaller and in a less expensive part of town, and your opportunities (such as education) were more limited. Social class affects one's comfort in interacting with others. We tend to select as friends and mates those with whom we feel most comfortable. One undergraduate from an upper-middle-class home said, "When he pulled out coupons at Subway for our first date, I knew this was going nowhere."

The **mating gradient** refers to the tendency for husbands to be more advanced than their wives with regard to age, education, and occupational success. Indeed, husbands are typically older than their wives, have more advanced education, and earn higher incomes (*Statistical Abstract of the United States, 2012–2013*, Table 702).

PHYSICAL APPEARANCE Homogamy is operative in regard to physical appearance in that people tend to become involved with those who are similar in degree of physical attractiveness. However, a partner's attractiveness may be a more important consideration for men than for women. Meltzer and McNulty (2014) emphasized that "body valuation by a committed male partner is positively associated with women's relationship satisfaction when that partner also values them for their nonphysical qualities, but negatively associated with women's relationship satisfaction when that partner is not committed or does not value them for their nonphysical qualities" (p. 68).

CAREER Individuals tend to meet and select others who are in the same career. Michelle and Barack Obama are both attorneys. Angelina Jolie and Brad Pitt are both movie celebrities. Danica Patrick and Ricky Stenhouse Jr. are both NASCAR drivers.

MARITAL STATUS Never-married people tend to select other never-married people as marriage partners; divorced people tend to select other divorced people; and widowed people tend to select other widowed people.

RELIGION/SPIRITUALITY/POLITICS Religion may be defined as a set of beliefs in reference to a supreme being which involves practices or rituals (e.g., communion) generally agreed upon by a group of people. Of course, some individuals view themselves as "not religious" but "spiritual," with spirituality defined as belief in the spirit as the seat of the moral or religious nature that guides one's decisions and behavior. Religious/spiritual homogamy is operative in that people of a similar religion or spiritual philosophy tend to seek out each other. Over a third (35%) of 2,293 undergraduate males and 43% of 7,406 undergraduate females agreed that "It is important that I marry someone of my same religion" (Hall & Knox, 2016).

Alford et al. (2011) emphasized that homogamy is operative in regard to politics. An analysis of national data on thousands of spousal pairs in the United States revealed that homogamous political attitudes were the strongest of all social, physical, and personality traits. Further, this similarity derived from initial mate choice "rather than persuasion and accommodation over the life of the relationship."

PERSONALITY Gonzaga et al. (2010) asked both partners of 417 eHarmony couples who married to identify the degree to which various personality trait terms reflected who they, as individuals, were. Examples of the terms included warm, clever, dominant, outgoing, quarrelsome, stable, energetic, affectionate, intelligent, witty, content, generous, wise, bossy, kind, calm, outspoken, shy, and trusting. Results revealed that those who were more similar to each other in personality characteristics were also more satisfied with their relationship.

CIRCADIAN PREFERENCE Circadian preference refers to an individual's preference for morningness–eveningness in regard to intellectual and physical activities. In effect, some prefer the morning while others prefer late afternoon or evening hours. In a study of 84 couples, Randler and Kretz (2011) found that partners in a romantic relationship tended to have similar circadian preferences. The couples also tended to have similar preferences as to when they went to bed in the evening and when they rose in the morning.

mating gradient the tendency for husbands to be more advanced than their wives with regard to age, education, and occupational success.

circadian preference refers to an individual's preference for morningness–eveningness in regard to intellectual and physical activities.

TRADITIONAL ROLES Partners who have similar views of what their marital roles will be are also attracted to each other. Abowitz et al. (2011) found that about a third of the 692 undergraduate women wanted to marry a "traditional" man—one who viewed his primary role as that of provider and who would be supportive of his wife staying home to rear the children.

GEOGRAPHIC BACKGROUND Haandrikman (2011) studied Dutch cohabitants and found that the romantic partners tended to have grown up within six kilometers of each other (**spatial homogamy**). While the university context draws people from different regions of the country, the demographics of state universities tend to reflect a preponderance of those from within the same state.

ECONOMIC VALUES, MONEY MANAGEMENT, AND DEBT Individuals vary in the degree to which they have money, spend money, and save money. Some are deeply in debt and carry significant educational debt. The average debt for those with a bachelor's degree is $23,000. Almost half (48%) of those who borrowed money for their undergraduate education report that they are burdened by this debt (Pew Research Center, 2011). Money becomes an issue in mate selection in that different economic values predict conflict. One undergraduate male noted, "There is no way I would get involved with this woman—she jokes about maxing out her credit cards. She is going to be someone else's nightmare."

4-8 PSYCHOLOGICAL FACTORS IN RELATIONSHIP DEVELOPMENT

Psychologists have focused on complementary needs, exchanges, parental characteristics, and personality types with regard to mate selection.

4-8a Complementary-Needs Theory

Complementary-needs theory (also known as "opposites attract") states that we tend to select mates whose needs are opposite yet complementary to our own. For example, some partners may be drawn to each other on the basis of nurturance versus receptivity. These complementary needs suggest that one person likes to give and take care of another, whereas the other likes to be the benefactor of such care. Other examples of complementary needs are responsibility versus irresponsibility, peacemaker versus troublemaker, and disorder versus order. Former *Tonight Show* host Jay Leno revealed in his autobiography that he and his wife of over 30 years are very different:

> We were, and are, opposites in most every way. Which I love. There's a better balance…I don't consider myself to have much of a spiritual side, but Mavis has almost a sixth sense about people and situations. She has deep focus, and I fly off in 20 directions at once. She reads 15 books a week, mostly classic literature. I collect classic car and motorcycle books. She loves European travel; I don't want to go anywhere people won't understand my jokes. (*Leno, 1996, pp. 214–215*)

4-8b Exchange Theory

Exchange theory in mate selection is focused on finding the partner who offers the greatest rewards at the lowest cost. The following five concepts help explain the exchange process in mate selection:

1. **Rewards.** Rewards are the behaviors (your partner looking at you with the eyes of love), words (saying "I love you"), resources (being beautiful or handsome, having a car, condo at the beach, and money), and services (cooking for you, typing for you) your partner provides that you value and that influence you to continue the relationship. Similarly, you provide behaviors, words, resources, and services for your partner that he or she values. Relationships in which the exchange is equal are happiest. Increasingly, men are interested in women who offer "financial independence" and women are interested in men who "cook and do the dishes."

2. **Costs.** Costs are the unpleasant aspects of a relationship. A woman identified the costs associated with being involved with her partner: "He abuses drugs, doesn't have a job, and lives nine hours away." The costs her partner associated with being involved with this woman included "she nags me," "she doesn't like sex," and "she insists that we live in the same town they live in if we marry."

3. **Profit.** Profit occurs when the rewards exceed the costs. Unless the couple described in the preceding

spatial homogamy the tendency for individuals to marry who grew up in close physical proximity.

complementary-needs theory tendency to select mates whose needs are opposite and complementary to one's own needs.

exchange theory theory that emphasizes that relations are formed and maintained between individuals offering the greatest rewards and least costs to each other.

paragraph derive a profit from staying together, they are likely to end their relationship and seek someone else with whom there is a higher profit margin. Biographer Thomas Maier (2009) said of Virginia Johnson (of the famous Masters and Johnson team) that she was motivated by money to marry Dr. William Masters. "I never wanted to be with him, but when you are making $200,000 a year, you don't walk," said Johnson (p. 235).

4. **Loss.** Loss occurs when the costs exceed the rewards. Partners who feel that they are taking a loss in their relationship are vulnerable to looking for another partner who offers a higher profit.

5. **Alternative.** Is another person currently available who offers a higher profit? Individuals on the marriage market have an understanding of what they are worth and whom they can attract (Bredow et al., 2011). Oberbeek et al. (2013) found that facially unattractive individuals with high body mass indexes were less selective in a speed dating context. In effect, they had less to offer so adjusted their expectations in terms of what they felt they could get. You will stay in a relationship where you have a high profit at a low cost. You will leave a relationship where your costs are high and you have an alternative partner who offers you a relationship with a higher profit margin.

4-8c Role Theory

Freud suggested that the choice of a love object in adulthood represents a shift in libidinal energy from the first love objects, the parents. **Role theory of mate selection** emphasizes that a son or daughter models after the parent of the same sex by selecting a partner similar to the one the parent selected as a mate. This means that a man looks for a wife who has similar characteristics to those of his mother and that a woman looks for a husband who is very similar to her father.

4-8d Attachment Theory

The **attachment theory of mate selection** emphasizes the drive toward psychological intimacy and a social and emotional connection. One's earliest experience as a child is to be emotionally bonded to one's parents (usually the

role theory of mate selection emphasizes that a son or daughter models after the parent of the same sex by selecting a partner similar to the one the parent selected as a mate.

attachment theory of mate selection emphasizes the drive toward psychological intimacy and a social and emotional connection.

The drive for intimate attachment is fueled by the comfort one experiences when in a reciprocal love relationship.

Courtesy of Chelsea Curry

mother) in the family context. The emotional need to connect remains as an adult and expresses itself in relationships with others, most notably the romantic love relationship. Children diagnosed with oppositional-defiant disorder (ODD) or post-traumatic stress disorder (PTSD) have had disruptions in their early bonding and frequently display attachment problems, possibly due to early abuse, neglect, or trauma. Children reared in Russian orphanages in the fifties where one caretaker was assigned to multiple children learned "no one cares about me" and "the world is not safe." Reversing early negative or absent bonding is difficult.

McClure and Lydon (2014) noted that anxiety attachment may express itself in meeting a new partner in the form of not knowing what to say and feeling socially awkward. The result is that would-be partners may be put off by this anxiety, disengage, and prevent a relationship from developing, the very context which could assist the anxious person in becoming more comfortable.

4-8e Undesirable Personality Characteristics of a Potential Mate

Researchers have identified several personality factors predictive of relationships which end in divorce or are unhappy (Burr et al., 2011; Foster, 2008). Potential partners who are observed to consistently display these characteristics might be avoided.

1. **Controlling.** The behavior that 60% of a national sample of adult single women reported as the most serious fault of a man was his being "too controlling" (Edwards, 2000).

2. **Narcissistic.** Individuals who are narcissistic view relationships in terms of what they get out of them. When satisfactions wane and alternatives are present, narcissists are the first to go. Because all relationships have difficult times, a narcissist is a high risk for a durable marriage relationship.

3. **Poor impulse control.** Lack of impulse control is problematic in relationships because such individuals are less likely to consider the consequences of their actions. Having an affair is an example of failure to control one's behavior to insure one's fidelity. Such people do as they please and worry about the consequences later.

4. **Hypersensitive.** Hypersensitivity to perceived criticism involves getting hurt easily. Any negative statement or criticism is received with a greater impact than a partner intended. The disadvantage of such hypersensitivity is that a partner may learn not to give feedback for fear of hurting the hypersensitive partner. Such lack of feedback to the hypersensitive partner blocks information about what the person does that upsets the other and what could be done to make things better. Hence, the hypersensitive one has no way of learning that something is wrong, and the partner has no way of alerting the hypersensitive partner. The result is a relationship in which the partners cannot talk about what is wrong, so the potential for change is limited.

5. **Inflated ego.** An exaggerated sense of oneself is another way of saying a person has a big ego and always wants things to be his or her way. A person with an inflated sense of self may be less likely to consider the other person's opinion in negotiating a conflict and prefer to dictate an outcome. Such disrespect for the partner can be damaging to the relationship.

6. **Perfectionist.** Individuals who are perfectionists may require perfection of themselves and others. They are rarely satisfied and always find something wrong with their partner or relationship. Living with a perfectionist will be a challenge since whatever one does will not be good enough.

7. **Insecure.** Feelings of insecurity also make relationships difficult. The insecure person has low self-esteem, constantly feels that something is wrong, and feels disapproved of by the partner.

The partner must constantly reassure him or her that all is well—a taxing expectation over time.

8. **Controlled.** Individuals who are controlled by their parents, former partner, child, or anyone else compromise the marriage relationship because their allegiance is external to the couple's relationship. Unless the person is able to break free of such control, the ability to make independent decisions will be thwarted, which will both frustrate the spouse and challenge the marriage. An example is a wife whose father dictated that she spend all holidays with him. The husband ultimately divorced her since he felt she was more of a daughter than a wife and that she had never emotionally left home. The late film critic Roger Ebert did not marry until he was 50—after his mother was dead—since he said she approved of none of the women he wanted to marry and he could not break free of her disapproval.

Individuals may also be controlled by culture. The example is a Muslim man who fell in love with a woman and she with him. They dated for four years and developed an intense emotional and sexual relationship. But he was not capable of breaking from his socialization to marry a woman of another faith.

9. **Substance abuser.** Heavy drug use does not predict well for relationship quality or stability.

10. **Unhappy.** Personal happiness is associated with relationship happiness. Stanley et al. (2012) noted that being unhappy in one's personal life is predictive of having an unhappy relationship once married. Conversely, having high life satisfaction before marriage is predictive of high relationship satisfaction once married. Hence, selecting an upbeat, optimistic, happy individual predicts well for a future marriage relationship with this person.

In addition to undesirable personality characteristics, Table 4.2 reflects some particularly troublesome personality disorders and how they may impact a relationship.

4-8f Female Attraction to "Bad Boys"

Carter et al. (2014) reviewed the **dark triad personality** in some men and confirmed that some women are attracted to these "bad boys." The dark triad is a term for intercorrelated traits of narcissism (sense of entitlement and

> **dark triad personality**
> term identifying traits of "bad boys" including narcissistic, deceptive, and no empathy.

TABLE 4.2 PERSONALITY DISORDERS PROBLEMATIC IN A POTENTIAL PARTNER

Disorder	Characteristics	Impact on Partner
Paranoid	Suspicious, distrustful, thin-skinned, defensive	Partners may be accused of everything.
Schizoid	Cold, aloof, solitary, reclusive	Partners may feel that they can never connect and that the person is not capable of returning love.
Borderline	Moody, unstable, volatile, unreliable, suicidal, impulsive	Partners will never know what their Jekyll-and-Hyde partner will be like, which could be dangerous.
Antisocial	Deceptive, untrustworthy, conscienceless, remorseless	Such a partner could cheat on, lie to, or steal from a partner and not feel guilty.
Narcissistic	Egotistical, demanding, greedy, selfish	Such a person views partners only in terms of their value. Don't expect such a partner to see anything from your point of view; expect such a person to bail in tough times.
Dependent	Helpless, weak, clingy, insecure	Such a person will demand a partner's full time and attention, and other interests will incite jealousy.
Obsessive-compulsive	Rigid, inflexible	Such a person has rigid ideas about how a partner should think and behave and may try to impose them on the partner.
Neurotic	Worries, obsesses about negative outcomes	This individual will impose negative scenarios on the partners and couple.

morrison/Shutterstock.com

grandiose self-view), Machiavellianism (deceptive and insincere), and psychopathy (callous and no empathy). These men are socially skilled and manipulative, have a high number of sex partners, and engage in mate poaching. The researchers analyzed data from 128 British undergraduate females and found that they were attracted to these bad boys. Explanations for such attraction was the self-confidence of the bad boys as well as their skill in manipulating the females. And there is the challenge. "I always knew I wasn't the only one, but I wanted to be the girl that changed him," said one undergraduate who dated a bad boy (he ended up breaking her heart).

engagement period of time during which committed, monogamous partners focus on wedding preparations and systematically examine their relationship.

4-9 ENGAGEMENT

Being identified as a couple occurs after certain events have happened. Chaney and Marsh (2009) interviewed 62 married and 60 cohabiting couples to find out when they first identified themselves as a couple. There were four markers: relationship events, affection/sex, having or rearing children, and time and money.

1. Relationship events included a specific event such as visiting the parents of one's partner, becoming engaged, or moving in together.

2. Affection/sexual events such as the first time the couple had sex. Losing one's virginity was a salient event.

3. Children—becoming pregnant, having a child together, or the first time the partner assumed a parenting role.

4. Time/money—spending a lot of time together, sharing funds, or exchanging financial support.

Some engagements happen very fast. Paul Jobs (father of Steve Jobs) and his wife, Clara, were engaged 10 days after they met (the marriage lasted over 40 years and ended by death). Mariah Carey and Nick Cannon married within two months of their first date (they divorced).

Engagement moves the relationship of a couple from a private love-focused experience to a public, parent-involved experience. Unlike casual dating, **engagement** is a time in which the romantic partners are sexually monogamous, committed to marry, and focused on wedding preparations. The engagement period molds the intimate relationship of the couple by means of the social support and expectations of family and friends. It is the last opportunity before marriage to systematically examine the relationship—to become confident in one's decision to marry a particular person. Johnson and Anderson (2011) studied 610 newly married couples and found that those spouses who were more confident in their decision to marry ended up investing more in their relationship with greater marital satisfaction.

4-9a Premarital Counseling

Jackson (2011) developed and implemented a unique evidence-informed treatment protocol for premarital counseling including six private sessions and two postmarital booster sessions. Some clergy require one or more sessions of premarital counseling before they agree to marry a couple. Premarital counseling is a process of discovery. Because partners might have hesitated to reveal information that they feel may have met with disapproval during casual dating, the sessions provide the context to be open with the other about their thoughts, feelings, values, goals, and expectations.

To examine your relationship, see the Involved Couples Inventory at the end of the chapter. By asking each other questions you can learn a great deal about each other and assess your compatibility.

4-9b Visiting Your Partner's Parents

Fisher and Salmon (2013) identified the reasons individuals take their potential partners home to meet their parents—to seek parental approval and feedback and to confirm to their partner that they are serious about the relationship. They also want to meet their partner's parents—to see how their potential mate will look when older, their future health, and potential familial resources that will be available.

Seize the opportunity to discover the family environment in which your partner was reared, and consider the implications for your subsequent marriage. When visiting your partner's parents, observe their standard of living and the way they interact (e.g., level of affection, verbal and nonverbal behavior, marital roles) with one another. How does their standard of living compare with that of your own family? How does the emotional closeness (or distance) of your partner's family compare with that of your family? Such comparisons are significant because both you and your partner will reflect your respective family or origins. "This is the way we did it in my family" is a phrase you will hear your partner say from time to time.

If you want to know how your partner is likely to treat you in the future, observe the way your partner's parent of the same sex treats and interacts with his or her spouse. If you want to know what your partner may be like in the future, look at your partner's parent of the same sex. There is a tendency for a man to become like his father and a woman to become like her mother. A partner's parent of the same sex and the parents' marital relationship are the models of a spouse and a marriage relationship that the person is likely to duplicate.

4-10 DELAY OR CALL OFF THE WEDDING IF…

"No matter how far you have gone on the wrong road, turn back" is a Turkish proverb. Behavioral psychologist B. F. Skinner noted that one should not defend a course of action that does not feel right, but stop and reverse directions. If your engagement is characterized by the following factors, consider delaying your wedding at least until the most distressing issues have been resolved. Alternatively, break the engagement (which happens in 30% of formal engagements), which will have fewer negative consequences and involve less stigma than ending a marriage.

4-10a Age 18 or Younger

The strongest predictor of getting divorced is getting married during the teen years. Individuals who marry at age 18 or younger have three times the risk of divorce than those who delay marriage into their late twenties or early thirties. Teenagers may be more at risk for marrying to escape an unhappy home and may be more likely to engage in impulsive decision making and behavior. Early marriage is also associated with an end to one's education, social isolation from close friends, early pregnancy or parenting, and locking oneself into a low income. Increasingly, individuals are delaying when they marry. As noted earlier, the median age at first marriage in the United States is 29 for men and 27 for women.

4-10b Known Partner Less Than Two Years

Twenty-nine percent of 2,290 undergraduate males and 31% of 7,391 undergraduate females agreed, "If I were really in love, I would marry someone I had known for only a short time" (Hall & Knox, 2016). Impulsive marriages in which the partners have known each other for less than a month are associated with a higher-than-average divorce rate. Indeed, partners who date each other for at least two years (25 months to be exact) before getting married report the highest level of marital satisfaction and are less likely to divorce (Huston et al., 2001). A short courtship does not allow partners enough time to learn about each other's background, values, and goals and does not permit opportunity to observe and scrutinize each other's behavior in a variety of settings (e.g., with one's close friends and family).

To increase the knowledge you and your partner have about each other, find out each other's answers to the questions in the Involved Couple's Inventory.

 Self-Assessment: Involved Couple's Inventory
Take the Involved Couple's Inventory self-assessment at the end of the chapter.

Take a five-day "primitive" camping trip, take a 15-mile hike together, wallpaper a small room together, or spend several days together when one partner is sick. If the couple plans to have children, they may want to offer to babysit a 6-month-old of their friends for a weekend.

4-10c Abusive Relationship

Abusive lovers become abusive spouses, with predictable negative outcomes. Though extricating oneself from an abusive relationship is difficult before the wedding, it becomes even more difficult after marriage, particularly when children are involved. Abuse is a serious red flag of impending relationship doom that should not be overlooked, and one should seek the exit ramp as soon as possible (see Chapter 10 on the details of leaving an abusive relationship).

4-10d High Frequency of Negative Comments/Low Frequency of Positive Comments

Markman et al. (2010) studied couples across the first five years of marriage and found that more negative and less positive communication before marriage tended to be associated with subsequent divorce. In addition, the researchers emphasized that "negatives tend to erode positives over time." Individuals who criticize each other end up damaging their relationship in a way which does not make it easy for positives to erase.

cyclical relationships when couples break up and get back together several times.

4-10e Numerous Significant Differences

Relentless conflict often arises from numerous significant differences. Though all spouses are different from each other in some ways, those who have numerous differences in key areas such as race, religion, social class, education, values, and goals are less likely to report being happy and to divorce.

4-10f On-and-Off Relationship

A roller-coaster premarital relationship is predictive of a marital relationship that will follow the same pattern. Partners in **cyclical relationships** (break up and get back together several times) have developed a pattern in which the dissatisfactions in the relationship become so frustrating that separation becomes the antidote for relief.

Vennum (2011) studied individuals in cyclical relationships and found that they reported lower-quality relationships compared to those in relationships which were uninterrupted. Partners in cyclical relationships tended to be African Americans in a long-distance dating relationship who expressed uncertainty about the future of the relationship and had less constructive communication.

4-10g Dramatic Parental Disapproval

Parents usually have an opinion of their son's or daughter's mate choice. Mothers disapprove of the mate choice of their daughters if they predict that he will be a lousy father, and fathers disapprove if they predict the suitor will be a poor provider (Dubbs & Buunk, 2010). When student and parent ratings of mate selection traits were compared, parents ranked religion higher than did their offspring, whereas offspring ranked physical attractiveness higher than did parents (Perilloux et al., 2011). Parents were also more focused on earning capacity and education (e.g., college graduate) in their daughter's mate selection than in their son's.

Indian and Asian parents who arrange the marriage of their offspring do so in terms of matching them with someone of the same religion, education, and social class which results in a higher frequency of more stable unions than those marriages in which American parents have less influence.

4-10h Low Sexual Satisfaction

Sexual satisfaction is linked to relationship satisfaction, love, and commitment. Sprecher (2002) followed 101 dating couples across time and found that low sexual satisfaction for both women and men was related to reporting low relationship quality, less love, lower commitment, and breaking up. Hence, couples who are dissatisfied with their sexual relationship might explore ways of improving it (alone or through counseling) or consider the impact of such dissatisfaction on the future of their relationship.

4-10i Limited Relationship Knowledge

Individuals and couples are most likely to have a positive future together if they have relationship knowledge. Bradford et al. (2012) validated the Relationship Knowledge Questionnaire as a way of assessing relationship knowledge. Such knowledge included knowing how to listen effectively, settle disagreements/solve problems/reach compromise, deepen a loving relationship, develop a strong friendship, and spend time together.

4-10j Wrong Reasons for Getting Married

Some reasons for getting married are more questionable than others. These reasons include the following:

REBOUND A rebound marriage results when you marry someone immediately after another person has ended a relationship with you. It is a frantic attempt on your part to reestablish your desirability in your own eyes and in the eyes of the partner who dropped you. To marry on the rebound is usually a bad decision because the marriage is made in reference to the previous partner and not to the current partner. In effect, you are using the person you intend to marry to establish yourself as the "winner" in the previous relationship.

Barber and Cooper (2014) used a longitudinal, online diary method to examine trajectories of psychological recovery and sexual experience following a romantic relationship breakup among 170 undergraduate students. Consistent with stereotypes about individuals on the rebound, those respondents who had been "dumped" used sex to cope with feelings of distress, anger, and diminished self-esteem. And those who had sex for these reasons were more likely (not initially, but over time) to continue having sex with different new partners. Caution about becoming involved with someone on the rebound may be warranted. One answer to the question, "How fast should you run from a person on the rebound?" may be "as fast as you can." Waiting until the partner has 12 to 18 months distance from the previous relationships provides for a more stable context for the new relationship.

ESCAPE A person might marry to escape an unhappy home situation in which the parents are oppressive, overbearing, conflictual, alcoholic, and/or abusive. Marriage

for escape is a bad idea. It is far better to continue the relationship with the partner until mutual love and respect become the dominant forces propelling you toward marriage, rather than the desire to escape an unhappy situation. In this way you can evaluate the marital relationship in terms of its own potential and not as an alternative to unhappiness.

UNPLANNED PREGNANCY Getting married because a partner becomes pregnant should be considered carefully. Indeed, the decision of whether to marry should be kept separate from decisions about a pregnancy. Adoption, abortion, single parenthood, and unmarried parenthood (the couple can remain together as an unmarried couple and have the baby) are all alternatives to simply deciding to marry if a partner becomes pregnant. Avoiding feelings of being trapped or later feeling that the marriage might not have happened without the pregnancy are two reasons for not rushing into marriage because of pregnancy. Couples who marry when the woman becomes pregnant have an increased chance of divorce.

PSYCHOLOGICAL BLACKMAIL Some individuals get married because their partner takes the position that "I will commit suicide if you leave me." Because the person fears that the partner may commit suicide, he or she may agree to the wedding. The problem with such a marriage is that one partner has been reinforced for threatening the other to get what he or she wants. Use of such power often creates resentment in the other partner, who feels trapped in the marriage. Escaping from the marriage becomes even more difficult. One way of coping with a psychological blackmail situation is to encourage the person to go with you to a therapist to discuss the relationship. Once inside the therapist's office, you can tell the counselor that you feel pressured to get married because of the suicide threat. Counselors are trained to respond to such a situation. Alternatively, another response to a partner who threatens suicide is to call the police and say, "Name, address, and phone number has made a serious threat on his or her own life." They police will dispatch a car to have the person picked up and evaluated.

INSURANCE BENEFITS In a poll conducted by the Kaiser Family Foundation, 7% of adults said someone in their household had married in the past year to gain access to insurance. In effect, marital decisions had been made to gain access to health benefits. "For today's couples, 'in sickness and in health' may seem less a lover's troth than an actuarial contract. They marry for better or worse, for richer or poorer, for co-pays and deductibles" (Sack, 2008). While selecting a partner who has resources (which may include health insurance) is not unusual, to select a partner solely because he or she has health benefits is dubious. Both parties might be cautious if the alliance is more about "benefits" than the relationship.

PITY Some partners marry because they feel guilty about terminating a relationship with someone whom they pity. The fiancée of an Afghanistan soldier reported that "when he came back with his legs blown off I just changed inside and didn't want to stay in the relationship. I felt guilty for breaking up with him...." Regardless of the reason, if one partner becomes brain-damaged or fails in the pursuit of a major goal, it is important to keep the issue of pity separate from the advisability of the marriage. The decision to marry should be based on factors other than pity for the partner.

FILLING A VOID A former student in the authors' classes noted that her father died of cancer. She acknowledged that his death created a vacuum, which she felt driven to fill immediately by getting married so that she would have a man in her life. Because she was focused on filling the void, she had paid little attention to the personality characteristics of the man who had asked to marry her. She discovered on her wedding night that her new husband had several other girlfriends whom he had no intention of giving up. The marriage was annulled.

In deciding whether to continue or terminate a relationship, listen to what your senses tell you ("Does it feel right?"), listen to your heart ("Do you love this person or do you question whether you love this person?"), and evaluate your similarities ("Are we similar in terms of core values, goals, view of life?"). Also, be realistic. Indeed, most people exhibit some negative and some positive indicators before they marry.

4-10k Letting Love Die and Moving On

Humans are serial monogamists (who typically mate with the same partner for years or even decades) but often mate with more than one partner over the life course (Boutwell et al., 2015). Given this trajectory, the researchers suggested that individuals have the capacity (evolutionary, cognitive, neurobiological, and genetic) which allows them to eject a mate and to move on.

> Primary mate ejection could exist as a functional device designed to transfer and focus resources from one mate to another. For males in need of making adjustments regarding where their resources are flowing, primary mate ejection could have evolved as an unconscious retraction of the affection felt between partners allowing for a redistribution of resources. (p. 33)

Females would have similar mechanisms that would allow them to refocus.

4-11 TRENDS IN LOVE RELATIONSHIPS

Love will continue to be one of the most treasured experiences in life. Love will be sought, treasured, and, when lost or ended, will be met with despair and sadness. After a period of recovery, a new search will begin. As our society becomes more diverse, the range of potential love partners will widen to include those with demographic characteristics different from our own. Romantic love will continue and love will maintain its innocence as those getting remarried love just as deeply and invest in the power of love all over again.

The development of a new love relationship will involve the same cultural constraints and sociological and psychological factors identified in the chapter. Individuals are not "free" to select their partner but do so from the menu presented by their culture. Once at the relationship buffet, factors of homogamy and exchange come into play. These variables will continue to be operative. Becoming involved with a partner with similar characteristics as one's own will continue to be associated with a happy and durable relationship.

STUDY TOOLS 4

READY TO STUDY? IN THE BOOK, YOU CAN:
- ☐ Rip out the chapter review card at the back of the book for a handy summary of the chapter and key terms.
- ☐ Assess yourself with the following self-assessments.

ONLINE AT CENGAGEBRAIN.COM YOU CAN:
- ☐ Collect StudyBits while you read and study the chapter.
- ☐ Quiz yourself on key concepts.
- ☐ Prepare for tests with M&F4 Flash Cards as well as those you create.

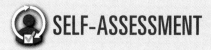

SELF-ASSESSMENT

Involved Couple's Inventory

The following questions are designed to increase your knowledge of how you and your partner think and feel about a variety of issues. Assume that you and your partner are considering marriage. Each partner should **ask each other** the following questions:

Partner's Thoughts and Feelings about Various Issues

1. If you could change one thing about me, what would it be?
2. On a scale of 0 to 10, how well do you feel I respond to criticism or suggestions for improvement?
3. What would you like me to say or not say that would make you happier?
4. What do you think of yourself? Describe yourself with three adjectives.
5. What do you think of me? Describe me with three adjectives.
6. What do you like best about me?
7. On a scale of 0 to 10, how jealous do you think I am? How do you feel about my level of jealousy?
8. How do you feel about me?
9. To what degree do you feel we each need to develop and maintain outside relationships so as not to focus all of our interpersonal expectations on each other? Does this include other-sex individuals?
10. Do you have any history of abuse or violence, either as an abused child or adult or as the abuser in an adult relationship?
11. If we could not get along, would you be willing to see a marriage counselor? Would you see a sex therapist if we were having sexual problems?
12. What is your feeling about prenuptial agreements?
13. Suppose I insisted on your signing a prenuptial agreement?
14. To what degree do you enjoy getting and giving a massage?
15. How important is it to you that we massage each other regularly?
16. On a scale of 0 to 10, how emotionally close do you want us to be?
17. How many intense love relationships have you had, and to what degree are these individuals still a part of your life in terms of seeing them or sending text messages?
18. Have you lived with anyone before? Are you open to our living together? What would be your understanding of the meaning of our living together—would we be finding out more about each other or would we be committed to marriage?
19. What do you want for the future of our relationship? Do you want us to marry? When?
20. On a 10-point scale (0 = very unhappy and 10 = very happy), how happy are you in general? How happy are you about us?
21. How depressed have you been? What made you feel depressed?
22. What behaviors that I engage in upset you and you want me to stop them?
23. What new behaviors do you want me to develop or begin to make you happier?
24. What quality for a future partner would be a requirement for you?
25. What quality for a future partner would be a deal breaker—you would not marry this person?
26. Why did your last relationship end?
27. What would your last partner say was your worst characteristic?
28. How many past sexual partners is too many for a person you would be interested in?

Parents and Family

1. How do you feel about your mother? Your father? Your siblings?
2. On a 10-point scale, how close are you to your mom, dad, and each of your siblings?
3. How close were your family members to one another? On a 10-point scale, what value do you place on the opinions or values of your parents?

4. How often do you have contact with your father or mother? How often do you want to visit your parents and/or siblings? How often would you want them to visit us? Do you want to spend holidays alone or with your parents or mine?

5. What do you like and dislike most about each of your parents?

6. What do you like and dislike about my parents?

7. What is your feeling about living near our parents? How would you feel about my parents living with us? How do you feel about our parents living with us when they are old and cannot take care of themselves?

8. How do your parents get along? Rate their marriage on a scale of 0 to 10 (0 = unhappy, 10 = happy).

9. To what degree do your parents take vacations together? What are your expectations of our taking vacations alone or with others?

10. To what degree did members of your family consult one another on their decisions? To what degree do you expect me to consult you on the decisions that I make?

11. Who was the dominant person in your family? Who had more power? Who do you regard as the dominant partner in our relationship? How do you feel about this power distribution?

12. What problems has your family experienced? Is there any history of mental illness, alcoholism, drug abuse, suicide, or other such problems?

13. What did your mother and father do to earn an income? How were their role responsibilities divided in terms of having income, taking care of the children, and managing the household? To what degree do you want a job and role similar to that of the same-sex parent?

Social Issues, Religion, and Children

1. How do you feel about the current President? Who did you vote for in the last election?

2. What are your feelings about women's rights, racial equality, and homosexuality?

3. To what degree do you regard yourself as a religious or spiritual person? What do you think about religion, a Supreme Being, prayer, and life after death?

4. Do you go to religious services? Where? How often? Do you pray? How often? How important is prayer to you? How important is it to you that we pray together? What do you pray about? When we are married, how often would you want to go to religious services? In what religion would you want our children to be reared? What responsibility would you take to ensure that our children had the religious training you wanted them to have?

5. How do you feel about abortion? Under what conditions, if any, do you feel abortion is justified?

6. How do you feel about children? How many do you want? When do you want the first child? At what intervals would you want to have additional children? What do you see as your responsibility in caring for the children—changing diapers, feeding, bathing, playing with them, and taking them to lessons and activities? To what degree do you regard these responsibilities as mine?

7. Suppose I did not want to have children or couldn't have them. How would you feel? How do you feel about artificial insemination, surrogate motherhood, in vitro fertilization, and adoption?

8. To your knowledge, can you have children? Are there any genetic problems in your family history that would prevent us from having normal children? How healthy (physically) are you? What health problems do you have? What health problems have you had? What operations have you had? How often have you seen a physician in the last three years? What medications have you taken or do you currently take? What are these medications for? Have you seen a therapist, psychologist, or psychiatrist? What for?

9. How should children be disciplined? Do you want our children to go to public or private schools?

10. How often do you think we should go out alone without our children? If we had to decide between the two of us going on a cruise to the Bahamas alone or taking the children camping for a week, what would you choose?

11. What are your expectations of me regarding religious participation with you and our children?

Sex

1. How much sexual intimacy of what kind do you feel is appropriate how soon in a relationship?

2. What does "having sex" mean to you? If a couple has experienced oral sex only, have they had sex?

3. What sexual behaviors do you most and least enjoy? How often do you need to have an orgasm, oral sex, intercourse? How do you feel about anal sex? Threesomes? How do you want me to turn you down when I don't want to have sex? How do you want me to approach you for sex? How do you feel about non-orgasm-focused intimacy: cuddling, massaging, holding?

4. By what method of stimulation do you experience an orgasm most easily?

5. What do you think about masturbation, homosexuality, sadism and masochism (S & M)?

6. What type of contraception do you suggest? Why? If that method does not prove satisfactory, what method would you suggest next?

7. What are your values regarding extramarital sex? An open relationship?

8. How often do you look at pornography? How do you feel about my doing so? How do you feel about our watching porn together? How do you feel about my going to a strip club? Our going together?

9. How important is our using a condom to you?

10. When is the last time you were tested for STIs? What were the results? If you have not been tested, what are your feelings about being tested? Do you want me to be tested for STIs?

11. What sexually transmitted infections (STIs) have you had?

12. How much do you want to know about my sexual behavior with previous partners?

13. How many friends with benefits relationships have you been in? What is your interest in our having such a relationship?

14. How much do you trust me in terms of my being faithful or monogamous with you?

15. How open do you want our relationship to be in terms of having emotional or sexual involvement with others, while keeping our relationship primary?

16. What things have you done that you are ashamed of?

17. What emotional, psychological, or physical health problems do you have? What issues do you struggle with?

18. What are your feelings about your sexual adequacy? What sexual problems do you or have you had?

19. What is your ultimate sexual fantasy?

20. To what degree have you cheated/been unfaithful in a relationship?

21. To what degree has a previous partner cheated/been unfaithful to you?

22. How important is monogamy to you?

Careers and Money

1. What kind of job or career will you have? What are your feelings about working in the evening versus being home with the family? Where will your work require that we live? How often do you feel we will be moving? How much travel will your job require?

2. To what degree did your parents agree on how to deal with money? Who was in charge of spending, and who was in charge of saving? Did working, or earning the bigger portion of the income, connect to control over money?

3. What are your feelings about a joint versus a separate checking account? Which of us do you want to pay the bills? How much money do you think we will have left over each month? How much of this do you think we should save?

4. When we disagree over whether to buy something, how do you suggest we resolve our conflict?

5. What jobs or work experience have you had? If we end up having careers in different cities, how do you feel about being involved in a commuter marriage?

6. What is your preference for where we live? Do you want to live in an apartment or a house? What are your needs for a car, television, cable service, phone plan, entertainment devices, and so on? What are your feelings about us living in two separate places, the living apart together idea whereby we can have a better relationship if we give each other some space and have plenty of room?

7. How do you feel about my having a career? Do you expect me to earn an income? If so, how much annually? To what degree do you feel it is your responsibility to cook, clean, and take care of the children? How do you feel about putting young children or infants in day care centers? When the children are sick and one of us has to stay home, who will that be?

8. To what degree do you want me to account to you for the money I spend? How much money, if any, do you feel each of us should have to spend each week as we wish without first checking with the other partner? What percentage of income, if any, do you think we should give to charity each year?

9. What assets or debts will you bring into the marriage (how much do you owe on student loans)? How do you feel about debt? How rich do you want to be?

10. If you have been married before, how much child support or alimony do you get or pay each month? Tell me about your divorce.

11. In your will, what percentage of your assets, holdings, and retirement will you leave to me versus anybody else (siblings, children of a previous relationship, and so on)?

Recreation and Leisure

1. What is your idea of the kinds of parties or social gatherings you would like for us to go to together?

2. What is your preference in terms of us hanging out with others in a group versus being alone?

3. What is your favorite recreational interest? How much time do you spend enjoying this interest? How important is it for you that I share this recreational interest with you?

4. What do you like to watch on television? How often do you watch television and for what periods of time?

5. What are the amount and frequency of your current use of alcohol and other drugs (for example, beer and/or wine, hard liquor, marijuana, cocaine, crack, meth, heroin)? What, if any, have been your previous alcohol and other drug behaviors and frequencies? What are your expectations of me regarding the use of alcohol and other drugs?

6. Where did you vacation with your parents? Where will you want us to go? How will we travel? How much money do you feel we should spend on vacations each year?

7. What pets do you own and what pets do you want to live with us? To what degree is it a requirement that we have one or more pets? To what degree can you adapt to my pets so that they live with us?

Relationships with Friends and Coworkers

1. How do you feel about my three closest same-sex friends?

2. How do you feel about my spending time with my friends or coworkers, such as one evening a week?

3. How do you feel about my spending time with friends of the opposite sex?

4. What do you regard as appropriate and inappropriate affection behaviors with opposite-sex friends?

Technology

1. What are your expectations in terms of our having complete access to each other's cell phone, email, computer passwords, etc.?

2. What are your expectations of whether we text others during our dinner or our time together?

3. What are your texting expectations—how often do you expect a text message from me? How soon after you text me do you expect a response?

4. When we are separated, how often do you want us to text each other—throughout the day or just now and then?

Note: This self-assessment is intended to be a guide to finding out about each other. It is not intended to be used as a clinical or diagnostic instrument.

 SELF-ASSESSMENT

Love Attitudes Scale

This scale is designed to assess the degree to which you are romantic or realistic in your attitudes toward love. There are no right or wrong answers.

Directions

After reading each sentence carefully, write the number that best represents the degree to which you agree or disagree with the sentence.

	1	2	3	4	5
	Strongly agree	*Mildly agree*	*Undecided*	*Mildly disagree*	*Strongly disagree*

_____ **1.** Love doesn't make sense. It just is.

_____ **2.** When you fall "head over heels" in love, it's sure to be the real thing.

_____ **3.** To be in love with someone you would like to marry but can't is a tragedy.

_____ **4.** When love hits, you know it.

_____ **5.** Common interests are really unimportant; as long as each of you is truly in love, you will adjust.

_____ **6.** It doesn't matter if you marry after you have known your partner for only a short time as long as you know you are in love.

_____ **7.** If you are going to love a person, you will "know" after a short time.

_____ **8.** As long as two people love each other, the educational differences they have really do not matter.

_____ **9.** You can love someone even though you do not like any of that person's friends.

_____ **10.** When you are in love, you are usually in a daze.

_____ **11.** Love "at first sight" is often the deepest and most enduring type of love.

_____ **12.** When you are in love, it really does not matter what your partner does because you will love him or her anyway.

_____ **13.** As long as you really love a person, you will be able to solve the problems you have with the person.

_____ **14.** Usually you can really love and be happy with only one or two people in the world.

_____ **15.** Regardless of other factors, if you truly love another person, that is a good enough reason to marry that person.

_____ **16.** It is necessary to be in love with the one you marry to be happy.

_____ **17.** Love is more of a feeling than a relationship.

_____ **18.** People should not get married unless they are in love.

_____ **19.** Most people truly love only once during their lives.

_____ **20.** Somewhere there is an ideal mate for most people.

_____ **21.** In most cases, you will "know it" when you meet the right partner.

_____ **22.** Jealousy usually varies directly with love; that is, the more you are in love, the greater your tendency to become jealous will be.

_____ **23.** When you are in love, you are motivated by what you feel rather than by what you think.

_____ **24.** Love is best described as an exciting rather than a calm thing.

_____ **25.** Most divorces probably result from falling out of love rather than failing to adjust.

_____ **26.** When you are in love, your judgment is usually not too clear.

_____ **27.** Love comes only once in a lifetime.

_____ **28.** Love is often a violent and uncontrollable emotion.

_____ **29.** When selecting a marriage partner, differences in social class and religion are of small importance compared with love.

_____ **30.** No matter what anyone says, love cannot be understood.

Scoring

Add the numbers you wrote to the left of each item. 1 (strongly agree) is the most romantic response and 5 (strongly disagree) is the most realistic response. The lower your total score (30 is the lowest possible score), the more romantic your attitudes toward love. The higher your total score (150 is the highest possible score), the more realistic are your attitudes toward love. A score of 90 places you at the midpoint between being an extreme romantic and an extreme realist. Of 45 undergraduate males, 85.3 was the average score; of 193 undergraduate females, 85.5 was the average score. These scores reflect a slight lean toward romanticism with no gender difference.

Source: Knox, D. "Conceptions of Love at Three Developmental Levels." Dissertation, Florida State University. Permission to use the scale for research available from David Knox at davidknox2@yahoo.com or by contacting Dr. Knox, Department of Sociology, East Carolina University, Greenville, NC 27858.

5 | Integrating Technology and Communication in Relationships

Madelyn Coates

SECTIONS

After finishing this chapter go to **PAGE 112** for **STUDY TOOLS**

Talking is out, texting is in.

— ANTHONY MUSSES, UNDERGRADUATE

 elationships are now begun, nurtured, and ended through texting. In this chapter we review communication basics and examine how technology impacts our relationships. We begin by defining interpersonal communication.

> Texting is not flirting, if you don't care about me enough to say the words then that's not love, I don't like it!
>
> —LAUREN GRAHAM, ACTRESS

5-1 COMMUNICATION: VERBAL AND NONVERBAL

Communication can be defined as the process of exchanging information and feelings between two people. Communication is both verbal and nonverbal. Although most communication is focused on verbal content, most (estimated to be as high as 80%) interpersonal communication is nonverbal. **Nonverbal communication** is the "message about the message," the gestures, eye contact, body posture, tone, and rapidity of speech. Even though a person says, "I love you and am faithful to you," crossed arms and lack of eye contact will

This woman is signaling an aggressive accusation by her body language/nonverbal communication.

convey a different meaning from the same words accompanied by a tender embrace and sustained eye-to-eye contact. The greater the congruence between verbal and nonverbal communication, the better. One aspect of nonverbal behavior is the volume of speech. The volume one uses when interacting with a partner has relevance for the relationship. When one uses a high frequency (yells), there are physiological (e.g., high blood pressure, higher heart rate, higher cortisol levels) and therapeutic (e.g., more limited gains in counseling—higher divorce rate) outcomes.

Flirting is a good example of both nonverbal and verbal behavior. **Flirting** may be defined as playful banter with the goal of eliciting the other person's response or interest. People flirt with their eyes (e.g., wink), voice (e.g., whisper), and hands (e.g., gentle touch or hug). Flirting in an established relationship may be the first in a sequence of behaviors toward intercourse (Frisby & Booth-Butterfield, 2015). Indeed, intercourse occurs at the end of a series of steps/stages. Traditionally, the female is responsible for signaling the male that she is interested so that he moves the interaction forward. For example, if the male holds the hand of the female, she must squeeze his hand before he can entwine their fingers. Females generally serve as sexual gatekeepers and control the speed of the interaction toward sex.

5-1a Words versus Action

A great deal of social discourse depends on saying things that sound good but that have no meaning in terms of behavioral impact. "Let's get together" or "let's hang out" sounds good since it implies an interest in spending time with each other. But the phrase has no specific plan so that the intent is likely never to happen—just the opposite. So let's hang out really means "we won't be spending any time together." Similarly, come over anytime means "never come."

> **communication** the process of exchanging information and feelings between two or more people.
>
> **nonverbal communication** the "message about the message," using gestures, eye contact, body posture, tone, volume, and rapidity of speech.
>
> **flirting** playful banter with the goal of eliciting the other person's response or interest.

CHAPTER 5: Integrating Technology and Communication in Relationships

Maria McDonald

Where there is behavioral intent, a phrase with meaning is "let's meet Thursday night at seven for dinner" (rather than "let's hang out") and "can you come over Sunday afternoon at four to play video games?" (rather than "come over any time"). With one's partner, "let's go camping sometime" means we won't ever go camping. "Let's go camping at the river this coming weekend" means you are serious about camping.

5-2 TECHNOLOGY AND COMMUNICATION IN ROMANTIC RELATIONSHIPS

The following scenario from one of our students reflects that technology has an enormous effect on romantic relationships.

> "I saw his photo on Tinder.com"
> "I typed his name into Facebook and friend requested him."
> "He accepted, messaged me and we began to text each other."
> "We were long distance so we began to have long talks on Skype."
> "To keep his interest I would sex text him ('What would you like me to do to you?')"
> "After we moved in together, I snooped, checked his cell phone—discovered other women."
> "I sent him a text message that it was over, and moved out."

Taylor et al. (2013) surveyed 1,003 emerging adults (18–25) about the use of technology in romantic

relationships. Both men and women reported that texting is appropriate with a potential romantic partner; however, neither agree with announcing a relationship on Facebook before having the "relationship talk" and becoming a committed couple.

Rappleyea et al. (2014) analyzed data on 1,003 young adults in regard to technology and relationship formation and found that the respondents believe that "talking," "hanging out," and "sharing intimate details" are more important when compared with using communication technologies to establish a relationship (p. 269).

Text messages have become a primary means for flirting (73% of 18–25-year-olds—Gibbs, 2012) and the initiation, escalation, and maintenance of romantic relationships (Bergdall et al., 2012). Some (to the disapproval of most) end a relationship with a text message (Gershon, 2010). Text messages and communication technology are also used by divorced parents in the coparenting of their children (Ganong et al., 2011).

5-2a Texting and Interpersonal Communication

Text messaging with cell phones has become commonplace in the lives of individuals as a way of staying connected with friends and partners. The youth of today are being socialized in a hyper-digital age where traditional modes of communication will be replaced by gadgets and texting will become the primary mode of communication (Bauerlein, 2010). This shift to greater use of technology affects relationships in both positive and negative ways. On the positive side, it allows for instant and unabated connection—individuals can text each other throughout the day so that they are "in effect, together all the time."

On the negative side, Su (2016) argues that the constant texting between lovers may be more bondage than bonding since it pushes one's personal boundaries to the limit and creates an intolerance for separation. Some partners get angry if they don't get a text message back in 10 minutes. In some cases, the use of

National and International Data

Based on a survey of 4,700 respondents in the United States and seven other countries (China, the United Kingdom, India, South Korea, South Africa, Indonesia, and Brazil), 9 in 10 carry a cell phone (1 in 4 checks it every 30 minutes; 1 in 5 checks it every 10 minutes) (Gibbs, 2012).

technology to communicate may create **nomophobia** where the individual is dependent on virtual environments to the point of having a social phobia (King et al., 2013). He or she finds personal interaction difficult.

Coyne et al. (2011) examined the use of technology by 1,039 individuals in sending messages to their romantic partner. The respondents were more likely to use their cell phones to send text messages than any other technology. The most common reasons were to express affection (75%), discuss serious issues (25%), and apologize (12%). There were no significant differences in use by gender, ethnicity, or religion. Pettigrew (2009) emphasized that **texting**, or text messaging (short typewritten messages—maximum of 160 characters sent via cell phone) is used to "commence, advance, maintain" interpersonal relationships and is viewed as more constant and private than talking on a cell phone. Women text more than men. On the negative side, these devices encourage the continued interruption of face-to-face communication between individuals and encourage the intrusion of one's work/job into the emotional intimacy of a couple and the family.

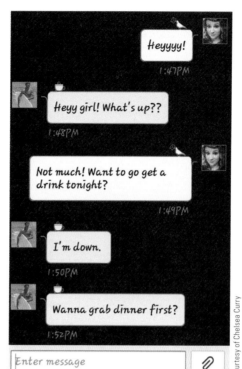

Courtesy of Chelsea Curry

Courtesy of Rachel Calisto

Huang and Leung (2010) studied instant messaging and identified four characteristics of "addiction" in teenagers: preoccupation with IM, loss of relationships due to overuse, loss of control, and escape. Results also showed that shyness and alienation from family, peers, and school were significantly and positively associated with levels of IM addiction. As expected, both the level of IM use and level of IM addiction were significantly linked to teenagers' poorer academic performance.

Technology is also used to convey both good and bad news to a romantic partner (see the What's New? section).

5-2b When Texting and Facebook Become a Relationship Problem

Schade et al. (2013) studied the effects of technology on romantic relationships. They analyzed data from 276 adults ages 18–25 in committed relationships and found that male texting frequency was negatively associated with relationship satisfaction and stability scores for both partners while female texting frequency was positively associated with their own relationship stability scores. Hence, females thrived on texting, which had a positive relationship effect. Males tolerated it, which had the opposite/negative effect.

Cell phones/text messaging may be a source of conflict (e.g., partner text messages while the lover is talking to him or her). Over 60% of Chinese respondents and a quarter of U.S. respondents noted that a mobile device had come between them and their spouse (Gibbs, 2012).

Norton and Baptist (2012) identified how social networking sites (e.g., Facebook, with over a billion users and 140 billion friendship connections) are problematic for couples—the sites are intrusive (e.g., partner surfs while lover is talking), and they encourage compulsive use (e.g., partner is always sending/receiving messages) and infidelity (e.g., flirting/cheating online). They studied how 205 married individuals mitigated the impact of technology on their relationship.

If you don't like what is being said, change the conversation.

—DON DRAPER, *MAD MEN*

nomophobia the individual is dependent on virtual environments to the point of having a social phobia.

texting text messaging (short typewritten messages—maximum of 160 characters sent via cell phone).

WHAT'S NEW?

Impact of Technology on Intimate Relationships

A random sample of 225 undergraduate and graduate students from a midsized southeastern university revealed via an Internet survey the ways technology had benefited and hurt their respective relationships.

Positive Aspects of Technology on Intimate Relationships

Improved communication was the primary benefit. The meaning of the term *benefits* included:

1. **Keeping in regular contact with each other throughout the day via texting.**
2. **Sharing news and information.**
3. **Multiple communication channels** (e.g., Skyping)
4. **Facilitating long-distance relationship** (texting and Skyping).
5. **Life management/planning.** Examples include knowing where each other is, online classes, and a quick text to pick up beer or milk on the way home.
6. **Intimacy and affection.** Text messages expressing love.

7. **Leisure and relaxation.** Downloading/watching movies, playing video games, enjoying apps (e.g., Yik Yak and Trivia Crack).
8. **Meeting someone new online.** Using various apps and Internet sites to find new partners.
9. **Learning about the partner.** Profiles on dating sites or Facebook provided information about the person and his or her interests.
10. **Connections to social support.** Staying connected to one's parents, siblings, and close friends.
11. **Preserving relationship memories.** Storing previous text messages, photographs of the couple, etc.

Three strategies included openness (e.g., each spouse knew the passwords and online friends and had access to each other's online social networking accounts, email, etc.), fidelity (e.g., flirting and online relationships were off limits), and appropriate people (e.g., knowing the friends of the partner and no former partners allowed). Proper cell phone etiquette is also important. We address this issue in the next section.

5-2c Cell Phone Etiquette

The frequency of cell phone use has challenged social norms and etiquette. According to the Pew Research Center, most Americans approve of cell phone use in public spaces including while walking in the street (77%), using public transportation (75%), and while waiting in line (74%). Social approval

decreases for cell phone use in social gatherings. Many frown upon cell phone use at church or worship service (96%), movie theater (95%), meetings (94%), family dinners (88%), and restaurants (62%) (Rainie & Zickuhr, 2015).

Tech etiquette, also known as netiquette or techniquette, has become increasingly important with the use of cell phones (Block, 2014; Dvorak, 2012). However, there is disagreement on what proper tech etiquette is (Allison, 2012). One's gender and age are associated with attitude toward cell phone use. Compared to men, women are less likely to consider cell phone use appropriate in all social situations. Older adults are also less approving of cell phone usage in social situations (Forgays et al., 2014).

People are more likely to notice the discourteous tech etiquette of others (such as talking loudly on the phone) than their own uncordial behaviors. A cross-cultural study reported that college students from both

tech etiquette social norms for cell phone use in public.

Negative Aspects of Technology on Intimate Relationships

The undergraduates also identified the negative impact of technology on relationships:

1. **Impaired, compromised communication and intimacy.** Texts can be misunderstood, and without the individuals being together, there can be upset feelings or frustration. Partners may also disagree about how often and how soon they should text each other; feelings can be hurt without intention or awareness.

2. **More superficial/inauthentic communication.** Some respondents felt texting was impersonal and not to be preferred to face-to-face communication.

3. **Privacy infringements.** Snooping into one's Internet history, emails, or text messages can cause feelings of having one's privacy invaded.

4. **Gossip and drama.** Some felt that their former partners could reach into their current relationship via Facebook and cause trouble by sending text messages to you/the new partner, start rumors, or gossip. Technology allowed for the invasion of one by others.

5. **Jealousy and trust issues.** Individuals can keep their email and cell phones private and secure, which causes the other to wonder why the secrecy and feel the partner has something to hide.

6. **Online pornography and infidelity.** Either partner can use the Internet to watch porno, to contact previous partners, or to develop new relationships online.

7. **Distracts from/infringes on the relationship.** The perception that one's partner cares more about texting someone else than talking with the partner or playing video games for hours rather than spending time together can be a major relationship problem.

8. **Overuse of technology.** Being obsessive about Play Station, video games, or checking one's email or text messages to the point that the person can't function without constant involvement with technology.

9. **Pet peeve with partner's use.** Answering the phone in a restaurant.

10. **Features of technology.** The cost of technology, video games, etc. can cause economic problems/disagreements, and breakdown of the equipment such as a bad connection on Skype can cause problems.

Source: Abridged and adapted from Murray, C. E., & E. C. Campbel. (2015). The pleasures and perils of technology in intimate relationships. *Journal of Couple & Relationship Therapy,* published online.

the United States (89%) and China (91%) considered themselves very courteous when using their cell phone. However, students from both countries stated other people (71% American and 67% Chinese) were discourteous and spoke loudly when using their cell phones (Rosenfeld & O'Connor Petruso, 2014).

The development of technology often outpaces the concomitant rise of social norms, manners, and laws. Nevertheless, respect, courtesy, and thoughtfulness remain important standards for tech etiquette in the 21st century. Some of the ideal cell phone etiquette norms today include:

▸ Safety and security. No cell phone use while driving and be concerned about network security (Simpson, 2010).

▸ Be attentive to those you are with and engage fully in the conversation (e.g., date or dinner) rather than check cell phone messages.

▸ Thumbs off, heads up, and look at people when they speak.

▸ When taking a phone call in public, lower your voice and speak softly. Try to be at least 12 feet away from people. Avoid discussing private matters and watch the language you use since everyone can hear you.

▸ Use a nonoffensive ring tone. Lock your phone to avoid pocket dialing.

▸ Before you answer your cell phone, get permission from people you are with.

▸ Treat others the way you want to be treated. No cell phone cameras in the locker room.

▸ Avoid talking on the phone in small enclosed spaces such as an elevator or restroom.

▸ Avoid cell phone use where it can be a distraction to others—in classrooms, concerts, theaters, churches, and at funerals.

5-2d Sexting

Another way in which technology affects communication, particularly in romantic relationships, is **sexting** (sending erotic text and photo images via a cell phone). Sexting begins in high school. Strassberg et al. (2013) surveyed 606 high school students and found that almost 20% reported having *sent* a sexually explicit image of themselves via cell phone while almost twice as many reported that they had *received* a sexually explicit picture via cell phone (of these, over 25% indicated that they had *forwarded* this picture to others). Of those who sent a sexually explicit cell phone picture, over a third did so despite believing that there could be serious legal consequences attached to the behavior.

Burke-Winkelman et al. (2014) reported that 65% of 1,652 undergraduates reported sending sexually suggestive texts or photos to a current or potential partner (69% reported receiving). Almost a third (31%) reported sending the text messages to a third party. In regard to how they felt about sending nude photos, less than half were positive, and females were more likely to feel pressure to send nude photos.

Dir et al. (2013) surveyed 278 undergraduates in regard to their receiving and sending sex text messages and sex photos. Gender and relationship status were significant predictors of specific sexting behaviors. Males reported sending more sex photos. In addition, those involved in a relationship (dating, serious relationship, cohabiting) sent more sexts than uninvolved singles. Males reported more positive outcomes of receiving sexts (e.g., sexual excitement); women were more likely to feel uncomfortable (e.g., embarrassed).

While undergraduates are not at risk as long as the parties are age 18 or older, sending erotic photos of individuals younger than 18 can be problematic. Sexting is considered by many countries as child pornography and laws related to child pornography have been applied in cases of sexting. Six high school students in Greensburg, Pennsylvania, were charged with child pornography after three teenage girls allegedly took nude or seminude photos of themselves and shared them with male classmates via their cell phones.

Some undergraduate females are under age 18. Having or sending nude images of underage individuals is a felony which can result in fines, imprisonment, and a record. We noted above that Strassberg et al. (2013) reported that a third of their high school respondents reported that they had forwarded a sexually explicit photo that could get them in serious legal trouble.

5-2e Video-Mediated Communication

Communication via computer between separated lovers, spouses, and family members is becoming more common. Furukawa and Driessnack (2013) assessed the use of **video-mediated communication (VMC)** in a sample of 341 online participants (ages 18 to 70-plus). Ninety-six percent reported that VMC was the most common method they used to communicate with their family, and 60% reported doing so at least once a week. VMC allows the person to see and hear what is going on; for example, while the grandparents can't be present Christmas morning they can see the excitement of their grandchildren opening their gifts. VMC is also valuable for transnational families (family members are separated by significant distances) in that the individuals can be copresent (be emotionally "there" for each other) via Skype and Face Time on one's cell phone/ computer. Baldassar (2016) noted that Australian migrants use communication technologies to remain together and support each other even though they are physically apart.

5-3 CHOICES FOR EFFECTIVE COMMUNICATION

> Not the power to remember, but its very opposite, the power to forget, is a necessary condition for our existence.
>
> —SHOLEM ASCH, *THE NAZARENE*

We continually make choices in how we communicate in our relationships. The following section identifies the various choices we can make to ensure that communication in our relationships has a positive outcome. First, you might want to take the Supportive Communication Scale at the end of this chapter to assess the degree to which your partner listens to you, helps you to clarify your thoughts, etc. The following identify the ways we can ensure effective communication in our relationships:

1. **Prioritize communication.** Communicating effectively implies making communication an important priority in a couple's relationship. When communication is a priority, partners make time for it to occur in a setting without interruptions:

sexting sending erotic text and photo images via a cell phone.

video-mediated communication (VMC) communication via computer between separated lovers, spouses, and family members.

they are alone; they are not texting or surfing the Internet; they do not answer the phone; and they turn the television off.

2. **Avoid negative and make positive statements to your partner.** Because intimate partners are capable of hurting each other so intensely, it is important to avoid brutal statements to the partner. Such negativity is associated with vulnerability to divorce (Woszidlo & Segrin, 2013). Indeed, be very careful how you give negative feedback or communicate disapproval to your partner. Markman et al. (2010a) noted that couples in marriage counseling

Emmanuel Hidalgo/Getty Images

Partners who look at each other when they are talking not only communicate an interest in each other but also are able to gain information about the partner's feelings and reaction to what is being said.

often will report "it was a bad week" based on one negative comment made by the partner. However, Velotti et al. (2016) studied emotional suppression by both husbands and wives in 229 newlywed couples at five months and two years after marriage and found that husbands' habitual use of suppression was the most consistent predictor of (lower) marital quality over time. Perhaps it is the way in which negative feelings are expressed (e.g. "I need for us to talk about an issue" rather than "I hate what you did") that impacts the relationship.

Markman et al. (2010a) also emphasized the need for partners to make positive comments to each other and that doing so was associated with more stable relationships. People like to hear others say positive things about them. These positive statements may be in the form of compliments ("You look terrific!") or appreciation ("Thanks for putting gas in the car"). Hiew et al. (2016) compared communication patterns in Chinese, Western, and intercultural Chinese-Western couples and found that a low frequency of negatives and a high frequency of positives were associated with relationship satisfaction across all of the couples.

3. **Establish and maintain eye contact.** Shakespeare noted that a person's eyes are the "mirrors to the soul." Partners who look at each other when they are talking not only communicate an interest in each other but also are able to gain information about the partner's feelings and responses to what is being said. Not looking at your partner may be interpreted as lack of interest and prevents you from observing nonverbal cues.

4. **Establish empathy. Empathy** is the ability to emotionally experience and cognitively understand another person and his or her experiences. To the degree that partners in a relationship have dyadic empathy (empathy with each other) they report satisfaction in their relationship (Kimmes et al., 2014).

5. **Ask open-ended questions.** When your goal is to find out your partner's thoughts and feelings about an issue, using **open-ended questions** is best. Such questions (e.g., "How do you feel about me?") encourage your partner to give an answer that contains a lot of information.

empathy the ability to emotionally experience and cognitively understand another person and his or her experiences.

open-ended questions questions that encourage answers that contain a great deal of information.

TABLE 5.1	NONJUDGMENTAL AND JUDGMENTAL RESPONSES TO A PARTNER'S SAYING, "I'D LIKE TO GO OUT WITH MY FRIENDS ONE NIGHT A WEEK"	
Nonjudgmental, Reflective Statements		**Judgmental Statements**
You value your friends and want to maintain good relationships with them.		You only think about what you want.
You think it is healthy for us to be with our friends some of the time.		Your friends are more important to you than I am.
You really enjoy your friends and want to spend some time with them.		You just want a night out so that you can meet someone new.
You think it is important that we not abandon our friends just because we are involved.		You just want to get away so you can drink.
You think that our being apart one night each week will make us even closer.		You are selfish.

Closed-ended questions (e.g., "Do you love me?"), which elicit a one-word answer such as "yes" or "no," do not provide the opportunity for the partner to express a range of thoughts and feelings.

6. **Use reflective listening.** Effective communication requires being a good listener. One of the skills of a good listener is the ability to use the technique of **reflective listening**, which involves paraphrasing or restating what the person has said to you while being sensitive to what the partner is feeling.

Reflective listening serves the following functions: (1) it creates the feeling for speakers that they are being listened to and are being understood; and (2) it increases the accuracy of the listener's understanding of what the speaker is saying. If a reflective statement does not accurately reflect what a speaker has just said, the speaker can correct the inaccuracy by saying it again.

An important quality of reflective statements is that they are nonjudgmental. For example, suppose two lovers are arguing about spending time with their respective friends and one says, "I'd like to spend one night

each week with my friends and not feel guilty about it." The partner may respond by making a statement that is judgmental (critical or evaluative), such as those exemplified in Table 5.1. Judgmental responses serve to punish or criticize people for what they think, feel, or want and often result in an argument.

Table 5.1 also provides several examples of nonjudgmental reflective statements.

7. **Use "I" statements. "I" statements** focus on the feelings and thoughts of the communicator *without* making a judgment on others. Because "I" statements are a clear and nonthreatening way of expressing what you want and how you feel, they are likely to result in a positive change in the listener's behavior. Making "I" statements reflects being authentic. Impett et al. (2010) emphasized the need to be authentic when communicating. Being **authentic** means speaking and acting in a manner according to what one feels. Being authentic in a relationship means being open with the partner about one's preferences and feelings about the partner's behavior. Being authentic has positive consequences for the relationship in that one's thoughts and feelings are out in the open (in contrast to being withdrawn and resentful).

"You" statements blame or criticize the listener and often result in increasing negative feelings and behavior in the relationship. For example, suppose you are angry with your partner for being late. Rather than say, "You are always late and irresponsible" (a "you" statement), you might respond with, "I get upset when you are late and ask that you call me when you will be delayed." The latter

closed-ended questions questions that allow for a one-word answer and do not elicit much information.

reflective listening paraphrasing or restating what a person has said to indicate that the listener understands.

"I" statements statements that focus on the feelings and thoughts of the communicator without making a judgment on others.

authentic speaking and acting in a manner according to what one feels.

"you" statements statements that blame or criticize the listener and often result in increasing negative feelings and behavior in the relationship.

focuses on your feelings and a desirable future behavior rather than blaming the partner for being late.

8. **Touch.** Touch may convey various meanings such as affection and approval or anger and disapproval. Endeavor to use touch to convey positive feelings.

> Conversation, like certain portions of the anatomy, always runs more smoothly when lubricated.
>
> —MARQUIS DE SADE

9. **Identify specific new behavior you want.** Focus on what you want your partner to do rather than on what you do not want. Rather than say, "You spend too much time with your Xbox playing Halo, Call of Duty, and Gears of War," an alternative might be "When I come home, please help me with dinner, ask me about my day and turn on your Xbox after 10 p.m.—after you have turned me on." Rather than say, "You never call me when you are going to be late," say, "Please call me when you are going to be late." Notice that you are asking your partner for what you want, not demanding.

> Couples who focus on the issue to get it resolved handle conflict with minimal relationship fallout.

10. **Stay focused on the issue. Branching** refers to going out on different limbs of an issue rather than staying focused on the issue. If you are discussing the overdrawn checkbook, stay focused on the checkbook. To remind your partner that he or she is equally irresponsible when it comes to getting things repaired or doing house work is to go off target. Stay focused.

11. **Make specific resolutions to disagreements.** To prevent the same issues or problems from recurring, agreeing on what each partner will do in similar circumstances in the future is important. For example, if going to a party together results in one partner's drinking too much and drifting off with someone else, what needs to be done in the future to ensure an enjoyable evening together? In this example, a specific resolution would be to decide how many drinks the partner will have within a given time period and make an agreement to stay together and dance only with each other.

12. **Give congruent messages. Congruent messages** are those in which the verbal and nonverbal behaviors match. A person who says, "Okay, you're right" and smiles while embracing the partner is communicating a congruent message. In contrast, the same words accompanied by leaving the room and slamming the door communicate a very different message.

13. **Share power. Power** is the ability to impose one's will on the partner and to avoid being influenced by the partner. One of the greatest sources of dissatisfaction in a relationship is a power imbalance and conflict over power (Knudson-Martin et al., 2015; Kurdek, 1994). Over half (63%) of 9,410 undergraduates from two universities reported that they had the same amount of power in the relationship as their partner. Sixteen percent felt that they had less power; 21% felt that they had more power (men reported that they had more power than women in 24% of cases versus 21%) (Hall & Knox, 2016a). Research on power and relationships also shows a positive relationship between equal power and relationship satisfaction (Hall & Knox, 2016b).

One way to assess power is to identify who has the least interest in the relationship. Waller and Hill (1951) observed that the person who has the least interest in continuing the relationship is in control of the relationship. This **principle of least interest** is illustrated by the woman who said, "He wants us to stay together more than I do so I am in control and when we disagree about something he gives in to me." Expressions of power in a relationship are numerous and include the following:

Withdrawal (not speaking to the partner)
Guilt induction ("How could you ask me to do this?")

branching in communication, going out on different limbs of an issue rather than staying focused on the issue.

congruent message one in which verbal and nonverbal behaviors match.

power the ability to impose one's will on one's partner and to avoid being influenced by the partner.

principle of least interest principle stating that the person who has the least interest in a relationship controls the relationship.

Being pleasant ("Kiss me and help me move the sofa.")

Negotiation ("We can go to the movie if we study for a couple of hours before we go.")

Deception (running up credit card debts of which the partner is unaware)

Blackmail ("I'll find someone else if you won't have sex with me.")

Physical abuse or verbal threats ("You will be sorry if you try to leave me.")

Criticism ("You are stupid and fat.")

Dominance ("I make more money than you so I will decide where we go.")

Power may also take the form of love and sex. The person in the relationship who loves less and who needs sex less has enormous power over the partner who is very much in love and who is dependent on the partner for sex. This pattern reflects the principle of least interest we discussed earlier in the text.

14. **Keep the process of communication going.** Communication includes both content (verbal and nonverbal information) and process (interaction). It is important not to allow difficult content to shut down the communication process. To ensure that the process continues, the partners should focus on the fact that talking is important and reinforce each other for keeping the communication process alive. For example, if your partner tells you something that you do that bothers him or her, it is important to thank your partner for telling you rather than becoming defensive. In this way, your partner's feelings about you stay out in the open rather than being hidden behind a wall of resentment. If you punish such disclosure because you do not like the content, disclosure will stop. For example, a wife told her husband that she felt his lunches with a woman at work were becoming too frequent and wondered if

Courtesy of Rachel Calisto

it were a good idea. Rather than the husband becoming defensive and saying he could have lunch with whomever he wanted he might say, "I appreciate your telling me how you feel about this…you're right…maybe it would be best to cut back."

15. **Conversation content on first dates.** Does it matter what you/your partner says or does on the first date in terms of how successful the date is regarded? Of course! Cohen (2016) asked 390 undergraduates to rate the verbal and nonverbal behaviors on the part of their date which signaled that their date was attracted to them.

Results revealed that there were differences between females and males. Behaviors females viewed as signaling that their date was attracted to them were making comments about their physical appearance ("You look nice"), centering the conversation on them ("Tell me about you"), making references to things in common ("We have the same major"), maintaining a lively conversation, making references to the future ("Maybe we could go to that concert"), paying for the meal, extending the date ("Want to take a walk?"), hugging/kissing you goodbye at the end of the date, and texting/calling shortly after the date.

Behaviors males viewed as signaling that their date was attracted to them was when the woman talked about themselves; in talking about her own life, interests, and hobbies, the man perceived this as the woman letting her guard down and revealing herself. Other first date behaviors men liked were steering the conversation to the topic of sex ("How do you feel about sex?") and hugging/kissing goodbye at the end of the date. The male did not want the woman to initiate contact after the date but to respond to his texts/calls.

Behaviors both genders noted that signaled that one's date was not attracted to them included waving hello and goodbye, talking about past relationships, focusing on differences, and no subsequent contact after the date.

5-4 GENDER AND COMMUNICATION

How individuals communicate with each other depends on which gender is talking/listening. Numerous jokes address the differences between how women and men communicate. One anonymous quote on the Internet follows:

When a woman says, "Sure . . . go ahead," what she means is "I don't want you to." When a woman says,

"I'm sorry," what she means is "You'll be sorry." When a woman says, "I'll be ready in a minute," what she means is "Kick off your shoes and start watching a football game on TV."

Women and men differ in their approach to and patterns of communication. Women are more communicative about relationship issues, view a situation emotionally, and initiate discussions about relationship problems. Deborah Tannen (1990, 2006) is a specialist in communication. She observed that, to women, conversations are negotiations for closeness in which they try "to seek and give confirmations and support, and to reach consensus" (1990, p. 25). To men, conversations are about winning and achieving the upper hand.

The genders differ in regard to emotionality. Garfield (2010) reviewed men's difficulty with emotional intimacy. He noted that their emotional detachment stems from the provider role which requires them to stay in control. Being emotional is seen as weakness. Men's groups where men learn to access and express their feelings have been helpful in increasing men's emotionality.

In contrast, women tend to approach situations emotionally. For example, if a child is seriously ill, wives will want their husbands to be emotional, to cry, to show that they really care that their child is sick. But a husband might react to a seriously ill child by putting pressure on the wife to be "mature" about the situation and by encouraging stoicism.

5-5 SELF-DISCLOSURE AND SECRETS

Shakespeare noted in *Macbeth* that "the false face must hide what the false heart doth know," suggesting that withholding information and being dishonest may affect the way one feels about oneself and relationships with others. All of us make decisions about the degree to which we disclose, are honest, and/or keep secrets.

5-5a Self-Disclosure in Intimate Relationships

One aspect of intimacy in relationships is self-disclosure, which involves revealing personal information and feelings about oneself to another person.

Relationships become more stable when individuals disclose themselves to their partners (Tan et al., 2012). Areas of disclosure include one's formative years, previous relationships (positive and negative), experiences of elation and sadness, and goals (achieved and thwarted). We noted in the discussion of love in Chapter 4 that self-disclosure is a psychological condition necessary for the development of love. To the degree that you disclose yourself to another, you invest yourself in and feel closer to that person. People who disclose nothing are investing nothing and remain aloof. One way to encourage disclosure in one's partner is to make disclosures about one's own life and then ask about the partner's life.

> The language of the heart is humankinds main common language.
>
> —SUZY KASSEM, *RISE UP AND SALUTE THE SUN: THE WRITINGS OF SUZY KASSEM*

5-5b Secrets in Romantic Relationships

Most lovers keep a secret or two from their partners. Oprah Winfrey's biographer revealed a secret that Oprah kept from her long-term boyfriend Stedman Graham. When the couple was vacationing at a resort and Stedman left for a round of golf, Oprah promptly called room service and ordered two whole pecan pies. She called room service back a short time later to come and remove the empty tin plates so that her partner would not know of her food binge (Kelley, 2010).

Stacy Huff

PERSONAL VIEW:

How Much Do You Tell Your Partner about Your Past?

Because of the fear of HIV infection and other sexually transmitted infections (STIs), some partners want to know the details of each other's previous sex life, including how many partners they have had sex with and in what contexts (e.g., hookups or stable relationships). Those who are asked will need to decide whether to disclose the requested information, which may include one's sexual orientation, present or past STIs, and any sexual preferences the partner might find bizarre (e.g., sadism). Ample evidence suggests that individuals are sometimes dishonest with regard to the sexual information about their past they provide to their partners. The "number of previous sexual partners" is the most frequent lie undergraduates report telling each other. One female undergraduate who has had more partners than she wants to reveal said that when she is asked about her number, she smiles and says, "A lady never kisses and tells." Another said, "Whatever number the person tells me, I double it."

In deciding whether or not to talk honestly about your past to your partner, you may want to consider the following questions: How important is it to your partner to know about your past? Do you want your partner to

The most frequent lie partners tell each other is the number of past sexual partners.

tell you (honestly) about her or his past? What impact on your relationship will open disclosure have? What impact will withholding such information have on the level of intimacy you have with your partner? Caughlin and Bassinger (2015) question whether "completely open and honest communication is really what we want." They suggest that the value of openness should be "balanced against other values, such as politeness, respectfulness and discretion" (p. f2).

College students also keep secrets from their partners. In a study of 431 undergraduates, Easterling et al. (2012) found the following:

1. **Most kept secrets.** Over 60% of the respondents reported having kept a secret from a romantic partner, and over one-quarter of respondents reported currently doing so.

2. **Females kept more secrets.** Sensitivity to the partner's reaction, desire to avoid hurting the partner, and desire to avoid damaging the relationship were the primary reasons why females were more likely than males to keep a secret from a romantic partner.

3. **Spouses kept more secrets.** Spouses have a great deal to lose if there is an indiscretion or if one partner does something the other will disapprove

of (e.g., hook up). Partners who are dating or "seeing each other" have less to lose and are less likely to keep secrets.

4. **Blacks kept more secrets.** Blacks are a minority who live in a racist society and are still victimized by the White majority. One way to avoid such victimization is to keep one's thoughts to oneself—to keep a secret. This skill of deception may generalize to one's romantic relationships.

5. **Homosexuals kept more secrets.** Indeed, the phrase "in the closet" means "keeping a secret."

Respondents were asked why they kept a personal secret from a romantic partner. "To avoid hurting the partner" was the top reason reported by 39% of the respondents. "It would alter our relationship" and "I feel so

Courtesy of Chelsea Curry

ashamed for what I did" were reported by 18% and 11% of the respondents, respectively.

Some secrets are embedded in technology—text messages, emails, and cell phone calls. Being deceptive with one's emails and cell phone is disapproved of by both women and men. In a study of 5,500 never-married individuals, 76% of the women and 53% of the men reported that being secretive with emails was a behavior they would not tolerate. Similarly, 69% of the women (47% of the men) said they would not put up with a partner who answered cell phone calls discretely (Walsh, 2013).

> One aspect of intimacy in relationships is self-disclosure, which involves revealing personal information and feelings about oneself to another person.

5-5c Family Secrets

Just as romantic partners have secrets, so do families. The family secret that takes the cake is the one Bernie Madoff kept from his wife and two adult sons—that he had defrauded almost 5,000 clients of over $50 billion over a number of years. Madoff's wife and sons were adamant that their husband and father had acted alone and without their knowledge. Sadly, Madoff's elder son, Mark, committed suicide in the wake of the intense public scrutiny.

Oprah Winfrey also had a family secret. At age 15 she gave birth to a son in her seventh month of pregnancy. The baby died a month later. When Oprah ran for Miss Black Tennessee she completed an application on which she stated that she had never had a child (Kelley, 2010).

5-6 DISHONESTY, LYING, AND CHEATING

Relationships are compromised by dishonesty, lying, and cheating.

5-6a Dishonesty

Dishonesty and deception take various forms. One is a direct lie—saying something that is not true (e.g., telling your partner that you have had 6 previous sexual partners when, in fact, you have had 13). Not correcting an assumption is another form of dishonesty (e.g., your partner assumes you are heterosexual but you are bisexual).

5-6b Lying in American Society

Lying, a deliberate attempt to mislead, is pervasive. Lance Armstrong was stripped of his seven Tour de France titles for lying about doping. Journalist Mike Daisey admitted to fabricating stories about oppressed workers at an Apple contractor's factory in China. He said of his deception, "It's not journalism. It's theater." Sixty-two percent of 125 Harvard students admitted to cheating on either tests or papers (Webley, 2012). Politicians routinely lie to citizens ("Lobbyists can't buy my vote"), and citizens lie to the government (via cheating on taxes). Teachers lie to students ("The test will be easy"), and students lie to teachers ("I studied all night"). Parents lie to their children ("It won't hurt"), and children lie to their parents ("I was at my friend's house"). Dating partners lie to each other ("I've had a couple of previous sex partners"), women lie to men ("I had an orgasm"), and men lie to women ("I'll call"). The price of lying is high—distrust and alienation. A student in class wrote:

> At this moment in my life I do not have any love relationship. I find hanging out with guys to be very hard. They lie to you about anything and you wouldn't know the truth. I find that college dating is mostly about sex and having a good time before you really have to get serious. That is fine, but that is just not what I am all about.

Catfishing refers to a process whereby a person makes up an online identity and an entire social facade to trick a person into becoming involved in an emotional relationship. The catfish is the lonely person on the Internet who is susceptible to being seduced into this fake relationship. University of Notre Dame football

catfishing process whereby a person makes up an online identity and an entire social facade to trick a person into becoming involved in an emotional relationship.

newphotoservice/Shutterstock.com

player Manti Te'o reported that he was a victim of an on-line hoax, fooled into a relationship by someone pretending to be a woman named Lennay Kekua. The creator of the pretend Lennay Kekua then conspired with others to lead Te'o to believe that Kekua had died of leukemia.

5-6c Lying and Cheating in Romantic Relationships

Lying is epidemic in college student romantic relationships. In response to the statement, "I have lied to a person I was involved with," 69% of 9,655 undergraduates (men more than women) reported "yes" (Hall & Knox, 2016a).

Cheating may be defined as having sex with someone else while involved in a relationship with a romantic partner. When 9,843 undergraduates were asked if they had cheated on a partner they were involved with, 30% reported that they had done so (no significant difference between women and men) (Hall & Knox, 2016a). Even in monogamous relationships, there is considerable cheating. Vail-Smith et al. (2010) found that of 1,341 undergraduates, 27.2% of the males and 19.8% of the females reported having oral, vaginal, or anal sex outside of a relationship that their partner considered monogamous.

People most likely to cheat in these monogamous relationships were men over the age of 20, those who were binge drinkers, members of a fraternity, male NCAA athletes, and those who reported that they were nonreligious. White et al. (2010) also studied 217 couples where both partners reported on their own risk behaviors and their perceptions of their partner's behavior; 3% of women and 14% of men were unaware that their partner had recently had a concurrent partner. Eleven percent and 12%, respectively, were unaware that their partner had ever injected drugs; 10% and 12% were unaware that their partner had recently received an STI diagnosis; and 2% and 4% were unaware that their partner was HIV-positive. These data suggest a need for people in committed relationships to reconsider their risk of STI and to protect themselves via condom usage. In addition, one of the ways in which college students deceive their partners is by failing to disclose that they have an STI. Approximately 25% of college students will contract an STI while they are in college (Purkett, 2014).

Strickler and Hans (2010) conceptualized infidelity (cheating) as both sexual and nonsexual. Sexual cheating was intercourse, oral sex, and kissing. Nonsexual cheating could be interpersonal (secret time together, flirting), electronic (text messaging, emailing), or solitary (sexual fantasies, pornography, masturbation). Of

400 undergraduates, 74% of the males and 67% of the females in a committed relationship reported that they had cheated according to their own criteria. Hence, in the survey, they identified a specific behavior as cheating and later reported whether they had engaged in that behavior.

5-7 THEORIES OF RELATIONSHIP COMMUNICATION

Symbolic interactionism and social exchange are theories that help explain the communication process.

5-7a Symbolic Interactionism

Interactionists examine the process of communication between two actors in terms of the meanings each attaches to the actions of the other. Definition of the situation, the looking-glass self, and taking the role of the other (discussed in Chapter 1) are all relevant to understanding how partners communicate. With regard to resolving a conflict over how to spend the semester break (e.g., vacation alone or go to see parents), the respective partners must negotiate their definitions of the situation (is it about their time together as a couple or their loyalty to their parents?). The looking-glass self involves looking at each other and seeing the reflected image of someone who is loved and cared for and someone with whom a productive resolution is sought. Taking the role of the other involves each partner's understanding the other's logic and feelings about how to spend the break.

5-7b Social Exchange

Exchange theorists suggest that the partners' communication can be described as a ratio of rewards to costs. Rewards are positive exchanges, such as compliments, compromises, and agreements. Costs refer to negative exchanges, such as critical remarks, complaints, and attacks. When the rewards are high and the costs are low, the outcome is likely to be positive for both partners (profit). When the costs are high and the rewards low, neither may be satisfied with the outcome (loss).

When discussing how to spend the semester break, the partners are continually in the process of exchange—not only in the words they use but also in the way they use them. If the communication is to continue, both partners need to feel acknowledged for their points of view and to feel a sense of legitimacy and respect. Communication in abusive relationships is characterized by the parties criticizing and denigrating each other, which usually results in a shutdown of the communication process and a drift toward ending the relationship.

5-8 FIGHTING FAIR: STEPS IN CONFLICT RESOLUTION

Resolving stress via conflict resolution is important for one's health. Lund et al. (2014) analyzed data from 9,875 Danish men and women aged 36–52 years to assess associations between stressful social relations with partner and with children and mortality. Results revealed that frequent worries/demands from partner or children were associated with 50–100% increased mortality risk.

When a disagreement begins, it is important to establish rules for fighting that will leave the partners and their relationship undamaged. Indeed, Lavner and Bradbury (2010) studied 464 newlyweds over a four-year period, noticed the precariousness of relationships (even those reporting considerable satisfaction divorced), and recommended that couples "impose and regularly maintain ground rules for safe and nonthreatening communication." Such guidelines for fair fighting/effective communication include not calling each other names, not bringing up past misdeeds, and not attacking each other.

Gottman (1994) identified destructive communication patterns to avoid which he labeled as "the four horsemen of the apocalypse"—criticism, defensiveness, contempt (the most damaging), and stonewalling. He also noted that being positive about the partner is essential—partners who said positive things to each other at a ratio of 5:1 (positives to negatives) were more likely to stay together. We have noted that "avoiding giving

> Fighting fairly also involves keeping the interaction focused and respectful, and moving toward a win-win outcome.

your partner a zinger" is also essential to maintaining a good relationship.

Fighting fairly also involves keeping the interaction focused and respectful, and moving toward a win–win outcome. If recurring issues are not discussed and resolved, conflict may create tension and distance in the relationship, with the result that the partners stop talking, stop spending time together, and stop being intimate. Developing and using skills for fair fighting and conflict resolution are critical for the maintenance of a good relationship.

Howard Markman is head of the Center for Marital and Family Studies at the University of Denver. He and his colleagues have been studying 150 couples at yearly intervals (beginning before marriage) to determine those factors most responsible for marital success. They have found that a set of communication skills that reflect the ability to handle conflict, which they call "constructive arguing," is the single biggest predictor of marital success over time (Marano, 1992). According to Markman, "Many people believe that the causes of marital problems are the differences between people and problem areas such as money, sex, and children. However, our findings indicate it is not the differences that are important, but how these differences and problems are handled, particularly early in marriage" (Marano, 1992, p. 53). Markman et al. (2010b) provide details for constructive communication in their book *Fighting for Your Marriage*. The following sections identify standard steps for resolving interpersonal conflict.

Stacy Huff

5-8a Address Recurring, Disturbing Issues

Addressing issues in a relationship is important. But whether partners do so is related to their level of commitment to the relationship. Partners who are committed to each other and to their relationship invest more time and energy to resolving problems. Those who feel stuck in relationships with barriers to getting out (e.g., children, economic dependence), avoid problem resolution (Frye, 2011). The committed are intent on removing relationship problems.

5-8b Identify New Desired Behaviors

Dealing with conflict is more likely to result in resolution if the partners focus on what they *want* rather than what they *don't want*. Tell your partner specifically what you want him or her to do. For example, if your partner routinely drives the car but never puts gas in it, rather than say, "Stop driving the gas out of the car," you might ask him or her to "always keep at least a fourth tank of gas in the car."

5-8c Identify Perceptions to Change

Rather than change behavior, changing one's perception of a behavior may be easier and quicker. Rather than expect one's partner to always be on time, it may be easier to drop this expectation and to stop being mad about something that doesn't matter. South et al. (2010) emphasized the importance of perception of behavior in regard to marital satisfaction.

5-8d Summarize Your Partner's Perspective

We often assume that we know what our partner thinks and why he or she does things. Sometimes we are wrong. Rather than assume how our partner thinks and feels about a particular issue, we might ask open-ended questions in an effort to learn our partner's thoughts and feelings about a particular situation. The answer to "How do you feel about me taking an internship abroad next semester?" will give you valuable information.

5-8e Generate Alternative Win–Win Solutions

Looking for win–win solutions to conflicts is imperative. Solutions in which one person wins means that the other person is not getting needs met. As a result, the person who loses may develop feelings of resentment, anger, hurt, and hostility toward the winner and may even look for ways to get even. In this way, the winner is also a loser. In intimate relationships, one winner really means two losers.

Generating win–win solutions to interpersonal conflict often requires **brainstorming**. The technique of brainstorming involves suggesting as many alternatives as possible without evaluating them. Brainstorming is crucial to conflict resolution because it shifts the partners' focus from criticizing each other's perspective to working together to develop alternative solutions.

Kurdek (1995) emphasized that conflict-resolution styles that stress agreement, compromise, and humor are associated with

brainstorming suggesting as many alternatives as possible without evaluating them.

> He mentioned the connection between us. He identified with me. These are the things that many people want to hear, that most "normal" people want to be able to truthfully say, but almost no one can.
>
> —RASMENIA MASSOUD, *HUMAN DETRITUS*

marital satisfaction, whereas conflict engagement, withdrawal, and defensiveness styles are associated with lower marital satisfaction. In his own study of 155 married couples, the style in which the wife engaged the husband in conflict and the husband withdrew was particularly associated with low marital satisfaction for both spouses.

Communicating effectively and creating a context of win–win in one's relationship contributes to a high-quality marital relationship, which is good for one's health.

5-8f Forgive

Too little emphasis is placed on forgiveness as an emotional behavior that can move a couple from a deadlock to resolution. Merolla and Zhang (2011) noted that offender remorse positively predicted forgiveness and that such forgiveness was associated with helping resolve the damage. Hill (2010) studied forgiveness and emphasized that it is less helpful to try to "will" oneself to forgive the transgressions of another than to engage a process of self-reflection—that one has also made mistakes, hurt others, and is guilty—and to empathize with the fact that we are all fallible and need forgiveness. In addition, forgiveness ultimately means letting go of one's anger, resentment, and hurt, and its power comes from offering forgiveness as an expression of love to the person who has betrayed him or her. Forgiveness also has a personal benefit—it reduces hypertension and feelings of stress. To forgive is to restore the relationship—to pump life back into it. Of course, forgiveness given too quickly may be foolish. A person who has deliberately hurt his or her partner without remorse may not deserve forgiveness.

It takes more energy to hold on to resentment than to move beyond it. One reason some people do not forgive a partner for a transgression is that one can use the fault to control the relationship. "I wasn't going to let him forget," said one woman of her husband's infidelity.

- Maria McDonald

A related concept to forgiveness is **amae**. Marshall et al. (2011) studied the concept of amae in Japanese romantic relationships. The term means expecting a close other's indulgence when one behaves inappropriately. Thirty Japanese undergraduate romantic couples kept a diary for two weeks that assessed their amae behavior (requesting, receiving, providing amae). Results revealed that amae behavior was associated with greater relationship quality and less conflict. "Cutting one some slack" may be another way of expressing amae.

5-8g Avoid Defense Mechanisms

Effective conflict resolution is sometimes blocked by **defense mechanisms**—techniques that function without awareness to protect individuals from anxiety and to minimize emotional hurt. The following paragraphs discuss some common defense mechanisms.

Escapism is the simultaneous denial of and withdrawal from a problem. The usual form of escape is avoidance. The spouse becomes "busy" and "doesn't have time" to think about or deal with the problem, or the partner may escape into recreation, sleep, alcohol, marijuana, or work. Denying and withdrawing from problems in relationships offer no possibility for confronting and resolving the problems.

Rationalization is the cognitive justification for one's own behavior that unconsciously conceals one's true motives. For example, one wife complained that her husband spent too much time at the health club in the evenings. The underlying reason for the husband's going to the health club was to escape an unsatisfying home life. However, the idea that he was in a dead marriage was too painful and difficult for the husband to face, so he rationalized to himself and his wife that he spent so much time at the health club because he made a lot of important business contacts there. Thus, the husband concealed his own true motives from himself (and his wife).

Projection occurs when one spouse unconsciously attributes individual feelings, attitudes, or desires to the partner. For example, the wife who desires to have an affair may accuse her husband of being unfaithful to her. Projection may be seen in such statements as "You spend too much money" (projection for "I spend too much money") and "You want to break up" (projection for "I want to break up"). Projection interferes with conflict resolution by creating a mood of hostility and defensiveness in both partners. The issues to be resolved in the relationship remain unchanged and become more difficult to discuss.

Displacement involves shifting your feelings, thoughts, or behaviors from the person who evokes them onto someone else. The wife who is turned down for a promotion and the husband who is driven to exhaustion by his boss may direct their hostilities (displace them) onto each other rather than toward their respective employers. Similarly, spouses who are angry at each other may displace this anger onto someone else, such as the children.

By knowing about defense mechanisms and their negative impact on resolving conflict, you can be alert to them in your own relationships.

 5-9 TRENDS IN COMMUNICATION AND TECHNOLOGY

The future of communication will increasingly involve technology in the form of texting, smartphones, Facebook, etc. Such technology will be used to initiate, enhance, and maintain relationships. Indeed, intimates today may text each other 60 times a day. Over 2,000 messages a month are not unusual. Binsahl et al. (2015) found that social networking sites such as Facebook were particularly valuable for international students in helping them to maintain a strong sense of connectivity and bonding while they are temporarily out of their home country.

amae expecting a close other's indulgence when one behaves inappropriately.

defense mechanisms unconscious techniques that function to protect individuals from anxiety and minimize emotional hurt.

escapism the simultaneous denial of and withdrawal from a problem.

rationalization the cognitive justification for one's own behavior that unconsciously conceals one's true motives.

projection attributing one's own feelings, attitudes, or desires to one's partner while avoiding recognition that these are one's own thoughts, feelings, and desires.

displacement shifting one's feelings, thoughts, or behaviors from the person who evokes them onto someone else.

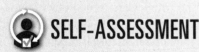 **SELF-ASSESSMENT**

Supportive Communication Scale (SCS)

This scale is designed to assess the degree to which partners experience supportive communication in their relationships. After reading each item, circle the number that best approximates your answer.

0	1	2	3	4
Strongly disagree	Disagree	Undecided	Agree	Strongly agree

	SD	D	UN	A	SA
1. My partner listens to me when I need someone to talk to.	0	1	2	3	4
2. My partner helps me clarify my thoughts.	0	1	2	3	4
3. I can state my feelings without my partner getting defensive.	0	1	2	3	4
4. When it comes to having a serious discussion, it seems we have little in common (reverse scored).	0	1	2	3	4
5. I feel put down in a serious conversation with my partner (reverse scored).	0	1	2	3	4
6. I feel discussing some things with my partner is useless (reverse scored).	0	1	2	3	4
7. My partner and I understand each other completely.	0	1	2	3	4
8. We have an endless number of things to talk about.	0	1	2	3	4

Scoring

Look at the numbers you circled. Reverse-score the numbers for questions 4, 5, and 6. For example, if you circled a 0, give yourself a 4; if you circled a 3, give yourself a 1, and so on. Add the numbers and divide by 8, the total number of items. The lowest possible score would be 0, reflecting the complete absence of supportive communication; the highest score would be 4, reflecting complete supportive communication. One hundred and eighty-eight individuals completed the scale. Thirty-nine percent of the respondents were married, 38% were single, and 23% were living together. The average age was just over 24. The average score of 94 male partners who took the scale was 3.01; the average score of 94 female partners was 3.07.

Source: Sprecher, S., S. Metts, B. Burelson, E. Hatfield, & A. Thompson. (1995). Domains of expressive interaction in intimate relationships: Associations with satisfaction and commitment. *Family Relations*, 44: 203–210. Published in 1995 by the National Council on Family Relations.

M&F
ONLINE

REVIEW FLASHCARDS
ANYTIME, ANYWHERE!

**Create Flashcards
from Your StudyBits**

**Review Key Term
Flashcards Already
Loaded on the
StudyBoard**

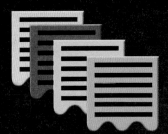

4LTR
PRESS

Access M&F ONLINE at www.cengagebrain.com

6 Enhancing Sexuality in Relationships

Hero Images/Getty Images

SECTIONS

After finishing this chapter go to **PAGE 130** for **STUDY TOOLS**

> When a couple's sex life is good, it is about 15% of the relationship;
> but when the sex is bad, it becomes a focus of the relationship.
>
> —ROBERT SAMMONS, PSYCHIATRIST

Think about the following situations:

Two people are at a party, drinking and flirting. Although they met only two hours ago, they feel a strong attraction to each other. Both are wondering whether they will hook up later that evening. Is this a good idea? What will be the effects on the respective individuals? Will it doom a future with the partner or be the start of a relationship?

***

Maria and Jose have been sexually intimate for a couple of months. While Maria has found that the use of a vibrator is helpful in her achieving an orgasm, she is challenged by how she should bring this up so that Jose has a positive reaction. What should she do?

***

While Melody was away for a weekend, her live-in partner had sex with his ex-girlfriend. He regretted his behavior, begged for forgiveness, and promised to be faithful in the future. What should Melody do?

***

A woman is married to a man whose career requires that he be away from home for extended periods. Although she loves her husband, she is lonely, bored, and sexually frustrated in his absence. She has been asked out by a colleague at work whose wife also travels. He, too, is in love with his wife but is lonely for emotional and sexual companionship. They are ambivalent about whether to hook up occasionally while their spouses are away. What advice would you give to this couple?

Sexual values are moral guidelines for sexual behavior in relationships. Values sometimes predict sexual behavior. One's sexual values may be identical to one's sexual behavior. For example, a person who values abstinence until marriage may not have sexual intercourse until marriage. But one's sexual behavior does not always correspond with one's sexual values. One explanation for the discrepancy between values and behavior is that a person may engage in a sexual behavior, then decide the behavior was wrong, and adopt a sexual value against it. We begin this chapter with an overview of various sexual values.

6-1 ALTERNATIVE SEXUAL VALUES

At least three sexual values guide choices in sexual behavior: absolutism, relativism, and hedonism. See Table 6.1 for the respective sexual values of almost 10,000 undergraduates. Individuals may have different sexual values at different stages of the family life cycle. For example, young and elderly individuals are more likely to be absolutist, whereas those in the middle years are more likely to be relativistic. Young unmarried adults are more likely to be hedonistic.

 Self-Assessment: Conservative-Liberal Sexuality Scale (CLSS)
To assess where your sexual values fall on a continuum from being ultraconservative to being ultraliberal, see the scale at the end of this chapter.

6-1a Absolutism

Absolutism is a sexual value system which is based on unconditional allegiance to tradition or religion (i.e., waiting until marriage to have sexual intercourse).

TABLE 6.1 SEXUAL VALUES OF 9,948 UNDERGRADUATES			
Respondents	**Absolutism, %**	**Relativism, %**	**Hedonism, %**
Male students (N = 2,376)	13	56	31
Female students (N = 7,572)	16	65	19

Source: Hall, S., & D. Knox. (2016). Relationship and sexual behaviors of a sample of 9,948 university students. Unpublished data collected for this text. Department of Family and Consumer Sciences, Ball State University and Department of Sociology, East Carolina University.

sexual values moral guidelines for sexual behavior in relationships.

absolutism belief system based on unconditional allegiance to the authority of religion, law, or tradition.

People who are guided by absolutism in their sexual choices have a clear notion of what is right and wrong. Parents influence sexual values. Adolescents who have high-quality relationships with their parents report having fewer sexual partners (Van de Bongardt et al., 2016).

The official creeds of fundamentalist Christian and Islamic religions encourage absolutist sexual values. Intercourse is solely for procreation, and any sexual acts that do not lead to procreation (masturbation, oral sex, homosexuality) are immoral and regarded as sins against God, Allah, self, and community. Waiting until marriage to have intercourse is also an absolutist sexual value. Unmarried religious individuals who report having sexual intercourse have higher levels of sexual guilt and lower levels of sexual satisfaction than nonreligious unmarried individuals engaging in sexual intercourse (Hackathorn et al., 2016). The wait until marriage value is often promoted in public schools.

Individuals conceptualize their virginity in one of three ways—as a process, a gift, or a stigma. The process view regards first intercourse as a mechanism of learning about one's self and one's partner and sexuality. The gift view regards being a virgin as a valuable positive status wherein it is important to find the right person since sharing the gift is special. The stigma view considers virginity as something to be ashamed of, to hide, and to rid oneself of. When 215 undergraduates were asked their view, 54% classified themselves as process oriented, 38% as gift oriented, and 8.4% as stigma oriented at the time of first coitus (Humphreys, 2013).

Madelyn Coates

This coed is an absolutist. She has never had oral, vaginal, or anal sex and plans to only be sexual with her spouse when she is married.

"True Love Waits" is an international campaign designed to challenge teenagers and college students to remain sexually abstinent until marriage. Under this program, created and sponsored by the Baptist Sunday School Board, young people are asked to agree to the absolutist position and sign a commitment to the following: "Believing that true love waits, I make a commitment to God, myself, my family, my friends, my future mate, and my future children to sexual purity including abstinence from this day until the day I enter a biblical marriage relationship." Since 1993, 2.4 million have taken the pledge (True Love Waits, 2016).

How effective is the "True Love Waits" and "virginity pledge" programs in delaying sexual behavior until marriage? Paik et al. (2016) revealed that approximately 12% of girls and young women in the United States pledge abstinence. Yet most break their pledges, engaging in first intercourse before marriage with few differences between pledge breakers and nonpledgers in sexually transmitted infections and nonmarital pregnancies. However, the author suggests that pledgers are at higher risk for human papillomavirus (HPV) and nonmarital pregnancies.

Some individuals still define themselves as virgins even though they have engaged in oral sex. Of 2,272 undergraduate males, 75% (71% of 7,333 undergraduate females) agreed with the statement "If you have oral sex, you are still a virgin." Hence, according to these undergraduates, having oral sex with someone is not really having sex (Hall & Knox, 2016). Persons most likely to agree that "oral sex is not sex" are freshmen/sophomores, those self-identifying as religious (Dotson-Blake et al., 2012). Individuals may engage in oral sex rather than sexual intercourse to avoid getting pregnant, to avoid getting an STI, to keep their partner interested, to avoid a bad reputation, and to avoid feeling guilty over having sexual intercourse (Vazonyi & Jenkins, 2010).

Indeed, rather than a dichotomous "one is or is not a virgin" concept that gets muddled by one's view of oral sex being "sex," a three-part view of virginity might be adopted—oral sex, vaginal sex, and anal sex. No longer might the term "virgin" be used to reveal sexual behaviors in these three areas. Rather, whether one has engaged in each of the three behaviors must be identified.

Hence, an individual would not say "I am a virgin" but "I am an oral virgin" (or intercourse virgin or anal virgin as the case may be).

Virginity loss for heterosexuals typically refers to vaginal sex (though some would say they are no longer virgins if there has been oral or anal sex). Lesbian and gay males typically refer to virginity loss if there has been oral or anal sex. Males who are virgins report that "my partner was not willing" as the most frequent reason for their virginity (Sprecher & Treger, 2015).

A subcategory of absolutism is **asceticism**. Ascetics believe that giving in to carnal lust is unnecessary and attempt to rise above the pursuit of sensual pleasure into a life of self-discipline and self-denial. Accordingly, spiritual life is viewed as the highest good, and self-denial helps one to achieve it. Catholic priests, monks, nuns, and some other celibate people have adopted the sexual value of asceticism.

It is not unusual that some sexually experienced individuals decide to stop having sex and withdraw from romantic relationship availability. Byers et al. (2016) surveyed 411 adolescents (16–21 years old, 56% female) and found that 27% had engaged in sexual avoidance (more females than males). The reason for sexual avoidance for females was often sexual coercion; for males, it was religion. Other reasons included lack of sexual pleasure/enjoyment, relationship reasons, and fear of negative outcomes. Almost half (47%) engaged in romantic avoidance (more females). Reasons included effects of previous relationship, not interested in commitment, wrong time, and other priorities.

6-1b Relativism

Fifty-six percent of 2,376 undergraduate males and 65% of 7,572 undergraduate females identified relativism as their sexual value (Hall & Knox, 2016). **Relativism** is a value system emphasizing that sexual decisions should be made in reference to the emotional, security, and commitment aspects of the relationship. Although absolutists might feel that having intercourse is wrong for unmarried people, relativists might feel that the moral correctness of sex outside marriage depends on the particular situation. For example, a relativist might say that marital sex between two spouses who are emotionally and

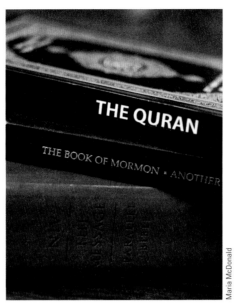

Maria McDonald

physically abusive to each other is not to be preferred over intercourse between two unmarried individuals who love each other, are kind to each other, and are committed to the well-being of each other.

Relativists apparently do value having a good sex partner. About half of never-married individuals want to stay in a relationship only if the sex is good. In a study of 5,500 never married people, half of the women and 44% of the men said that "bad sex would be a deal-breaker" (Walsh, 2013).

A disadvantage of relativism as a sexual value is the difficulty of making sexual decisions on a relativistic case-by-case basis. The statement "I don't know what's right anymore" reflects the uncertainty of a relativistic view. Once a person decides that mutual love is the context justifying intercourse, how often and how soon is it appropriate for the person to fall in love? Can love develop after some alcohol and two hours of conversation? How does one know that love feelings are genuine? The freedom that relativism brings to sexual decision making requires responsibility, maturity, and judgment. In some cases, individuals may convince themselves that they are in love so that they will not feel guilty about having intercourse.

> The sexual embrace can only be compared with music and with prayer.
>
> —MARCUS AURELIUS

FRIENDS WITH BENEFITS RELATIONSHIP

Friends with benefits is often part of the relational sexual landscape. Mongeau et al. (2013) defined the **friends with benefits relationship (FWBR)** as platonic friends (i.e., those not involved in a romantic relationship) who engage in some degree of sexual intimacy on multiple occasions.

asceticism the belief that giving in to carnal lusts is wrong and that one must rise above the pursuit of sensual pleasure to a life of self-discipline and self-denial.

relativism sexual decisions are made in reference to the emotional, security, and commitment aspects of the relationship.

friends with benefits relationship a relationship between nonromantic friends who also have a sexual relationship.

A Script for Delaying Intercourse in a Relationship

It is sometimes the case where one partner wants to de-escalate or slow down the sex in a relationship. Communicating this desire to the partner is tricky—one wants to communicate interest in sex but not allow the relationship to become sex focused. The script to a partner follows:

I need to talk about sex in our relationship. I am anxious talking about this and not sure exactly what I want to say so I have written it down to try and help me get the words right. I like you, enjoy the time we spend together, and want us to continue seeing each other. The sex is something I need to feel good about to make it good for you, for me, and for us.

I need for us to slow down sexually. I need to feel an emotional connection that goes both ways—we both have very strong emotional feelings for each other. I also need to feel secure that we are going somewhere—that we have a future and that we are committed to each other. We aren't there yet so I need to wait till we get there to be sexual (have intercourse) with you.

How long will this take? I don't know—the general answer is "longer than now." This may not be what you have in mind and you may be ready for us to increase the sex now. I'm glad that you want us to be sexual and I want this too but I need to feel right about it. So, for now, let me drive the bus sexually . . . when I feel the emotional connection and that we are going somewhere, I'll be the best sex partner you ever had. But let me move us forward. If this is too slow for you or not what you have in mind, maybe I'm not the girl for you. It is certainly OK for you to tell me you need more and move on. Otherwise, we can still continue to see each other and see where the relationship goes.

So . . . tell me how you feel and what you want . . . don't feel like you need to tell me you love me and want us to get married . . . ha! I'm not asking that . . . I'm just asking for time. . . .

This sexual activity could range from kissing to sexual intercourse and is a repeated part of a friendship, not just a one-night hookup. Fifty-one percent of 2,318 undergraduate males reported that they had been in an FWBR (45% of 7,474 undergraduate females). These undergraduates were primarily first- and second-year students (Hall & Knox, 2016). Mongeau et al. (2013) identified seven types of friends with benefits relationships:

1. **True friends.** Close friends who have sex on multiple occasions (similar to but not labeled as romantic partner). The largest percent (26%) of the 258 respondents reported this type of FWBR.

2. **Network opportunism.** Part of same social networks who just hang out and end up going home to have sex together since there is no better option; a sexual fail-safe. Fifteen percent reported this type of FWBR.

3. **Just sex.** Focus is sex, serial hookup with same person. Do not care about person other than as sexual partner. Twelve percent reported this type of FWBR.

4. **Transition out.** The couple were romantic, the relationship ended, but the sexual relationship continued. Eleven percent reported this type of FWBR.

5. **Successful transition.** Intentional use of friends with benefits relationship to transition into a romantic relationship. Eight percent reported this type of FWBR.

6. **Unintentional transition.** Sexual relationship morphs into romantic relationship without intent. Relationship results from regular sex, hanging out together, etc. Eight percent reported this type of FWBR.

7. **Failed transition.** One partner becomes involved while the other does not. The relationship stalls. The lowest percentage (7%) of the 258 respondents reported this type of FWBR.

Advantages to having sex with one's former partner include having a "safe" sexual partner, having a predictably "good" sexual partner who knows likes/dislikes and does not increase the number of lifetime sexual partners,

> A strong friendship doesn't need daily conversation, doesn't always need togetherness, as long as the relationship lives in the heart, true friends will never part...
>
> —NIX

and "fanning sexual flames might facilitate rekindling partners' emotional connections" (Mongeau et al., 2013). Disadvantages include developing a bad reputation as someone who does not really care about emotional involvement, coping with discrepancy of becoming more or less involved than the partner, and losing the capacity to give oneself emotionally.

Lehmiller et al. (2014) analyzed data on 376 individuals in a relationship and compared those who were in a friends with benefits relationship (50.5%) with those who were romantically involved but not in an FWB relationship (49.5%). Differences included that FWB partners were less likely to be sexually exclusive, were less sexually satisfied, more likely to practice safe sex, and generally communicated less about sex than romantic partners who were not in an FWB relationship.

Concurrent sexual partnerships are those in which the partners have sexual relationships with several individuals with whom they have a relationship. Jolly et al. (2016) studied African American relationships and found that men were more likely to engage in concurrent sexual relationships than women. They were also more likely to use a condom with casual than with stable partners. Wester and Phoenix (2013) studied relationships at the "talking" phase and noted that men were much more likely to approve of all forms of sexual behavior in multiple relationships than women.

CONSENSUALLY NONMONOGAMOUS RELATIONSHIPS Cohen (2016) studied 122 consensually nonmonogamous (CNM) partners in which the partners agreed that each could become involved with others outside the dyad. Almost two-thirds (73%) of the CNM were by mutual agreement. The greatest advantage was "to experience something new," to be "free," and to not be "tied down." Males were attracted by the opportunity to have sex with others; females were attracted by the notion of not being stuck in a relationship. The greatest disadvantage was the stigma associated with the lifestyle followed by problems in communication, jealousy and trust. Following the rules such as not seeing the same person twice was important for involvement in CNN.

SWINGING **Swinging relationships** consist of focused recreational sex. These relationships involve married/pair-bonded individuals agreeing that they may have sexual encounters with others.

Kimberly and Hans (2012) reviewed the literature on swinging couples. There are about 3 million swinging couples in the United States with most reporting positive emotional and sexual relationships. Swinging for them is a mutually agreeable recreational behavior that has positive benefits for the relationships. Kimberly (2016) conducted 32 formal interviews with married spouses at a swinging convention to assess how they introduced the idea of swinging and negotiated the practice of swinging into their relationship.

Fourteen percent of 2,146 undergraduate males and 9% of 6,784 undergraduate females reported that they were comfortable with their partner being emotionally and sexually involved with someone else (Hall & Knox, 2016).

6-1c Hedonism

Hedonism is the belief that the ultimate value and motivation for human actions lie in the pursuit of pleasure and the avoidance of pain. Thirty-one percent of 2,376 undergraduate males and 19% of 7,572 undergraduate females defined hedonism as their primary sexual value (Hall & Knox, 2016).

Men, compared to women, reported higher sexual desire (Dosch et al., 2016). Bersamin and colleagues (2014) analyzed data on single, heterosexual college students (N = 3,907) ages 18 to 25 from 30 institutions across the United States. A greater proportion of men (18.6%) compared to women (7.4%) reported having had casual sex in the month prior to the study. The researchers also found that casual sex was negatively associated with psychological well-being (defined in reference to self-esteem, life satisfaction, and eudaimonic well-being—having found oneself). Casual sex was also positively associated with psychological distress

concurrent sexual partnerships those in which the partners have sex with several individuals concurrently.

swinging relationships involve married/pair-bonded individuals agreeing that they may have sexual encounters with others.

hedonism belief that the ultimate value and motivation for human actions lie in the pursuit of pleasure and the avoidance of pain.

(e.g., anxiety, depression). There were no gender differences. Sandberg-Thoma and Kamp Dush (2014) also found suicide ideation and depressive symptoms associated with casual sexual relationships (sample of 12,401 adolescents). Fielder et al. (2014) studied hookups in first-year college women and found an association with experiencing depression, sexual victimization, and STIs.

The **sexual double standard**, more prevalent among males and those adhering to traditional religious scripts (Emmerink et al., 2016), is the view that encourages and accepts sexual expression of men more than women. Men can be promiscuous but women cannot (Sohn, 2016). Table 6.1 reveals that men are almost two times more hedonistic than women (Hall & Knox, 2016).

Acceptance of the double standard is evident in the words used to describe hedonism: hedonistic men are thought of as "studs" but hedonistic women as "sluts." Indeed, Porter (2014) emphasized the double standard in her presentation on "slut-shaming" which she defined as "the act of making one feel guilty or inferior for engaging in certain sexual behaviors that violate traditional dichotomous gender roles." She pointed out that Charlie Sheen was a national celebrity for his flagrant debauchery but Kristen Stewart was shamed for her infidelity. Porter surveyed 240 undergraduates and found that 81% of the females reported having been slut-shamed in contrast to 7% of the males.

Fulle et al. (2016) reported that hedonistic females develop various strategies to mitigate their exposure to disapproval/stigma: detach from religion, withhold information about their sexual behavior from significant others, and reduce their expectations of a future relationship developing from a hookup encounter.

The double standard is also reflective of the gendered sexual scripting of female sexual behavior. Fahs (2016) noted that women give the "gift" of virginity and "direct attention away from their own needs/prioritize their partners' resulting in gendered inequalities such as faking orgasm, giving in to unwanted sex, sexual assault, tolerating sexual pain and prioritization of their partner's pleasure over their own."

Finally, Jones (2016) also revealed that the double standard is evident in regard to the sexual past of a man or woman, respectively. Whereas a man's sexual promiscuity in the past may be "forgiven," particularly if he decides to commit to monogamy, a woman's sexual past may haunt her in that her "reputation" is damaged.

sexual double standard
the view that encourages and accepts sexual expression of men more than women.

6-1d Themes in Women Making Sexual Decisions

Two researchers (Cooper & Gordon, 2015) studied the sexual decision making (SDM) of a group of women who had previously participated in casual sex without a condom. In interviews with 11 women, four major themes of sexual decision making emerged.

The first theme was "the importance of being in a relationship."

> I have sex with someone to date them . . . and hope they will call again . . . the idea that you're having casual sex with a guy . . . and then it will turn into a relationship . . . a lot of girls see it as a way into a relationship with someone.

A second theme was the influence of alcohol.

> It loosens you up, and your inhibitions run wild . . . you're freer...more confident and flirt a bit more . . . you sort of think you can do anything when you're drunk, there's no consequences.

Research on threesomes and anal sex reveal that both behaviors were associated with the use of alcohol (Morris et al., 2016; Molinares et al., 2016).

A third theme was the need to be seen as normal.

> Like when all your friends are having sex you feel like you are missing out cause you are not doing it . . . you're not cool because you are not doing . . . it kind of felt ok to do it because everyone else was doing it.

A final theme was a feeling of powerlessness in negotiating condom use.

> Where if you say no to them they might not like you; or think oh if I say no, that's going to be the end of our night . . . and then they won't call me next day, or whatever.

6-2 SOURCES OF SEXUAL VALUES

The sources of one's sexual values are numerous and include one's education, religion, and family, as well as technology, television, social movements, and the Internet. Public schools in the United States typically promote absolutist sexual values through abstinence education.

Religion is a particularly important influence. Thirty-seven percent of 2,386 undergraduate males (44% of 7,591 undergraduate females) self-identified as being "very" or "moderately" religious (Hall & Knox, 2016). In regard to sexual behavior, researchers have found that religiously active young adults are more likely to agree that sexting and sexual intercourse are inappropriate activities to engage in before being in a committed dating relationship (Miller et al., 2011).

Parents are also influential in one's sexual values. Van de Bongardt et al. (2016) found that adolescents who have high-quality relationships with their parents report having fewer sexual partners than adolescents with estranged parental relationships. Similarly, Wetherill et al. (2010) found that for individuals with parents who were aware of what their children were doing and cared about them, their behavior reported engaging in less frequent sexual behaviors.

Dusan Zidar/Shutterstock.com

Purity Balls, which are events where fathers and daughters alike pledge purity—the fathers pledge that they will be faithful to their wives and the daughters pledge (both sign "pledge cards") that they will wait until marriage to have sexual intercourse—are held in 48 states.

Konstantin L/Shutterstock.com

Purity Balls have their basis in evangelical conservative religious families. The documentary *Virgin Tales* focuses on one family in Colorado and their involvement in Purity Balls. You can read other examples of familial influences on one's sexuality in the What's New? section.

Peers, particularly same-sex friends, are major sources of sexual values. Trinh (2016) surveyed the sexual socialization of women by their female friends—translation, what their girlfriends tell them about their sexual choices. Examples of what they were told include:

You should enjoy being a female and not feel hindered by stereotypes and really enjoy your sexuality but do it in secret. Don't be outward with sexual promiscuity.

—A 21-year-old student, on what her female friends told her about sex and relationships

If you aren't having sex within the first month, he is going to dump you. Guys like you based on how much you pleasure them.

—A 20-year-old student, on what her male friends told her about sex and relationships

While these messages from female friends were laced with the admonition of "be careful," the messages from their male friends were to "have fun."

Reproductive technologies such as birth control pills, the morning-after pill, and condoms influence sexual values by affecting the consequences of behavior. Being able to reduce the risk of pregnancy and HIV infection with the pill and condoms allow one to consider a different value system than if these methods of protection did not exist.

Television also influences sexual values. A television advertisement shows an affectionate couple with minimal clothes on in a context where sex could occur. "Be ready for the moment" is the phrase of the announcer, and Levitra, the new quick-start Viagra, is the product for sale. The advertiser used sex to get the attention of the viewer and punch in the product to elicit buying behavior.

The women's movement affects sexual values by empowering women with an egalitarian view of their sexuality. This view translates into encouraging women to be more assertive about their own sexual needs and giving them the option to experience sex in a variety of contexts (e.g., without love or commitment) without self-deprecation. The net effect is a potential increase in the frequency of recreational, hedonistic sex. The gay liberation movement has also been influential in encouraging values that are accepting of sexual diversity.

Finally, the Internet has an influence on sexual values. The Internet features erotic photos, videos, and "live" sex acts/stripping by webcam sex artists. Individuals can exchange nude photos, have explicit sex dialogue, arrange to have phone sex or meet in person, or find a prostitute. Pornography has been criticized as having the potential for destroying both individuals and relationships (Luscombe, 2016).

Undergraduates Report What They Learned from Family about Sex

One's family (both nuclear and extended) is a major source of learning about sexuality. A team of researchers conducted an online survey of 101 undergraduates (from a midwest, northeast, and southern campus) who identified a memory or event from their family that had an impact on their current sexual behavior.

Key Findings

The narratives reflected a balance of negative (37.6%), positive (34.7%), and neutrally framed (27.7%) familial messages about sex. The five themes included: (1) practice safe sex, (2) premarital sex is wrong, (3) wait until you are ready/for the right person, (4) sex as natural or pleasurable, and (5) sex as negative, abusive, and/or taboo. Examples follow:

Practice Safe Sex

My mother had an abortion when she was 18 years old. She has always been very open with me about her decision as well has how I should practice safe sex so I would never have to make that decision.

Premarital Sex is Wrong

From my mother and others I was always told to wait until I was married to have sex—I was actually kind of scared out of it completely . . .

Wait Until You Are Ready/ for the Right Person

I have decided to sustain from any sexual activity until I am in a committed relationship because of a promise I made to my aunt. My aunt Crystal and I are extremely close and my promise to her will remain sacred until I am in a committed and respectable relationship.

Sex as Natural or Pleasurable

When I was 9 years old I wanted to sleep in my mother's bed. She allowed it and after a minute I felt something weird. I had a used condom stuck to my leg. My mother called her boyfriend and they laughed hysterically. I guess I learned early that sex is fun and lighthearted.

SW Productions/Photodisc/Getty Images

Sex as Negative, Abusive, and/or Taboo

My father was arrested for a sexual offense when I was 10 years old. He had solicited a girl just three years older than me online, sent her explicit material, and made plans to meet. During the custody battle, my sister and I had to endure a rape kit. Although I have no recollection of sexual abuse, the tests revealed heavy sexual abuse from extraneous objects, which revealed why I had been ridden with infection as a young child. The wounds were mostly healed, and despite no memory of the indicated events, to this day it takes me a very long time and a lot of trust to take steps towards more intimacy.

Source: Kauffman, L., M. P. Orbe, A. L. Johnson, & A. Cooke-Jackson. (2013, June 20). Memorable familial messages about sex: A qualitative content analysis of college student narratives. *Electronic Journal of Human Sexuality, 16.* Online at www.ejhs.org.

6-3 SEXUAL BEHAVIORS

We have been discussing the various sources of sexual values. We now focus on what people report that they do sexually.

6-3a What Is Sex?

Horowitz and Spicer (2013) asked 124 emerging adults (40 male heterosexuals, 42 female heterosexuals, and 42 lesbians) to identify various sexual behaviors on a six-point scale (from "definitely" to "definitely not") as "having sex." There was agreement that vaginal and anal sex were "definitely" sex while kissing was "definitely not" sex. Ratings of heterosexual males and females did not differ significantly, but gays were more likely than heterosexuals to rate various forms of genital stimulation as "having sex."

Some individuals are **asexual**, which means there is an absence of arousal or interest in having sex with someone else (the person may still masturbate, have orgasms, etc.). About 4% of females and 11% of males reported being asexual in the last 12 months (DeLamater & Hasday, 2007). In contrast, most individuals report engaging in various sexual behaviors. Penhollow et al. (2010) found that, for both male and female students, participation in recreational sexual behaviors (with or without a partner) enhanced their overall sexual satisfaction. Sexual behavior is dictated by **social scripts**—the identification of the roles in a social situation, the nature of the relationship between the roles, and the expected behaviors of those roles. In regard to kissing, two individuals kiss because they are in a relationship where the expectation is such that they are expected to kiss.

6-3b Masturbation

Masturbation involves stimulating one's own body with the goal of experiencing pleasurable sexual sensations. Ninety-seven percent of 2,312 undergraduate males (69% of 7,420 undergraduate females) reported having masturbated (Hall & Knox, 2016). Masturbation is relevant to couples in that individuals with a history of masturbation report greater sexual/relationship satisfaction than those in which a masturbatory history is absent.

Alternative terms for masturbation include *autoeroticism, self-pleasuring, solo sex,* and *sex without a partner.* An appreciation of the benefits of masturbation has now replaced various myths about it (e.g., it causes blindness).

Courtesy of Rachel Calisto

Most health care providers and therapists today regard masturbation as a normal and healthy sexual behavior. Masturbation is safe sex in that it involves no risk of transmitting diseases (such as HIV) or producing unintended pregnancy.

6-3c Oral Sex

Fellatio is oral stimulation of the man's genitals; cunnilingus is oral stimulation of the woman's genitals by her partner. In a sample of undergraduate females, 77% or 7,441 undergraduate females reported having given oral sex; of 2,312 undergraduate males, 72% reported having given oral sex (Hall & Knox, 2016). In many states, legal statutes regard

Maria McDonald

asexual an absence of sexual behavior with a partner and oneself.

social scripts the identification of the roles in a social situation, the nature of the relationship between the roles, and the expected behaviors of those roles.

masturbation stimulating one's own body with the goal of experiencing pleasurable sexual sensations.

fellatio as a "crime against nature." "Nature" in this case refers to reproduction, and the "crime" is sex that does not produce babies.

Wood et al. (2016) found that over two-thirds of 899 male and female university students reported that their last sexual encounter included giving and/or receiving oral sex. Most men (73%) and women (69%) reported that receiving oral sex was "very pleasurable." However, men were significantly more likely than women to report that giving oral sex was very pleasurable (52% vs. 28%). Overall, ratings of pleasure for giving oral sex were higher for men, but no gender differences were found for overall pleasure ratings of receiving oral sex.

There is the mistaken belief that only intercourse carries the risk of contracting an STI. However, STIs as well as HIV can be contracted orally. Use of a condom or dental dam, a flat latex device that is held over the vaginal area, is recommended.

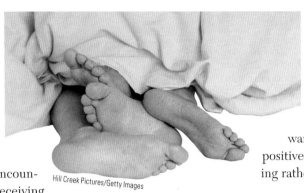

Hill Creek Pictures/Getty Images

6-3d Vaginal Intercourse

Vaginal intercourse, or **coitus**, refers to the sexual union of a man and woman by insertion of the penis into the vagina (the preferred sexual behavior of men) (Hill, 2016). Brenot and Wunsch (2016) assessed the sexual needs of 5,000 men and women and found that men needed higher sexual frequency and a partner who is more active, erotic, faithful, and understanding. In contrast, women needed a partner who is gentle, caring, and attentive to the conditions in which lovemaking takes place. In regard to university students, each academic year, there are fewer virgins.

Vasilenko et al. (2012) reported on the consequences of vaginal sex for 209 first-year undergraduates at a large northeastern university. Students kept a diary for 28 days on their sexual behavior and the personal and interpersonal consequences. The most commonly reported (81%) positive consequence of having vaginal sex was feeling physically satisfied; the most commonly reported negative consequence was worry about pregnancy (17%).

coitus sexual union of a man and woman by insertion of the penis into the vagina.

sexual readiness determining when one is ready for first intercourse in reference to contraception, autonomy of decision, consensuality, and absence of regret.

In regard to interpersonal consequences, the most common consequence was feeling closer to the partner (89%); the most common negative consequence was worrying if the partner wanted more commitment. More positive outcomes resulted from dating rather than casual partners.

6-3e First Intercourse

Seventy-three percent of 7,470 undergraduate females (69% or 2,317 undergraduate males) reported having had sexual intercourse (Hall & Knox, 2016). A study of first intercourse experience of 475 young Canadian adults revealed orgasm for 6% of females and 62% of males with alcohol/drugs associated with fewer positive experiences and higher sexual regret (Reissing et al., 2012). Having first intercourse "early" in adolescence (age 14) was remembered as a positive experience when there was an emotional relationship with the partner and when the experience was physically pleasurable. Early negative experiences were associated with no relationship involvement, physical pain/discomfort, and little preparation. It was not uncommon for the early debut adolescents to report that they were drunk. These findings are based on quantitative data (N = 705) and in-depth interviews (24 young people ages 16–18 years) (Symons et al., 2014).

Sprecher (2014) examined data from 5,769 respondents over a 23-year period in regard to gender differences in pleasure, anxiety, and guilt in response to first intercourse. Men reported more pleasure and anxiety than women, and women reported more guilt than men. Anxiety decreased over the three decades for men; pleasure increased and guilt decreased for women. The result is that "although gender differences in emotional reactions to first intercourse have decreased over time, the first intercourse experience continues to be a more positive experience for men than for women."

Hawes et al. (2010) emphasized that **sexual readiness** is helpful in determining when one is ready for first intercourse. Such readiness can be determined in reference to contraception, autonomy of decision (not influenced by alcohol or peer pressure), consensuality (both partners equally willing), and the absence of regret (the right time for me). Using these criteria, the negative consequences of first intercourse are minimized.

6-3f Cybersex

Cybersex is any consensual sexual experience mediated by a computer that involves at least two people. In this context, sexual experience includes sending text messages or photographic images that are sexual. Individuals typically send sex text and photos with the goal of arousal or looking at each other naked or masturbating when viewing each other on a webcam.

6-3g Kink

Individuals enjoy a range of sex play including what is referred to as a **kink**. Examples include sadism (a partner enjoys giving pain to another) and masochism (a partner enjoys receiving pain), which are sometimes viewed as pathological. However, Dr. Julie Fennell (2014) noticed that such behaviors are often pathologized by the psychiatric community (e.g., DSM-5).

> In much the same way that gays and lesbians feel that their sexual desires were unfairly pathologized by the medical establishment prior to the removal of homosexuality as a mental disorder from the DSM, people who participate in BDSM (Bondage & Discipline/Dominance & Submission/Sadism & Masochism) feel that they have been unfairly pathologized for their sexual desires. People who engage in BDSM apply principles of consent to their practices—meaning that there are no victims or abusers, only "tops" and "bottoms." As explained by the National Coalition for Sexual Freedom, when BDSM is practiced correctly, only people who want to get hurt get hurt. People who have medical disorders associated with sadism and masochism are not engaging in consensual behaviors, and most people in the BDSM community view the diagnoses of "fetishism" and "transvestism" as obsolete and heteronormative, respectively.

 ## 6-4 SEXUALITY IN RELATIONSHIPS

Sexuality occurs in a social context that influences its frequency and perceived quality.

6-4a Sexual Relationships among Never-Married Individuals

Never-married individuals and those not living together report more sexual partners than those who are married or living together. The never married also report the lowest level of sexual satisfaction. One-third of a national sample of people who were not married and not living with anyone reported that they were emotionally satisfied with their sexual relationships. In contrast, 85% of the married and pair-bonded individuals reported emotional satisfaction in their sexual relationships. Hence, although never-married individuals have more sexual partners, they are less emotionally satisfied (Michael et al., 1994).

6-4b Sexual Relationships among Married Individuals

Marital sex is distinctive for its social legitimacy, declining frequency, and satisfaction (both physical and emotional).

1. **Social legitimacy.** In our society, marital intercourse is the most legitimate form of sexual behavior. Those who engage in homosexual, premarital, and extramarital intercourse do not experience as high a level of social approval as do those who engage in marital sex. It is not only OK to have intercourse when married, it is expected. People assume that married couples make love and that something is wrong if they do not.

2. **Declining frequency.** Sexual intercourse between spouses occurs about six times a month, which declines in frequency as spouses age. Pregnancy also decreases the frequency of sexual intercourse (Lee et al., 2010). In addition to biological changes due to aging and pregnancy, satiation also contributes to the declining frequency of intercourse between spouses and partners in long-term relationships. Psychologists use the term **satiation** to mean that repeated exposure to a stimulus results in the loss of its ability to reinforce. The thousandth time that a person has sex with the same partner is not as new and exciting as the first few times. Polyamorists use the term **new relationship energy (NRE)** to refer to the euphoria of a new emotional/sexual relationship that dissipates over time. Polyamorists often talk with a long-term partner about the NRE they are feeling, and

> **cybersex** any consensual sexual experience mediated by a computer that involves at least two people.
>
> **kink** typically refers to BDSM (bondage and discipline/dominance and submission/sadism and masochism).
>
> **satiation** the state in which a stimulus loses its value with repeated exposure.
>
> **new relationship energy (NRE)** refers to the euphoria of a new emotional/sexual relationship that dissipates over time.

both watch its eventual decline. Hence, polyamorists don't get upset when they see their partner experiencing NRE with a new partner since they view it as having a cycle that will not last forever (Starr, 2016).

3. **Satisfaction (emotional and physical).** Despite declining frequency and less satisfaction over time, marital sex remains a richly satisfying experience. As noted above, in a national sample, 88% of married people said they received great physical pleasure from their sexual lives, and almost 85% said they received great emotional satisfaction (Michael et al., 1994). Individuals least likely to report being physically and emotionally pleased in their sexual relationships are those who are not married, not living with anyone, or not in a stable relationship with one person. The higher reported satisfaction is not related to a high frequency of sexual intercourse. Muise et al. (2015) noted that once a week (the norm for most couples in long-term relationships), not less or more, is associated with reported satisfaction; hence, more is not better. Finally, Fallis et al. (2016) found that sexual satisfaction was related to relationship satisfaction, particularly for men.

6-4c Sexual Relationships among Divorced Individuals

Of the almost 2 million people getting divorced, most will have intercourse within one year of being separated from their spouses. The meanings of intercourse for separated or divorced individuals vary. For many, intercourse is a way to reestablish—indeed, repair—their crippled self-esteem. Questions such as "What did I do wrong?" "Am I a failure?" and "Is there anybody out there who will love me again?" loom in the minds of divorced people. One way to feel loved, at least temporarily, is through sex. Being held by another and being told that it feels good give people some evidence that they are desirable. Because divorced people may be particularly vulnerable, they may reach for sexual encounters.

Because divorced individuals are usually in their mid-thirties or older, they may not be as sensitized to the danger of contracting HIV as are people in their twenties. Divorced individuals should always use a condom to lessen the risk of an STI, including HIV infection and autoimmune deficiency syndrome (AIDS).

6-4d Sexual Problems: General

Sexual relationships are not without sexual problems. Hendrickx and Enzlin (2014) analyzed data on an Internet survey of 35,132 heterosexual Flemish men and women (aged 16 to 74 years). In men, the most common sexual difficulties (impairment in sexual function regardless of level of distress) were hyperactive sexual desire (frequent sexual urges or activity) (27.7%), premature ejaculation (12.2%), and erectile difficulty (8.3%). For women, the most common sexual difficulties were absent or delayed orgasm (20.1%), hypoactive sexual desire (19.3%), and lack of responsive desire (13.7%).

iStockphoto.com/PhotoEuphoria

6-4e Sexual Problems: Pornography

While not typically regarded as a "sexual problem," the discrepancy in pornography use by men and women creates a context for conflict. All research reports higher pornography use by men than women. Brown et al. (2013) analyzed national data and found that the discrepancy drops as men move into more committed relationships. For example, among casually dating individuals, over half of men reported regular pornography use (weekly or more frequent) while only 1% of women report similar patterns—45% of men and 43% of women reported conflict over pornography use. Among married couples, the pornography gap was less with 20% for men and 3% for women reporting regular pornography use—21% of men and 27% of women reported conflict over pornography use. Whether reduction in conflict about porn use as relationship seriousness increased was due to lower frequency of use as a result of the partner's surveillance or the partner was more secure as relationship commitment increased remains an open question.

Pornography has been blamed for creating unrealistic expectations for sexuality in a real relationship that is unrealistic and for destroying individuals' and couples' sex lives. A lead article in *Time Magazine* featured the ill effects of pornography (Luscombe, 2016). Data for widespread negative consequences are nonexistent.

6-5 SEXUAL FULFILLMENT: SOME PREREQUISITES

There are several prerequisites for having a good sexual relationship.

6-5a Self-Knowledge, Body Image, and Health

Sexual fulfillment involves knowledge about yourself and your body. Such information not only makes it easier for you to experience pleasure but also allows you to give accurate information to a partner about pleasing you. It is not possible to teach a partner what you do not know about yourself.

Sexual fulfillment also implies having a positive body image. To the degree that you have positive feelings about your body, you will regard yourself as a person someone else would enjoy touching, being close to, and making love with. If you do not like yourself or your body, you might wonder why anyone else would. Woertman and Van den Brink (2012) found sexual arousal, initiating sex, sexual satisfaction, and orgasm related to a positive body image in women.

Effective sexual functioning also requires good physical and mental health. This means regular exercise, good nutrition, lack of disease, and lack of fatigue. Performance in all areas of life does not have to diminish with age—particularly if people take care of themselves physically.

Good health also implies being aware that some drugs may interfere with sexual performance. Alcohol is the drug most frequently used by American adults (including college students). Although a moderate amount of alcohol can help a person become aroused through a lowering of inhibitions, too much alcohol can slow the physiological processes and deaden the senses. Shakespeare may have said it best: "It [alcohol] provokes

the desire, but it takes away the performance" (*Macbeth*, act 2, scene 3). The result of an excessive intake of alcohol for women is a reduced chance of orgasm; for men, overindulgence results in a reduced chance of attaining an erection.

The reactions to marijuana are less predictable than the reactions to alcohol. Though some individuals report a short-term enhancement effect, others say that marijuana just makes them sleepy. In men, chronic use may decrease sex drive because marijuana may lower testosterone levels.

> Nothing says "I respect you" quite like a 2 A.M. "what's up" text.
>
> —YIK YAK POSTING

6-5b A Committed Loving Relationship

A guideline among therapists who work with couples who have sexual problems is to treat the relationship before focusing on the sexual issue. The sexual relationship is part of the larger relationship between the partners, and what happens outside the bedroom in day-to-day interaction has a tremendous influence on what happens inside the bedroom. Indeed, relationship satisfaction is associated with sexual satisfaction (Stephenson et al., 2013). The statement "I can't fight with you all day and want to have sex with you at night" illustrates the social context of the sexual experience. Partners in committed relationships reported the highest sexual satisfaction (Galinsky & Sorenstein, 2013).

In the chapter on love, we reviewed the concept of alexithymia or the inability to experience and express emotion. Scimeca et al. (2013) studied a sample of 300 university students who revealed that higher alexithymia scores were associated with lower levels of sexual satisfaction and higher levels of sexual detachment for females, and with sexual shyness and sexual nervousness for both genders. Conversely, being able to experience and express emotion has positive outcomes for one's sexual relationship.

6-5c An Equal Relationship

Sanchez et al. (2012) emphasized that traditional gender roles interfere with and inhibit a sexually fulfilling relationship. These roles dictate that the woman not initiate sex, be submissive, disregard her own pleasure, and not give accurate feedback to the male. By disavowing these roles,

Maria McDonald

adopting an egalitarian perspective, and engaging in new behavior (initiating sex, taking the dominant role, insisting on her own sexual pleasure, and informing her partner about what she needs), the couple are on the path to a new and more fulfilling sexual relationship. Of course, such a change in the woman requires that the male give up that he must always initiate sex and belief in the double standard (e.g., the belief that women who love sex are sluts), and delight in not having to drive the sexual bus all the time.

6-5d Condom Assertiveness

Wright et al. (2012) reviewed the concept of **condom assertiveness**—the unambiguous messaging that sex without a condom is unacceptable—and identified the characteristics of undergraduate women who are more likely to insist on condom use. Compared with less condom-assertive females, more condom-assertive females have more faith in the effectiveness of condoms, believe more in their own condom communication skills, perceive that they are more susceptible to STIs, believe there are more relational benefits to being condom assertive, believe their peers are more condom assertive, and intend to be more condom assertive.

Condom assertiveness is important not only for sexual and anal intercourse but also for oral sex. Not to use a condom or dental dam is to increase the risk of contracting an STI. Indeed, individuals think "I am on the pill and won't get pregnant" or "No way I am getting pregnant by having oral sex" only to discover Human papillomavirus (HPV) or another STI in their mouth or throat.

Also known as sexually transmitted disease, or STD, **STI** refers to the general category of sexually transmitted infections such as chlamydia, genital herpes, gonorrhea, and syphilis. The most lethal of all STIs is that caused by the human immunodeficiency virus (HIV), which attacks the immune system and can lead to AIDS.

6-5e Open Sexual Communication (Sexual Self-Disclosure) and Feedback

Sexually fulfilled partners are comfortable expressing what they enjoy and do not enjoy in the sexual experience. Unless both partners communicate their needs, preferences, and expectations to each other, neither is ever sure what the other wants. In essence, the Golden Rule ("Do unto others as you would have them do unto you") is *not* helpful, because what you like may not be the same as what your partner wants.

condom assertiveness the unambiguous messaging that sex without a condom is unacceptable.

STI sexually transmitted infection.

Amy: Sheldon, are we ever going to have an intimate relationship?
Sheldon: Oh, my. That's an uncomfortable topic. Amy, before I met you, I never had any interest in being intimate with anyone.
Amy: And now?
Sheldon: And now what?
Amy: Do you have any interest now?
Sheldon: I have not ruled it out.
Amy: Wow. Talk dirty to me.

—THE BIG BANG THEORY

Sexually fulfilled partners take the guesswork out of their relationship by communicating preferences and giving feedback. Women may be less assertive about what they want sexually than men, particularly when they want oral sex. In a study of 237 sexually active women, the researchers observed that if they perceived that their partners would not be open to giving them oral sex, they were less likely to ask them to do so (Satinsky & Jozkowski, 2015).

6-5f Frequent Initiation of Sexual Behavior

Simms and Byers (2013) assessed the sexual initiation behaviors of 151 individuals (33% men and 66% women) who were 18–25 years of age, had been in an exclusive, heterosexual, noncohabitating dating relationship between 3 and 18 months, had seen their dating partners

Maria McDonald

at least 3–4 days per week over the previous month, and had engaged in genitally focused sexual activities. The researchers found that both men and women who reported initiating sex more frequently and who perceived their partner as initiating more frequently reported greater sexual satisfaction.

6-5g Having Realistic Expectations

To achieve sexual fulfillment, expectations must be realistic. A couple's sexual needs, preferences, and expectations may not coincide. It is unrealistic to assume that your partner will want to have sex with the same frequency and in the same way that you do on all occasions. It may also be unrealistic to expect the level of sexual interest and frequency of sexual interaction to remain consistently high in long-term relationships.

Sexual fulfillment means not asking things of the sexual relationship that it cannot deliver. Failure to develop realistic expectations will result in frustration and resentment. One's age, health (both mental and physical), sexual dysfunctions of self and partner, and previous sexual experiences will have an effect on one's sexuality and one's sexual relationship and sexual fulfillment (McCabe & Goldhammer, 2012).

Each partner brings to a sexual encounter, sometimes unconsciously, a motive (pleasure, reconciliation, procreation, duty), a psychological state (love, hostility, boredom, excitement), and a physical state (tense, exhausted, relaxed, turned on). The combination of these factors will change from one encounter to another. Tonight one partner may feel aroused and loving and seek pleasure, but the other partner may feel exhausted and hostile and have sex only out of a sense of duty. Tomorrow night, both partners may feel relaxed and have sex as a means of expressing their love for each other.

6-5h Sexual Compliance

Given that partners may differ in sexual interest and desire, Vannier and O'Sullivan (2010) identified the concept of **sexual compliance** whereby an individual willingly agrees to participate in sexual behavior without having the desire to do so. The researchers studied 164 heterosexual young (18–24) adult couples in committed relationships to assess the level of sexual compliance. Almost half (46%) of the respondents reported at least one occasion of sexual compliance with sexual compliance comprising 17% of all sexual activity recorded over a three-week period. Indeed, sexual compliance was a mechanism these individuals used in their committed relationships to resolve the issue of different levels of sexual desire that is likely to happen over time in a stable couple's relationship. Others felt guilty they did not desire sex, and still others did it because their partner provided sex when the partner was not in the mood.

There were no gender differences in differences of sexual desire and no gender difference in providing sexual compliant behavior. The majority of participants reported enjoying the sexual activity despite not wanting to engage in it at first.

6-5i Avoiding Spectatoring

One of the obstacles to sexual functioning is **spectatoring**, which involves mentally observing your sexual performance and that of your partner. When the researchers in one extensive study observed how individuals actually behave during sexual intercourse, they reported a tendency for sexually dysfunctional partners to act as spectators by mentally observing their own and their partners' sexual performance. For example, the man would focus on whether he was having an erection, how complete it was, and whether it would last. He might also watch to see whether his partner was having an orgasm (Masters & Johnson, 1970). Just focusing on one's own body can have an effect. Van den Brink et al. (2013) confirmed that body image self-consciousness was negatively associated with sexual functioning and frequency of sexual activity with a partner. Spectatoring,

Milos Luzanin/Shutterstock.com

Diversity in Other Countries

Nagao et al. (2014) surveyed 5,665 Japanese women who were involved with a male partner and were interested in sexual activity. In general, the women reported a desire for longer foreplay and after play as well as more influence over when sex occurred and what sexual positions were experienced. Their partner's unilateral action during sexual activity negatively affected the quality of their sexual life with their partner. These findings emphasize the need for more sexual communication between the partners.

sexual compliance an individual willingly agrees to participate in sexual behavior without having the desire to do so.

spectatoring mentally observing one's own and one's partner's sexual performance.

as Masters and Johnson conceived it, interferes with each partner's sexual enjoyment because it creates anxiety about performance, and anxiety blocks performance. A man who worries about getting an erection reduces his chance of doing so. A woman who is anxious about achieving an orgasm probably will not. Montesi et al. (2013) confirmed the negative effect of anxiety on a couple's sexual relationship. The desirable alternative to spectatoring is to relax, focus on and enjoy your own pleasure, and permit yourself to be sexually responsive.

6-5j Female Vibrator Use, Orgasm, and Partner Comfort

It is commonly known that vibrators (also known as sex toys and novelties) are beneficial for increasing the probability of orgasmic behavior in women. During intercourse, women typically report experiencing orgasm less than 10% of the time (Mintz, 2017); vibrator use increases orgasmic reports to over 90%. Herbenick et al. (2010) studied women's use of vibrators within sexual partnerships. They analyzed data from 2,056 women aged 18–60 years in the United States. Partnered vibrator use was common among heterosexual-, lesbian-, and bisexual-identified women. Most vibrator users indicated comfort using them with a partner and related using them to positive sexual function. In addition, partner knowledge and perceived liking of vibrator use was a significant predictor of sexual satisfaction for heterosexual women.

That men are accepting of using a vibrator with their female partners was confirmed by Reece et al. (2010), who surveyed a nationally representative sample of heterosexual men in the United States. Forty-three percent reported having used a vibrator. Of those who had done so, most vibrator use had occurred within the context of sexual interaction with a female partner. Indeed, 94% of male vibrator users reported that they had used a vibrator during sexual play with a partner, and 82% reported that they had used a vibrator during sexual intercourse. In another study which used a national sample, women and men held positive attitudes about female vibrator use (Herbenick et al., 2011). These data support recommendations of therapists and educators who often suggest the incorporation of vibrators into partnered relationships.

6-6 TRENDS IN SEXUALITY IN RELATIONSHIPS

The future of sexual relationships will involve continued individualism as the driving force in sexual relationships. Numerous casual partners (hooking up) will continue

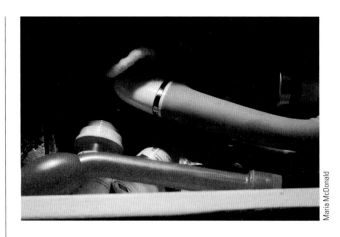

Maria McDonald

to characterize about 75% of individuals in late adolescence and early twenties. As these persons reach their late twenties, the goal of sexuality begins to transition to seeking a partner—not just to hook up with and have fun with but to settle down with. This new goal is accompanied by new sexual behaviors such as delayed first intercourse in the new relationship, exclusivity, and movement toward marriage. The monogamous move toward the marriage context creates a transitioning of sexual values from hedonism to relativism to absolutism, where strict morality rules become operative in the relationship (expected fidelity).

Sexual robots will also become more visible and their use will continue. Artificial intelligence expert Noel Sharkey reported that teenagers risk losing their virginity to sophisticated humanoid robots (Roxxxy or Rocky True Companion) (Bodkin, 2016).

STUDY TOOLS 6

READY TO STUDY? IN THE BOOK, YOU CAN:

☐ Rip out the chapter review card at the back of the book for a handy summary of the chapter and key terms.

☐ Assess yourself with the following self-assessment.

ONLINE AT CENGAGEBRAIN.COM YOU CAN:

☐ Collect StudyBits while you read and study the chapter.

☐ Quiz yourself on key concepts.

☐ Prepare for tests with M&F4 Flash Cards as well as those you create.

 **SELF-ASSESSMENT**

Conservative–Liberal Sexuality Scale (CLSS)

This scale is designed to assess the degree to which you are conservative or liberal in your attitudes toward sex. There are no right or wrong answers. After reading each sentence carefully, select the number that best represents the degree to which you agree or disagree with the sentence.

1	2	3	4	5
Strongly agree	*Mildly agree*	*Undecided*	*Mildly disagree*	*Strongly disagree*

____ **1.** Abortion is wrong.

____ **2.** Homosexuality is immoral.

____ **3.** Couples should wait to have sexual intercourse until after they are married.

____ **4.** Couples who are virgins at marriage have more successful marriages.

____ **5.** Watching pornography is harmful.

____ **6.** Kinky sex is something to be avoided.

____ **7.** Having an extramarital affair is never justified.

____ **8.** Masturbation is something an individual should try to avoid doing.

____ **9.** One should always be in love when having sex with a person.

____ **10.** Transgender people are screwed up and "not right."

____ **11.** Sex is for youth, not for the elderly.

____ **12.** There is entirely too much sex on TV today.

____ **13.** The best use of sex is for procreation.

____ **14.** Any form of sex that is not sexual intercourse is wrong.

____ **15.** Our society is entirely too liberal when it comes to sex.

____ **16.** Sex education gives youth ideas about sex they shouldn't have.

____ **17.** Promiscuity is the cause of the downfall of an individual.

____ **18.** Too much sexual freedom is promoted in our country today.

____ **19.** The handicapped probably should not try to get involved in sex.

____ **20.** The movies in America are too sexually explicit.

Scoring

Add the numbers you circled. 1 (strongly agree) is the most conservative response and 5 (strongly disagree) is the most liberal response. The lower your total score (20 is the lowest possible score), the more sexually conservative your attitudes toward sex. The higher your total score (100 is the highest possible score), the more liberal your attitudes toward sex. A score of 60 places you at the midpoint between being the ultimate conservative and the ultimate liberal about sex. Of 191 undergraduate females, the average score was 69.85. Of 39 undergraduate males the average score was 72.89. Hence, both women and men tended to be more sexually liberal than conservative with men more sexually liberal than women.

Source: Knox, D. (2014)."The Conservative–Liberal Sexuality Scale" was developed for this text. The scale is intended to be thought provoking and fun. It is not intended to be used as a clinical or diagnostic instrument.

7 | Examining GLBTQIA Relationships

SECTIONS

After finishing
this chapter go
to **PAGE 149** for
STUDY TOOLS

> My sexual orientation? Horizontal, usually.
>
> —BUMPER STICKER

In April 2016, North Carolina passed a law that requires schools and public agencies to have gender-segregated bathrooms. The goal was to prevent people from using a bathroom that does not correspond to their biological sex. A similar law has been considered by an additional seven states.

The law is seen as discriminatory and against the GLBT community. Bruce Springsteen and other artists canceled a concert scheduled in the state in protest of the law. Professional organizations such as the Southern Sociological Society confirmed that they would no longer hold their conventions in the state unless such legislation was repealed.

One effect of the "transgender bathroom law" was to bring into cultural awareness the issues of the GLBT community—the focus of this chapter.

In the following pages, we discuss concerns experienced by LGBTQIA individuals. **LGBTQIA** is a term that has emerged to refer collectively to **l**esbians, **g**ays, **b**isexuals, **t**ransgender individuals, those **q**uestioning their sexual orientation/sexual identity (the term may also refer to queer), those who are **i**ntersexed, and **a**sexual (some also refer to the A as ally/friend of the cause and asexual).

The term **asexual** means that there is an absence of sexual attraction/arousal to a partner. However, the person may form emotional attachments, masturbate, and experience sexual pleasure (Hille, 2014) and orgasm (Van Houdenhove et al., 2015).

Asexuality may be regarded as a sexual orientation. Just as asexuality individuals may be emotionally attracted to the other or same sex, they may be emotionally attracted to neither. The Asexual Visibility and Education Network (AVEN) facilitates awareness of asexuality as an explicit identify category. In this chapter, we begin by clarifying some terms.

7-1 TERMINOLOGY AND IDENTIFICATION

Sexual orientation (also known as **sexual identity**) is a classification of individuals as heterosexual, bisexual, or gay, based on their emotional, cognitive, and sexual attractions and self-identity. **Heterosexuality** refers to the predominance of cognitive, emotional, and sexual attraction to individuals of the other sex. **Homosexuality** refers to the predominance of cognitive, emotional, and sexual attraction to individuals of the same sex, and **bisexuality** is cognitive, emotional, and sexual attraction to members of both sexes. The term **lesbian** refers to women who prefer same-sex partners; **gay** can refer to either women or men who prefer same-sex partners. Of U.S. adults, about 1% of females self-identify as lesbian, 2% of males self-identify as gay, and 1.5% of adults self-identify as bisexual. Hence, about 3.5% or about 10 million individuals in the United States are LGB (Mock & Eibach, 2012). Of 9,970 undergraduates, 1.4% identified as lesbian, 1.6% as gay male, 5.7% as bisexual, and 1.2% as other (Hall & Knox, 2016).

Moser (2016) noted that there is disagreement on the definition of sexual orientation. While most agree that the definition involves one's heterosexual or homosexual orientation (or some combination), others suggest that asexuality, pedophilia, and polyamory are definitions. Sexual configurations theory has been used to help understand diverse partnered sexuality.

The word **transgender** is a generic term for a person of one biological sex who displays characteristics of the other sex. Kuper et al. (2012) identified 292 transgendered individuals online. Most self-identified as gender queer (their gender identity was neither

LGBTQIA a term that has emerged to refer collectively to **l**esbians, **g**ays, **b**isexuals, **t**ransgender individuals, those **q**uestioning their sexual orientation/sexual identity (the term may also refer to queer), those who are **i**ntersexed, and **a**sexual (some also refer to the A as ally/friend of the cause and asexual).

asexual means that there is an absence of sexual attraction/arousal to a partner.

sexual orientation (sexual identity) a classification of individuals as heterosexual, bisexual, or homosexual, based on their emotional, cognitive, and sexual attractions and self-identity.

heterosexuality the predominance of emotional and sexual attraction to individuals of the other sex.

homosexuality predominance of emotional and sexual attraction to individuals of the same sex.

bisexuality emotional and sexual attraction to members of both sexes.

lesbian homosexual woman.

gay homosexual women or men.

transgender individuals who express their masculinity and femininity in nontraditional ways consistent with their biological sex.

male nor female) and pansexual/queer (they were attracted to men, women, bisexuals) as their sexual orientation. An estimated 0.3% adults or about 700,000 individuals in the United States self-identify as transgender (Gates, 2011).

Transsexuals are individuals with the biological and anatomical sex of one gender (e.g., male) but the self-concept of the other sex (e.g., female). In the Kuper et al. (2012) sample of 292 transgendered individuals, most did not desire to (or were unsure of their desire to) take hormones or undergo sexual reassignment surgery.

"I am a woman trapped in a man's body" reflects the feelings of the male-to-female transsexual (MtF), who may take hormones to develop breasts and reduce facial hair and may have surgery to artificially construct a vagina. Such a person lives full time as a woman. The female-to-male transsexual (FtM) is one who is a biological and anatomical female but feels "I am a man trapped in a woman's body." This person may take male hormones to grow facial hair and deepen her voice and may have surgery to create an artificial penis. This person lives full time as a man. Individuals need not take hormones or have surgery to be regarded as transsexuals. The distinguishing variable is living full time in the role of the other biological sex. A man or woman who presents full time as the other gender is a transsexual by definition.

Johnson et al. (2014) noted the complexity of gender, sexuality, and sexual orientation issues as experienced by transgender, queer, and questioning individuals. One of the participants in their study who identified themselves as TQQ, explained:

> I would consider myself to be bi-gendered or gender fluid. Which is probably like the most complicated thing or decision that I have ever made . . . because there aren't very many people that understand it. Being bi-gendered makes a lot more sense for me just because like my sexuality in general is just really fluid and it's really hard to identify myself in one particular box for very long at all 'cause it's always changing.

In addition to GLBT, sometimes the acronym GLBTQIA is used. The letter Q stands for questioning, I stands for inner sex (individuals are part female and part male), and A refers to an ally of the movement; the A may also refer to asexual.

Cross-dresser is a broad term for individuals who may dress or present themselves in the gender of the other sex. Some cross-dressers are heterosexual adult males who enjoy dressing and presenting themselves as women. Cross-dressers may also be women who dress as men and present themselves as men. Cross-dressers may be heterosexual, homosexual, or bisexual.

The term **queer** is typically used by a male (but it could be used by a female) as a self-identifier to indicate that the person has a sexual orientation other than heterosexual (**genderqueer** means that the person does not identify as either male or female since he or she does not feel sufficiently like one or the other). Traditionally, the term *queer* was used to denote a gay person, and the connotation was negative. More recently, individuals have begun using the term *queer* with pride, much the same way African Americans called themselves Black during the 1960s civil rights era as part of building ethnic pride and identity. Hence, GLBT people took the term *queer*, which was used to demean them, and started to use it with pride. The term also has shock value, which some people who identify strongly with being queer seem to savor when they introduce themselves as being queer.

Queer theory refers to a movement or theory dating from the early 1990s. Queer theorists advocate for less labeling of sexual orientation and a stronger "anyone can be anything he or she wants" attitude. The theory is that society should support a more fluid range of sexual orientations and that individuals can move through the range as they become more self-aware. Queer theory may be seen as a very specific subset of gender and human sexuality studies.

transsexual individual with the biological and anatomical sex of one gender but the self-concept of the other sex.

cross-dresser broad term for individuals who may dress or present themselves in the gender of the other sex.

queer a self-identifier to indicate that the person has a sexual orientation other than heterosexual.

genderqueer the person does not identify as either male or female since he or she does not feel sufficiently like one or the other.

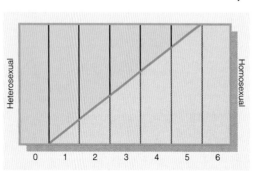

Based on both psychologic reactions and overt experience, individuals rate as follows:
0. Exclusively heterosexual with no homosexual
1. Predominantly heterosexual, only incidentally homosexual
2. Predominantly heterosexual, but more than incidentally homosexual
3. Equally heterosexual and homosexual
4. Predominantly homosexual, but more than incidentally heterosexual
5. Predominantly homosexual, but incidentally heterosexual
6. Exclusively homosexual

7-1a Kinsey Scale

Early research on sexual behavior by Kinsey and his colleagues (1948, 1953) found that, although 37% of men and 13% of women had had at least one same-sex sexual experience since adolescence, few of the individuals reported exclusive homosexual behavior. Kinsey suggested that heterosexuality and homosexuality represent two ends of a sexual-orientation continuum and that most individuals are neither entirely homosexual nor entirely heterosexual, but fall somewhere along this continuum. The Heterosexual–Homosexual Rating Scale (see previous page) that Kinsey et al. (1953) developed allows individuals to identify their sexual orientation on a continuum. Very few individuals are exclusively a 0 (exclusively heterosexual) or 6 (exclusively homosexual), prompting Kinsey to believe that most individuals are bisexual.

7-1b Difficulty in Identifying Sexual Orientation

Lyons et al. (2014) investigated the accuracy of one's "gaydar" or the ability to identify sexual orientation by looking at a person. In a study of heterosexual (N = 80) and homosexual (N = 71) women who rated the faces of heterosexual/homosexual men and women, detection accuracy was better than chance but male targets were more likely to be falsely labeled as homosexual than were female targets.

Some researchers have also emphasized that sexual orientation of women is sometimes fluid and noted that social context impacts self-identify development as a lesbian. Davis-Delano (2014) interviewed 56 women to explore the range of activities which influenced the development of their same-sex attractions and relationships. These included activities described as involving lesbians, were primarily composed of women, affirmed women, facilitated bonding, featured a climate of acceptance of lesbians/gays/bisexuals, and did not emphasize heteronormativity.

7-2 SEXUAL ORIENTATION

Same-sex behavior has existed throughout human history. Much of the biomedical and psychological research on sexual orientation attempts to identify one or more "causes" of sexual-orientation diversity. The driving question behind this research is this: "Is sexual orientation inborn or is it learned or acquired from environmental influences?" Although a number of factors have been correlated with sexual orientation, including genetics, gender role behavior in childhood,

Maria McDonald

fraternal birth order, and child sex abuse (Roberts et al., 2013), no single theory can explain diversity in sexual orientation.

7-2a Beliefs about What "Causes" Homosexuality

Aside from what "causes" homosexuality, most gay people believe that homosexuality is an inherited, inborn trait. Overby (2014) analyzed Internet data of over 20,000 respondents (primarily heterosexual) and found that roughly half (52%) thought of homosexuality as being based primarily in "biological make-up" compared to 32% who saw sexual orientation as more of a lifestyle choice.

The terms *sexual preference* and *sexual orientation* are often used interchangeably. However, those who believe that sexual orientation is inborn more often use the term *sexual orientation*, and those who think that individuals choose their sexual orientation tend to use the term *sexual preference*. The term *sexual identity* is, increasingly, being used since it connotes more about the whole person than does sexuality.

7-2b Can Homosexuals Change Their Sexual Orientation?

Individuals who believe that homosexual people choose their sexual orientation tend to think that homosexuals can and should change their sexual orientation. While about 2% of U.S. adults report that there has been a change

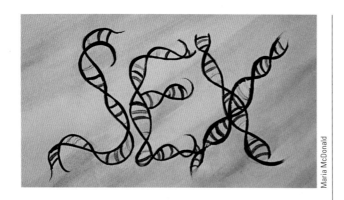

Maria McDonald

in their sexual orientation (Mock & Eibach, 2012), various forms of **conversion therapy (reparative therapy)** are focused on changing homosexuals' sexual orientation. Data confirm that conversion therapy is ineffective and misguided. Gay people are not the problem; social disapproval is the problem. The National Association for the Research and Therapy of Homosexuality (NARTH) has been influential in moving public opinion from "gays are sick" to "society is judgmental." The American Psychiatric Association, the American Psychological Association, the American Academy of Pediatrics, the American Counseling Association, the National Association of School Psychologists, the National Association of Social Workers, and the American Medical Association agree that homosexuality is not a mental disorder and needs no cure.

At present, California, New Jersey, Oregon, Illinois, Vermont, Washington, DC., and the Canadian Province of Ontario have passed legislation banning conversion therapy for minors and an increasing number of U.S. States are considering similar bans. In April 2015, the Obama administration also called for a ban on conversion therapies for minors.

7-3 HETEROSEXISM, HOMONEGATIVITY, ETC.

conversion therapy (reparative therapy) therapy designed to change a person's homosexual orientation to a heterosexual orientation.

heterosexism the denigration and stigmatization of any behavior, person, or relationship that is not heterosexual.

homophobia negative (almost phobic) attitudes toward homosexuality.

The United States, along with many other countries throughout the world, is predominantly heterosexist. **Heterosexism** refers to "the institutional and societal reinforcement of heterosexuality as the privileged and powerful norm." Heterosexism is based on the belief that heterosexuality is superior to homosexuality.

Of 9,677 undergraduates, 26% agreed (men more than women) with the statement "It is better to be heterosexual than homosexual" (Hall & Knox, 2016). Heterosexism results in prejudice and discrimination against homosexual and bisexual people. The word *prejudice* refers to negative attitudes, whereas *discrimination* refers to behavior that denies equality of treatment for individuals or groups.

Woodford et al. (2015) used the term *microaggressions* to refer to subtle and covert discrimination against sexual minorities. Examples of microaggressions include hearing a joke about LGBQ people, hearing someone say "That's so gay" to describe something negative/stupid/uncool or limiting information about sexual health to heterosexual sex.

7-3a Attitudes toward Homosexuality: Homonegativity and Homophobia

Adolfsen et al. (2010) noted that there are five dimensions of attitudes about homosexuality:

1. **General attitude.** Is homosexuality considered to be normal or abnormal? Do people think that homosexuals should be allowed to live their lives just as freely as heterosexuals?

2. **Equal rights.** Should homosexuals be granted the same rights as heterosexuals in regard to marriage and adoption?

3. **Close quarters.** Feelings in regard to having a gay neighbor or a lesbian colleague.

4. **Public display.** Reactions to a gay couple kissing in public.

5. **Modern homonegativity.** Feeling that homosexuality is accepted in society and that all kinds of special attention are unnecessary.

The term **homophobia** is commonly used to refer to negative attitudes and emotions toward homosexuality and those who engage in homosexual behavior. Homophobia is not necessarily a clinical phobia (i.e., one

 Self-Assessment: Self-Report of Behavior Scale (SRBS)

Take the Self-Report of Behavior Scale in the self-assessment section at the end of this chapter to identify your behavior during past encounters with people you thought were homosexuals and provide information in regard to the level of negative attitudes toward homosexuals.

New American Family? Do Gays Constitute a "Real" Family?

To what degree are gay individuals, couples, and those with children regarded by mainstream adults in the United States as having "real" families? The Pew Research Center surveyed attitudes toward gay and lesbian couples raising one or more children via landline and cell phone interviews with 2,691 adults (Becker & Todd, 2013).

Almost two-thirds of the respondents (63%) agreed that a gay or lesbian couple living together raising one or more children constitute a family. In contrast, other household arrangements with children received broader public support: (1) an unmarried man and woman who live together with one or more children (80% said this is a family), (2) a single parent living with one or more children (86% said this is a family), and (3) a husband and wife with one or more children (99% say this is a family). And only 45% of respondents indicate that they define "a gay or lesbian couple living together with no children" as a family. Hence, the presence of children in households led by gay and lesbian couples has an influence on attitudes.

involving a compelling desire to avoid the feared object despite recognizing that the fear is unreasonable). Other terms that refer to negative attitudes and emotions toward homosexuality include **homonegativity** (attaching negative connotations to being gay) and antigay bias.

Homophobia and homonegativity are sometimes expressed as **hate crimes** or violence against homosexuals. Such crimes include verbal harassment (the most frequent form of hate crime experienced by victims), vandalism, sexual assault and rape, physical assault, and murder. Hate crimes also target transsexuals (more so than gay individuals).

The Sex Information and Education Council of the United States (SIECUS) notes that "individuals have the right to accept, acknowledge, and live in accordance with their sexual orientation, be they bisexual, heterosexual, gay or lesbian. The legal system should guarantee the civil rights and protection of all people, regardless of sexual orientation" (SIECUS, 2016).

Characteristics associated with positive attitudes toward homosexuals and gay rights include females, Whites, supporters of egalitarian gender roles, younger age, advanced education, no religious affiliation, liberal political party affiliation, and personal contact with homosexual individuals (Daboin et al., 2015; Lee & Hicks, 2011). Women also tend to have more positive attitudes toward homosexuality (Wright & Bae, 2013).

Negative social meanings associated with homosexuality can affect the self-concepts of LGBT individuals.

Internalized homophobia is a sense of personal failure and self-hatred among lesbians and gay men resulting from social rejection and the stigmatization of being gay. Hu et al. (2016) compared lesbian, gay, and bisexual adults with heterosexual adults and found lower self-esteem and higher loneliness in the former groups. However, life satisfaction was similar. Being gay and growing up in a religious context that is antigay may be particularly difficult (Lalicha & McLaren, 2010). Gonzales (2014) noted that many LGBT people report "worse physical and mental health conditions than heterosexual and nontransgender populations, largely as a result of the stress caused by being a member of a stigmatized minority group or because of discrimination due to sexual orientation or gender nonconformity. Discriminatory environments and public policies stigmatize LGBT people and engender feelings of rejection, shame, and low self-esteem, which can negatively affect people's health-related behavior as well as their mental health. LGBT people living in states that ban same-sex marriage, for instance, are more likely than their counterparts in other states to report symptoms of depression, anxiety, and alcohol use disorder" (p. 1374).

homonegativity a construct that refers to antigay responses such as negative feelings (fear, disgust, anger), thoughts ("homosexuals are HIV carriers"), and behavior ("homosexuals deserve a beating").

hate crime instances of violence against homosexuals.

internalized homophobia a sense of personal failure and self-hatred among lesbians and gay men resulting from the acceptance of negative social attitudes and feelings toward homosexuals.

Barbara Alper/Getty Images

7-3b Biphobia and Transphobia

An **ally development model** has been suggested as a means of providing a new learning context for homophobic heterosexist students (Zammitt et al., 2015). Such a model is multilayered and involves school counselors, school social workers, and school psychologists providing programs to expose children K–12 to the nature of prejudice/discrimination toward GLBT individuals. In addition, GLBT individuals should be provided with a framework to react/perceive prejudice and discrimination. In some schools the whole culture is GLBT aware and supportive.

College is another context where acceptance toward GLBT individuals can increase. Research has demonstrated that interaction with gays/lesbians and taking courses related to these issues are associated with more accepting attitudes regarding same-sex relationships, voting for a gay presidential candidate, being friends with a feminine man/masculine woman, and comfort with a gay/lesbian roommate (Sevecke et al., 2015).

Just as the term *homophobia* is used to refer to negative attitudes toward homosexuality, gay men, and lesbians, **biphobia** (also referred to as **binegativity**) refers to a parallel set of negative attitudes toward bisexuality/those identified as bisexual. Just as bisexuals are often rejected by heterosexuals (men are more rejecting than women) they are also rejected by many homosexual individuals (Yost & Thomas, 2012). Thus, bisexuals experience "double discrimination" and reveal worse mental health than their heterosexual and gay/lesbian counterparts. Minority stress and lifetime adversity contribute to this outcome (Persson & Pfaus, 2015).

Transsexuals are targets of **transphobia**, a set of negative attitudes toward transsexuality or those who self-identify as transsexual. As was noted at the beginning of the chapter, transgendered individuals were targets of the "bathroom laws" and do not have protection in the workplace in about half the states. Blosnich et al. (2016) found that transgender individuals who lived in states with employment nondiscrimination protection (about half) had a 26% lower incidence of mood disorders (e.g., depression).

7-3c Effects of Antigay/Trans Bias and Discrimination on Heterosexuals

The antigay and heterosexist social climate of our society is often viewed in terms of how it victimizes the gay population. Indeed, Fredriksen-Goldsen et al. (2015) confirmed that the negative effects (impaired physical and mental health) of discrimination continue as GLBT members age. However, heterosexuals are also victimized by heterosexism and antigay prejudice and discrimination. Some of these effects follow:

1. **Homocide victims of hate crimes.** Extreme homophobia contributes to instances of violence against homosexuals—acts known as hate crimes. The National Coalition of Anti-Violence Programs (2015) reported that, in 2014, there were 20 homicides. In June 2016, around 50 individuals were gunned down at a gay nightclub in Orlando, Florida. Other hate crimes included verbal harassment (the most frequent form of hate crime experienced by victims), vandalism, sexual assault and rape, and physical assault. Hate crimes also target transsexuals (more so than gay individuals). And sometimes heterosexuals may be victims in that they may be partying at a gay bar and be victimized as others are.

2. **Concern, fear, and grief over well-being of gay or lesbian family members and friends.** Many heterosexual family members and friends of homosexual people experience concern, fear, and grief over the mistreatment of their gay or lesbian friends and/or family members. Heterosexual parents who have a gay or lesbian teenager often worry about how the harassment, ridicule, rejection, and violence experienced at school might affect their gay or lesbian child. Will their child be traumatized/make bad grades or drop out of school to escape the harassment, violence, and alienation they endure there? Will the gay or

ally development model professionals provide consistent exposure to the discriminatory patterns against GLBT individuals.

biphobia (binegativity) refers to a parallel set of negative attitudes toward bisexuality and those identified as bisexual.

transphobia negative attitudes toward transsexuality or those who self-identify as transsexual.

lesbian child respond to the antigay victimization by turning to drugs or alcohol? Newcomb et al. (2014) compared national samples of gay and straight youth and found higher drug use among sexual minorities. Peter and Taylor (2014) analyzed data from of 1,205 university students. Findings showed, compared to non-LGBTQ respondents, sexual minority youth are at a greater risk for serious suicidal ideation (8.9% versus 23%, respectively) and suicide attempt (3.5% versus 26.2%).

3. **Restriction of intimacy and self-expression.** Because of the antigay social climate, heterosexual individuals, especially males, are hindered in their own self-expression and intimacy in same-sex relationships. Males must be careful about how they hug each other so as not to appear gay. Homophobic scripts also frighten youth who do not conform to gender role expectations, leading some youth to avoid activities—such as arts for boys, athletics for girls—and professions such as elementary education for males.

4. **Early sexual behavior.** Homonegativity also encourages early sexual activity among adolescent men. Adolescent male virgins are often teased by their male peers, who say things like "You mean you don't do it with girls yet? What are you, a fag or something?" Not wanting to be labeled and stigmatized as a "fag," some adolescent boys "prove" their heterosexuality by having sex with girls.

5. **School shootings.** Antigay harassment has also been a factor in many of the school shootings in recent years. For example, 15-year-old Charles Andrew Williams fired more than 30 rounds in a San Diego, California, suburban high school, killing 2 and injuring 13 others. A woman who knew Williams reported that the students had teased him and called him gay.

6. **Public bathrooms.** As noted at the beginning of the chapter, North Carolina passed an antitransgender bathroom law which required that everyone must use the bathroom matching the sex on their birth certificate. This law is fueled by the fear that male sexual predators would pretend to be transgender women to gain access to women's rooms to prey on young targets.

The bathroom law sends the message that transgender people are deviants who are dangerous to girls and young women. Hence, individuals are socialized to fear transgender people.

In response to the "Bathroom Laws" some states have developed gender neutral bathrooms.

Clinton Kernen/Cengage

7-4 COMING OUT

> I consider being gay among the greatest gifts God has given me.
>
> —TIM COOK, APPLE CEO

Coming out is a major decision with which GLBT individuals struggle. Svab and Kuhar (2014) studied the coming out process of 443 gay men and lesbians. Over three-fourths (77%) came out first to their friends in comparison to 7% who first came out to their mother, 5% to their brother/sister, and 3% to their father. Coming out to grandparents is a cautious decision based on the perception of their having nonconservative values (Scherrer, 2016).

Coming out is often a matter of degree. In interviews with gay men about how they dressed, the overriding theme was that they were not "hiding or shouting" but were just presenting their authentic selves (Clarke & Smith, 2015). A new context for coming out is on YouTube. Shawn Dawson did so for 7 million viewers (https://www.yahoo.com/katiecouric/shane-dawson-come-out-youtube-its-one-stop-125399663913.html). GLBT individuals may also "go back into the closet"

PERSONAL VIEW:

A Coming Out Letter to One's Parents and Parental Reactions

Below is a letter one of our former students wrote to her parents disclosing her being gay.

Dear Mom and Dad:

I love you very much and would give you the world if I could. You've always given me the best. You've always been there when I needed you. The lessons of love, strength, and wisdom you've taught me are invaluable. Most importantly, you've taught me to take pride and stand up for what I believe. In the past six months I've done some very serious thinking about my goals and outlook on life. It's a tough and unyielding world that caters only to those who do for themselves. Having your help and support seems to make it easier to handle. But I've made a decision that may test your love and support. Mom and Dad, I've decided to live a gay lifestyle.

I'm sure your heads are spinning with confusion and disbelief right now but please try to let me finish. As I said before, I've given this decision much thought. First and foremost, I'd like for you to know that I'm happy. All my life as a sexual being has been spent frustrated in a role I could not fulfill. Emotionally and mentally, I'm

relieved. Believe me, this was not an easy decision to make. (What made it easier was having the strength to accept myself). Who I choose to sleep with does not make me more or less of a human being. My need for love and affection is the same as anyone else's; it's just that I fulfill this need in a different way. I'm still the same person I've always been.

It's funny I say I'm still the same person, yet society seems to think I've changed. They seem to think that I don't deserve to be treated as a respectable citizen. Instead, they think I should be

Courtesy of Rachel Calisto

---

when they enter a new context. Research on gay women and men in long-term care facilities reveal that they may fear prejudice and discrimination by staff and

other patients and may hide their minority sexual status (Green & Humble, 2015).

In regard to how others reacted to a gay person coming out, 74% of the 443 gay men and lesbians reported experiencing a positive and supportive reaction by others to their first coming out, 18% reported neutral, and 4% reported negative reactions. Negative reactions included religious talk, criticism, and shaming statements (Manning, 2015). Baiocco et al. (2015) found no differences between mothers and fathers in their reaction to the coming out of their son or daughter.

7-4a Risks and Benefits of Coming Out

In a society where heterosexuality is expected and considered the norm, heterosexuals do not have to choose whether or not to tell others that they are heterosexual.

treated as a deranged maniac needing constant supervision to prevent me from molesting innocent children. I have the courage and strength to face up to this opposition, but I can't do it alone. Oh, what I would give to have your support!

I realize I've thrown everything at you rather quickly. Please take your time. I don't expect a response. And please don't blame yourselves, for there is no one to blame. Please remember that I'm happy and I felt the need to share my happiness with two people I love with all my heart.

Your loving daughter,
Maria

Below are examples of the reactions of parents to their child's coming out (Grafsky, 2014).

He came downstairs and said he had to talk to me. I'm like, okay, and popped off the TV. He just sat down and said that he had something to tell me and he didn't want me to worry about him. Then he told me he was bisexual. And I said, "Okay. What does that mean?" So then we talked a lot of that kind of stuff over…. I asked him pretty personal questions. (Hannah, age 55)

***

Everything that I had envisioned, you know parents have this like little ball of fantasy in their head for their children, the white picket fence, the

dog, the kids, the wife. [Gay son]'s popped [snaps fingers] and it was like this void…. And it's really scary 'cause you don't know how to fill it…. I've spent twenty-some years with this whole reality for him and now there's this empty void and I don't know how to fill it. (Alice, age 42)

***

I was afraid. Fear, fear was my biggest thing. I was petrified. I thought somebody would hurt him, I mean, all the horrors of um, people not accepting him. Is life gonna be hard? Afraid of him being harassed at school. How do I tell people? How are people going to treat him? (Eve, age 47)

It is often thought that coming out to parents is a one-time event. But data by Denes and Afifi (2014) revealed that approximately one-fourth of 106 GLBQ individuals (ages 18 to 55) reported coming out a second time. The reason for doing so was to reinforce their sexual orientation (e.g., not going through a "phase"), to clarify aspects of their identity (e.g., from "bi" to "gay"), and to share more information about their GLBQ lifestyle (e.g., their partner). The more individuals perceived their parents to react to their first coming out with denial and the lower their reported relationship satisfaction with their parents after their first coming out, the more likely they were to come out again.

However, decisions about **coming out**, or being open and honest about one's sexual orientation and identity (particularly to one's parents), are agonizing for GLBT individuals. As noted above, friends, mothers, siblings, and fathers, in that order, are those to whom disclosure is first made (Svab & Kuhar, 2014).

> Never be bullied into silence. Never allow yourself to be made a victim. Accept no one's definition of your life; define yourself.
>
> —HARVEY FIERSTEIN, ACTOR

RISKS OF COMING OUT Whether GLBT individuals come out is influenced by how tired they have become hiding their sexual orientation, how much they feel they need to be "honest" about who they are, and their prediction of how others will respond. Some of the risks involved in coming out include disapproval and rejection by parents and other family members, harassment and discrimination at school, discrimination and harassment in the workplace, and hate crime victimization.

1. **Parental and family members' reactions.** Rothman et al. (2012) studied 177 LBG individuals who reported that two-thirds of the parents to whom they first came out responded with social and emotional support.

coming out being open and honest about one's sexual orientation and identity.

Their research is in contrast to that of Mena and Vaccaro (2013), who interviewed 24 gay and lesbian youth about their coming out experience to their parents. All reported a less than 100% affirmative "we love you"/"being gay is irrelevant" reaction which resulted in varying degrees of sadness or depression (three became suicidal).

Svab and Kuhar (2014) identified the concept of the "transparent closet" to describe a situation in which parents are informed about a child's homosexuality but do not talk about it…a form of rejection. The "family closet" refers to the wider kinship system having knowledge of a child's homosexuality but "keeping it quiet" (a form of rejection).

Because Black individuals are more likely than White individuals to view homosexual relations as "always wrong," African Americans who are gay or lesbian are more likely to face disapproval from their families than are White lesbians and gays (Glass, 2014). *The Resource Guide to Coming Out for African Americans* (2011) is a useful model. Because most parents are heavily invested in their children, they find a way not to make an issue of their son or daughter being gay. "We just don't talk about it," said one parent.

Parents and other family members can learn more about homosexuality from the local chapter of Parents, Families, and Friends of Lesbians and Gays (PFLAG) and from books and online resources, such as those found at Human Rights Campaign's National Coming Out Project (http://www.hrc.org/). Mena and Vaccaro (2013) emphasized the importance of parents educating themselves about gay/lesbian issues and to know the importance of loving and accepting their son or daughter at this most difficult time.

2. **Harassment and discrimination at school.** GLBT students are more vulnerable to being bullied, harassed, and discriminated against. The negative effects are predictable including "a wide range of health and mental health concerns, including sexual health risk, substance abuse, and suicide, compared with their heterosexual peers" (Russell et al., 2011). Some communities offer charter schools which are "GLBT friendly" and which promote tolerance. Google "charter schools for GLBT youth" for examples of such schools offering a safe haven from the traditional bullying.

3. **Discrimination and harassment at the workplace.** The workplace continues to be a place where the 8 million GLBT individuals experience discrimination and harassment. Specifically, gay men are paid less than heterosexual men, GLBT individuals feel their potential for promotion is less than the heterosexual majority, and many remain closeted for fear of retribution. There is no federal law that explicitly prohibits sexual orientation and gender identity discrimination against GLBTs (Pizer et al., 2012). McIntyre et al. (2014) noted that being a racial minority and a sexual minority is associated with more stigma and psychological distress than just being a sexual minority.

4. **Hate crime victimization.** Another risk of coming out is being victimized by antigay hate crimes against individuals or their property that are based on bias against the victim because of his/her perceived sexual orientation.

> But when a son, daughter, brother, sister, or close friend comes out it is no longer an "issue," it becomes a person. They realize everything they'd said was painfully targeted at someone they love. Then…everything changes.
>
> —ANTHONY VENN-BROWN, *A LIFE OF UNLEARNING: ONE MAN'S JOURNEY TO FIND THE TRUTH*

BENEFITS OF COMING OUT Coming out to parents is associated with decided benefits. D'Amico and Julien (2012) compared 111 gay, lesbian, and bisexual youth who disclosed their sexual orientation to their parents with 53 who had not done so. Results showed that the former reported higher levels of acceptance from their parents, lower levels of alcohol and drug consumption, and fewer identity and adjustment problems. Similarly, Rothman et al. (2012) noted that for lesbian and bi females (not

Stephen Orsillo/Shutterstock.com

males), higher levels of illicit drug use, poorer self-reported health status, and being more depressed were associated with nondisclosure to parents.

One of the most difficult contexts to come out in is professional football. Defensive lineman Michael Sam is an example of an openly gay male in this macho context. Since U.S culture is becoming more accepting, gays in all sports, including football, will eventually (and increasingly) come out.

The basic trajectory of reacting to one's romantic partner coming out is not unlike learning of the death of one's beloved. Life as one knew it is altered. The stages of this transition are shock, disbelief, numbness, and mourning for the partner/life that was, readjustment, and moving on. The last two stages may involve staying in the relationship with the gay partner (the choice of about 15% of straight spouses) or divorcing/ending the relationship (the choice of 85%).

7-5 GLBT RELATIONSHIPS

Interviews with 36 GLBT couples in regard to their relationship histories revealed that GLBT individuals and couples noted more stress in reference to coming out as individuals and as a couple (if and when), greater hesitancy to commit, and less family/institutional support for their relationship (hence, more vulnerable to breaking up) (Macapagal et al., 2015). Otherwise, gay and heterosexual couples are amazingly similar in regard to having equal power and control, being emotionally expressive, perceiving many attractions and few alternatives to the relationship, placing a high value on attachment, and sharing decision making (Kurdek, 1994). In a comparison of relationship quality of cohabitants over a 10-year period involving both partners from 95 lesbian, 92 gay male, and 226 heterosexual couples living without children, and both partners from 312 heterosexual couples living with children, the researcher found that lesbian couples showed the highest level of relationship quality (Kurdek, 2008).

Individuals who identify as bisexual have the ability to form intimate relationships with both sexes. However, research has found that the majority of bisexual women and men tend toward primary relationships with the other sex (McLean, 2004). Contrary to the common myth that bisexuals are, by definition, nonmonogamous, some bisexuals prefer monogamous relationships (especially in light of the widespread concern about HIV). Some gay and bisexual men have monogamous relationships in which both men have agreed that any sexual activity with casual partners must happen when both members of the couple are present and involved (e.g., three-ways or group sex) (Parsons et al., 2013).

7-5a Older Gay Males Speak of Dating Concerns

What are the thoughts of older gay males in regard to dating? Suen (2015) interviewed 25 gay males over the age of 50 who revealed the factors which encouraged or discouraged them from dating. Factors which encouraged dating included the social pressure to do so, the joy of rejecting the social norm of monogamy by having casual sex with multiple partners, wanting a companion to engage in social events with, meeting one's emotional needs, and variety of sexual partner. Factors discouraging older gays from dating included their joy of being free, feeling no need to have someone take care of them, and not wanting to take care someone else's needs.

7-5b Conflict Resolution and Intimate Partner Violence

Some same-sex relationships involve interpersonal violence. Finneran and Stephenson (2014) analyzed national Internet data from 1,575 men who had had sex with men. Nine percent reported that they had experienced some form of physical violence from a male partner in the previous 12 months.

7-5c Sexuality

Like many heterosexual women, most gay women value stable, monogamous relationships that are emotionally as well as sexually satisfying. Gay and heterosexual women in U.S. society are taught that sexual expression should occur in the context of emotional or romantic involvement.

Courtesy of Chelsea Curry

A common stereotype of gay men is that they prefer casual sexual relationships with multiple partners versus monogamous, long-term relationships. Van Eeden-Moorefield et al. (2015) studied a small sample (43) of gay men and found that 72% reported a preference for traditional monogamy. In contrast, Gotta et al. (2011) found that gay men reported greater interest in casual sex than did heterosexual men. The degree to which gay males engage in casual sexual relationships is better explained by the fact that they are male than by the fact that they are gay. In this regard, gay and straight men have a lot in common: they both tend to have fewer barriers to engaging in casual sex than do women (heterosexual or lesbian). While given little cultural visibility, some gay men are in long-term monogamous relationships. Interviews with 36 gay men committed to monogamy in their relationships revealed the benefits of emotional/sexual satisfaction, trust, security, etc. (Duncan et al., 2015).

7-5d Love and Sex

Rosenberger et al. (2014) analyzed data from 24,787 gay and bisexual men who were members of online websites facilitating social or sexual interactions with other men. Over half of those who completed the questionnaire (61.4%) reported that they did not love their sexual partner during their most recent sexual encounter (28.3% reported being in love with their most recent sexual partner). Hence, most of these men did not require love as a context to having sex. However, they were mostly accurate in identifying their own feelings and those of their partners. Over 90% (91%) were matched by presence ("I love him/he loves me"), absence ("I don't love him/he doesn't love me"), or uncertainty ("I don't know if I do/I don't know if he does") of feelings of love with their most recent sexual partner.

7-5e Division of Labor

Kelly and Hauck (2015) interviewed 30 queer participants who were cohabitating with a partner to examine how they negotiated the household division of labor in their relationship. Results revealed that their roles in reference to housework and child care were shaped by time availability and personal preferences as well as labor force participation and citizenship. The authors suggested that queer couples are "redoing gender" by challenging normative gender roles. Similarly, Umberson et al. (2015) noted that in regard to "emotion work" (e.g., caring about how the other is feeling and keeping the emotional relationship stable)

lesbian relationships were more egalitarian than in heterosexual relationships and in male same-sex relationships (Umberson et al., 2015).

7-5f Mixed-Orientation Relationships

Mixed-orientation couples are those in which one partner is heterosexual and the other partner is lesbian, gay, or bisexual. A study of 38 mixed-orientation couples (Yarhouse et al., 2015) revealed the progression through the five stages following disclosure—initial shock/denial, facing/accepting reality, letting go, healing, and transformation. Forgiveness was an important factor in moving forward. Reinhardt (2011) studied a sample of bisexual women in heterosexual relationships and found that these women maintained a satisfactory relationship with the male partner. One-half of these women were maintaining sexual relationships with other women while in primary heterosexual relationships. Their average sexual contact with another female was 1½ times per month. The majority of the women were satisfied with their sexual experiences with their male partner, and they were having sexual intercourse, on average, three times per week.

Gay and bisexual men are also in heterosexual relationships. Peter Marc Jacobson is gay and was married

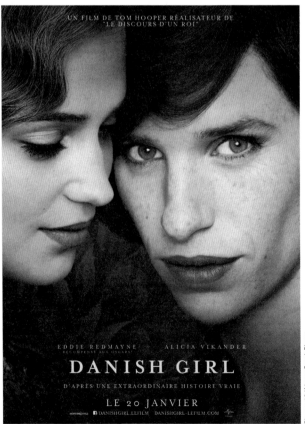

UN FILM DE TOM HOOPER RÉALISATEUR DE "LE DISCOURS D'UN ROI"

EDDIE REDMAYNE   ALICIA VIKANDER

DANISH GIRL

D'APRÈS UNE EXTRAORDINAIRE HISTOIRE VRAIE

LE 20 JANVIER

DANISHGIRL-LEFILM DANISHGIRL-LEFILM.COM

to Fran Drescher (actress in *The Nanny*) for 21 years. They report a wonderful relationship/friendship during and after the marriage. The Straight Spouse Network (www.straightspouse.org) provides support to heterosexual spouses or partners, current or former, of GLBT mates.

Some males are on the down low. Men on the **down low** (nongay-identifying men who have sex with men and women meet their partners out of town, not in predictable contexts—e.g., park—or on the Internet) (Schrimshaw et al., 2013). There is considerable disruption in the marriage if their down low behavior is discovered by the straight spouse.

7-5g Transgender Relationships

The Danish Girl is a 2015 movie which focused on the relationship between Lili Elbe, a male to female transgender person (born in 1882), and Gerda Wegener, his wife. The film depicts some of the individual and couple issues involved in transitioning. While a great deal is known about transgender individuals, little is known about transgender relationships. The exception is the research by Iantiffi and Bockting (2011) who reported on an Internet study of 1,229 transgender individuals over the age of 18 living in the United States. Fifty-seven percent were transwomen (MtF); 43%, transmen (FtM). The median age was 33 and most were White (80%). The average income was $32,000. Almost 70% (69.2%) of the transwomen were living together; 57% of the transmen. While those who were living together were in a relationship, another 15% of the transwomen were in a couple relationship, but not living together; 29% of the transmen—hence around 85% of the transwomen and transmen were involved in a relationship. In regard to sexual fidelity 65% of the transwomen were monogamous (26% were not); 70% of the transmen (21% were not). Some of the partners of the transgender individuals did not know their partner was trans—8% of transwomen and 2% of transmen. Transgender individuals live in fear they will not be accepted. Twenty-five percent of transwomen and 9% of transmen reported that they were afraid to tell their partner they were trans (which is required to a future marriage partner in Europe) (Sharpe, 2012). Having sex in the dark/giving oral sex were strategies used to avoid discovery that one's genitals do not match their presentation of self (if they had not had surgery). Indeed, the whole subject of the feminine/masculine parts of one's body is a subject to be avoided (56% of transwomen; 51% of transmen). Sexual-orientation attractions were predictable. Transgendered individuals

who were mostly lesbian, gay, or bisexual in sexual orientation were mostly attracted to women, men, and both sexes.

What is it like to be a spouse of a partner who is transitioning? Chase (2011) interviewed partners of transgendered individuals. One wife commented on what it was like to watch her male to female transgendered husband transition:

> He's more girly than I am! Which [chuckles] is kind of frustrating at times. You know, he'll want to wear all these bracelets and you know jewelry and stuff. Oh, I just think sometimes he kind of goes overboard on it. And he'll always ask, I mean he asks me a lot my opinion on what he wears, you know, if I think this is going to look good or not and things like that. So, he's always asking about that, does this go with this and everything. [And] he's probably bought more makeup through the years than I have. (p. 436)

7-6 SAME-SEX MARRIAGE

In June 2015, the Supreme Court ruled that same-sex marriage was legal in all 50 states. The decision was 5–4. Justice Anthony Kennedy, the pivotal swing vote, wrote the majority opinion. "They ask for equal dignity in the eyes of the law," Kennedy wrote of same-sex couples in the case. "The Constitution grants them that right."

Earlier, also by a 5–4 decision, the Supreme Court declared the **Defense of Marriage Act (DOMA)** unconstitutional on equal protection grounds, thus giving same-sex married couples federal recognition and benefits. These include:

▸ The right to inherit from a spouse who dies without a will.

▸ The benefit of not paying inheritance taxes upon the death of a spouse.

▸ The right to make crucial medical decisions for a spouse and to take care of a seriously ill spouse or a parent of a spouse under current provisions in the federal Family and Medical Leave Act.

▸ The right to collect Social Security survivor benefits.

down low nongay-identifying men who have sex with men and women meet their partners out of town, not in predictable contexts, or on the Internet.

Defense of Marriage Act (DOMA) legislation passed by Congress denying federal recognition of homosexual marriage and allowing states to ignore same-sex marriages licensed by other states.

Tiffany Beaver

▶ The right to receive health insurance coverage under a spouse's insurance plan.

Other rights bestowed on married (or once-married) partners include assumption of a spouse's pension, bereavement leave, burial determination, domestic violence protection, reduced-rate memberships, divorce protections (such as equitable division of assets and visitation of partner's children), automatic housing lease transfer, and immunity from testifying against a spouse. All of these advantages are now available to same-sex married couples because of the Supreme Court decision.

> To me, marriage is really important and what we build families on. That's why gay marriage is really important.
>
> —MARGARET CHO

Diversity in Other Countries

Same-sex marriage has been legal in Canada since 2005. Humble (2013) interviewed 28 individuals (including lesbians, gay men, and bisexuals) aged 26 to 72 about their wedding experience. Overwhelmingly, the respondents reported a positive response from family, friends, and the community. The one caveat is that they felt that gay weddings were absent in wedding magazines.

7-7 GLBT PARENTING ISSUES

Undergraduate females, friends of gays, individuals supportive of same-sex marriage, and former students of a marriage/family class where same-sex issues were discussed are more likely to report favorable attitudes toward same-sex parenting (Schoephoerster & Aamlid, 2016).

7-7a Gay Families: Lesbian Mothers and Gay Fathers

Between 20% and 25% of gay individuals are rearing over a quarter of a million children (Van Willigen, 2015). Some gay and lesbian individuals and couples had children from prior heterosexual relationships or marriages (Gates, 2015). Some of these individuals married as a "cover" for their homosexuality; others discovered their interest in same-sex relationships after they married. Children with mixed-orientation parents may be raised by a gay or lesbian parent, a gay or lesbian stepparent, a heterosexual parent, and a heterosexual stepparent. A gay or lesbian individual or couple may have children through the use of assisted reproductive technology, including in vitro fertilization, surrogate mothers, and donor insemination. Researcher Hanssen (2015) noted that having a gay mom and a father via donor insemination is about "handling dilemmas related to cultural and heteronormative discourses about reproduction and sexuality." The researcher interviewed donor children to assess their feelings about not having a father in the traditional sense. One of the male respondents said: "It is difficult to say what a father is, but I have never missed a father. I have never said 'wah-wah, I want to have a father like everyone else.' Not ever. It has always been natural for me to have two mothers. They are my parents."

Other gay couples adopt or become foster parents. Less commonly, some gay fathers are part of an emergent family form known as the hetero-gay family. In a hetero-gay family, a heterosexual mother and a gay father conceive and raise a child together but reside separately.

Gay male parents are often viewed negatively. Researcher Vinjamuri (2015) interviewed 20 gay adoptive fathers about their parenting experiences as gay men. Although the fathers led fulfilling lives as parents, many of them faced uninvited questions which reminded them of their place in the heterosexual society. These reminders of heteronormativity included scrutiny about their parenting, concerns about the well-being of their children, and decisions regarding disclosing information about their families. Some comments by the participants follow:

> Before even asking us if [she] was hot or to take off some layers, she asked about mom. . . . We started to recognize that when people say, "Where's mommy?" that they just assume there's a mom and they think a man with a child by themselves must need help, or that he couldn't possibly do it . . . whether he was gay or straight.

***

> There is a level of not wanting to deal with it . . . I always find it's difficult to say, "There's no mother." It was easier when she was younger—now that she understands the conversation, I don't want to say that she doesn't have a mother, because she does have a mother. . . . I don't think that I have figured out what to say yet.

Brittany Bolen

Panozzo (2015) studied 76 gay fathers who brought children into their relationship after the primary relationship had been formed and revealed that the male partner who made less money and who had more limited career goals tended to have a higher desire for children. This partner was also more likely to function in the mothering role (e.g., take care of the child).

Padovano-Janik et al. (2015) interviewed seven women (aged 20 to 28) who were reared by lesbian mothers about how being reared in a gay home shaped core aspects of themselves. Findings included that the participants felt an openness to differences, felt like a strong person, and had them identify as an advocate. As an example of the latter, Jamie noted a desire to be an advocate for traditionally stigmatized minority groups:

> So I think my childhood—it was like I was very, very conscious of what it meant to be part of any persecuted or formally persecuted group. And that really kind of dominated the way in which I thought about my interaction with other people. . . . It gave me a very different perception and made me, like, hyper aware of when people were being discriminated against and it also has made me a real advocate for groups that have historically or currently continued to be challenged by society.

In regard to how LGBTQ parents differ from heterosexual parents, Averett (2016) found that while heterosexual parents believe that children are or should be heterosexual and encourage traditional gender socialization (e.g., ribbon in hair for female babies), LGBTQ parents provide their children with a variety of gendered options for clothing, toys, and activities (e.g., the gender buffet). Below is an example of "the gender buffet" revealed in comments by Latisha and Maria about their 3-year-old daughter Alivia's interest in both "boy" and "girl" things (p. 200).

Latisha:

> Once Maria bought her an imitation tool set, because that's what she was interested in at the time. But she also has microphones, and she also has dolls. But, even like, with her puzzles—she is interested in castles and dragons and things like that. And so that's the puzzle that we're going to get, and we don't think about [whether it is for boys or girls].

Maria:

> But then there's people's view on it, like when we bought that tool set. The cashier—it was man—was like, "Oh, you buying this for your son?" And I was like "Actually, no, my daughter." And he was like, "Whoa! Oh, okay, that's cool!" But it like, takes people a minute.

7-7b Bisexual Parents

Power et al. (2013) surveyed 48 bisexuals who were parenting inside a variety of family structures (heterosexual relationships, same-sex relationships, coparenting with ex-partners or nonpartners, sole parenting) and revealed issues relevant to all parents—discipline, combining work/parenting, etc. The dimension of bisexuality rarely surfaced. When it did, it was in the form of being closeted to help prevent their child being subjected to prejudice and dealing with prejudiced ex-partners, in-laws, and grandparents.

> Exposing "innocent" children to gay relationships won't make them gay. . . . I was exposed to straight relationships, and yet, I'm still gay!
>
> —ANONYMOUS

7-7c Development and Well-Being of Children with Gay or Lesbian Parents

While critics suggest that children reared by same-sex parents are disadvantaged (Kirby & Michaelson, 2015), there are no data to support this fear. Sasnett (2015) interviewed 20 adults with gay and lesbian parents who revealed that the sexual orientation of their parents was not an issue for them; instead the reactions of others was the factor which influenced how they were able to create meanings in their lives—their identities were reinforced by positive interactions, and challenged by negative interactions.

Some children of lesbian parents report appreciation for being connected to a unique group: "I've always been grateful for the queer community I was raised in, which provided me with lots of adults to be close to and lots of different models for how to be a person" (Leddy et al., 2012, p. 247).

7-7d Development and Well-Being of Children in Transgender Families

Research on children in transgender families is virtually nonexistent (Biblarz & Savci, 2010). What is known focuses on the stress transgender children experience as they try to "fit in" to please parents and society at the expense of personal depression and loss of well-being. Meanwhile, children of transgender parents struggle with new definitions of who their parents are and how this affects them. Male children of male-to-female transsexuals may have a particularly difficult time adapting.

7-7e Discrimination in Child Custody, Visitation, and Adoption

A student in one of our classes reported that, after she divorced her husband, she became involved in a lesbian relationship. She explained that she would like to be open about her relationship to her family and friends, but she was afraid that if her ex-husband found out that she was in a lesbian relationship, he might take her to court and try to get custody of their children. Although several respected national organizations including the American Academy of Pediatrics, the Child Welfare League of America, the American Bar Association, the American Medical Association, the American Psychological Association, the American Psychiatric Association, and the National Association of Social Workers have gone on record in support of treating gays and lesbians without prejudice in parenting and adoption decisions, lesbian and gay parents are often discriminated against in child custody, visitation, adoption, and foster care.

Despite the research confirming positive outcomes for children reared by gay or lesbian parents, and despite the support for gay adoption by child advocacy organizations, placing children for adoption with gay or lesbian parents remains controversial. Of 9,680 undergraduates, 13% agreed (men more than women) with the statement "Children reared by same-sex parents are more likely to be homosexual as adults than children reared by two parents of different sexes" (Hall & Knox, 2016).

Prejudice against same-sex adoptions is not unique to America. In a study of Portuguese undergraduates, Gato and Fontaine (2016) found both women and men expressing more negative attitudes toward adoption by gays, with increased disapproval for adoption of males into gay families.

7-7f When LGB Relationships End: Reaction of the Children

How do children react to the ending of the relationship of their LGB parents? Goldberg and Allen (2013) interviewed 20 young adults who experienced their LGB parents' relationship dissolution and/or the formation of a new LGB stepfamily. Almost all families negotiated relational transitions informally and without legal intervention; the relationship with one's biological mother was the strongest tie from breakup to repartnering and stepfamily formation; and geographic distance from their nonbiological parents created hardships in interpersonal closeness. Overall, "young people perceived their families as strong and competent in handling familial transitions" (p. 529).

7-8 TRENDS

While heterosexism, homonegativity, biphobia, and transphobia have historically been entrenched in American society, moral acceptance and social tolerance/acceptance of gays, lesbians, bisexuals, and transsexuals as individuals, couples, and parents will increase. Indeed, Mahaffey and Bryan (2016) confirmed that GLBT attitudes are responsive to social influence. As a result of a more accepting culture, more GLBTIA individuals will come out, their presence will become more evident, and tolerance, acceptance, and support will increase. A change in policy by the Boy Scouts allowing gays and lesbians to be members is another example of change/increased acceptance (Pynes, 2016).

STUDY TOOLS 7

READY TO STUDY? IN THE BOOK, YOU CAN:

☐ Rip out the chapter review card at the back of the book for a handy summary of the chapter and key terms.

☐ Assess yourself with the following self-assessment.

ONLINE AT CENGAGEBRAIN.COM YOU CAN:

☐ Collect StudyBits while you read and study the chapter.

☐ Quiz yourself on key concepts.

☐ Prepare for tests with M&F4 Flash Cards as well as those you create.

SELF-ASSESSMENT

Self-Report of Behavior Scale (SRBS)

This questionnaire is designed to examine which of the following statements most closely describes your behavior during past encounters with people you thought were homosexuals. Rate each of the following self-statements as honestly as possible using the following scale. Write each value in the provided blank.

1	2	3	4	5
Never	*Rarely*	*Occasionally*	*Frequently*	*Always*

_____ **1.** I have spread negative talk about someone because I suspected that the person was gay.

_____ **2.** I have participated in playing jokes on someone because I suspected that the person was gay.

_____ **3.** I have changed roommates and/or rooms because I suspected my roommate was gay.

_____ **4.** I have warned people who I thought were gay and who were a little too friendly with me to keep away from me.

_____ **5.** I have attended antigay protests.

_____ **6.** I have been rude to someone because I thought that the person was gay.

_____ **7.** I have changed seat locations because I suspected the person sitting next to me was gay.

_____ **8.** I have had to force myself to keep from hitting someone because the person was gay and very near me.

_____ **9.** When someone I thought to be gay has walked toward me as if to start a conversation, I have deliberately changed directions and walked away to avoid the person.

_____ **10.** I have stared at a gay person in such a manner as to convey my disapproval of the person being too close to me.

_____ **11.** I have been with a group in which one (or more) person(s) yelled insulting comments to a gay person or group of gay people.

_____ **12.** I have changed my normal behavior in a restroom because a person I believed to be gay was in there at the same time.

_____ **13.** When a gay person has checked me out, I have verbally threatened the person.

_____ **14.** I have participated in damaging someone's property because the person was gay.

_____ **15.** I have physically hit or pushed someone I thought was gay because the person brushed against me when passing by.

_____ **16.** Within the past few months, I have told a joke that made fun of gay people.

_____ **17.** I have gotten into a physical fight with a gay person because I thought the person had been making moves on me.

_____ **18.** I have refused to work on school and/or work projects with a partner I thought was gay.

_____ **19.** I have written graffiti about gay people or homosexuality.

_____ **20.** When a gay person has been near me, I have moved away to put more distance between us.

Scoring

Determine your score by adding your points together. The lowest score is 20 points, the highest 100 points. The higher the score, the more negative the attitudes toward homosexuals.

Comparison Data

Sunita Patel (1989) originally developed the Self-Report of Behavior Scale in her thesis research in her clinical psychology master's program at East Carolina University. College men (from a university campus and from a military base) were the original participants (Patel et al., 1995). The scale was revised by Shartra Sylivant (1992), who used it with a coed high school student population, and by Tristan Roderick (1994), who involved college students to assess its psychometric properties. The scale was found to have high internal consistency. Two factors were identified: a passive avoidance of homosexuals and active or aggressive reactions.

In a study by Roderick et al. (1998), the mean score for 182 college women was 24.76. The mean score for 84 men was significantly higher, at 31.60. A similar-sex difference, although with higher (more negative) scores, was found in Sylivant's high school sample (with a mean of 33.74 for the young women, and 44.40 for the young men).

The following table provides the scores of the college students in Roderick's sample (from a mid-sized state university in the southeast):

	N	Mean	Standard Deviation
Women	182	24.76	7.68
Men	84	31.60	10.36
Total	266	26.91	9.16

Source: By Ms. Shartra Sylivant M.A., L.P.A. Clinical, H.S.P. The cognitive, affective, and behavioral components of adolescent homonegativity. Master's thesis, East Carolina University, 1992. The SBS-R is reprinted by the permission of S. Sylivant.

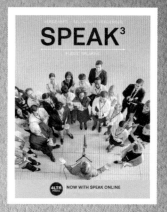

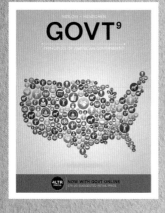

8 | Exploring Diversity in Marriage Relationships

SECTIONS

8-1 Motivations, Functions, and Transition to Egalitarian Marriage

8-2 Weddings and Honeymoons

8-3 Changes after Marriage

8-4 Diversity in Marriage

8-5 Marriage Success

8-6 Trends in Marriage Relationships

After finishing this chapter go to **PAGE 172** for **STUDY TOOLS**

Hill Street Studios/Getty Images

> A journey is like marriage. The certain way to be wrong is to think you control it.
>
> —JOHN STEINBECK, NOVELIST

With the media proclaiming that more people are single, that cohabitation rates are increasing and that marriage is obsolete, one is left with the view that only the few get married. Look again. Of all adults (women and men) over the age of 85, 96% have married at least once (*Proquest Statistical Abstract of the United States, 2016*, Table 57). While it is unlikely that the current generation will marry at that high a percentage, the overwhelming majority will do so. Indeed, they will marry have children as did most of their parents.

The title of this chapter, Exploring Diversity in Marriage Relationships (with plural "relationships"), confirms that marriages are different. *Diversity* is the term that best describes relationships, marriages, and families today. No longer is there a one-size-fits-all cultural norm of what a relationship, marriage, or family should be. In this chapter, we review the diversity of relationships. We begin by looking at some of the different reasons people marry.

8-1 MOTIVATIONS, FUNCTIONS, AND TRANSITION TO EGALITARIAN MARRIAGE

In this section, we discuss both why people marry and the functions that getting married serve for society.

8-1a Motivations to Marry

We have defined marriage in the United States as a legal contract between two adults that regulates their economic and sexual interaction. However, individuals in the United States tend to think of marriage in personal more than legal terms. The following are some of the reasons people give for getting married.

1. **Love.** Unlike individuals in Iceland who are *not* focused on marriage, Americans view marriage as the ultimate expression of their love for each other—the desire to spend their lives together in a secure, legal, committed relationship. In U.S. society, love is expected to precede marriage—thus, only couples in love consider marriage. Those not in love are ashamed to admit it.

> Love is life. And if you miss love, you miss life.
>
> —LEO BUSCAGLIA, LOVE GURU

2. **Personal fulfillment.** Americans also marry because they anticipate a sense of personal fulfillment by doing so. As Americans, we were born into a family (family of origin) and want to create a family of our own (family of procreation). We remain optimistic that our marriage will be a good one. Even if our parents divorced or we have friends who have done so, we feel that our relationship will be different.

3. **Companionship.** Although marriage does not ensure it, companionship is the greatest expected benefit of marriage in the United States. Coontz (2016) noted that companionship has become the legitimate goal of marriage.

4. **Parenthood.** Most people want to have children. Although some people are willing to have children outside marriage (e.g., in a cohabiting relationship or in no relationship at all), most Americans prefer to have them in a marital context. Previously, a strong norm existed in our society (particularly among Whites) that individuals should be married before they have children. This norm is becoming more relaxed, with more individuals willing to have children without being married.

5. **Economic security.** Married people report higher household incomes than do unmarried people. Indeed, almost 80% of wives work outside the home so that two incomes are available to the couple. One of the disadvantages of remaining single is that the lifestyle is associated with lower income. The median income for a single female household is $31,770; for a married couple, $99,983 (*Proquest Statistical Abstract of the United States, 2016*, Table 721).

6. **Psychological well-being.** Being married is associated with positive mental health—happier, less

TABLE 8.1 TRADITIONAL VERSUS EGALITARIAN MARRIAGES

Traditional Marriage	Egalitarian Marriage
Limited expectation of husband to meet emotional needs of wife and children.	Husband is expected to meet emotional needs of his wife and children.
Wife is not expected to earn income.	Wife is expected to earn income.
Emphasis is on ritual and roles.	Emphasis is on companionship.
Couples do not live together before marriage.	Couples often live together before marriage.
Wife takes husband's last name.	Wife may keep her maiden name. In some cases, he will take her last name.
Husband is dominant; wife is submissive.	Neither spouse is dominant.
Roles for husband and wife are rigid.	Roles for spouses are flexible.
Husband initiates sex; wife complies.	Either spouse initiates sex.
Wife takes care of children.	Fathers more involved in child rearing.
Education is important for husband, not for wife.	Education is important for both spouses.
Husband's career decides family residence.	Career of either spouse may determine family residence.

anxiety, etc. (Amato, 2015a). Spouses not only in the United States but in the UK and Germany report being happier than the unmarried (Chapman & Guven, 2016).

8-1b Functions of Marriage

As noted in Chapter 1, important societal functions of marriage are to bind a male and a female together who will reproduce, provide physical care for their dependent young, and socialize them to be productive members of society who will replace those who die (Murdock, 1949). Marriage helps protect children by giving the state legal leverage to force parents to be responsible to their offspring whether or not they stay married. If couples did not have children, the state would have no interest in regulating marriage.

Additional functions of marriage include regulating sexual behavior (spouses are expected to be faithful, which results in less exposure to sexually transmitted infections than being single) and stabilizing adult personalities by providing a companion and "in-house" counselor. As noted in the section on motivations for marriage, in the past, marriage and family served protective, educational, and religious functions for its members. These functions have been taken over by the legal, educational, and religious institutions of our society. Only the companionship-intimacy function of marriage/family has remained virtually unchanged.

forced marriages those in which the parents force the child to marry a person of the parents choosing.

rite of passage an event that marks the transition from one social status to another.

8-1c Transition to Egalitarian Marriage

The very nature of the marriage relationship has also changed from being very traditional or male-dominated to being very modern or egalitarian. A summary of these differences is presented in Table 8.1. Keep in mind that these are stereotypical marriages and that only a small percentage of today's modern marriages have all the traditional or egalitarian characteristics that are listed.

8-1d Forced Marriages

To this point in the text, we have discussed marriage as a choice. But some marriages are **forced marriages** in that one of the individuals has no choice in the person they marry. About 1,500 marriages annually in the United States are forced marriages (Alanen, 2016). An example of a forced marriage is the case of 8-year-old Mannal who was sold by her father for $8,000 to marry a 59-year-old man. Poverty, save the "honor" of the family, and religious cults are reasons for forced marriages. The outcome is predictable: physical and psychological consequences are disastrous and enduring.

8-2 WEDDINGS AND HONEYMOONS

A **rite of passage** is an event that marks the transition from one social status to another. Starting school, getting a driver's license, and graduating from high school or college are events that mark major transitions in status (to student, to driver, and to graduate). The wedding itself is another rite of passage that marks the transition from fiancée and

The wedding is a rite of passage that transforms the lovers into spouses.

fiancé to spouse. Preceding the wedding is the traditional bachelor party for the soon to be groom. Somewhat new on the cultural landscape is the bachelorette party (sometimes wilder than the bachelor party), which conveys the message that both soon to be spouses can have their version of a premarital celebration—their last hurrah!

> I have great hopes that we shall love each other all our lives as much as if we had never married at all.
>
> —LORD BYRON

8-2a Weddings

The wedding is a rite of passage that is both religious and civil. To the Catholic Church, marriage is a sacrament that implies that the union is both sacred and

Maria McDonald

indissoluble. According to Jewish and most Protestant faiths, marriage is a special bond between the husband and wife sanctified by God, but divorce and remarriage are permitted.

Wedding ceremonies still reflect traditional cultural definitions of women as property. For example, the father of the bride usually walks the bride down the aisle and "gives her away" to her husband. In some cultures, the bride is not even present at the time of the actual marriage. For example, in the upper-middle-class Muslim Egyptian wedding, the actual marriage contract signing occurs when the bride is in another room with her mother and sisters. The father of the bride and the new husband sign the actual marriage contract (identifying who is marrying whom, the families they come from, and the names of the two witnesses). The father will then place his hand on the hand of the groom, and the maa'zun, the presiding official, will declare that the marriage has transpired.

That marriage is a public event is emphasized by weddings in which the couple invites their family and friends to participate. The wedding is a time for the respective families to learn how to cooperate with each other for the benefit of the couple.

Brides often wear traditional **artifacts** (concrete symbols that reflect the existence of a cultural belief or activity): something old, new, borrowed, and blue. The old wedding artifact represents the durability of the impending marriage (e.g., an heirloom gold locket). The new wedding artifact, perhaps in the form of new undergarments, emphasizes the new life to begin. The borrowed wedding artifact is something that has already been worn by a currently

artifact concrete symbol that reflects the existence of a cultural belief or activity.

Increasingly, the terms *marriage* and *wedding* refer to same-sex individuals. The wedding marks a rite of passage from the role of lover to spouse.

happy bride (a wedding veil). The blue wedding artifact represents fidelity. When the bride throws her floral bouquet, the single woman who catches it will be the next to be married; the rice thrown by the guests at the newly married couple signifies fertility.

Couples now commonly have weddings that are neither religious nor traditional. In the exchange of vows, the couple's relationship may be spelled out by the partners rather than by tradition, and neither partner may promise to obey the other. Vows often include the couple's feelings about equality, individualism, humanism, and openness to change.

honeymoon the time following the wedding whereby the couple becomes isolated to recover from the wedding and to solidify their new status change from lovers to spouses.

In 2015, the average cost of a wedding was $32,461 (www.theknot.com). Ways in which couples lower the cost of their wedding include marrying any day but Saturday, or marrying off season (not June) or off locale (in Mexico or on a Caribbean Island where fewer guests will attend). They may also broadcast their wedding over the Internet through websites such as webcastmywedding.net. Streaming capability means that the couple can get married in Hawaii and have their ceremony beamed back to the mainland where well-wishers can see the wedding without leaving home.

> Everyday's a honeymoon. Cuz darling, I love you to the moon.
>
> —CRYSTAL WOODS, *WRITE LIKE NO ONE IS READING*

8-2b Honeymoons

Traditionally, another rite of passage follows immediately after the wedding—the **honeymoon** (the time following the wedding whereby the couple isolates themselves to recover from the wedding and to solidify their new status change from lovers to spouses). The functions of the honeymoon are both personal and social.

The personal function is to provide a period of recuperation from the usually exhausting demands of preparing for and being involved in a wedding ceremony and reception. The social function is to provide a time for the couple to be alone to solidify their new identity from that of an unmarried to a married couple.

A caveat in taking a honeymoon is to avoid an extensive travel schedule too close to the wedding day.

Now that they are married, their sexual expression and childbearing with each other achieves full social approval and legitimacy.

8-3 CHANGES AFTER MARRIAGE

After the wedding and honeymoon, the new spouses begin to experience changes in their legal, personal, and marital relationship.

> When marrying, ask yourself this question: Do you believe that you will be able to converse well with this person into your old age? Everything else in marriage is transitory.
>
> —FRIEDRICH NIETZSCHE

8-3a Legal Changes

Unless the partners have signed a prenuptial agreement specifying that their earnings and property will remain separate, the wedding ceremony makes each spouse part owner of what the other earns in income and accumulates in property. Although the laws on domestic relations differ from state to state, courts typically award to each spouse half of the assets accumulated during the marriage (even though one of the partners may have contributed a smaller proportion).

For example, if a couple buys a house together, even though one spouse invested more money in the initial purchase, the other will likely be awarded half of the value of the house if they divorce. Having children complicates the distribution of assets because the house is often awarded to the custodial parent. In the case of death of the spouse, the remaining spouse is legally entitled to inherit between one-third and one-half of the partner's estate, unless a will specifies otherwise.

8-3b Mental/Physical Health Changes

New spouses experience an array of personal changes in their lives. One consequence of getting married is an enhanced sense of self-esteem and sense of mastery (Chen et al., 2016). The strong evidence that your spouse approves of you and is willing to spend a lifetime with you also tells you that you are a desirable person.

Amato (2015a) confirmed that marriage is good for one's mental health. With marriage there is often the assumption of home ownership that facilitates a sense of mastery or feeling in control of one's life (Tyndall & Christie-Mizell, 2016).

Averett et al. (2013) also confirmed that being married is associated with lower alcohol use and a higher BMI. In effect, spouses put on weight after they say "I do." Weight gain occurs for both women and men (Teachman, 2016).

8-3c Friendship Changes

Marriage affects relationships with others. Burton-Chellew and Dunbar (2015) observed that a couple in love withdraws from other relationships (both related and nonrelated). However, abandoning one's friends after marriage may be problematic because one's spouse cannot be expected to satisfy all of one's social needs. Because almost half of marriages end in divorce, friendships that have been maintained throughout the marriage can become a vital source of support for a person going through divorce. "Don't forget your friends on your way up, you'll need them on your way down" reflects the sentiment of maintaining one's friends after getting married.

> Keep your eyes wide open before marriage, half shut afterwards.
>
> —BEN FRANKLIN

8-3d Relationship Changes

A couple happily married for 45 years spoke to our class and began their presentation with, "Marriage is one of life's biggest disappointments." They spoke of the difference between all the hype and the cultural ideal of what marriage is supposed to be . . . and the reality.

One effect of getting married is **disenchantment** (also known as **disillusionment**)—the transition from a state of newness and high expectation to a state of mundaneness tempered by reality. It may not happen in the first few weeks or months of marriage, but it is almost inevitable. Although courtship is the anticipation of a life together, marriage is the day-to-day reality of that life together—and reality does not always fit the dream. "Moonlight and

> **disenchantment (disillusionment)**
> the transition from a state of newness and high expectation to a state of mundaneness tempered by reality.

roses become daylight and dishes" is an old adage reflecting the realities of marriage. In a national study of married (N = 752) and cohabiting (N = 323) couples, Niehuis et al. (2015) confirmed that disillusionment occurred in both sets of couples with the greater the disillusionment, the greater the predicted breakup. Cohabitation relationships were more vulnerable than married relationships due to fewer constraints from ending the relationship. **Satiation**, which occurs when a stimulus loses its value with repeated exposure, speeds disenchantment. Individuals tire of each other because they are no longer new. Happy long-term spouses unaffected by the principle of satiation do not require newness for excitement and contentment.

Disenchantment after marriage is also related to the partners shifting their focus away from each other to work or children; each partner usually gives and gets less attention in marriage than in courtship. College students are not oblivious to the change after marriage. Twenty-eight percent of 2,285 undergraduate males and 20% of 7,372 undergraduate females agreed that "most couples become disenchanted with marriage within five years" (Hall & Knox, 2016). Looking for a positive future may be helpful. Casad et al. (2015) surveyed 99 women in heterosexual relationships and found that those who believed in marriage myths (e.g., "We will live happily ever after") were predicted to have more positive relationship outcomes.

In addition to disenchantment/disillusionment, a couple will experience numerous changes once they marry:

1. **Loss of freedom.** Single people do as they please. They make up their own rules and answer to no one.

2. **More responsibility.** Single people are responsible for themselves only. Spouses are responsible for the needs of each other and sometimes resent it.

3. **Less alone time.** Aside from the few spouses who live apart, most live together. They wake up together, eat their evening meals together, and go to bed together. Each may feel too much togetherness. "This altogether, togetherness thing is something I don't like," said one spouse.

4. **Change in how money is spent.** Entertainment expenses in courtship become allocated to living expenses and setting up a household together.

5. **Sexual changes.** The frequency with which spouses have sex with each other decreases after marriage (Hall & Adams, 2011).

6. **Power changes.** The power dynamics of the relationship

satiation a stimulus loses its value with repeated exposure.

change after marriage with men being less patriarchal/collaborating more with their wives while women change from deferring to their husbands' authority to challenging their authority (Huyck & Gutmann, 1992). In effect, with marriage, men tend to lose power and women gain power. This shift to a more egalitarian relationship is associated with marital happiness. Wives' perception of power may be assessed by asking questions about the degree to which one's husband "tries to dominate and control," "expects me to play a dependent role," "treats me as an equal," and "makes the major decisions."

8-3e Parents and In-Law Changes

Marriage affects relationships with parents. Time spent with parents and extended kin radically increases when a couple has children. Indeed, a major difference between couples with and without children is the amount of time they spend with relatives. Parents and kin rally to help with the newborn and are typically there for birthdays and family celebrations.

Don't let your in-laws become outlaws is a guideline for relationships with parents.

8-3f Financial Changes

An old joke about money in marriage is that "two can live as cheaply as one as long as one doesn't eat." The reality behind the joke is that marriage involves the need for spouses to discuss and negotiate how they are going to get and spend money in their relationship. Some spouses bring considerable debt into the marriage or amass great debt during the marriage. Such debt affects marital interaction.

Marriage is also associated with the male becoming more committed to earning money. Ashwin and Isupova (2014) noted that husbands "implicitly commit themselves to a 'responsible' version of masculine identity" (e.g., rather than hard drinking) and that wives monitor their behavior to ensure a productive outcome. One example is a wife who made it clear that she did not want her husband to quit his job regardless of how unhappy he was. Her focus on keeping the family income coming in and her desire to avoid the "my husband is unemployed" stigma kept her husband on the job.

8-4 DIVERSITY IN MARRIAGE

Any study of marriage relationships emphasizes the need to understand the diversity of marriage/family life. Researchers (Ballard & Taylor, 2012; Wright et al., 2012) have emphasized the various racial, ethnic, structural, geographic location, and contextual differences in marriage and family relationships. In this section, we review Hispanic, Mormon, and military families. We also look at other examples of family diversity: interracial, interreligious, international, and age discrepant.

> I love you not for who you are, but for who I am when I am with you.
>
> —GABRIEL GARCIA MARQUEZ

8-4a African American Families

Black families, like families in general, are diverse. There are African American families, Caribbean Black families, and African Black families. In the literature, the terms *Black* and *African American families* are used interchangeably (Bough & Coughlin, 2012). Blacks represent about 46 million individuals in the United States or 15% of the U.S. population (*Proquest Statistical Abstract of the United States, 2016*, Table 7). Black

Flashon Studio/Shutterstock.com

families include husband-wife families, gay families, single-parent families, and families headed by grandparents. Black families also are large and extended with generations of close and distant relatives (blood and nonblood) helping each other.

African American families have been described in terms such as being low income, having high birthrates among unmarried mothers, being one-parent families, and having absentee fathers. Such a perspective, seen by some as a pathological view, is a result of researchers looking at the African American family as a deviation from the White family norm rather than viewing African American families in terms of their historical uniqueness and resilience as a cultural variant (the emergent model).

Pellebon (2012) reviewed the historical and contemporary aspects of the African American family. The inhumane treatment of Blacks by many slave owners contributed to supportive family structures, spiritual expression, and social community. Family structures evolved that emphasized the mother, who remains the core of the Black family. Related is the fact that the Black woman, independent of being a mother, is known as "strong and empowered" (Williams et al., 2016). Spiritual expression emerged to provide hope and an outlet for the oppressive context of slavery. Social community developed out of survival needs to help each other to cope with the unconscionable treatment during slavery. The collectivist nature of Black families emphasizes that they are a network of support and resources for both blood and nonblood relatives (Bough & Coughlin, 2012).

The majority of African American married couples live in one household. Although higher rates of Black female single-parent families (compared to White female single-parent families) exist, this does not reflect a disregard for marriage, but is a response to the economic reality of Black men. Black men experience higher rates of incarceration, unemployment, and lower income (which thus reduces income to the household). Longitudinal data on an all African American sample of 422 found the impact of economic distress on adolescent conduct problems was negative due to effects on the parents' depression and conflict (Simons et al., 2016).

Unique aspects of African American families reviewed by Pellebon (2012) include:

1. **Cultural collective.** A functional network of individuals based on their shared history, group experiences, and struggles provides a sense of cultural pride and identification. African Americans who do not know each other may greet each other with cultural handshakes (bump) and words ("Whassup!").

2. **Ethnic socialization.** Blacks emphasize their own self-respect, dignity, and pride, which counters negative stereotypes of Blacks. Parents are focused on building a strong sense of Black pride in their children.

3. **Prominence of motherhood.** Noted earlier, as a key person in Black families, mothers not only look after their own but cooperate with other Black mothers in the rearing of their children. Illustrative of the value of community mothering was a story from slavery of Hannah who escaped and left her daughter. She was criticized as being "inhumane" for leaving an infant daughter, but cultural norms were in place and a network of mothers was always available to take care of both blood and nonblood children in the community. Even today, the mother remains a key figure. One example of a football coach who said that he told one of his star Black players that "I am sending airline tickets to your mother to attend the game on Saturday" since the coach knew that the mother's attendance would guarantee a superb performance.

4. **Firm child rearing strategies.** In addition to shared parenting, Black families are known for their firm disciplining. "My mother would smack my lips off if I even thought about sassing her," said a Black undergraduate.

5. **Social justice training of children.** To prepare children for the reality of racism, Black parents socialized their children to be alert to the cultural entrenchment of racism, and to look to their own group for understanding and pride. Parents of White children are oblivious to racism and the need to socialize their children in this regard.

6. **Religion.** In spite of the fact that religion was used to justify slavery, Blacks have embraced religion and socialize their children to do so. The church provided a coping mechanism during slavery and today is a source of hope and a context to be spiritually expressive and to bond with other Blacks and Black families.

The above factors do not mention the Black male. Research has found that his presence is important to the outcome for children and adolescents. Data by Langley (2016) revealed that African American adolescents reporting a father figure had lower rates of sexual debut than those youth reporting no father figure.

8-4b Hispanic Families

The panethnic term *Hispanic* refers to both immigrants and U.S. natives with an ancestry to one of 20 Spanish-speaking countries in Latin America and the Caribbean. By 2020, Hispanics will represent 19% of the U.S. population (*Proquest Statistical Abstract of the United States, 2016*, Table 13). Hispanic families vary not only by where they are from but by whether they were born in the United States. About 40% of U.S. Hispanics are foreign born and immigrated here, 32% have parents who were born in the United States, and 28% were born here of parents who were foreign born.

Great variability exists among Hispanic families. Although it is sometimes assumed that immigrant Hispanic families come from rural impoverished Mexico where family patterns are traditional and unchanging, immigrants may also come from economically developed urbanized areas in Latin America (Argentina, Uruguay, and Chile), where family patterns include later family formation, low fertility, and nuclear family forms.

Hispanics tend to have higher rates of marriage, early marriage, higher fertility, nonmarital child rearing, and prevalence of female householder. They also have two micro family factors: male power and strong familistic values.

1. **Male power.** The husband and father is the head of the family in most Hispanic families.

2. **Strong familistic values.** The family is the most valued social unit in the society—not only the parents and children but also the extended family. Hispanic families have a moral responsibility to help family members with money, health, or transportation needs. Children are taught to respect their parents as well as the elderly. Indeed, elderly parents may live with the Hispanic family where children may address their grandparents in a formal way. Spanish remains the language spoken in the home as a way of preserving family bonds.

8-4c Mormon Families

There are about 6 million Mormons in the United States (and 14 million worldwide). Also known as the Church of Jesus Christ of Latter-day Saints, the Mormons have been associated with polygyny. But this practice was disavowed in 1890 by mainstream Mormons. Sects of the Mormon Church continuing the practice are not included in the following discussion (Dollahite & Marks, 2012).

Unique characteristics of Mormon beliefs/families include:

1. **Eternal marriage.** Mormon doctrine holds that Mormon spouses are married not only until death but throughout eternity. Mormon spouses also believe that their children become a permanent part of their family both in this life and in the afterlife. Hence, the death of a spouse or child is viewed as a family member who has gone to heaven only to be reunited with other family members at their earthly death.

2. **Family rituals.** Mormons are expected to pray both as spouses and as a family, to study the scripture (*Book of Mormon*), and to observe family home evening every Monday night. The latter involves the family praying, singing, having a lesson taught by a parent or older child, experiencing a fun activity (e.g., board game/charades), and enjoying refreshments (e.g., homemade cookies).

3. **Frequent prayer.** While most religions encourage prayer, the Mormon faith encourages the family to pray together three times a day—morning, at mealtimes, and at bedtime. The ritual provides an emotional bond of family members to each other.

Art Directors & TRIP/Alamy Stock Photo

4. **Substance prohibitions.** Mormons avoid alcohol, tobacco, coffee, and some teas (e.g., caffeinated). The health benefits include lower cancer rates and increased longevity (8 to 11 years).

5. **Extended family/intergeneration support.** Family reunions, family web pages, and ties with parents and grandparents are core to Mormon family norms. The result is a close family system of children, parents, and grandparents.

6. **Intramarriage.** Selecting another Mormon to marry is encouraged. Only devout members of the church may be married in the temple, which seals the couple for this life and for eternity.

7. **Early marriage/large families.** Mormons typically marry younger (remember, no sex before marriage so there is some incentive to marry soon) and have a higher number of children than the national average. One result of larger families is that adults stay in the role of parents for a longer period of their lives.

8. **Lower divorce rate.** It comes as no surprise that the Mormon emphasis on family rituals and values

results in strong family ties and a lower divorce rate. While 40% to 50% of marriages in general in the United States end in divorce, only about 10% of Mormon marriages do so.

8-4d Poly Families

Polyamory refers to multiple intimate sexual and/or loving relationships with the knowledge and consent of all partners involved. The term is different from polygamy which means multiple spouses. Multi-partner relationships that raise children and function as families are known as **poly families**.

One study of polyamory by Elizabeth Sheff (2014) included about 500 participants whom Sheff observed, and 131 persons whom she interviewed. The majority were White, college educated, and had a professional job (e.g., teacher, health care professional).

BENEFITS OF POLY FAMILIES The following are benefits of poly families:

1. **Shared resources.** Sharing resources was the most important advantage of living in a poly family. "From shared income to increased personal time for adults and more attention for children, having numerous adults in the family allows members to distribute tasks so that (ideally) no one person has to take the brunt of family care" (p. 196).

2. **Honesty and emotional intimacy among family members.** In Sheff's study, "Parents emphasized honesty with their children as a key element of their overall relationship philosophy and parenting strategy" and "characterize honesty as the primary factor that cultivates emotional intimacy...." (p. 191). Sheff interviewed children and teens who valued the open and honest relationships they had with their parents. Speaking of her relationship with her parents, one girl said,

> We have a good dialog, there is nothing I would keep from them. We are just very open people; there is no need to hide anything.... Some of my friends, things are bad for them at home, they can't and don't want to talk to their parents. It is kinda sad; they don't think they can trust their parents. (pp. 194–195)

3. **Multiple role models for children.** Children in poly families benefit from the multiple role models available in poly families. "Many parents say that their children's lives, experiences, and self-concepts are richer for the multiple loving adults in their families" (p. 201).

DIFFICULTIES IN POLY FAMILIES The following are difficulties in poly families:

1. **Social stigma.** Due to the social stigma associated with polyamory, members of poly families may experience rejection from other family members (e.g., parents/siblings) and risk discrimination in the workplace, housing, and child custody matters. Sheff noted that, "people in poly families were...aware that the stigma of being a sexual minority made them more vulnerable to accusations of poor parenting or questionable family situations from relatives, neighbors, teachers, and Child Protective Services . . . ." (p. 225). Although children ages 5 to 8 generally were not aware that their family was different from other families, older children and teens knew that their families were different, and were aware of the potential for social stigma. One child reported he did not invite friends to his house because he did not want to explain the multiple adults living in his household. A 15-year-old male said, "It's kind of weird to live with a secret, something you can't tell any of your friends cause they wouldn't understand" (p. 144).

2. **Teenagers' leverage against poly parents.** Raising teenagers can be challenging for any parent, but poly parents have the additional possibility that a disgruntled teen can blackmail their parents, threatening to reveal their unconventional lifestyle to authorities, employers, or teachers.

Sheff concludes that polyamory is "a legitimate relationship style that can be tremendously rewarding for adults and provide excellent nurturing for children" (p. x). She also notes that "polyamory is not for everyone. Complex, time-consuming, and potentially fraught with emotional booby traps, polyamory is tremendously rewarding for some people and a complete disaster for others" (p. ix). Sheff's investigation of poly families highlights that the nonsexual emotional ties that bind people in poly families together are far more important than the sexual connections between the adults (Sheff, 2014):

> While the sexual relationships polys establish with each other get the most attention from the media . . . they are not the . . . most important aspect of poly relationships. . . . Much like heterosexual families, poly families spend far more time hanging out together, doing homework, making dinner, carpooling, folding

polyamory refers to multiple intimate sexual and/or loving relationships with the knowledge and consent of all partners involved.

poly families multi-partner relationships that raise children and function as families.

laundry, and having family meetings or relationship talks than they do having sex." (pp. 206–207)

Sheff found that the children in the poly families she studied "seemed remarkably articulate, intelligent, self-confident, and well adjusted" . . . and "appeared to be thriving with the plentiful resources and adult attention their families provided" (p. 135). The well-being of the children could also be due, in part, to their privileged upper-middle-class, predominantly White background.

Does being raised in a poly family lead children to reject monogamy in their own lives? Sheff found that some teens were definitely not interested in polyamory in their own relationships, others envisioned trying polyamory in their adult lives, and still others were undecided, but "none of them reported feeling pressured to become polyamorous in the future or feeling like their choices were constrained" (p. 158).

8-4e Military Families

American Sniper, which premiered in 2014, focused on U.S. Navy SEAL Chris Kyle whose mission was to save his comrades in battle. The film also revealed the dramatic impact of deployment on the stay-at-home wife and children. Approximately 2.6 million members of the U.S. military were deployed in recent U.S. interventions with 40% being deployed more than once. Over half (52%) of service members are married; of those married, 69% have children (Sherman et al., 2015).

There are three main types of military marriages. In one type, an individual falls in love, gets married, and subsequently joins the military. A second type of military marriage is one in which one or both of the partners are already members of the military before getting married. The final and least common type is known as a **military contract marriage**, in which a military person will marry a civilian to get more money and benefits from

the government, such as additional housing allowance. Contract military marriages are not common but they do exist.

Some ways in which military families are unique include:

1. **Traditional sex roles.** Although both men and women are members of the military service, the military has considerably more men than women (85% versus 15%). In the typical military family, the husband is deployed (sent away to serve) and the wife is expected to understand his military obligations and to take care of the family in his absence. The wife often has to sacrifice her career to follow (or stay behind in the case of deployment) and support her husband in his fulfillment of military duties.

   There are also circumstances in which both parents are military members, and this can blur traditional sex roles because the woman has already deviated from a traditional "woman's job." Military families in which both spouses are military personnel are rare.

2. **Loss of control—deployment.** Military families have little control over their lives as the chance of deployment is ever present. Where one of the spouses will be next week and for how long are beyond the control of the spouses and parents. Spierling (2015) emphasized the need to plan ahead for deployment including anticipating a "new normal" and adjusting one's expectations in regard to stress and marshaling support. Frequent communication during deployment between the parents increases feelings of closeness and facilitates reintegration on return (O'Neal et al., 2015).

   Adjusting to the return of the deployed spouse has its own challenges. Some deployed spouses who were exposed to combat have had their brain chemistry permanently altered and are never the same again. "These spouses rarely recover completely—they need to accept that their symptoms (e.g., depression, anxiety) can be managed but not cured," noted Theron Covin, who specializes in treating PTSD among the combat deployed (Covin, 2013). Researchers have observed an increased incidence of PTSD, depression, sleep problems, substance abuse, and risky behaviors (e.g., unsafe driving) among those who have been deployed (Sherman et al., 2015). Indeed, the mental health of

Deployment is a major challenge for military couples.

Courtesy of Almotis Austin

military contract marriage
a military person will marry a civilian to get more money and benefits from the government.

the returning soldier impacted the mental health of the at home partner upon return (Gorman et al., 2015) with deployment to combat assignments being associated with subsequent divorce (Foran et al., 2013).

3. **Infidelity.** Although most spouses are faithful to each other, being separated for months (sometimes years) increases the vulnerability of both spouses to infidelity. The double standard may also be operative, whereby "men are expected to have other women when they are away" and "women are expected to remain faithful and be understanding." Separated spouses use various strategies to bridge the time they are apart with text messages, emails, Skype, and phone calls.

4. **Frequent moves and separation from extended family or close friends.** Because military couples are often required to move to a new town, parents no longer have doting grandparents available to help them rear their children. And although other military families become a community of support for each other, the consistency of such support may be lacking.

5. **Lower marital satisfaction and higher divorce rates among military families.** Wick and Nelson Goff (2014) reaffirmed the challenge military marriages experience when a deployed spouse returns with PTSD. Lucier-Greer and Mancini (2014) studied 234 couples in which the partner had been deployed. Spouses reporting that they experienced marital warmth (partner acted lovingly toward them) reported less stress, greater self-efficacy, and lower levels of anxiety/depression (Lucier-Greer & Mancini, 2014).

8-4f Interracial Marriages

Just under 5% of the over 62 million couples in the United States are interracial (*Proquest Statistical Abstract of the United States, 2016,* Table 60). Hispanic and non-Hispanic are the most frequent interracial/interethnic unions.

In discussing interracial marriages, a complicating factor is that one's racial identity may be mixed. Tiger Woods refers to his race as "Cablinasian," which combines Caucasian, Black, Native American (Indian), and Asian origins—he is one-quarter Chinese, one-quarter Thai, one-quarter Black, one-eighth Native American, and one-eighth Dutch.

Black–White marriages are the most infrequent. In spite of the cultural visibility of the interracial

Less than 1% of the 62 million married couples in the United States consist of a White and a Black spouse.

marriage of Kim Kardashian and Kanye West, fewer than 1% of the over 62 million marriages in the United States are between a Black person and a White person. Segregation in religion (the races worship in separate churches), housing (White and Black neighborhoods), and education (White and Black colleges), not to speak of parental and peer endogamous pressure to marry within one's own race, are factors that help to explain the low percentage of interracial Black and White marriages.

The spouses in Black and White couples are more likely to have been married before, to be age discrepant, to live far away from their families of orientation, to have been reared in racially tolerant homes, and to have educations beyond high school. Some may also belong to religions that encourage interracial unions. The Baha'i religion, which has more than 6 million members worldwide and 84,000 in the United States, teaches that God is particularly pleased with interracial unions. Finally, interracial spouses may tend to seek contexts of diversity. "I have been reared in a military family, been everywhere, and met people of different races and nationalities throughout my life. I seek diversity," noted one student.

Black–White interracial marriages are likely to increase—slowly. Not only has White prejudice against African Americans in general declined, but also segregation in school, at work, and in housing has decreased, permitting greater contact between the races. One-third of 2,295 undergraduate males (39% of 7,380 undergraduate females) reported that they had dated interracially (Hall & Knox, 2016).

Self-Assessment: Attitudes toward Interracial Dating Scale

Take the Attitudes toward Interracial Dating Scale in the self-assessment section at the end of this chapter to assess your attitude toward dating individuals of a different race.

8-4g Interreligious Marriages

Of married couples in the United States, 37% have an interreligious marriage (Pew Research, 2008). Although religion may be a central focus of some individuals and their marriage, Americans in general have become more secular, and as a result religion has become less influential as a criterion for selecting a partner. In a survey of 2,293 undergraduate males and 7,406 undergraduate females, 36% and 43%, respectively, reported that marrying someone of the same religion was important for them (Hall & Knox, 2016).

Are people in interreligious marriages less satisfied with their marriages than those who marry someone of the same faith? The answer depends on a number of factors. First, people in marriages in which one or both spouses profess "no religion" tend to report lower levels of marital satisfaction than those in which at least one spouse has a religious tie. People with no religion are often more liberal and less bound by traditional societal norms and values; they feel less constrained to stay married for reasons of social propriety.

The impact of a mixed religious marriage may also depend more on the devoutness of the partners than on the fact that the partners are of different religions. If both spouses are devout in their respective religious beliefs, they may expect some problems in the relationship. Less problematic is the relationship in which one spouse is

devout but the partner is not. If neither spouse in an interfaith marriage is devout, problems regarding religious differences may be minimal or nonexistent. In their marriage vows, one interfaith couple who married (he was Christian, she was Jewish) said that they viewed their different religions as an opportunity to strengthen their connections to their respective faiths and to each other. "Our marriage ceremony seeks to celebrate both the Jewish and Christian traditions, just as we plan to in our life together."

8-4h International Marriages

With increased globalization, international matchmaking Internet opportunities, and travel abroad programs, there is greater opportunity to meet/marry someone from another country.

Over three-fourths of 2,291 undergraduate males (78%) and over two-thirds of 7,383 undergraduate females (69%) reported that they would be willing to marry someone from another country (Hall & Knox, 2016). The opportunity to meet that someone is increasing, as upwards of 900,000 foreign students are studying at American colleges and universities.

Tili and Barker (2015) studied Caucasian Americans married to Asians and noticed a common theme of these intercultural relationships—the perception of personal growth both felt that they derived from their union. One of the respondents noted:

> Intercultural marriages open you up to a whole new outlook on life. They say if you learn an instrument or learn another language that boosts your IQ. I feel, as a

This couple met in graduate school in the United States. The husband is 100% Taiwanese and the wife is 50% Chinese and 50% Taiwanese. The husband's parents, radical supporters of Taiwan independence, disapprove of their offspring marrying anyone of Chinese descent.

Maria McDonald

Courtesy of Joyce Chang

couple, we are growing in acceptance, in intelligence, in many different ways as we learn something totally new. It is more than just culturally understanding something.

Some people from foreign countries marry an American citizen to gain citizenship in the United States, but immigration laws now require the marriage to last two years before citizenship is granted. If the marriage ends before two years, the foreigner must prove good faith (that the marriage was not just to gain entry into the country) or he or she will be asked to leave the country.

Cultural differences may sometimes surface. An American woman fell in love with and married a man from Fiji. She was unaware of a norm from his culture that anyone from his large kinship system could visit at any time and stay as long as they liked—indeed it would be impolite to ask them to leave. On one occasion two "cousins" showed up unannounced at the home of the couple. The wife was in the last week of exams for her medical degree and could not tolerate visitors. The husband told her, "I cannot be impolite." But with the marriage threatened, the husband told his cousins they had to leave.

8-4i Immigrant Families

National news is replete with families fleeing one country/immigrating to another. Researchers Murray et al. (2015) interviewed immigrants who noted that their new home was not a panacea—that they worried about their safety, discrimination, and legal institutions in the new country. Positive coping was facilitated by focusing on the advantages for their children, viewing their situation as temporary, and having hope for improvement.

8-4j Age-Discrepant Relationships and Marriages

Although people in most pairings are of similar age, sometimes the partners are considerably different in age. In marriage, these are referred to as ADMs (age-dissimilar marriages) and are in contrast to ASMs (age-similar marriages). ADMs are also known as

May–December marriage
age-dissimilar marriage (ADM) in which the woman is typically in the spring of her life (May) and her husband is in the later years (December).

rtguest/Shutterstock.com

May–December marriages. Typically, the woman is in the spring of her youth (May) whereas the man is in the later years of his life (December). There have been a number of May–December celebrity marriages, including that of Celine Dion, who is 26 years younger than René Angelil (in 2015, they were aged 47 and 73). Michael Douglas is 25 years older than his wife, Catherine Zeta-Jones, and Ellen DeGeneres is 15 years older than her spouse, Portia de Rossi.

Sociobiology suggests that men select younger women since doing so results in healthier offspring. Women benefit from obtaining sperm from older men who have more resources for their offspring.

In a study of 433 spouses where the husband was older, marital effects were less time spent together and more marital problems. Having less in common was the presumed reason for the negative effects (Wheeler et al., 2012).

Perhaps the greatest example of a May–December marriage that worked is of Oona and Charles Chaplin. She married him when she was 18 (he was 54). Their alliance was expected to last the requisite six months, but they remained together for 34 years (until his death at 88) and raised eight children, the last of whom was born when Chaplin was 73.

Although less common, some age-discrepant relationships are those in which the woman is older than her partner. Mariah Carey was 11 years older than her former husband, Nick Cannon. Valerie Gibson (2002),

This wife is 6 years older than her husband.

U.S. and Icelandic College Student Attitudes toward Relationships

It is easy to forget that people in other countries may not believe as do American youth. Iceland became part of U.S. consciousness in 2010 when the Eyjafjallajökull volcano erupted on April 14 causing the cancellation of thousands of flights across Europe and to Iceland. Anyone in the United States trying to fly to Europe was likely affected. Iceland was on the nightly national news for a week.

It is axiomatic that societies differ in regard to norms regarding relationships and sexuality. Iceland and the United States represent two diverse societies/cultures. Iceland is one of five Nordic countries (the others are Denmark, Finland, Sweden, and Norway) representing over 40,000 square miles with a population of 320,000, mostly of Norwegian and Irish origins. In contrast, the United States is 3.79 million square miles with a population of around 330 million.

The Study

A team of American and Icelandic researchers compared the responses of 722 undergraduates from a large southeastern university in the United States on 100 items about relationships with the responses of

Johann Herbertsson was born and reared in Iceland. He is pointing to the town of Reykjavik where he lives and where the Icelandic data were collected.

368 undergraduates from the University of Iceland in Reykjavik, Iceland. The sample consisted of 813 females and 277 males. The proportion of males and females in the respective countries was very similar—74% of the U.S. sample was female compared to 76% of the Icelandic students. The racial composition of the sample differed between the two countries. The U.S. sample was 76% White, 15% Black, 3% Asian, 2% mixed, and 2% reporting "other." The Icelandic sample was 98% White and 2% Black.

To test for differences in the responses of the U.S. and Icelandic students when responses were made on a five-point response scale, the test for mean differences between independent groups was used. When two point yes/no responses were analyzed, t-tests for differences in proportions were used.

Results

Several significant differences were found between U.S. and Icelandic undergraduates:

▸ **Desire to marry.** Students were presented with the item "Someday I want to marry" and asked to respond on a five-point scale from "strongly agree" (1) to "strongly disagree" (5), the lower the score the more important the goal to marry and the higher the score the lower the importance of getting married. Scores for the U.S. and Icelandic students were .97 and .89, respectively (significant at the .01 level), revealing that U.S. students have a higher desire to marry than Icelandic students. Explanation of the data include that Icelandics have long held the tradition of cohabitation independent of marriage, hence, their lower desire to marry.

▸ **Interracial marriage.** Students were presented with the item "It is important to me that I marry of someone my race" and asked to respond on a five-point scale. Scores for the U.S. and Icelandic students were 2.78 and 4.27, respectively (significant at the .01 level), revealing that U.S. students were much more open to interracial marriage with few Icelandic students reporting a willingness to cross racial lines to marry. Explanation of the data include that the

(Continued)

United States is a much larger country with a more diverse population compared to Iceland. Icelandic undergraduates have had limited exposure to those outside their own group.

▶ **Interreligious marriage.** Students were presented with the item "It is important to me that I marry someone of my same religion" and asked to respond on a five-point scale. Scores for the U.S. and Icelandic students were 2.77 and 3.80, respectively (significant at the .01 level), revealing that marrying someone of the same faith was more important to U.S. than Icelandic students. This finding is not a surprise since the U.S. sample is from the southern region of the United States where conservative religion has, traditionally, been dominant. Hence, these students are simply reflecting their heritage whereas Icelandic students are more moderate in their religious views and more open to diversity.

▶ **Impulsiveness about love.** Students were presented with the item "If I were really in love, I would marry someone I had known for only a short time" and asked to respond on a five-point scale. Scores for the U.S. and Icelandic students were 2.77 and 3.80, respectively (significant at the .01 level), revealing that a higher number of the U.S. students would be willing to marry someone they were madly in love with even though they had only known that person for a short time. Icelanders are simply not in a hurry to get married, and being in love doesn't propel them along the way.

▶ **Cheating on a partner.** Students were presented with the item "I have cheated on a partner I was involved with" and asked to respond on a five-point scale. Scores for the U.S. and Icelandic students were 3.46 and 4.18, respectively (significant at the .01 level), revealing that U.S. undergraduates were much more likely to have cheated whereas Icelandic students were more likely to be faithful. The explanation for this finding is that Icelandic students were more likely to be in cohabitation relationships (e.g., more committed relationships) than U.S. students. With less commitment/structure among U.S. relationships, greater infidelity would be expected.

Additional Results

Other findings included that, compared to Icelandics, U.S. undergraduates were less likely to have lived together, less likely to have had sex without love, and more likely to view marriage as a goal. However, there were no differences between U.S. and Icelandic students in desire to have children (both had high desire to have children), in openness to marry someone outside of their own country (both were moderately open), in commitment to end a relationship with a partner who cheated on them, in willingness to see a marriage counselor before seeing a lawyer (both were moderately willing), and in condom use (both did not use consistently).

Source: Adapted and abridged from Halligan, C., D. Knox, F. J. Freysteinsdottir, & S. Skulason. (2014, March). U.S. and Icelandic college student attitudes toward relationships. Poster, Annual Meeting of the Southern Sociological Society, Charlotte, NC.

---

the author of *Cougar: A Guide for Older Women Dating Younger Men*, notes that the current use of the term **cougars** refers to "women, usually in their thirties and forties, who are financially stable and mentally independent and looking for a younger man to have fun with." Gibson noted that one-third of women between the ages of 40 and 60 are dating younger men. Financially independent women need not select a man in reference to his breadwinning capabilities. Instead, these women are looking for men not to marry but to enjoy. The downside of such relationships comes if the man gets serious and wants to have children, which may spell the end of the relationship.

cougar a woman, usually in her thirties or forties, who is financially stable and mentally independent and looking for a younger man with whom to have fun.

8-4k College Marriages

Cottle et al. (2013) analyzed data from 429 currently and formerly married college students. The ages ranged from 18 to 62. The newlyweds reported significantly greater life satisfaction, marital satisfaction, relationships with in-laws, communication about sex, working out problems, etc., than the older college-married students. A major finding was that students who quit college were less likely to report satisfaction in these areas.

8-5 MARRIAGE SUCCESS

A successful marriage is the goal of most couples. But what is a successful marriage and what are its characteristics?

8-5a Definition and Characteristics of Successful Marriages

Marital success refers to the quality of the marriage relationship measured in terms of stability and happiness. Stability refers to how long the spouses have been married and how permanent they view their relationship to be, whereas happiness refers to more subjective/emotional aspects of the relationship. In describing marital success, researchers have used the terms *satisfaction, quality, adjustment, lack of distress,* and *integration.* Marital success is often measured by asking spouses how happy they are, how often they spend their free time together, how often they agree about various issues, how easily they resolve conflict, how sexually satisfied they are, how equitable they feel their relationship is, and how often they have considered separation or divorce.

Are wives or husbands happier? Jackson et al. (2014) reported data on 226 independent samples comprising 101,110 participants and found statistically significant yet very small gender differences in marital satisfaction between wives and husbands, with wives slightly less satisfied than husbands. However, the researchers noted that this difference was due to the inclusion of clinical samples, with wives in marital therapy 51% less likely to be satisfied. When

Ron Dale/Shutterstock.com

nonclinical community-based samples were used, no significant gender differences were observed in marital satisfaction among couples in the general population.

Chapman and Guven (2016) reported that wives were happier than husbands across their national samples from the United States, the UK, and Germany.

Researchers have also identified characteristics associated with successful marriages (Buri et al., 2014; Harris et al., 2016; Olson et al., 2014; Stafford, 2016). Their findings and those of other researchers include the following:

1. **Time together/attachment.** Spending time together is basic. Flood and Genadek (2016) reviewed data from 46,883 individuals over a seven-year period and confirmed that greater happiness and less stress were associated with spending time with one's spouse rather than spending time apart. In addition, securely emotionally attached spouses report the highest levels of relationship satisfaction (Kilmann et al., 2013).

2. **Communication/humor.** Gottman and Carrere (2000) studied the communication patterns of couples over an 11-year period and emphasized that those spouses who stayed together were five times more likely to lace their arguments with positives ("I'm sorry I hurt your feelings") and to consciously choose to say things to each other that nurture the relationship. Successful spouses also feel comfortable telling each other what they want and not being defensive at feedback from the partner.

3. **Common interests/positive self-concepts.** Spouses who have similar interests, values, and goals, as well as positive self-concepts, report higher marital success. Spending time together is also associated with marital satisfaction (Luu, 2014).

4. **Not materialistic.** Being nonmaterialistic is characteristic of happily married couples (Carroll et al., 2011).

5. **Role models.** Successfully married couples speak of having positive role models in their parents.

RossHelen/Shutterstock.com

marital success the quality of the marriage relationship measured in terms of stability and happiness.

Good marriages beget good marriages—good marriages run in families (Amato, 2015b). It is said that the best gift you can give your children is a good marriage.

6. **Religiosity.** Strong religious values, religious homogamy, and viewing marriage as sacred are associated with marital satisfaction and a lower divorce rate (Olson et al., 2014; Prabu & Stafford, 2015; Stafford, 2016). Religion provides spouses with a common value. In addition, religion provides social, spiritual, and emotional support from church members and with moral guidance in working out problems.

7. **Trust.** Trust in the partner provides a stable floor of security for the respective partners and their relationship (Harris et al., 2016). Neither partner fears that the other partner would leave or become involved in another relationship. "She can't take him anywhere he doesn't want to go" is a phrase from a country-and-western song that reflects the trust that one's partner will be faithful.

8. **Personal and emotional commitment to stay married.** Divorce was not considered an option. The spouses were committed to each other for personal reasons rather than societal pressure.

9. **Sexual satisfaction.** Barzoki et al. (2012) studied wives and found that marital dissatisfaction leads to sexual dissatisfaction but that this connection can become reciprocal—sexual dissatisfaction can lead to marital dissatisfaction.

10. **Equitable relationships.** Partners in equitable/ egalitarian relationships report higher relationship quality than those in traditional relationships (where one partner has more power than the other) (Simpson et al., 2015).

11. **Marriage/connection rituals. Marriage rituals** are deliberate repeated social interactions that reflect emotional meaning to the couple. **Connection rituals** are those which occur daily in which the couple share time and attention. Campbell et al. (2011) studied 129 unmarried individuals (involved with a partner) who identified 13 different types of rituals (average of 6). The most frequent was enjoyable activities (23%) such as having meals together and watching TV together.

marriage rituals deliberate repeated social interactions that reflect emotional meaning to the couple.

connection rituals habits which occur daily in which the couple share time and attention.

Intimacy expressions (19%) included "taking a shower together every morning and washing each other's hair." Communication ritual (14%) examples were sending frequent text messages and having pet names for each other.

12. **Absence of negative statements and attributions.** Not making negative remarks to the spouse is associated with higher marital quality (Woszidlo & Segrin, 2013). Biological anthropologist Helen Fisher (2015) noted that happily married spouses have mastered the quality of "positive illusion" whereby they consciously choose to focus on the positive aspects of their partner and relationship and overlook the negatives.

13. **Forgiveness.** At some time in all marriages, each spouse engages in behavior that hurts or disappoints the partner. Forgiveness, rather than harboring and nurturing resentment allows spouses to move forward. Researchers have found that forgiving and being forgiven are related to higher marital quality (Aalgaard et al., 2016; Prabu & Stafford, 2015). Indeed, spouses who do not "drop the lowest test score" (an academic metaphor) of their partner find that they inadvertently create an unhappy marital context which they endure. However, Woldarsky and Greenberg (2014) noted that it is not forgiveness but the perception that the partner experiences shame for the transgression that is restorative to the couple. Perhaps the two work in combination?

> You hurt yourself more by not forgiving than any hurt ever caused you by another.
>
> —WILLIAM FERGUS MARTIN

14. **Economic security.** Although money does not buy happiness, having a stable, secure economic floor is associated with marital quality (Amato et al., 2007) and marital happiness (Mitchell, 2010). Indeed, higher incomes are associated with marital happiness (Choi & Marks, 2013).

15. **Physical/emotional health.** One's physical and emotional health and the control of one's stress positively impact one's marriage (Fisher, 2015).

And a good marriage has positive effects on one's health and emotional well-being (Choi & Marks, 2013; Miller et al., 2014).

16. **Flexibility.** Flexibility is an important quality for long-term stability. Flexible couples make mutual decisions, accommodate as necessary to each other's schedule, and ensure that they spend time together. Hence, whatever the issue of contention, their relationship is more important.

17. **Mindset of marriage success.** Marital success may be viewed from a "growth" (a dynamic/transformative process) or a "fixed" (a soul mate) mindset. A team of researchers confirmed that "growth" view was associated with greater romantic love for the partner and greater hope for resolving marital conflict than a "fixed" view (Buri et al., 2014).

18. **Exchange minded.** Happily married spouses ensure a high rate of positive behavior exchange with each other. Each partner is eager to do things for each other. Examples include one cooks and the other does the dishes/cleans the kitchen. Or one takes the spouse's car to have it serviced while the other cleans the partner's study. In effect, both are givers that results in a balance—neither feels exploited.

19. **Empathy.** Being able to empathize with one's partner and what the partner is experiencing is one of the hallmarks of a successful relationship (Fisher, 2015). This quality is particularly important for husbands (McDonald et al., 2015). To feel a partner's empathy is to feel understood. Since intimacy is a primary reason individuals marry, empathy in one's relationship is a factor associated with both quality and longevity.

 Self-Assessment: Satisfaction with Marriage Scale

Take the Satisfaction with Marriage Scale in the self-assessment section at the end of this chapter to assess your feelings about your marriage.

8-5b Theoretical Views of Marital Happiness and Success

Interactionists, developmentalists, exchange theorists, and functionalists view marital happiness and success differently. Symbolic interactionists emphasize the subjective nature of marital happiness and point out that the definition of the situation is critical. Indeed, a happy marriage exists only when spouses define the verbal and nonverbal behavior of their partner as positive, and only when they label themselves as being in love and happy. Marital happiness is not defined by the existence of specific criteria (time together) but by the subjective definitions of the respective partners. Indeed, spouses who work together may spend all of their time together but define their doing so as a negative. Shakespeare's phrase "Nothing is either good or bad but thinking makes it so" reflects the importance of perception.

Family developmental theorists emphasize developmental tasks that must be accomplished to enable a couple to have a happy marriage. These tasks include separating emotionally from one's parents, building a sense of "we-ness," establishing an imaginative and pleasurable sex life, and making the relationship safe for expressing differences.

Exchange theorists focus on the exchange of behavior of a kind and at a rate that is mutually satisfactory to both spouses. When spouses exchange positive behaviors at a high rate (with no negatives), they are more likely to feel marital happiness than when the exchange is characterized by high-frequency negative behavior (and no positives).

Structural functionalists regard marital happiness as contributing to marital stability, which is functional for society. When two parents are in love and happy, the likelihood that they will stay together to provide for the physical care and emotional nurturing of their offspring is increased. Furthermore, when spouses take care of their own children, society is not burdened with having to pay for their care through welfare payments, paying foster parents, or paying for institutional management (group homes).

> Marriage is a coming together for better or for worse, hopefully enduring, and intimate to the degree of being sacred.
>
> —WILLIAM O. DOUGLAS

8-5c Marital Happiness across Time

Anderson et al. (2010) analyzed longitudinal data of 706 individuals over a 20-year period. Over 90% were in their first marriage; most had two children and 14 years of education. Reported marital happiness, marriage problems, time spent together, and economic hardship were assessed. Five patterns emerged:

1. **High stable 2** (started out happy and remained so across time) = 21.5%

2. **High stable 1** (started out slightly less happy and remained so across time) = 46.1%

3. **Curvilinear** (started out happy, slowly declined, followed by recovery) = 10.6%

4. **Low stable** (started out not too happy and remained so across time) = 18.3%

5. **Low declining** (started out not too happy and declined across time) = 3.6%

The researchers found that, for couples who start out with a high level of happiness, they are capable of rebounding if there is a decline. But for those who start out at a low level, the capacity to improve is more limited.

Spencer and Amato (2011) emphasized the importance of using a number of variables such as interaction and conflict rather than just marital happiness in the examination of marital relationships over time. Based on data from couples married over 20 years they found that marital happiness shows a U-shape distribution but interaction declined across time. The researchers hypothesized that couples do not interact less because they are unhappy but because they have other interests.

Other studies on marital happiness over time show, in general, a progressive decline in satisfaction. Based on an analysis of marital data on women across 35 years of marriage, researcher James (2015) found evidence supporting a continuous decline in marital happiness with about 35% of marriages recovering in the later years, but never to the early marriage level. A "flat fishhook" was used to describe the pattern.

Finkel (2015) suggested that in order to achieve marital happiness, three conversations must occur. The first is about what each partner expects of marriage (e.g., level of emotional intimacy, commitment, fidelity, autonomy, support). The second conversation is about one's commitment of personal resources (e.g., time, flexibility) to achieve the expectations. The third conversation involves recalibration that occurs across time (e.g., investing more resources or asking less).

 ## 8-6 TRENDS IN MARRIAGE RELATIONSHIPS

Diversity will continue to characterize marriage relationships of the future. The traditional model of the husband provider, stay-at-home mom, and two children will continue to transition to other forms including more women in the workforce, single parent families, and smaller families. What will remain is the intimacy/companionship focus that spouses expect from their marriages.

Openness to interracial, interreligious, cross-national, and age-discrepant relationships will increase. The driving force behind this change will be the U.S. value of individualism which minimizes parental disapproval. An increased global awareness, international students, and study abroad programs will facilitate increased opportunities and a mindset of openness to diversity in terms of one's selection of a partner.

STUDY TOOLS 8

READY TO STUDY? IN THE BOOK, YOU CAN:

☐ Rip out the chapter review card at the back of the book for a handy summary of the chapter and key terms.

☐ Assess yourself with the following self-assessments.

ONLINE AT CENGAGEBRAIN.COM YOU CAN:

☐ Collect StudyBits while you read and study the chapter.

☐ Quiz yourself on key concepts.

☐ Prepare for tests with M&F4 Flash Cards as well as those you create.

SELF-ASSESSMENT

Attitudes toward Interracial Dating Scale

Interracial dating or marrying is the dating or marrying of two people from different races. The purpose of this survey is to gain a better understanding of what people think and feel about interracial relationships. Please read each item carefully, and in each space, score your response using the following scale. There are no right or wrong answers to any of these statements.

1	2	3	4	5	6	7
Strongly disagree						*Strongly agree*

_____ **1.** I believe that interracial couples date outside their race to get attention.

_____ **2.** I feel that interracial couples have little in common.

_____ **3.** When I see an interracial couple, I find myself evaluating them negatively.

_____ **4.** People date outside their own race because they feel inferior.

_____ **5.** Dating interracially shows a lack of respect for one's own race.

_____ **6.** I would be upset with a family member who dated outside our race.

_____ **7.** I would be upset with a close friend who dated outside our race.

_____ **8.** I feel uneasy around an interracial couple.

_____ **9.** People of different races should associate only in nondating settings.

_____ **10.** I am offended when I see an interracial couple.

_____ **11.** Interracial couples are more likely to have low self-esteem.

_____ **12.** Interracial dating interferes with my fundamental beliefs.

_____ **13.** People should date only within their race.

_____ **14.** I dislike seeing interracial couples together.

_____ **15.** I would not pursue a relationship with someone of a different race, regardless of my feelings for that person.

_____ **16.** Interracial dating interferes with my concept of cultural identity.

_____ **17.** I support dating between people with the same skin color, but not with a different skin color.

_____ **18.** I can imagine myself in a long-term relationship with someone of another race.

_____ **19.** As long as the people involved love each other, I do not have a problem with interracial dating.

_____ **20.** I think interracial dating is a good thing.

Scoring

First, reverse the scores for items 18, 19, and 20 by switching them to the opposite side of the spectrum. For example, if you selected 7 for item 18, replace it with a 1; if you selected 3, replace it with a 5; and so on. Next, add your scores and divide by 20. Possible final scores range from 1 to 7, with 1 representing the most positive attitudes toward interracial dating and 7 representing the most negative attitudes toward interracial dating.

Norms

The norming sample was based upon 113 male and 200 female students attending Valdosta State University. The participants completing the Attitudes toward Interracial Dating Scale (IRDS) received no compensation for their participation. All participants were U.S. citizens. The average age was 23.02 years (standard deviation [SD] = 5.09), and participants ranged in age from 18 to 50 years. The ethnic composition of the sample was 62.9% White, 32.6% Black, 1% Asian, 0.6% Hispanic, and 2.2% others. The classification of the sample was 9.3% freshmen, 16.3% sophomores, 29.1% juniors, 37.1% seniors, and 2.9% graduate students. The average score on the IRDS was 2.88 (SD = 1.48), and scores ranged from 1.00 to 6.60, suggesting very positive views of interracial dating. Men scored an average of 2.97 (SD = 1.58), and women, 2.84 (SD = 1.42). There were no significant differences between the responses of women and men.

Source: The Attitudes toward Interracial Dating Scale. (2004). Mark Whatley, Ph.D., Department of Psychology, Valdosta State University, Valdosta, GA 31698.

SELF-ASSESSMENT

Satisfaction with Marriage Scale

Below are five statements with which you may agree or disagree. Using the 1–7 scale below, indicate your agreement with each item by circling the appropriate number on the line following that item. Please be open and honest in responding to each item.

1	2	3	4	5	6	7
Strongly disagree	Disagree	Slightly disagree	Neither agree nor disagree	Slightly agree	Agree	Strongly agree

	SD	D	SD	N	SA	A	SA
1. In most ways my married life is close to ideal	1	2	3	4	5	6	7
2. The conditions of my married life are excellent.	1	2	3	4	5	6	7
3. I am satisfied with my married life.	1	2	3	4	5	6	7
4. So far I have gotten the important things I want in my married life.	1	2	3	4	5	6	7
5. If I could live my married life over, I would change almost nothing.	1	2	3	4	5	6	7

Scoring

Add the numbers you circled. The marital satisfaction score will range from 5 to 35. For purposes of this study a couple's combined marital satisfaction score was calculated by summing both partners' scores, resulting in a possible score range of 10 to 70, with higher scores indicating greater marital satisfaction for the couple. The internal consistency of the SWML has been reported with a Cronbach's alpha of .92 along with some evidence of construct validity (Johnson et al., 2006).

Source: Johnson, H. A., Zabriskie, R. B., & Hill, B. (2006). The contribution of couple leisure involvement, leisure time, and leisure satisfaction to marital satisfaction. *Marriage and Family Review, 40:* 69–91. Publisher by Taylor & Francis Ltd.

9 | Integrating Work and Relationships

Rob Marmion/Shutterstock.com

SECTIONS

After finishing this chapter go to **PAGE 188** for **STUDY TOOLS**

Two-earner families yearned to simplify their lives yet felt that they were caught on a treadmill from which neither parent could afford to step off.

—STEPHANIE COONTZ, FAMILY HISTORIAN

i ho, hi ho, it's off to work we go" are Disney lyrics we learned as children. As adults we quickly learned that work is relentless, mundane, and impacts us and our relationships. The focus of this chapter is how money affects individuals, marriages, and families. We begin by looking at money and relationships.

9-1   MONEY AND RELATIONSHIPS

> All I ask is the chance to prove that money can't make me happy.
>
> —SPIKE MILLIGAN, ENGLISH COMEDIAN

Money is major for both individuals and couples. Ruberton et al. (2016) found that the amount of "cash on hand" is related to one's reported life satisfaction. Fales et al. (2016) found significant gender differences in what men and women want in regard to money in the partners they marry. In two national U.S. samples, men and women indicated it was "essential" that their potential partner had a steady income (74% versus 97%) and that the partner made or would make a lot of money (47% versus 69%).

Just the presence of money and the security of it impact relationship formation. Lewchuk et al. (2016) studied the social and economic effects of precarious employment in the Greater Toronto-Hamilton area and found that low earnings and economic uncertainty translated into delayed formation of relationships, lower marriage rates for workers under the age of 35, and fewer households with children.

Money also impacts a couple's interaction and happiness in that it is a gateway to more problems in the relationship, such as spending less time together and having disagreements about sex (Wheeler & Kerpelman, 2013).

Money is also tied to one's physical health. Williams et al. (2016) found that spending money on others in contrast to one's self is associated with a reduction of one's own blood pressure. This finding was repeated in several studies.

Bankruptcy is associated with declines in physical, psychological, and marital health. Maroto (2015) noted that bankruptcy does not come suddenly (e.g., job loss) but through a series of events such as accumulating medical debt, marital dissolution, and lack of savings. Not being materialistic and having sufficient savings are associated with weathering negative economic times (e.g., job loss) (Wheeler et al., 2015).

> I married for love and got a little money along with it.
>
> —ROSE KENNEDY

Difficult economic times are also associated with positive consequences such as causing individuals to become less consumer oriented, more engaged in their relationships, and more involved in transcendental activities (religious, contemplative) (Etzioni, 2011). Indeed, the entrenched value of **consumerism**—to buy everything and to have everything now—has come under fire. The real stress that money inflicts on relationships is the result of internalizing the societal expectations of who one is, or should be, in regard to the pursuit of money.

9-1a   Money as Power in a Couple's Relationship

Money is a central issue in relationships because of its association with power, control, and dominance. Generally, the

Consumerism to buy everything and to have everything now.

more money a partner makes, the more power that person has in the relationship. Males in general make considerably more money than females and generally have more power in relationships. The median annual income of a male with a bachelor's degree is $58,170 compared with $39,201 for a female with the same education (*Proquest Statistical Abstract of the United States, 2016*, Table 724).

When a wife earns an income, her power in the relationship increases. The author of your text knows a married couple in which the wife began to earn considerably more than her husband. Prior to her raise, her husband's fishing boat was stored in the couple's protected carport. Her higher income resulted in her having more power in the relationship, as reflected in her parking her car in the carport and her husband putting his fishing boat underneath the pine trees to the side of the house.

A record 40% of all households with children under the age of 18 include mothers who are either the sole or primary source of income for the family. These "breadwinner moms" are made up of two very different groups: 5.1 million (37%) are married mothers who have a higher income than their husbands, and 8.6 million (63%) are single mothers (Wang et al., 2013).

To some individuals, money means love. While admiring the engagement ring of her friend, a woman said, "What a big diamond! He must really love you." The cultural assumption is that a big diamond equals expense and a lot of sacrifice and love. Similar assumptions are often made when gifts are given or received.

Maria McDonald

9-1b Money and the Wife's Happiness

Sohn (2016) found a direct relationship between the husband's income and the wife's happiness. Indeed, a 100% increase in the husband's income was related to a 72% increase in the wife expressing that she was "very happy."

 ## 9-2 WORK AND MARRIAGE

> [T]hey told me all about the pretty girls and the wine and the money and the good times…no mention of all the wear and tear on an old honky-tonker's heart. I might of known it…but nobody told me about this part.
>
> —GEORGE STRAIT, *NOBODY TOLD ME ABOUT THIS PART*

A couple's marriage is organized around the work of each spouse. Where the couple live is determined by where the spouses can get jobs. Jobs influence what time spouses eat, which family members eat with whom, when they go to bed, and when, where, and for how long they vacation. In this section, we examine some of the various influences of work on a couple's relationship. We begin by looking at the skills identified by dual earner spouses to manage their work/job/career so as to provide income for the family but minimal expense to their relationship.

9-2a Basic Rules for Managing One's Work Life to Have a Successful Marriage

Määttä and Uusiautti (2012) analyzed data from 342 married couples who explained their secrets for maintaining a successful relationship in the face of the demands of work. These secrets included turning a negative into a positive, being creative, tolerating dissimilarity (accepting the partner), and being committed to the relationship. Some jobs are more challenging for spouses than others (e.g., police officer). Karaffa et al. (2015) found that both officers and spouses generally agreed on the stressors (work hours are long/constantly changing, role of the controlling interrogating police officer may be incompatible with the listening nurturing spouse, high stress such as being shot at) and positives such as being a family of a police officer.

Work is often tiresome and relentless.

Courtesy of Brittany Bolen

9-2b Employed Wives

Driven primarily by the need to provide income for the family, most wives who have children are in the labor force. The time wives are most likely to be in the labor force is when their children are teenagers (between the ages of 14 and 17), the time when food and clothing expenses are the highest. Seventy-four percent are in the labor force at this time (*Proquest Statistical Abstract of the United States, 2016*, Table 617).

Traditional conceptions of the role of mother are that she will work part-time, give priority to her child, and be pair bonded with someone who has an additional source of income. But this pattern may vary. African American mothers assume that they will be gainfully (full-time) employed, that they will be financially independent, and that they will look to kin and community for help with their child caregiving (Marie Dow, 2016).

Treas et al. (2011) found that homemakers (in 28 countries) were happier than full-time wives. Bean et al. (2016) interviewed full-time stay-at-home moms. What was critical to their life/marital satisfaction was the knowledge of and support for by the spouse of the enormous work parenting is and the appreciation to the mother for her role. One respondent said:

> I've worked all day too. You know, I'd like to just sit all evening and watch sports, but I'm still doing laundry, and I'm still and you know, I don't think he thinks that I'm working. I mean I know he does. (*Annie*)

Hoffnung and Williams (2013) assessed 200 female college seniors, most of whom wanted both a career and children, and followed up on them 16 years later. Though they could be divided into three role-status outcome groups—Have It All (mothers, employed full-time), Traditional (mothers, employed part-time or not at all), and

Employed Only (childfree, employed full-time)—most of the women still wanted to "have it all." Many traditional women looked forward to returning to employment, and many of the employed only women wanted to have children. Some parents wonder if the money a wife earns by working outside the home is worth the sacrifices to earn it. Not only is the mother away from her children, but she must pay for others to care for the children.

Some parents wonder if the money a wife earns by working outside the home is worth the sacrifices to earn it. Not only is the mother away from her children, but she had to pay for others to care for the children. The value of a stay-at-home mother was about $52,000 per year in 2016 in terms of what a dual-income family spends to pay for all the services that she provides (domestic cleaning, laundry, meal planning and preparation, shopping, providing transportation to activities, taking the children to the doctor, and running errands) (Sefton, 1998, provided original data, updated to account for inflation). The value of a house husband would be the same. However, because males typically earn higher incomes than females, the loss of income would be greater than for a female.

Of interest is that working mothers give themselves slightly higher ratings than nonworking mothers for the job they are doing as parents. Among mothers with children under age 18 who work full-time or part-time, 78% say they are doing an excellent or very good job as parents. Among mothers who are not employed, 66% say the same (Parker & Wang, 2013).

Research on outcomes of mothers who spend time with their children suggests that the amount of time mothers spend engaged with their children or are accessible to them (3 to 11 years old) seems unrelated to emotional, behavioral, or academic outcome for the children. However, positive outcomes do occur when the question is time spent with adolescents (Milkie et al., 2015).

The **mommy track** (stopping paid employment to spend time with young children) is another potential cost to those women who want to build a career. Taking time out to rear children in their formative years can derail a career. Unless a young mother has a supportive partner with a flexible schedule, family who live close and who can take care of her children, or money to pay for child care, she will discover that corporations need the work done and do not care about the kids. Kahn et al. (2014) reconfirmed that motherhood is costly to women's careers, but mostly to women who have three children. Those who have one or two children experience

mommy track stopping paid employment to be at home with young children.

Spencer Grant/PhotoEdit

the greatest expense when the woman is young, but this disadvantage is eliminated by their forties and fifties. Although most couples are two earner families, some couples struggle with whether one spouse, usually the wife, will work outside the home.

Self-Assessment: Maternal Employment Scale (MES)

Take the Maternal Employment Scale in the self-assessment section at the end of this chapter to assess your attitude toward working mothers.

dual-career marriage one in which both spouses pursue careers.

HIS/HER career marriage a husband's and wife's careers are given equal precedence.

commuter marriages a type of long-distance marriage where spouses live in different locations during the workweek (and sometimes for longer periods of time) to accommodate the careers of the respective spouses.

9-2c **Office Romance**

The office or workplace is where people earn money. It is also a place where they meet and establish relationships, including love and sexual relationships. Faith Hill and Tim McGraw toured together, and while she was engaged to someone else, sparks flew. They subsequently married and had three children. In a survey of over a thousand employees in the workplace, half said that they had been involved in an office romance (Vault Office Romance Survey, 2016). Jane Merrill interviewed 70 adults who had been involved in an office romance. Of these interviews, she reported that "…the office is still a scene of seduction and amorality. The hallmark of office romances is secrecy—either hiding a steamy short or long love relationship between two single people or where one or both is married or in a serious relationship" (Merrill & Knox, 2010). Undergraduates have also experienced romance on the job (see What's New? section).

9-2d **Types of Dual-Career Marriages**

A **dual-career marriage** is defined as one in which both spouses pursue careers and may or may not include dependents. A career is different from a job in that the former usually involves advanced education or training, full-time commitment, long hours/night/weekend work "off the clock," and a willingness to relocate. Dual-career couples typically operate without a person (e.g., a "wife") who stays home to manage the home and children. However, some couples hire a nanny.

Types of dual-career marriages include those in which both careers are equally important (**HIS/HER career marriage**). About 6 in 10 wives work today, nearly double the percentage in 1960. Sixty-two percent endorse the modern marriage (HIS/HER career marriage) in which the husband and wife both work and both take care of the household and children (Parker & Wang, 2013).

Some HIS/HER career marriages are **commuter marriages**, a type of long-distance marriage where spouses live in different locations during the workweek (and sometimes for longer periods of time) to accommodate the careers of the respective spouses. The estimated number of commuter marriages is about 3.5 million—50 of the wives from which had been in a commuter marriage

Undergraduate Love and Sex on the Job

Seven-hundred seventy-four undergraduates in North Carolina, Florida, and California completed an Internet survey on office romance. The purpose was to identify the percent of the sample who had fantasized about love and sex on the job and the percent who actually experienced their fantasies. Other objectives included the percent reporting having kissed a coworker, whether the involvement was with someone of equal or higher status, how often they disclosed an office relationship to others, and the outcome of the office romance.

Over three-fourths (78%) of the respondents were female; 22% were male. Forty-seven percent were employed in a service job such as sales, fast food, or retail; 9% worked in an academic context; 12% in an office; and 4% in a medical context. Most (73%) regarded where they worked as a job, not a career, and 13% saw it as a place to meet a future spouse.

Over 40% of the student employees reported fantasies of both love and sex with a coworker in contrast to a quarter who *actually experienced* love and sex with a coworker.

FANTASIES AND REALITIES ON THE JOB (N = 774)

	Fantasized About, %	Actually Experienced, %
Love relationship at the office	43	25
Sexual relationship at the office	41	24

Other findings included:

Kissing
Almost 30% (28.6%) reported that they had kissed a fellow employee at work.

Rank of Person Undergraduate Had Sex With
Almost 80% (79%) reported having had sex with a peer/coworker; 11% of those surveyed had sex with a boss, supervisor, or someone above them.

Telling Others about the Office Romance
About 30% (28.1%) reported that they told someone else about their office romance.

After the Office Romance Ends
Of the workplace romances that had ended, almost three-quarters (73%) ended positively with over half (54%) remaining friends. Thirteen percent still see each other, 5% are married to each other, and 1% live together. Less than 2% (1.7%) ended up losing their job at the place where they had the office romance.

The Society for Human Resources Management conducted a survey in which they interviewed 380 human resource professionals about office romance policies. Over half (54%) had no policy; 36% had a written policy; and 6% had a verbal policy (Carey & Trapp, 2013).

Source: Merrill, J., & D. Knox. (2010). *Finding love from 9 to 5: Trade secrets of an office love.* Santa Barbara, CA: Praeger.

at least a year and were interviewed (another 25 wives were in focus groups) by McBridge and Bergen (2014).

One issue spouses coped with was the physical separation from the partner. One spouse said, "Say you have something great happen to you at work, and the first person you want to walk in and see is your husband or your wife and tell them what happened. Well, we don't have them at home." Another issue is the lack of understanding others have of such a "weird" arrangement ("If they really loved each other, they would not get jobs apart from each other" is the thinking). A third issue is managing fidelity. One wife warned, "Be sure that your

marriage can take this…because if you have any doubt in your mind that he's not going to be faithful to you…or that the marriage is strong enough that it's going to make it through this commute…don't do it."

For couples who do not have traditional gender role attitudes, the wife's career may take precedence (**HER/HIS career marriage**). In such marriages, the husband is willing to relocate and to subordinate his career for his wife's. Such a pattern is also likely to occur when a wife earns considerably more

HER/HIS career marriage
a wife's career is given precedence over her husband's career.

money than her husband. In some cases, the husband who is downsized by his employer or who prefers the role of full-time parent becomes "Mr. Mom." Not only may the wife benefit in terms of her career advancement, the relationship of the father with his children will be closer than that of fathers in traditional marriages who spend less time with their children. Indeed, some fathers no longer need to be an economic provider but are valued as the front line caretaker and nurturer (Stykes et al., 2015).

Some dual-career marriages are those in which the careers of both the wife and husband are given equal status in the relationship (HIS/HER career). About 6 in 10 wives work today, nearly double the percentage in 1960. More than 62% of survey respondents endorse the modern marriage (HIS/HER career marriage) in which the husband and wife both work and both take care of the household and children (Parker & Wang, 2013). About half (54%) of parents in households where both the mother and the father work full-time say that, in their family, the mother does more when it comes to managing the children's schedules (Pew Research Center, 2015). In some cases, both spouses share a career or work together (**THEIR career marriage**). Some news organizations hire both spouses to travel abroad to cover the same story. These careers are rare.

In the following sections, we look at the effects on women, men, their marriage, and their children when a wife is employed outside the home.

9-3 EFFECTS OF THE MOTHER'S EMPLOYMENT ON THE SPOUSES AND MARRIAGE

A major challenge is for women to combine a career and motherhood. While some new mothers enjoy their work role and return to work soon after their children are born, others anguish over leaving their baby to return to the workforce.

The new mother discovers that there are now two spheres to manage—work and family—which may result in **role overload**—not having the time or energy to meet the demands of their responsibilities in the roles of wife, parent, and worker. Because women have traditionally been responsible for

THEIR career marriage a career shared by a couple who travel and work together (e.g., journalists).

role overload not having the time or energy to meet the demands of their responsibilities in the roles of wife, parent, and worker.

second shift housework and child care that are done when the parents return home after work.

role conflict being confronted with incompatible role obligations.

most of the housework and child care, employed women come home from work to what Hochschild (1989) calls the second shift, housework and child care that have to be done after work. According to Hochschild, the **second shift** has the following result:

> Women tend to talk more intently about being over-tired, sick, and "emotionally drained." Many women could not tear away from the topic of sleep. They talked about how much they could "get by on" . . . six and a half, seven, seven and a half, less, more . . . . Some apologized for how much sleep they needed . . . . They talked about how to avoid fully waking up when a child called them at night, and how to get back to sleep. These women talked about sleep the way a hungry person talks about food. (p. 9)

The short answer to the effects of maternal employment on the mother is stress. Research by Westrupp et al. (2016) has confirmed the reciprocal relationships between employed mothers' work–family conflict and psychological distress across 8 years of the child's life (0 to age 9). Associations persisted after controlling for family socioeconomic status, maternal age, or job quality.

While some new mothers enjoy their work role and return to work soon after their children are born, others anguish over leaving their baby to return to the workforce. One new mother who went back to work after the birth of her daughter said, "You go through periods of guilt for leaving her, sadness, missing her, worrying to death and even a slight bit of anger at your spouse. 'Hey, if you made more money, we could afford for me to stay home.'"

Another stressful aspect of employment for employed mothers in dual-earner marriages is **role conflict**, being confronted with incompatible role obligations. For example, the role of a career woman is to stay late and prepare a report for the following day. However, the role of a mother is to pick up her child from day care at 5 p.m. When these roles collide, there is role conflict. Although most women resolve their role conflicts by giving

Going Back to Work—A New Mother's View

Some mothers anguish over leaving their newborn and returning to full-time employment.

You probably get the most advice of your life during pregnancy, especially if it's your first. Some advice is very welcome and some, not so much. Actually, I wanted as much advice as possible about anything and everything baby. I figured it would better prepare me ... HA! "Be prepared" is something I heard repeatedly after I answered yes to "Are you going back to work?" I knew I would be very sad, but I also knew there was no other choice. I was too busy worrying about making sure all the cute pink things were washed and folded (and refolded) in her drawer as I anticipated her arrival. Thinking about having her and then having to leave her were distant thoughts. I mean, 8 to 10 weeks of time off is a really long time isn't it? More time off than a summer between grade school. It seemed like an eternity. But there is no way to prepare yourself for the reality. She is born, your life is forever different. Your time in the hospital is a whirlwind. You blow in, and blow out.

Then you are home, with your precious baby and you have 10 weeks ... 10 long weeks. But no matter how much time you take with your newborn, it flies by. It's never enough time. You are trying to heal from delivery and learn about being a new mother at the same time. You're losing sleep and using more energy. A spinning tornado of being tired and falling in love ... and POOF ... it's gone. You go through periods of guilt for leaving her, sadness, missing her, worrying to death and even a slight bit of anger at your spouse. Hey, "if you made more money, we could afford for me to stay home."

Your first day back at work will be very hard. If you work somewhere with many employees like I did, I had people coming to my office every few minutes, "It's nice to have you back!" What can you possibly say to that? It's good to be back ... hell no. But you are not going to tell them how much you would rather be home with your baby. If you are lucky, you have an amazing mother who always says the right thing at the right time. When I was pouring my heart out to her over the phone my last day at the house with my daughter she said, "Yes, I couldn't imagine leaving my babies with anyone else. It's going to be really hard when she does everything first with them and not with you. I sure hope she says mama before her caregiver's name." Talk about a freak-out.

The best thing you can do if going back to work is hard for you is to talk to other mothers that went through it. One of my friends stayed home for a year before she put her son in day care. She says now that she would feel like a bad mother if she took him out of his day care because he learns so much and really enjoys it. When I'm feeling really sad about being at work I try to think of all the things we will be able to afford for her because I work. Like sports teams, music lessons, dance, vacations, etc., that are also important for her growth and development. Also remember that no matter what, you will always be mommy, and no one can take that away.

—Amanda Kinsch
(Subsequent to writing the above, Amanda quit her job and she and her husband had two more children.

---

preference to the mother role, some give priority to the career role and feel guilty about it.

Role strain, the anxiety that results from being able to fulfill only a limited number of role obligations, occurs for both women and men in dual-earner marriages. No one is at home to take care of housework and children while they are working, and they feel strained at not being able to do everything.

role strain the anxiety that results from being able to fulfill only a limited number of role obligations.

9-3a Effects of the Wife's Employment on Her Husband

Husbands also report benefits from their wives' employment. These include being relieved of the sole responsibility for the financial support of the family and having more freedom to quit his job, change jobs, or go to school. Since men traditionally had no options but to work full-time, they now benefit by having a spouse with whom to share the daily rewards and stresses of employment.

9-3b Effects of the Wife's Employment on the Marriage

Helms et al. (2010) analyzed the relationship between employment patterns and marital satisfaction of 272 dual-earner couples and found that coprovider couples (in contrast to those where there were distinct primary and secondary providers) reported the highest marital satisfaction. In addition, these couples reported the most equitable division of housework. However, Minnotte et al. (2013) found reduced marital satisfaction for more egalitarian husbands and wives, suggesting that husbands may have resented the intrusion of family life into their work roles. More traditional relationships were also associated with higher sex frequency (Kornrich et al., 2013).

Are marriages in which the wife has her own income more vulnerable to divorce? Not if the wife is happy. But if she is unhappy, her income will provide her a way to take care of herself when she leaves. Schoen et al. (2002) wrote, "Our results provide clear evidence that, at the individual level, women's employment does not destabilize happy marriages but increases the risk of disruption in unhappy marriages" (p. 643). Hence, employment would not affect a happy marriage but it can affect an unhappy one.

9-4 WORK AND FAMILY: EFFECTS ON CHILDREN

Independent of the effect on the wife, husband, and marriage, what is the effect on the children of the wife earning an income outside of the home? Abundant research confirms that maternal employment has no significant negative effects on young children (Coontz, 2016). In general, women expect that they will more often be employed part-time and that they will be more involved in child care (Gartzia & Fetterolf, 2016). Some parents have different views on the effects of maternal employment on children.

The concept of intensive mothering reflects the belief that mothers must prioritize their time to take care of their children, which is incompatible with full-time employment; hence, "good mothers are not employed" (Walls et al., 2016). In their study of 2015 full-time employed mothers of infants, researchers Walls et al. (2016) found that they did not endorse the beliefs of intensive mothering.

Indeed, mothers with young children are the least likely to be in the labor force. Mothers most likely to be in the workforce are those with children between the ages of 14 and 17—the teen years. Teenagers are no longer dependent on the physical care of their mother, and they create more expenses, often requiring a second income.

There is a positive effect of wife's employment on the relationship of the father with his children. Meteyer and Perry-Jenkins (2012) confirmed that the more hours the wife worked, the greater the father was involved with his children. However, a disadvantage for children of two-earner parents is that they receive less supervision. Letting children come home to an empty house is particularly problematic. The issue of self-care children is discussed shortly.

9-4a Quality Time with Children

The term *quality time* has become synonymous with good parenting. Dual-income parents struggle with not having enough quality time with their children. Mormons typically set aside "Monday home evenings" as a time to bond, pray, and sing together. Other parents (child-centered parents) noted that quality time occurred when they were having heart-to-heart talks with their children. Still other parents believed that all the time they were with their children was quality time. Whether they were having dinner together or riding to the post office, quality time was occurring if they were together. As might be expected, mothers assumed greater responsibility for quality time.

9-4b Day Care Considerations

About two-thirds of women in the workforce have children under 6 years old (Liu, 2015). Day care options include a center, a home-based day care, or care by a relative. The younger the child the more likely the child will be placed with a relative. While most mothers prefer relatives (spouse or partner or another relative) for the day care arrangement for their children, 23% of 1- to 2-year-old children and 18% of children 3 to 4 are in center-based day care programs (*Proquest Statistical Abstract of the United States, 2016*, Table 587).

Day care quality is indexed by the ratio of adults to children, training of adult day care workers, stability of

Parents are always apprehensive about the care their babies and children are getting when they are in day care.

day care workers, and salary of day care workers. The latter is associated with attracting educated, engaged individuals to care for one's children.

"Day care children do as well or better than their at home counterparts in the areas of sociability, social competence, problem solving, achievement, language skills, empathy, and self-confidence" (Coontz, 2016, p. 291). And while some research suggests that day care children are less compliant, perhaps this is because they are learning to think for themselves (p. 291).

Day care quality is highest with relatives, then center-based, then home-based contexts (Liu, 2015). The best context is a stable, warm, engaging person to take care of one's child. Such a context is variable since workers may earn minimum wage, are exhausted, and have high turnover rates. Vigilence can also be a problem. The authors of your text know of a child in a day care context who ate a pebble that lodged in the

windpipe and the child died. While tragic, such events are rare (and could happen at the parents' home); most children survive and turn out more than OK. The authors also know of a day care that provides detailed information on each child, each day, what the child ate, the length of the child's nap, and bathroom behavior (BMs or wet). Gentile and Pierce (2014) surveyed adults who, themselves, were placed in day care and compared them with adults not exposed to day care. Those who went to day care as a child were more likely to display flexibility in their thinking and to be more comfortable in public speaking and interacting with others.

Day care costs are a factor in whether a low-income mother seeks employment, because the cost can absorb her paycheck. Even for dual-earner families, cost is a factor in choosing a day care center. Day care costs vary widely from nothing, where friends trade off taking care of the children, to very expensive institutionalized day care in large cities. The cost of high-quality day care can be as high as $3,000 per month. One such day care provides continuous web cam video for parents and daily reports on the eating, sleeping, and elimination behavior of their child. These costs are for one child; most spouses have two children. Do the math.

9-5 BALANCING WORK AND FAMILY LIFE

Work is definitely stressful on individuals, spouses, and relationships. Economic challenges in general (e.g., unemployment, low wages, debt) have been linked to relationship distress, depression, partner's discord, parenting stress, and coparenting dysfunction (Williams et al., 2015).

Hoser (2012) examined work and family life and found that the **spillover thesis** worked in only one direction—work spread into family life in the form of doing

spillover thesis work spreads into family life in the form of the worker/parent doing overtime, taking work home, attending seminars organized by the company, being "on call" on the weekend/during vacation, and always being on the computer in reference to work.

overtime, taking work home, attending seminars organized by the company, and being "on call" on the weekend/during vacation. Rarely did one's family life dictate the work role.

> There is no such thing as work-life balance. Everything worth fighting for unbalances your life.
>
> —ALAIN DE BOTTON, SWISS PHILOSOPHER

Virtual work is one answer. Based on a survey of 2,500 adults age 18 and older conducted by Ricoh Americas and Harris International, 64% of the respondents reported a preference for working "virtually" compared to 34% who preferred to work in an office (Yang & Gonzalez, 2013).

One of the major concerns of employed parents and spouses is how to juggle the demands of work and family. When there is conflict between work and family, various strategies are employed to cope with the stress of role overload and role conflict, including (1) the superperson strategy, (2) cognitive restructuring, (3) delegation of responsibility, (4) planning and time management, and (5) role compartmentalization (Stanfield, 1998).

superperson strategy involves working as hard and as efficiently as possible to meet the demands of work and family.

superwoman (supermom) a cultural label that allows a mother who is experiencing role overload to regard herself as particularly efficient, energetic, and confident.

third shift the emotional energy expended by a spouse or parent in dealing with various family issues.

9-5a Superperson Strategy

The **superperson strategy** involves working as hard and as efficiently as possible to meet the demands of work and family. A superperson often skips lunch and cuts back on sleep and leisure to have more time available for work and family. Women are particularly vulnerable because they feel that if they give too much attention to child care concerns, they will be sidelined into lower-paying jobs with no opportunities.

Hochschild (1989) noted that the terms **superwoman** or **supermom** are cultural labels that allow a woman to regard herself as very efficient, bright, and confident. However, Hochschild noted that this is a "cultural cover-up" for an overworked and/or frustrated woman. As noted earlier, not only does the woman have a job in the workplace (first shift), she comes home to another set of work demands in the form of house care and child care (second shift). Finally, she has a third shift (Hochschild, 1997).

The **third shift** is the expense of emotional energy by a spouse or parent in dealing with various issues in family living. Although young children need time and attention, responding to conflicts and problems with teenagers also involves a great deal of emotional energy. Minnottea et al. (2010) studied 96 couples and found that women perform more "emotion work." Opree and Kalmijn (2012) noted that employed women who also take care of an adult child or aging parents are more likely to report negative changes in their own mental health.

What about the husband contributing to housework? How does equality of housework translate into frequent sex? "There is no association" according to Johnson et al. (2016), who examined housework division of labor and sexual frequency. However, the researchers noted that it is the perception of fairness that is the key. If the female partner perceives that she is being treated fairly, which may include occasional dishes, sexual frequency and reported sexual satisfaction increases.

Sometimes a parent (more often the mother) takes a child into work when other options are not available.

Who does what chores in the house is also negotiated and outsourced (Carlson & Hans, 2015). When neither partner wants to do something, the one who didn't do it the last time is often "it."

9-5b Cognitive Restructuring

Another strategy used by some women and men experiencing role overload and role conflict

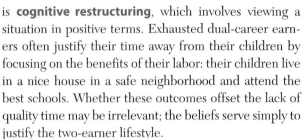
Christopher Boswell/Shutterstock.com

is **cognitive restructuring**, which involves viewing a situation in positive terms. Exhausted dual-career earners often justify their time away from their children by focusing on the benefits of their labor: their children live in a nice house in a safe neighborhood and attend the best schools. Whether these outcomes offset the lack of quality time may be irrelevant; the beliefs serve simply to justify the two-earner lifestyle.

9-5c Delegation of Responsibility and Limiting Commitments

A third way couples manage the demands of work and family is to delegate responsibility to others for performing certain tasks. Because women tend to bear most of the responsibility for child care and housework, they may choose to ask their partner to contribute more or to take responsibility for these tasks.

Another form of delegating responsibility involves the decision to reduce one's current responsibilities and not take on additional ones. For example, women and men may give up or limit committing to volunteer responsibilities. One woman noted that her life was being consumed by the responsibilities of her church; she had to change churches because the demands were relentless. In the realm of paid work, women and men can choose not to become involved in professional activities beyond those that are required.

photosync/Shutterstock.com

9-5d Time Management

While two-thirds of women prefer to work part-time as opposed to full-time, Vanderkam (2010) argues that women who work part-time end up spending just 41 more minutes daily on child care and 10 minutes more per day playing with the child than if they worked full-time. By working full-time, she says the woman affords high-quality day care and can focus on the child when she is not at work. The full-time worker is not exhausted from being with the children all day but may be more "emotionally ready" to spending dinner, bath, and reading time with their children at night.

Other women use time management by prioritizing and making lists of what needs to be done each day. This method involves trying to anticipate stressful periods, planning ahead for them, and dividing responsibilities with the spouse. Such division of labor allows each spouse to focus on an activity that needs to be done (grocery shopping, picking up children at day care) and results in a smoothly functioning unit.

Having flexible jobs and/or careers is particularly beneficial for two-earner couples. Being self-employed, telecommuting, or working in academia permits flexibility of schedule so that individuals can cooperate on what needs to be done. Alternatively, some dual-earner couples attempt to solve the problem of child care by having one parent work during the day and the other parent work at night so that one of them can always be with the children. Shift workers often experience sleep deprivation and fatigue, which may make fulfilling domestic roles as a parent or spouse difficult for them. Similarly, **shift work** may have a negative effect on a couple's relationship because of their limited time together.

9-5e Role Compartmentalization

Some spouses use **role compartmentalization** separating the roles of work and home so that they do not think about or dwell on the problems of one when they are at the other. Spouses unable to compartmentalize their work and home feel role strain, role conflict, and role overload, with the result that their efficiency

cognitive restructuring viewing a situation in positive terms.

shift work having one parent work during the day and the other parent work at night so that one parent can always be with the children.

role compartmentalization separating the roles of work and home so that an individual does not dwell on the problems of one role while physically being at the place of the other role.

> Sometimes we just have to suck it up and do what we have to do, until we are able to do what we want to do.
>
> —MARK W. BOYER, PROFESSIONAL FOOTBALL PLAYER

drops in both spheres. Some families look to the government and their employers for help in balancing the demands of family and work.

9-5f Finding Balance: Work and Play

Finding a balance between work and leisure is challenging. For starters, workers want more leisure time. In a Robert Half Survey of 1,000 workers, "additional vacation days" was the more desirable nonmonetary perk at work, valued even more than "health/wellness benefits" (Yang & Trap, 2016). And more time together is associated with increased marital happiness (Flood & Genadek, 2016).

9-6 TRENDS IN MONEY, WORK, AND FAMILY LIFE

Families will continue to be stressed by work. Employers will, increasingly, ask employees to work longer and do more without the commensurate increases in salary or benefits. Businesses are struggling to stay solvent and workers will take the brunt of the instability.

The number of wives who work outside the home will increase—the economic needs of the family will demand that they do so. Husbands will adapt, most willingly, some reluctantly. Children will become aware that budgets are tight, tempers are strained, and leisure with the family in the summer may not be as expansive as previously. As children go to college they can benefit from exposure to financial management information—being careful about credit card debt and how they spend money (Fiona et al., 2012).

While the percent of wives in the workforce may increase, the percent of mothers who do not work outside the home is increasing. The percent in 2012 was 29%, up from 23% in 1999 (Cohn et al., 2014). Difficulty finding employment and concerns about the employment effects on children are explanations.

 **SELF-ASSESSMENT**

Maternal Employment Scale (MES)

Directions

Using the following scale, please mark a number on the blank next to each statement to indicate how strongly you agree or disagree.

1	2	3	4	5	6
Disagree very strongly	Disagree strongly	Disagree slightly	Agree slightly	Agree strongly	Agree very strongly

____ 1. Children are less likely to form a warm and secure relationship with a mother who works full-time outside the home.

_____ **2.** Children whose mothers work are more independent and able to do things for themselves.

_____ **3.** Working mothers are more likely to have children with psychological problems than mothers who do not work outside the home.

_____ **4.** Teenagers get into less trouble with the law if their mothers do not work full-time outside the home.

_____ **5.** For young children, working mothers are good role models for leading busy and productive lives.

_____ **6.** Boys whose mothers work are more likely to develop respect for women.

_____ **7.** Young children learn more if their mothers stay at home with them.

_____ **8.** Children whose mothers work learn valuable lessons about other people they can rely on.

_____ **9.** Girls whose mothers work full-time outside the home develop stronger motivation to do well in school.

_____ **10.** Daughters of working mothers are better prepared to combine work and motherhood if they choose to do both.

_____ **11.** Children whose mothers work are more likely to be left alone and exposed to dangerous situations.

_____ **12.** Children whose mothers work are more likely to pitch in and do tasks around the house.

_____ **13.** Children do better in school if their mothers are not working full-time outside the home.

_____ **14.** Children whose mothers work full-time outside the home develop more regard for women's intelligence and competence.

_____ **15.** Children of working mothers are less well-nourished and don't eat the way they should.

_____ **16.** Children whose mothers work are more likely to understand and appreciate the value of a dollar.

_____ **17.** Children whose mothers work suffer because their mothers are not there when they need them.

_____ **18.** Children of working mothers grow up to be less competent parents than other children because they have not had adequate parental role models.

_____ **19.** Sons of working mothers are better prepared to cooperate with a wife who wants both to work and have children.

_____ **20.** Children of mothers who work develop lower self-esteem because they think they are not worth devoting attention to.

_____ **21.** Children whose mothers work are more likely to learn the importance of teamwork and cooperation among family members.

_____ **22.** Children of working mothers are more likely than other children to experiment with alcohol, other drugs, and sex at an early age.

_____ **23.** Children whose mothers work develop less stereotyped views about men's and women's roles.

_____ **24.** Children whose mothers work full-time outside the home are more adaptable; they cope better with the unexpected and with changes in plans.

Scoring

Items 1, 3, 4, 7, 11, 13, 15, 17, 18, 20, and 22 refer to "costs" of maternal employment for children and yield a Costs Subscale score. High scores on the Costs Subscale reflect strong beliefs that maternal employment is costly to children. Items 2, 5, 6, 8, 9, 10, 12, 14, 16, 19, 21, 23, and 24 refer to "benefits" of maternal employment for children and yield a Benefits Subscale score. To obtain a total score, reverse the score of all items in the Benefits Subscale so that 1 = 6, 2 = 5, 3 = 4, 4 = 3, 5 = 2, and 6 = 1. The higher one's total score, the more one believes that maternal employment has negative consequences for children.

Source: E. Greenberger, W. A. Goldberg, T. J. Crawford, and J. Granger, Beliefs about the consequences of maternal employment for children in *Psychology of Women Quarterly, Maternal Employment Scale, 12:* 35–59, 1988.

10 Reacting to Abuse in Relationships

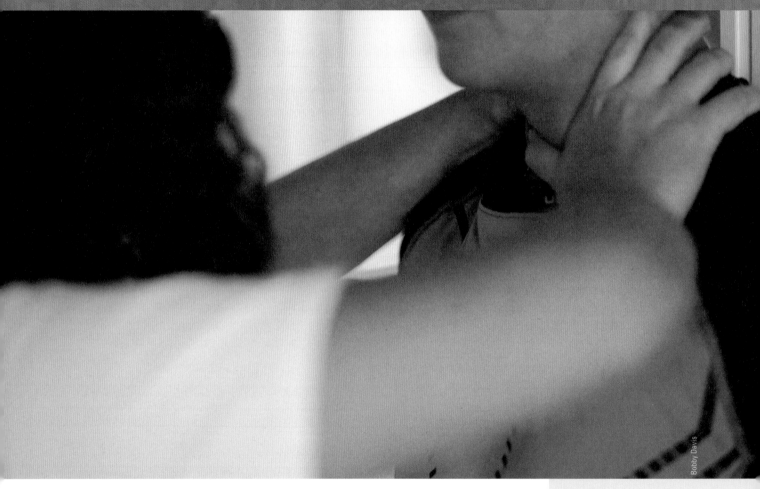

Bobby Davis

SECTIONS

After finishing this chapter go to **PAGE 205** for **STUDY TOOLS**

> Why are you afraid of women? I asked a group of men.
> We're afraid they'll laugh at us, replied the men.
> Why are you afraid of men? I asked a group of women.
> We're afraid they'll kill us, replied the women.
>
> —MARGARET ATWOOD, POET/NOVELIST

The brutality of Isis has a constant media presence. Bombs also regularly explode at parades, airports, and malls. What goes unnoticed is the brutality of how intimate partners inflict violence on each other.

What begins as an intimate love relationship can become emotional and physical abuse, even murder. Such abuse can begin early (e.g., in teen relationships between 13 and 19) (Murray et al., 2016). In this chapter, we examine the other side of intimacy in relationships—the types, causes, and outcomes of intimate partner violence (IPV). We begin by looking at the nature of abuse and defining some terms.

Maria McDonald

10-1 TYPES OF RELATIONSHIP ABUSE

There are several types of abuse in relationships.

10-1a Violence as Abuse

Also referred to as physical abuse, **violence** is defined as physical aggression with the purpose of controlling or intimidating the partner. Examples of physical violence include pushing, throwing something at the partner, slapping, hitting, and forcing the partner to have sex. Eleven percent of 7,572 undergraduate females and 4% of 2,376 undergraduate males reported that they had been in a physically abusive relationship (Hall & Knox, 2016). Twenty people per minute are victims of IPV in the United States (Centers for Disease Control and Prevention, 2016, pp. 2–16). One in four women in the United States experiences interpersonal partner violence in her lifetime (Liu et al., 2013). While men are more often the perpetrator, Stith (2015) examined violence in relationships in the military and found that 15% of the females (independent of which branch of service) were the offender. **Intimate partner violence** (IPV) is an all-inclusive term that refers to crimes committed against current or former spouses, boyfriends, or girlfriends.

There are two types of violence. One type is **situational couple violence** (SCV) where conflict escalates over an issue (e.g., money, sex) and one or both partners lose control. The person feels threatened and seeks to defend himself or herself. Control is lost and the partner strikes out. Both partners may lose control at the same time, so it is symmetrical. A second type of violence, referred to as **intimate terrorism** (IT), is designed to control the partner (Brownridge, 2010).

Battered woman syndrome (also referred to as **battered woman defense**) is a legal term used in court that the person accused of murder was suffering from abuse so as to justify his or her behavior ("I shot him because he raped me"). While there is no medical or psychological term, the "syndrome" refers to frequent, severe maltreatment which often requires medical treatment.

Klipfel et al. (2014) assessed the occurrence of emotional, physical, and sexual interpersonal aggression reported by 161 individuals

violence physical aggression with the purpose to control, intimidate, and subjugate another human being.

intimate partner violence an all-inclusive term that refers to crimes committed against current or former spouses, boyfriends, or girlfriends.

situational couple violence conflict escalates over an issue and one or both partners lose control.

intimate terrorism behavior designed to control the partner.

battered woman syndrome (battered woman defense) legal term used in court that the person accused of murder was suffering from to justify their behavior. Therapists define battering as physical aggression that results in injury and accompanied by fear and terror.

Bobby Davis

within various levels of relationships. The relationship and percent of reported intimate partner violence in the various relationships follow: committed romantic relationships (69%), casual dating relationships (33%), friends with benefits relationships (31%), booty calls (36%), and one-night stands (35%). The take home message is that the greater the commitment in the relationship, the greater the reported IPV (intimate partner violence).

Battering may lead to murder. **Uxoricide** is the murder of a woman by a romantic partner. **Intimate partner homicide** is the murder of a spouse. Cunha and Goncalves (2016) compared moderate violent partners with severely violent partners (murderers) and found that the latter were more likely to use weapons, to be involved in a separation/breakup, and to be of high socioeconomic status (SES).

Other forms of murder in the family are **filicide** (murder of an offspring by a parent), **parricide** (murder of a parent by an offspring), and **siblicide** (murder of a sibling). Regarding filicide, parental mental illness, domestic violence, and alcohol/substance abuse are common contexts (Sidebotham, 2013).

A great deal more abuse occurs than is reported. As few as 5% of rapes are reported to the authorities (Heath et al., 2013). The primary reasons rape victims do not report their experience to the police are not wanting others to know, nonacknowledgment

---

uxoricide the murder of a woman by a romantic partner.

intimate partner homicide murder of a spouse.

filicide murder of an offspring by a parent.

parricide murder of a parent by an offspring.

siblicide murder of a sibling.

emotional abuse nonphysical behavior designed to denigrate the partner, reduce the partner's status, and make the partner feel vulnerable to being controlled by the partner.

revenge porn posting nude photos of ex; a form of emotional and sexual abuse; some states considering legislation against this behavior.

---

of rape (e.g., "It wasn't really rape…I just gave in") and criminal justice concerns ("It won't do any good," "I will be blamed") (Cohn et al., 2013).

Self-Assessment: Abusive Behavior Inventory

To assess the frequency of abuse in a current or past relationship, take the Abusive Behavior Inventory at the end of this chapter.

10-1b Emotional Abuse

Emotional abuse (also known as psychological abuse, verbal abuse, or symbolic aggression) is nonphysical behavior designed to denigrate and control the partner. Examples of emotionally abusive behaviors of one's partner include refusal to talk to the partner as a way of punishing the partner, making personal decisions for the partner (e.g., what to wear, what to eat, whether to smoke), throwing a temper tantrum and breaking things to frighten the partner, criticizing/belittling the partner to make him or her feel bad, and acting jealous when the partner is observed talking or texting a potential romantic partner. Other emotionally abusive behaviors include:

Yelling and screaming—as a way of intimidating
Staying angry/pouting—until the partner gives in
Requiring an accounting—of the partner's time
Ridicule—making the partner feel stupid
Isolation—prohibiting the partner from spending time with friends, siblings, and parents
Threats—threatening the partner with abandonment or threats of harm to oneself, family, or partner's pets
Public demeaning behavior—insulting the partner in front of others
Demanding behavior—requiring the partner to do as the abuser wishes (e.g., have sex)

A final example of emotional abuse is **revenge porn**—posting on the Internet nude photos of one's

---

> An emotionally abusive relationship, in very simplistic terms, is much like standing up in a too hot bath and sinking back in so as not to feel so dizzy.
>
> —JACKIE HAZE, *BORDERLESS*

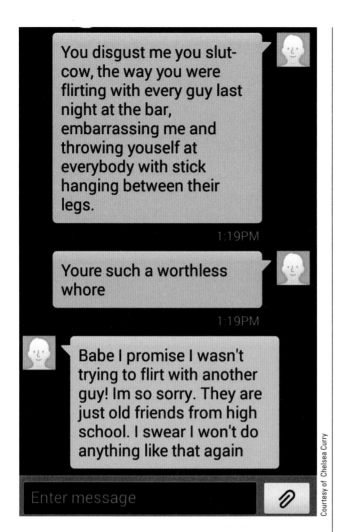

You disgust me you slut-cow, the way you were flirting with every guy last night at the bar, embarrassing me and throwing youself at everybody with stick hanging between their legs.

1:19PM

Youre such a worthless whore

1:19PM

Babe I promise I wasn't trying to flirt with another guy! Im so sorry. They are just old friends from high school. I swear I won't do anything like that again

Enter message

Courtesy of Chelsea Curry

ex-partner. This is both emotional and sexual abuse. Some states are considering legislation against this behavior.

Thirty-seven percent of 7,573 undergraduate females (and 23% of 2,375 undergraduate males) reported that they "had been involved in an emotionally abusive relationship" (Hall & Knox, 2016). Emotional abuse may also be cyber abuse such as threatening text messages and posting embarrassing content on social media. Temple et al. (2016) revealed that adolescents who have experienced interpersonal physical abuse (e.g., slapping, hitting, choking) were also likely to report cyber abuse; hence the same person may experience multiple layers of abuse.

Based on a sample of 338 university students (122 male and 216 female), one-third reported at least one type of dating abuse: 33.1% psychological, 9.5% physical, 10.4% sexual, and 9.8% technological violence (Cho & Huang, 2016).

Once abused, who do people tell or who do they seek for help? Of the victims of dating abuse in the Cho and Huang (2016) study, abuse victims were more likely to seek informal help from friends and family than formal help from professionals.

10-1c Mutual or Unilateral Abuse?

Marcus (2012) assessed the frequency of unilateral or mutual partner violence in a sample of 1,294 young adults. A quarter of the couples reported a mutually violent pattern compared to three-quarters who evidenced a unilateral pattern. Mathes (2013) noted that among those couples where violence is a part of their relationship, individuals select each other to play their game—to be violent. In all cases, the more violence, the lower the relationship quality.

10-1d Female Abuse of Partner

Nybergh et al. (2016) interviewed 20 men who had been subjected to IPV (most by female partners). They reported that the violence was not physical but more emotional/psychological. Their partners were described as jealous, disliked their friends, made them pay for things, excluded them from family events, or belittled, humiliated, and/or called them names, etc.

When women did express violence, Whitaker (2014) noted that they often did so for reasons of losing their temper, to try to get their partner to listen, to make their partner do as they wanted, or to punish the partner. Their motives may be mixed. When women are abusive, they are rarely arrested by the police. Men do not want others to know that they "aren't man enough" to stand up to an abusive woman.

10-1e Stalking

Abuse may take the form of stalking. **Stalking** is defined as unwanted following or harassment that induces fear in the victim. Twenty-eight percent of 7,509 undergraduate females and 19% of 2,340 undergraduate males reported that they had been stalked (followed and harassed)

Mike Focus/Shutterstock.com

stalking (unwanted pursuit behavior) unwanted following or harassment of a person that induces fear in the victim.

(Hall & Knox, 2016). Most (77%) stalkers are male (Lyndon et al., 2012).

Another term for stalking is **unwanted pursuit behavior** (UPB). DeSmet et al. (2015) studied the UPB in 631 adult ex-partners and found an average of five to six UPBs after their separation. Male and female and same- and opposite-gender ex-partners reported an equal number of UPBs. Frequency was related to breakup characteristics (ex-partner initiation of the breakup), relationship characteristics (anxious attachment to former partner), and individual perpetrator characteristics (borderline traits/past delinquent behaviors).

Less threatening than stalking is **obsessive relational intrusion** (ORI), the relentless pursuit of intimacy with someone who does not want it. The person becomes a nuisance but does not have the goal of harm as does the stalker. People who cross the line in terms of pursuing an ORI relationship or responding to being rejected (stalking) engage in a continuum of behavior from telling the person they are beautiful to **cyber victimization** to **cyber control**.

10-1f Reacting to the Stalker

Being very controlling in an existing relationship is predictive that the partner will become a stalker when the relationship ends. Ending a relationship with a potential stalker in a way that does not spark stalking is important. Some guidelines include:

> **obsessive relational intrusion** the relentless pursuit of intimacy with someone who does not want it.
>
> **cyber victimization** harassing behavior which includes being sent threatening email, unsolicited obscene email, computer viruses, or junk mail (spamming); can also include flaming (online verbal abuse) and leaving improper messages on message boards.
>
> **cyber control** use of communication technology, such as cell phones, email, and social networking sites, to monitor or control partners in intimate relationships.
>
> **corporal punishment** the use of physical force with the intention of causing a child to experience pain, but not injury, for the purpose of correction or control of the child's behavior.

1. Make a direct statement to the person ("I am not interested in a relationship with you, my feelings about you will not change, and I know that you will respect my decision and direct your attention elsewhere").

2. Seek protection through formal channels (police or court restraining order).

3. Avoid the perpetrator (ignore text messages/ emails, do not walk with or talk to, hang up if the person calls).

4. Use informal coping methods (block text messages/phone calls).

5. Stay away. Do not offer to be friends since the person may misinterpret this as a romantic overture.

> But even when I stop crying, even when we fall asleep and I'm nestled in his arms, this will leave another scar. No one will see it. No one will know. But it will be there. And eventually all of the scars will have scars, and that's all I'll be—one big scar of a love gone wrong.
>
> —AMANDA GRACE, *BUT I LOVE HIM*

10-2 REASONS FOR VIOLENCE AND ABUSE IN RELATIONSHIPS

Research suggests that numerous factors contribute to violence and abuse in intimate relationships. These factors operate at the cultural, community, individual, and family levels.

10-2a Cultural Factors

In many ways, American culture tolerates and even promotes violence. Violence in the family stems from the acceptance of violence in our society as a legitimate means of enforcing compliance and solving conflicts at interpersonal, familial, national, and international levels. Violence and abuse in the family may be linked to such cultural factors as violence in the media, acceptance of corporal punishment, gender inequality, and the view of women and children as property.

VIOLENCE IN THE MEDIA One need only watch boxing matches, football, or the evening news to see the violence in war, school shootings, and domestic murders. Wright and Tokunaga (2016) noted that male violence against women is related to men's magazines (e.g., *Maxum* and *Esquire*), reality TV (e.g., *Jersey Shore*), and pornography, which objectify women as targets for men.

CORPORAL PUNISHMENT OF CHILDREN The use of physical force with the intention of causing a child pain, but not injury, for the purposes of correcting or controlling the child's behavior and/or making the child obedient is **corporal punishment**. In the United States,

Radius Images/Getty Images

corporal punishment in the form of spanking, hitting, whipping, and paddling or otherwise inflicting pain on the child is legal in all states (as long as the corporal punishment does not meet the individual state's definition of child abuse). Seventy percent of U.S. respondents agreed that spanking is necessary to discipline children (Ma et al., 2012). Unlike Sweden, Italy, Germany, and 12 other countries which have banned corporal punishment in the home, violence against children has become a part of U.S. cultural heritage.

Corporal punishment is associated with negative outcomes. Ward et al. (2015) found that parental use of corporal punishment was associated with children's internalizing (depression and anxiety) and externalizing (rule breaking and aggression) symptoms. In addition, according to a meta-analysis of five decades of research on spanking (defined as an open-handed hit on the behind or extremities), parents should seek alternatives to spanking (e.g., time-out). The more children are spanked, the more likely they are to defy their parents, experience mental health issues and cognitive difficulties, and exhibit a spectrum of problem behaviors such as antisocial and aggression (Gershoff & Grogan-Kaylor, 2016).

vvvita/Shutterstock.com

Child development specialists recommend an end to corporal punishment to reduce the risk of physical abuse, harm to other children, and to break the cycle of abuse.

GENDER INEQUALITY Domestic violence and abuse may also stem from traditional gender roles. Traditionally, men have also been taught that they are superior to women and that they may use their aggression toward women, believing that women need to be "put in their place." The greater the inequality and the more the woman is dependent on the man, the more likely the abuse. Adams and Williams (2014) emphasized that

violence among Mexican American adolescents is sometimes normative in the context of jealousy. Hence the partner is seen as property and when who has access to this property is violated, violence may be legitimized.

Some occupations, such as police officers and military personnel, lend themselves to contexts of gender inequality. In military contexts, men notoriously devalue, denigrate, and sexually harass women. In spite of the rhetoric about gender equality in the military, women in the Army, Navy, and Air Force academies continue to be sexually harassed. In 2012, according to the Department of Defense, there were 26,000 sexual assaults in the military, yet only about 14% filed a complaint. Holland et al. (2016) noted that military sexual trauma occurs from sexual assault in the military coupled with the feeling of being unsafe from sexual assault—individuals feel that they would be viewed as weak, that leaders would treat them differently, and that coworkers would have less confidence in them if they became visible.

10-2b Community Factors

Community violence itself presents in the form of robberies, stabbings, and shootings. Kennedy and Ceballo (2016) found that urban youth become desensitized to such events over time. Nevertheless, factors that contribute to violence and abuse in the family include social isolation, poverty, and inaccessible or unaffordable health care, day care, elder care, and respite care services and facilities.

SOCIAL ISOLATION Living in social isolation from extended family and community members increases the risk of being abused. Spouses whose parents live nearby are least vulnerable.

POVERTY Abuse in adult relationships occurs among all socioeconomic groups. However, poverty and low socioeconomic status are a context of high stress which lends itself to expression of this stress by violence and abuse in interpersonal relationships.

INACCESSIBLE OR UNAFFORDABLE COMMUNITY SERVICES Failure to provide medical care to children and elderly family members sometimes results from the lack of accessible or affordable health care services in the community. Without elder care and respite care facilities, families living in social isolation may not have any help with the stresses of caring for elderly family members and children.

10-2c Individual Factors

Elmquist et al. (2016) studied individuals' motivations for physical dating violence. The researchers found that 29.4% of their sample of male (163) and female (319) college students reported being the perpetrator of dating violence. Of the various motivations, including power/control, self-defense, expression of negative emotion—anger, communication difficulties, retaliation, jealousy, and other (e.g., sexually arousing, influence of alcohol or drugs), communication and self-defense were the most frequently identified motives by both women and men.

Individual factors also associated with domestic violence and abuse include psychopathology, personality characteristics, and alcohol or substance abuse. A number of personality characteristics have also been associated with people who are abusive in their intimate relationships. Some of these characteristics follow:

honor crime (honor killing) refers to unmarried women who are killed because they bring shame on their parents and siblings; occurs in Middle Eastern countries such as Jordan.

1. **Dependency.** Therapists who work with batterers have observed that they are overly dependent on their partners. Because the thought of being left by their partners induces panic and abandonment anxiety, batterers use physical aggression and threats of suicide to keep their partners with them.

2. **Jealousy.** Along with dependence, batterers exhibit jealousy, possessiveness, and suspicion. An abusive husband may express his possessiveness by isolating his wife from others; he may insist she stay at home, not work, and not socialize with others. His extreme, irrational jealousy may lead him to accuse his wife of infidelity and to beat her for her presumed affair.

3. **Need to control.** Abusive partners have an excessive need to exercise power over their partners and to control them. The abusers do not let their partners make independent decisions (including what to wear), and they want to know where their partners are, whom they are with, and what they are doing. Abusers like to be in charge of all aspects of family life, including finances and recreation.

4. **Unhappiness and dissatisfaction.** Abusive partners often report being unhappy and dissatisfied with their lives, both at home and at work. Many abusers have low self-esteem and high levels of anxiety, depression, and hostility. They may take out their frustration with life on their partner.

5. **History of aggressiveness.** Abusers often have a history of interpersonal aggressive behavior. They have poor impulse control and can become instantly enraged and lash out at the partner. Battered women report that episodes of violence are often triggered by minor events, such as a late meal or a shirt that has not been ironed.

6. **Quick involvement.** Because of feelings of insecurity, the potential batterer will rush his partner quickly into a committed relationship. If the woman tries to break off the relationship, the man will often try to make her feel guilty for not giving him and the relationship a chance.

7. **Blaming others for problems.** Abusers take little responsibility for their problems and blame everyone else.

Andris Torms/Shutterstock.com

8. **Jekyll-and-Hyde personality.** Abusers have sudden mood changes so that a partner is continually confused. One minute an abuser is nice, and the next minute angry and accusatory. Explosiveness and moodiness are the norm.

9. **Isolation.** An abusive person will try to cut off a partner from all family, friends, and activities. Ties with anyone are prohibited. Isolation may reach the point at which an abuser tries to stop the victim from going to school, church, or work.

10. **Alcohol and other drug use.** Whether alcohol reduces one's inhibitions to display violence, allows one to avoid responsibility for being violent, or increases one's aggression, it is associated with violence and abuse (Foshee et al., 2016). Being antisocial and having no empathy are also associated with violence/abuse (Romero-Martinez et al., 2016).

11. **Criminal/psychiatric background.** Eke et al. (2011) examined the characteristics of 146 men who murdered or attempted to murder their intimate partner. Of these, 42% had prior criminal charges, 15% had a psychiatric history, and 18% had both Shorey et al. (2012) identified the mental health problems in men arrested for domestic violence and found high rates of PTSD, depression, generalized anxiety disorder (GAD), panic disorder, and social phobia.

12. **Impulsive.** Miller et al. (2012) identified one of the most prominent personality characteristics associated with aggression/abuse. "Impulsive behavior in the context of negative affect" was consistently related to aggression across multiple indices.

10-2d Relationship Factors

Halpern-Meekin et al. (2013) studied a sample of 792 relationships and found that "relationship churning" was associated with both physical and emotional violence. The researchers compared relationships which had ended, those which were still together, and those which had an on-and-off pattern (churners). Individuals in the latter type relationship were twice as likely to report physical violence and half again as likely to report emotional abuse compared to the other two patterns.

10-2e Family Factors

Family factors associated with domestic violence and abuse include being abused as a child, having parents who abused each other, and not having a father in the home.

CHILD ABUSE IN FAMILY OF ORIGIN Individuals who were abused as children are more likely to be abusive toward their intimate partners as adults. Indeed, they feel that violence in dating relationships is both normative and acceptable (Lee et al., 2016).

FAMILY CONFLICT Children learn abuse from their family context. Children whose fathers were not affectionate were more likely to be abusive to their own children.

PARENTS WHO ABUSE EACH OTHER Parents who are aggressive toward each other create a norm of aggression in the family and are more likely to be aggressive toward their children (Graham et al., 2012). While most parents are not aggressive toward each other in front of their children (Pendry et al., 2011), Dominguez et al. (2013) reconfirmed the link between witnessing parental abuse (either father or mother abusive toward the other) and being in an abusive relationship as an adult. However, a majority of children who witness abuse do not continue the pattern—a family history of violence is only one factor out of many associated with a greater probability of adult violence.

Finally, Cascardi (2016) also found that being the victim of violence in the home and observing the violence between one's parents were associated with being the victim of violence by one's partner. The author suggested that such violence may reduce one's feelings of self-esteem in one's own relationships and undermine one's acuity to a harmful relationship. However, a majority of children who experience or witness abuse do not continue the pattern—a family history of violence is only one factor out of many associated with a greater probability of adult violence.

10-3 SEXUAL ABUSE IN UNDERGRADUATE RELATIONSHIPS

Based on data from the National Crime Victimization Survey (NCVS) of rape and sexual assault victimization against females aged 18 to 24 who are enrolled and not enrolled in college, rape and sexual assault were 1.2 times higher for nonstudents (7.6 per 1,000) than for students (6.1 per 1,000), but the rate of not reporting sexual victimization to police was higher among students than nonstudents (80% versus 67%) (Langston & Sinozich, 2014).

The Hunting Ground is a 2015 documentary on rape crimes on U.S. college and university campuses, the

WHAT'S NEW?

Technology and Intimate Partner Violence

Technology has been used to inflict harassment, abuse, and violence against women (Stoleru & Costescu, 2014). Survivors of intimate partner violence (IPV) report being stalked by abusers through the use of cameras, GPS tracking, and spyware (Southworth et al., 2007). Small cameras can be placed in the victim's home. GPS tracking devices can be placed on the victim's car.

Spyware allows unauthorized monitoring of an individual's activities via computer and/or phone and can be installed remotely by sending an email, photo, or instant message. The presence of spyware is usually undetectable and difficult to eliminate (NNEDV, 2009). Unwanted calls can be blocked, but there are applications that allow callers to falsify or "spoof" their identities so that blocked calls may still pass through. Other technologies such as texting can be a significant barrier for leaving an abusive relationship. Halligan et al. (2013) found that rejected lovers would "blow up" the victim's cell phone (send repeated text messages all day) by accusing and threatening the victim so that "moving on" became difficult. Although technology can be used for stalking and intimidation, it can also enhance investigation and prosecution of IPV. Digital forensics and virtual investigation have aided in better understanding perpetrator behaviors (al-Khateeb & Epiphaniou, 2016).

The stigma of IPV including shame, guilt, and fear may hinder disclosure (McCleary-Sills et al., 2016). Instead of calling a hotline or contacting professionals face to face, survivors have turned to websites. Caution must be taken when using the Internet to reach out for help since one's computer records online activity automatically and one's search history may be uncovered by abusers. Therefore, safety measures such as using a public computer or enabling the private browsing mode should be considered. The private browsing mode is available on most web browsers such as Safari (private browsing) and Google Chrome (incognito). The private browsing mode cannot fend off computer viruses, but can protect private information from being tracked and any websites visited while using the private browsing mode would not be stored in the computer search history.

The National Network to End Domestic Violence launched the Safety Net Project to address issues surrounding the intersection of technology and IPV. This project offers resources such as "Who's spying on your computer?" and "Technology safety quick tips" to enhance safety, privacy, and confidentiality. Smartphone apps have played an increasingly active role in the fight against assault and violence.

Personal safety apps such as bSafe, Guardly, and Circle of 6 attempt to assist various safety issues such as walking alone, dating violence, abusive relationships, and stalking (Bouman, 2013; Lee, 2011). The One Love MyPlan app, sponsored by the National Institute of Health and Centers for Disease Control, enables access to a trained advocate 24/7 through live chat. In addition, this app provides a decision aid for friends who are concerned about the safety of a friend's relationship (Glass et al., 2015; Kaiser Permanente, 2016). These apps empower users and bystanders by providing easy access to resources, help, safety networks, and real-time GPS location tracking.

Although these technological innovations are brilliant additions to expand services, they cannot rescue people from life-threatening situations. Technological advances have simultaneously encouraged different manifestations of violence, such as obsession and control, while also providing innovative resources and interventions to survivors.

institutional cover-ups, and the devastation on the lives of the victims. The title comes from the fact that males on campus can "hunt" for and rape their prey with relative impunity (20% of university coeds are sexually assaulted with less that 5% of the alleged rapists prosecuted).

Sexual coercion, which involves using force (actual or threatened) to engage a person in sexual acts against that person's will, may be of four types: verbal coercion until the person gives in, someone does something sexual to a partner without asking for her or his consent, someone does something sexual to the person while she or he is intoxicated/asleep, or someone uses or threatens to use physical force so that the sex happens under duress (Mustapha & Muehlenhard, 2014; Raghavan et al., 2015). Some sexual assaults begin as flirting at parties in the context of alcohol that result in hooking up. The cues about how much sex the partner is willing to engage in are ambiguous (Yazedjian & Toews, 2015).

Sexual coercion often takes place in the context of an abusive relationship (referred to as covictimization) (Katz & Rich, 2015). Indeed, emotional, physical, and sexual aggression are more likely to occur in committed relationships (69%) but may also occur in casual sexual relationships (31–36%) such as friends with benefits, booty calls, and hooking up relationships (Klipfel et al., 2014). A study of individuals who persisted in obtaining sex after an initial refusal noted that verbal pressure, existing intoxication, and promoting intoxication were the primary tactics to get a partner to relent (Smeaton & Anderson, 2014).

Tasteless and odorless, Rophypnol, the "date rape" drug, results in victims losing their memory for 8 to 10 hours.

Rommel Canlas/Shutterstock.com

10-3a Acquaintance and Date Rape

About 85% of rapes are perpetrated by someone the woman knows (12% of victims have been raped by both an acquaintance and a stranger—**double victims**) (Hall & Knox, 2012). The type of rape by someone the victim knows is referred to as **acquaintance rape**, which is defined as nonconsensual sex between adults (of the same or other sex) who know each other. The behaviors of sexual coercion occur on a continuum from verbal pressure and threats to use of physical force to obtain sexual acts, such as oral sex, sexual intercourse, and anal sex. The event is traumatic and associated with the use of marijuana the following day by the female victim of date rape (Shorey et al., 2016).

The perpetrator of a rape is likely to believe in various rape myths. **Female rape myths** are beliefs about the female that deny that she was raped or cast blame on the woman for her own rape. These beliefs are false, widely held, and justify male aggression. Examples include: "women deserve to be raped" (particularly when they drink too much and are provocatively dressed); "women fantasize about and secretly want to be raped"; and "women who really don't want to be raped resist more—they could stop a guy if they really wanted to." Carroll et al. (2016) confirmed that men are more likely to accept female rape myths than women.

There are also **male rape myths** such as "men can't be raped" and "men who are raped are gay."

One type of acquaintance rape is **date rape**, which refers to nonconsensual sex between people who are dating or on a date. The woman (while both women and men may be raped on a date, we will refer to the female since male–female rape is more prevalent) has no idea that rape is on the agenda. She may have gone out to dinner, had a pleasant evening, and gone back to her apartment with her date only to be raped. Whether she reports the rape is related to her perceptions of perceived norms on campus—do peers who are raped report the incidence (Rodgers et al., 2015)?

10-3b Sexual Abuse in Same-Sex Relationships

Rape also occurs in same-sex relationships. Gay, lesbian, and bisexual individuals are not immune to experiencing sexual abuse in their relationships. Rothman et al. (2011) reviewed studies which involved a total sample of 139,635 gay, lesbian, and bisexual women and men and found that the highest estimates reported for lifetime sexual assault were for lesbian and bisexual women (85%). In regard to childhood sexual assault of lesbian and bisexual women the percentage was 76%. For childhood sexual assault of gay and bisexual men, it was 59%.

10-3c Alcohol and Rape

Alcohol is the most common rape drug. A person under the influence cannot give consent. Hence, a person who has sex with someone who is impaired is engaging in rape. Some bars encourage female drinking. Results of a study by Buvik and Baklien (2016) revealed that intoxicated females were more likely to be served alcohol than intoxicated men. One explanation is that intoxicated women are good for

double victims individuals who report being a victim of forced sex by both a stranger and by a date or acquaintance.

acquaintance rape nonconsensual sex between adults (of same or other sex) who know each other.

female rape myths beliefs that deny victim injury or cast blame on the woman for her own rape.

male rape myths beliefs that deny victim injury or make assumptions about his sexual orientation.

date rape one type of acquaintance rape which refers to nonconsensual sex between people who are dating or are on a date.

business in that men are more likely to remain in the bar and to spend money. In addition, intoxicated women are viewed as more available to have sex not only with the patrons but with the bar staff.

10-3d Rophypnol: The Date Rape Drug

Rophypnol—also known as the date rape drug, rope, roofies, Mexican Valium, or the "forget (me) pill"—causes profound, prolonged sedation and short-term memory loss. Similar to Valium but 10 times as strong, Rophypnol is a prescription drug used as a potent sedative in Europe. It is sold in the United States for about $5, is dropped in a drink (where it is tasteless and odorless), and causes victims to lose their memory for 8 to 10 hours. During this time, victims may be raped yet be unaware until they notice signs of it (e.g., blood in panties) the next morning.

The Drug-Induced Rape Prevention and Punishment Act of 1996 makes it a crime to give a controlled substance to anyone without his or her knowledge and with the intent of committing a violent crime (such as rape). Violation of this law is punishable by up to 20 years in prison and a fine of $250,000.

10-3e Reducing Sexual Violence on Campus

Eggett and Irvin (2016) reviewed 29 research articles on sexual violence prevention programs on campus. While all claimed "success" (e.g., reduced rape myths, increased bystander effectiveness), only one reported a reduction of the sexual assaults on campus. The researchers concluded that colleges and universities need to reduce parental anxiety by showing that the administration is engaged in keeping the campus safe. The reality is that almost none of programs reduce sexual violence on campus.

10-3f Male Rape

Rape is usually discussed as a female issue. O'Brien et al. (2016) studied rape in the military and confirmed that half of military sexual assault survivors are men. Men are restrained by culture from making visible their abuse due to myths such as real men can't be raped, rape is a homosexual issue, and rape by a woman is not serious. Nevertheless, men are traumatized by the experience and have limited healing venues.

Rophypnol causes profound, prolonged sedation and short-term memory loss; also known as the date rape drug, roofies, Mexican Valium, or the "forget (me) pill."

marital rape forcible rape by one's spouse—a crime in all states.

ABUSE IN MARRIAGE RELATIONSHIPS

The chance of abuse in a relationship increases with marriage. Indeed, the longer individuals know each other and the more intimate their relationship, the greater the abuse.

10-4a General Abuse in Marriage

Abuse in marriage may differ from unmarried abuse in that the husband may feel ownership of the wife and feel the need to control her. But the behaviors of abuse are the same—belittling the spouse, controlling the spouse, physically hurting the spouse, etc. The Personal View section provides the horror of abuse inside one marriage.

10-4b Men Who Abuse

Henning and Connor-Smith (2011) studied a large sample of men who were recently convicted of violence toward a female intimate partner (N = 1,130). More than half of the men (59%) reported that they were continuing or planning to continue the relationship with the partner they had abused. Reasons included being older (e.g., too late to start over), being married to the victim, having children together, attributing less blame to the victim for the recent offense, and having a childhood history of family violence.

10-4c Rape in Marriage

Marital rape, now recognized in all states as a crime, is forcible rape (includes vaginal, oral, anal) by one's spouse. Some states (Washington) recognize a marital defense exception for third-degree rape in which force is not used even though there is no consent. Over 30 countries (e.g., China, Afghanistan, Pakistan) have no laws against marital rape.

There are many who don't wish to sleep for fear of nightmares. Sadly, there are many who don't wish to wake for the same fear.

—RICHELLE E. GOODRICH,
DANDELIONS: THE DISAPPEARANCE OF ANNABELLE FANCHER

Not 12 Years a Slave but 13 Years an Abused Wife

I was verbally, physically, and sexually abused for 13 years in my marriage from ages 22–34. I never had any hint during the two years we were dating that the man I loved (he was my soul mate) would end up making my life a living hell. He was a little jealous but I thought this was cute and that he cared about me. In fact he made me feel special . . . he made me feel LOVED . . . we could talk for hours and hours.

The very next day after we were married, when I came home from work he had put all my dresses and skirts on the bed with the hem taken out of them . . . I wondered what in the world I had gotten myself into.

The abuse occurred mostly when he had been drinking:

- **Accusations** . . . accusing me of sleeping with any-one breathing.
- **Fear** . . . he jumped at me . . . got into my face . . . he threatened me with bodily harm . . . anything to intimidate me.
- **Shame** . . . he belittled me, called me names, cussed at me.
- **Control** . . . he got mad at me for visiting my family
- **Physical abuse** . . . he pushed, pinched, squeezed, spit, and pulled a gun on me.
- **Rape** . . . he forced me to have sex with him (when he was drunk he would last forever).

He would stay out all night; come home and wake me up . . . and accuse me of going out and being with someone else . . . (looked for stamps on my hand from a club).

Black eyes were common . . . I kept sunglasses on for about 5–6 years . . . I will never forget one night when he was on top of me . . . he had me pinned down just hitting me in the face with his fist just as hard as he could.

He once backhanded me and knocked four of my front teeth loose (they later died and had to be pulled). I now have a plate in my mouth.

Another time he picked me up and slung me across the room with both of my legs hitting the coffee table and seriously bruising the front shins of my legs. Today, I still have problems . . . broken veins and poor circulation in my lower legs.

I left him many times . . . he would always talk me into coming back . . . buying me back . . . he would start back to church with me and we would go to church for months . . . then he would start his drinking again.

I once called the police and he was arrested . . . but I dropped the charges. The reason I stayed is because I loved him and when he wasn't drinking he was perfect and treated me right. But his abuse was changing my personality and one time I lost it and pulled a gun on him . . . so I knew it was time to go . . . I have since forgiven him and moved on. The message to my daughter and other young people is to make a deliberate choice to get out immediately after the abuse starts.

Source: Abridged and used with the permission of Teresa Carol Wimberly.

10-5 EFFECTS OF ABUSE

Abuse has devastating effects on the physical and psychological well-being of victims. Abuse between parents also affects the children.

10-5a Effects of Partner Abuse on Victims

Abuse has devastating consequences. Being a victim of intimate partner violence is associated with symptoms of depression, anxiety, fear, feeling detached from others, inability to sleep, and irritability. Victims may become involved in individual therapy or couple therapy or both (Maharaj, 2016).

10-5b Effects of Partner Abuse on Children

The most dramatic effects of abuse occur on pregnant women, which include increased risk of miscarriage, birth defects, low birth weight, preterm delivery, and neonatal death. Negative effects may also accrue to children who witness domestic abuse (e.g., depression).

Bobby Davis

10-6 THE CYCLE OF ABUSE

The cycle of abuse begins when a person is abused and the perpetrator feels regret, asks for forgiveness, and engages in positive behavior (gives flowers). The victim, who perceives few options and feels anxious terminating the relationship with the abusive partner, feels hope for the relationship at the contriteness of the abuser and does not call the police or file charges.

After the forgiveness, couples usually experience a period of making up or honeymooning, during which the victim feels good again about the partner and is hopeful for a nonabusive future. However, stress, anxiety, and tension mount again in the relationship, which the abuser relieves by violence toward the victim. Such violence is followed by the familiar sense of regret and pleadings for forgiveness, accompanied by a new round of positive behavior (flowers and candy).

> To not have your suffering recognized is an almost unbearable form of violence.
>
> —ANDREI LANKOV

As the cycle of abuse reveals, some victims do not prosecute their partners who abuse them. In response to this problem, Los Angeles has adopted a zero tolerance policy toward domestic violence. Under the law, an arrested person is required to stand trial and his victim required to testify against the perpetrator. The sentence in Los Angeles County for partner abuse is up to six months in jail and a fine of $1,000.

Figure 10.1 illustrates this cycle, which occurs in clockwise fashion. In the rest of this section, we discuss reasons why people stay in an abusive relationships and how to get out of them.

10-6a Why Victims Stay in Abusive Relationships

The primary reason female victims of abuse return again and again to an abusive relationship is the emotional attachment to her partner—she is in love. While someone who criticizes ("you're ugly/stupid/pitiful"), is dishonest (sexually unfaithful), or

FIGURE 10.1 THE CYCLE OF ABUSE

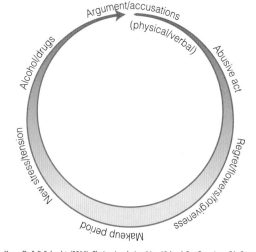

Source: Knox, D., & C. Schacht. (2016). *Choices in relationships*, 12th ed. San Francisco, CA: Cengage.

physically harms a partner will create a context of interpersonal misery, the victim might still love that person.

Other reasons were identified by Cravens et al. (2015), who conducted a content analysis of Twitter posts in the wake of the abuse by Ray Rice and his fiancé:

▶ Rationalization ("I felt like it was my fault . . . I should have listened to him more.)"

▶ Fear ("I was afraid of him—he'd make leaving an ugly drawn out nightmare.")

▶ Savior ("I believed I could love the abuse out of him.")

▶ Commitment ("I was determined to make it work.")

▶ Help partner ("He needed me to make his life better.")

▶ Children ("I was afraid if he wasn't beating me, he would beat the children.")

Still other reasons identified by our students included:

▶ Fear of loneliness ("I'd rather be with someone who abuses me than alone.")

▶ Emotional dependency ("I needed him.")

▶ Hope ("He will stop being abusive—he's just not himself lately.")

▶ A view of violence as legitimate ("All relationships include some abuse.")

▶ Guilt ("I can't leave a sick man.")

▶ Economic dependence ("I have no money and no place to go.")

▶ Isolation ("I don't know anyone who can help me.")

▶ No alternative ("I have nowhere to go/no one else to go to.")

▶ Negative self-concept ("I am not such a good catch . . . this is the best I can do.")

▶ Deserve abuse ("I deserve to be abused.")

Another explanation for why some people remain with abusive partners is that the abuse is only one part of the relationship. When such partners are not being abusive, they are kind, caring, and loving. It is these positive behaviors which keep the victim hooked. The psychological term is a **periodic reinforcement** which means that every now and then the abusive person "floods" the partner with strong love/positives which keep the partner in the relationship. In effect, the person who is abused stays in the relationship since it includes positives such as flowers, gifts, or declarations of love to entice a partner to stay in the relationship.

Halligan et al. (2013) noted the impact of technology on the maintenance of abusive relationships. She and her colleagues found that undergraduates in abusive relationships could not stop themselves from checking their text messages—even if the message was from an abusive partner. Some of the messages from the abusive partners included an apology, a promise to never be abusive again, and a request to resume the relationship.

Battered women also stay in abusive relationships because they rarely have escape routes related to educational or employment opportunities, they do not want to disrupt the lives of their children, and they may be so emotionally devastated by the abuse (anxious, depressed, or suffering from low self-esteem) that they feel incapable of planning and executing their departure.

Disengaging from an abusive relationship is a process that takes time. One should not be discouraged when they see a friend return to an abusive context but recognize that progress in disengagement is occurring (she did it once) and that positive movement is predictive of eventually getting out.

10-6b Fighting Back? What Is the Best Strategy?

How might a partner respond when being physically abused? First, the goal is to avoid serious physical injury. Such injury is increased if the partner is drunk, on drugs, or has a weapon so forceful physical resistance (pushing, striking, struggling) to the mind-altered partner should be avoided.

periodic reinforcement reinforcement that occurs every now and then (unpredictable). The abused victim never knows when the abuser will be polite and kind again (e.g., flowers and candy).

Nordling/Shutterstock.com

Verbal resistance (pleading, crying, or trying to assuage the offender) or nonforceful physical resistance (fleeing or hiding) might be more helpful in avoiding injury. Fortunately, the frequency of severe injury is low (7%) with most (69%) abusive incidents resulting in no injury (Powers & Simpson, 2012). Of course, any abuse in an intimate relationship may be too much and should be avoided or the relationship ended.

10-6c Triggers for Leaving an Abusive Relationship

A study of 123 survivors of past abusive relationships revealed the triggers operative for their decision to end an abusive relationship (Murray et al., 2015). These were (1) facing the threat of severe violence (e.g., the victims felt their life or that of their child was in danger); (2) changing their perspective about the relationship, abuse, and/or their partner (e.g., concluding that things would never improve but would only get worse); (3) learning about the dynamics of abuse (e.g., cycle of abuse); (4) experiencing an intervention from external sources (e.g., friend told me I was being destroyed and should leave); (5) realizing the impact of the violence on children (e.g., children were learning to be aggressive); and (6) the relationship being terminated by the abuser (e.g., husband had affair and left). Some of the respondents could not identify a trigger.

> I never had a turning point but always knew I needed to get out of the situation, I just didn't know how without having to move away from my family who was my main support. Therefore I felt "stuck" in my situation. (p. 236)

Cravens et al. (2015) noted that clarity about self ("I deserve better"), partner ("It was not up to me to change him"), or relationship ("Someone who loves you will make an effort instead of excuses") were related to leaving. In addition, some abused women felt it important that they be a good role model for their children and not stay in an abusive relationship since children might think this was OK.

10-6d How to Leave an Abusive Relationship

Couple therapy to reduce abuse in an abusive relationship is hampered by the fact of previous abuse. Being a victim of previous psychological aggression (female or male) is related to fear of speaking in front of the partner and fear of being in therapy with the partner (O'Leary et al., 2013). Hence, gains may be minimal.

> Sure relationships include arguments, but pain is not a side-effect of love.
>
> —TYLER OAKLEY, *BINGE*

Leaving an abusive partner begins with the person making a plan and acting on the plan—packing clothes/belongings, moving in with a sister, mother, or friend, or going to a homeless shelter. If the new context is better than being in the abusive context, the person will stay away. Otherwise, the person may go back and start the cycle all over. As noted previously, this leaving and returning typically happens seven times.

Sometimes the woman does not leave while the abuser is at work but calls the police and has the man arrested for violence and abuse. While the abuser is in jail, she may move out and leave town. In either case, disengagement from the abusive relationship takes a great deal of courage. Calling the National Domestic Violence Hotline (800-799-7233 [SAFE]), available 24 hours, is a point of beginning.

Taking out a protective order whereby the accused is prohibited from being within close proximity of the victim partner is one option some abused partners take. While Kothari et al. (2012) confirmed that taking out such an order against a partner who has engaged in intimate partner violence was associated with a reduced frequency of repeated violence against the victim, other research is less clear. Ward et al. (2014) studied the effect of involving the police when interpersonal abuse occurs and found a different answer. When there was a history of abuse, there was an increased likelihood of future violent offending subsequent to police contact. When there was no history of abuse, there seemed to be no change, no increase in violence. So what is a person in an abusive relationship to do? The best answer seems to be to take the position that the abusive behavior will continue and to removing oneself from the abusive context and stay in a safe context.

10-6e Treatment of Abusers

In the typical situation where men perpetrate violence on women, Satyanarayana et al. (2016) confirmed the effectiveness of integrative cognitive behavioral intervention in group therapy contexts designed to reduce subsequent violent acts against one's partner. Relaxation techniques, anger management, and cognitive reframing were skills the previous perpetrators found helpful.

However, Armenti and Babcock (2016) emphasized that men-only treatment groups miss at least a third of the perpetrators of violence and abuse—women.

10-7 TRENDS IN ABUSE IN RELATIONSHIPS

Prevention of relationship violence/abuse is a daunting task. Just as the causes are cultural (culture of violence), gender scripted (aggressive males) with drugs available (e.g., alcohol), singular workshops/training prevention programs might be expected to have little impact. Fellmeth et al. (2015) assessed the efficacy of educational and skills-based interventions to prevent relationship and dating violence in adolescents and young adults across a broad spectrum of research (38 studies involving 15,903 participants) and found no evidence of effectiveness of interventions on episodes of violence, attitudes, or behaviors.

However, progress toward reducing sexual assaults on college and university campuses is under way. Title IX is designed to empower students to combat campus violence/rape. The law requires colleges and universities receiving federal funding to take seriously a complaint of violence/rape either by filing a federal complaint or a civil lawsuit. Schools in violation would be fined $150,000 per violation and up to 1% of their operating budget for failure to investigate reports of sexual assault on campus. The reality of universities taking rape on campus seriously is slow to take hold. Brock Turner, a Stanford undergraduate, served three months in jail for raping an unconscious female on campus—a slap on the wrist for a heinous crime.

Reducing family violence through education involves altering aspects of American culture that contribute to such violence. For example, violence in the media must be curbed (not easy, with nightly news clips of bombing assaults in other countries, gun shootings, violent films, etc.).

Bennett et al. (2014) emphasized the need for bystander intervention programs, which sensitizes individuals to be aware of abuse and to intervene. Hines and Palm-Reed (2015) found that such bystander programs led by peer educators are more effective in altering attitudes.

Finally, Lippy and DeGue (2016) suggested that since most campus rapes occur in the context of alcohol, tightening alcohol policies is one path to reducing campus rapes.

Abuse in relationships will continue to occur behind closed doors, in private contexts where the abuse is undetected. Reducing such abuse will depend on prevention strategies focused at three levels: the general population, specific groups at high risk for abuse, and individuals/couples who have already experienced abuse. Public education and media campaigns aimed at the general population will continue to convey the criminal nature of domestic assault, suggest ways the abused might learn escape from abuse, and identify where abuse victims and perpetrators can get help.

Another important cultural change is to reduce violence-provoking stress by reducing poverty and unemployment and by providing adequate housing, nutrition, medical care, and educational opportunities for everyone. Integrating families into networks of community and kin would also enhance family well-being and provide support for families under stress.

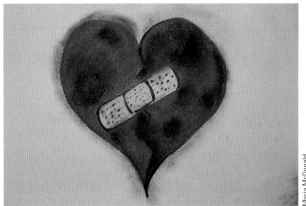

Maria McDonald

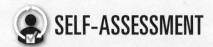

SELF-ASSESSMENT

Abusive Behavior Inventory

Circle the number that best represents your closest estimate of how often each of the behaviors have happened in the relationship with your current or former partner during the previous six months.

1.	Called you a name and/or criticized you	1	2	3	4	5
2.	Tried to keep you from doing something you wanted to do (e.g., going out with friends or going to meetings)	1	2	3	4	5
3.	Gave you angry stares or looks	1	2	3	4	5
4.	Prevented you from having money for your own use	1	2	3	4	5
5.	Ended a discussion and made a decision without you	1	2	3	4	5
6.	Threatened to hit or throw something at you	1	2	3	4	5
7.	Pushed, grabbed, or shoved you	1	2	3	4	5
8.	Put down your family and friends	1	2	3	4	5
9.	Accused you of paying too much attention to someone or something else	1	2	3	4	5
10.	Put you on an allowance	1	2	3	4	5
11.	Used your children to threaten you (e.g., told you that you would lose custody or threatened to leave town with the children)	1	2	3	4	5
12.	Became very upset with you because dinner, housework, or laundry was not done when or how it was wanted	1	2	3	4	5
13.	Said things to scare you (e.g., told you something "bad" would happen or threatened to commit suicide)	1	2	3	4	5
14.	Slapped, hit, or punched you	1	2	3	4	5
15.	Made you do something humiliating or degrading (e.g., begging for forgiveness or having to ask permission to use the car or do something)	1	2	3	4	5
16.	Checked up on you (e.g., listened to your phone calls, checked the mileage on your car, or called you repeatedly at work)	1	2	3	4	5
17.	Drove recklessly when you were in the car	1	2	3	4	5
18.	Pressured you to have sex in a way you didn't like or want	1	2	3	4	5
19.	Refused to do housework or child care	1	2	3	4	5
20.	Threatened you with a knife, gun, or other weapon	1	2	3	4	5
21.	Spanked you	1	2	3	4	5
22.	Told you that you were a bad parent	1	2	3	4	5
23.	Stopped you or tried to stop you from going to work or school	1	2	3	4	5
24.	Threw, hit, kicked, or smashed something	1	2	3	4	5
25.	Kicked you	1	2	3	4	5
26.	Physically forced you to have sex	1	2	3	4	5
27.	Threw you around	1	2	3	4	5
28.	Physically attacked the sexual parts of your body	1	2	3	4	5
29.	Choked or strangled you	1	2	3	4	5
30.	Used a knife, gun, or other weapon against you	1	2	3	4	5

Add the numbers you circled and divide the total by 30 to determine your score. The higher your score (5 is the highest score), the more abusive your relationship.

The inventory was given to 100 men and 78 women equally divided into groups of abusers or abused and nonabusers or nonabused. The men were members of a chemical dependency treatment program in a veterans' hospital and the women were partners of these men. Abusing or abused men earned an average score of 1.8; abusing or abused women earned an average score of 2.3. Nonabusing, abused men and women earned scores of 1.3 and 1.6, respectively.

Source: Shepard, M. F., & J. A. Campbell. The Abusive Behavior Inventory: A measure of psychological and physical abuse. *Journal of Interpersonal Violence, 7*(3):291–305, 1992.

11 | Deciding about Children

Bobby Davis

After finishing
this chapter go
to **PAGE 223** for
STUDY TOOLS

> Everything I thought I'd hate about having children—the crying, the screaming—nothing fazes me. I love it all, and it's relaxed me.
>
> —ELTON JOHN

"That's when our marriage fell off a cliff," recalled a couple on the impact of children on their marriage. "You have to live through having a child to know what doing so is all about—no book, documentary, or advice from other parents can prepare you for what having children is like." Most individuals want children. In a sample of 9,711 undergraduates, 91% (a similar percent for both women and men) reported wanting children (Hall & Knox, 2016). And most individuals have the number of children that they want (Gunther et al., 2016). Part of the impact of having children is related to the planning of children—the subject of this chapter.

While individuals may feel there is no need for family planning, since individual choices impact others, there remains a need

karen roach/Shutterstock.com

for individual responsibility. Marcell et al. (2016) surveyed young unmarried men aged 15 to 44 in the United States and concluded that 60% of men were in need of family planning—they were having vaginal sex, were fecund (capable of reproducing), and had fecund partner(s). Yet only a fourth consistently used condoms; only 41% had parents who consistently used contraception. Unintended pregnancies do occur—reported 40% of a national sample of women and men in Australia (Rowe et al., 2016).

Planning when to become pregnant has benefits for both the mother and the child. Having several children at short intervals increases the chances of premature birth, infectious disease, and death of the mother or the baby. Would-be parents can minimize such risks by planning fewer children with longer intervals.

11-1 DO YOU WANT TO HAVE CHILDREN?

Beyond a biological drive to reproduce (which not all adults experience), societies socialize their members to have children. Unless children are born, the society will cease to exist. In this section, we examine the social influences that motivate individuals to have children, the lifestyle changes that result from such a choice, and the costs of rearing children.

11-1a Social Influences Motivating Individuals to Have Children

Our society tends to encourage childbearing, an attitude known as **pronatalism**. Our family, friends, religion, and government encourage positive attitudes toward parenthood. Cultural observances also function to reinforce these attitudes.

FAMILY Our experience of being reared in families encourages us to have families of our own. Our parents are our models. They married; we marry. They had children; we have children. We also expect to have a "happy family."

FRIENDS Our friends who have children influence us to do likewise. Decisions are made in social context. Notice how many of your decisions are identical to those of your close friends—if you want to know, whether, when, and how many children a person will have, find out what decisions their three closest friends have made. Most undergraduates just out of high school have no interest in being married and having children while in school—a value shared by almost 100% of their peers.

RELIGION Religion is a strong influence on an individual's decision to have children. Catholics are taught that having children is the basic purpose (procreation) of marriage and gives meaning to the union. Mormons and ultra-Orthodox Jews also have a strong interest in having and rearing children.

RACE Hispanics have the highest fertility rate of any racial/ethnic category.

GOVERNMENT The taxes (or lack of them) that our federal and state governments impose support parenthood. Although individuals have children for more emotional than financial reasons, married couples with children pay lower taxes than married couples without children. Assume there are two couples (one married couple with two children and one childfree married couple), each making $100,000. The couple with children would pay $1,950 less in federal tax than the childfree couple.

pronatalism cultural attitude which encourages having children.

The smile of a new baby cancels thoughts of costs and lifestyle changes for new parents.

CULTURAL OBSERVANCES Our society reaffirms its value for having children by identifying special days for Mom and Dad. Each year on Mother's Day and Father's Day (and now Grandparents' Day), parenthood is celebrated across the nation with cards, gifts, and embraces. People choosing not to have children have no cultural counterpart (e.g., Childfree Day). In addition to influencing individuals to have children, society and culture also influence feelings about the age parents should be when they have children. Recently, couples have been having children at later ages. Is this a good idea?

11-1b Individual Motivations for Having Children

While social influences are important, so are individual motivations in the decision to have children. Some of these inducements are obvious as in the desire to love and to be loved by one's own child, companionship, and the desire to be personally fulfilled as an adult by having a child. Some people also want to recapture their own childhood and youth by having a child. Motives that are less obvious may also be operative—wanting a child to avoid career tracking (e.g., "I'd rather have a baby than tenure") and to gain the acceptance and approval of one's parents and peers.

11-1c Evaluation of Lifestyle Changes

Becoming a parent often involves changes in lifestyle. Daily living routines become focused around the needs of the children. Living arrangements change to provide space for another person in the household.

procreative liberty the freedom to decide to have children or not.

Some parents change their work schedule to allow them to be home more. Food shopping and menus change to accommodate the appetites of children. A major lifestyle change is the loss of freedom of activity and flexibility in one's personal schedule. Lifestyle changes are particularly dramatic for women. The time and effort required to be pregnant and rear children often compete with the time and energy needed to finish one's education or build one's career. Parents learn quickly that being both an involved parent and climbing the career ladder are difficult. The careers of women may suffer most.

11-1d Awareness of Financial Costs

Meeting the financial obligations of parenthood is difficult for many parents. The costs begin with prenatal care and continue at childbirth. For an uncomplicated vaginal delivery, with a two-day hospital stay, the cost may total $10,000, whereas a Cesarean section birth will cost around $16,000. The annual cost of a child less than 2 years old for a family making less than $63,530 is $9,480 with the largest expense for housing. For families with a joint income from $63,530 to $106,540, the annual cost is $12,940. For families with an income above $106,540 the annual cost is $21,430 (*Proquest Statistical Abstract of the United States, 2016*, Table 711). These costs do not include the wages lost when a parent drops out of the workforce to provide child care. Indeed, a woman with a child (particularly a heterosexual woman) is less likely to be hired (Baumle, 2013). Lifetime costs of rearing a child from birth to age 18 is $245,340 (U.S. Department of Commerce, 2016).

11-1e Parenthood: Positives and Negatives Over Time

The positives and negatives of having children continue throughout one's life. Fingerman et al. (2016) analyzed diaries of 247 midlife parents, 96% of whom revealed that they had weekly contact/joy/laughter with their grown children. But more than half the parents reported that their children were also sources of stress ("they get on my nerves") and were sources of their worrying.

11-2 HOW MANY CHILDREN DO YOU WANT?

Procreative liberty is the freedom to decide whether or not to have children. More women are deciding not to have children or to have fewer children.

Do Parents Have Higher Life Satisfaction than Nonparents?

Since most individuals/couples have children, what is the outcome in terms of effect on life satisfaction? Data from Germany on 1,220 women and 1,107 men who became first-time parents and who reported their life satisfaction over a six-year period help answer the question.

Researcher Matthias Pollmann-Schult (2014) noted that during the first five years, children provide enormous positive emotional rewards and "psychological stimulation as well as pleasure, fun and excitement." They also "form the basis for relationships with other parents and thereby contribute to a sense of social connectedness."

Over time, however, children incur heavy burdens in terms of time costs, psychosocial stress, and financial costs which suppress life satisfaction for parents. Significant variables affecting life satisfaction include age of the child (higher life satisfaction with children under 5), marital status of the couple (higher for married couples than single parents), and financial arrangements (higher in male breadwinning households than dual-earner households). Additional children seem to further suppress the life satisfaction associated with parenting.

> I'm a childless woman, yet I felt no maternal urges whatsoever. The prospect of years of broken nights and nappy changes holds no appeal for me.
>
> —KIKI DEE, ENGLISH SINGER

11-2a Childfree Marriage?

In a national sample of adult women, 16% said that they were neither trying to have a child, nor did they want a child (Greil et al., 2016). Some avoid having children because of the Zika virus. Of 753 consumers, 25% said they would avoid getting pregnant because of the Zika virus (Byrne & Bravo, 2016).

What is the process of deciding to remain childfree? Lee and Zvonkovic (2014) interviewed 20 childfree couples. The driving force behind most decisions to remain childfree was the importance the spouses gave to their relationship and the strength of their conviction. Three phases of the decision-making process were identified—agreement, acceptance, and closing the door (e.g., no longer capable of having a child). One of the respondents noted the difference between agreement and acceptance:

> Agreeing was the first, really the first thing. Acceptance was the second thing . . . now that I think about it. It's like, true because she said, "I'm not gonna have kids" and I would go, "Okay." That's me agreeing. Accepting it took a little bit longer . . . I mean, I accept that's what it is, right? . . . the accepting means, we should not have kids. I mean, like by the time we are 30, it's like, "It's never going to happen." It's really total acceptance. "This is never gonna happen."

Stereotypes about couples who deliberately elect not to have children include that they do not like kids, are immature, and are not fulfilled because they do not have a

Rearing a child is a relentless series of tasks that parents engage in out of love for their children. Rearing children is hard work and often a thankless job.

Self-Assessment: Childfree Lifestyle Scale (CLS)
Take the self-assessment on choosing a childfree lifestyle at the end of the chapter.

child to make their lives "complete." The reality is that such individuals may enjoy children and some deliberately choose careers to work with them (e.g., elementary school teacher). But they do not want the full-time emotional and economic responsibility of having their own children.

Childlessness concerns is a concept which refers to the idea that holidays and family gatherings may be difficult because of not having children or feeling left out or sad that others have children. To what degree are childfree individuals less happy than those who have children? It depends on where the individuals live. Those living in pronatalist countries (70% or more believe motherhood is necessary) are more unhappy and report less life satisfaction than those living in countries with weak pronatalist values (30% or less believe motherhood is necessary). This finding is a result of examining the data from 36 nations (Tanaka & Johnson, 2016).

McQuillan et al. (2012) studied a representative sample of 1,180 women without children from the National Survey of Fertility Barriers and found that the degree to which women report these concerns is related to their reason for being childless; women who were voluntarily childless reported few concerns. Those most reactive were the childless due to biomedical causes or having delayed parenthood until they could no longer get pregnant.

Some people simply do not like children. Celebrity Bill Maher states, "I hate kids." Aspects of our society reflect **antinatalism** (a perspective against children). Indeed, there is a continuous fight for corporations to implement or enforce any family policies (from family leaves to flex time to on-site day care). Profit and money—not children—are priorities. In addition, although people are generally tolerant of their own children, they often exhibit antinatalistic behavior in reference to the children of others. Notice the unwillingness of some individuals to sit next to a child on an airplane. Asia Air has responded to this need by offering the first 12 rows in coach only for individuals ages 12 and above.

Laura Scott (2009), a childfree wife, set up the Childless by Choice Project and surveyed 171 childfree adults (ages 22 to 66, 71% female, 29% male) to identify their motivations for not having children. The categories of her respondents and the percentage of each follow:

Early articulators (66%)—these adults knew early that they did not want children
Postponers (22%)—adults who kept delaying when they would have children and remained childless
Acquiescers (8%)—those who made the decision to remain childless because their partner did not want children
Undecided (4%)—those who are childless but still in the decision-making process

childlessness concerns
the idea that holidays and family gatherings may be difficult because of not having children or feeling left out or sad that others have children.

antinatalism opposition to children.

Diversity in Other Countries

Beginning in 1979 and continuing until 2015, China had a one-child policy, which dictated that, with some exceptions, citizens could have only one child. Consequences for having a second child were forced (sometimes) abortions, reduced salary, a smaller home, and a less desirable job. Seccombe (2015) noted a positive outcome was reducing China's population by preventing 400 million births. The negative outcome was fewer children to take care of aging parents (China has no Social Security or Medicare) and an oversupply of males (150 males to 100 females).

Most parents have two children. One advantage is that they can enjoy life together.

Some of Scott's interviewees also had an aversion to children, having had a bad childhood or concerns about childbirth. But other individuals love children, enjoy them, and benefit from having them. Hoffnung and Williams (2013) analyzed data on 200 women and found that being a mother was associated with higher life satisfaction than being childfree.

11-2b Nonheterosexuals: Preferences for or against Children

Most research on deciding for or against having children has been conducted on heterosexuals. A team of researchers (Kleinert et al., 2015) assessed the preferences for a sample of 1,283 nonheterosexuals who took an online survey. Most respondents (80%) reported that they did not have children. However, among this group, 43% stated that they had decided to have children later in their lives, 24% were undecided, and 11% had already decided against having children. These percentages are similar to heterosexual preferences. Negative experiences as a result of sexual orientation and internalized stigma had no impact on the decisions regarding parenthood.

11-2c One Child?

Sixteen percent of married couples in the United States have one child (*Proquest Statistical Abstract of the United States, 2016*, Table 64). Those who have only one child may do so because they want the experience of parenthood without children markedly interfering with their lifestyle

and careers. Still others have an only child because of the difficulty in pregnancy or birthing the child. One mother said, "I threw up every day for nine months including on the delivery table. Once is enough for me." There are also those who have only one child because they can't get pregnant a second time.

11-2d Two Children?

Women and men want a similar number of children—two being the most preferred number (Morita et al., 2016). Indeed, the most preferred family size in the United States (for non-Hispanic White women) is the two-child family (1.9 to be exact!). Reasons for this preference include feeling that a family is "not complete" without two children, having a companion for the first child, having a child of each sex, and repeating the positive experience of parenthood enjoyed with their first child. Caspi et al. (2014) confirmed that siblings may provide a positive

Bobby Davis

influence in terms of academic engagement, prosocial behavior, and social competence. However, siblings may also provide a negative influence such as drug use, sibling violence/abuse, and delinquency.

11-2e Three Children?

Nine percent of married couples in the United States have three or more children (*Proquest Statistical Abstract of the United States, 2016*, Table 64). Couples are more likely to have a third child, and to do so quickly, if they already have two girls rather than two boys. They are least likely to bear a third child if they already have a boy and a girl. One male said, "I have 12 older sisters…my parents kept having children till they had me."

Having a third child creates a middle child. This child is sometimes neglected because parents of three children may focus more on the baby and the firstborn than on the child in between. However, an advantage to being a middle child is the chance to experience both a younger and an older sibling. Each additional child also has a negative effect on the existing children by reducing the amount of parental time available to the other children. The economic resources available for each child are also affected by each subsequent child.

competitive birthing
having the same number (or more) of children in reference to one's peers.

11-2f Four or More Children

More than three children are often born to parents who are immersed in a religion which encourages procreation. Catholics, Mormons, and ultra-Orthodox Jews typically have more children than Protestants. When religion is not a factor, **competitive birthing** may be operative whereby individuals have the same number (or more) of children as their peers.

The addition of each subsequent child dramatically increases the possible relationships in the family. For example, in a one-child family, four interpersonal relationships are possible: mother–father, mother–child, father–child, and father–mother–child. In a family of four, eleven relationships are possible.

11-2g Contraception

To achieve the desired family size and to prevent unwanted pregnancies, see Table 11.1 for the various types, effectiveness, and costs.

Even though there is willingness to use contraception, there may be difficulty in obtaining what is desired. Grindlay and Grossman (2016) found that 29% of a nationally representative sample of women at risk for unintended pregnancy (ages 18 to 44) reported having problems obtaining a prescription for the pill, patch, or ring. These problems included lack of money/insurance, challenges getting an appointment, and the requirement to have a regular doctor. Nevertheless, the availability of family planning services into lower income areas has been linked to the decrease in teenage motherhood (Colen et al., 2016).

Pill use in middle age is another consideration. The use of the hormonal pill among young women is common and with limited medical restrictions/concern. But what about use of the pill in middle-age women? Mendoza et al. (2016) found that risks of the pill and thrombosis increase with age. Women in middle age might select an alternative contraceptive.

Assuming that access to contraception has been achieved, a good beginning is to be sober, plan whether or not sexual intercourse will be part of your relationship, and discuss contraception. Having a conversation about birth control is important for sharing responsibility for contraception.

Men can also share responsibility by purchasing and using condoms, paying for medical visits and the pharmacy bill, reminding their partner to use the method, assisting with insertion of barrier methods, checking contraceptive supplies, and having a vasectomy if that is what the couple decide on. The partners should also

TABLE 11.1 | METHODS OF CONTRACEPTION EFFECTIVENESS AND COST

Method	Rates, %[1]	STI Protection	Benefits	Disadvantages	Cost[2]
Oral contraceptive (the pill)	91	No	High effectiveness rate, 24-hour protection, and menstrual regulation	Daily administration, side effects possible, medication interactions	
Nexplanon/Implanon NXT or Implanon (3-year implant)	99.95	No	High effectiveness rate, long-term protection	Side effects possible, menstrual changes	
Depo-Provera (3-month injection) or Depo-subQ Provera 104	94	No	High effectiveness rate, long-term protection	Decreases body calcium, not recommended for use longer than 2 years for most users, side effects likely	
Transdermal patch	91	No	Same as oral contraceptives except use is weekly, not daily	Patch changed weekly, side effects possible	$15–$32 per month
NuvaRing (vaginal ring)	91	No	Same as oral contraceptives except use is monthly, not daily	Must be comfortable with body for insertion	$15–$48 per month
Male condom	82	Yes	Few or no side effects, easy to purchase and use	Can interrupt spontaneity	$2–$10 a box
Female condom	79	Yes	Few or no side effects, easy to purchase	Decreased sensation and insertion takes practice	$4–$10 a box
Spermicide	72	No	Many forms to choose, easy to purchase and use	Can cause irritation, can be messy	$8–$18 per box/tube/can
Today Sponge	76–88[3]	No	Few side effects, effective for 24 hours after insertion	Spermicide irritation possible	$3–$5 per sponge
Diaphragm and cervical cap	88 (diaphragm)	No	Few side effects, can be inserted within 2 hours before intercourse	Can be messy, increased risk of vaginal/UTI infections	$50–$200 plus spermicide
Intrauterine device (IUD): Paraguard or Mirena	99.2	No/little maintenance, longer term protection	Risk of PID increased, chance of expulsion		$150–$300
Withdrawal	78	No	Requires little planning, always available	Pre-ejaculatory fluid can contain sperm	
Periodic abstinence	76	No	No side effects, accepted in all religions/cultures	Requires a lot of planning, need ability to interpret fertility signs	
Emergency contraception		No	Provides an option after intercourse has occurred	Must be taken within 72 hours, side effects likely	$10–$32
Abstinence		Yes	No risk of pregnancy or STIs	Partners both have to agree to abstain	

[1]Effectiveness rates are listed as percentages of women not experiencing an unintended pregnancy during the first year of typical use. Typical use refers to use under real-life conditions. Perfect use effectiveness rates are higher.

[2]Costs may vary.

[3]Lower percentages apply to parous women (women who have given birth). Higher rates apply to nulliparous women (women who have never given birth).

remember that contraception provides no protection against STIs and to use condoms/dental dams.

Sometimes there is a question of how hormonal contraceptives influence mood and sexual desire. In one study of sexual desire, sexual behavior, and mood in 89 women taking one of four contraceptive methods (including nonhormonal and hormonal) no cycle effects of sexual desire were established in the hormonal group but frequency of sexual intercourse declined in the last days of active pill taking (e.g., the woman was having her period). Negative effects did not vary with sexual desire (Elaut et al., 2016).

11-2h Emergency Contraception

Emergency contraception (also called **postcoital contraception**) refers to various types of combined estrogen-progesterone morning-after pills or post-coital IUD insertion used primarily in three circumstances: when a woman has unprotected intercourse, when a contraceptive method fails (such as condom breakage, which occurs 7% of the time, or slippage), and when a woman is raped. "Better safe than sorry" requires immediate action because the sooner the EC pills are taken, the lower the risk of pregnancy—12 hours is best, and 72 hours at the latest (Tal et al., 2014).

While emergency contraception medication is available over the counter—no prescription is necessary (and no pregnancy test is required) for women age 17 and above—some parents feel their parental rights are being undermined. For females under age 17, a prescription is required. Although side effects (nausea, vomiting, and so on) may occur, they are typically over in a couple of days and the risk of being pregnant is minimal.

Emergency contraception is usually discussed in terms of use by females. Research on male awareness of EC was conducted by Richards et al. (2016) who found that only 42% of their convenience sample of males aged 13–24 had heard of emergency contraception. Those who were aware of EC were more likely to have spoken with a health care provider, and 97% felt that they should participate in contraceptive decisions in a relationship.

11-2i Sex Selection

Some couples use sex selection technologies to help ensure a boy or a girl. MicroSort is the new preconception sperm-sorting technology, which allows parents to increase the chance of having a girl or a boy baby. The procedure is also called "family balancing" since couples that already have several children of one sex often use it. The eggs of a woman are fertilized and the sex of

Courtesy of Michelle North

the embryos three to eight days old is identified. Only embryos of the desired sex are then implanted in the woman's uterus.

Puri and Nachtigall (2010) examined ethical considerations in regard to sex selection. One perspective held by sex selection technology providers argues that sex selection is an expression of reproductive rights and a sign of female empowerment to prevent unwanted pregnancies and abortions. A contrasting view is that sex selection contributes to gender stereotypes that could result in neglect of children of the lesser-desired sex. Whatever the cause, the numbers are alarming. Bongaarts and Guilmoto (2015) noted that the annual number of newly "missing females" due to sex selection reached 3.4 million in 2010 and is expected to remain above 3 million every year until 2050.

11-3 INFERTILITY

> It's frustrating to watch everyone else's dreams come true while knowing your own are slipping farther and farther away from becoming a reality.
>
> —ANONYMOUS

Infertility is the inability to achieve a pregnancy after at least one year of regular sexual relations without birth control, or the inability to carry a pregnancy to a live birth. Six percent of adult women in the United States meet the criteria for infertility (of these 84% want to get pregnant) (Greil et al., 2016).

11-3a Types of Infertility

Different types of infertility include the following:

1. **Primary infertility.** The woman has never conceived even though she wants to and has had regular sexual relations for the past 12 months.

---

emergency contraception (postcoital contraception) refers to various types of morning-after pills.

infertility the inability to achieve a pregnancy after at least one year of regular sexual relations without birth control, or the inability to carry a pregnancy to a live birth.

2. **Secondary infertility.** The woman has previously conceived but is currently unable to do so even though she wants to and has had regular sexual relations for the past 12 months.

3. **Pregnancy wastage.** The woman has been able to conceive but has been unable to produce a live birth.

Shapiro (2012) emphasized the importance of conceiving in one's twenties rather than delaying pregnancy until one's thirties or forties. The chance of conceiving per month in one's thirties is 20%; in one's forties, it is 10%. Dougall et al. (2013) interviewed women who delayed getting pregnant until age 40 or later—44% reported that they were "shocked" to learn that the difficulty in getting pregnant declines so steeply as a woman moves into her mid to late thirties. Schmidt et al. (2012) also noted that delaying pregnancy until 35 and beyond is associated with higher risk of preterm births and stillbirths.

11-3b Causes of Infertility

Although popular usage does not differentiate between the terms *fertilization* and the *beginning of pregnancy*, fertilization or **conception** refers to the fusion of the egg and sperm, whereas **pregnancy** is not considered to begin until five to seven days later, when the fertilized egg is implanted (typically in the uterine wall). Hence, not all fertilizations result in a pregnancy. An estimated 30% to 40% of conceptions are lost prior to or during implantation. Forty percent of infertility problems are attributed to the woman, 40% to the man, and 20% to both of them. Some of the more common causes of infertility in men include low sperm production, poor semen motility, effects of STIs (such as chlamydia, gonorrhea, and syphilis), and interference with passage of sperm through the genital ducts due to an enlarged prostate. Additionally, there is some association between high body mass index in men and sperm that is problematic in impregnating a female (Sandlow, 2013).

Infertility in the woman is related to her age, not having been pregnant before, blocked fallopian tubes, endocrine imbalance that prevents ovulation, dysfunctional ovaries, chemically hostile cervical mucus that may kill sperm, and effects of STIs (Van Geloven et al., 2013). Obesity in the woman is also related to her infertility. Frisco and Weden (2013) analyzed national data on 1,658 females at two different time periods and found that young women who were obese at baseline had higher odds of remaining childless and increased odds of underachieving fertility intentions than young women

who were normal weight at baseline. The researchers concluded that obesity has long-term ramifications for women's childbearing experiences with respect to whether and how many children women have in general relative to the number of children they want. Brandes et al. (2011) noted that unexplained infertility is one of the most common diagnoses in fertility care and is associated with a high probability of achieving a pregnancy—most spontaneously.

Luk and Loke (2015) reviewed 20 articles on infertility that revealed inconclusive evidence for the effect on marital relationships and quality of life. Regarding infertility and its association with sexual dysfunction, in a study of 142 infertile women, when the cause was due to the woman, 43% evidenced female sexual dysfunction. When the cause was due to the man, 55% of the women reported female sexual dysfunction; when the cause was unexplained, 52% reported female sexual dysfunction (Kucur Suna et al., 2016).

An at-home fertility kit, Fertell, allows women to measure the level of their follicle-stimulating hormone on the third day of their menstrual cycles. An abnormally high level means that egg quality is low. The test takes 30 minutes and involves a urine stick. The same kit allows men to measure the concentration of motile sperm. Men provide a sample of sperm (e.g., masturbation) that swim through a solution similar to cervical mucus. This procedure takes about 80 minutes. Fertell has been approved by the Food and Drug Administration (FDA). No prescription is necessary and the cost for the kit is about $100.

11-3c Success Using Assisted Reproductive Technologies (ART)

Some infertile women seek various reproductive technologies to get pregnant. The cost of treating infertility is enormous. Katz et al. (2011) examined the costs for 398 women in eight infertility practices over an 18-month period. For the half who pursued IVF, the median per-person medication costs ranged from $1,182 for medications only to $24,373 and $38,015 for IVF and IVF-donor egg groups, respectively. In regard to the costs of successful outcomes (delivery or ongoing pregnancy by 18 months) for IVF, the cost was $61,377. Within the time frame of the study, costs were not significantly different for women whose outcomes were successful

conception refers to the fusion of the egg and sperm. Also known as fertilization.

pregnancy when the fertilized egg is implanted (typically in the uterine wall).

and women whose outcomes were not. Only 28% of couples who invest in a fertility clinic end up with a live birth (Lee, 2006). The sooner an infertility problem is suspected the more successful the intervention.

Researchers continue to investigate the reason for low birth weight in babies which result from ART. It is not known if such is due to ART procedures or to the fact of infertility itself (Kondapalli & Perales-Puchalt, 2013).

11-4 ADOPTION

> Biology is the least of what makes someone a mother.
>
> —OPHRA WINFREY

Angelina Jolie and Brad Pitt are celebrities who have given national visibility to adopting children. They are not alone in their desire to adopt children. The various routes to adoption are public (children from the child welfare system), private agency (children placed with nonrelatives through agencies), independent adoption (children placed directly by birth parents or through an intermediary such as a physician or attorney), kinship (children placed in a family member's home), and stepparent (children adopted by a spouse). Motives for adopting a child include an inability to have a biological child, a desire to give an otherwise unwanted child a permanent loving home, or a desire to avoid contributing to overpopulation by having more biological children.

Maria McDonald

Bobby Davis

Some couples may seek adoption for all of these motives. Most (70%) adoptions are by a married couple, 23% by a single female, and 6% by a single male. Eighty-seven percent of parents who adopt a child report that they would do so again (Adoption USA, 2015).

11-4a Characteristics of Children Available for Adoption

Burge et al. (2016) assessed the child profile preferences of 5,830 adults seeking to adopt a child. While the most preferred (and least often adopted) were younger children, between 43% to 60% indicated a willingness to consider adopting children with degrees of learning disabilities, emotional behavioral disorders, and physical disabilities. The most preferred, among 20 categories of available children's possible exposures and health diagnoses, were those children who had been abused in the past.

11-4b Children Who Are Adopted

Children who are adopted have an enormous advantage over those who are not adopted. Juffer et al. (2011) examined 270 research articles including more than 230,000 children to compare the physical growth, attachment, cognitive development, school achievement, self-esteem, and behavioral problems of adopted and nonadopted children. Results revealed that adopted children outperformed their nonadopted peers who remained in institutions and they showed a dramatic recovery in practically all areas of development.

"Who are your real parents?," "Why did your mother give you up?," and "Are those your real parents?" are questions children who are adopted must sometimes cope with. These are microaggressions reflecting that adopted children are stigmatized (Baden, 2016). W.I.S.E. UP is a tool provided to adopted children to help them cope with these intrusive, sometimes uncomfortable questions (Singer, 2010). W.I.S.E. is an acronym for: **W**alk away, **I**gnore or change the subject, **S**hare what you are comfortable sharing, and **E**ducate about adoption in general. The tool emphasizes that adopted children are wiser about adoption than their peers and can educate them or remove themselves from the situation.

11-4c Costs of Adoption

The cost of an adoption varies by the type of adoption. The least expensive (no cost) adoption is adoption via being a foster parent which comprises 56% of no cost adoptions. The most expensive adoptions are international, costing over $10,000 (Adoption USA, 2015). We know of a couple who adopted a child from Moldavia at a cost of $30,000. Private adoptions, through an agency, range in price from $1,000 to over $10,000 with a third costing over $10,000 (Adoption USA, 2015).

While being a foster parent is the least expensive route to adopting a child, the foster parents run the risk of the parents resurfacing and claiming the child after the foster parents get emotionally attached. Stepparent and kinship adoptions are also (usually) without cost and have less risk of the child being withdrawn.

11-4d Open versus Closed Adoptions

Another controversy is whether adopted children should be allowed to obtain information about their biological parents. In general, there are considerable benefits for having an open adoption, especially the opportunity for the biological parent to stay involved in the child's life. Adoptees learn early that they are adopted and who their biological parents are. Birth parents are more likely to avoid regret and to be able to stay in contact with their child. Adoptive parents have information about the genetic background of their adopted child.

However, Jones (2016) emphasized that there are difficulties faced by members of the adoption triad that are likely to threaten rather than promote further progress regarding openness in adoption. These difficulties include the management of emotions by each party in regard to who belongs to whom, where the alliances are, and a continual process of redefining an arrangement that is ambiguous. Goldberg et al. (2011) studied lesbian, gay, and heterosexual couples who were involved in an open adoption. While there were some tensions with the birth parents over time, most of the 45 adoptive couples reported satisfying relationships.

Black et al. (2014) emphasized the role of social media and technology in reference to adoptive and birth families. The researchers interviewed 36 individuals within 18 couples who had adopted a child in the past five years. The individuals reported both active contact with birth families via Skype/email or passive contact in that they had seen the birth family on Facebook but had not made contact. Results revealed ambivalence about the availability of technology—the advantage was the ease with which adoptive families might find/interact with birth families; the disadvantage was that such technology might become intrusive. And partners might disagree about the use of technology.

Some adopted children want to find their birth parents but face policies that prohibit giving them information.

11-5 FOSTER PARENTING

> Treat people as if they were what they ought to be and you will help them become what they are capable of becoming.
>
> —JOHANN WOLFGANG VON GOETHE

Some individuals seek the role of parent via foster parenting. A **foster parent**, also known as a family caregiver, is neither a biological nor an adoptive parent but is one who takes care of and fosters a child taken into custody. Foster care may be temporary or long term. A foster parent has made a contract with the state for the service, has judicial status, and is reimbursed by the state. Foster parents are screened for previous arrest records and child abuse and neglect. They are licensed by the state; some states require a "foster parent orientation" program.

11-5a Internet Adoption

Some couples use the Internet to adopt a baby. The Donaldson Adoption Institute surveyed 2,000 adoptees, adoptive parents,

foster parent neither a biological nor an adoptive parent but a person who takes care of and fosters a child taken into custody.

Bobby Davis

birth parents, and adoption professionals. The survey revealed the Internet's value of being able to make connections and provide information for parents seeking to adopt (Healy, 2013). The Internet's use to adopt a baby can pose serious problems of potential fraud, exploitation, and, most important, lack of professional consideration of the child's best interest. Couples should proceed with great caution. Policymakers should also be aware of the practice of "rehoming" where parents who have adopted a child use the Internet to place unwanted adopted children in new families. There is no monitoring or regulation of this practice (Healy, 2013).

11-6 ABORTION

Abortion remains a controversial issue in the United States. Among American women, half will have an unintended pregnancy and 40% will have an abortion (Guttmacher Institute, 2016). An abortion may be either an **induced abortion**, which is the deliberate termination of a pregnancy through chemical or surgical means, or a **spontaneous abortion (miscarriage)**, which is the unintended termination of a pregnancy. Miscarriages often represent a significant loss which is associated with depression/anxiety (Geller et al., 2010) and marital unhappiness (Sugiura-Ogasawara et al., 2013).

In this text the term *abortion* refers to induced abortion. In general, abortion is legal in the United States but it was challenged under the Bush administration.

11-6a Incidence of Abortion

When this country was founded abortion was legal and accepted by the public up until the time of "quickening"—the moment when a woman can feel the fetus inside her. By the time of the Civil War, one in five pregnancies was terminated by an abortion. Opposition to abortion grew in the 1870s, led by the American Medical Association launching a fierce campaign to make abortion illegal unless authorized and performed by a licensed physician. Abortion was made illegal in 1880, which did not stop the practice; a million abortions were performed illegally by the 1950s. In 1973, the Supreme Court upheld in *Roe v. Wade* the right of a woman to have a legal abortion. However, the law is continually challenged. In May 2016, the senate in Oklahoma passed a bill that would make it a felony for a physician to perform a licensed abortion (and the person would lose his or her license to practice medicine). Governor Fallin vetoed the bill.

> Why am I the foster parent of 7 children? Because someone has to give a dam.
>
> —FOSTER PARENT

About 1.2 million abortions are performed annually in the United States. Although the number of abortions has been increasing among the poor (lower access to health care and health education), there has been a decrease among higher income women (due to increased acceptability of having a child without a partner and increased use of contraception). Two-thirds of abortions occur within the first two months of pregnancy (Guttmacher Institute, 2016).

The **abortion rate** in 2011 was 16.9 per 1,000 women aged 15–44, down 13% from 19.4 per 1,000 in 2008. This is the lowest rate observed since abortion became legal in the United States in 1973 (Guttmacher Institute, 2016). About 40% of abortions are repeat abortions (Ames & Norman, 2012).

The **abortion ratio** refers to the number of abortions per 1,000 live births. Abortion is affected by the need for parental consent and parental notification. **Parental consent** means that a woman needs permission from a parent to get an abortion if she is under a

induced abortion the deliberate termination of a pregnancy through chemical or surgical means.

spontaneous abortion (miscarriage) the unintended termination of a pregnancy.

abortion rate the number of abortions per thousand women aged 15 to 44.

abortion ratio refers to the number of abortions per 1,000 live births. Abortion is affected by the need for parental consent and parental notification.

parental consent a woman needs permission from a parent to get an abortion if under a certain age, usually 18.

Diversity in Other Countries

There are wide variations in the range of cultural responses to the abortion issue. On one end of the continuum is the Kafir tribe in Central Asia, where an abortion is strictly the choice of the woman. In this preliterate society, there is no taboo or restriction with regard to abortion, and the woman is free to exercise her decision to terminate her pregnancy. One reason for the Kafirs' approval of abortion is that childbirth in the tribe is associated with high rates of maternal mortality. Because birthing children may threaten the life of significant numbers of adult women in the community, women may be encouraged to abort. Such encouragement is particularly strong in the case of women who are viewed as too young, too old, too sick, or too small to bear children.

A tribe or society may also encourage abortion for a number of other reasons, including practicality, economics, lineage, and honor. Abortion is practical for women in migratory societies. Such women must control their pregnancies, because they are limited in the number of children they can nurse and transport. Economic motivations become apparent when resources are scarce—the number of children born to a group must be controlled. Abortion for reasons of lineage or honor involves encouragement of an abortion in those cases in which a woman becomes impregnated in an adulterous relationship. To protect the lineage and honor of her family, the woman may have an abortion.

certain age, usually 18. **Parental notification** means that a woman has to tell a parent she is getting an abortion if she is under a certain age, usually 18, but she does not need parental permission. Laws vary by state. Call the National Abortion Federation Hotline at 1-800-772-9100 to find out the laws in your state.

11-6b Reasons for an Abortion

In a survey of 1,209 women who reported having had an abortion, the most frequently cited reasons were that having a child would interfere with a woman's education, work, or ability to care for dependents (74%); that she could not afford a baby now (73%); and that she did not want to be a single mother or was having relationship problems (48%). Nearly 4 in 10 women said they had completed their

childbearing, and almost one-third of the women were not ready to have a child (Finer et al., 2005). Falcon et al. (2010) confirmed that the use of drugs was related to unintended pregnancy and the request for an abortion. Clearly, some women get pregnant when high on alcohol or other substances, regret the pregnancy, and want to reverse it.

Abortions performed to protect the life or health of the woman are called **therapeutic abortions**. However, there is disagreement over this definition. Garrett et al. (2001) noted, "Some physicians argue that an abortion is therapeutic if it prevents or alleviates a serious physical or mental illness, or even if it alleviates temporary emotional upsets. In short, the health of the pregnant woman is given such a broad definition that a very large number of abortions can be classified as therapeutic" (p. 218).

Some women with multifetal pregnancies (a common outcome of the use of fertility drugs) may have a procedure called *transabdominal first-trimester selective termination*. In this procedure, the lives of some fetuses are terminated to increase the chance of survival for the others or to minimize the health risks associated with multifetal pregnancy for the woman. For example, a woman carrying five fetuses may elect to abort three of them to minimize the health risks of the other two.

11-6c Pro-Life Abortion Position

A dichotomy of attitudes toward abortion is reflected in two opposing groups of abortion activists. Individuals and groups who oppose abortion are commonly referred to as "pro-life" or "antiabortion."

Of 9,662 undergraduates at two large universities, 23% reported that abortion is not acceptable under certain conditions (Hall & Knox, 2016). Pro-life groups favor abortion policies or a complete ban on abortion. They essentially believe the following:

1. The unborn fetus has a right to live and that right should be protected.

2. Abortion is a violent and immoral solution to unintended pregnancy.

3. The life of an unborn fetus is sacred and should be protected, even at the cost of individual difficulties for the pregnant woman.

Foster et al. (2013) studied the effect of pro-life protesters outside of abortion clinics on those individuals who came to the clinic to get an abortion. The researchers

parental notification
a woman has to tell a parent she is getting an abortion if she is under a certain age, usually 18, but she does not need parental permission.

therapeutic abortions
abortions performed to protect the life or health of the woman.

interviewed 956 women, 16% of whom said that they were very upset by the protesters. However, exposure to the protesters was not associated with differences in emotions one week after the abortion.

11-6d Pro-Choice Abortion Position

In the sample of 9,662 undergraduates referred to above, 63% reported that abortion is acceptable under certain conditions (Hall & Knox, 2016). Pro-choice advocates support the legal availability of abortion for all women. They essentially believe the following:

1. Freedom of choice is a central value—the woman has a right to determine what happens to her own body.

2. Those who must personally bear the burden of their moral choices ought to have the right to make these choices.

3. Procreation choices must be free of governmental control.

Although many self-proclaimed feminists and women's organizations, such as the National Organization for Women (NOW), have been active in promoting abortion rights, not all feminists are pro-choice.

Mark Wilson/Getty Images

11-6e Physical Effects of Abortion

Part of the debate over abortion is related to its presumed effects. In regard to the physical effects, legal abortions, performed under safe medical conditions, are safer than continuing the pregnancy. The earlier in the pregnancy the abortion is performed, the safer it is. Vacuum aspiration, a frequently used method in early pregnancy, does not increase the risks to future childbearing. However, late-term abortions do increase the risks of subsequent miscarriages, premature deliveries, and babies of low birth weight.

Weitz et al. (2013) compared the outcome of 11,487 early aspiration abortions depending on who performed the abortion—nurse, certified nurse midwife, physician's assistant, and physician and found a complication rate of 1.8% with insignificant variation. These data support the adoption of policies to allow these providers to perform early aspirations to expand access to abortion care.

11-6f Psychological Effects of Abortion

Of equal concern are the psychological effects of abortion. Steinberg et al. (2016) found that the greatest amount of depression, anxiety, and stress regarding an abortion decision occurred *before* the abortion. The stigma associated with having an abortion was a significant factor associated with these psychological states. The researchers suggested that addressing stigma among women seeking abortions may significantly lower their psychological distress. The American Psychological Association reviewed all outcome studies on the mental health effects of abortion and concluded, "Based on our comprehensive review and evaluation of the empirical literature published in peer-reviewed journals since 1989, this Task Force on Mental Health and Abortion concludes that the most methodologically sound research indicates that among women who have a single, legal, first-trimester abortion of an unplanned pregnancy for nontherapeutic reasons, the relative risks of mental health problems are no greater than the risks among women who deliver an unplanned pregnancy" (Major et al., 2008, p. 71).

Canario et al. (2013) analyzed data on 50 women (and 15 partners) one and six months after abortion and found a decrease in emotional disorder for all etiologies of abortion and an increase in perceived quality of a couple's relationship in therapeutic abortion over time. The researchers concluded that the psychological adjustment of an individual after abortion seems to be influenced by factors such as the couple's relationship.

 11-7 ## TRENDS IN DECIDING ABOUT CHILDREN

As birthrates in the United States and Western Europe continue to fall (Dervin, 2016), being childfree will lose some of its stigma. Indeed, the pregnancy rate for women aged 15–29 has dropped steadily since 1990 (Curtin et al., 2013). Individualism and economics are the primary factors responsible for reducing the obsession to have children. To quote Laura Scott, "having children will change from an assumption to a decision." Once the personal, social, and economic consequences of having children come under close scrutiny the automatic response to have children will be tempered.

For the infertile, "google baby" will increasingly be considered as an option for having a child. *Google Baby* is the name of a documentary showing how infertile couples with a credit card can submit an order for a baby—the firm will find donor egg and donor sperm, fertilize the egg, and implant it in a surrogate mother in India. The couple need only fly to India, pick up their baby, and return to the states.

STUDY TOOLS 11

READY TO STUDY? IN THE BOOK, YOU CAN:

☐ Rip out the chapter review card at the back of the book for a handy summary of the chapter and key terms.

☐ Assess yourself with the following self-assessments.

ONLINE AT CENGAGEBRAIN.COM YOU CAN:

☐ Collect StudyBits while you read and study the chapter.

☐ Quiz yourself on key concepts.

☐ Prepare for tests with M&F4 Flash Cards as well as those you create.

SELF-ASSESSMENT

Childfree Lifestyle Scale (CLS)

The purpose of this scale is to assess your attitudes toward having a childfree lifestyle. After reading each statement, select the number that best reflects your answer, using the following scale:

1	2	3	4	5	6	7
Strongly disagree						*Strongly agree*

_____ **1.** I do not like children.

_____ **2.** I would resent having to spend all my money on kids.

_____ **3.** I would rather enjoy my personal freedom than have it taken away by having children.

_____ **4.** I would rather focus on my career than have children.

_____ **5.** Children are a burden.

_____ **6.** I have no desire to be a parent.

_____ **7.** I am too "into me" to become a parent.

_____ **8.** I lack the nurturing skills to be a parent.

_____ **9.** I have no patience for children.

_____ **10.** Raising a child is too much work.

_____ **11.** A marriage without children is empty.

_____ **12.** Children are vital to a good marriage.

_____ **13.** You can't really be fulfilled as a couple unless you have children.

_____ **14.** Having children gives meaning to a couple's marriage.

_____ **15.** The happiest couples that I know have children.

_____ **16.** The biggest mistake couples make is deciding not to have children.

_____ **17.** Childfree couples are sad couples.

_____ **18.** Becoming a parent enhances the intimacy between spouses.

_____ **19.** A house without the "pitter patter" of little feet is not a home.

_____ **20.** Having a child means your marriage is successful.

Scoring

Reverse score items 11 through 20. For example, if you wrote a 7 for item 20, change this to a 1. If you wrote a 7, change to a 1. If you wrote a 2, change to a 6, etc. Add the numbers. The higher the score (140 is the highest possible score), the greater the value for a childfree lifestyle. The lower the score (20 is the lowest possible score), the less the desire to have a childfree lifestyle. The midpoint between the extremes is 80: Scores below 80 suggest less preference for a childfree lifestyle, and scores above 80 suggest a desire for a childfree lifestyle. The average score of 52 male and 138 female undergraduates at Valdosta State University was below the midpoint (M = 68.78, SD = 17.06), suggesting a tendency toward a lifestyle that included children. A significant difference was found between males, who scored 72.94 (SD = 16.82), and females, who scored 67.21 (SD = 16.95), suggesting that males are more approving of a childfree lifestyle. There were no significant differences between Whites and Blacks or between students in different ranks (freshman, sophomore, junior, senior, etc.).

Source: "The Childfree Lifestyle Scale," 2010, by Mark A. Whatley, Ph.D., Department of Psychology, Valdosta State University, Valdosta, Georgia 31698-0100. Used by permission. Other uses of this scale by written permission of Dr. Whatley only (mwhatley@valdosta.edu). Information on the reliability and validity of this scale is available from Dr. Whatley.

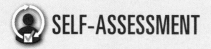 **SELF-ASSESSMENT**

Abortion Attitude Scale (AAS)

This is not a test. There are no wrong or right answers to any of the statements, so just answer as honestly as you can. The statements ask your feelings about legal abortion (the voluntary removal of a human fetus from the mother during the first three months of pregnancy by a qualified medical person). Tell how you feel about each statement by selecting only one response. Use the following scale for your answers:

5	4	3	2	1
Strongly agree	*Slightly agree*	*Agree*	*Slightly disagree*	*Strongly disagree*

_____ **1.** The Supreme Court should strike down legal abortions in the United States.

_____ **2.** Abortion is a good way of solving an unwanted pregnancy.

_____ **3.** A mother should feel obligated to bear a child she has conceived.

_____ **4.** Abortion is wrong no matter what the circumstances are.

_____ **5.** A fetus is not a person until it can live outside its mother's body.

_____ **6.** The decision to have an abortion should be the pregnant mother's.

_____ **7.** Every conceived child has the right to be born.

_____ **8.** A pregnant female not wanting to have a child should be encouraged to have an abortion.

_____ **9.** Abortion should be considered killing a person.

_____ **10.** People should not look down on those who choose to have abortions.

_____ **11.** Abortion should be an available alternative for unmarried pregnant teenagers.

_____ **12.** People should not have the power over the life or death of a fetus.

_____ **13.** Unwanted children should not be brought into the world.

_____ **14.** A fetus should be considered a person at the moment of conception.

Scoring and Interpretation

As its name indicates, this scale was developed to measure attitudes toward abortion. Sloan (1983) developed the scale for use with high school and college students. To compute your score, first reverse the point scale for items 1, 3, 4, 7, 9, 12, and 14. For example, if you selected a 5 for item one, this becomes a 0; if you selected a 1, this becomes a 4. After reversing the scores on the seven items specified, add the numbers you circled for all the items. Sloan provided the following categories for interpreting the results:

70–56 Strong proabortion

54–44 Moderate proabortion

43–27 Unsure

26–16 Moderate pro-life

15–0 Strong pro-life

Reliability and Validity

The AAS was administered to high school and college students, Right to Life group members, and abortion service personnel. Sloan (1983) reported a high total test estimate of reliability (0.92). Construct validity was supported in that the mean score for Right to Life members was 16.2; the mean score for abortion service personnel was 55.6; and other groups' scores fell between these values.

Source: Sloan, L. A. (May/June 1983). Abortion Attitude Scale. *Journal of Health Education, 14*(3). The *Journal of Health Education* is a publication of the American Alliance for Health, Physical Education, Recreation and Dance, 1900 Association Drive, Reston, VA 20191.

12 | Rearing Children

SECTIONS

After finishing this chapter go **to PAGE 245** for **STUDY TOOLS**

> Before I got married I had six theories about raising children; now,
> I have six children and no theories.
>
> — JOHN WILMOT

E lementary and high school teachers regularly complain that the behavior of children today is a challenge. Children who are disruptive, noncompliant, and aggressive toward authority plague teachers who question whether lack of parental involvement is the culprit. In this chapter we focus on rearing children. But first we look at parenting as a matter of choices.

12-1 PARENTING: A MATTER OF CHOICES

Parents endeavor to make the best decisions in rearing their children. Their choices have a profound impact on their children. In this section, we review the nature of parenting choices and identify some of the basic choices parents make.

12-1a Nature of Parenting Choices

Parents might keep the following points in mind when they make choices about how to rear their children:

1. **Not to make a parental decision is to make a decision.** Parents are constantly making choices even when they think they are not doing so. When a child makes a commitment ("I'll text you when I get to my friend's house") and does not do as promised, unless the parent addresses the issue (and provides a consequence such as grounding the child) the child learns nothing about taking commitments seriously.

2. **All parental choices involve trade-offs.** The decision to take on a second job or to work overtime to afford the larger house will come at the price of having less time to spend with one's children and being more exhausted when such time is available. The choice to enroll a younger child in the highest-quality day care will mean less money for an older child's karate lessons. Parents should increase their awareness that no choice is without a trade-off and should evaluate the costs and benefits of making such decisions.

3. **Reframe "regretful" parental decisions.** All parents regret a previous parental decision (e.g., they should have held their child back a year in school

or not done so; they should have intervened in a bad peer relationship; they should have handled their child's drug use or coming out differently). Whatever the issue, parents chide themselves for their mistakes. Rather than berate themselves as parents, they might emphasize the positive outcome of their choices (e.g., not holding the child back made the child the first to experience some things among his or her peers; they made the best decision they could at the time).

4. **Parental choices are influenced by society and culture.** In the United States, parents are continually assaulted by commercial interests to get them to buy products for their children. Corporations regularly market to young parents to get them to buy the latest learning aid for their child, which promises a genius by age 5.

    Worldwide, parental choices are influenced by the education of the parents. In a study of 227,431 parents from 90 nations, child independence was more popular in nations with more highly educated populations. In contrast, obedience was more popular in nations with lower percentages of educated and urban populations (Park & Lau, 2016).

12-1b Seven Basic Parenting Choices

The seven basic choices parents make include deciding (1) whether or not to have a child, (2) the number of children to have, (3) the interval between children, (4) the method of discipline, (5) the degree to which they will invest time with their children, (6) whether or not to coparent (the parents cooperate in the development of the lives of their children), and (7) how much technological exposure they will allow their children at what age. In regard to the latter, technology is culturally pervasive, and unlimited access at young ages is an important parental consideration. Dervin (2016) noted the temptation of parents to use technology to entertain their children that focuses them on in-house solitary interaction with a digital screen rather than social interaction with humans. The researcher also noted that parks for children to play outdoors are also disappearing since children now prefer to be inside playing their video games.

Though all of the above decisions are important, the relative importance one places on parenting as opposed to one's career will have implications for the parents, their children, and their children's children.

12-2 ROLES OF PARENTS

Although finding one definition of **parenting** is difficult, there is general agreement about the various roles parents play in the lives of their children. New parents assume at least seven roles.

12-2a Caregiver

A major role of parents is the physical care of their children. From the moment of birth, when infants draw their first breath, parents stand ready to provide nourishment (milk), cleanliness (diapers), and temperature control (warm blanket). The need for such sustained care in terms of a place to live/eat continues into adulthood as one-fourth of 18- to 34-year-olds have moved back in with their parents after living on their own.

12-2b Emotional Resource

Beyond providing physical care, parents are sensitive to the emotional needs of children in terms of their need to belong, to be loved, and to develop positive self-concepts. In hugging, holding, and kissing an infant, parents not only express their love for the infant but also reflect awareness that such displays of emotion are good for the child's sense of self-worth.

Parents also provide "emotion work" for children—listening to

parenting defined in terms of roles including caregiver, emotional resource, teacher, and economic resource.

boomerang generation adult children who return to live with their parents.

Maria McDonald is the artist

their issues, helping them figure out various relationships they are struggling with, etc.

12-2c Teacher

All parents think they have a philosophy of life or set of principles their children will benefit from. Parents soon discover that their children may not be interested in their religion or philosophy and, indeed, may rebel against it. This possibility does not deter parents from their role as teacher.

12-2d Economic Resource

New parents are also acutely aware of the costs for medical care, food, and clothes for infants, and seek ways to ensure that such resources are available to their children. Working longer hours, taking second jobs, and cutting back on leisure expenditures are attempts to ensure that money is available to meet the needs of the children.

Boomerang generation children are those young adults who leave home for college or marriage and come back, primarily for economic reasons. The What's New? section details how much money parents provide for their adult children.

How Much Money Do Parents Give Their Adult Children?

One of the roles of parents is to provide financial assistance to their children. Indeed, 62% of young adults (ages 19–22) report that they receive money from their parents—mostly to pay bills. How much assistance are parents providing? A great deal, is the general answer—an average of $12,185 annually (Wightman et al., 2012). Padilla-Walker et al. (2012) studied a sample of 401 undergraduates and at least one of their parents and discovered that over half reported paying between $5,000 and $30,000 (30% paid $30,000 or more and 20% paid less than $5,000) yearly. Most felt it was their obligation as parents to help their children financially, particularly while their children were "emerging adults" (between 18 and late twenties).

When the parents were asked how long they should provide financial support, about half (49%) said until their offspring gets a job, about a quarter (23%) said when they graduate from college, and 6% said never. It seems that "lower levels of financial support may indeed facilitate a greater perception of oneself as an adult and promote more adult-like behaviors including fewer risky behaviors (e.g., drinking/binge drinking), greater identity development (at least in the domain of occupational identity), and higher numbers of work hours per week" (Padilla-Walker et al., 2012, p. 56). Hence, underwriting children completely seemed to interfere with the transition of those children to more responsible adult behavior.

12-2e Protector

Parents also feel the need to protect their children from harm. This role may begin in pregnancy in that the pregnant mother to be may stop smoking. Other expressions of the protective role include insisting that children wear seatbelts in cars and jackets in cold weather, protecting them from violence or nudity in the media, and protecting them from strangers. Increasingly, parents are joining the technological age and learning how to text message. In their role as protector, this ability allows parents to text message their children to tell them to come home, to phone home, or to work out a logistical problem—"meet me at the food court in the mall."

12-2f Health Promoter

The family is a major agent for health promotion—not only in promoting healthy food choices, responsible use of alcohol, nonuse of drugs, and safe driving skills, but also in ending smoking behavior.

12-2g Ritual Bearer

To build a sense of family cohesiveness, parents often foster rituals to bind members together in emotion and in memory. Prayer at meals and before bedtime, birthday, and holiday celebrations, and vacations at the same place (beach, mountains, and so on) provide predictable times of togetherness and sharing.

> Over and over again, cross-cultural research on infancy teaches the exact same lesson: infants can tolerate— and thrive under—care that most any Western parent would assume would end very badly.
>
> —NICHOLAS DAY, *BABY MEETS WORLD: SUCK, SMILE, TOUCH, TODDLE*

There is no shortage of books for parents on how to rear their children.

12-3 TRANSITION TO PARENTHOOD

The **transition to parenthood** refers to that period from the beginning of pregnancy through the first few months after the birth of a baby. The mother, father, and two of them as a couple undergo changes and adaptations during this period.

> Women may give lip service to wanting husbands who take on an equal role in raising children, but many will pull rank when an important decision, like how to discipline or what baby sitter to hire, has to be made.
>
> —PEPPER SCHWARTZ

12-3a Transition to Motherhood

Being a mother, particularly a biological or adoptive mother (in contrast to a stepmother), is a major social event for a woman. Research reveals that mothers are under intense pressure to be the perfect mother and often feel guilty for not living up to the cultural expectations (Henderson et al., 2016). While mothers of infants are, in general, very involved and committed to their infants, those who feel that they should not be employed (be away from their infant) are younger and less educated (Walls et al., 2016).

While a baby changes a woman's life forever, her initial reaction is influenced by whether the baby was intended. Su (2012) studied 825 women and found that unintended births were associated with decreased happiness among mothers. Nevertheless, whatever her previous focus, her decisions in life will now include her baby.

One woman expressed: "Our focus shifts from our husbands to our children, who then take up all our energy. We become angry and lonely and burdened... and that's if we LIKE it."

Sociobiologists suggest that the attachment between a mother and her offspring has a biological basis (one of survival). The mother alone carries the fetus in her body for nine months, lactates to provide milk, and, during the expulsive stage of labor, produces **oxytocin**, a hormone from the pituitary gland that has been associated with the onset of maternal behavior in lower animals. Most new mothers become emotionally bonded with their babies and resist separation.

Not all mothers feel joyous after childbirth. Naomi Wolf uses the term "the conspiracy of silence" to note motherhood is "a job that sucks 80 percent of the time" (quoted in Haag, 2011, p. 83). Some mothers do not bond immediately and feel overworked, exhausted, mildly depressed, and irritable; they cry, suffer loss of appetite, and have difficulty in sleeping. Many new mothers experience **baby blues**—transitory symptoms of depression 24 to 48 hours after the baby is born.

Parents learn to enjoy the work of parenting.

transition to parenthood period from the beginning of pregnancy through the first few months after the birth of a baby during which the mother and father undergo changes.

oxytocin hormone from the pituitary gland during the expulsive stage of labor that has been associated with the onset of maternal behavior in lower animals.

baby blues transitory symptoms of depression in a mother 24 to 48 hours after her baby is born.

About 10% to 15% of mothers experience **postpartum depression**, a more severe reaction than baby blues (usually occurs within a month of the baby's birth) (Brummelte & Galea, 2016). Gelabert et al. (2012) looked at various personality traits that were associated with postpartum depression. They found that women who were perfectionist (characterized by concern over mistakes, personal standards, parental expectations, parental criticism, doubt about actions and organization) were more likely to report postpartum depression. Women with anxiety prior to childbirth may also be vulnerable to depression (Hipwell et al., 2016).

To minimize baby blues and postpartum depression, antidepressants such as Zoloft and Prozac are used. Most women recover within a short time. With prolonged negative feelings, a clinical psychologist should be consulted.

Postpartum psychosis, a reaction in which a woman wants to harm her baby, is even more rare than postpartum depression. While having misgivings about a new infant is normal, the parent who wants to harm the infant should make these feelings known to the partner, a close friend, and a professional.

Some parents become so despondent they consider killing or abandoning their child. Each state provides an alternative **safe haven (Baby Moses law)**, which allows overwhelmed despondent parents to give their baby to someone who will take care of him or her with no criminal prosecution (http://www.nationalsafehavenalliance.org/law.php). The rules in Texas for the parent are:

▸ Your baby *must* be 60 days old or younger and unharmed and safe.

▸ You may take your baby to *any* hospital, fire station, or emergency medical services (EMS) station in Texas.

▸ You need to give your baby to an employee who works at one of these safe places and tell this person that you want to leave your baby at a safe haven.

▸ You may be asked by an employee for family or medical history to make sure that your baby receives the care he or she needs. If you leave your unharmed infant at a safe haven, you will not be prosecuted for abandonment or neglect. See http://www.nationalsafehavenalliance.org/law.php for more information.

Aside from these feelings sometimes experienced in the early days of parenting, how do women feel about the role of mother and how is it related to their sense of personal and parental well-being over time? When personal well-being is defined in terms of lack of anxiety, depression, and stress as well as being satisfied ("full" and "fulfilled") and parental well-being is defined in terms of absence of stress, role overload, and guilt, and experiencing joy in the role, Luthar and Ciciolla (2016) analyzed Internet survey data of 2,200 mostly well-educated mothers with children ranging from infants to adults. They found a curvilinear pattern across children's developmental stages, with mothers of middle-schoolers faring the most poorly, and mothers of adult children and infants faring the best in terms of personal and parental well-being.

Mothers sometimes feel isolated. Momstown.ca is a website/context that allows Canadian moms to connect/share their experiences. Valtchanov et al. (2016) interviewed 22 member moms who revealed that they felt less visible, socially relevant, and isolated. However, the website allowed them to transcend their isolation via technology and enjoy an alternate online leisure reality.

Senior (2014) confirmed that mothers (and fathers) spend more time with their children than they did in 1965. While 40% of mothers are the primary or sole breadwinner, they focus on time with their children when they are not at work. The house is a mess and there are fewer home-cooked meals—time with the kids is a priority.

> I always thought I was born to be a musician, but I realize now that I was born to be a dad.
>
> —DAVE JOHNSON (ON THE BIRTH OF EVIE AND JOY)

12-3b Transition to Fatherhood

Kings et al. (2016) noted that men receive limited socialization for the role of father. Nevertheless, there has been a major cultural shift in how fatherhood is conceptualized. While economic provider remains an important factor in how men view their role as fathers, increasingly, men are becoming more active in the physical care of and emotional engagement with their children (Stykes, 2015).

postpartum depression a more severe reaction following the birth of a baby which occurs in reference to a complicated delivery as well as numerous physiological and psychological changes occurring during pregnancy, labor, and delivery; usually in the first month after birth but can be experienced after a couple of years have passed.

postpartum psychosis a reaction in which a woman wants to harm her baby.

safe haven (Baby Moses law) place where mother of infant can take her baby and leave it without fear of prosecution.

A favorite activity some children enjoy is reading with their dad.

Such engagement begins with fathers being present at the ultrasound where they report increased feelings of attachment and a sense of pride (Harpel & Gentry, 2014). Another event that increases the father's involvement is a second child—he spends more time with the older child while the mother takes care of the infant (Kuo & Volling, 2014). Finally, fathers who have wives who work part- or full-time and with whom they have a romantic attachment report more involvement with their infants (Roubinov et al., 2016).

Some fathers experience postpartum depression following the birth of a baby. The personal reaction of the male to the role of becoming a new father is related to whether the birth of the baby was intended. Su (2012) studied 889 men and found that unintended

gatekeeper role term used to refer to the influence of the mother on the father's involvement with his children.

births were associated with depressive symptoms among fathers, particularly where financial strain was involved. Brown et al. (2015) did not find evidence for postpartum depression among a sample of low SES African American fathers.

Regardless of whether the father gets depressed or the birth was intended, there is an economic benefit to the family for the husband becoming a father. Killewald (2013) noted that fathers who live with their wives and biological children become more focused and committed to work, and their wage gains increase 4%. Adler and Lenz (2014) noted that the value of fatherhood in the United States is primarily in reference to being a good provider for the family. Men who become fathers and who remain in the role for at least five years are less likely to become involved in crime (Theobald et al., 2015).

Puhlman and Pasley (2015) emphasized that mothers are the gatekeepers of the father's involvement with his children. Fathers who perceived mothers as more encouraging and less discouraging/controlling reported higher quality and more frequent involvement with their children. The **gatekeeper role** is particularly pronounced after a divorce in which the mother receives custody of the children (the role of the father may be severely limited). Sweeney et al. (2015) compared child care gatekeeping in couples representing different sexual identities and found that lesbians have more egalitarian relationships than heterosexual women and are less likely to display gatekeeping behavior. However, men (particularly those whose career is not salient) in same-sex relationships may display more gatekeeping behavior than men in other sex relationships.

The importance of the father in the lives of his children is enormous and goes beyond his economic

Maria McDonald

Mothers can be the gatekeepers of the father's involvement with his children.

contribution (Dearden et al., 2013; Gordon & Hull, 2014; Levtov et al., 2015). Seinfeld's biographer noted the enormous influence his salesman father had on him in terms of being an assertive-make-your-own-life-happen man (Oppenheimer, 2002). Children who have a father who maintains active involvement in their lives tend to:

- Make good grades
- Be less involved in crime
- Have good health/ self-concept
- Have a strong work ethic
- Have durable marriages
- Have a strong moral conscience
- Have higher life satisfaction

- Have higher incomes as adults
- Have higher education levels
- Have higher cognitive functioning
- Have stable jobs
- Have fewer premarital births
- Have lower incidences of child sex abuse
- Exhibit healthier/on time physical development

Daughters may have an extra benefit of a close relationship with fathers. Byrd-Craven et al. (2012) noted that such a relationship was associated with the daughters' having lower stress levels which assisted them in coping with problems and in managing interpersonal relationships. To foster the relationship between fathers and daughters, the Indian Princess program has emerged. Google Indian Princess program for an organization in your community.

12-3c **Transition from a Couple to a Family**

Children impact a couple's marriage by reducing the amount of time the spouses spend together. Flood and Genadek (2016) reviewed data from 46,883 individuals over a seven-year period and confirmed that having children resulted in spouses spending less time together to the detriment of the happiness of their marriage (nonparents in the sample spent more time with their spouses and reported greater happiness).

The degree to which the birth of a baby has a negative impact on parents and their relationship is due, in part, to the negative emotionality (e.g., fusses, cries, easily upset) of the infant. Berryhill et al. (2016) found that parents of infants perceived to display negative emotionality reported higher stress levels as parents and lower relationship quality. New parenting stress, particularly for the mother, also has a negative effect on the reported sexual satisfaction of both the mother and the father (Leavitt et al., 2015).

The physical health of the child can also impact the experience of parents. Davis and Manago (2016) revealed that parents with children with disabilities are stigmatized. For example, Marsha, a mother of a 5-year-old son with a rare blood disorder, noted:

> Ummm . . . with our own friends, (long pause—deep exhale) it's like we have the plague. And, you know, it's not because they don't like us, it's . . . they feel awkward around us now. You can only ask "how's your son doing?" so many times before, you . . . people don't really want to know how is your son doing [laugh]. But, you know, so it got to the point where the invites stopped coming.

Finally, mindful of the effect children may have on today's couples, Moroney (2016) noted that the value parents assign to parenting is reflected in housing construction. Nineteenth- to mid-20th-century house designs situated a "parents' room" within close proximity to other bedrooms, keeping the marital couple near their children. Beginning in the mid-20th century, the "master bedroom" grew in size and importance. "Modern marriages require sanctuary from the stresses of family life and must have privacy to achieve happiness and fulfillment."

Not all couples report problems when they have a baby. Holmes et al. (2013) studied 125 couples as they transitioned to parenthood and found that although many parents reported declines in love and increases in conflict, 23% of mothers and 37% of fathers reported equal or increased love; 20% of mothers and 28% of fathers reported equal or lower conflict. Durtschi and Soloski (2012) found that coparenting was associated with less parental stress and greater relationship quality. However, coparenting may not mean an equal share of hours at the parental wheel as women typically do more child care than men, particularly in the early transition phase of parenting (Yavorsky et al., 2015).

What about satisfaction in the role of parents over time? Coparenting satisfaction increases the first decade of the marriage, peaking around 10 to 12 years, and levels off and declines the second half of the second decade of the marriage. When the child reaches adolescence and asserts his or her independence and desire for more freedom, satisfaction with the parental role declines, marital conflict increases, and marital satisfaction drops. This pattern was observed by Riina and McHale (2015), who studied 145 African American dyads. The results are similar to those found in White families.

FIGURE 12.1 PERCENTAGE OF COUPLES GETTING DIVORCED BY NUMBER OF CHILDREN

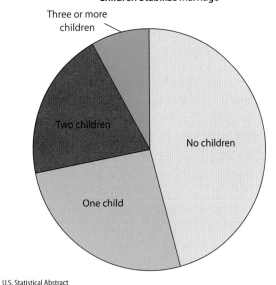

Children Stabilize Marriage

Three or more children

Two children

One child

No children

U.S. Statistical Abstract

Regardless of how children affect relationship satisfaction, spouses report more commitment to their relationship once they have children. Figure 12.1 illustrates that the more children a couple has, the more likely the couple will stay married. A primary reason for this increased commitment is the desire on the part of both parents to provide a stable family context for their children. In addition, parents of dependent children may keep their marriage together to maintain continued access to and a higher standard of living for their children. Finally, people (especially mothers) with small children feel more pressure to stay married (if the partner provides sufficient economic resources) regardless of how unhappy they may be. Hence, though children may decrease happiness, they increase stability, because pressure exists to stay together (the larger the family is, the more difficult the economic postdivorce survival is).

 12-4 PARENTHOOD: SOME FACTS

Parenting is only one stage in an individual's or couple's life (children typically live with an individual 30% of that person's life and with a couple 40% of their marriage). Parenting involves responding to the varying needs of children as they grow up, and parents require help from family and friends in rearing their children.

Some additional facts of parenthood follow.

helicopter parents parents who seek to manage the lives of their children long beyond childhood/early adolescence.

12-4a Views of Children Differ Historically

The concept of childhood, like gender, is a social construct rather than a fixed life stage. From the 13th through 16th centuries, children were viewed as innocent, sweet, and a source of amusement for adults. From the 16th through the 18th centuries, they were viewed as being in need of discipline and moral training. In the 19th century, whippings were routine as a means of breaking a child's spirit and bringing the child into submission. Although remnants of both the innocent and moralistic views of children exist today, the lives of children are greatly improved. Child labor laws in the United States protect children from early forced labor; education laws ensure a basic education; and modern medicine has been able to increase the life span of children.

Children of the millennial generation have grown up as the focus of parental attention to the extreme. In some families, everything children did was "fantastic" and deserved a gold star. The result was a generation of young adults who felt that they were special and entitled. Some of their parents (the number has been overestimated) (Lowe et al., 2015) were **helicopter parents** (HP) (also referred to as PFH—Parents from Hell), defined as parents who make important decisions for their children (e.g., where they live, work, classes they take), intervene in settling disputes with roommates/friends/employers/professors, and resolve problems and/or look for jobs for their offspring to ensure their child's success (Willoughby et al., 2015).

The result of HP may not be good for offspring. Nelson et al. (2015) found that children of helicopter parents (in contrast to free-range children) were more likely to have lower levels of self-worth and more likely to delay marriage. The latter finding is from researchers Willoughby et al. (2015) who noted:

> Although most helicopter parents are over involved because they want to protect their children, results from this study suggest that this type of parenting behavior may actually have the opposite effect. Specifically, rather than ameliorating the chance of their children being harmed, by possibly contributing to an extended period of singleness parents may actually be placing their children at greater long-term risk.

12-4b Millennials as Parents

As millennials have become parents, the 22 million spawn about 9,000 babies per day. Reacting to their own overscheduled childhoods, these millennials take a less directorial approach and want their children to try new things. Rather than "helicopter" parents they are "drone" parents whereby they don't hover but follow and respond to the needs of their children (Steinmetz, 2015).

Millennials as parents also feel intense pressure, generated by social media, to be the perfect parents they see posted on Facebook, Twitter, blogs, and apps. No longer do they just ask mom how to parent but they Google for answers and are barraged with different opinions. Indeed, 58% of millennials feel that the amount of parenting information available on the Internet is overwhelming compared to 46% of those of Generation X and 43% of baby boomers (Steinmetz, 2015).

Mary Jane LaNeave

12-4c Parents Are Only One Influence in a Child's Development

Although parents often take the credit and the blame for the way their children turn out, they are only one among many influences on child development. Peer influence, siblings, teachers, media, and the Internet influence the development of children. Regarding the Internet, although parents may encourage their children to conduct research and write term papers using the Internet, they may fear their children are also looking at pornography. Parental supervision of teenagers and their privacy rights on the Internet remain potential sources of conflict.

12-4d Teaching One's Children to Think for Themselves Has a Trade-Off

How do parents manage the issue of teaching their children to be independent thinkers yet reflect the values of the parents? Dill (2015) revealed in his research on 101 parents of school-age children that most valued socializing their children to "think for themselves" by which they wanted their children to internalize the moral code from the parents and to resist negative influences. In effect, "think for yourself" means "think like me" (obedience and conformity). The result is that parents are very ambivalent—they want to instill in their children a sense of individualism and freedom but want them to "choose wisely." Being an independent thinker might involve an interracial relationship, alcohol/drug use, or eschewing education. One father lamented that his

son wanted to drop out of college and be a musician playing nightly gigs (clearly the value of the son).

12-4e Each Gender Is Unique

Wiseman (2013) reminds parents that the genders are also different and encourages them not to assume that boys are always emotionally resilient. Just because girls are socialized to be more open about their feelings (e.g., sad and depressed), boys may have these same feelings without a way to cope with them. She recommends that parents stay close to the emotional worlds of boys too—their falling in love, having their hearts broken, being bullied.

Gray et al. (2016) interviewed parents of transgender children who expressed their fear, support, and continued engagement with their children and related issues. An example is a parent who said:

> I considered the issue that all parents consider about him being stealth…and it's about safety. And I was really scared about that, like all parents are, and then, I realized that he didn't want to be stealth, and I realized that I could probably respect that, but it would be a harder way to go. (p. 11)

12-4f Parenting Styles Differ

Diana Baumrind (1966) developed a typology of parenting styles that has become classic in the study of parenting. She noted that parenting behavior has two dimensions: responsiveness and demandingness. **Responsiveness** refers to the extent to which parents respond to and meet the emotional needs of their children. In other words, how supportive are the parents? Warmth, reciprocity, person-centered communication, and attachment are all aspects of responsiveness. **Demandingness**, on the other hand, is the manner in which parents place demands on children in regard to expectations and discipline. How much control do they exert over their children? Monitoring and confrontation are also aspects of demandingness. Categorizing parents in

responsiveness refers to the extent to which parents respond to and meet the needs of their children.

demandingness the manner in which parents place demands on children in regard to expectations and discipline.

My Children Are the Yin and the Yang

My daughter as a baby was the type of child who would be categorized as "spirited" or "strong willed." The real definition without the fluff is that she was difficult to parent most of the time. As a baby, she had colic and reflux and was hard to soothe. She did not sleep well and she demanded a great deal of attention. As a toddler, she was dramatic and intense in her play. She did not like to be told "no" and she liked to have control over her environment. She was also funny, loving, bright, and very creative.

Today, my daughter (age 13) is the epitome of a teen. She is moody, intense, entitled, and concerned that her peers like her. She is also amazingly creative and smart, has a good sense of humor, is loving, and craves my attention and affection after being at school all day. She is becoming more responsible and contributing to the family. I am able to reframe in my own mind that some of her traits that almost put me over the edge (e.g., assertiveness) will serve her well as she matures into an adult.

My son was born when my daughter was 4 years old, and I often wonder how I have another child that is completely different than my daughter. My son was

an "easy" baby. He had no eating or sleeping difficulties and his temperament was very laid back. When I tell people my son literally slept through the night every night from 6 months onward, they find it hard to believe. My son could play in his playpen without being entertained, he was the type of baby that you could take out to a dinner, and he was not fussy or disruptive. He was the preschool teacher's "favorite" student. Parenting him almost felt easy.

Now, age 9, my son remains very easy to parent. He is goofy and smart and loves video games and doing creative things. Because he is so well behaved, I have to remind myself to give him as much attention as his sister. I can see him as a young man, and I think that he will make a wonderful husband and father because he has so many amazing and warm qualities. On days when I am feeling overwhelmed or the kids are being loud when I've already had a rough day at work, I try to remind myself that I have the best of both worlds. They both help me grow in different ways. I have a girl and a boy— I have my yin and a yang.

—VICKI OLIVER

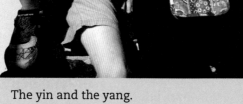
The yin and the yang.

Vicki Oliver

terms of their responsiveness and their demandingness creates four categories of parenting styles: permissive (also known as indulgent), authoritarian, authoritative, and uninvolved:

1. **Permissive parents are high on responsiveness and low on demandingness.** These parents are very lenient and allow their children to largely regulate their own behavior. Walcheski and Bredehoft (2010) found that the permissive parenting style is associated with overindulgence. For example, these parents state punishments but do not follow through; they give in to their children. These parents act out of fear that disciplining the child will cause the child to dislike his or her parents. The parents are controlled by the potential disapproval of the child.

2. **Authoritarian parents are high on demandingness and low in responsiveness.** Authoritarian parents feel that children should obey their parents no matter what. King et al. (2016) provided data on 17,399 youth to confirm that they were more likely to be depressed if they had parents who displayed an authoritarian parenting style. Surjadi et al. (2013) confirmed that harsh, inconsistent discipline from parents was later related to poor relationship quality with romantic partners during cohabitation or the early years of marriage.

3. **Authoritative parents are both demanding and responsive.** They impose appropriate limits on their children's behavior but emphasize reasoning and communication. Authoritative parenting offers a balance of warmth and control and is associated

with the most positive outcome for children. Examples of this style include parents telling the child their expectations of the child's behavior before the child engages in the activity, giving the child reasons why rules should be obeyed, talking with the child when he or she misbehaves, and explaining consequences (Walcheski & Bredehoft, 2010). Panetta et al. (2014) studied outcomes of various parenting styles of mothers and fathers on 195 seventh to eleventh grade adolescents. Temperament of adolescent (e.g., mood, flexibility–rigidity) explained half of the variance in adolescent outcomes. Parenting styles contributed a smaller but significant role. When both parents were authoritative, it was associated with more optimal outcomes in adolescents' personal adjustment than any other parenting style combination. In addition, when both parents were permissive and neglectful, these parenting styles were associated with poorer adolescent outcomes. Similar positive outcomes for authoritative parenting were observed in Japanese children by Uji et al. (2014).

4. **Uninvolved parents are low in responsiveness and demandingness.** These parents are not invested in their children's lives. Beato et al. (2016) conceptualized parenting styles as disengaged, overinvolved, and supportive, and found that the children of disengaged mothers were more likely to report higher levels of anxiety. Panetta et al. (2014) confirmed that permissive and neglectful parenting has negative outcomes for adolescents.

McKinney and Renk (2008) identified the differences between maternal and paternal parenting styles, with mothers tending to be authoritative and fathers tending to be authoritarian. Mothers and fathers also use different parenting styles for their sons and daughters, with fathers being more permissive with their sons than with their daughters. Overall, this study emphasized the importance of examining the different parenting styles on adolescent outcome and suggested that having at least one authoritative parent may be a protective factor for older adolescents. In summary, the authoritative parenting style is the combination of warmth, guidelines, and discipline— "I love you but you need to be in by midnight or you'll lose the privileges of having a cell phone and a car."

To be an authoritative parent is reflected in some of the qualities of mindfulness. Mindfulness (focused, calm, empathetic, compassionate) has been found to be a positive quality in relating to children. Corthorn and Milicic (2016) studied 62 mothers (of preschool children) who practiced mindful parenting and found that doing so was associated with less depression, anxiety, and

Diversity in Other Countries

Petrovic et al. (2016) examined parenting practices in several transnational eastern European countries (Bosnia and Herzegovina, Macedonia and Serbia, a total of 9,973 respondents) and found that 27% of the respondents practiced only nonviolent child discipline. Parents from more affluent households were more likely than those from less affluent households to be against physical punishment of children and more likely to practice only nonviolent discipline.

general stress. Mindful abilities such as being nonjudgmental about herself as a person and as a mother were particularly helpful in relating to children.

> Each time your child or teenager comes to talk with you about something important or interesting in their lives, you are auditioning to have another conversation down the road.
>
> —KAREN RAYNE, *BREAKING THE HUSH FACTOR*

12-5 PRINCIPLES OF EFFECTIVE PARENTING

Numerous principles are involved in being effective parents (Keim & Jacobson, 2011). We begin with the most important of these principles, which involves giving time/love to your children as well as praising and encouraging them.

12-5a Give Time, Love, Praise, Encouragement, and Acceptance

Children need to feel that they are worth spending time with and that they are loved. Because children depend first on their parents for the development of their sense

Children never forget the time you spend with them.

Lisa Knox

of emotional security, it is critical that parents provide a warm emotional context in which the children develop. Feeling loved as an infant also affects one's capacity to become involved in adult love relationships.

Abundant evidence from children reared in institutions where nurses attended only to their physical needs testify to the negative consequences of early emotional neglect. **Reactive attachment disorder** is common among children who were taught as infants that no one cared about them. Such children have no capacity to bond emotionally with others since they have no learning history of the experience and do not trust adults/caretakers/parents. A 5:1 ratio of positive to negative statements to the child is also associated with positive outcomes for the child (Armstrong & Clinton, 2012). The value of a positive family context continues into middle school. Researchers Williams and Anthony (2015) analyzed data on 20,749 adolescents in middle school and found that family togetherness

reactive attachment disorder common among children who were taught as infants that no one cared about them; these children have no capacity to bond emotionally with others since they have no learning history of the experience and do not trust adults, caretakers, or parents.

overindulgence defined as more than just giving children too much; includes overnurturing and providing too little structure.

and parental behavioral expectations were associated with less school misbehavior.

12-5b Avoid Overindulgence

Overindulgence may be defined as more than just giving children too much; it includes overnurturing and not providing enough structure. Using this definition, a study of 466 participants revealed that those who are overindulged tend to hold materialist values for success, are not able to delay gratification, and are less grateful for things and to others. Another result of overindulgence is that children grow up without consequences so they avoid real jobs where employers expect them to show up at 8:00 A.M. Indeed, not being overindulged promotes the ability to delay gratification, be grateful, and experience a view (nonmaterialism) that is associated with happiness (Slinger & Bredehoft, 2010).

12-5c Monitor Child's Activities/Drug Use

Parents who monitor their children and teens and know where their children are, who they are with, and what they are doing are less likely to report that their adolescents receive low grades, or are engaged in early sexual activity, delinquent behavior, and alcohol or drug use. Indeed, Henchoz et al. (2016) found that chronic adult marijuana users began smoking marijuana an average of two years earlier than those with no use or moderate use. "Keep your eye on your children" is the takeaway message for parents. Crutzen et al. (2012) assessed the effects of parental approval of children's drinking alcohol at home on their subsequent drinking behavior. Of 1,500 primary school children, those who were allowed to drink alcohol around their parents were less likely to consume alcohol when they were away from their parents.

Parents who drank alcohol under age and who used marijuana or other drugs wonder how to go about encouraging their own children to be responsible alcohol users and drug free. Drugfree.org has some recommendations for parents, including being honest with their children about previous alcohol and drug use, making clear that they do not want their children to use alcohol or drugs, and explaining that although not all alcohol or drug use leads to negative consequences, staying clear of alcohol/drug use is the best course of action.

12-5d Monitor Pornography Exposure

The negative effects of pornography exposure among children include their developing sexist and unhealthy notions of sex and relationships. Pornography teaches unrealistic expectations (e.g., females are expected to have bodies like porn stars, to enjoy "facials," and to have anal sex) and is devoid of integrating intimacy in sexual expression (Knox & Milstein, 2017).

12-5e Use Technology to Monitor Cell Phone/ Text Messaging Use

"Technological advances" was identified by 2,000 parents as the top issue (violence was second) that makes parenting children today tougher than in previous years (Payne & Trapp, 2013). Some parents are concerned about their child's use of a cell phone, texting, and sexting. Not only may predators contact children/teenagers without the parents' awareness, but also 39% of teens report having sent sexually suggestive text messages, and 20% have sent nude or seminude photos or videos of themselves. New technology called SMS Tracker for Android permits parents to effectively take over their child's mobile phone. A parent can see all incoming and outgoing calls, text messages, and photos. Another protective device on the market is MyMobileWatchdog (known as MMWD), which monitors a child's cell phone use and instantly alerts the parents online if their son or daughter receives unapproved email, text messages, or phone calls. SecuraFone can reveal how fast the car in which the cell phone of the user is moving and alert parents. If a teen is speeding, the parents will know. One version shuts the texting capability

lucadp/Fotolia

down if the phone is going faster than 5 miles an hour. Mobiflock for Android allows parents to lock their child's phone for a predetermined time (e.g., 7 to 10 P.M. when studying is scheduled). In effect, these smartphones have web filters (which can block inappropriate websites), app filters (which make sure apps are kid-friendly), and contact filters (which can prevent harassing calls or texts by blocking certain numbers), which allow parents to monitor their child's location, texts, calls, browsing histories, app downloads, and photos they send and receive.

Dangerous apps that parents should not allow their children to have on their phones include Snapchat (photos disappear), Kik Messenger (hides content from parents), Yik Yak (has GPS so predator can locate), Poof (hides apps), O Mengle (can't track who is messaging your child), and Down (sex focused). Children/adolescents may say "you are invading my privacy" and "you don't trust me." The parents response is "I'm the parent, I love you, and I am responsible for you. When you are 18, you will have privacy. Until then, I'm on duty."

12-5f Provide Guidance and Discipline

The goal of setting limits and disciplining children is their self-control. Parents want their children to be able to control their own behavior and to make good decisions on their own. Parental guidance involves reinforcing desired behavior and punishing undesirable behavior. Unless parents levy negative consequences for lying, stealing, and hitting, children can grow up to be dishonest, to steal, and to be inappropriately aggressive. **Time-out** (a noncorporal form of punishment that involves removing the child from a context of reinforcement to a place of isolation for one minute for each year of the child's age) has been shown to be an effective consequence for inappropriate behavior. Withdrawal of privileges (use of cell phone, watching television, being with friends), pointing out the logical consequences of the

> I think that the best thing we can do for our children is to allow them to do things for themselves, allow them to be strong, allow them to experience life on their own terms, allow them to take the subway… let them be better people, let them believe more in themselves.
>
> —C. JOYBELL C.

time-out a noncorporal form of punishment that involves removing the child from a context of reinforcement to a place of isolation.

misbehavior ("you were late; we won't go"), and positive language ("I know you meant well but . . .") are also effective methods of guiding children's behavior.

Physical punishment is less effective in reducing negative behavior; it teaches the child to be aggressive and encourages negative emotional feelings toward the parents. When using time-out or the with-

Brand X Pictures/Thinkstock

drawal of privileges, parents should make clear to the child that they disapprove of the child's behavior, not the child. A review of some of the alternatives to corporal punishment includes the following:

1. **Be a positive role model.** Children learn behaviors by observing their parents' actions, so parents must model the ways in which they want their children to behave. If a parent yells or hits, the child is likely to do the same.

2. **Set rules and consequences.** Make rules that are fair, realistic, and appropriate to a child's level of development. Explain the rules and the consequences of not following them. If children are old enough, they can be included in establishing the rules and consequences for breaking them.

3. **Encourage and reward good behavior.** When children are behaving appropriately, give them verbal praise and reward them with tangible objects (occasionally), privileges, or increased responsibility.

4. **Use charts.** Charts to monitor and reward behavior can help children learn appropriate behavior. Charts should be simple and focus on one behavior at a time, for a certain length of time.

5. **Use time-out.** Time-out involves removing children from a situation following a negative behavior. This can help children calm down, end an inappropriate behavior, and reenter the situation in a positive way. Explain what the inappropriate behavior is, why the time-out is needed, when it will begin, and how long it will last. Set an appropriate length

of time for the time-out based on age and level of development, usually one minute for each year of the child's age. Awareness of these alternatives is associated with a reduction in the use of spanking. Implementation of these principles results in behavior change in the desired direction—children become more compliant, less disruptive, etc. (Yu et al., 2015).

12-5g Have Family Meals

Parents who stay emotionally connected with their children build strong relationships with them and report fewer problems. The family ritual of having dinner together is associated with fewer behavioral symptoms and lower family stress. Females seem to benefit the most (Yoon et al., 2015).

12-5h Encourage Responsibility

Giving children increased responsibility encourages the autonomy and independence they need to be assertive and self-governing. Giving children more responsibility as they grow older can take the form of encouraging them to choose healthy snacks and letting them decide what to wear and when to return from playing with a friend (of course, the parents should praise appropriate choices).

Children who are not given any control over, and responsibility for, their own lives remain dependent on others. A dependent child is a vulnerable child. Successful parents can be defined in terms of their ability to rear children who can function as independent adults.

Parents also recognize that there is a balance they must strike between helping their children and impeding their own growth and development. One example is making decisions on how long to provide free room and board for an adult child.

Self-Assessment: Spanking versus Time-Out Scale

See the Spanking versus Time-Out Scale at the end of this chapter to assess your views.

> But kids don't stay with you if you do it right. It's the one job where, the better you are, the more surely you won't be needed in the long run.
>
> —BARBARA KINGSOLVER, *PIGS IN HEAVEN*

12-5i Adult Children Living with Parents: Boomerang Children/Accordion Family

Children of the boomerang generation are not unusual as 22% of young adults return to the parental home at least once (Sandberg-Thoma et al., 2015). Jang and Mernitz (2015) found that 40% will return home. Some remain in the home, preferring the advantages of living in a well-equipped home with a large flat "smart" TV, regular meals, etc., than living in an apartment with three roommates in a less desirable section of town. Hence, they will trade their independence for living under their parents' roof/rules to maintain a higher standard of living (Newman, 2015).

Reasons for 8,162 adult youth (average age 24) leaving and returning to the parental home were revealed by Sandberg-Thoma et al. (2015). Emotional distress was a primary reason for both leaving and returning to the parental home. Alcohol problems were also related to returning to the parental home.

Jang and Mernitz (2015) found that emerging adults elect to live close to or farther away from parents depending on their need for emotional/financial support versus their need to avoid parental control. Needs of the parents (e.g., divorce, unemployment) as well as changes in the life of the offspring (e.g., they have a baby) are also associated with the offspring moving closer to the parents. About 26% will remain in the area of their parents; 18% will move away.

Regardless of the motivations, when adult children move back into the home, parents and children negotiate the length of stay, employment, education, and curfew (Otters & Hollander, 2015).

Another issue is who does the housework when adult children return home? It depends on whether the offspring have a job and are in school. Being employed and being in school are associated with doing less housework (Craig et al., 2015).

12-5j Establish Norm of Forgiveness

Carr and Wang (2012) emphasized the importance of forgiveness in family relationships and the fact that forgiveness is a complex time-involved process rather than a one-time cognitive event (e.g., "I forgive you"). Respondents revealed in interviews with the researchers that forgiveness involved head over heart (finding ways to explain the transgression), time (sometimes months and years), and distance (giving the relationship a rest and coming back with renewed understanding).

12-5k Teaching Emotional Competence/Empathy

Wilson et al. (2012) emphasized the importance of teaching children **emotional competence**—experiencing, expressing, and regulating emotion. Being able to label when one is happy or sad (experiencing emotion), expressing emotion ("I love you"), and regulating emotion (e.g., reducing anger) assists children in getting in touch with their feelings and being empathetic with others. Wilson et al. (2012) reported on "Tuning in the Kids," a training program for parents to learn how to teach their children to be emotionally competent. Follow-up data on parents who took the six-session, two-hour-a-week program revealed positive outcomes/changes.

Children also need to learn empathy. While narcissism ("it's all about me") is the current cultural mantra, Borba (2016) emphasized the benefits (happier, more cooperative, engaging) of learning to see the world from another's point of view. It's a win–win for all.

12-5l Provide Sex Education

Hyde et al. (2013) interviewed 32 mothers and 11 fathers about the sexuality education of their children. Most gave little to no explicit information about safe sex—they assumed that the school had done so and that their son or daughter was not in a romantic relationship. Some felt that talking to their children about sex might be viewed as encouraging sexual behavior.

12-5m Express Confidence

"One of the greatest mistakes a parent can make," confided one mother, "is to be anxious all the time about your child, because the child interprets this as your lack of confidence in his or her ability to function independently." Rather, this mother noted that it is best to convey to one's child that you know that he or she will be fine because you have confidence in him/her. "The effect on the child," said this mother, "is a heightened sense of self-confidence." Another way to conceptualize this parental principle is to think of the self-fulfilling prophecy as a mechanism that facilitates self-confidence. If parents show their child that they have confidence in him or her, the child begins to accept these social definitions as real and becomes more self-confident.

12-5n Respond to the Teen Years Creatively

Parenting teenage children presents challenges that differ from those in parenting infants and young

emotional competence teaching the child to experience emotion, express emotion, and regulate emotion.

children. Conflicts between parents and teenagers often revolve around money and independence. The desired cell phone, designer clothes, and car can outstrip the budgets of many parents. Teens also want increasingly more freedom. However, neither of these issues need result in conflict. When they do, the effect on the parent–child relationship may be inconsequential. One parent tells his children, "I'm just being the parent, and you're just being who you are; it is okay for us to disagree but you can't go." Metler and Small (2015) emphasize a "wise parenting" approach to conflict with teenagers. This involves finding out the teenager's point of view, identifying what needs the teen is trying to meet, and finding a solution that does not alienate the teen. The following suggestions are standard aspects of relating to teens.

> Teenagers only have to focus on themselves—it's not until we get older that we realize that other people exist.
>
> —JENNIFER LAWRENCE

1. **Catch them doing what you like rather than criticizing them for what you do not like.** Adolescents are like everyone else—they do not like to be criticized, but they do like to be noticed for what they do that is exemplary.

2. **Be direct when necessary.** Though parents may want to ignore some behaviors of their children, addressing certain issues directly is necessary. Regarding the avoidance of sexually transmitted infections (STIs) or HIV infection and pregnancy, parents should inform their teenagers of the importance of using a condom or dental dam before sex.

3. **Provide information rather than answers.** When teens are confronted with a problem, try to avoid making a decision for them. Rather, provide information on which they may base a decision. What courses to take in high school and what college to apply to are decisions that might be made primarily by the adolescent. The role of the parent might best be to listen.

4. **Be tolerant of high activity levels.** Some teenagers are constantly listening to loud music, going

to each other's homes, and talking on cell phones for long periods of time. Parents often want to sit in their easy chairs in peace. Recognizing that it is not realistic to always expect teenagers to be quiet and sedentary may be helpful in tolerating their disruptions.

5. **Engage in leisure activity with your teenagers.** In an analysis of data on mothers of 778 adolescents (aged 12–18), spending engaged time with their adolescent had positive behavioral/emotional/academic outcomes as well as lower frequencies of adolescent risky behavior (e.g., drug use). Engaged time with the father also had positive outcomes for the adolescent (Milkie et al., 2015). Parental time with teenagers (e.g., riding in the car, meals together) is also associated with the adolescent's higher self-esteem and lower substance abuse (Irving & Richardson, 2014) as well as fewer depressive symptoms (Zeiders et al., 2016). Bottom line: whether renting a DVD, eating together, or taking a camping trip, structuring activities with your teenagers is important.

   Sometimes teenagers present challenges with which their parents feel unable to cope. Mothers seem more able to stay connected to their children during the teen years than fathers (Doty, 2015). Aside from monitoring their behavior closely, family therapy may be helpful. Two major goals of such therapy are to increase the emotional bond between the parents and the teenagers and to encourage positive consequences for desirable behavior (e.g., cell phone for good grades) and negative consequences for undesirable behavior (e.g., loss of cell phone/car privileges).

6. **Use technology to encourage safer driving.** GPS devices are now available that can tell a parent where their teenager is, record any sudden stops, and record speed. Some teenagers scream foul and accuse their parents of not trusting them. One answer is that of a father who required his daughter to pay for her car insurance but told her she could get a major discount if the GPS device was installed. She then thought the GPS was a good idea (Copeland, 2012).

All of the above are helpful in rearing teenagers some of the time. Janssen et al. (2016) confirmed that parental behavior has an impact on adolescent delinquency (e.g., vandalism, robbery), but the factors are beneficial in combination, not alone.

Teaching children to exercise self-control, monitoring their time/associations with peers, and restricting their access to problematic contexts (e.g., no curfew, party) in combination is associated with low frequencies of delinquent behavior in a way that just one of these parental behaviors has a limited impact.

Sometimes parents ask for help in responding to emotional and behavioral problems of their children. One such program is the Triple P Positive Parenting Program, which was founded by Professor Matt Sanders of Brisbane, Australia. The evidenced-based Triple P parenting system has been used by over 4 million children and their families in 25 countries. More than 55,000 practitioners have been trained in its delivery, some of whom may be available in your community. Ozyurt et al. (2016) found that the program was effective in reducing emotional and behavioral problems in children with anxiety disorder as well as providing a sense of well-being in parents.

> Being a single parent is twice the work, twice the stress and twice the tears but also twice the hugs, twice the love and twice the pride.
>
> —UNKNOWN

12-6 SINGLE-PARENTING ISSUES

Forty percent of births in the United States are to unmarried mothers. Distinguishing between a single-parent "family" and a single-parent "household" is important. A **single-parent family** is one in which there is only one parent—the other parent is completely out of the child's life through death or complete abandonment or as a result of sperm donation, and no contact is ever made. In contrast, a **single-parent household** is one in which one parent typically has primary custody of the child or children, but the parent living out of the house is still a part of the child's life. This arrangement is also referred to as a binuclear family. In most divorce cases in which the mother has primary physical custody of the child, the child lives in a single-parent household because the child is still connected to the father, who remains part of the child's life. In cases in which one parent has died,

the child or children live with the surviving parent in a single-parent family because there is only one parent. Single-parent households may be headed by a mother or a father (Coles, 2015).

12-6a Single Mothers by Choice

Single parents enter their role through divorce or separation, widowhood, adoption, or deliberate choice to rear a child or children alone. Diane Keaton, never married, has two adopted daughters.

An organization for women who want children and who may or may not marry is Single Mothers by Choice. Golombok et al. (2016) compared the well-being of children born to single mothers by choice with children born to two-parent families (all children by donor insemination). There were no differences in child adjustment. However, the researcher did observe lower mother–child conflict in solo mother families.

12-6b Challenges Faced by Single Parents

The single-parent lifestyle involves numerous challenges. See singleparent.lifetips.com for some interesting advice. Challenges associated with being a single parent include the following:

1. **Responding to the demands of parenting with limited help.** Perhaps the greatest challenge for single parents is taking care of the physical, emotional, and disciplinary needs of their children alone. Depression and stress are common among single parents (Hong & Welch, 2013). Daryanani et al. (2016) suggested that one explanation for more negative outcomes in children/adolescents (e.g., depression) of single-parent mothers are the demands and stresses of the role.

2. **Resolving the issue of adult sexual needs.** Some single parents regard their parental role as interfering with their sexual relationships. They may be concerned that their children will find out if they have a sexual encounter at home or be frustrated if they have to go away from home to enjoy a sexual relationship. Gray et al. (2015) analyzed data from

single-parent family family in which there is only one parent and the other parent is completely out of the child's life through death, sperm donation, or abandonment, and no contact is made with the other parent.

single-parent household one parent has primary custody of the child/children with the other parent living outside of the house but still being a part of the child's family; also called binuclear family.

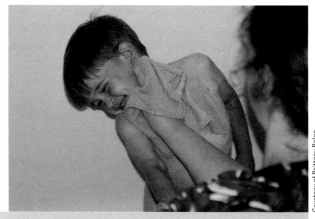

Single parenting involves one person doing all the work of parenting, including feeding and bathing children every day.

over 2,000 young single parents and found that the presence of young children under the age of 5 did not impact sexual frequency or dating of the parent negatively. Some choices with which they are confronted include, "Do I wait until my children are asleep and then ask my lover to leave before morning?" or "Do I openly acknowledge my lover's presence in my life to my children and ask them not to tell anybody?" and "Suppose my kids get attached to my lover, who may not be a permanent part of our lives?"

3. **Coping with lack of money.** Single-parent families, particularly those headed by women, report that money is always lacking. The median income of a single-woman householder is $26,425, much lower than that of a single-man householder ($36,876) or a married couple ($76,509) (*Proquest Statistical Abstract of the United States, 2016,* Table 714).

4. **Ensuring guardianship.** If the other parent is completely out of the child's life, the single parent needs to appoint a guardian to take care of the child in the event of the parent's death or disability.

5. **Obtaining prenatal care.** Single women who decide to have a child have poorer pregnancy outcomes than married women. Their children are likely to be born prematurely and to have low birth weight (Mashoa et al., 2010). The reason for such an association may be the lack of economic funds (no male partner with economic resources available) as well as the lack of social support for the pregnancy or the working conditions of the mothers.

6. **Coping with the absence of a father.** Another consequence for children of single-parent mothers is that they often do not have the opportunity to develop an emotionally supportive relationship with their father. Andersson (2016) noted the positive effect on the male child's own health as an adult of having grown up in an emotionally warm relationship with one's father in an intact traditional family. Often the mother in the single-parent family is no longer involved with the father of her child. In a study of 788 teen mothers, 45% were not romantically involved with the baby's father a year after the birth of the baby (Thompson & Beckmeyer, 2015).

7. **Perpetuating a single-family structure.** Growing up in a single-family home increases the likelihood that the adult child will have a first child while unmarried and in a cohabitation relationship, thus perpetuating the single-family structure.

8. **Developmentally delayed child of teen mothers.** In those cases where the single mother is a teen mother, there is an added risk to the child. Lehr et al. (2016) confirmed that a third of the young children of stressed (e.g., feeling less confident, restricted, socially isolated) teen mothers were developmentally delayed (e.g., fine motor skills, personal-social interaction).

Though the risk of negative outcomes is higher for children in single-parent homes, most are happy and well adjusted. Maier and McGeorge (2013) emphasized that single parents (both mothers and fathers) are victims of negative stereotyping. The reality is that there are numerous positives associated with being a single parent. These include having a stronger bonding experience with one's children since they "are" the family, a sense of pride and self-esteem for being independent, and being a strong role model for offspring who observe their parent being able to "wear many hats."

 ## 12-7 TRENDS IN PARENTING

For the first time in more than 130 years, adults ages 18 to 34 were more likely to be living in their parents' home (32.1%) than they were to be living with a spouse or partner in their own household (31.6%). Fourteen percent were living alone or with a child as a single parent and 22% other (Fry, 2016).

As parents face increasing difficulty with rearing their children who are growing up amid massive exposure via the Internet/social media to an ever-changing society, they may reach out for help with parenting. Tully and Hunt (2016) reviewed eight research projects reflecting 836 families in five countries and found that parents who took part in a training program (8 to 12 sessions) to help them manage the externalizing behavior of their children (e.g., aggression, defiance, hostility, and poor impulse control) reported improvements in these behaviors, their own skills as parents, and their sense of self-efficacy. Incredible Years is an example of an effective parenting program (Edwards et al., 2016). A final trend in parenting is increased time fathers spend with their children, particularly young children. Adler and Lenz (2014) found that fathers are, increasingly, the primary care arrangement for preschoolers.

SELF-ASSESSMENT

Spanking versus Time-Out Scale

Parents discipline their children to help them develop self-control and correct misbehavior. Some parents spank their children; others use time-out. Spanking is a disciplinary technique whereby a mild slap (i.e., a "spank") is applied to the buttocks of a disobedient child. Time-out is a disciplinary technique whereby, when a child misbehaves, the child is removed from the situation. The purpose of this survey is to assess the degree to which you prefer spanking versus time-out as a method of discipline. Please read each item carefully and select a number from 1 to 7, which represents your belief. There are no right or wrong answers; please give your honest opinion.

1	2	3	4	5	6	7
Strongly disagree						Strongly agree

_____ **1.** Spanking is a better form of discipline than time-out.

_____ **2.** Time-out does not have any effect on children.

_____ **3.** When I have children, I will more likely spank them than use a time-out.

_____ **4.** A threat of a time-out does not stop a child from misbehaving.

_____ **5.** Lessons are learned better with spanking.

_____ **6.** Time-out does not give a child an understanding of what the child has done wrong.

_____ **7.** Spanking teaches a child to respect authority.

_____ **8.** Giving children time-outs is a waste of time.

_____ **9.** Spanking has more of an impact on changing the behavior of children than time-out.

_____ **10.** I do not believe "time-out" is a form of punishment.

_____ **11.** Getting spanked as a child helps you become a responsible citizen.

_____ **12.** Time-out is only used because parents are afraid to spank their kids.

_____ **13.** Spanking can be an effective tool in disciplining a child.

_____ **14.** Time-out is watered-down discipline.

Scoring

If you want to know the degree to which you approve of spanking, reverse the number you selected for all odd-numbered items (1, 3, 5, 7, 9, 11, and 13) after you have selected a number from 1 to 7 for each of the 14 items. For example, if you selected a 1 for item 1, change this number to a 7 (1 = 7; 2 = 6; 3 = 5; 4 = 4; 5 = 3; 6 = 2; 7 = 1). Now add these 7 numbers. The lower your score (7 is the lowest possible score), the lower your approval of spanking; the higher your score (49 is the highest possible score), the greater your approval of spanking. A score of 21 places you at the midpoint between being very disapproving of or very accepting of spanking as a discipline strategy.

If you want to know the degree to which you approve of using time-out as a method of discipline, reverse the number you selected for all even-numbered items (2, 4, 6, 8, 10, 12, and 14). For example, if you selected a 1 for item 2, change this number to a 7 (i.e., 1 = 7; 2 = 6; 3 = 5; 4 = 4; 5 = 3; 6 = 2; 7 = 1). Now add these 7 numbers. The lower your score (7 is the lowest possible score), the lower your approval of time-out; the higher your score (49 is the highest possible score), the greater your approval of time-out. A score of 21 places you at the midpoint between being very disapproving of or very accepting of time-out as a discipline strategy.

Scores of Other Students Who Completed the Scale

The scale was completed by 48 male and 168 female student volunteers at East Carolina University. Their ages ranged from 18 to 34, with a mean age of 19.65 (SD = 2.06). The ethnic background of the sample included 73.1% White, 17.1% African American, 2.8% Hispanic, 0.9% Asian, 3.7% from other ethnic backgrounds; 2.3% did not indicate ethnicity. The college classification level of the sample included 52.8% freshman, 24.5% sophomore, 13.9% junior, and 8.8% senior. The average score on the spanking dimension was 29.73 (SD = 10.97), and the time-out dimension was 22.93 (SD = 8.86), suggesting greater acceptance of spanking than time-out.

Time-out differences. In regard to sex of the participants, female participants were more positive about using time-out as a discipline strategy (M = 33.72, SD = 8.76) than were male participants (M = 30.81, SD = 8.97; p = .05). In regard to ethnicity of the participants, White participants were more positive about using time-out as a discipline strategy (M = 34.63, SD = 8.54) than were non-White participants (M = 28.45, SD = 8.55; p = .05). In regard to year in school, freshmen were more positive about using spanking as a discipline strategy (M = 34.34, SD = 9.23) than were sophomores, juniors, and seniors (M = 31.66, SD = 8.25; p = .05).

Spanking differences. In regard to ethnicity of the participants, non-White participants were more positive about using spanking as a discipline strategy (M = 35.09, SD = 10.02) than were White participants (M = 27.87, SD = 10.72; p = .05). In regard to year in school, freshmen were less positive about using spanking as a discipline strategy (M 5 28.28, SD = 11.42) than were sophomores, juniors, and seniors (M = 31.34, SD = 10.26; p = .05). There were no significant differences in regard to sex of the participants (p = .05) in the opinion of spanking.

Overall differences. There were no significant differences in overall attitudes to discipline in regards to sex of the participants, ethnicity, or year in school.

Source: "The Spanking vs. Time-Out Scale," 2004, by Mark Whatley, Ph.D., Department of Psychology, Valdosta State University, Valdosta, Georgia 31698-0100. Information on the reliability and validity of this scale is available from Dr. Whatley (mwhatley@valdosta.edu).

Nicki Pardo/Getty Images

After finishing
this chapter go
to **PAGE 265** for
STUDY TOOLS

> "Life is a shipwreck, but we must not forget to sing in the lifeboats."
>
> — VOLTAIRE, PHILOSOPHER

"The course of true love never did run smooth" wrote Shakespeare. There is no reason why love relationships should be anything but stressful/turbulent. Meshing the needs, desires, personalities, and work/school schedules of two individuals over a lifetime is like the huddling of two porcupines on a cold winter night—there is need for constant adjustment each to the other so that the maximum amount of warmth is achieved with a minimum of pricking. We begin our discussion with how stress and crisis in relationships are defined.

13-1 DEFINITIONS AND SOURCES OF STRESS AND CRISIS

Stress is a reaction of the body to substantial or unusual demands (physical, environmental, or interpersonal). Stress is often accompanied by irritability, high blood pressure, and depression.

Lee et al. (2016) assessed the stress level of a national sample of adults aged 25 to 64. On a scale of 0 to 6 (with 6 being very much) the respondents averaged a 4.5 when asked to identify their "no stress" level—hence, most were not highly stressed.

While major stress events such as loss of one's job or a partner getting cancer have been the target of most individual and relationship studies, Falconier et al. (2015) focused on daily stress hassles and the effects. They analyzed data from 110 heterosexual couples and found that daily stress resulted in anxiety and physical exhaustion, while relationship stress more often resulted in depression and a drop in relationship satisfaction.

Stress is a process rather than a state. For example, a person will experience different levels of stress throughout the breakup with one's live-in partner—acknowledging that the relationship is over, telling one's friends/family of the breakup, and moving to another place all result in varying levels of stress.

> It is not stress that kills us, it is our reaction to it.
>
> — HANS SELYE, PSYCHOLOGIST

Parenting is stressful for both the parent and the child.

> The more you cut the branches of a tree, the higher and stronger it grows.... Therefore I am happy that you have had great tribulations and difficulties.
>
> — ABDU'L-BAHA, HEAD OF THE BAHÁ'Í FAITH

A **crisis** is a situation that requires changes in normal patterns of response behavior. A family crisis is a situation that upsets the normal functioning of the family and requires a new set of responses to the stressor. Sources of stress and crises can be external, such as the hurricanes that annually hit our coasts or devastating tornadoes in the spring. Other examples of an external crisis are economic recession, downsizing, or military deployment.

The source of stress and crisis events may also be internal (e.g., alcoholism, an extramarital affair, or Alzheimer's disease of one's spouse or parents). Another internal source of a crisis event is inheriting money from one's deceased parents. One spouse reported a dramatic change in the relationship when the partner suddenly "became rich" and did not "share the wealth."

stress reaction of the body to substantial or unusual demands (physical, environmental, or interpersonal).

crisis a crucial situation that requires change in one's normal pattern of behavior.

Bouncing back and staying back is the modus operandi of this man who has continued an involved and meaningful life in spite of a diving accident that resulted in his being in a wheelchair for more than 20 years.

Stressors or crises may also be categorized as expected or unexpected. Expected family stressors include the need to care for aging parents and the death of one's parents. Unexpected stressors include contracting a sexually transmitted infection, becoming aware of an unplanned pregnancy, or experiencing the death/suicide of a friend.

Both stress and crisis events are normal aspects of family life and sometimes reflect a developmental sequence. Pregnancy, childbirth, job change or loss, children's leaving home, retirement, and widowhood are predictable for most couples and families. Crisis events may have a cumulative effect: the greater the number in rapid succession, the greater the stress.

Maria McDonald is artist

13-1a Resilient Families

Just as the types of stress and crisis events vary, individuals and families vary in their abilities to respond successfully to crisis events. **Resiliency** refers to a family's strengths and ability to respond to a crisis in a positive way. Hence, resiliency is both about bouncing back and the factors associated with doing so (Rodriguez-Rey et al.,

resiliency a family's strength and ability to respond to a crisis in a positive way.

family resiliency the successful coping of family members under adversity that enables them to flourish with warmth, support, and cohesion.

2016). Lane et al. (2012) identified the various aspects of **family resiliency** as beliefs (e.g., finding meaning in diversity, a positive outlook, spirituality), organizational patterns (e.g., flexibility, connectedness), and communication process (e.g., clarity, open emotional sharing). A family's ability to bounce back from a crisis (from negative health diagnosis, loss of one's job to the death of a family member) reflects its level of resiliency.

> Life doesn't get easier or more forgiving, we get stronger and more resilient.
>
> —STEVE MARABOLI, *LIFE, THE TRUTH, AND BEING FREE*

13-1b A Family Stress Model

Various theorists have explained how individuals and families experience and respond to stressors. The ABCX model of family stress was developed by Reuben Hill in the 1950s. The model can be explained as follows:

A = stressor event
B = family's management strategies, coping skills
C = family's perception, definition of the situation
X = family's adaptation to the event

A is the stressor event, which interacts with B, the family's coping ability or crisis-meeting resources. Both A and B interact with C, the family's appraisal or perception of the stressor event. X is the family's adaptation to the crisis. Thus, a family that experiences a major stressor (e.g., a spouse with a spinal cord injury) but has great coping skills (e.g., religion or spirituality, love, communication, and commitment) and perceives the event to be manageable will experience a moderate crisis. However, a family that experiences a less critical stressor event (e.g., their child makes Cs and Ds in school) but has minimal coping skills (e.g., everyone blames everyone else) and perceives the event to be catastrophic will experience an extreme crisis.

Reed et al. (2014) found that one's perception of support/help is more important than the actual availability or amount of support. Persons who belong to a church community who perceive that help is available seem to benefit before any help is actually provided.

13-2 POSITIVE STRESS-MANAGEMENT STRATEGIES

Researchers Burr and Klein (1994) administered an 80-item questionnaire to 78 adults to assess how families experiencing various stressors such as bankruptcy, infertility, a disabled child, and a troubled teen used various coping strategies and how they felt these strategies worked. In the following sections, we detail some helpful stress-management strategies.

> The oak fought the wind and was broken, the willow bent when it must and survived.
>
> —ROBERT JORDAN, *THE FIRES OF HEAVEN*

13-2a Choosing a Positive Perspective

How an event is perceived is crucial. In response to a financial setback, Adolf Merckle threw himself in front of a train. He was a billionaire who had lost hundreds of millions of Euros on Volkswagen shares.

The strategy that most respondents reported as being helpful in coping with a crisis was choosing a positive view of the crisis situation. Survivors of hurricanes, tornados, and earthquakes routinely focus on the fact that they and their loved ones are alive rather than the loss of their home or material possessions. Buddhists have the saying, "Pain is inevitable; suffering is not." This perspective emphasizes that how one views a situation, not the situation itself, determines its impact on you. One Chicago woman said after a pipe burst and caused $30,000 worth of damage to her home: "If it's not about your health, it's irrelevant." A team of researchers (Baer et al., 2012) confirmed the importance of selecting positive cognitions for 87 adults who enrolled/participated in an eight-week program on mindfulness-based stress reduction (MBSR). Mindfulness can be thought of as choosing how you view a phenomenon. These adults were coping with chronic illness and chronic pain and reduced their stress by being mindful to frame their situation positively: "we are alive," "we are coping," and "we have each other." Reiser et al. (2016) confirmed the value of mindfulness in stress reduction.

Regardless of the crisis event, one can view the crisis positively. A betrayal can be seen as an opportunity for

> It all depends on how we look at things, and not on how they are in themselves.
>
> —CARL G. JUNG, FOUNDER OF JUNGIAN ANALYSIS

forgiveness, unemployment as a stage to spend time with one's family, and ill health as a chance to appreciate one's inner life.

13-2b Exercise

The Centers for Disease Control and Prevention (CDC) and the American College of Sports Medicine (ACSM) recommend that people ages 6 years and older engage regularly, preferably daily, in light to moderate physical activity for at least 30 minutes at a time. These recommendations are based on research that has shown the physical, emotional, and cognitive benefits of exercise.

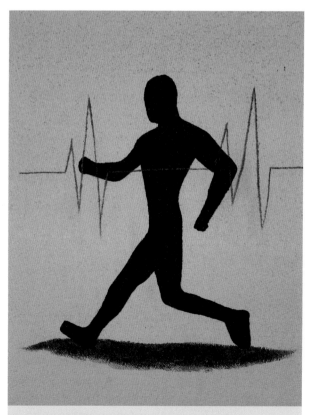

Exercise has an enormous positive effect on cutting stress.

> If you are in a bad mood go for a walk. If you are still in a bad mood go for another walk.
>
> —HIPPOCRATES

13-2c Family Cohesion, Friends, and Relatives

Being immersed in a context of relationships with one's parents/siblings, friends, and extended family is associated with positive adjustment to a crisis event. A team of researchers (Boterhoven de Haan et al., 2015) identified ways in which families provide an aid to managing a crisis: availability to each other for support, being accepted, expressing feelings, and confiding in each other.

Self-Assessment: Family Hardiness Scale (FHS)
Take the self-assessment at the end of the chapter to better understand your family's hardiness.

13-2d Love

A love relationship also helps individuals cope with stress. Being emotionally involved with another and sharing the crisis experience with that person helps insulate individuals from being devastated by a traumatic event. Love is also viewed as helping resolve relationship problems. Over 86% of 9,684 undergraduates (more females than males) agreed with the statement, "A deep love can get a couple through any difficulty or difference" (Hall & Knox, 2016).

13-2e Religion and Spirituality

A strong religious belief is associated with coping with stress/loss (Walker et al., 2015). Ellison et al. (2011) examined the role of religion and marital satisfaction/coping with stress. They found that **sanctification** (viewing the marriage as having divine character or significance) was associated with

sanctification viewing the marriage as having divine character or significance.

both predicting positive marital quality and providing a buffer for financial stress and general stress on the marriage.

Religion has also been identified as a coping mechanism for parents of children who have been diagnosed with a rare disease (Picci et al., 2015).

> Problems are not the problem; coping is the problem.
>
> —VIRGINIA SATIR, THERAPIST

13-2f Laughter and Play

A sense of humor is related to lower anxiety (Grases et al., 2012). Humor has also been used to cope with aging (Berk, 2015), adjusting to divorce (Frisby et al., 2016), and coping with caring for a mentally ill person (Power et al., 2016).

13-2g Sleep

Adequate sleep is necessary for optimum health. Mrug et al. (2016) confirmed that sleep problems (getting to sleep, staying asleep, not enough sleep) were related to higher stress and academic, behavioral, and health problems in a sample of adolescents.

13-2h Pets

Kanat-Maymon et al. (2016) surveyed 206 owners of a dog or cat and found that the presence of a dog or cat was associated with psychological well-being. Pets have also demonstrated their value in promoting empathy/healthy relationships (Thomas & Matusitz, 2016).

Pets are companions and associated with stress reduction.

13-3 HARMFUL STRESS-MANAGEMENT STRATEGIES

Some coping strategies not only are ineffective for resolving family problems but also add to the family's stress by making the problems worse. Respondents in the Burr and Klein (1994) research identified several strategies they regarded as harmful to overall family functioning. These included keeping feelings inside, taking out frustrations on or blaming others, and denying or avoiding the problem.

Burr and Klein's research also suggested that women and men differ in their perceptions of the usefulness of various coping strategies. Women were more likely than men to view as helpful such strategies as sharing concerns with relatives and friends, becoming more involved in religion, and expressing emotions. Men were more likely than women to use potentially harmful strategies such as using alcohol, keeping feelings inside, or keeping others from knowing how bad the situation was.

13-4 FIVE INDIVIDUAL, COUPLE, AND FAMILY CRISIS EVENTS

Some of the more common crisis events that spouses and families face include physical illness, mental illness, an extramarital affair, unemployment, substance abuse, and death.

13-4a Physical Illness

While most spouses are healthy most of the time, when one partner has a debilitating illness there are profound changes in the roles of the respective partners and their relationship. Stroke is the leading cause of disability in the United States. Interviews with both spouses (aged 31 to 93) by McCarthy and Bauer (2015) revealed the impact of the stroke on their own life, their spouse's life, and their relationship. Changes included practical and emotional challenges (e.g., helping the partner, feeling nurtured/burdened) and relationship changes (e.g., recreation, sexuality). Sitnick et al. (2016) studied the impact of a spouse's physical illness and found that it was associated with increased incidence of depression.

Individuals often have disabilities that are not visible. These include chronic back pain, rheumatoid arthritis, and chronic fatigue syndrome. These illnesses are particularly invasive in that conventional medicine has little to offer besides pain medication. For example, spouses with chronic fatigue syndrome may experience financial consequences ("I could no longer meet the demands of my job so I quit"), gender role loss ("I couldn't cook for my family" or "I was no longer a provider"), and changed perceptions by their children ("They have seen me sick for so long they no longer ask me to do anything").

In those cases in which the illness is fatal, **palliative care** is helpful. This term describes the health care for the individual who has a life-threatening illness (focusing on relief of pain and suffering) and support for the individual and his or her loved ones. Such care may involve the person's physician or a palliative care specialist who works with the physician, nurse, social worker, and chaplain. Pharmacists or rehabilitation specialists may also be involved. The goals of such care are to approach the end of life with planning (how long should life be sustained on machines?) and forethought to relieve pain (medication) and provide closure.

We have been discussing reacting to the crisis of a spouse with a physical illness or disability. Children may also become physically ill resulting in stress and crisis for the family. Parents are devastated emotionally by a serious physical illness of their child. They also experience the burden and interference of the illness in their lives. In a study of 126 parents of children with malignant cancer, the parents reported high levels of caregiving burden and interference in the quality of life (Salvador et al., 2015).

palliative care health care for the individual who has a life-threatening illness which focuses on relief of pain/suffering and support for the individual.

Black Hole: A Spouse Talks about Being Depressed

If you have experienced life in the Black Hole, then you don't need an explanation of it. If you have never experienced life in the Black Hole, it is impossible for anyone to explain it to you, and even if someone could explain it to you, you still wouldn't understand it.

The Black Hole is, by definition, an irrational state. The only thing you can comprehend about it is that you cannot comprehend it. Offering ANY advice, judgmental comments, suggestions like—"If you would only…," "You've got to want to help yourself…,""I know you are depressed, BUT…,""You are not being rational…"—to someone who is in the Black Hole is not helpful.

On the contrary, offering advice is very destructive. It may temporarily relieve YOUR frustration with the person, but all it does for them is to give them a serving of guilt to deal with as they wait for the Black Hole to pass. If you really want to help somebody who is in the Black Hole, there IS one thing you can do—and that one thing is NOTHING.

After living in the Black Hole for a lifetime, a person has pretty much heard everything that you plan to tell them about it. Eventually, people who visit the Black Hole learn that it is a Monster, which comes without warning or invitation, it stays for a while, and it leaves when it is ready. The Monster doesn't time its visits to avoid holidays, vacations, or rainy days. It just barges in.

A person also knows what works for them while they are in the Black Hole. For some it may be exercise, or fishing, or sex (if they are still physically able), or music, or going to the beach, or talking about it, or employing logic to deal with it, or prayer, or reciting positive affirmations. For others, like me, there are only two things that help—complete solitude and sleep. Those two things do not provide a cure, but they do help you cope with the Monster until he leaves.

Nobody asks why you wear glasses. They just assume that you wear glasses because you need to, they don't ask questions about it, they don't offer suggestions and they don't try to fix it. And they don't assume that you wear glasses because of something they did. What a blessing it would be, if people treated those who struggle with clinical depression with the same respect.

Source: Former student of the author. Name withheld by request.

13-4b Mental Illness

Mental illness is defined as a state in which one's thoughts or behavior result in distress and impaired functioning. Eight percent of adults 18–29 have a serious mental illness. This percentage drops as individuals age to 1.4% of those over the age of 65 (Hudson, 2012). Thomeer (2016) noted that the husband's number of chronic health conditions is associated with the wife's depressive symptoms. For couples in which both spouses reported mental health problems, rates of marital disruption reflected the additive combination of each spouse's separate risk. See the Black Hole for insight into depression.

Children also experience mental illness that impacts the parents. Preyde et al. (2015) analyzed data on parental reactions to the emotional and behavioral disorders of their children (who were in treatment). Results revealed that the respondents' parental sense of competency was negatively associated with the severity of the internalizing (e.g., depression) and externalizing (e.g., drug use) behaviors of their children.

iofoto/Shutterstock.com

13-4c Extramarital Affair

Affairs are not unusual. Of spouses in the United States, about one-fourth of husbands and one-fifth of wives report ever having had intercourse with someone to whom they were not married (Russell et al., 2013).

What is a profile of those who do have sex outside of their pair-bonded relationship? Analysis of data from a sample of 512 adults revealed that being unfaithful was associated with being a male, favorable attitudes toward infidelity, an approving social network, lower levels of religiosity, having cheated before, being cheated on in the past, and displaying high levels of self-efficacy (e.g., feeling that one

> Husband's text: *Darling, I've been hit by a car outside the office. Paula brought me to the hospital. They have been making tests and taking X-rays. The blow to my head has been very strong but fortunately it seems that did not cause any serious injury. However, I have three broken ribs, a compound fracture in the left leg, and they may have to amputate the right foot.*
>
> Wife's response: *Who's Paula?*
>
> —INTERNET HUMOR

is attractive and can interact with ease with others) (Jackman, 2015). Power is also associated with infidelity (e.g., Bill Clinton). Lammers and Maner (2016) found that power "releases people from the inhibiting effects of social norms and thus increases their appetite for counternormative forms of sexuality."

> The issue here was my repeated irresponsible behavior. I was unfaithful. I had affairs. I cheated.
>
> —TIGER WOODS

TYPES OF EXTRAMARITAL AFFAIRS The term **extramarital affair** refers to a spouse's sexual involvement with someone outside the marriage. Affairs are of different types, which may include the following:

1. **Brief encounter.** A spouse meets and hooks up with a stranger. In this case, the spouse is usually out of town, and alcohol is often involved.

2. **Paid sex.** A spouse seeks sexual variety with a prostitute who will do whatever he wants. These encounters usually go undetected unless there is an STI, the person confesses, or the prostitute exposes the client. In some cases, customers are "outed." In 2015 the Ashley Madison website was hacked revealing the names of 31 million married men.

3. **Instrumental or utilitarian affair.** This is sex in exchange for a job or promotion, to get back at a spouse, to evoke jealousy, or to transition out of a marriage.

4. **Coping mechanism.** Sex can be used to enhance one's self-concept or feeling of sexual inadequacy, compensate for failure in business, cope with the death of a family member, or test one's sexual orientation.

5. **Paraphiliac affairs.** In these encounters, the on-the-side sex partner acts out sexual fantasies or participates in sexual practices that the spouse considers bizarre or abnormal, such as sexual masochism, sexual sadism, or transvestite fetishism.

6. **Office romance.** Two individuals who work together may drift into an affair. David Petraeus (former CIA director) and John Edwards (former presidential candidate) became involved in affairs with women they met on the job.

7. **Internet use.** Although, legally, an extramarital affair does not exist unless two people (one being married) have intercourse, Internet use can be disruptive to a marriage or a couple's relationship.

8. **Facebook infidelity.** While Internet affairs via Match.com is common (persons in a "monogamous" relationship simply look for someone new), Facebook (boasting 1.2 billion active users) allows one to connect with old partners, friends of friends, persons at work, etc. and start a relationship.

While men and women agree that actual kissing, touching breasts/genitals, and sexual intercourse constitute infidelity, they disagree about the degree to which online behaviors constitute cheating.

Computer friendships may move to feelings of intimacy, involve secrecy (one's partner does not know the level of involvement), include sexual tension (even though there is no overt sex), and take time, attention, energy, and affection away from one's partner. Carter (2016) emphasized that spouses who communicate with the other sex on Facebook are doing so at a risk to their marriage relationship.

Extradyadic involvement, or extrarelational involvement, refers to the sexual involvement of a pair-bonded individual with someone other than the partner. Extradyadic involvements are not uncommon. Of 2,339 undergraduate males, 29% agreed with the statement, "I have cheated on a partner I was involved with" (30% of 7,504

> **extramarital affair** refers to a spouse's sexual involvement with someone outside the marriage.
>
> **extradyadic involvement** refers to sexual involvement of a pair-bonded individual with someone other than the partner; also called extrarelational involvement.

Maria McDonald

TABLE 13.1	TILL DEATH DO US PART?		
Monogamy	**Cheating**	**Swinging**	**Polyamory**
Spouse is only sex partner	Husband and/or wife cheats	Spouses agree to multiple sex partners	Spouses agree to multiple love and sex partners

undergraduate females). When the statement was "A partner I was involved with cheated on me," 52% of the males and 58% of the females agreed (Hall & Knox, 2016).

One-third of 655 individuals (both heterosexual and homosexual) reported that they had been unfaithful in their current monogamous relationship (Swan & Thompson, 2016). The researchers titled their article "Monogamy: The Protective Fallacy." Traditional marriage scripts fidelity. Traditional wedding vows state, "Hold myself only unto you as long as we both should live."

Traditional marriage scripts fidelity. Traditional wedding vows state, "Hold myself only unto you as long as we both should live." Table 13.1 identifies the alternatives for resolving the transition from multiple to one sexual partner till death.

Unless a couple have a polyamorous or swinging relationship, if they are to have sex outside their marriage, it is via cheating.

REASONS FOR EXTRAMARITAL AFFAIRS Reasons spouses give for becoming involved with someone other than their mate include (Jeanfreau et al., 2014; MaddoxShaw et al., 2013; Omarzu et al., 2012):

1. **Variety, novelty, and excitement.** Most spouses enter marriage having had numerous sexual partners. Extradyadic sexual involvement may be motivated by the desire for continued variety, novelty, and excitement. One of the characteristics of sex in long-term committed relationships is the tendency for it to become routine. Early in a relationship, the partners cannot seem to have sex

often enough. However, with constant availability, partners may achieve a level of satiation, and the attractiveness and excitement of sex with the primary partner seem to wane.

The **Coolidge effect** is a term used to describe this waning of sexual excitement and the effect of novelty and variety on sexual arousal:

One day President and Mrs. Coolidge were visiting a government farm. Soon after their arrival, they were taken off on separate tours. When Mrs. Coolidge passed the chicken pens, she paused to ask the man in charge if the rooster copulated more than once each day. "Dozens of times," was the reply. "Please tell that to the President," Mrs. Coolidge requested. When the President passed the pens and was told about the rooster, he asked, "Same hen every time?" "Oh no, Mr. President, a different one each time." The President nodded slowly and then said, "Tell that to Mrs. Coolidge." (*Bermant, 1976, pp. 76–77*)

Whether or not individuals are biologically wired for monogamy continues to be debated. Monogamy among mammals is rare (from 3% to 10%), and monogamy tends to be the exception more often than the rule (Morell, 1998).

2. **Workplace friendships.** Drifting from being friends to lovers is not uncommon in the workplace. We noted in the last chapter that about 60% of persons in the workforce reported having become involved with someone at work. Coworkers share the same world 8 to 10 hours a day and, over a period of time, may develop good feelings for each other that eventually lead to a sexual relationship. Tabloid reports regularly reflect that romances develop between married actors making a movie together (e.g., Brad Pitt and Angelina Jolie met on a movie set).

Michelle North

Coolidge effect term used to describe waning of sexual excitement and the effect of novelty and variety on increasing sexual arousal.

Tiger Woods admitted to numerous affairs and asked forgiveness from his wife and fans.

3. **Relationship dissatisfaction.** It is commonly believed that people who have affairs are not happy in their marriage. Spouses who feel misunderstood, unloved, and ignored sometimes turn to another who offers understanding, love, and attention. An affair is a context where a person who feels unloved and neglected can feel loved and important.

4. **Sexual dissatisfaction.** Some spouses engage in extramarital sex because their partner is not interested in sex. Others may go outside the relationship because their partners will not engage in the sexual behaviors they want and enjoy. The unwillingness of the spouse to engage in oral sex, anal intercourse, or a variety of sexual positions sometimes results in the other spouse's looking elsewhere for a more cooperative and willing sexual partner. Commenting on the Ashley Madison hacking/exposure, Klein (2015) noted that "the question is NOT why do 31 million men want to cheat," but rather "why are so many men inhibited from talking about sexual or emotional issues with their partners?"

5. **Revenge.** Some extramarital sexual involvements are acts of revenge against one's spouse for having an affair. When partners find out that their mate has had or is having an affair, they are often hurt and angry. One response to this hurt and anger is to have an affair to get even with the unfaithful partner.

6. **Homosexual relationship.** Some individuals marry as a front for their homosexuality. Cole Porter, known for such songs as "I've Got You Under My Skin," "Night and Day," and "Every Time We Say Goodbye," was a homosexual who feared no one would buy his music if his sexual orientation were known. He married Linda Lee Porter (alleged to be a lesbian), and their marriage lasted until Porter's death 30 years later.

Other gay individuals marry as a way of denying their homosexuality. These individuals are likely to feel unfulfilled in their marriage and may seek involvement in an extramarital homosexual relationship. Other individuals may marry and then discover later in life that they desire a homosexual relationship. Such individuals may feel that (1) they have been homosexual or bisexual all along, (2) their sexual orientation has changed from heterosexual to homosexual or bisexual, (3) they are unsure of their sexual orientation and want to explore a homosexual relationship, or (4) they are predominantly heterosexual but wish to experience a homosexual relationship for variety. The term **down low** refers to African American married men who have sex with men and hide this behavior from their spouse.

7. **Aging.** A frequent motive for intercourse outside marriage is the desire to return to the feeling of youth. Ageism, which is discrimination against the elderly, promotes the idea that being young is good and being old is bad. Sexual attractiveness is equated with youth, and having an affair may confirm to older partners that they are still sexually desirable. Also, people may try to recapture the love, excitement, adventure, and romance associated with youth by having an affair.

8. **Absence from partner.** One factor that may predispose a spouse to an affair is prolonged separation from the partner. Some wives whose husbands are away for military service report that the loneliness can become unbearable. Some husbands who are away say that remaining faithful is difficult. Partners in commuter relationships may also be vulnerable to extradyadic sexual relationships.

REVEALING ONE'S AFFAIR BY CONFESSION/ PARTNER SNOOPING Walters and Burger (2013) identified how individuals revealed their infidelity— in person (38%), over the phone (38%), by a third partner (12%), via email (6%), and through text messaging (6%). A primary motivation for disclosure was respect either for the primary partner or for the history of the

> **down low** term refers to African American married men who have sex with men and hide this from their spouse.

primary relationship. While some felt the need to confess because they were guilty or felt the need to be honest, others felt the relationship would benefit from openness/ honesty.

In other cases, the cheating was discovered by snooping. **Snooping**, also known as covert intrusive behavior, is defined as investigating (without the partner's knowledge or permission) a romantic partner's private communication (e.g., text messages, email, and cell phone use) motivated by concern that the partner may be hiding something. Derby et al. (2012) analyzed snooping behavior in 268 undergraduates and found that almost two-thirds (66%) reported that they had engaged in snooping behavior, most often when the partner was taking a shower. Primary motives were curiosity and suspicion that the partner was cheating. Being female, being jealous, and having cheated were associated with higher frequencies of snooping behavior.

> How can I be reasonable? To me our love was everything and you were my whole life. It is not very pleasant to realize that to you it was only an episode.
>
> —W. SOMERSET MAUGHAM, *THE PAINTED VEIL*

OTHER EFFECTS OF AN AFFAIR Reactions to the knowledge that one's unfaithfulness vary. Some relationships end. Negash et al. (2014) found that 36% of 539 young adult females reported emotional or sexual extradyadic involvement (EDI) in the last two months. Such behavior was particularly predictive of ending one's primary relationship if the partner thought the relationship was of high quality and felt particularly disillusioned and betrayed by the EDI.

snooping investigating (without the partner's knowledge or permission) a romantic partner's private communication (e.g., text messages, email, and cell phone use) motivated by concern that the partner may be hiding something.

alienation of affection law which gives a spouse the right to sue a third party for taking the affections of a spouse away.

Seven states (Hawaii, Illinois, North Carolina, Mississippi, New Mexico, South Dakota, and Utah) recognize **alienation of affection** lawsuits which give a spouse the right to sue a third party for taking the affections of a spouse away. Alienation of affection claims evolved from common law, which considered women property of their husbands. The reasoning was if another man was accused of stealing his "property," a husband could sue him for damages. The law applies to both women and men, so a woman who steals another woman's man can be sued for taking her property away. Such was the case of Cynthia Shackelford who sued Anne Lundquist in 2010 for "alienating" her husband from her and breaking up her 33-year marriage. A jury awarded Cynthia Shackelford $4 million in punitive damages and $5 million in compensatory damages. The decision has been appealed. In North Carolina, about 200 alienation of affection lawsuits are filed annually. The infraction must have occurred while the couple was still married (not during the separation period) and there is a three-year statute of limitations.

SUCCESSFUL RECOVERY FROM INFIDELITY While an affair is a high-frequency cause of a couple deciding to divorce, keeping the relationship together (with forgiveness and time) is the most frequent outcome. Abrahamson et al. (2012) interviewed seven individuals who had experienced an affair in their relationship and who were still together two years later. The factors involved in rebuilding their relationship included:

1. **Motivation to stay together.** Having been together several years, having children, having property jointly, not wanting to "fail," and fearing life alone were factors which motivated the partners to stay together. The basic feeling is that we have a lot to gain by working this out.

2. **Taking joint responsibility.** The betrayed partner found a way to acknowledge she or he had contributed to the affair so that there was joint responsibility for the affair.

3. **Forgiveness, counseling, and not referring to the event again.** Forgiveness involved letting go of one's resentment, anger, and hurt; accepting that we all need forgiveness; and moving forward (Hill, 2010). Aalgaard et al. (2016) emphasized the value of forgiveness for getting over an affair, for marital satisfaction, and for one's own health and well-being. See the Personal View section, which asks if an affair warrants a divorce.

4. **Vicarious learning.** Noting that others who ended a relationship over an affair were not necessarily happier/better off.

5. **Feeling pride in coming through a difficult experience.** An affair is a major crisis. Coming through it together can actually strengthen the couple's relationship. One wife whose husband had had an

WHAT'S NEW?

Reactions to Discovering One's Partner Is Cheating

"How could you?" asked an angry wife who had discovered her husband in a secluded parked car with a woman from his office. The scene was on *Cheaters*, a television program which features spouses caught in the act of cheating on their mates. Cheating also occurs in undergraduate relationships. The purpose of this research was to identify how undergraduates react to the knowledge that one's romantic partner has cheated—had sexual intercourse with someone else.

The Survey
A 47-item questionnaire was posted on the Internet and completed by 244 undergraduates (83% of the survey respondents were female, 69% were White, and 52% were in their first year).

Results: Gender Differences in Reactions
Significantly more women than men (55% versus 31%) reported that a romantic partner had cheated on them.

In addition to a significant gender difference with men cheating more than women, there were significant gender differences in the reactions to a partner's cheating. Women were more likely to cry, put their partner under surveillance, confront their partner, and get tested for an STI.

Results: Differences in "Unhealthy" and "Healthy" Reactions by Gender
A subset of 19 "unhealthy" and 9 "healthy" reactions to a partner's cheating were identified to ascertain if there were gender differences. For example, increasing one's alcohol consumption, becoming suicidal, and having an affair out of revenge were identified as "unhealthy" reactions, while confronting the partner, forgiving the partner, and seeing a therapist were regarded as more "healthy" reactions. For each item, participants were assigned a score of 1 point if they agreed (somewhat agree, agree, strongly agree) with the reaction (e.g., "I drank more alcohol" or "I forgave my partner"). Scores

on the unhealthy and healthy reactions were summed to create an overall count of demonstrated unhealthy and healthy reactions.

Females reported a significantly higher percentage of healthy reactions/behaviors than males; females averaged 3.71 healthy behaviors (SD = 1.46) compared to males, who averaged 2.44 healthy behaviors (SD = 1.58).

Theoretical Framework and Discussion
Symbolic interaction theory and social exchange theory provide frameworks for understanding reactions to the knowledge that one's partner has cheated. In reference to cheating, partners in a relationship have definitions about the meaning of one partner having sexual intercourse with someone outside the dyad.

The social exchange framework views the interaction between partners in a romantic relationship in terms of profit and cost. When one partner does not exchange fidelity for fidelity, there is a significant cost to the faithful partner for remaining in a relationship where the partner has been unfaithful.

Implications of the Study
There are three implications of this study. One, cheating in romantic relationships among undergraduates is not uncommon. Over half (51%) reported having been cheated on. Two, the knowledge that one's partner has cheated is traumatic. Feeling betrayed (6.24 out of 7) was the most common reaction and was often accompanied by crying (5.81 out of 7), depression (4.65 out of 7), and increased drinking (2.92 out of 7). Three, the range of alternative reactions to the knowledge of infidelity was extensive, including many healthy alternatives including forgiveness, exercise, and seeing a therapist (with women more likely than men to select healthy alternatives).

Source: Abridged and adapted from Barnes, H., D. Knox, & J. Brinkley. (March 2012). CHEATING: Gender differences in reactions to discovery of a partner's cheating. Paper, Annual Meeting of the Southern Sociological Society, New Orleans, LA.

affair was told by their counselor: "You're going to need to resolve this in a way that it does not wreck your life whether or not you stay married…one option is to resolve it AND stay married…to keep

your family together." The couple worked it out, improved their relationship, and are still together.

Scuka (2015) provided guidelines for the involved partner, for the hurt partner, and for the couple in getting over an affair. A rewording and summary of these guidelines follow:

Tasks for the partner who had the affair. Acknowledge the hurt to the partner, express sorrow/contriteness, give up all interaction/contact with the affair person, provide complete information about whereabouts/text messages, get tested for STI/report results to partner, and be tolerant of the partner's moods/suspicions/struggle to get over the infidelity.

Tasks for the partner who was hurt. Acknowledge the contriteness of the partner, have compassion for the partner's imperfection/be mindful of one's own imperfections, make a commitment to forgive/get over one's anger/resentment.

Tasks for the couple. Accept that the healing will take time, maintain hope, be kind to each other (don't attack), listen/make reflective statements to each other, spend time together doing things of mutual enjoyment, reestablish sexual intimacy, be sensitive in different timetables of recovery.

Positive outcomes of having experienced and worked through infidelity include a closer marital relationship, placing higher value on each other, and realizing the importance of good marital communication. Spouses who remain faithful to their partners have decided to do so. They avoid intimate conversations with members of the other sex and a context (e. g., being alone in a hotel room) that is conducive to physical involvement. The best antidote to an affair is a strong emotional/sexual connection with one's spouse and avoiding contexts conducive to external involvement.

13-4d Unemployment

The unemployment rate is defined as the number of people actively looking for a job divided by the labor force. Changes in unemployment depend mostly on inflows made up of non-employed people starting to look for jobs, of employed people who lose their jobs and look for new ones, and of people who stop looking for employment.

Ricardo Reitmeyer/Shutterstock.com

Unemployment is associated with subsequent long-term earnings losses, lower job quality (in subsequent jobs), declines in psychological/physical well-being, social withdrawal, divorce, and lower levels of children's attainment and well-being. Although reemployment mitigates some of the negative effects of job loss, it does not eliminate them (Brand, 2015).

When spouses or parents lose their jobs as a result of physical illness or disability, the family experiences a double blow—loss of income combined with higher medical bills. Unless an unemployed spouse is covered by the partner's medical insurance, unemployment can result in loss of health insurance for the family. Insurance for both health care and disability is very important to help protect a family from an economic disaster.

> But here I am again mixing misery and gin/Sittin' with all my friends and talkin' to myself.
>
> —MERLE HAGGARD, "MISERY AND GIN"

13-4e Alcohol/Substance Abuse

A person has a problem with alcohol or a substance if it interferes with the person's health, job, or relationships. Twelve percent of 2,059 male undergraduates and 9% of 6,430 female undergraduates reported that "I have a problem with alcohol" (Hall & Knox, 2016).

Spouses, parents, and children who abuse alcohol contribute to the stress experienced in their respective marriages and families. Parental abuse of alcohol is also related to externalizing behaviors (e.g., aggression, delinquency, substance abuse) in adolescents (Finan et al., 2014).

Although some individuals abuse drugs to escape from unhappy relationships or the stress of family problems, substance abuse inevitably adds to the individual's marital and family problems when it results in health and medical problems, legal problems, loss of employment, financial ruin, school failure, emotionally distant relationships (Cox et al., 2013; Lotspeich-Younkin & Bartle-Haring, 2012), and divorce.

My Husband and I Survived His Affair

My husband had an extended affair with my best friend for seven years. I found out by reading a text message she had sent him. I was devastated. We had three children.

We went to a marriage counselor who told me, "You're going to need to resolve this in a way that it does not wreck your life whether or not you stay married . . . one option is to resolve it AND stay married . . . to keep your family together." This was probably the best advice I could have received. I was bitterly angry, hurt that he would deceive me, and wanted revenge. But the cost would be breaking up our family and messing up the lives of my children with their father.

While he is the one who had the affair, I was not without blame. When the children came, I put them first and our lives as lovers came to a halt. My husband asked me for time together alone but I told him we should always do things as a family. Since I was not there for him, he sought someone else . . . could I blame him completely? . . . I think not.

He ended the relationship with the other woman (as did I) and we resolved to devote time to ourselves as well as to our children. The result is that we avoided a divorce, our family remains together, and we showed our children "you can work through anything if you want to." No question but what this was the right decision for us.

—NAME WITHHELD BY REQUEST

Diversity in Other Countries

Vladimirov et al. (2016) studied alcohol consumption patterns of 5,621 Finish adults at ages 31 and 46 and found that daily alcohol consumption rose by 30% for men and 40% for women with the unemployed, single, or those with a low level of education consuming the most. Seventy percent of the sample were classified as steady drinkers, with only 10% drinking less across time.

TABLE 13.2	CURRENT DRUG USE BY TYPE OF DRUG AND AGE GROUP		
Type of Drug Used	Age 12 to 17, %	Age 18 to 25, %	Age 26 to 34, %
Marijuana and hashish	7.1	19.1	5.6
Cocaine	.2	1.1	.5
Alcohol	11.6	59.6	55.9
Cigarettes	5.6	30.6	21.6

Source: Adapted from *Proquest Statistical Abstract of the United States, 2016,* Table 220. Washington, DC: U.S. Bureau of the Census.

Hall (2015) reviewed evidence in the last 20 years on regular marijuana use and found that it doubles one's risk of a car crash, that 1 in 10 develop dependence, and that its use is associated with the use of other illicit drugs. Other researchers contend these associations are related to other risk factors. Table 13.2 reflects substance use at various age categories.

13-4f Death of Family Member

Even more devastating than drug abuse are family crises involving death—of one's child, parent, or loved one (we discuss the death of one's spouse in Chapter 15 on relationships in the later years). The crisis is particularly acute when the death is a suicide. Hottes et al.

(2016) noted 4% of suicide attempts for heterosexual individuals and 11% for LGB individuals. See A Mother's Grief in reference to the suicide of a mother's son.

DEATH OF ONE'S CHILD A parent's worst fear is the death of a child. Most people expect the death of their parents but not the death of their children. Grief feelings may be particularly acute on the anniversary of the death of an individual with whom one was particularly close.

> The room fills up with my absent child.
>
> —SHAKESPEARE

A Mother's Grief

I remember the day—the hour—the minute
the split second—when my real life ended
and became an illusion
when was that you ask?
the day the world was right for the
   last time
the day my son gasped for the last time
just a split second
a millisecond really
when a life—my son's life—Ryan's precious life
spilled over the edge of the universe
and entered Eternity—beyond all Time

"I'm sorry," my husband said
and I said "no."
"I'm so sorry," he said yet again
and my anguished screams, oh, the screams . . .
   came loud and raw and primal.
and they've never ceased… not really.

grief . . . merely a word . . .
just a grouping of five simple letters
but such an ugly, desperate, heart-wrenching word.
I want to be able to cope with it, live with it,
   befriend it, be at peace with it.
yet it crushes my very soul still
like a drumbeat pounding, pounding—without
   a rhythm
it strikes, scrambling coherent thought
thrumming, vibrating,
always just under the surface
and inside I shriek . . .

It can't be real.
Tell me it isn't true.

I went home.
such a dream-like state
alone in my agony
and crazed beyond reason . . .
I know a part of me died that night too
torment; forevermore my companion.

and the doorbell keeps ringing
and the phone just keeps ringing.

family came to sit with me
friends came to comfort me
pastors came to pray with me
neighbors came with food for me

me—a shell, nothing more
a blank page—yet a captive to
the notes he scribbled to himself
the pillboxes on the counter
the pack of cigarettes he left on the fence post
his sandals by the back door
these ghostly reminders scattered throughout
the house
these, his last good-byes
shattering my soul at every turn, over and over
   and over again.

I know there is no turning back
I know you are gone forever

days are endless; barren for me
memories . . . wracked with pain for me
sleep . . . no longer comes to me
and hope is a long lost dream for me.

I so needed you to hold on . . .

—Katie Basile

Katie Basile

Albuquerque et al. (2016) examined the effect of a child's death on the couple's marriage and found it can cause cohesive as well as detrimental effects. Pre-death characteristics of the relationship, communication, incongruent grieving, social support, and religious affiliation were factors involved in each parent's adjustment.

Maple et al. (2013) interviewed 22 parents following the death of a young adult child and found that the parents needed to maintain a relationship with their child including public and private memorials to internal dialogues. Mothers and fathers sometimes respond to the death of their child in different ways. When they do, the respective partners may interpret these differences in negative ways, leading to relationship conflict and unhappiness. To deal with these differences, spouses need to be patient and practice tolerance in allowing each to grieve in her or his own way.

DEATH OF ONE'S PARENT Terminally ill parents may be taken care of by their children. Such care over a period of years can be emotionally stressful, financially draining, and exhausting. Hence, by the time the parent dies, a crisis has already occurred.

Reactions to the death of a loved one (whether parent or partner) is not something one "gets over." Burke et al. (1999) noted that grief is not a one-time experience that people adjust to and move on. Rather, for some, there is **chronic sorrow**, where grief-related feelings occur periodically throughout the lives of those left behind. Burke et al. (1999) noted that 97% of the individuals in one study who had experienced the death of a loved one 2 to 20 years earlier met the criteria for chronic sorrow.

Boss (2013) also noted that closure may not be a realistic goal but to learn to cope with the death of a loved one by finding meaning and dropping the expectation that one should "get over it." Particularly difficult are those cases of ambiguous loss where the definitions of death become muddled, as when a person disappears or has a disease such as Alzheimer's.

13-5 RELATIONSHIP/MARRIAGE THERAPY

All couples might consider consulting a relationship/marriage therapist about their relationship rather than remaining in an unhappy relationship or ending a relationship that can be improved. Signs to look for in your own relationship that suggest you might consider seeing a therapist include chronic arguing, feeling distant/avoiding each other, being unable or unwilling to address issues which create tension/dissatisfaction, feeling depressed, drifting into a relationship with someone else, increased drinking, and privately contemplating separation or breaking up. Relationship therapy may help identify behaviors which create unhappiness for the respective partners, identify new behaviors to replace negative ones, make commitments to change, and begin new behaviors so that the partners can start feeling better about each other.

13-5a Availability of Marriage/Relationship Therapists

There are around 50,000 marriage and family therapists in the United States. Whatever marriage therapy costs, it can be worth it in terms of improved relationships. If divorce can be averted, both spouses and children can avoid the trauma and thousands of dollars will be saved. Effective marriage therapy usually involves seeing the spouses together (conjoint therapy).

> Tweeting lovebirds turn into roaring bears after marriage.
>
> —JUNAID E MUSTAFA

13-5b Effectiveness of Relationship/Marriage Therapy

Research on the effectiveness of various approaches to couple therapy shows that no one approach is superior (Kim et al., 2016). Indeed, the problem of the couple, their age, the number of years they have been in a relationship, their motivation, and the skill/personality of the therapist are all involved in whether a couple report improvement.

chronic sorrow grief-related feelings that occur periodically throughout the lives of those left behind.

Behavior Contract for Partners

Name of Partners _____ *Date:*_Week of June 8–14
Behaviors each partner agrees to engage in and days of week:

	Mon	Tues	Wed	Thurs	Fri	Sat	Sun
1. No negative statements to partner.	☐	☐	☐	☐	☐	☐	☐
2. Compliment partner twice each day.	☐	☐	☐	☐	☐	☐	☐
3. Hug or hold partner once a day.	☐	☐	☐	☐	☐	☐	☐
4. Out to dinner Saturday night.	☐	☐	☐	☐	☐	☐	☐

Source: From Crisp, B., & D. Knox. (2009). *Behavioral family therapy.* Durham, NC: Carolina Academic Press.

Two moderately motivated partners with numerous conflicts over several years are less likely to work out their problems than a highly motivated couple with minor conflicts of short duration.

Severe depression, alcoholism on the part of either spouse, or an affair are factors that will limit positive marital and family gains. In general, these issues must be resolved individually before the spouses can profit from marital therapy. Johnson and Bradbury (2015) emphasized that effective therapy must address the contextual issues of the couple: job loss, financial strain, heal issues, in-laws, etc.

In regard to marital and family therapy in general, Kanewisher and Harris (2015) interviewed 12 women (who sought marital therapy) who were contemplating divorce but who changed their mind. All reported that therapy was a helpful experience. The benefits of therapy they emphasized were creating a space (the therapist's office was a place to talk with the partner about the relationship), accountability (when decisions were made by the spouses to change behavior, the therapist was there to follow up and make sure the changes happened), and feeling understood (the clients felt that their positions in the marriage were understood and accepted).

13-5c Behavioral Couple Therapy

Most therapists (31%) report that they use either a behavioral or cognitive-behavioral approach. A behavioral approach—also referred to as **behavioral couple therapy (BCT)**—means that the therapist focuses on behaviors the respective spouses want increased or decreased, initiated or terminated, and then negotiates behavioral exchanges between the partners.

Some therapists use behavior contracts which are agreements partners make of new behaviors to engage in between sessions. The following is an example and assumes that the partners argue frequently, never compliment each other, no longer touch each other, and do not spend time together. The contract calls for each partner to make no negative statements to the other, give two compliments per day to the other, hug or hold each other at least once a day, and allocate Saturday night to go out to dinner alone with each other. On the contract, under each day of the week, the partners check that they did what they agreed to; the contract is given to the therapist at the next appointment. Partners who change their behavior toward each other often discover that the partner changes also and there is a new basis for each to feel better about each other and their relationship.

Sometimes clients do not like behavior contracts and say to the behavior therapist, "I want my partner to compliment me and hug me because my partner wants to, not because you wrote it down on this silly contract." The behavior therapist acknowledges the desire for the behavior to come from the heart of the partner and points out that the partner is making a choice to engage in new behavior to please the partner.

13-5d Telerelationship (Skype) Therapy

An alternative to face-to-face therapy is **telerelationship therapy**, which uses the Internet (Skype). Both therapist and couple log on to Skype, where each can

behavioral couple therapy therapeutic focus on behaviors the respective spouses want increased or decreased, initiated or terminated.

telerelationship therapy therapy sessions conducted online, often through Skype, where both therapist and couple can see and hear each other.

Increasingly, therapists are seeing more clients online and couples are discovering that online relationship therapy is just as effective as face-to-face sessions.

see and hear the other while the session is conducted online. Terms related to telerelationship therapy are telepsychology, telepsychiatry, virtual therapy, and video interaction guidance (VIG) (Magaziner, 2010; Doria et al., 2014). Telerelationship therapy allows couples to become involved in relationship therapy independent of where they live (e.g., isolated rural areas), the availability of transportation, and time (i.e., sessions can be scheduled outside the 9 to 5 block).

Doria et al. (2014) provided content analysis of 15 therapeutic sessions (by three therapists in Europe) which improved family happiness, parental self-esteem and self-efficacy, and attitude–behavior change. These data emphasize that therapy can be effectively conducted over the Internet. Kincaid (2015) noted that a major advantage of online therapy is that it provides access to those who live in areas where there are few mental health providers. Challenges include lack of computer skills/privacy fears (Aboujaoude et al., 2015) as well as questionable therapist credentials and the management of crisis situations online (e.g., client becomes suicidal) (Hertlein et al., 2015).

13-5e Online Therapy: OurRelationship Program

An alternative to face-to-face and telerelationship therapy is online therapy. The OurRelationship program is an 8-hour online program whereby couples complete online activities and have four 15-minute calls with the project staff. Doss et al. (2016) reported on 300 heterosexual couples (N = 600 participants)

throughout the United States who participated in a study whereby couples were randomly assigned to begin the program immediately or to a two-month wait-list control group.

Compared to the wait-list group, intervention couples reported significant improvements in relationship satisfaction, relationship confidence, and relationship quality. Gains were also noted including a decrease in depressive and anxious symptoms and an increase in perceived health, work functioning, and quality of life. Hence, distressed couples can benefit significantly from online couple therapy, specifically the low-cost, web-based OurRelationship program (https://www.ourrelationship.com).

13-6 TRENDS REGARDING STRESS AND CRISIS IN RELATIONSHIPS

Stress and crisis will continue to be a part of relationships. No spouse, partner, marriage, family, or relationship is immune. A major source of stress will be economic—the difficulty in securing and maintaining employment and sufficient income to take care of the needs of the family.

Relationship partners will be challenged by whatever crisis events occur. The greater the number of crisis events, the shorter the time between the events and the severity of the events, the more difficult the adjustment. Ann Landers is known for her admonition to "expect trouble and rise above it."

STUDY TOOLS 13

READY TO STUDY? IN THE BOOK, YOU CAN:

☐ Rip out the chapter review card at the back of the book for a handy summary of the chapter and key terms.

☐ Assess yourself with the following self-assessment.

ONLINE AT CENGAGEBRAIN.COM YOU CAN:

☐ Collect StudyBits while you read and study the chapter.

☐ Quiz yourself on key concepts.

☐ Prepare for tests with M&F4 Flash Cards as well as those you create.

 **SELF-ASSESSMENT**

Family Hardiness Scale (FHS)

This scale is designed to identify the degree to which your family has the characteristics of hardiness, which is defined as resistance to stress, having internal strength, and having a sense of control over life events and hardships. Read each statement and decide to what degree each describes your family. Choices include false, mostly false, mostly true, or totally true about your family. Write a 0 to 3 (or NA) next to each statement.

0	1	2	3	NA
False	*Mostly false*	*Mostly true*	*Totally true*	*Not applicable*

In our family…

_____ **1.** Trouble results from mistakes we make.

_____ **2.** It is not wise to plan ahead and hope because things do not turn out anyway.

_____ **3.** Our work and efforts are not appreciated no matter how hard we try and work.

_____ **4.** In the long run, the bad things that happen to us are balanced by the good things that happen.

_____ **5.** We have a sense of being strong even when we face big problems.

_____ **6.** Many times I feel I can trust that even in difficult times things will work out.

_____ **7.** While we don't always agree, we can count on each other to stand by us in times of need.

_____ **8.** We do not feel we can survive if another problem hits us.

_____ **9.** We believe that things will work out for the better if we work together as a family.

_____ **10.** Life seems dull and meaningless.

_____ **11.** We strive together and help each other no matter what.

_____ **12.** When our family plans activities we try new and exciting things.

_____ **13.** We listen to each other's problems, hurts, and fears.

_____ **14.** We tend to do the same things over and over…it's boring.

_____ **15.** We seem to encourage each other to try new things and experiences.

_____ **16.** It is better to stay at home than go out and do things with others.

_____ **17.** Being active and learning new things are encouraged.

_____ **18.** We work together to solve problems.

_____ **19.** Most of the unhappy things that happen are due to bad luck.

_____ **20.** We realize our lives are controlled by accidents and luck.

Scoring

Reverse score items 1, 2, 3, 8, 10, 14, 16, 19, and 20. For example, if for number 1 you wrote down a 0, replace the 0 with a 3 and vice versa. Now add all the numbers from 1 to 20.

Norms

A "low" score indicating very low hardiness is 0 and a "high" score indicating very high hardiness is 60. The overall average of 304 families who took the scale scored 47.4 (SD = 6.7).

Source: The authors of the scale are Marilyn A. McCubbin, Hamilton I. McCubbin, and Anne I. Thompson. See McCubbin, H. I., & A. I. Thompson (Eds.). (1991). *Family assessment inventories for research and practice.* Madison, WI: University of Wisconsin.

14 | Coping with Divorce and Getting Remarried

Bacho/Shutterstock.com

SECTIONS

After finishing this chapter go to **PAGE 289** for **STUDY TOOLS**

> Sometimes the best and worst times of your life can coincide.
>
> —SHANNON L. ADLER, INSPIRATIONAL AUTHOR

Everyone who marries does so with the goal of continuing the love feelings and relationship that they have on their wedding day. The reality is that 40% to 50% of brides and grooms transition from the altar to the courtroom. Just as one's wedding is often a day of great joy and hope, one's divorce is a day of great sadness and despair. **Divorce** (there are about 1 million divorces each year in the United States) is the legal ending of a valid marriage contract. The often quoted statistic that half of all marriages end in divorce is not true. Some marriages, such as those by teenagers who drop out of high school, end at the 50% plus rate. But for college graduates married at age 26 or later, 82% were still married 20 years later (hence, less than 20% divorced). Race (Whites) and religion (more devout) are also associated with a lower divorce rate (Coontz, 2016).

The divorce rate has dropped for the last three years. In 2015, there were 16.9 divorces per 1000 married women. This rate is the lowest in more than 35 years (Anderson, 2016). A primary reason for the declining divorce rate is that people are delaying marriage so that they are older at the time of marriage. Indeed, the older a person at the time of marriage, the less likely the person is to divorce.

14-1 DECIDING WHETHER TO CONTINUE OR END A RELATIONSHIP/GET A DIVORCE

Several factors are predictive of maintaining a relationship or letting it go. In addition, there is a process in terms of what should be considered before deciding to end a relationship/divorce.

14-1a Deal-Breakers in Relationships

In a Match.com's survey of 5,500 singles, women identified deal-breakers as dating someone who was secretive with their texts (77%), lazy (72%), shorter than them (71%), or a virgin (51%). Deal-breakers for men were

Bobby Davis

> Divorce isn't such a tragedy. A tragedy's staying in an unhappy marriage, teaching your children the wrong things about love. Nobody ever died of divorce.
>
> —JENNIFER WEINER, *FLY AWAY HOME*

dating someone who was disheveled/unclean (63%), lazy (60%), or no career path/ambition (46%) (Fisher & Garcia, 2016).

Hansson and Ahborg (2016) identified the reasons 39 parents gave who were separated and headed toward divorce. These reasons included strains from parenthood, stressful conditions, lack of intimacy, insufficient communication, differing personalities and interests, no commitment, and negative effects of addiction.

14-1b Issues to Consider before Ending a Relationship

Eighty-seven percent of 353 university students reported that they had experienced the breakup of a romantic relationship. Of these, 39% said that they initiated the break (30% of the breakups were initiated by the partner and 23% mutually) (Brenner & Knox, 2016). Issues to consider before making a decision to end a romantic relationship follow:

1. **Consider improving the relationship rather than ending it.** In some cases, people end relationships and later regret having done so. Setting unrealistically high standards may end a marriage prematurely. Particularly in our individualistic society with the fun/love/sex focus of relationships, anything that deviates is considered justification for divorce. James (2015) examined longitudinal data from a nationally representative sample of divorced women who "looked backward" from the time of divorce

divorce the legal ending of a valid marriage contract.

to reveal their perceptions of the marriage. Almost two-thirds reported relatively high levels of both happiness and communication and either low or moderate levels of conflict.

Indeed, not all persons who begin divorce proceedings are completely on board with the idea. Doherty et al. (2016) surveyed 624 parents who had filed for divorce. One-quarter reported that they are ambivalent about going through with the divorce; 8% did not want the divorce.

Given the uncertainty of a larger number of persons contemplating divorce, it may be wise to contact a marriage therapist before an attorney as many relationships cannot just be salvaged but can flourish (of course, we do not recommend giving an abusive relationship more time, as abuse, once started, tends to increase in frequency and intensity). Kanewisher and Harris (2015) reported data on 15 women who entered therapy with the idea that divorce was likely. All 15 decided to stay married. Don't end a relationship without a great deal of thought and consideration.

> The ability to leave a marriage more easily has helped not only those escaping bad marriages but also many who remain married, because it gives the partner who wants change, more negotiating power.
>
> —STEPHANIE COONTZ, FAMILY HISTORIAN

2. **Acknowledge and accept that terminating a relationship will be difficult and painful.** The self-concept of the person getting divorced is typically shaken (e.g., "How could I have become involved with someone like that?" or "Why did I stay in such an unfulfilling relationship?"). The longer and more intense the relationship, the more intense the negative outcome and the longer it takes for the person getting divorced to heal (Graham et al., 2014).

The ending of a love relationship is also associated (for about half of undergraduates who experience a breakup) with depression, sleep disturbances, intrusive thoughts, and increased use of medications (for sleep) or alcohol. When a divorce is involved, the risk of suicide also increases (Stack & Scourfield, 2015).

3. **Select your medium of breaking up.** While some break up face to face, others do so in a text message, in an email, or on Facebook. Most prefer that their partner break up with them face to face, not in a text message (Faircloth et al., 2012).

Another alternative is just fading away. After a five-year relationship with Caryn Trager, Jerry Seinfeld ended the relationship by "avoiding her, seeing her less often, so their breakup was spread out until she got the message, rather than be concentrated in one nuclear moment" (Oppenheimer, 2002, p. 144).

4. **In talking with your partner, blame yourself for the breakup.** It is important to blame yourself for the reason you want to break up (e.g., "I need for us to take a break," "I want to go to graduate school," or "I am not ready to settle down"). If you blame your partner, you may feel obligated to continue the relationship if your partner agrees to change. For example, if you say, "You drink too much," your partner can reply, "I have stopped drinking and joined AA... let's have dinner tonight."

5. **Cut off the relationship completely.** While you may wish to continue to see your ex-partner (e.g., due to missing "your friend" or wanting to prove that you are still important to the person) (Var et al., 2014), doing so will have different consequences depending on whether you are the "dumper" or "dumpee." If you are the person who ended the relationship (dumper), it will be easier for you to transition into a friendship without difficulty. However, the other person (dumpee) will heal faster if he or she does not see you again (and hopes of reconciliation are ended). Tan et al. (2015) studied post relationships with one's partner

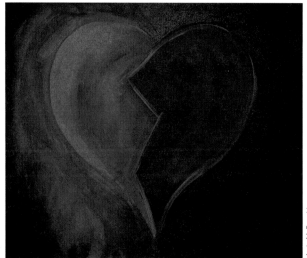

Maria McDonald

after a romantic breakup and found that the stronger the pre-breakup commitment/emotional investment, the more the couple was able to transition to a friendship four months later.

6. **Learn from the terminated relationship.** Among the reasons for ending a relationship are behaviors of being too controlling; being oversensitive, jealous, or too picky; cheating; fearing commitment; or being unable to compromise/negotiate conflict. Since few breakups are completely one person's fault, you might consider recognizing your own contribution to the breakup and work on behaviors that might be a source of problems in future relationships.

7. **Allow time to heal.** Ending a love relationship is painful and will take time to heal. Recovering from a divorce often takes 12 to 18 months. In the sample of 353 who reported on their broken romantic relationship, about half (47%) reported that they had made a "complete" recovery and that time and support from friends was very helpful (Brenner & Knox, 2016). Focusing on the negative qualities of the ex-partner/relationship and becoming involved with a new partner helped to speed the recovery.

8. **Clean your Facebook page.** Angry spouses sometimes post nasty notes about their ex on their Facebook page that can be viewed by the ex's lawyer. Also, if there are any incriminating photos of indiscreet encounters, drug use, wild parties, or the like, these can be used in court and should be purged. Twitter and blog postings should also be scrutinized.

14-1c Separations Don't Always Become Divorces

Separation is often thought of as resulting in divorce. But some separations are permanent (the couple remain legally married but may no longer function as spouses) while others may result in reconciliation. For example, in analysis of various national data sets, 32% of women who were separated were still married three years later. About 12% of the separations resulted in reconciliations. African Americans were more likely to reconcile a separation (Tumin et al., 2015).

14-1d Divorce: The Most Likely Year

Based on a large longitudinal data set, Kulu (2015) found that the probability of divorce rises with each year of marriage, reaches a peak about the fifth year, and gradually declines. Since most of the respondents lived together before marriage, the year of dissolution from the onset of a relationship was closer to seven years.

Break It to Me Gently

Researcher Sprecher and her colleagues (2014) surveyed 335 undergraduates and identified compassionate strategies for breaking up. Two of the most commonly used strategies were "I verbally explained to my partner in person my reasons for desiring to break up," and "I told my partner that I didn't regret the time we had spent together in the relationship." Both of these were compassionate strategies which more often resulted in the partners remaining friends. More brutal ways of breaking up included manipulation (e.g., starting an argument/blaming it on the partner) or distant communication (e.g., text message).

Iakov Filimonov/Shutterstock.com

14-2 MACRO FACTORS CONTRIBUTING TO DIVORCE

Sociologists emphasize that social context creates outcome. This concept is best illustrated by the fact that from 1639 to 1760, the Puritans in Massachusetts averaged only one divorce per year (Morgan, 1944). The social context of that era involved strong profamily values and strict divorce laws, with the result that divorce was almost nonexistent for over 100 years. In contrast, divorce occurs more frequently today as a result of various structural and cultural factors, also known as macro factors.

14-2a Economic Factors Associated with Divorce

Marriages and families live in an economic context. Unemployment is not only associated with spouses' decreased marital satisfaction and increased arguments, but the parents are also more critical/negative toward their children (Fonseca et al., 2016). And, while a happy wife who is economically independent is not more likely to divorce (Killewald, 2016), such economic independence for the unhappy wife will expedite her leaving the relationship (Kesselring & Bremmer, 2006).

14-2b Social and Psychological Consequences of Divorce for Spouses

Divorce is associated with a decrease in psychological and physical well-being for both women and men (Zella, 2016). However, most adjust. In a study of adjustment to divorce from long-term marriages (over 25 years) the researchers found that most (80%) of the 306 respondents were satisfactorily adjusted with a new spouse or cohabiting partner. Those individuals who had resilient/adaptive personalities were the most likely to rebound (Perrig-Chiello et al., 2015). Lawson and Satti (2016) noted that there is a stereotype of the divorced female as "passive, inactive, and despairing victims waiting to be rescued by Prince Charming." However, their research on divorced Black and White women in the United States revealed that they were resilient, as they used the coping strategies of keeping busy, relying on family support, and being involved in religious/spiritual activities. Spiritual well-being has also been associated with positive divorce adjustment (Steiner et al., 2015). Finally, where there was considerable unhappiness in the previous marriage (particularly for women), divorce was sweet. Bourassa et al. (2015) analyzed data from a sample of 1,639 divorced women and found that those who came from very low quality marriages gained in life satisfaction following divorce.

14-2c Calling Off the Divorce

After getting a glimpse at the devastation divorce can cause, some separated spouses change their minds and get back together. Plauche et al. (2016) interviewed 7 couples (14 spouses, mostly White, around age 40, marriage average of 8 years with children) who filed for divorce but who reconciled their marriage before the divorce was finalized. Themes of getting back together included:

1. **Pulling together during difficult times.** Often there was an event which happened during the separation period that brought the couple back together. One respondent said:

   > With me it was a severe injury that she was with me every step of the way. . . . Elizabeth went with me the last time to see my general practitioner and that day, it was, devastating for me, but she was there

   with me. I think it scared her a little bit, too…I guess we've learned that, unlike our previous spouses, that we weren't going to run out on each other.

2. **Growth from separation and reconciliation.**

   > I think that time apart from each other helped us think, even though it was a rocky road, . . . just leaving and clearing my head and trying to pick myself back up, I think that was the best decision I ever made . . . that separation.

3. **Multiple attempts and rough starts.**

   > I guess the first two times that we tried to reconcile, I . . . was thinking, "The children are gonna grow up without a father, or [without] their father and . . . I don't want that for my children." . . . I didn't want them to go through that. The first few times I think we tried because of different reasons. But the very last time it had nothing to do with financial or any . . . of the, what you might call . . . logical reasons.

4. **It's worth the hard work.**

   > It was not gonna happen overnight. . . . We made that decision not knowing what was going to be ahead of us. We knew it was gonna be hard, [but] we did not know it was gonna be a roller coaster ride. It really took both of us . . . being real humble [to make it].

5. **Big moves and grand gestures.**

   > Literally, we were sitting in the courtroom and they called my name and I looked at my attorney. . . . I got up and walked out into the ladies room. My sister followed me. I was crying. I said, "I can't do it." She said, "[Then] don't do it. . . ." And, we left. We went and had breakfast and I sent Kyle a text and said, "I can't do it." And we had not spoken in probably six months.

14-2d Changing Family Functions and Structure

Many of the protective, religious, educational, and recreational functions of the family have been largely taken over by outside agencies. Family members may now look to the police for protection, the church or synagogue for meaning, the school for education, and commercial recreational facilities for fun rather than to each other within the family for fulfilling these needs. The result is that, although meeting emotional needs remains an important and primary function of the family, fewer reasons exist to keep a family together.

In addition to the change in functions of the family brought on by the Industrial Revolution, family structure has changed from that of the larger extended family in a rural community to a smaller nuclear family in an urban community. In the former, individuals could turn to a lot of people in times of stress; in the latter, more stress necessarily falls on fewer shoulders. Also, with marriages more isolated and scattered, kin may not live close enough to express their disapproval for the breakup of a marriage. With fewer social consequences for divorce, Americans are more willing to escape unhappy unions.

14-2e Liberal Divorce Laws/ Social Acceptance

All states recognize some form of **no-fault divorce** in which neither party is identified as the guilty party or the cause of the divorce (e.g., committing adultery). In effect, divorce is granted after a period of separation (typically 12 months). Nevada requires the shortest waiting period of six weeks. Most other states require from 6 to 12 months. The goal of no-fault divorce is to make divorce less acrimonious. However, this objective has not been achieved as spouses who divorce may still fight over custody of the children, child support, spouse support, and division of property. Nevertheless, social acceptability as well as legal ease may affect the frequency of divorce. Konstam et al. (2016) confirmed that the stigma of divorce (while lessening) is still operative in the thinking and behavior of emerging adult women.

14-2f Prenuptial Agreements and the Internet

New York family law attorney Nancy Chemtob notes that those who have prenuptial agreements are more likely to divorce, since one can cash out without economic devastation. In addition, she suggested that the Internet contributes to divorce since a bored spouse can go online to the various dating sites and see what alternatives are out there. Spinning up a new relationship online before dumping the spouse of many years is not uncommon.

14-2g Fewer Moral and Religious Sanctions

While previously some churches denied membership to the divorced, today many priests and clergy recognize

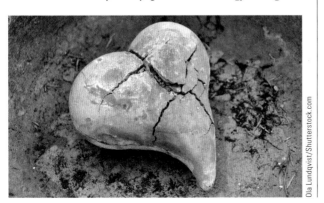
Ola Lundqvist/Shutterstock.com

that divorce may be the best alternative in particular marital relationships. Churches increasingly embrace single and divorced or separated individuals, as evidenced by divorce adjustment groups.

Beginning in 2015 Pope Francis recommended annulments via the Catholic Church be expedited from 18 months to 45 days. About half of all annulments sought by Catholics are sought by citizens of the United States. These annulments impact the perception of Church law, so the Catholic who has been married who gets an annulment is free to remarry and remain in good standing with the Catholic Church (e.g., still able to take communion). Annulments granted by the Catholic Church have no effect on the legal marital status of a couple.

14-2h More Divorce Models

The prevalence of divorce today means that most individuals know someone who is divorced. The more divorced people a person knows, the more normal divorce will seem to that person. The less deviant the person perceives divorce to be, the greater the probability the person will divorce if that person's own marriage becomes strained. Divorce has become so common that numerous websites for the divorced are available.

14-2i Mobility and Anonymity

When individuals are highly mobile, they have fewer roots in a community and greater anonymity. Spouses who move away from their respective families and friends often discover that they are surrounded by strangers who do not care if they stay married or not. Divorce thrives when promarriage social expectations are not operative. In addition, the factors of mobility and anonymity also result in the removal

no-fault divorce neither party is identified as the guilty party or the cause of the divorce.

of a consistent support system to help spouses deal with the difficulties they may encounter in marriage.

14-2j Ethnicity and Culture

Asian Americans and Mexican Americans have lower divorce rates than other Americans because the former consider the family unit to be of greater value (familism) than their individual interests (individualism).

Unlike familistic values in Asian cultures, individualistic values in American culture emphasize the goal of personal happiness in marriage. When spouses stop having fun (when individualistic goals are no longer met), they sometimes feel no reason to stay married. Of 9,650 undergraduates, only 9% agreed that "I would not divorce my spouse for any reason" (Hall & Knox, 2016).

14-3 MICRO FACTORS CONTRIBUTING TO DIVORCE

Macro factors are not sufficient to cause a divorce. Micro factors are the reasons spouses end relationships. A discussion of micro factors follows.

14-3a Growing Apart/Differences

The top reason for seeking divorce given by a sample of 886 divorcing individuals was "growing apart" (55%) (Hawkins et al., 2012). The individuals found that they no longer had anything in common.

Extensive video game playing interferes with couple interaction and time together.

Growing apart is also a reason for divorce among arranged marriages. Bromfield et al. (2016) interviewed 21 Arab Muslims from the United Arab Emirates who divorced from a marriage that was arranged by their parents. Age at marriage (19.5 for females, 24 for males), disrespect/violence/abuse, and problems with extended kin were themes of divorce among the respondents. One divorced male noted:

> My wife did not like to socialize with my family . . . because of hijab [head cover], she does not feel comfortable to be covered while she is staying with the family [the bride had to wear hijab in the presence of her husband's brothers who lived in the house]. . . . My mother and sisters did not like her and encouraged me to divorce her. Her mother was influencing her and pushed her to ask for a separate house . . . she needs privacy and therefore she needs a separate house. I was not financially prepared for that . . . we have been quarrelling often on these issues.

14-3b Falling Out of Love

In her book *Boys in the Trees*, Carly Simon (2015) recounts her marriage/divorce with James Taylor. She notes, "He never criticized me, he just grew cold. The heartbeat went out of our house, the rhythm went out of our romance . . ." Indeed, 4 in 10 (43%) of 9,959 undergraduates reported that they would divorce a spouse they no longer loved (Hall & Knox, 2016). No couple is immune to falling out of love and getting divorced.

14-3c Limited Time Together: Video Game Addict Widow

Some spouses do not make time to be together/nurture their relationship. Time devoted to children and career interferes with couple time. Partners who spend little time together doing things they mutually enjoy often feel estranged from each other and have little motivation to stay together. However, how much time spouses need/prefer to be together to define their relationship as nurturing and fulfilling varies. Both Jay Leno and Jerry Seinfeld reported that they are constantly on the road doing standup and have no interest in staying home every night. Their partners agree that "constant togetherness" (e.g., altogether togetherness) is not what they bargained for. So there is limited time together if both agree.

However, some partners are online video game addicts and the partner does not like it. Northrup and Shumway (2014) interviewed 10 wives who revealed that their game-addicted husbands spent 40 plus hours a week online playing video games—to the exclusion of themselves, their children, and their friends. The impact on their marriage was devastating since their husbands flew into a rage whenever their wives confronted them about their video gaming.

14-3d Low Frequency of Positive Behavior

People marry because they anticipate greater rewards from being married than from being single. During courtship, each partner engages in a high frequency of positive verbal (compliments) and nonverbal (eye contact, physical affection) behavior toward the other. The good feelings the partners experience as a result of these positive behaviors encourage them to marry to "lock in" these feelings across time. Just as love feelings are based on partners making the choice to engage in a high frequency of positive behavior toward each other, negative feelings (e.g., abandonment, loneliness) result when these positive behaviors stop and negative behaviors begin. Thoughts of divorce may then begin (to escape the negative behavior).

14-3e Having an Affair

In a survey of U.S. individuals, half of those who reported having participated in extramarital sex also reported that they were either divorced or separated (Allen & Atkins, 2012).

14-3f Poor Communication/Conflict Resolution Skills

The second most frequent reason for seeking divorce given by a sample of 886 divorcing individuals was "not able to talk together" (Hawkins et al., 2012). Not only do individuals distance themselves from each other by not talking, they further complicate their relationship since they have no way to reduce conflict.

Managing differences and conflict in a relationship helps to reduce the negative feelings that develop in a relationship. Some partners respond to conflict by withdrawing emotionally from their relationship; others respond by attacking, blaming, and failing to listen to their partner's point of view.

14-3g Changing Values

Both spouses change throughout the marriage. "He's not the same person I married" is a frequent observation of people contemplating divorce. One minister married and decided seven years later that he did not like the confines of his religious or marital role. He left the ministry, earned a PhD, and began to drink and have affairs. His wife now found herself married to a clinical psychologist who spent his evenings at bars with other women. The couple divorced.

Because people change throughout their lives, the person selected at one point in life may not be the same partner one would select at another point. Margaret Mead, the famous anthropologist, noted that her first marriage was a student marriage; her second, a professional partnership; and her third, an intellectual marriage to her soul mate, with whom she had her only child. At each of several stages in her life, she experienced a different set of needs and selected a mate who fulfilled those needs.

14-3h Onset of Satiation

Satiation, also referred to as habituation, refers to the state in which a stimulus loses its value with repeated exposure. Spouses may tire of each other. Their stories are no longer new, their sex is repetitive, and their presence for each other is no longer exciting as it was at the beginning of the relationship. Some people who feel trapped by the boredom of constancy decide to divorce and seek what they believe to be more excitement by returning to singlehood and new partners. One man said, "I traded something good for something new." A developmental task of marriage is for couples to enjoy being together and not demand a constant state of excitement (which is not possible over a 50-year period). The late comedian George Carlin said, "If all of your needs are not being met, drop some of your needs." If spouses did not expect so much of marriage, maybe they would not be disappointed.

> I don't miss him, I miss who I thought he was.
>
> —UNKNOWN

14-3i Having the Perception That One Would Be Happier If Divorced

Women file most divorce applications. Their doing so may be encouraged by their view that they will achieve greater power over their own life. They feel that by getting a divorce they will have their own money (in the form of child support and/or alimony) without having a man they do not want in the house. In addition, they will have greater control over their children, since women are more often awarded custody (see Section 14-9 of this chapter which reveals that this is changing).

satiation a stimulus loses its value with repeated exposure; also called habituation.

College Student Romances That Ended: Reasons and Reactions

Most undergraduates have experienced the end of a romantic relationship. The purpose of this study was to investigate the strategies they used or were subjected to in regard to the end of their last romantic relationship and to identify the outcomes for the individuals and their relationship. Basically we wanted to know why relationships ended (e.g., infidelity, boredom), how (e.g., face to face or text message), and the post-breakup relationship outcomes (e.g., enemies, friends).

Sample
A convenience sample from a large southeastern university completed a voluntary, anonymous 25-item online survey on relationship breakups. The sample (N = 478) was predominately female (70%), White (71%), and heterosexual (80%).

Research Questions and Findings
Two major questions guided this research.

Research Question 1
What reasons did undergraduates give for ending their last romantic relationship? See Table 14.1 for the reasons given by 478 respondents. There was no significant difference between sex of the respondent and the reason given for ending the relationship.

Research Question 2
Following the ending of the romantic relationship, what were the effects and feelings associated with the breakup (e.g., depression, guilt, relief)? And to what degree did these vary by sex of respondent (see Table 14.2)?

TABLE 14.1	MAIN REASONS FOR BREAKING UP (N = 478)		
	Male, %	Female, %	Total, %
Bored in the relationship/not happy	32	22	23
Betrayal of partner	9	17	14
Different interests	11	11	11
I met someone new	12	10	10
Different values	13	7	8
Moved away	6	9	8

"Feeling initially upset but recognizing the breakup was for the best" was the primary reaction to breaking up. "I was glad it was over" was the second most frequent response. Chi-square analysis showed that for females there was a significant difference between who initiated the breakup and the reactions to those breakups ($\chi^2 = 55.51$, df = 8, p < .001). For example, if the woman ended the relationship she was more likely to report "I'm glad it was over" and "I was initially upset but felt it was for the best." In contrast, males showed no significant difference in effect regardless if they were the initiators of the breakup or not.

Theoretical Framework
Symbolic interactionism provided the theoretical framework for viewing the findings of this study. Symbolic interactionism is a micro-level theory that focuses on the meanings individuals attribute to phenomena. Symbolic interactionists focus on the importance of symbols, subjective versus objective reality, and the definition of social

14-3j Top 20 Factors Associated with Divorce

Researchers have identified the characteristics of those most likely to divorce (Amato, 2015; Djamba et al., 2012; Park & Raymo, 2013). Some of the more significant associations include the following:

1. Less than two years of hanging out together (partners know little about each other)

2. Having little in common (similar interests serve as a bond between people)

3. Marrying at age 17 and younger (associated with low education and income and lack of maturity)

4. Being different in race, education, religion, social class, age, values, and libido (widens the gap between spouses)

5. Not being religiously devout (less bound by traditional values)

6. Having a cohabitation history with different partners (pattern of establishing and breaking relationships)

TABLE 14.2 REACTIONS TO THE BREAKUP

	I Ended the Relationship		My Partner Ended the Relationship		It Was Mutual		Total
	Male	Female	Male	Female	Male	Female	
I was glad it was over	16	44	2	4	9	9	84
I was initially upset but feel it was for the best	27	78	11	43	16	48	223
I was depressed	5	11	3	30	5	7	61
I saw a counselor to help with the breakup	0	0	1	2	0	0	3
I felt suicidal	0	2	0	1	0	1	4
Total	48	135	17	80	30	65	375

situations. The respondents identified "feeling bored/unhappy" and "betrayal of partner" as reasons to terminate a relationship. The fact that Americans are socialized to think in individualist rather than Asian familistic terms emphasizes the cultural backdrop on which romantic breakup decisions are made. In addition, U.S. youth are taught to get upset and end a romantic relationship in response to a partner's cheating. French lovers are less quick to end a relationship over an indiscretion or an affair.

Similarly, these undergraduates viewed the ending of their romantic relationships as an undesirable event which resulted in the culturally scripted response—being sad, being upset, being depressed. Older individuals might take another view—that the end of an unfulfilling romantic relationship is an opportunity to meet a new partner and create a more fulfilling relationship.

Implications
There are three implications of the data. First, the ending of romantic relationships is filled with angst.

Respondents spoke of feeling unhappy, betrayed, and replaced by another lover. They also revealed feelings of anger and jealousy.

Second, the aftermath of a romantic relationship may have negative consequences. Thirty percent of the females reported feeling depressed when their partner ended the relationship. Over 40% reported that they were initially upset.

Third, romantic breakups are not serious enough to induce thoughts of suicide or to seek counseling. Only 4 of the 478 respondents revealed that they felt suicidal; only three sought counseling. Indeed, most undergraduates were resilient and moved on. Almost half (46%) said that while they were initially upset, they believed the ending of the romantic relationship was for the best.

Source: Updated, abridged, and adapted from "Saying goodbye in romantic relationships: Strategies and outcomes," by Brackett, A., J. Fish, & D. Knox. (February 21–23, 2013). Poster, Southeastern Council on Family Relations, Birmingham, AL.

7. Having been previously married (less fearful of divorce)

8. Having no children or fewer children (less reason to stay married)

9. Having limited education (associated with lower income, more stress, less happiness)

10. Falling out of love (spouses have less reason to stay married)

11. Being unfaithful (broken trust, emotional reason to leave relationship)

12. Growing up with divorced parents (models for ending rather than repairing relationship; may have inherited traits such as alcoholism that are detrimental to staying married)

13. Having poor communication skills (issues go unresolved and accumulate)

14. Having mental problems (bipolar, depression, anxiety) or physical disability (chronic fatigue syndrome)

15. Having seriously ill child (impacts stress, finances, couple time)

16. Having premarital pregnancy or unwanted child (spouses may feel pressure to get married; stress of parenting unwanted child)

17. Emotional/physical abuse (relationship is aversive)

18. Lacking commitment (for nontraditional spouses, divorce is seen as an option if the marriage does not work out)

19. Unemployment (finances decrease, stress increases)

20. Alcoholism/substance abuse (partner no longer dependable)

The more of these factors that exist in a marriage, the more vulnerable a couple is to divorce. Regardless of the various factors associated with divorce, there is debate about the character of people who divorce. Are they selfish, amoral people who are incapable of making good on a commitment to each other and who wreck the lives of their children? Or are they individuals who care a great deal about relationships and would not settle for a bad marriage? Indeed, they may divorce precisely because they value marriage and want to rescue their children from being reared in an unhappy conflict ridden home.

14-3k Physical Illness of Wife

How does "In sickness and in health" play out as related to divorce? Researchers Karraker and Latham (2015) found that divorce was more likely if the wife developed heart problems, cancer, stroke, or lung disease in midlife. No increased divorce was associated with the husband getting sick. Hence "health is a determinant of marital dissolution in later life via both biological and gendered social pathways."

 14-4 CONSEQUENCES OF DIVORCE FOR SPOUSES/PARENTS

My parents' divorce left me with a lot of sadness and pain and acting, and especially humour, was my way of dealing with all that.

—JENNIFER ANISTON

In a study of adjustment to divorce from long-term marriages (over 25 years) the researchers found that most (80%) of the 306 respondents were satisfactorily adjusted with a new spouse or cohabiting partner. Those individuals who had resilient/adaptive personalities were the most likely to rebound (Perrig-Chiello et al., 2015). Spiritual well-being was also associated with positive divorce adjustment, particularly among men (Steiner et al., 2015). And, where there was considerable unhappiness in the previous marriage (particularly for women), divorce was sweet. Bourassa et al. (2015) analyzed data from a sample of 1,639 divorced women and found that those who came from very low quality marriages gained in life satisfaction following divorce. Since same-sex marriages only became legal in 2015, data on same-sex divorces is not available. Herman (2016) noted that use of first names in litigation of same-sex partners (rather than husband and wife) is one of the changes that will occur. He also predicted that when one of the partners has a child, custody/partner maintenance issues will need to be negotiated.

14-4a Importance of Choosing One's Perspective/Thoughts in Getting Over a Past Love

Sometimes it is difficult to get over a partner. The lyrics to Don Henley's "You Must Not Be Drinking Enough" reflect the dilemma of telling yourself you are over your love but emotionally you are still involved. Brenner and Vogel (2014) emphasized that recovery from a terminated romantic relationship is related to being selective about one's thoughts—not dwelling on positive memories of the former relationship (e.g., "we were such good friends and loved each other") and focusing on negative aspects of the relationship (e.g., "cheating, drug abuse, disrespect"). The self-assessment at the end of the chapter provides a way to assess the degree to which one is selective in reviewing one's past relationship.

Maintaining one's positive self-identity is associated with a positive recovery from a romantic relationship that has ended (Mason et al., 2012). Individuals who define themselves solely in reference to their ex-partner experience more difficulty in getting over and moving on (e.g., more likely to remain in love with the ex). These individuals may also use Facebook to find out current information about the ex-partner in regard to their involvement in a new relationship (Tong, 2013).

As an alternative to focusing on a previous partner's negatives/avoiding dwelling on the ex's positives as a mechanism to get over the partner, some individuals find meaning in viewing positively the relationship they enjoyed while married. Although Carly Simon's divorce with James Taylor was over 30 years ago (1983), she noted in her memoir:

> I've stopped trying to stop loving. If the rules decree that you are allowed to love only if that love is reciprocated, then whoever made up those rules is cutting an important part of their authenticity away . . . that heart might have been broken, but brokenness doesn't stop it from loving. [She still lives in the same house and sleeps in the same bed they slept in on Martha's Vinyard.] (*Simon, 2015, pp. 369–370*)

Is breaking up harder on spouses or cohabitants? Tavares and Aassve (2013) compared those who were married with those who were living together to assess the level of psychological distress due to a breakup. When children are involved, the breakup is more difficult, but controlling for children, the distress for spouses and cohabitants is similar.

14-4b Financial Consequences of Divorce

Both women and men experience a drop in income following divorce, but women may suffer more (Warrener et al., 2013). However, the economic bloodletting for divorced women has slowed in recent years due to the employment earnings of wives, child support payments, and income from personal networks (Tach & Eads, 2015).

How money is divided at divorce depends on whether the couple had a prenuptial agreement or a **postnuptial agreement**. Such agreements are most likely to be upheld if an attorney insists on four conditions—full disclosure of assets by both parties, independent representation by separate counsel, absence of coercion or duress, and terms that are fair and equitable.

14-4c Friends with One's Ex?

What about staying friends with an ex? Mogilski and Welling (2016) examined the nature of the relationship with one's ex in two studies of 348 and 513 participants, respectively. The primary reasons for staying friends were that the ex-partner was regarded as reliable, trustworthy, and of sentimental value (i.e., reliability/sentimentality). Reasons of less importance were pragmatism and sex, with men more often maintaining the

One unforeseen positive outcome of divorce is that children may spend more time with their dad.

relationship for these reasons. The researchers concluded that maintaining a connection with one's ex provides an opportunity for ex-partners to exchange desirable resources (e.g., love, status, information, money, sex, parenting) after romantic relationship dissolution.

14-5 NEGATIVE AND POSITIVE CONSEQUENCES OF DIVORCE FOR CHILDREN

The act of separation/divorce is a major adverse childhood experience (ACE) (Soares et al., 2016). In a study of 3,951 adolescents, when seven types of ACEs were identified—physical abuse, sexual abuse, physical neglect, emotional neglect, domestic violence, parental separation, and parental death—the most common type was parental separation (42%). Baglivio and Epps (2016) found that 79% of 64,329 juveniles who had been arrested in the state of Florida between 2007 and 2012 had experienced the separation or divorce of their parents.

But there are both negative and positive outcomes. Negative outcomes include economic hardship, lack of concentration in school, sleeping disorders, and an increase in challenging the parent/being stubborn (Al-Gharaibeh, 2015). Weaver and Schofield (2015) analyzed national data on children aged 5 to 15 and

postnuptial agreement
an agreement about how money is to be divided should a couple later divorce, which is made after the couple marry.

found that children of divorced parents had more internalized (e.g., depression) and externalized (e.g., grades) behavior than children whose parents were together. Higher income moderated the effects.

Most research on reactions of children to divorce has focused on young children. Jensen and Bowen (2015) analyzed data on 283 adults who divorced after age 40 to assess their perceptions of the reactions to divorce of their emerging adult children. Just over half of emerging adult children were perceived as being unsupportive, somewhat upset, or very upset in response to their parents' divorce. One in five was devastated. Fathers perceived that their adult children were having greater difficulty adjusting to divorce than mothers, race of parents did not make a difference in reaction, and the longer parents had been married, the more difficult the adjustment.

Self-Assessment: Children's Beliefs about Parental Divorce Scale
Take the self-assessment at the end of the chapter to explore childhood feelings about divorce.

But there are also positive aspects of divorce. Halligan et al. (2014) analyzed data from 336 undergraduates who were asked to identify positive outcomes they experienced from the divorce of their parents. Table 14.3 provides the percentages "agreeing" or "strongly agreeing" with various outcomes.

Table 14.3 also reflects that children of divorce may choose to notice the positive aspects of divorce rather than buy into the cultural script that "divorce is terrible and my life will be ruined because of my parent's divorce." South

Wavebreakmedia Ltd/Wavebreak Media/Getty Images

TABLE 14.3 TWENTY POSITIVE EFFECTS OF DIVORCE: PERCENTAGE OF UNDERGRADUATE RESPONDENTS' AGREEMENT	
	Percent
Since my parents' divorce, I am more compassionate for people who are going through a difficult time.	65.63
I have greater tolerance for people with different viewpoints since my parents' divorce.	63.16
Since my parents' divorce, I have been exposed to different family values, tradition, and lifestyles.	60.01
I have liked spending time alone with my mother since my parents' divorce.	57.71
My mother is happier since the divorce.	57.20
I rely less on my parents for making decisions since my parents' divorce.	53.51
I have liked spending time alone with my father since my parents' divorce.	45.61
My mother has made a greater effort to spend quality time with me since the divorce.	45.61
I can spend more time with the parent I prefer since my parents' divorce.	45.37
Since my parents' divorce, I have felt closer to my mother.	44.98
My relationship with my mother has improved since my parents' divorce.	44.74
My father is happier since the divorce.	43.85
My parents' divorce has made me closer to my friends.	42.54
Since my parents' divorce, I have greater appreciation for my siblings.	40.78
My father has made a greater effort to spend quality time with me since the divorce.	38.60
Since my parents' divorce, I feel closer to my siblings.	35.96
After my biological parents' divorce, I noticed that I was exposed to less conflict between my parents on a daily basis.	34.93
My relationship with my father has improved since my parents' divorce.	34.65
I think my parents have a "good" divorce.	34.35
My parents are more civil to each other since the divorce.	34.21

PERSONAL VIEW:

What a Mother Told Her Sons about the Impending Divorce

The following are the words of a mother of two children (8 and 12) as she tells her children of the pending divorce. It assumes that both parents take some responsibility for the divorce and are willing to provide a united front to the children. The script should be adapted for one's own unique situation.

Daddy and I want to talk to you about a big decision that we have made. A while back we told you that we were having a really hard time getting along, and that we were having meetings with someone called a therapist who has been helping us talk about our feelings, and deciding what to do about them.

We also told you that the trouble we are having is not about either of you. Our trouble getting along is about our grown-up relationship with each other. That is still true. We both love you very much, and love being your parents. We want to be the best parents we can be.

Daddy and I have realized that we don't get along so much, and disagree about so many things all the time, that we want to live separately, and not be married to each other anymore. This is called getting divorced. Daddy and I care about each other but we don't love each other in the way that happily married people do. We are sad about that. We want to be happy, and want each other to be happy. So to be happy we have to be true to our feelings.

It is not your fault that we are going to get divorced. And it's not our fault. We tried for a very long time to get along living together but it just got too hard for both of us.

We are a family and will always be your family. Many things in your life will stay the same. Mommy will stay living at our house here, and Daddy will move to an apartment close by. You both will continue to live with mommy and daddy but in two different places. You will keep your same rooms here, and will have a room at Daddy's apartment. You will be with one of us every day, and sometimes we will all be together, like to celebrate somebody's birthday, special events at school, or scouts. You will still go to your same school, have the same friends, go to soccer, baseball, and so on. You will still be part of the same family and will see your aunts, uncles, and cousins.

The most important things we want you both to know are that we love you, and we will always be your mom and dad . . . nothing will change that. It's hard to understand sometimes why some people stop getting along and decide not to be friends anymore, or if they are married decide to get divorced. You will probably have lots of different feelings about this. While you can't do anything to change the decision that daddy and I have made, we both care very much about your feelings. Your feelings may change a lot. Sometimes you might feel happy and relieved that you don't have to see and feel daddy and me not getting along. Then sometimes you might feel sad, scared, or angry. Whatever you are feeling at any time is OK. Daddy and I hope you will tell us about your feelings, and it's OK to ask us about ours. This is going to take some time to get used to. You will have lots of questions in the days to come. You may have some right now. Please ask any question at any time.

Daddy and I are here for you. Today, tomorrow, and always. We love you with our heart and soul.

(2013) also found that some children of divorced parents are very deliberate in trying not to repeat the mistakes of their parents. Some of their respondents reported that "they were hard on their romantic partners," meaning that they were unwilling to let issues slide but addressed them quickly even though doing so might cause conflicts. Overall, the negative outcomes of divorce for children are balanced by positives (Gatins et al., 2015). Spouses in highly conflictual, loveless marriages should *not* stay married for the children (Gager et al., 2016).

Divorce Mediation Not Litigation

Divorce mediation is a process in which spouses who have decided to separate or divorce meet with a neutral third party (mediator) to negotiate four issues: (1) how they will parent their children, which is referred to as child custody and visitation; (2) how they are going to financially support their children, referred to as child support; (3) how they are going to divide their property, known as property settlement; and (4) how each one is going to meet their financial obligations, referred to as spousal support. Another term for involving a range of professionals in a divorce is **collaborative practice** or **collaborative divorce**, a process that brings a team of professionals (lawyer, psychologist, mediator, social worker, financial counselor) together to help a couple separate and divorce in a humane and cost-effective way (Alba-Fisch, 2016).

goodluz/Shutterstock.com

Benefits of Mediation

There are enormous benefits from avoiding litigation and mediating one's divorce:

1. **Better relationship.** Spouses who choose to mediate their divorce have a better chance for a more civil relationship because they cooperate in specifying the conditions of their separation or divorce. Mediation emphasizes negotiation and cooperation between the divorcing partners. Such cooperation is particularly important if the couple has children, in that it provides a positive basis for discussing issues in reference to the children and how they will be parented across time.

2. **Economic benefits.** Mediation is less expensive than litigation. The combined cost (total cost to both spouses) of hiring attorneys and going to court over issues of child custody and division of property is around $35,000.

A mediated divorce typically costs less than $5,000.

3. **Less time-consuming process.** Although a litigated divorce can take two to three years, a mediated divorce takes two to three months; for highly motivated individuals, a "mediated settlement conference"". . . can take place in one session from 8:00 A.M. until both parties are satisfied with the terms" (Amato).

4. **Avoidance of public exposure.** Some spouses do not want to discuss their private lives and finances in open court. Mediation occurs in a private and confidential setting.

5. **Greater overall satisfaction.** Mediation results in an agreement developed by the spouses, not one imposed by a judge or the court system. A comparison of couples who chose mediation with couples who chose litigation found that those who mediated their own settlement were more satisfied with the conditions of their agreement. In addition, children of mediated divorces were exposed to less marital conflict, which may facilitate their long-term adjustment to divorce.

Basic Mediation Guidelines

Divorce mediators conduct mediation sessions with certain principles in mind:

1. **Children.** What is best for a couple's children should be the major concern of the parents

divorce mediation
meeting with a neutral professional who negotiates child custody, division of property, child support, and alimony directly with the divorcing spouses.

collaborative practice (collaborative divorce) a process that brings a team of professionals (lawyer, psychologist, mediator, social worker, financial counselor) together to help a couple separate and divorce in a humane and cost-effective way.

because they know their children far better than a judge or a mediator. Children of divorced parents adjust best under three conditions: (1) that both parents have regular and frequent access to the children; (2) that the children see the parents relating in a polite and positive way; and (3) that each parent talks positively about the other parent and neither parent talks negatively about the other to the children.

Sometimes children are included in the mediation. They may be interviewed without the parents present to provide information to the mediator about their perceptions and preferences. Such involvement of the children has superior outcomes for both the parents and the children (McIntosh et al., 2008).

2. **Fairness.** It is important that the agreement between the soon to be ex-spouses be fair, with neither party being exploited or punished. It is fair for both parents to contribute financially to the children and to have regular access to their children.

3. **Open disclosure.** The spouses will be asked to disclose all facts, records, and documents to ensure an informed and fair agreement regarding property, assets, and debts.

4. **Other professionals.** During mediation, spouses may be asked to consult an accountant regarding tax laws. In addition, each spouse is encouraged to consult an attorney throughout the mediation and to have the attorney review the written agreements that result from the mediation. However, during the mediation sessions, all forms of legal action by the spouses against each other should be stopped.

5. **Confidentiality.** The mediator will not divulge anything spouses say during the mediation sessions without their permission. The spouses are asked to sign a document stating that, should they not complete mediation, they agree not to empower any attorney to subpoena the mediator or any records resulting from the mediation for use in any legal action. Such an agreement is necessary for spouses to feel free to talk about all aspects of their relationship without fear of legal action against them for such disclosures.

Divorce mediation is not for every couple. It does not work where there is a history of spouse abuse, where the parties do not disclose their financial information, where one party is controlled by someone else (e.g., a parent of one of the divorcing spouses) or where there is the desire for revenge. Mediation should be differentiated from **negotiation** (where spouses discuss and resolve the issues themselves), **arbitration** (where a third party, an arbitrator, listens to both spouses and makes a decision about custody, division of property, and so on), and **litigation** (where a judge hears arguments from lawyers representing the respective spouses and decides issues of custody, child support, division of property, and spousal support).

The following chart identifies a continuum of consequences from negotiation to litigation.

negotiation identifying both sides of an issue and finding a resolution that is acceptable to both parties.

arbitration third party listens to both spouses and makes a decision about custody, division of property, child support, and alimony.

litigation a judge hears arguments from lawyers representing the respective spouses and decides issues of custody, child support, division of property, etc.

Negotiation	Mediation	Arbitration	Litigation
Cooperative			Competitive
Low cost			High cost
Private			Public
Protects relationships			Damages relationships
Focus on the future			Focus on the past
Parties in control			Parties lose control

14-6 PREREQUISITES FOR HAVING A "SUCCESSFUL" DIVORCE

The following are some of the behaviors spouses can engage in to achieve a "successful" divorce (minimize the negative consequences of divorce for their children):

1. **Mediate rather than litigate the divorce.** Divorce mediators encourage a civil, cooperative, compromising relationship while moving the couple toward an agreement on the division of property, custody, and child/spousal support. In contrast, attorneys make their money by encouraging hostility so that spouses will prolong the conflict, thus running up higher legal bills. The couple cannot divide money spent on divorce attorneys (average is $20,000 for each side so a litigated divorce cost will start at $40,000). Spouses who hire an expensive attorney to destroy the ex end up in a protracted court fight where no one wins—the result is less money to split, the ex-spouses develop an intense hatred for each other, and the children must cope with the acrimonious relationship between their parents for years. Divorce mediation results in a quicker, less expensive divorce with children who benefit from an amicable relationship between their parents. Some states require divorce mediation to encourage parental civility and to clear the court calendar of protracted legal battles. If one of the parties does not "require their day in court" due to revenge or punishment (Sullivan, 2016), divorce mediation should be considered.

2. **Coparent with your ex-spouse.** Setting aside negative feelings about your ex-spouse so as to cooperatively coparent not only facilitates parental adjustment but also takes children out of the line of fire. Such coparenting translates into being cooperative when one parent needs to change a child care schedule, sitting together during a school performance by the children, and showing appreciation for the other parent's skill in parenting. While there is 100% agreement among professionals as to the importance of divorcing parents developing and maintaining a positive relationship, training programs for ex-spouses to be effective coparents are difficult to find/obtain. The exception is Successful Co-Parenting After Divorce (https://coparenting.fsu.edu/), which has an online training course.

Some divorced parents use technology—email and text messaging—to discuss issues and handle scheduling. McCann et al. (2015) reported that over half (52%) of their divorcing sample reported use of these technologies, which spared them face-to-face contact that might be more difficult/volatile.

3. **Take some responsibility for the divorce.** Because marriage is an interaction between spouses, one person is seldom totally to blame for a divorce. Rather, both spouses share reasons for the demise of the relationship. Take some responsibility for what went wrong. What did *you* do wrong that you could correct in a subsequent relationship?

> Divorce is never a pleasant experience. You look upon it as a failure. But I learned to be a different person once we broke up. Sometimes you learn more from failure than you do from success.
>
> —MICHAEL CRAWFORD

> Whether life finds us guilty or not guilty, we ourselves know we are not innocent.
>
> —SÁNDOR MÁRAI, JUDIT . . . ÉS AZ UTÓHANG

4. **Avoid alcohol and other drugs.** The stress and despair that some people feel during and following the divorce process sometimes make them vulnerable to the use of alcohol or other drugs. These should be avoided because they produce an endless negative cycle. For example, stress is relieved by alcohol; alcohol produces a hangover and negative feelings; the negative feelings are relieved by more alcohol, producing more negative feelings, etc.

5. **Engage in aerobic exercise.** Exercise helps one to not only counteract stress but also avoid it. Jogging, swimming, riding an exercise bike, or engaging in other similar exercise for 30 minutes every

day increases oxygen to the brain and helps facilitate clear thinking. In addition, aerobic exercise produces endorphins in the brain, which create a sense of euphoria (runner's high).

6. **Continue interpersonal connections.** Adjustment to divorce is facilitated by continuing relationships with friends and family. These individuals provide emotional support and help buffer the feeling of isolation and aloneness. First Wives World (www.firstwivesworld.com) is a new interactive website that provides an Internet social network for women transitioning through divorce.

7. **Let go of the anger for your ex-partner.** Former spouses who stay negatively attached to an ex by harboring resentment and trying to get back at the ex prolong their adjustment to divorce. The old adage that "you can't get ahead by getting even" is relevant to divorce adjustment.

8. **Allow time to heal.** Because self-esteem usually drops after divorce, a person is often vulnerable to making commitments before working through feelings about the divorce. Most individuals need between 12 and 18 months to adjust to the end of a marriage. Although being available to others may help to repair one's self-esteem, getting remarried during this time should be considered cautiously. Two years between marriages is recommended.

AISPIX by Image Source/Shutterstock.com

14-7 REMARRIAGE

I don't care if I'm your first love—I just want to be your last.

—GRETCHEN WILSON

Divorced spouses are not sour on marriage. Although they may want to escape from the current spouse, they are open to having a new spouse. Of 353 undergraduates who reported on their end of a romantic relationship, 81% felt that that they would be able to love again (Brenner & Knox, 2016).

Most of the divorced remarry and do so for many of the same reasons as those in their first marriage—love, companionship, emotional security, and a regular sex partner. Other reasons are unique to remarriage and include financial security (particularly for a woman with children), help in rearing one's children, the desire to provide a "social" father or mother for one's children, escape from the stigma associated with the label "divorced person," and legal threats regarding the custody of one's children. With regard to the latter, the courts view a parent seeking custody of a child more favorably if the parent is married. The religiously devout remarry, in part because religion is pro-family and members of a religious congregation seek the context that reflects these religious values (Brown & Porter, 2013).

Knopfli et al. (2016) noted the benefits among the divorced who remarry who are more likely to report a more positive state of health than those who remain single. Indeed the repartnered are as healthy as the continuously married.

If a single mother's goal is to be remarried, how does the involvement of the nonresident father with her children impact the likelihood of remarriage? The answer from 882 divorced mothers is that such involvement increases her chances of remarriage. A team of researchers (McNamee et al., 2014) noted that such nonresident father contact creates leisure time for the mother and opportunities for her to develop new relationships "by providing private time (without children) on a regular basis. Moreover, men may be more willing to adopt the stepfather role when biological fathers remain physically present in their children's lives because this signals fewer parenting responsibilities for the stepfather."

14-7a Issues for Those Who Remarry

Several issues challenge people who remarry (Ganong & Coleman, 1999; Goetting, 1982; Kim, 2011; Martin-Uzzi & Duval-Tsioles, 2013; Scarf, 2013):

1. **Boundary maintenance.** Ghosts of the first marriage, in terms of the ex-spouse, must be dealt with. A parent must decide how to relate to an ex-spouse to maintain a good parenting relationship for the biological children while keeping an emotional distance from the ex to prevent problems from developing with the new partner.

   Some spouses continue to be emotionally attached to and have difficulty breaking away from an ex-spouse. These former spouses have what Masheter (1999) terms a **negative commitment** whereby such individuals "have decided to remain [emotionally] in this relationship and to invest considerable amounts of time, money, and effort in it . . . [T]hese individuals do not take responsibility for their own feelings and actions, and often remain 'stuck,' unable to move forward in their lives" (p. 297).

2. **Emotional remarriage.** Remarriage involves beginning to trust and love another person in a new relationship. Such feelings may come slowly as a result of negative experiences in a previous marriage.

3. **Psychic remarriage.** Divorced individuals considering remarriage may find it difficult to give up the freedom and autonomy of being single and to develop a mental set conducive to pairing.

4. **Community remarriage.** This aspect involves a change in focus from single friends to a new mate and other couples with whom the new pair will interact.

5. **Parental remarriage.** Because most remarriages involve children, people must work out the nuances of living with someone else's children. Mothers are usually awarded primary physical custody, and this circumstance translates into a new stepfather adjusting to the mother's children and vice versa.

6. **Economic and legal remarriage.** A second marriage may begin with economic responsibilities to a first marriage. Alimony and child support often threaten the harmony and sometimes even the economic survival of second marriages. Although the income of a new wife is not used legally to decide the amount her new husband is required to pay in child support for his children of a former marriage, his ex-wife may petition the court for more child support. The ex-wife may do so, however, on the premise that his living expenses are reduced with a new wife and that, therefore, he should be able to afford to pay more child support. Although an ex-wife is not likely to win, she can force the new wife to go to court and to disclose her income (all with considerable investment of time and legal fees for a newly remarried couple).

   There may also be a need for a marriage contract to be drawn up before the wedding. Suppose a wife moves into the home of her new husband. If he has a will stating that his house goes to his children from a former marriage at his death and no marriage contract that either gives his wife the house or allows her to stay in the house rent free until her death, his children can legally throw her out of the house. The same is true for their beach house which he brought into the marriage. If his will gives the beach house to his children, his wife may have no place to live.

negative commitment spouses who continue to be emotionally attached to and have difficulty breaking away from ex-spouses.

> Marriage is like wine. It is not to be properly judged until the second glass.
>
> —DOUGLAS JERROLD

14-7b Stability of Remarriages

Jensen et al. (2014) found that 40% of second marriages compared to 32% of first marriages ended within the first 10 years of marriage. They compared 410 individuals in second marriages with 1,679 individuals in first marriages—data from the RELATE Institute.

Mirecki et al. (2013) confirmed lower marital satisfaction of spouses in second marriages. Since 65% of second marriages include the presence of stepchildren, integrating the various individuals into a functioning family is challenging. Higher education on the part of the spouses seemed to help (higher education is associated with higher income). That second marriages, in general, are more susceptible to divorce than first marriages may also be related to the fact that divorced individuals are less fearful of divorce (e.g., they know they can survive divorce) than individuals who have never divorced.

Though remarried people are more vulnerable to divorce in the early years of their subsequent marriage, they are less likely to divorce after 15 years of staying in the second marriage than those in first marriages (Clarke & Wilson, 1994). Hence, these spouses are likely to remain married because they want to, not because they fear divorce.

14-8 STEPFAMILIES

Stepfamilies, also known as blended, binuclear, remarried, or reconstituted families, represent the fastest-growing type of family in the United States. A **blended family** is one in which spouses in a new marriage relationship blend their respective children from at least one other spouse from a previous marriage. The term **binuclear family** refers to a family that spans two households; when a married couple with children divorce, their family unit typically spreads into two households. There is a movement away from the use of the term *blended* because stepfamilies really do not blend. The term **stepfamily** (sometimes referred to as step relationships) is the term currently in vogue. Although there are various types of stepfamilies, the most common is a family in which the partners bring children from previous relationships into the new home, where they may also have a child of their own. The couple may be married or living together, heterosexual or homosexual, and of any race. Nuru and Wang (2014) emphasized the need to include step relationships for those in cohabiting relationships.

Various myths abound regarding stepfamilies, including that new family members will instantly bond emotionally, that children in stepfamilies are damaged and do not recover, that stepmothers are "wicked home-wreckers," that stepfathers are uninvolved with their stepchildren, and that stepfamilies are not "real" families. Garneau et al. (2016) also identified various beliefs about remarriage/stepfamilies including the degree to which stepfamilies are as valuable to children as biological families, how quickly emotional ties should develop, and prioritizing the couple or the children. Stepfamilies are also stigmatized. **Stepism** is the assumption that stepfamilies are inferior to biological families. Like racism, heterosexism, sexism, and ageism, stepism involves prejudice and discrimination.

Stepfamilies differ from nuclear families in a number of ways. These are identified in Table 14.4. These

The spouses of this remarried couple both brought children into their marriage.

changes impact the parents, their children, and their stepchildren and require adjustment on the part of each member.

14-8a Developmental Tasks for Stepfamilies

A **developmental task** is a skill that, if mastered, allows a family to grow as a cohesive unit. Developmental tasks that are not mastered will move the family closer to the point of disintegration. Some of the more important developmental tasks for stepfamilies are discussed in this section. Most of these suggestions are included in workshops designed for stepfamilies (Zeleznikow & Zeleznikow, 2015). In an analysis of data on 390 stepparents, higher levels of relationship satisfaction and stability were

blended family family wherein spouses in a remarriage bring their children to live with the new partner and at least one other child.

binuclear family family that lives in two households as when parents live in separate households following a divorce.

stepfamily family in which spouses in a new marriage bring children from previous relationships into the new home.

stepism the assumption that stepfamilies are inferior to biological families.

developmental task a skill that, if mastered, allows a family to grow as a cohesive unit.

TABLE 14.4   DIFFERENCES BETWEEN NUCLEAR FAMILIES AND STEPFAMILIES

Nuclear Families	Stepfamilies
1. Children are (usually) biologically related to both parents.	1. Children are biologically related to only one parent.
2. Both biological parents live together with children.	2. As a result of divorce or death, one biological parent does not live with the children. In the case of joint physical custody, children may live with both parents, alternating between them.
3. Beliefs and values of members tend to be similar.	3. Beliefs and values of members are more likely to be different because of different backgrounds.
4. The relationship between adults has existed longer than relationship between children and parents.	4. The relationship between children and parents has existed longer than the relationship between adults.
5. Children have one home they regard as theirs.	5. Children may have two homes they regard as theirs.
6. The family's economic resources come from within the family unit.	6. Some economic resources may come from an ex-spouse.
7. All money generated stays in the family.	7. Some money generated may leave the family in the form of alimony or child support.
8. Relationships are relatively stable.	8. Relationships are in flux: new adults adjusting to each other; children adjusting to a stepparent; a stepparent adjusting to stepchildren; stepchildren adjusting to each other.
9. No stigma is attached to nuclear family.	9. Stepfamilies are stigmatized.
10. Spouses had a childfree period.	10. Spouses had no childfree period.
11. Inheritance rights are automatic.	11. Stepchildren do not automatically inherit from stepparents.
12. Rights to custody of children are assumed if divorce occurs.	12. Rights to custody of stepchildren are usually not considered.
13. Extended family networks are smooth and comfortable.	13. Extended family networks become complex and strained.
14. Nuclear family may not have experienced loss.	14. Stepfamily has experienced loss.
15. Families experience a range of problems.	15. Stepchildren tend to be a major problem.
16. Parents obligated to provide support to biological children.	16. Stepparents not obligated to provide support to stepchildren.

associated with fewer stepparenting issues (Jensen et al., 2015).

1. Be patient for stepparent/stepchild relationships to develop.
2. Have realistic expectations.
3. Accept your stepchildren.
4. Give parental authority to your spouse/coparent.
5. Establish your own family rituals.
6. Support the children's relationship with their absent parent.

Sometimes the absent parent may be an occasion for jealousy by the new stepparent. DeGreeff and Platt (2016) noted that a stepmother may feel jealous of the biological mother.

When the kids were little and they were seeing their mom on a regular basis, I had a mixture of both, um, jealousy and anger. I was jealous when the kids went there because it upset me, it was like she was the fun mom, and she was the vacation mom, and she didn't have to do the day-to-day stuff.

7. Use living apart together (LAT) to reduce the strain and conflict of stepfamily living.

LAT is a structural solution to many of the problems of stepfamily living (see Chapter 2 for a more thorough discussion). By getting two condos (side by side or one on top of the other), a duplex, or two small houses and having the respective biological parents live in each of the respective units with their respective children, everyone wins. The children and biological parent will experience minimal disruption as the spouses transition to the new marriage. This arrangement is particularly useful where both spouses have children ranging in age from 10 to 18. Situations where only one spouse has children from a former relationship or those in which the children are very young will have limited benefit. The new spouses can still spend plenty of time together to nurture their relationship without spending all of their time trying to manage the various issues that come up with the stepchildren.

14-9 TRENDS IN DIVORCE AND REMARRIAGE

As divorce continues to be stigmatized in our society (as evidenced by the term **divorcism**—the belief that divorce is a disaster), a number of attempts will continue to be made to reduce the sting of divorce.

"The Rise of the Good Divorce" (Schrobsdorff, 2015) reflects the "conscious uncoupling" (a phrase used by Gwyneth Paltrow and Chris Martin in their divorce of 2014). The term was developed by psychotherapist Katherine Woodward Thomas (2015) and is the title of her book. The theme is "living happily even after" and emphasizes "a new way to end a failing relationship that isn't bitter and needlessly painful, but is, instead, characterized by goodwill, generosity, and respect. With its precepts, couples learn how to do minimal damage to themselves, each other, and their children."

Celebrities Ben Affleck and Jennifer Garner also attempted the conscious uncoupling pattern for their three children when they vacationed together in the Bahamas as a family as they announced their divorce (the so-called divorce moon). Such conscious uncoupling will not be easy as new partners, division of property, and scheduling time with the children test the new plan with the reality of divorce. But the conscious attempt to make divorce easier for children is clearly evident. And divorce may be becoming easier for adults. Van Tilburg et al. (2015) emphasized, that compared to earlier decades, the divorced of today are less lonely.

Other attempts to mitigate the negatives of divorce are workshops/education programs focused on communication, conflict resolution, and parenting skills for the divorced. Lawick and Visser (2015) noted a new program designed to keep children out of conflict from divorcing parents by keeping the child in mind and stopping the legal process. Lucier-Greer et al. (2012) found positive outcomes for remarried couples with children who were involved in these programs.

divorcism the belief that divorce is a disaster.

STUDY TOOLS 14

READY TO STUDY? IN THE BOOK, YOU CAN:
- ☐ Rip out the chapter review card at the back of the book for a handy summary of the chapter and key terms.
- ☐ Assess yourself with the following Self-Assessment.

ONLINE AT CENGAGEBRAIN.COM YOU CAN:
- ☐ Collect StudyBits while you read and study the chapter.
- ☐ Quiz yourself on key concepts.
- ☐ Prepare for tests with M&F4 Flash Cards as well as those you create.

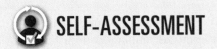

SELF-ASSESSMENT

Children's Beliefs about Parental Divorce Scale

The following are some statements about children and their separated parents. Some of the statements are **true** about how you think and feel, so you will want to check **yes**. Some are **not true** about how you think or feel, so you will want to check **no**. There are no right or wrong answers. Your answers will just indicate some of the things you are thinking now about your parents' separation.

1. It would upset me if other kids asked a lot of questions about my parents. ___ Yes ___ No
2. It was usually my father's fault when my parents had a fight. ___ Yes ___ No
3. I sometimes worry that both my parents will want to live without me. ___ Yes ___ No
4. When my family was unhappy, it was usually because of my mother. ___ Yes ___ No
5. My parents will always live apart. ___ Yes ___ No
6. My parents often argue with each other after I misbehave. ___ Yes ___ No
7. I like talking to my friends as much now as I used to. ___ Yes ___ No
8. My father is usually a nice person. ___ Yes ___ No
9. It's possible that both my parents will never want to see me again. ___ Yes ___ No
10. My mother is usually a nice person. ___ Yes ___ No
11. If I behave better, I might be able to bring my family back together. ___ Yes ___ No
12. My parents would probably be happier if I were never born. ___ Yes ___ No
13. I like playing with my friends as much now as I used to. ___ Yes ___ No
14. When my family was unhappy, it was usually because of something my father said or did. ___ Yes ___ No
15. I sometimes worry that I'll be left all alone. ___ Yes ___ No
16. Often I have a bad time when I'm with my mother. ___ Yes ___ No
17. My family will probably do things together just like before. ___ Yes ___ No
18. My parents probably argue more when I'm with them than when I'm gone. ___ Yes ___ No
19. I'd rather be alone than play with other kids. ___ Yes ___ No
20. My father caused most of the trouble in my family. ___ Yes ___ No
21. I feel that my parents still love me. ___ Yes ___ No
22. My mother caused most of the trouble in my family. ___ Yes ___ No
23. My parents will probably see that they have made a mistake and get back together again. ___ Yes ___ No
24. My parents are happier when I'm with them than when I'm not. ___ Yes ___ No
25. My friends and I do many things together. ___ Yes ___ No
26. There are a lot of things I like about my father. ___ Yes ___ No
27. I sometimes think that one day I may have to go live with a friend or relative. ___ Yes ___ No
28. My mother is more good than bad. ___ Yes ___ No
29. I sometimes think that my parents will one day live together again. ___ Yes ___ No
30. I can make my parents unhappy with each other by what I say or do. ___ Yes ___ No
31. My friends understand how I feel about my parents. ___ Yes ___ No
32. My father is more good than bad. ___ Yes ___ No
33. I feel my parents still like me. ___ Yes ___ No

34. There are a lot of things about my mother I like. ___ Yes ___ No

35. I sometimes think that my parents will live together again once they realize
how much I want them to. ___ Yes ___ No

36. My parents would probably still be living together if it weren't for me. ___ Yes ___ No

Scoring

The Children's Beliefs about Parental Divorce Scale (CBAPS) identifies problematic responding. A ***yes*** response on items 1, 2, 3, 4, 6, 9, 11, 12, 14–20, 22, 23, 27, 29, 30, 35, and 36, and a ***no*** response on items 5, 7, 8, 10, 13, 21, 24–26, 28, and 31–34 indicate a problematic reaction to one's parents divorcing. A total score is derived by adding the number of problematic beliefs across all the items, with a total score of 36. The higher the score, the more problematic the beliefs about parental divorce.

Norms

A total of 170 schoolchildren whose parents were divorced completed the scale; of the children, 84 were boys and 86 were girls, with a mean age of 11. The mean for the total score was 8.20, with a standard deviation of 4.98.

Source: From Table 1 (adapted), p. 715, from Kurdek, L. A., & Berg, B. (1987). Children's Beliefs About Parental Divorce Scale: Psychometric characteristics and concurrent validity. *Journal of Consulting and Clinical Psychology, 55*(5), 712–718.

15 | Enjoying the Later Years

SECTIONS

After finishing this chapter go to **PAGE 307** for **STUDY TOOLS**

The later years are fraught with stereotypes—ill health, limited income, loneliness, and death. The reality is that while health declines it does so slowly so that individuals are able to live as they did in their younger days until their mid to late eighties. And, while income may decline, so does the need for money—the children are gone, the house is paid for, and the desire for expensive travel has been replaced by enjoying one's home and friends. However, there is great variability in what people experience in the later years—the subject of this chapter.

15-1 AGE AND AGEISM

In 2015, about 15% of the 347 million individuals in the United States were age 65 and older. By 2020, this percentage will grow to 17%. By 2040, one in five Americans (88 million) will be over the age of 65 (*Proquest Statistical Abstract of the United States, 2016*, Table 8). Researcher Amy Rauer (2013) noted that we are moving toward a society of more "walkers than strollers."

All societies have a way to categorize their members by age. And all societies provide social definitions for particular ages.

> You don't stop laughing when you grow old, you grow old when you stop laughing.
>
> —GEORGE BERNARD SHAW

15-1a Defining Age

A person's **age** may be defined chronologically, physiologically, psychologically, sociologically, and culturally. Chronologically, an "old" person is defined as one who has lived a certain number of years. The concept has obvious practical significance in everyday life. Bureaucratic organizations and social programs identify chronological age as a criterion of certain social rights and responsibilities. One's age determines the right to drive, vote, buy alcohol or cigarettes, and receive Social Security and Medicare benefits.

Age has meaning in reference to the society and culture of the individual. In ancient Greece and Rome, where the average life expectancy was 20 years, an individual was old at 18; similarly, one was old at 30 in medieval Europe and at 40 in the United States in 1850. In the United States today, however, people are usually not considered old until they reach age 65. However, our society is moving toward new chronological definitions of "old." Three groups of the elderly have emerged—the "young-old," the "middle-old," and the "old-old." The young-old are typically between the ages of 65 and 74; the middle-old, 75 to 84; and the old-old, 85 and beyond. Current life expectancy is shown in Table 15.1.

There are different ways of defining age. In the following sections we look at several ways.

1. **Physiologically.** People are old when their auditory, visual, respiratory, and cognitive capabilities decline significantly. Becoming disabled is associated with being old. Sleep changes also occur for the elderly, including going to bed earlier, waking up during the night, and waking up earlier in the morning, as well as such disorders such as snoring and obstructive sleep apnea.

2. **Physical dependence.** People who need full-time nursing care for eating, bathing, and taking medication properly and who are placed in nursing homes are thought of as being old. Indeed, successful aging is culturally defined as maintaining one's health, independence, and cognitive ability. It is not death but the slow deterioration from aging that brings the most fear.

> **age** term which may be defined chronologically (number of years), physiologically (physical decline), psychologically (self-concept), sociologically (roles for the elderly/retired), and culturally (meaning age in one's society).

TABLE 15.1	LIFE EXPECTANCY			
Year	White Males	Black Males	White Females	Black Females
2015	77.7	72.9	82.2	78.9
2020	78.6	74.0	82.9	79.8

Source: *Proquest Statistical Abstract of the United States, 2016*, online ed., Table 115. Washington, DC: U.S. Bureau of the Census.

3. **Psychologically.** A person's self-concept is important in defining how old that person is. Once they see themselves as old, they are.

4. **Sociologically.** Once individuals occupy roles such as retiree, grandparent, and Social Security recipient, others begin to see them as old.

5. **Culturally.** The society in which an individual lives defines when and if a person becomes old and what being old means. In U.S. society, the period from age 18 through 64 is generally subdivided into young adulthood, adulthood, and middle age. Cultures also differ in terms of how they view and take care of their elderly. Spain is particularly noteworthy in terms of care for the elderly, with most elderly people receiving care from family members and other relatives.

> Aging is not just decay, you know. It's growth. It's more than the negative that you're going to die, it's also the positive that you understand you're going to die, and that you live a better life because of it.
>
> —MITCH ALBOM, *TUESDAYS WITH MORRIE*

ageism the systematic persecution and degradation of people because they are old.

ageism by invisibility when older adults are not included in advertising and educational materials.

gerontophobia fear or dread of the elderly, which may create a self-fulfilling prophecy.

gerontology the study of aging.

15-1b Ageism

Every society has some form of **ageism**—the systematic persecution and degradation of people because they are old. Ageism is reflected in negative stereotypes of the elderly—forgetful, lonely, impoverished. Ageism also occurs when older individuals are treated differently because of their age, such as when they are spoken to loudly in simple language, when it is assumed they cannot understand normal speech, or when they are denied employment due to their age.

Another form of ageism—**ageism by invisibility**—occurs when older adults are not included in advertising and educational materials. Ageism is similar to sexism, racism, and heterosexism. The elderly are shunned, discriminated against in employment, and sometimes victims of abuse.

Negative stereotypes and media images of the elderly engender **gerontophobia**—a shared fear or dread of the elderly. Such a negative view may create a self-fulfilling prophecy. For example, an elderly person forgets something and attributes forgetting to age. A younger person, however, is unlikely to attribute forgetfulness to age, given cultural definitions surrounding the age of the onset of senility.

The negative meanings associated with aging underlie the obsession of many Americans to conceal their age by altering their appearance. Chonody and Teater (2016) noted that the stigma associated with aging is related to the outward appearance that stems from fears about social identity and death. A wrinkled slow-moving person occupies social roles that youth wants to delay and the associations with death bring further retreat. With the hope of holding on to youth a little bit longer, aging Americans spend billions of dollars each year on plastic surgery, exercise equipment, hair products, facial creams, and Botox injections.

Sex creams are also marketed to the elderly. The pharmaceutical drug Osphena has been heralded as an innovative, hormone-free therapeutic option to cure two dysfunctions associated with menopausal women's bodies: vaginal atrophy and dyspareunia. Women are told that their sexual bodies could return to youth—"the Osphena campaign is a clear contemporary illustration that the age-old rhetoric of women's bodies as requiring medical intervention to resist aging is far from passé" (Bedor, 2016).

> Forty is the old age of youth, fifty is the youth of old age.
>
> —HOSEA BALLOU

15-1c Theories of Aging

Gerontology is the study of aging. Various theories may be conceptualized as macro or micro. Table 15.2 identifies the theory, the assumptions, and the criticisms.

TABLE 15.2 THEORIES OF AGING

Name of Theory	Level of Theory	Theorists	Basic Assumptions	Criticisms
Disengagement	Macro	Elaine Cumming, William Henry	The gradual and mutual withdrawal of the elderly and society from each other is a natural process. It is also necessary and functional for society that the elderly disengage so that new people can be phased in to replace them in an orderly transition.	Not all people want to disengage; some want to stay active and involved. Disengagement does not specify what happens when the elderly stay involved.
Activity	Macro	Robert Havighurst	People continue the level of activity they had in middle age into their later years. Though high levels of activity are unrelated to living longer, they are related to reporting high levels of life satisfaction.	Ill health may force people to curtail their level of activity. The older a person, the more likely the person is to curtail activity.
Conflict	Macro	Karl Marx, Max Weber	The elderly compete with youth for jobs and social resources such as government programs (Medicare).	The elderly are presented as disadvantaged. Their power to organize and mobilize political resources such as the American Association of Retired Persons is underestimated.
Age stratification	Macro	M. W. Riley	The elderly represent a powerful cohort of individuals passing through the social system that both affect and are affected by social change.	Too much emphasis is put on age, and little recognition is given to other variables within a cohort such as gender, race, and socioeconomic differences.
Modernization	Macro	Donald Cowgill	The status of the elderly is in reference to the evolution of the society toward modernization. The elderly in premodern societies have more status because what they have to offer in the form of cultural wisdom is more valued. The elderly in modern technologically advanced societies have low status because they have little to offer.	Cultural values for the elderly, not level of modernization, dictate the status of the elderly. Japan has high respect for the elderly and yet is highly technological and modernized.
Symbolic	Micro	Arlie Hochschild	The elderly socially construct meaning in their interactions with others and society. Developing social bonds with other elderly can ward off being isolated and abandoned. Meaning is in the interpretation, not in the event.	The power of the larger social system and larger social structures to affect the lives of the elderly is minimized.
Continuity	Micro	Bernice Neugarten	The earlier habit patterns, values, and attitudes of the individual are carried forward as a person ages. The only personality change that occurs with aging is the tendency to turn one's attention and interest on the self.	Other factors than one's personality affect aging outcomes. The social structure influences the life of the elderly rather than vice versa.
Interpersonal	Micro	Julian Palmore III, Jean-Pierre Langlois	Negative assumptions based on physical appearance (droopy eyes means sad person).	Some elderly are in good physical condition.

15-2 CAREGIVING FOR THE FRAIL ELDERLY: THE "SANDWICH GENERATION"

Thirty percent of adults in the United States provide care for a loved one, often the elderly frail (Murphy et al., 2015b). An elderly parent is defined as **frail** if he or she has difficulty with at least one personal care activity or other activity related to independent living; the severely disabled are unable to complete three or more personal care activities. These personal care activities include bathing, dressing, getting in and out of bed, shopping for groceries, and taking medications. Most (over 90%) frail elderly do not have long-term health care insurance.

Most children choose to take care of their elderly parents. The term children typically means female adult *children* (usually employed) taking care of their mothers (fathers often have a spouse or are deceased) (Leopold et al., 2014). These women provide **family caregiving** and are known as the

> **frail** term used to define elderly people if they have difficulty with at least one personal care activity (feeding, bathing, toileting).
>
> **family caregiving** adult children providing care for their elderly parents.

What's New?

Anger of Family Caretakers When Taking Care of Elderly Relatives

Researchers Crespo and Fernandez-Lansac (2014) interviewed 129 caregivers who had primary responsibility for taking care of an elderly (age 60 or older) dependent family member for a period of at least six months. Most of the caregivers were women and were ether an older adult child or the spouse of the care recipient. The diagnosis of the person they took care of was most often dementia, Alzheimer's type.

The caregiving experience was extensive—about 16 hours a day for about 4.5 years. Most of these caregivers had some help from other family members or some kind of formal service.

The purpose of the research was to find out how often the caregivers felt mad/furious and how often they expressed their anger. Results revealed that around 40% of the caregivers could be categorized as having moderate to severe anger levels and a similar percent showed moderate to severe levels of anger expressions. Higher levels of anger were evident if there was a nonloving or negative relationship with the elderly person they were taking care of. Over time, feelings of resentment about taking care of the elderly family member could lead to interpersonal conflict and further deterioration of the bond between the caregiver and the care recipient. Particularly problematic was the cognitive confusions of the care recipient and repetitive questions to the caregiver which made anger control challenging.

On most occasions, the caregivers controlled their expressions of anger since they felt their own anger was an unacceptable emotion. Indeed, the caregivers made an effort to deliberately control and suppress their anger. Both children and spouses who cared for the elderly patient had similar levels of anger or anger expression. The research emphasized the difficulty of caring for an elderly family member, the struggle family members experience in doing so and the effort they expend to try and do the right thing. Also, evident is the degree to which help from other family members or formal services are valuable in reducing anger.

---

sandwich generation because they take care of their parents and their children simultaneously. Wiemers and Bianchi (2015) emphasized the increase in having both children and aging parents to care for is a result of the increase in life expectancy.

Caregiving for an elderly parent has two meanings. One form of caregiving refers to providing personal help with the basics of daily living, such as getting in and out of bed, bathing, toileting, and eating. A second form of caregiving refers to performing instrumental activities, such as shopping for groceries, managing money (including paying bills), and driving the parent to the doctor.

The number of individuals in the sandwich generation will increase for the following reasons:

> **sandwich generation**
> generation of adults who are "sandwiched" between caring for their elderly parents and their own children.

1. **Longevity.** The over-85 age group, the segment of the population most in need of care, is the fastest-growing segment of our population.

2. **Chronic disease.** In the past, diseases took the elderly quickly. Today, diseases such as arthritis and Alzheimer's are associated not with an immediate death sentence but with a lifetime of managing the illness and being cared for by others.

3. **Fewer siblings to help.** The current generation of elderly have fewer children than the elderly in previous generations. Hence, the number of siblings available to help look after parents is more limited. Children without siblings are more likely to feel the weight of caring for elderly parents alone.

4. **Commitment to parental care.** Contrary to the myth that adult children in the United States

This daughter visits her mother in the nursing home daily. She is getting her mother ready to walk to the dining room so they can eat together.

abrogate responsibility for taking care of their elderly parents, most children institutionalize their parents only as a last resort. Indeed, most adult children want to take care of their aging parents either in the parents' own home or in the adult child's home. When parents can no longer be left alone and can no longer cook for themselves, full-time nursing care is sought. Asian children, specifically Chinese children, are socialized to expect to take care of their elderly in the home.

5. **Lack of support for the caregiver.** Caring for a dependent, aging parent requires a great deal of effort, sacrifice, and decision making on the part of more than 20 million adults in the United States

who are challenged with this situation. The emotional toll on the caregiver may be heavy. Guilt (over not doing enough), resentment (over feeling burdened), and exhaustion (over the relentless care demands) are common feelings. In regard to the marriages of caregivers, Murphy et al. (2015) analyzed data from 191 family caregivers and found that those who were spiritual/religious and hopeful reported greater marital satisfaction.

Some people reduce the strain of caring for an elderly parent by arranging for home health care. This involves having a nurse go to the home of a parent and provide such services as bathing and giving medication.

What are the outcomes of placing elderly parents in a nursing home versus allowing them to stay in their own home and getting home health care? Blackburn et al. (2016) analyzed data on 1,291 pairs—admitted to either context. After one year, 77.7% of home health beneficiaries were alive compared with 76.2% of nursing home beneficiaries (p < .001).

15-3 ISSUES CONFRONTING THE ELDERLY

Numerous issues become concerns as people age. In middle age, the issues are early retirement (sometimes forced), job layoffs (recession-related cutbacks), **age discrimination** (older people are often not hired and younger workers are hired to take their place), separation or divorce from a spouse, and adjustment to children leaving home. For some in middle age, grandparenting is an issue if they become the primary caregiver for their grandchildren. As couples move from the middle to the later years, the issues become more focused on income, health, retirement, and sexuality.

> Old age is no place for sissies.
>
> —BETTE DAVIS

15-3a Income

A regret of many retirees is that they did not save enough money for retirement—that they spent more than they should have during their peak earning years. Indeed, for most elderly, the end of life is characterized by reduced income. Social Security and pension benefits,

age discrimination
a situation where older people are often not hired and younger workers are hired to take their place.

when they exist, are rarely equal to the income a retired person formerly earned. Many elderly continue working since they cannot afford to quit. The median annual income of men aged 65 and older is $29,327; women, $16,301 (*Proquest Statistical Abstract of the United States, 2016*, Table 724).

Elderly women are particularly disadvantaged because their out-of-home employment has often been discontinuous, part-time, and low-paying. Social Security and private pension plans favor those with continuous, full-time work histories. Hence, their retirement incomes are considerably lower than the retirement income of males.

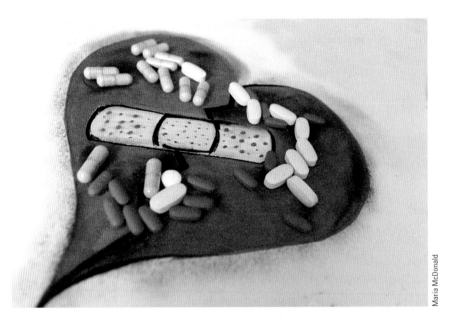

Maria McDonald

> In fact, Social Security is the only source of income nationwide for 29 percent of unmarried elderly women.
>
> —GINNY BROWN-WAITE

15-3b Physical Health

There is a gradual deterioration in physical well-being as one ages. Of 8,875 old-old individuals (85 years or older) in home health care, nursing homes, or hospice, two-thirds needed assistance in performing three or more activities of daily living (ADLs) and were bladder incontinent. Hypertension and heart disease were the two most common chronic health conditions. Read et al. (2016) reviewed 71 studies and found that poorer socioeconomic position was associated with poorer subjective health and well-being.

Chao (2016) studied 2,660 older adults over a 12-year period and found that declines in physical activity were related to increased somatic complaints, higher scores on depression, and lower positive affect scores.

Good physical health is the single most important determinant of an elderly person's reported happiness. Being in good health when entering the hospital for an acute illness is related to positive outcomes at discharge—being able to take care of one's self, such as toileting, dressing, and bathing, and avoiding institutionalization (Parlevliet et al., 2016). Johnson et al. (2014)

reconfirmed the association between greater activity and higher quality of life.

> I don't feel old. I don't feel anything till noon. That's when it's time for my nap.
>
> —BOB HOPE

Good physical health has an effect on marital quality. Iveniuk et al. (2014) noted that wives with husbands in fair or poor physical health were more likely to report higher levels of marital conflict, but the reverse was not true. The authors suggested that men with compromised health have limited leverage (in terms of reduced resources and status) to resist changes expected by their wives, so the wives are asked to give in with fewer rewards.

15-3c Cognitive Changes/ Mental Health

An individual's cognitive abilities may decline with age. But such a decline is not inevitable, and specific activities are associated with mental alertness. Lee and Chi (2016) studied 704 individuals aged 70 or older and found that those who engaged in cognitive leisure activities (e.g., reading newspapers, magazines, books) or visuospatial activities (e.g., crossword puzzles, cards, board games) were more likely to have no cognitive impairment or dementia compared to those who did not evidence such activities.

Aside from possible cognitive changes, mood disorders, with depression being the most frequent, are more common among the elderly. Scheetz et al. (2012) found higher rates of depression among centenarians. Bereavement over the death of a spouse, loneliness, physical illness, and institutionalization may be the culprits. Spirituality helps to provide meaning in life in spite of symptoms of depression (Bamonti et al., 2016). Nguyen et al. (2016) studied the well-being (e.g., life satisfaction, happiness) of 837 elderly and found an association with subjective closeness with family and friends.

Dementia, which includes Alzheimer's disease, is the mental disorder most associated with aging. *Still Alice* is the 2014 academy award winning movie for which Julianne Moore won best actress. She portrayed a university professor's slow descent into Alzheimer's and the impact of the disease on her, her husband, and her children. Worldwide, 36 million individuals live with dementia-like disease (Hogsnes et al., 2014). The self-assessment feature at the end of the chapter reflects some of the misconceptions about Alzheimer's disease.

There has been considerable cultural visibility in regard to the medical use of marijuana. Ahmed et al. (2014) reported data on older adults in regard to its use with Alzheimer's patients; behavioral disturbances and nighttime agitation were reduced.

Hogsnes et al. (2014) interviewed 11 spouses of persons with dementia before and after relocating them to a nursing home. Feelings of shame and guilt and feelings of isolation preceded relocating the spouse to a nursing home. The event which triggered the move was threats and physical violence (some with a knife) directed toward the caring partner. After relocating the spouse to a nursing home, partners described feelings of both guilt and freedom, living with grief, feelings of loneliness in the spousal relationship, and striving for acceptance despite a lack of completion.

15-3d Divorce

Middle-aged and older adults do not always live "happily ever after." According to Brown and Lin (2012), there is a gray divorce revolution occurring in that the divorce rate for those age 50 and older doubled from 1990 to 2009 (now one in four divorces or 600,000 annually). Blacks, formerly married, noncollege, and those married less than 10 years were most likely to divorce. Reasons include that older people are more likely to be remarried and this group is more likely to divorce, greater acceptance of divorce (e.g., friends likely to be divorced), and wife more likely to be economically independent. Other reasons for later life divorce may include that children are grown (less concern about the effect of divorce on them), health (time left for a second life), prenuptial agreements (limit one's economic liability to spouse being divorced), and dating sites (find a new partner quickly).

Some spouses are literally dumped as they age. According to son and biographer Peter Ford, Cynthia Hayword, the third wife of Glenn Ford (famous movie star of the fifties), enjoyed being on his arm for 11 years of traveling the world and parties with the rich and famous in Hollywood. When he became ill in his mid-eighties, she checked him into a dependency care facility (Pasadena Las Encinas Hospital) and divorced him (Ford, 2011).

15-3e Retirement

Retirement represents a rite of passage through which most elderly pass. Reasons for retirement include wanting to enjoy life without the constraints of employment, availability of income from sources other than employment (e.g., Social Security, pension), and job satisfaction or lack of it. Lumsdaine and Vermeer (2015) observed that the presence of a grandchild also hastens the decision of a female to retire.

The retirement age in the United States for those born after 1960 is 67. Individuals can take early retirement at age 62, with reduced benefits. Retirement affects an individual's status, income, privileges, power, and prestige. One retiree noted that he was being waited on by a clerk who looked at his name on his check, thought she recognized him and said, "Didn't you use to be somebody?"

People least likely to retire are unmarried, widowed, single-parent women who need to continue working because they have no pension or even Social Security benefits—if they do not work or continue to work, they will have no income, so retirement is

> **dementia** loss of brain function that occurs with certain diseases. It affects memory, thinking, language, judgment, and behavior.

Fishing is a favorite pastime for the retired elderly.

> Just like going to high school, the military, college, or your first job, know that the learning curve is very sharp. Don't think retirement is a continuation of what you did a few years earlier. Learn fast or you will be bored.

> For every 10 phone calls you make expect about 1 back; your status has dwindled and you have less to offer those who want something from you.

> Have at least three to five hobbies that you can do almost any time and any place. Feed your hobbies or they will die.

> Having several things to look forward to is so much more exciting than looking backward. If you looked backward to high school while in college, your life would be boring.

> Develop a new physical exercise program that you want to do. Don't expect others to support your activities. The "pay off" in retirement is vastly different from what colleagues expected of you.

> Find new friends who have time to share (colleagues are often too busy).

> Retirement is a *new* time to live and *new* things have to happen.

> Travel—we have traveled to seven new countries in the past few years.

Some retired individuals volunteer—giving back their time and money to attack poverty, illiteracy, oppression, crime, and so on. Examples of volunteer organizations are the Service Corps of Retired Executives, known as SCORE (www.score.org), Experience Works (www.experienceworks.org), and Generations United (www.gu.org).

15-3f Housing

The stereotype of the elderly residing in an assisted living facility has been replaced by the concept of "niche aging," whereby retirement communities are set up for those with a particular interest (Barovick, 2012). For those into country music, there is a community in Franklin, Tennessee, which offers not only the array of housing alternatives but also recording studios and performance venues; for Asian Americans, there is Aegis Gardens in Freemont, California; for gay and lesbian retirees, there is Fountaingrove Lodge in Santa Rosa, California. There are now 100 such communities including those set up close to universities so individuals can continue to take classes (Oberlin and Dartmouth). Some adults seek these contexts and check in as early as age 40.

not an option. Some workers experience what is called **blurred retirement** rather than a clear-cut one. A blurred retirement means the individual works part-time before completely retiring or takes a "bridge job" that provides a transition between a lifelong career and full retirement. Others may plan a **phased retirement** whereby an employee agrees to a reduced work load in exchange for reduced income. This arrangement is beneficial to both the employee and employer.

Individuals who have a positive attitude toward retirement are those who have a pension waiting for them, are married (and thus have social support for the transition), have planned for retirement, are in good health, and have high self-esteem (Wang et al., 2011). Identifying interests to share in retirement is also important for couple satisfaction (Price & Nesteruk, 2013).

Paul Yelsma is a retired university professor. For a successful retirement, he recommends the following:

blurred retirement
an individual working part-time before completely retiring or taking a "bridge job" that provides a transition between a lifelong career and full retirement.

phased retirement
an employee agreeing to a reduced work load in exchange for reduced income.

Some elderly grandparents live in granny pods, a small prefabricated house (12 by 24 feet), referred to as a medcottage, which is hooked up to the water and electricity of the main house. Grandparents not only live on the premises to be close to their children/grandchildren, but the adult children have them close by to take care of them as they age.

> The trouble with retirement is that you never get a day off.
>
> —ABE LEMONS

15-3g Sexuality

Negative stereotypes abound in regard to sex and the elderly—they are unattractive/undesirable sexually, they are not interested in sex, they are not capable of sex, they are asexual, and they should not want to have sex (Yelland, 2016). However, the stigma associated with sexuality in the later years is decreasing, with men more likely to hold on to stigmatic beliefs (Syme & Cohn, 2016). There are numerous changes in the sexuality of men and women as they age (see Table 15.3). For men, erections take longer to achieve, are less rigid, and it takes longer for the man to recover so that he can have another erection. "It now takes me all night to do what I used to do all night" is the adage aging men become familiar with.

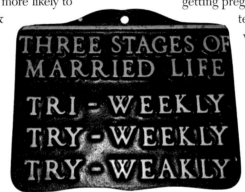

> You don't appreciate a lot of stuff in school until you get older. Little things like being spanked every day by a middle-aged woman.
>
> —EMO PHILLIPS, COMEDIAN

Levitra, Cialis, and Viagra (prescription drugs that help a man obtain and maintain an erection) are helpful for about 50% of men. Others with erectile dysfunction may benefit from a pump that inflates two small banana-shaped tubes that have been surgically implanted into the penis. Still others benefit from devices placed over the penis to trap blood so as to create an erection.

Women also experience changes including menopause, which is associated with a surge of sexual libido, an interest in initiating sex with her partner, and greater orgasmic capacity. Not only are they free from worry about getting pregnant, but also estrogen levels drop and testosterone levels increase. A woman's vaginal walls become thinner and less lubricating; the latter issue can be resolved by lubricants like KY Jelly.

Table 15.3 describes these and other physiological sexual changes that occur as individuals age.

Some spouses are sexually inactive. Karraker and DeLamater (2013) analyzed data on 1,502 men and women ages 57 to 85 and found that 29% reported no sexual activity for the

TABLE 15.3 PHYSIOLOGICAL SEXUAL CHANGES AS INDIVIDUALS AGE	
Physical Changes in Sexuality as Men Age	**Physical Changes in Sexuality as Women Age**
1. Delayed and less firm erection.	1. Reduced or increased sexual interest.
2. More direct stimulation needed for erection.	2. Possible painful intercourse due to menopausal changes.
3. Extended refractory period (12 to 24 hours before rearousal can occur).	3. Decreased volume of vaginal lubrication.
4. Fewer expulsive contractions during orgasm.	4. Decreased expansive ability of the vagina.
5. Less forceful expulsion of seminal fluid and a reduced volume of ejaculate.	5. Possible pain during orgasm due to less flexibility.
6. Rapid loss of erection after ejaculation.	6. Thinning of the vaginal walls.
7. Loss of ability to maintain an erection for a long period.	7. Shortening of vaginal width and length.
8. Decrease in size and firmness of the testes.	8. Decreased sex flush, reduced increase in breast volume, and longer postorgasmic nipple erection.

Source: Adapted from Janell L. Carroll, *Sexuality Now: Embracing Diversity*, 4th ed., p. 273. © 2012. Wadsworth, a part of Cengage Learning, Inc. Reproduced by permission. www.cengage.com/permissions.

Maria McDonald

past 12 months or more. The longer the couple had been married, the older the spouse, and the more compromised the health of the spouse, the more likely the individual was to report no sexual activity. Syme and Cohn (2016) reported on the sexuality of adults aged 63 to 67. Factors associated with lack of sexual satisfaction included spouse in poor health, history of diabetes, and fatigue. Elderly women were less sexually satisfied than men.

As noted earlier, the most sexually active are in good health. Diabetes and hypertension are major causes of sexual dysfunction. Incontinence (leaking of urine) is particularly an issue for older women and can be a source of embarrassment. The most frequent sexual problem for men is erectile dysfunction; for women, the most frequent sexual problem is the lack of a partner.

Age is a case of mind over matter.
If you don't mind, it don't matter.

—SATCHEL PAIGE

 **15-4 SUCCESSFUL AGING**

Healthy aging has been defined by the World Health Organization as developing and maintaining functional ability in the later years including physical, mental, and psychosocial. It is recognized that these abilities interact in environments (physical, social, and policy) that facilitate these abilities (Sadana et al., 2016). Paramount in the definition of successful aging is health. Having interpersonal, community, physical, and psychological well-being is associated with individuals who have a high income, are married, are a white- collar professional, and own their own home (Ribenstein et al., 2016).

Claudia Kawas of the National Institutes of Health studied 1,600 plus individuals who were over the age of 90. The goal of the research was to find out those factors

associated with successful aging (Stahl, 2014). These included not smoking, exercising 45 minutes a day, being socially active (book clubs, being with friends), drinking alcohol moderately, drinking coffee (1–3 cups a day), and maintaining or gaining weight. Taking vitamins was not associated with longevity.

Having a happy marriage was also important for successful aging. Indeed, the elderly who were identified as being "happy and well" were six times more likely to be in a good marriage than those who were identified as "sad and sick."

The society/culture in which the elderly person lives also impacts the aging experience. Fuller-Iglesias and Antonucci (2016) emphasized that the elderly in Mexico live in a context of familism where the elderly are included and revered. Indeed, higher familism is associated with better psychological and physical well-being.

15-5 RELATIONSHIPS AND THE ELDERLY

Relationships in the later years vary. Some elderly men and women are single and date.

15-5a Dating

Brown and Shinohara (2013) studied the dating behavior of 3,005 individuals ages 57–85 and found that 14% of singles were in a dating relationship. Dating was more common among men than women and declined with age. Compared to nondaters, daters were more socially advantaged, college educated, and had more assets, better health, and more social connectedness. Some elderly seek dating partners through Internet sites which cater to older individuals. Ourtime.com is an example.

Alterovitz and Mendelsohn (2013) noted the importance of health in seeking a partner for the elderly. In their study of 450 personal ads, they compared the middle aged (40–45), young-old (60–74), and old-old (75 plus) and found that the two younger cohorts focused on a partner for adventure, romance, sex, and a soul mate; the older group was more likely to mention the importance of a healthy partner. We (authors of your text) know of an example where a woman in her sixties met a man in his sixties via Match.com. On their second date she asked him to walk with her, which ended up being 1.5 miles. She later said, "I was testing to see how healthy he was…if he could not walk a mile and a half it would have been our last date."

About 3.2 million individuals over the age of 50 are cohabiting. One of the motivations for older females cohabiting with a partner rather than marrying the partner is to avoid becoming a caretaker—there are no "in sickness and in health" expectations (Manning & Brown, 2015).

> A person is not old until regrets take the place of dreams.
>
> —JOHN BARRYMORE, ACTOR

> As time goes by and you're getting older and stuff like that—getting older sucks. You know, I hear all this crap about, "Oh, you can age with dignity." Really?
>
> —MICKEY ROURKE

15-5b Relationships between Elderly Spouses

Marriages that survive into late life are characterized by little conflict, considerable companionship, and mutual supportiveness. Rauer (2013) reported on 64 older couples (married an average of 42 years) and emphasized that being married in late life was the best of all contexts in terms of social/emotional, economic, and behavioral resources (e.g., taking care of each other). She noted that taking care of a spouse actually benefits the caregiver with feelings of self-esteem (but the outcome for the spouse being cared for may be negative since he or she may feel dependent).

Koren et al. (2016) noted that when widowed individuals repartner in late life they talk of caregiving issues. One woman in the Koren et al. study told the interviewer:

> I went through radiation, but I told my partner: "Listen, I don't think you need such a punishment, to deal twice with such a story, you had your share, keep your distance, you don't have to," and he said: "There's no such thing, it's for better or for worse." So there is also beauty in late-life repartnering, it's not shallow, and you know, in the course of time, if he'll need it, I'll be there. . . . When he had to have a catheterization, I was with him; when he goes to the doctor, I go with him. I don't believe in withdrawal of responsibility in late-life repartnering. I'm there with his children.

Only a small percentage (8%) of individuals older than 100 are married. Most married centenarians are men in their second or third marriage. Many have outlived some of their children. Marital satisfaction in these elderly marriages is related to a high frequency of expressing love feelings to one's partner. Though it is assumed that spouses who have been married for a long time should know how their partners feel, this is often not the case. Telling each other "I love you" is very important to these elderly spouses.

15-5c Grandparenthood

Another significant role for the elderly is that of grandparent. Among adults aged 40 and older who had children, close to 95% are grandparents and most have, on average, five or six grandchildren.

Margolis (2016) studied the amount of time grandparents in Canada spend in the role. They found that due to increased childlessness and fertility postponement the time spent in grandparenting was 24.3 years for women and 18.9 years for men.

Some grandparents actively take care of their grandchildren full-time, provide supplemental help in a multigenerational family, assist on an occasional part-time basis, or occasionally visit their grandchildren. Grandparents see themselves as caretakers, emotional and/or economic resources, teachers, and historical connections on the family tree.

15-5d Grandfamilies

Grandfamilies—families in which children reside with and are being raised by grandparents—include multigenerational families where grandparents care for grandchildren so the parent(s) can work or go to school. Grandfamilies also form in response to the parent(s) experiencing job loss, out of state employment, military deployment, divorce, deportation, illness, death, substance abuse, incarceration, or mental illness.

Just over 2% (2.2%) of all children in the United States are being reared in grandfamilies. About half of grandfamilies consist of both grandparents, 46% consist of the grandmother only, and 5% consist of just the

grandfamilies families in which children reside with and are being raised by grandparents.

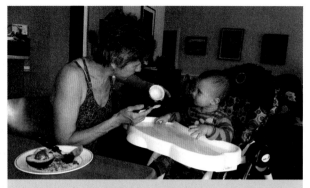

Grandmothers are the workhorses of the family. They often cherish their role.

grandfather (Pilkauskas & Dunifon, 2016). The number of children in grandfamilies is almost 8 million children (7.8) who live in grandfamilies where the grandparents or other relatives are householders (*The State of Grandfamilies in America, 2015*). Most biological parents see their children two or three times a week.

Children in grandfamilies usually enter a more economically advantaged home than their parents' home. However, the incidence of ADD/ADHD is much higher among children in grandfamilies than those in other households, and this likely spills over into school interactions, as teacher-reported levels of cooperation are lower, and oppositional behavior and inattention are higher, among grandfamily children (Pilkauskas & Dunifon, 2016).

15-5e Effect of Divorce on the Grandparent-Child Relationship

Divorce often has a negative effect on grandparents seeing their grandchildren. The situation most likely to produce this outcome is when the children are young, the wife is granted primary custody, and the relationship between the spouses is adversarial.

This 92-year-old grandfather delights in watching his grandson work in garden.

A Grandma Kind of Love

What kind of love is bigger than the sky above?
It's that very, very, very, special kind of Grandma love.

What kind of love is sweeter than honey? finer than fine? better than best?
You're right if "Grandma's love" is what you guessed!

What kind of love is playful and fun?
It's Grandma's love that shines like the sun.

What kind of love sticks like glue?
It's the love that Grandma has for you.

What kind of love stays sure and strong?
It's Grandma's love that lasts so long.

What kind of love is off the chart?
It's the love that comes from Grandma's heart.

What kind of love is always there?
It's the love that you and Grandma share.

Will Grandma's love ever end?
The answer to that is "never"
Because Grandma's special kind of love is a love that lasts forever.

Source: Caroline Schacht

Some grandparents are not allowed to see their grandchildren. In all 50 states, the role of the grandparent has limited legal and political support. By a vote of six to three, the Supreme Court (*Troxel v. Granville*) sided with the parents and virtually denied 60 million grandparents the right to see their grandchildren. The court viewed parents as having a fundamental right to make decisions about with whom their children could spend time—including keeping them from grandparents. However, some courts have ruled in favor of grandparents. Stepgrandparents have no legal rights to their stepgrandchildren.

15-5f Benefits of Grandparents to Grandchildren

Grandchildren report enormous benefits from having a close relationship with grandparents, including development of a sense of family ideals, moral beliefs, and a work ethic. Feeling loved is also a major benefit. This poem reflects the love of a grandmother.

15-6 THE END OF ONE'S LIFE

> But one thing I could never get use to was how we treat our old and frail—leaving them to a life alone or isolating them in a series of anonymous facilities, their last conscious moments spent with nurses and doctors who barely know their names.
>
> —ATUL GWANDE, *BEING MORTAL*

Thanatology is the examination of the social dimensions of death, dying, and bereavement. The end of one's life sometimes involves the death of one's spouse.

> The biggest problems in our lives are the ones that we inevitably have to face, like old age, illness, and death.
>
> —THE DALAI LAMA, *THE ART OF HAPPINESS*

15-6a Death of One's Spouse

While the death of one's parents is often one's first encounter with death (and most devastating for females to lose their mother) (Leopold & Lechner, 2015), the death of one's spouse happens later in life and is one of the most stressful adult life events a person experiences. Compared to both the married and the divorced, the widowed are the most lonely and have the lowest life satisfaction (Ben-Zur, 2012; Hensley et al., 2012). Because women tend to live longer than men (81.2 versus 76.4) (Murphy et al., 2015b), they are more likely to experience the widowed role.

Although individual reactions and coping mechanisms for dealing with the death of a loved one vary, several reactions to death are common. These include shock, disbelief and denial, confusion and disorientation, grief and sadness, anger, numbness, physiological symptoms such as insomnia or lack of appetite, withdrawal from activities, immersion in activities, depression, and guilt. Eventually, surviving the death of a loved one involves the recognition that life must go on, the need to make sense out of the loss, and the establishment of a new identity. Such a new life is difficult—widows generally report less well-being than spouses due to the "greedy marriage" hypothesis (married interact among themselves and isolate widows) (Ory & Huijts, 2015).

Women and men tend to have different ways of reacting to and coping with the death of a loved one. Women are more likely than men to express and share feelings with family and friends and are also more likely to seek and accept help, such as attending grief support groups. Initial responses of men are often cognitive rather than emotional. From early childhood, males are taught to be in control, to be strong and courageous under adversity, and to be able to take charge and fix things. Showing emotions is labeled weak.

Men sometimes respond to the death of their spouse in behavioral rather than emotional ways. Sometimes they immerse themselves in work or become involved in physical action in response to the loss. For example, a widower immersed himself in repairing a beach cottage he and his wife had recently bought. Later, he described this activity as crucial to getting him through those first two months. Another coping mechanism for men is the increased use of alcohol and other drugs.

The age at which one experiences the death of a spouse is also a factor in one's adjustment. People in their eighties may be so consumed with their own health and disability that they have little emotional energy to grieve. But even after the spouse's death, the emotional relationship with the deceased may continue. Some widows and widowers report a feeling that their spouses are with them for years after the death of their beloved. Some may also dream of their deceased spouses, talk to their photographs, and remain interested in carrying out their wishes. Such continuation of the relationship may be adaptive by providing meaning and purpose for the living or maladaptive in that it may prevent the surviving spouse from establishing new relationships.

15-6b Use of Technology and Death of One's Partner

Just as technology has changed the way relationships begin (e.g., text messaging), its use in memorializing the deceased is increasing. Some spouses are so distraught over the death of their partner that they cannot weather a traditional funeral. But they can upload a eulogy and videos to a website where others may pay their respects, post their own

thanatology the examination of the social dimensions of death, dying, and bereavement.

photos of the deceased, and blog comments of various experiences with the deceased. One such website for the deceased is http://www.respectance.com.

15-6c Preparing for Death

What is it like for those near the end of life to think about death? To what degree do they go about actually preparing for death? Cheng et al. (2013) discussed anticipatory grief therapy where one comes to terms with his or her own death. Johnson and Barer (1997) interviewed 48 individuals with an average age of 93 to find out their perspectives on death. Most interviewees were women (77%); of those, 56% lived alone, but 73% had some sort of support from their children or from one or more social support services. The following findings are specific to those who died within a year after the interview:

1. **The last year of life.** Most of the respondents had thought about death and saw their life as one that would soon end. Most did so without remorse or anxiety. With their spouses and friends dead and their health failing, they accepted death as the next stage in life. They felt like the last leaf on the tree (see Personal View section).

   The major fear these respondents expressed was not the fear of death but of the dying process. Dying in a nursing home after a long illness is a dreaded fear. Sadly, almost 60% of the respondents died after a long, progressive illness. They had become frail, fatigued, and burdened by living. They identified dying in their sleep as the ideal way to die. Some hastened their death by no longer taking their medications; others wished they could terminate their own life. Competent adults have the legal right to refuse or discontinue medical interventions. For incompetent individuals, decisions are made by a surrogate—typically a spouse or child (McGowan, 2011).

2. **Behaviors in the last year of life.** Aware that they are going to die, most simplify their life, disengage from social relationships, and leave final instructions. In simplifying their life, they sell their home and belongings and move to smaller quarters. One 81-year-old woman sold her home, gave her car away to a friend, and moved into a nursing home. The extent of her belongings became a chair, a lamp, and a TV.

   Some divorce just before they die. Upon learning he had terminal cancer, actor Dennis Hopper filed for divorce from his fifth wife. One explanation for this behavior is that divorce removes a spouse from automatically getting part of a deceased spouse's estate and allows control of dispensing one's assets (often to one's own children) while one is alive.

Disengaging from social relationships is selective. Some maintain close relationships with children and friends but others "let go." They may no longer send out Christmas cards and stop sending letters. Phone calls become the source of social connections. Some leave final instructions in the form of a will or handwritten note expressing wishes of where to be buried, handling costs associated with disposal of the body (e.g., cremation), and directives about pets. One of Johnson and Barer's (1997) respondents left $30,000 each to specific caregivers to take care of several pets (p. 204).

Elderly who may have counted on children to take care of them may find that their children have scattered because of job changes, divorce, or both, and may be unavailable for support. Some children simply walk away from their parents or leave their care to their siblings. The result is that the elderly may have to fend for themselves.

Some of the elderly live full lives up until the very end. Ted Kennedy died of brain cancer at age 77. Up until the last week of his life, he was active in politics (he

The waning days of our lives are given over to treatments that addle our brains and sap our bodies for a sliver's chance of benefit. They are spent in institutions—nursing homes and intensive care units—where regimented, anonymous routines cut us off from all the things that matter to us in life.

—ATUL GAWANDE, *BEING MORTAL*

Thoughts at the End of Life

Individuals with an average age of 93 were interviewed and shared their thoughts as they reached the end of life (Johnson & Barer, 1997).

If I die tomorrow, it would be all right. I've had a beautiful life, but I'm ready to go. My husband is gone, my children are gone, and my friends are gone.

***

That's what is so wonderful about living to be so old. You know death is near and you don't even care.

***

I've just been diagnosed with cancer, but it's no big deal. At my age, I have to die of something.

For some, the end is frightening. Movie star Glenn Ford spoke into a tape recorder at the end of his life:

Is this the way my life is going to end up, in deep sadness? I don't know if I'm even capable of working. I'm very insecure. I think I've lost it. I don't know if I can handle memorizing lines. My mind is so shook up, I don't know.... I've thought about taking my own life. It's a drastic thing to do—a horrible thing to do. But I don't think I can go on living like I am now...I'm lost. I'm just completely washed up. I'm finished. (Ford, 2011, p. 296)

had sponsored over 300 bills in his Senate career). His words resonate, "For all those whose cares have been our concern, the work goes on, the cause endures, the hope still lives, and the dream must never die."

inside a more approving cultural context (Benson & Coleman, 2016).

Finally, robotic companions for the elderly are being used in Asian countries such as Japan (Bodkin, 2016). They will soon make their way to America.

15-7 TRENDS AND THE ELDERLY IN THE UNITED STATES

By 2020, 17% of the U.S. population will be over the age of 65. Between 2015 and 2040 the percent of the population age 85 and over will almost double (*Proquest Statistical Abstract of the United States, 2016,* Table 8). As the aging population increases in size, greater acceptance of aging will occur.

There will also be a new emphasis on physical exercise as the pathway to physical, psychological, and social health in the later years (Bauman et al., 2016). This will include a focus on the freedom of the elderly to pursue areas of interest, staying busy, and enjoying recreational activities (Denmark & Zarbiv, 2016).

Living apart together (LAT), discussed in Chapter 2, will increasingly become a lifestyle option for the elderly who are single, widowed, or divorced. LAT provides the autonomy that they desire and occurs

STUDY TOOLS 15

READY TO STUDY? IN THE BOOK, YOU CAN:

☐ Rip out the chapter review card at the back of the book for a handy summary of the chapter and key terms.

ONLINE AT CENGAGEBRAIN.COM YOU CAN:

☐ Collect StudyBits while you read and study the chapter.

☐ Quiz yourself on key concepts.

☐ Prepare for tests with M&F4 Flash Cards as well as those you create.

REFERENCES

Chapter 1

Amato, P. R. (2015a). Claiming more than we know. *National Council on Family Relations Report*, Fall/60.3: 3.

———. (2015b). Is marriage becoming passé? *National Council on Family Relations Report*, Summer/60.2: 3.

Andersen, S. H., L. S Andersen, & P. E. Skov. (2015). Effect of marriage and spousal criminality on recidivism. *Journal of Marriage and the Family*, 77: 496–509.

Asadi, M. (2015). The sexuality transition: Premarital sex, the nuclear family, and "doing" gender. *Women's Studies: An Interdisciplinary Journal*, 44: 23–53.

Busby, D., & K.Yoshida. (2015). Challenges with online research for couples and families: Evaluating nonrespondents and the differential impact of incentives. *Journal of Child and Family Studies*, 24: 505–513.

Byrne, T., & K. Gelles. (January 11, 2016). American Student Assistance Life delayed survey. *USA Today*.

Cohen, M. (2016). An exploratory study of individuals in non-traditional, alternative relationships: How 'open' are we? *Sexuality and Culture*, 20: 295–315.

Cohn, D. (2013). Love and marriage. Pew Research Center. Retrieved January 12, 2014, from http://www.pewsocialtrends.org/2013/02/13/love-and-marriage/

Coontz, S. (2016). *The way we never were: American families and the nostalgia trap*, 2nd ed. New York: Basic Books.

Cottle, N. R., B. K. Burr, D. S. Hubler, P. B. Payne, & B. Kern. (November 13, 2015). Assessing unique perceptions of couple relationship education programs. Annual Meeting of the National Council on Family Relations, Vancouver, Canada.

Cottle, N.R., A. K. Thompson, B. K. Burr, & D. S. Hubler. (2014). The effectiveness of relationship education in the college classroom. *Journal of Couple & Relationship Therapy*, 13: 267–283.

Cravens, J. D. (2015). Couples' communication of rules and boundaries for technology and the Internet. *Family Focus*, Summer/60.2: F17.

Darnton, K. (February 12, 2012). Deception at Duke. *Sixty Minutes*/CBS Television.

Dragojlovic, A. (2016). "Playing family": Unruly relationality and transnational motherhood. *Gender, Place and Culture: A Journal of Feminist Geography*, 23: 243–256.

Erichsen, E. & P. Dignam. (April 2016). From hookup to husband: Transitioning hookups to committed relationships. Paper, Southern Sociological Society Annual Meeting, Atlanta, GA.

Forsberg, H., & R. Natkin. (2016). Families in the future: Stories of Finnish students. *Journal of Comparative Family Studies*, 47: 27–43.

Hall, S., & D. Knox. (2016). Relationship and sexual behaviors of a sample of 9,974 undergraduates. Unpublished data collected for this text.

Department of Family and Consumer Sciences, Ball State University and Department of Sociology, East Carolina University.

———. (2017). Relationship power in emerging adults' romantic relationships. Unpublished manuscript. Email knoxd@ecu.edu since article submitted for publication.

Hawkins, A. J., & S. E. Erickson. (2015). Is couple and relationship education effective for lower income participants? A meta-analytic study. *Journal of Family Psychology*, 29: 59–68.

Hertlein, K. M., & M. L. C. Blumer. (2013). *The couple and family technology framework: Intimate relationships in a digital age.* New York: Routledge.

Incerti, L., C. Henderson-Wilson, & M. Dunn. (2015). Challenges in the family. *Family Matters*, 96: 29–38.

Kanat-Maymon, Y., A. Antebi, & S. Zilcha-Mano. (2016). Basic psychological need fulfillment in human-pet relationships and well-being. *Personality and Individual Differences*, 92: 69–73.

Karpowitz, C. F., & J. C. Pope. (2015). Summary report: Marriage and family attitudes, practices, & policy opinions. *American Family Survey*. Center for the Study of Elections and Democracy. Retrieved from http://national.deseretnews.com/american-family-survey

Kopystynska, O., T. L. Spinrad, D. M. Seay, & N. Eisenberg. (November 12–14, 2015). Parent child relationship quality predict child affect. Annual Meeting of the National Council on Family Relations, Vancouver, Canada.

Lee, G. R. (2015). *The limits of marriage*. Blue Ridge Summit, PA: Lexington Books.

Lorber, J. (1998). *Gender inequality: Feminist theories and politics*. Los Angeles: Roxbury.

Lucier-Greer, M., F. Adler-Baeder, S. A. Ketring, K. T. Harcourt, & T. Smith. (2012). Comparing the experiences of couples in first marriages and remarriages in couple and relationship education. *Journal of Divorce and Remarriage*, 53: 55–75.

Ma, Y., J. Pittman, J. Kerpelman, & F. Adler-Baeder. (November 5–9, 2013). Relationship education and classroom climate impact on faulty relationship views. Annual Meeting of the National Council on Family Relations, San Antonio, TX.

Marshall, J. (November 5–9, 2013). Can we understand that which we cannot define? How marriage and family therapists define the family. Annual Meeting of the National Council on Family Relations, San Antonio, TX.

McHale, S. M., K. A. Updegraff, & S. D. Whiteman (2012). Sibling relationships and influences in childhood and adolescence. *Journal of Marriage and Family*, 74: 913–930.

Ogolsky, B. G., C. A. Surra, & J. K. Monk. (2016). Pathways of commitment to wed: The development and dissolution of romantic relationships. *Journal of Marriage and Family*, 78: 293–310.

Proquest Statistical Abstract of the United States, 2016, online ed. Washington, DC: U.S. Bureau of the Census.

Salvatore, J., & D. M. Dick. (2015). Gene-environment interplay: Where we are, where we are going. *Journal of Marriage and Family*, 77: 344–350.

Schramm, D. G., S. M. Harris, J. B. Whiting, A. J. Hawkins, M. Brown, & R. Porter. (2013). Economic costs and policy implications associated with divorce: Texas as a case study. *Journal of Divorce and Remarriage*, 54: 1–24.

Shelton, L. G. (November 13, 2015). Teaching an ecological perspective on family transitions. Annual Meeting of the National Council on Family Relations, Vancouver, Canada.

Silverstein, L. B., & C. F. Auerbach. (2005). (Post) modern families. In Jaipaul L. Roopnarine & U. P. Gielen (Eds.), *Families in global perspective* (pp. 33–48). Boston: Pearson Education.

Spuhler, B., L. Skogrand, K. Bradford, & B. Higginbotham. (November 19, 2014). Relationship education for low-income job seekers. Paper, Annual Meeting of the National Council on Family Relations, Baltimore, MD.

Toews, M. L., & A. Yazedjian. (November 5–9, 2013). An evaluation of a relationship education program for adolescent parents. Poster, Annual Meeting of the National Council on Family Relations, San Antonio, TX.

Wilmoth, J. D., & A. D. Blaney. (2016). African American clergy involvement in marriage preparation. *Journal of Family Issues*, 37: 855–876.

Yang, X. (2015). Chinese college students' risk attitude to moving abroad to study. *Social Behavior and Personality: An International Journal*, 43: 795–802.

Zemanek, L. J. (November 2014). The impact of animals on prosocial behaviors in children with autism spectrum disorders: A critical literature review. Paper, Annual Meeting of the National Council on Family Relations, Baltimore, MD.

Chapter 2

Allison, R. (2016). Gendered jocks or equal players? Athletic affiliation and hooking up among college students. *Sociological Spectrum*, 36: 255–270.

Ashwin, S., & O. Isupova. (2014). "Behind every great man....": The male marriage wage premium examined qualitatively. *Journal of Marriage and Family*, 76: 37–55.

Aubrey, J. S., & S. E. Smith. (2013). Development and validation of the endorsement of the Hookup Culture Index. *Journal of Sex Research*, 50: 435–448.

Benson, J. J., & M. Coleman. (2016). Older adults developing a preference for living apart together. *Journal of Marriage and Family*, 78: 797–812.

Birger, J. (2015). *Date onomics: How dating became a lopsided numbers game*. New York: Workman Publishing.

Bradshaw, C., A. S. Kahn, & B. K. Saville. (2010). To hook up or date: Which gender benefits? *Journal Sex Roles*, 62: 661–669.

Brown, S. L., W. D. Manning, K. K. Payne, & H. Wu. (March 30–April 2, 2016). Living apart together (LAT) relationships in the U.S. Presented at the Population Association of America, Washington, DC.

Budgeon, S. (2016). The "problem" with single women: Choice, accountability and social change. *Journal of Social and Personal Relationships, 33*: 401–418.

Chang, I. J., & Kennedy, G. E. (2001). Pick up lines: Gender differences in meeting initiation. Paper, Annual Conference of the National Council of Family Relations, Irvine, CA.

Chang, J., R. Ward, D. Padgett, & M. F. Smith. (November 1, 2012). Do feminists hook up more? Examining pro-feminism attitude in the context of hooking-up. Paper, National Council on Family Relations, Phoenix, AZ.

Cook, J. (April 2015). Tinder would be worth $1.6 billion as a standalone business. *Business Insider.* Retrieved from http://www.businessinsider.com/jmp-securities-analyst-note-on-tinder-2015-4?r=UK&IR=T

Coontz, S. (2016). *The way we never were: American families and the nostalgia trap, 2nd ed.* New York: Basic Books.

Dargie, E., K. L. Blair, C. Goldfinger, & C. F. Pukall. (2015). Outcomes in long-distance relationships. *Journal of Sex & Marital Therapy, 41*: 181–202.

Denney, J. T. (2010). Family and household formations and suicide in the United States. *Journal of Marriage and the Family, 72*: 202–213.

Du Bois, S. N., T. G. Sher, K. Grotkowski, T. Aizenman, N. Slesinger, & M. Cohen. (2016). Going the distance. *Family Journal, 24*: 5–14.

Eck, B. A. (2013). Identity twists and turns: How never-married men make sense of an unanticipated identity. *Journal of Contemporary Ethnography, 42*: 31–33.

Erichsen, K., & P. Dignan (April 2016). From hookup to husband: Transitioning hookups to committed relationships. Paper, Annual Meeting of the Southern Sociological Society, Atlanta, GA.

Finkel, E. (February 2015). In defense of Tinder. *New York Times.* Retrieved from http://www.nytimes.com/2015/02/08/opinion/sunday/in-defense-of-tinder.html

Guzzo, K. B. (2014). Trends in cohabitation outcomes: Compositional changes and engagement among never-married young adults. *Journal of Marriage and Family, 76*: 826–842.

Hall, J. A., N. Park, M. J. Cody, & H. Song. (2010). Strategic misrepresentation in online dating: The effects of gender, self-monitoring, and personality traits. *Journal of Social and Personal Relationships, 27*: 117–135.

Hall, S., & D. Knox. (2016). Relationship and sexual behaviors of a sample of 9,974 undergraduates. Unpublished data collected for this text. Department of Family and Consumer Sciences, Ball State University and Department of Sociology, East Carolina University.

Hess, J. (2012). Personal communication. Appreciation is expressed to Judye Hess for the development of this section. For more information about Judye Hess, see http://www.psychotherapist.com/judyehess/

Holden, M. (September 12, 2015). Dating with Tinder: The definitive guide to doing Tinder right. Retrieved from http://www.askmen.com/dating/curtsmith/dating-with-tinder.html

Jacinto, E., & J. Ahrend. (2012). Living apart together. Unpublished data provided by Jacinto and Ahrend.

Jankowiak, W., & M. Escasa-Dorne. (2016) Bisexual and straight females' preferences voiced on an adult sex dating site. *Current Anthropology, 57*: 104–112.

Jayson, S. (February 14, 2013). The end of online dating. *USA Today,* p. 1A et passim.

Jose, A., K. D. O'Leary, & A. Moyer. (2010). Does premarital cohabitation predict subsequent marital stability and marital quality? A meta-analysis. *Journal of Marriage and Family, 72*: 105–116.

Jurkane-Hobein, I. (2015). When less is more: On time work in long distance relationships. *Qualitative Sociology, 38*: 185–203.

Kamiya, Y., M. Doyle, J. C. Henretta, et al. (2013). Depressive symptoms among older adults: The impact and later life circumstances and marital status. *Aging and Mental Health, 17*: 349–357.

Kilpi, F., H. Konttinen, K. Silventoinen, & P. Martikainen. (2015). Living arrangements as determinants of myocardial infarction incidence and survival: A prospective register study of over 300,000 Finnish men and women. *Social Science & Medicine, 133*: 93–100.

Klinenberg, E. (2012). *Going solo: The extraordinary rise and surprising appeal of living alone.* New York: Penguin.

Kotlyar, I., & D. Ariely. (2013). The effect of nonverbal cues on relationship formation. *Computers in Human Behavior, 29*: 544–551.

Kuperberg, A. (2014). Age at coresidence, premarital cohabitation, and marital dissolution, 1985–2009. *Journal of Marriage and the Family, 76*: 352–369.

LaBrie, J. W., J. F. Hummer, T. M. Gaidarov, A. Lac, & S. R. Kenney. (2014). Hooking up in the college context: The event-level effects of alcohol use and partner familiarity on hookup behaviors and contentment. *Journal of Sex Research, 51*: 62–73.

Lewis, M. A., D. C. Atkins, J. A. Blayney, D. V. Dent, & D. L. Kaysen. (2013). What is hooking up? Examining definitions of hooking up in relation to behavior and normative perceptions. *Journal of Sex Research, 50*: 757–766.

Lo, S. K., A. Y. Hsieh, & Y. P. Chiu. (2013). Contradictory deceptive behavior in online dating. *Computers in Human Behavior, 29*: 1755–1762.

Manning, W. D., & S. L. Brown. (2015). Aging cohabitation couples and family policy: Different sex and same-sex couples. *Public Policy Aging Report, 25*: 94–97.

Manning, W. D., & J. A. Cohen. (2012). Premarital cohabitation and marital dissolution: An examination of recent marriages. *Journal of Marriage and the Family, 74*: 377–387.

Miller, A. J., S. Sassler, & D. Kusi-Appouh. (2011). The specter of divorce: Views from working- and middle-class cohabiters. *Family Relations, 60*: 602–616.

Miss Your Mate, Loving from a Distance, IVillage. (2015). Retrieved from http://www.statisticbrain.com/long-distance-relationship-statistics/

Munsch, C. (August 2015). Stigma, status, and singles: The effect of marital status on perceptions of the unmarried. Paper, Annual Meeting of the American Sociological Association, Chicago.

Muraco, J. A., & M. A. Curran. (2012). Associations between marital meaning and reasons to delay marriage for young adults in romantic relationships. *Marriage and Family Review, 48*: 227–247.

Murray, C. (2012). *Coming apart: The state of white America, 1960–2010.* New York: Crown Forum.

Oppenheimer, J. (2002). *Seinfeld: The making of an American icon.* New York: HarperCollins.

Proquest Statistical Abstract of the United States, 2016, online ed. Washington, DC: U.S. Census Bureau.

Rauer, A. (February 22, 2013). From golden bands to the golden years: The critical role of marriage in older adulthood. Annual Meeting of the Southeastern Council on Family Relations, Birmingham, AL.

Rhoades, G. K., S. M. Stanley, & H. J. Markman. (2012). A longitudinal investigation of commitment dynamics in cohabiting relationships. *Journal of Family Issues, 33*: 369–390.

Roberts, J. (March 30, 2016). Relationship norms in Iceland. Presentation to Courtship and Marriage class.

Ruiz, M. (March 2014). Do you have dating ADD? *Cosmopolitan.* Retrieved September 17, 2015, from http://www.cosmopolitan.com/sex-love/advice/a5895/dating-add/

Sales, N. J. (August 2015). Tinder and the dawn of dating apocalypse. *Vanity Fair.* Retrieved September 15, 2015, from http://www.vanityfair.com/culture/2015/08/tinder-hook-up-culture-end-of-dating

Sarkisian, N., & N. Gerstel. (2016). Does singlehood isolate or integrate? Examining the link between marital status and ties to kin, friends and neighbors. *Journal of Social and Personal Relationship, 33*: 361–384.

Sassler, S., K. Michelmore, & J. A. Holland. (2016). The progression of sexual relationships. *Journal of Marriage and Family, 78*: 587–597.

Smith, A., & M. Duggan. (October 21, 2013). Dating, social networking, mobile online dating & relationships. Pew Research Center. Retrieved from http://pewinternet.org/Reports/2013/Online-Dating.aspx

Sobal, J., & K. L. Hanson. (2011). Marital status, marital history, body weight, and obesity. *Marriage & Family Review, 47*: 474–504.

Sommers, P., S. Whiteside, & K. Abbott. (November 5–9, 2013). Cohabitation: Perspectives of undergraduate students. Poster, Annual Meeting of the National Council on Family Relations, San Antonio, TX.

Trenholm, R. (September 2015). Tinder adds super like when swiping right just isn't romantic enough. CNET. Retrieved September 13, 2015, from http://www.cnet.com/news/tinder-adds-super-like-when-swiping-right-just-isnt-enough/

Trost, J. (2016). Marriage, cohabitation and LAT relationships *Journal of Comparative Family Studies, 47*: 17–26.

Uecker, J., & M. Regnerus. (2011). *Premarital sex in America: How young Americans meet, mate, and think about marrying.* United Kingdom: Oxford University Press.

United Nations. (December 2011). World marriage patterns. *Population Facts.* Retrieved October 2, 2013, from http://www.un.org/en/development/desa/population/publications/pdf/popfacts/PopFacts_2011-1.pdf

Upton-Davis, K. (2015). Subverting gendered norms of cohabitation: Living Apart Together for women over 45. *Journal of Gender Studies, 24*: 104–116.

Valle, G., & K. H. Tillman. (2014). Childhood family structure and romantic relationships during the transition to adulthood. *Journal of Family Issues, 35:* 97–124.

Walsh, S. (2013). Match's 2012 singles in America survey. Retrieved from http://www .hookingupsmart.com/2013/02/07 /hookinguprealities/matchs-2012-singles -in-america-survey/

Wang, W., & K. Parker. (September 24, 2014). Record share of Americans have never married. Pew Research Center. Retrieved from http:// www.pewsocialtrends.org/2014/09/24/chapter -4-never-married-young-adults-on-the -marriage-market/

Willoughby, B. J., & D. Belt. (2016). Marital orientation and relationship well-being among cohabiting couples. *Journal of Family Psychology, 30:* 181–192.

Willoughby, B. J., J. S. Carroll, & D. M. Busby. (2012). The different effects of "living together": Determining and comparing types of cohabiting couples. *Journal of Social and Personal Relationships, 29:* 397–419.

Wu, P., & W. Chiou. (2009). More options lead to more searching and worse choices in finding partners for romantic relationships online: An experimental study. *CyberPsychology & Behavior, 12:* 315–318.

Vespa, J. (2014). Historical trends in the marital intentions of onetime and serial cohabitors. *Journal of Marriage and Family, 76:* 207–217.

Chapter 3

Abboud, P. (2013). The third gender: Samoa's Fa'afafine people. Retrieved September 29 from http://www.pedestrian.tv/features/arts -and-culture/meet-the-third-gender-samoas -faafafine-people/70b3c7c8-66fc-4453-9f06 -1de911d249ee.htm

Barnes, H., D. Knox, & J. Brinkley. (March 23, 2012). CHEATING: Gender differences in reactions to discovery of a partner's cheating. Poster, Southern Sociological Society, New Orleans, LA.

Brook, H. (2015). Bros before ho(mo)s: Hollywood bromance and the limits of heterodoxy. *Men and Masculinities, 18:* 249–266.

Bulanda, J. R. (2011). Gender, marital power, and marital quality in later life. *Journal of Women and Aging, 23:* 3–22.

Clemans, K. H., & J. A. Graber. (2016). Young adolescents' gender, ethnicity, and popularity based social schemas of aggressive behavior. *Youth and Society, 48:* 303–317.

Craig, L., & K. Mullan. (2010). Parenthood, gender and work-family time in the United States, Australia, Italy, France, and Denmark. *Journal of Marriage and Family, 72:* 1344–1361.

DeMaris, A., L. A. Sanchez, & K. Knivickas. (2012). Developmental patterns in marital satisfaction: Another look at covenant marriage. *Journal of Marriage and Family, 74:* 989–1004.

East, L., D. Jackson, L. O'Brien, & K. Peters. (2011). Condom negotiation: Experiences of sexually active young women. *Journal of Advanced Nursing, 67:* 77–85.

Eubanks Fleming, C. J., & J. V. Córdova. (2012). Predicting relationship help seeking prior to a marriage checkup. *Family Relations, 61:* 90–100.

Fernandez-Cornejo, J. A., L. Escot, J. Kabubo-Mariara, B. Kinyanjui Kinuthia, G. B. Eydal, & T. Bjarnason. (2016). Gender differences in young adults' inclination to sacrifice career opportunities in the future for family reasons: Comparative study with university students from Nairobi, Madrid, and Reykjavik. *Journal of Youth Studies, 19:* 457–482.

Flynn, M. A., C. M. Craig, C. N. Anderson, & K. J. Holody. (2016). Objectification in popular music lyrics: An examination of gender and genre differences. *SexRoles, 75:* 164–176.

Garfield, R. (2010). Male emotional intimacy: How therapeutic men's groups can enhance couples therapy. *Family Process, 49:* 109–122.

Gerding, A., & N. Signorielli. (2014). Gender roles in tween television programming: A content analysis of two genres. *Sex Roles, 70:* 43–56.

Haag. P. (2011). *Marriage confidential.* New York: Harper Collins.

Hall, S., & D. Knox. (2016). Relationship and sexual behaviors of a sample of 2,388 undergraduate males and 7,586 undergraduate females. Unpublished data collected for this text. Department of Family and Consumer Sciences, Ball State University and Department of Sociology, East Carolina University.

Jasper, M. (March 27, 2015). The influence of pop songs on the promotion of rape culture and sexism. Poster, Annual Meeting of the Southern Sociological Society, New Orleans, LA.

Kohlberg, L. (1966). A cognitive-developmental analysis of children's sex-role concepts and attitudes. In E. E. Macoby (Ed.), *The development of sex differences.* Stanford, CA: Stanford University Press.

———. (1969). State and sequence: The cognitive developmental approach to socialization. In D. A. Goslin (Ed.), *Handbook of socialization theory and research* (pp. 347–480). Chicago: Rand McNally.

Krisch, A. C., & S. K. Murnen. (2015). "Hot" girls and "cool dudes": Examining the prevalence of the heterosexual script in American children's television media. *Psychology of Popular Media Culture, 4:* 18–30.

Kronz, V. (2016). Women with beards and men with frocks: Gender nonconformity in modern American film. *Sexuality & Culture, 20:* 85–110.

Kuhle, B. X., D. K. Melzer, C. A. Cooper, A. J. Merkle, N. A. Pepe, A. Ribanovic, A. L. Verdesco, & T. L. Wettstein. (2015). The "birds and the bees" differ for boys and girls: Sex differences in the nature of sex talks. *Evolutionary Behavioral Sciences, 9:* 107–115.

Maltby, L E., M. E. L. Hall, T. L. Anderson, & K. Edwards. (2010). Religion and sexism: The moderating role of participant gender. *Sex Roles, 62:* 615–622.

Martin, C. L., R. E. Cook, & N. C. Z. Andrews. (March 2016). Reviving androgyny: A modern day perspective on flexibility of gender identity and behavior. *Sex Roles,* online. Retrieved from http://link.springer.com.jproxy.lib.ecu.edu/article /10.1007/s11199-016-0602-5/fulltext.html

Mead, M. (1935). *Sex and temperament in three primitive societies.* New York: William Morrow.

Meliksah, D., O. Simsek, & A. Procsa. (2013). I am so happy 'cause my best friend makes me feel unique: Friendship, uniqueness and happiness. *Journal of Human Happiness Studies,14:* 1201–1224.

Michniewicz, K.S., J.A. Vandello, & J. K. Bosson. (2014). Men's (Mis)perceptions of the gender threatening consequences of unemployment. *Sex Roles, 70:* 88–97.

Minnottea, K. L., D. E. Pedersena, S. E. Mannonb, & G. Kiger. (2010). Tending to the emotions of children: Predicting parental performance of emotion work with children. *Marriage & Family Review, 46:* 224–241.

Monro, S. (2000). Theorizing transgender diversity: Towards a social model of health. *Sexual and Relationship Therapy, 15:* 33–42.

Myers, J. (2016). *The future of men: Masculinity in the twenty-first century.* Oakland, CA: Inkshares.

National Science Foundation, National Center for Science and Engineering Statistics. (2015). Doctorate recipients from U.S. universities. 2014. Special Report NSF 16-300. Arlington, VA.

Nelms, B. J., D. Knox, & B. Easterling. (2012). The relationship talk: Assessing partner commitment. *College Student Journal, 46:* 178–182.

Pew Research Center. (2012). A gender reversal on career trends. Young women now top young men in valuing a high-paying career. Retrieved April 19 from http://pewresearch.org /pubs/2248/gender-jobs-women-men-career -family-educational-attainment-labor-force -participation?src=prc-newsletter

———. (2015). America's changing religious landscape. Retrieved from http://www.pewforum .org/2015/05/12/americas-changing-religious -landscape/

Prickett, K., A. Martin-Storey, & R. Crosnoe. (2015). A research not on time with children in different and same sex two parent families. *Demography, 52:* 905–918.

Proquest Statistical Abstract of the United States, 2016, online ed. Washington, DC: U.S. Bureau of the Census.

Senden, M. G., S. Sikstrom, & T. Lindholm. (2015). "She" and "He" in news media messages: Pronoun use reflects gender biases in semantic contexts. *Sex Roles, 72:* 40–49.

Sherman, A. M., & E. L. Zurbriggen. (2014). "Boys can be anything": Effect of Barbie play on girls' career cognitions. *Sex Roles, 70:* 195–208

Swanson, A. (June 4, 2015). The number of Fortune 500 companies led by women is at an all-time high: 5 percent. *The Washington Post.* Retrieved from https://www.washingtonpost .com/news/wonk/wp/2015/06/04/the-number -of-fortune-500-companies-led-by-women-is -at-an-all-time-high-5-percent/

Way, N. (2013). Boys' friendships during adolescence: Intimacy, desire, and loss. *Journal of Research on Adolescence, 23:* 201–213.

Weisgram, E. S., R. S. Bigler, & L. S. Liben. (2010). Gender, values, and occupational interests among children, adolescents, and adults. *Child Development, 81:* 778–796.

Chapter 4

Abowitz, D., D. Knox, & K. Berner. (March 2011). Traditional and non-traditional husband preference among college women. Annual Meeting of the Eastern Sociological Society, Philadelphia, PA.

Alford, J. J., P. K. Hatemi, J. R. Hibbing, N. G. Martin, & L. J. Eaves. (2011). The politics of mate choice. *The Journal of Politics, 73:* 362–379.

Allendorf, K. (2013). Schemas of marital change: From arranged marriages to eloping for love. *Journal of Marriage and Family, 75:* 453–469.

Barber, L. L., & M. L. Cooper. (2014). Rebound sex: Sexual motives and behaviors following a relationship breakup. *Archives of Sexual Behavior, 43*: 251–265.

Blomquist, B. A., & T. A. Giuliano. (2012). Do you love me, too? Perceptions of responses to "I love you." *North American Journal of Psychology, 14*: 407–418.

Boutwell, B. B., J. C. Barnes, & K. M. Beaver. (2015). When love dies: Further elucidating the existence of a mate ejection module. *Review of General Psychology, 19*: 30–38.

Bradford, K., W. Stewart, B. Higginbotham, L. Skogrand, & C. Broadbent. (November 1, 2012). Validating the Relationship Knowledge Questionnaire. Poster, Annual Meeting of the National Council on Family Relations. Phoenix, AZ.

Bredow, C. A., T. L. Huston, & G. Noval. (2011). Market value, quality of the pool of potential mates, and singles, confidence about marrying. *Personal Relationships, 18*: 39–57

Burr, B. K, J. Viera, B. Dial, H. Fields, K. Davis, & D. Hubler. (November 18, 2011). Influences of personality on relationship satisfaction through stress. Poster, Annual Meeting of National Council on Family Relations, Orlando, FL.

Carter, C. S., & S. W. Porges. (2013). The biochemistry of love: An oxytocin hypothesis. *Science & Society, 14*: 12–16.

Carter, G. L., A. C. Campbell, & S. Muncer. (2014). The dark triad personality: Attractiveness to women. *Personality and Individual Differences, 56*: 57–61.

Chaney, C., & K. Marsh. (2009). Factors that facilitate relationship entry among married and cohabiting African Americans. *Marriage & Family Review, 45*: 26–51.

Chapman, G. (2010). *The five love languages: The secret to love that lasts.* Chicago: Northfield Publishing.

Diamond, L. M. (2003). What does sexual orientation orient? A biobehavioral model distinguishing romantic love and sexual desire. *Psychological Review, 110*: 173–192.

Dijkstra, P., D. P. H. Barelds, H. A. K. Groothof, S. Ronner, & A. P. Nautal. (2012). Partner preferences of the intellectually gifted. *Marriage & Family Review, 48*: 96–108.

Dubbs, S. L., & A. P. Buunk. (2010). Sex differences in parental preferences over a child's mate choice: A daughter's perspective. *Journal of Social and Personal Relationships, 27*: 1051–1059.

Edwards, T. M. (August 28, 2000). Flying solo. *Time*, pp. 47–53.

Elliott, L., B. Easterling, & D. Knox. (March 2012). Taking chances in romantic relationships. Poster, Annual Meeting of the Southern Sociological Society, New Orleans, LA.

Erichsen, K., P. Dignam, & D. Knox. (April 2016) From hookup to husband: Transitioning a casual to a committed relationship. Paper, Annual Meeting of the Southern Sociological Society, Atlanta, GA.

Fehr, B., C. Harasymchuk, & S. Sprecher. (2014). Compassionate love in romantic relationships: A review of some new findings. *Journal of Social and Personal Relationships, 31*: 575–600.

Finkenauer, C. (2010). Although it helps, love is not all you need: How Caryl Rusbult made me discover what relationships are all about. *Personal Relationships, 17*: 161–163.

Fisher, H. E., L. L. Brown, A. Aron, G. Strong, & D. Mashek. (2010). Reward, addiction, and emotion regulation systems associated with rejection in love. *Journal of Neurophysiology, 104*: 51–60.

Fisher, M. L., & C. Salmon. (2013). Mom, dad, meet my mate: An evolutionary perspective on the introduction of parents and mates. *Journal of Family Studies, 19*: 99–107.

Foster, J. D. (2008). Incorporating personality into the investment model: Probing commitment processes across individual differences in narcissism. *Journal of Social and Personal Relationships, 25*: 211–223.

Freud, S. (1905/1938). Three contributions to the theory of sex. In A. A. Brill (Ed.), *The basic writings of Sigmund Freud.* New York: Random House.

Frye-Cox, N. (November 2012). Alexithymia and marital quality: The mediating role of loneliness. Paper, National Council on Family Relations, Phoenix, AZ.

Gonzaga, G. C., S. Carter, & J. Galen Buckwalter. (2010). Assortative mating, convergence, and satisfaction in married couples. *Personal Relationships, 17*: 634–644.

Greitemeyer, T. (2010). Effects of reciprocity on attraction: The role of a partner's physical attractiveness. *Personal Relationships, 17*: 317–330.

Haandrikman, K. (2011). Spatial homogamy: The geographical dimensions of partner choice. *Journal of Economic and Social Geography, 102*: 100–110.

Hall, S., & D. Knox. (2016). Relationship and sexual behaviors of a sample of 9,677 university students. Unpublished data collected for this text. Department of Family and Consumer Sciences, Ball State University and Department of Sociology, East Carolina University.

———. (2017). Relationship power in emerging adults' romantic relationships. Unpublished manuscript.

Harris, V. W., K. Bedard, D. Moen, & P. Alvarez-Perez. (2016). The role of friendship: Trust and love in happy German marriages. *Marriage and Family Review, 52*: 262–304.

Huston, T. L., J. P. Caughlin, R. M. Houts, S. E. Smith, & L. J. George. (2001). The connubial crucible: Newlywed years as predictors of marital delight, distress, and divorce. *Journal of Personality and Social Psychology, 80*: 237–252.

Jackson, J. (November 2011). Premarital counseling: An evidence-informed treatment protocol. Presentation, Annual Meeting of the National Council on Family Relations, Orlando, FL.

Jenks, R. J. (2014). An on-line survey comparing swingers and polyamorists. *Electronic Journal of Human Sexuality, 17*: July 7.

Johnson, M. D., & J. R. Anderson. (November 2011). The longitudinal association of marital confidence, time spent together and marital satisfaction. Presentation, National Council on Family Relationship, Orlando, FL.

Kem, J. (2010). Fatal lovesickness in Marguerite de Navarre's Heptaméron. *Sixteenth Century Journal, 41*: 355–370.

Kennedy, D. P., J. S. Tucker, M. S. Pollard, M. Go, & H. D. Green. (2011). Adolescent romantic relationships and change in smoking status. *Addictive Behaviors, 36*: 320–326.

Lambert, N. M., S. Negash, T. F. Stillman, S. B. Olmstead, & F. D. Fincham. (2012). A love that doesn't last: Pornography consumption and weakened commitment to one's romantic partner. *Journal of Social & Clinical Psychology, 31*: 410–438.

Langeslag, S. J. E., P. Muris, & I. H. A. Fraken. (2013). Measuring romantic love: Psychometric properties of the infatuation and attachment scales. *Journal of Sex Research, 50*: 739–774.

Lee, J. A. (1973). *The colors of love: An exploration of the ways of loving.* Don Mills, Ontario: New Press.

———. (1988). Love-styles. In R. Sternberg & M. Barnes (Eds.), *The psychology of love* (pp. 38–67). New Haven, CN: Yale University Press.

Lenhart, A. (2012). Teens, smartphones & texting. Retrieved July 26, 2015, from http://www.pewinternet.org/2012/03/19/teens-smartphones-texting/

Leno, J. (1996). *Leading with my chin.* New York: Harper Collins.

Maier, T. (2009). *Masters of Sex.* New York: Perseus Books.

Markman, H. J., G. K. Rhoades, S. M. Stanley, E. P. Ragan, & S. W. Whitton. (2010). The premarital communication roots of marital distress and divorce: The first five years of marriage. *Journal of Family Psychology, 24*: 289–298.

McClure, M. J., & J. E. Lydon. (2014). Anxiety doesn't become you: How attachment anxiety compromises relational opportunities. *Journal of Personality and Social Psychology, 106*: 89–111.

Meltzer, A. L., & J. K. McNulty. (2014). "Tell me I'm sexy . . . and otherwise valuable": Body valuation and relationship satisfaction. *Personal Relationships, 21*: 68–87.

Milne, C. (2015). Texting etiquette explained. Retrieved July 23, 2015, from http://www.match.com/magazine/article/6802/Texting-Etiquette-Explained/

Neto, F. (2012). Perceptions of love and sex across the adult life span. *Journal of Social and Personal Relationships,* September 29: 760–775.

Northrup, J., & J. Smith. (2016). Effects of Facebook maintenance behaviors on partners' experience of love. *Contemporary Family Therapy: An International Journal, 38*: 245–253.

Oberbeek, G., S. A. Nelemans, J. Karremans, & R. C. M. E. Engels. (2013). The malleability of mate selection in speed-dating events. *Archives of Sexual Behavior, 42*: 1163–1171.

Ozay, B., D. Knox, & B. Easterling. (March 2012). You're dating who? Parental attitudes toward interracial dating. Poster, Annual Meeting of the Southern Sociological Society, New Orleans, LA.

Pande, R. (2016). Becoming modern: British-Indian discourses of arranged marriages. *Social & Cultural Geography, 17*: 380–400.

Perilloux, C., D. S. Fleischman, & D. M. Buss. (2011). Meet the parents: Parent-offspring convergence and divergence in mate preferences. *Personality & Individual Differences, 50*: 253–258.

Pew Research Center. (2011). The burden of student debt. Retrieved from http://pewresearch.org/databank/dailynumber/?NumberID=1257

———. (2015). U.S. smartphone use. Retrieved from Pew Research Center at http://www.pewinternet.org/2015/04/01/us-smartphone-use-in-2015/

Proquest Statistical Abstract of the United States, 2016, online ed. Washington, DC: U.S. Bureau of the Census.

Przbylski, A., & Weinstein, N. (2012). Can you connect with me now? How the presence of mobile communication technology influences face-to-face conversation quality. *Journal of Social and Personal Relationships.* doi: 10.1177/0265407512453827

Randler, C., & S. Kretz. (2011). Assortative mating in morningness-eveningness. *International Journal of Psychology, 46:* 91–96.

Rauer, A. J., A. Sabey, & J. F. Jensen. (2014). Growing old together: Compassionate love and health in older adulthood. *Journal of Social and Personal Relationships, 31:* 677–696.

Reis, H. T., M. R. Maniaci, & R. D. Rogge. (2014). The expression of compassionate love in everyday compassionate acts. *Journal of Social and Personal Relationships, 31:* 651–676.

Reiss, I. L. (1960). Toward a sociology of the heterosexual love relationship. *Journal of Marriage and Family Living, 22:* 139–145.

Reynaud, M., L. Blecha, & A. Benyamina. (2011). Is love passion an addictive disorder? *American Journal of Drug & Alcohol Abuse, 36:* 261–267.

Riela, S., G. Rodriguez, A. Aron, X. Xu, & B. P. Acevedo. (2010). Experiences of falling in love: Investigating culture, ethnicity, gender, and speed. *Journal of Social and Personal Relationships, 27:* 473–493.

Robert, J., & B. H. Williams. (2012). Cellphone addiction is an increasingly realistic possibility. Baylor study of college students reveals. Retrieved July 22, 2015, from http://www.baylor.edu/mediacommunications/news.php?action=story&story=145864

Ross, C. B. (March 24, 2006). An exploration of eight dimensions of self-disclosure on relationship. Paper, Southern Sociological Society, New Orleans, LA.

Sack, K. (August 12, 2008). Health benefits inspire rush to marry, or divorce. *The New York Times.*

Scheff, E. (2014). *The polyamorists next door.* Lanham, MD: Rowman & Littlefield.

Sprecher, S. (2002). Sexual satisfaction in premarital relationships: Associations with satisfaction, love, commitment, and stability. *Journal of Sex Research, 39:* 190–196.

Stanik, C. E., S. M. McHale, & A. C. Couter. (2013). Gender dynamics predict changes in marital love among African-American couples. *Journal of Marriage and Family, 75:* 795–798.

Stanley, S. M., E. P. Ragan, G. K. Rhoades, & H. J. Markman. (2012). Examining changes in relationship adjustment and life satisfaction in marriage. *Journal of Family Psychology, 26:* 165–170.

Stanton, S.C. E., & L. Campbell. (2014). Psychological and physiological predictors of health in romantic relationships: An attachment perspective. *Journal of Personality, 82:* 528–538.

Starr, L. R., J. Davila, C. B. Stroud, P. C. Clara Li, A. Yoneda, R. Hershenberg, & M. Ramsay Miller. (2012). Love hurts (in more ways than one): Specificity of psychological symptoms as predictors and consequences of romantic activity among early adolescent girls. *Journal of Clinical Psychology, 68:* 373–381.

Statistical Abstract of the United States, 2012–2013, 131th ed. Washington, DC: U.S. Bureau of the Census.

Sternberg, R. J. (1986). A triangular theory of love. *Psychological Review, 93:*119–135.

Stinehart, M. A., D. A. Scott, & H. G. Barfield. (2012). Reactive attachment disorder in adopted and foster care children: Implications for mental health professionals. *The Family Journal: Counseling and Therapy for Couples and Families, 20:* 355–360.

Toufexis, A. (February 15, 1993). The right chemistry. *Time,* p. 49–51.

Tsunokai, G. T., & A. R. McGrath. (2011). Baby boomers and beyond: Crossing racial boundaries in search for love. *Journal of Aging Studies, 25:* 285–294.

Turkle, S. (2011). Along together: Why we expect more from technology and less from each other. New York: Basic Books.

Tzeng, O. C. S., K. Wooldridge, & K. Campbell. (2003). Faith love: A psychological construct in intimate relations. *Journal of the Indiana Academy of the Social Sciences, 7:* 11–20.

Vedes, A., P. Hilpert, F. W. Nussbeck, A. K. Randall, G. Bodenmann, & W. R. Lind. (2016). Love styles, coping and relationship satisfaction: A dyadic approach. *Personal Relationships, 23:* 84–97.

Vennum, A. (2011). Understanding young adult cyclical relationships. Dissertation, Florida State University, College of Home Economics.

Warren, J. T., S. M. Harvey, & C. R. Agnew. (2012). One love: Explicit monogamy agreements among heterosexual young couples at increased risk of sexually transmitted infections. *Journal of Sex Research, 49:* 282–289.

Watkins, S., & S. D. Boon. (2016). Expectations regarding fidelity in dating relationships. *Journal of Social and Personal Relationships, 33:* 237–256.

Yodanis, C., S. Lauer, & R. Ota. (2012). Interethnic romantic relationships: Enacting affiliative ethnic identities. *Journal of Marriage and Family, 74:* 1021–1037.

Yoo, H. C., M. F. Steger, & R. M. Lee. (2010). Validation of the subtle and blatant racism scale for Asian American college students (SABR-A²). *Cultural Diversity and Ethnic Minority Psychology, 16:* 323–334.

Chapter 5

Allison, J. (2012). Netiquette 101. *Huffington Post.* Retrieved January 6, 2016, from http://www.huffingtonpost.com/julia-allison/internet-etiquette_b_1238286.html

Baldassar, L. (2016). De-demonizing distance in mobile family lives: Co-presence, care circulation and polymedia as vibrant matter. *Global Networks, 16:* 145–163.

Bauerlein, M. (2010). Literary learning in the hyperdigital age. *Futurist, 44:* 24–25.

Bergdall, A. R., J. M. Kraft, K. Andes, M. Carter, K. Hatfield-Timajchy, & L. Hock-long. (2012). Love and hooking up in the new millennium: Communication technology and relationships among urban African American and Puerto Rican young adults. *Journal of Sex Research, 49:* 570–582.

Binsahl, H., S. Chang, & R. Bosua. (2015). Identify and belonging: Saudi female international students and their use of social networking sites. *Crossings: Journal of Migration & Culture, 6:* 81–102.

Block, D. G. (2014). The sound of one phone ringing. *Teaching Music, 4:* 50.

Burke-Winkelman, S., K. Vail-Smith, J. Brinkley, & D. Knox. (2014). Sexting on the college campus. *Electronic Journal of Human Sexuality, 17* (February 3).

Caughlin, J. P., & E. D. Bassinger. (2015). Completely open and honest communication: Is this really what we want? *Family Focus,* Issue FF64. Minneapolis, MN: National Council on Family Relations.

Cohen, M. (2016). It's not you, It's men. . . . No, Actually it's you: Perceptions of what makes a first date successful or not. *Sexuality & Culture, 20:* 173–191.

Coyne, S. M., L. Stockdale, D. Busby, B. Iverson, & D. M. Grant. (2011). "I luv u :)!": A descriptive study of the media use of individuals in romantic relationships. *Family Relations, 60:* 150–162.

Dir, A. L., A. Coskunpinar, J. L. Steiner, & M. A. Cyders. (2013). Understanding differences in sexting behaviors across gender, relationship status, and sexual identity, and the role of expectancies in sexting. *Cyberpsychology, Behavior, and Social Networking, 16:* 568–574.

Dvorak, J. (January, 2012). Losing the culture war to the cell phone. *PC Magazine,* p. 1-1.

Easterling, B., D. Knox, & A. Brackett. (2012). Secrets in romantic relationships: Does sexual orientation matter? *Journal of GLBT Family Studies, 8:* 198–210.

Forgays, D. K., I. Hyman, & J. Shreiber. (2014). Texting everywhere for everything: Gender and the age differences in cell phone etiquette and use. *Computers in Human Behavior, 31:* 314–321.

Frisby, B. N., & M. Booth-Butterfield. (2015). The "how" and "why" of flirtatious communication between marital partners. *Communication Quarterly, 60:* 465–480.

Frye, N. E. (2011). Responding to problems: The roles of severity and barriers. *Personal Relationships, 18:* 471–486.

Furukawa, R., & M. Driessnack. (2013). Video-mediated communication to support distant family connectedness. *Clinical Nursing Research, 22:* 82–94.

Ganong, L. H., M. Coleman, R. Feistman, T. Jamison, & M. S. Markham. (November 18, 2011). Communication technology and post-divorce co-parenting. Poster, Annual Meeting of the National Council on Family Relations, Orlando, FL.

Garfield, R. (2010). Male emotional intimacy: How therapeutic men's groups can enhance couples therapy. *Family Process, 49:* 109–122.

Gershon, I. (2010). *The breakup 2.0.* New York: Cornell University Press,

Gibbs, N. (August 27, 2012). Your life is fully mobile: Time Mobility Survey. *Time Magazine,* p. 32 and following.

Gottman, J.. (1994). *Why marriages succeed or fail.* New York: Simon & Schuster.

Hall, S., & D. Knox. (2016a). Relationship and sexual behaviors of a sample of 9,410 university students. Unpublished data collected for this text. Department of Family and Consumer Sciences, Ball State University and Department of Sociology, East Carolina University.

———. (2016b). Relationship power in emerging adults' romantic relationships. Unpublished manuscript.

Hiew, D. N., W. K. Halford, & F. J. R. van de Vijver. (2016). Communication and relationship satisfaction in Chinese, Western and intercultural

Chinese-Western couples. *Journal of Family Psychology, 30:* 193–202.

Hill, E. W. (2010). Discovering forgiveness through empathy: Implications for couple and family therapy. *Journal of Family Therapy, 32:* 169–185.

Huang, H., & L. Leung. (2010). Instant messaging addiction among teenagers in China: Shyness, alienation and academic performance decrement. *CyberPsychology & Behavior, 12:* 675–679.

Impett, E. A., J. B. Breines, & A. Strachman. (2010). Keeping it real: Young adult women's authenticity in relationships and daily condom use. *Personal Relationships, 17:* 573–584.

Kelley, K. (2010). *Oprah: A biography.* New York: Crown Publishers.

Kimmes, J. G., A. B. Edwards, J. L. Wetchler, & J. Bercik. (June 18, 2014). Self and other ratings of dyadic empathy as predictors of relationship satisfaction. *The American Journal of Family Therapy,* online.

King, A. L. S., A. M. Valenca, A. C. O. Silva, T. Baczynski, M. R. Carvalho, & A. E. Nardi. (2013). Nomophobia: Dependency on virtual environments or social phobia? *Computers in Human Behavior, 29:* 140–144.

Knudson-Martin, C., D. Huenergardt, K. Lafontant, L. Bishop, J. Schaepper, & M. Wells. (2015). Competencies for addressing gender and power in couple therapy: A socioemotional approach. *Journal of Marital & Family Therapy, 41:* 205–220.

Kurdek, L. A. (1994). Areas of conflict for gay, lesbian, and heterosexual couples: What couples argue about influences relationship satisfaction. *Journal of Marriage and Family, 56:* 923–934.

———. (1995). Predicting change in marital satisfaction from husbands' and wives' conflict resolution styles. *Journal of Marriage and Family, 57:* 153–164.

Lavner, J. A., & T. N. Bradbury. (2010). Patterns of change in marital satisfaction over the newlywed years. *Journal of Marriage and Family, 72:* 1171–1187.

Lund, R., U. Christensen, C. J. Nilsson, M. Kriegbaum, & N. H. Rod. (May 2014). Stressful social relations and mortality: A prospective cohort study. *Journal of Epidemiology and Community Health,* online.

Marano, H. E. (January/February 1992). The reinvention of marriage. *Psychology Today,* p. 49.

Markman, H. J., G. K. Rhoades, S. M. Stanley, E. P. Ragan, & S. W. Whitton. (2010a). The premarital communication roots of marital distress and divorce: The first five years of marriage. *Journal of Family Psychology, 24:* 289–298.

Markman, H. J., S. M. Stanley, & S. L. Blumberg. (2010b). *Fighting for your marriage,* 3rd ed. San Francisco: Jossey-Bass.

Marshall, T. C., K. Chuong, & A. Aikawa. (2011). Day-to-day experiences of amae in Japanese romantic relationships. *Asian Journal of Social Psychology, 14:* 26–35.

Merolla, A. J., & S. Zhang. (2011). In the wake of transgressions: Examining forgiveness communication in personal relationships. *Personal Relationships, 18:* 79–95.

Norton, A. M., & J. Baptist. (November 2012). Couple boundaries for social networking: Impact of trust and satisfaction. Paper, National Council on Family Relations, Phoenix, AZ.

Pettigrew, J. (2009). Text messaging and connectedness within close interpersonal relationships. *Marriage & Family Review, 45:* 697–716.

Purkett, T. (Fall 2014). Sexually transmitted infections. Presented to Courtship and Marriage class, Department of Sociology, East Carolina University.

Rainie, L., & K. Zickuhr. (August 2015). Americans' views on mobile etiquette. Pew Research Center. Retrieved from http://www.pewinternet.org/2015/08/26/americans-views-on-mobile-etiquette/

Rappleyea, D., A. C. Taylor, & X. Fang. (2014). Gender differences in communication technology among emerging adults in the initiation of dating relationships. *Marriage and Family Review, 50:* 269–284.

Rosenfeld, B., & S. A. O'Connor-Petruso. (2014). East vs. west: A comparison of mobile phone use by Chinese and American college students. *College Student Journal, 48:* 312–321.

Schade, L. C., J. Sandberg, R. Bean, D. Busby, & S. Coyne. (2013). Using technology to connect in romantic relationships: Effects on attachment, relationship satisfaction, and stability in emerging adults. *Journal of Couple & Relationship Therapy: Innovations in Clinical and Educational Interventions, 12:* 314–338.

Simpson, M. (2010). Tech etiquette is just common sense. *Common Ground Journal, 7:* 81–88. Retrieved January 18, 2015, from http://edcot.com/ecampus/elearning/Tech%20Etiquette%20is%20Just%20Common%20Sense.pdf

South, S. C., B. D. Doss, & A. Christensen. (2010). Through the eyes of the beholder: The mediating role of relationship acceptance in the impact of partner behavior. *Family Relations, 59:* 611–622.

Strassberg, D. S., R. K. McKinnon, M. A. Sustaita, & J. Rullo. (2013). Sexting by high school students: An exploratory and descriptive study. *Archives of Sexual Behavior, 42:* 15–21.

Strickler, B. L., & J. D. Hans. (November 3–5, 2010). Defining infidelity and identifying cheaters: An inductive approach with a factorial design. Poster, Annual Meeting of the National Council on Family Relations, Minneapolis, MN.

Su, H. (2016). Constant connection as the media condition of love: Where bonds become bondage. *Media, Culture & Society, 38:* 232–247.

Tan, R., N. C. Overall, & J. K. Taylor. (2012). Let's talk about us: Attachment, relationship-focused disclosure, and relationship quality. *Personal Relationships, 19:* 521–534.

Tannen, D. (1990). *You just don't understand: Women and men in conversation.* London: Virago.

———. (2006). *You're wearing that? Understanding mothers and daughters in conversation.* New York: Random House.

Taylor, A. C., D. L. Rappelea, X. Fang, & D. Cannon. (2013). Emerging adults' perceptions of acceptable behaviors prior to forming a committed, dating relationship. *Journal of Adult Development, 20:* 173–184.

Vail-Smith, K., L. MacKenzie, & D. Knox. (2010). The illusion of safety in "monogamous" undergraduates. *American Journal of Health Behavior, 34:* 15–20.

Velotti, P., S. Balzarotti, S. Tagliabue, T. English, G. C. Zavattini, & J. J. Gross. (2016). Emotional suppression in early marriage. *Journal of Social & Personal Relationships, 33:* 277–302.

Waller, W., & R. Hill. (1951). *The family: A dynamic interpretation.* New York: Holt, Rinehart and Winston.

Walsh, S. (2013). Match's 2012 singles in America survey. Retrieved from http://www.hookingupsmart.com/2013/02/07/hookinguprealities/matchs-2012-singles-in-america-survey/

Webley, K. (September 17, 2012). Cheating Harvard. *Time,* p. 22.

White, S. S., N. El-Bassel, L. Gilbert, E. Wu, & M. Chang. (2010). Lack of awareness of partner STD risk among heterosexual couples. *Perspectives on Sexual & Reproductive Health, 42:* 49–55.

Woszidlo, A., & C. Segrin. (2013). Negative affectivity and educational attainment as predictors of newlyweds' problem solving communication and marital quality. *Journal of Psychology, 147:* 49–73.

Chapter 6

Bodkin, H. (June 9, 2016). Sex robots to storm into the British bedroom within ten years. *The Telegraph News.* Retrieved from http://www.telegraph.co.uk/news/2016/06/09/sex-robots-to-storm-into-the-british-bedroom-within-ten-years/

Brenot, P. S., & S. Wunsch. (2016). Sexual needs of women in response to the needs of their partners. *Sexologies: European Journal of Sexology and Sexual Health, 25:* 20–23.

Brown, C. C., J. S. Carroll, D. M. Busby, B. J. Willoughby, & RELATE Institute Brigham Young University. (November 2013). The pornography gap: Differences in men's and women's pornography patterns in couple relationships. Poster, Annual Meeting of the National Council on Family Relations, San Antonio, TX. Contact first author at cameronbrownbyu@gmail.com for more information.

Byers, E. S., L. F. O'Sullivan, & L. A. Brotto. (2016). Time out from sex or romance: Sexually experienced adolescents' decisions to purposefully avoid sexual activity or romantic relationships. *Journal of Youth and Adolescence, 45:* 831–845.

Cooper, A., & B. Gordon (2015). Young New Zealand woman's sexual decision making in casual sex situations: A qualitative study. *Canadian Journal of Human Sexuality, 24:* 69–76.

DeLamater, J., & M. Hasday. (2007). The sociology of sexuality. In Clifton D. Bryant & Dennis L. Peck (Eds.), *21st century sociology: A reference handbook* (pp. 254–264). Thousand Oaks, CA: Sage.

Dosch, A., S. Belayachi, & M. Van der Linden. (2016). Implicit and explicit sexual attitudes: How are they related to sexual desire and sexual satisfaction? *Journal of Sex Research, 53:* 251–264.

Dotson-Blake, K. P., D. Knox, & M. Zusman. (2012). Exploring social sexual scripts related to oral sex: A profile of college student perceptions. *The Professional Counselor, 2:* 1–11. Online journal at http://tpcjournal.nbcc.org/

Emmerink, P. M., I. Vanwesenbeeck, R. J. J. M. Vanden Eijinden, & T. F. M. ter Bogt. (2016). Psychological correlates of sexual double standard endorsement in adolescent sexuality. *Journal of Sex Research, 53:* 286–297.

Fahs, B. (May 30, 2016). Methodological mishaps and slippery subjects: Stories of first sex, oral sex, and sexual trauma in qualitative sex research. *Qualitative Psychology,* online.

Fallis, E. E., U. S. Rehman, E. Z. Woody, & C. Purdon. (April 14, 2016). The longitudinal association of relationship satisfaction and sexual satisfaction in long-term relationships. *Journal of Family Psychology*, online.

Fennell, J. (March 18, 2014) Dungeon rules: Normalizing kinky desires. Presentation to Sociology of Human Sexuality class, Department of Sociology, East Carolina University, Greenville, NC.

Fielder, R. L., J. L. Walsh, K. B. Carey, & M. P. Carey. (2014). Sexual hookups and adverse health outcomes: A longitudinal study of first year college women. *The Journal of Sex Research, 51:* 131–144.

Fulle, A., D. Knox, & J. Chang. (2016). Female sexual hedonism: Navigating stigma. *College Student Journal, 50:* 29–34.

Galinsky, A. M., & Sorenstein, F. L. (2013). Relationship commitment, perceived equity, and sexual enjoyment among young adults in the United States. *Archives of Sexual Behavior, 42:* 93–104.

Hackathorn, J., B. Ashdown, & S. Rife. 2016. The Sacred Bed: Sex guilt mediates religiosity and satisfaction for unmarried people. *Sexuality and Culture, 20:* 153–172.

Hall, S., & D. Knox. (2016). Relationship and sexual behaviors of a sample of 9,948 university students. Unpublished data collected from 2009 to 2016 for this text. Department of Family and Consumer Sciences, Ball State University and Department of Sociology, East Carolina University.

Hawes, Z. C., K. Wellings, & J. Stephenson. (2010). First heterosexual intercourse in the United Kingdom: A review of the literature. *Journal of Sex Research, 47:* 137–152.

Hendrickx, L. G., & P. Enzlin. (2014). Associated distress in heterosexual men and women: Results from an internet survey in Flanders. *The Journal of Sex Research, 51:* 1–12.

Herbenick, D., et al. (2010). Sexual behavior in the United States: Results from a national probability sample of men and women ages 14–94. *Journal of Sexual Medicine, 7:* 255–265.

Herbenick, D., M. Reece, V. Schick, K. N. Jozkowski, S. E. Middelstadt, S. A. Sanders, B. S. Dodge, A. Ghassemi, & J. D. Fortenberry. (2011). Beliefs about women's vibrator use: Results from a nationally representative probability survey in the United States. *Journal of Sex & Marital Therapy, 37:* 329–345.

Hill, C. A. (2016) Implicit and explicit sexual motives as related, but distinct characteristics. *Basic & Applied Social Psychology, 38:* 59–88.

Horowitz, A. D., & L. Spicer. (2013). Definitions among heterosexual and lesbian emerging adults in the U.K. *Journal of Sex Research, 50:* 139–150.

Humphreys, T. P. (2013). Cognitive frameworks of virginity and first intercourse. *Journal of Sex Research,50:* 664–675.

Jolly, D. H., L. Alston, M. Hawley, M. P. Mueller, M. Chen, E. Okumu, N. T. Eley, K. M. MacQueen, & T. Stancil. (2016). Concurrency and other sexual risk behaviors among Black young adults in a Southeastern city. *AIDS Education & Prevention, 28:* 59–76.

Jones, D. N. (2016). The "Chasing Amy" bias in past sexual experiences: Men can change, women cannot. *Sexuality & Culture, 20:* 24–37.

Kimberly, C. (2016). Permission to cheat: Ethnography of a swingers' convention. *Sexuality & Culture, 20:* 56–68.

Kimberly, C., & J. Hans. (November 2012). Sexual self-disclosure and communication among swinger couples. Poster, National Council on Family Relations, Phoenix, AZ.

Lee, J. T., C. L. Lin, G. H. Wan, & C. C. Liang. (2010). Sexual positions and sexual satisfaction of pregnant women. *Journal of Sex & Marital Therapy, 36:* 408–420.

Lehmiller, J. J., L. E. VanderDrift, & J. R. Kelly. (2014). Sexual communication, satisfaction, and condom use behavior in friends with benefits and romantic partners. *Journal of Sex Research, 51:*74–85.

Luscombe, B. (April 15, 2016). Porn: Why young men who grew up with Internet porn are becoming advocates for turning it off. *Time Magazine*, pp. 40–47.

Masters, W. H., & V. E. Johnson. (1970). *Human sexual inadequacy.* Boston: Little, Brown.

McCabe, M. P., & D. L. Goldhammer. (2012). Demographic and psychological factors related to sexual desire among heterosexual women in a relationship. *Journal of Sex Research, 49:* 78–87.

Michael, R. T., J. H. Gagnon, E. O. Laumann, & G. Kolata. (1994). *Sex in America: A definitive survey.* Boston: Little, Brown.

Miller, S., A. Taylor, & D. Rappleyea. (April 4–8, 2011). The influence of religion on young adult's attitudes of dating events. Poster, Fifth Annual Research & Creative Achievement Week, East Carolina University.

Mintz, L. (2017). *Cliteracy.* New York: Harper One.

Molinares, C., I. Kolobava, & D. Knox. (April 2016). This one's for you: Anal sex as a gift. Poster, Annual Meeting of the Southern Sociological Society, Atlanta, GA.

Mongeau, P. A., K. Knight, J. Williams, J. Eden, & C. Shaw. (2013). Identifying and explicating variation among friends with benefits relationships. *Journal of Sex Research, 50:* 37–47.

Montesi, J., B. Conner, E. Gordon, R. Fauber, K. Kim, & R. Heimberg. (2013). On the relationship among social anxiety, intimacy, sexual communication, and sexual satisfaction in young couples. *Archives of Sexual Behavior, 42:* 81–91.

Morris, H., I. J. Chang, & D. Knox. (April 2016). Threesomes: Data on negotiation and engagement. Poster, Southern Sociological Society, Atlanta, GA.

Muise, A., U. Schimmack, & E. A. Impett. (November 18, 2015). Sexual frequency predicts greater well being, but more is not always better. *Social Psychological and Personality Service*, online.

Nagao, S., K. T. Tai, R. Saigo, M. Kimura, Y. Ozaki, N. Tanaka, H. Kobayashi, & K. Nakajima. (2014). Gaps between actual and desired sex life: Web survey of 5,665 Japanese women. *Journal of Sex & Marital Therapy, 40:* 33–42.

Paik, A., K. J. Sanchagrin, and K. Heimer. (2016). Broken promises: Abstinence pledging and sexual and reproductive health. *Journal of Marriage and Family, 78:* 546–561.

Penhollow, T. M., A. Marx, & M. Young. (March 31, 2010). Impact of recreational sex on sexual satisfaction and leisure satisfaction. *Electronic Journal of Human Sexuality, 13.*

Porter, Nora. (April 2014). Slut-shamming: The double standard on campus. Paper, Annual Meeting of the Southern Sociological Society, Charlotte, NC.

Reece, M., D. Herbenick, B. Dodge, S. A. Sanders, A. Ghassemi, & D. Fortenberry. (2010). Vibrator use among heterosexual men varies by partnership status: Results from a nationally representative study in the United States. *Journal of Sex & Marital Therapy, 36:* 389–407.

Reissing, E. D., H. L. Andruff, & J. J. Wentland. (2012). Looking back: The experience of first sexual intercourse and current sexual adjustment in young heterosexual adults. *Journal of Sex Research, 49:* 27–35.

Sanchez, D. T., J. C. Fetterolf, & L. A. Rudman. (2012). Eroticizing inequality in the United States: The consequences and determinants of traditional gender role adherence in intimate relationships. *Journal of Sex Research, 49:* 168–183.

Sandberg-Thoma, S. E., & C. M. Kamp Dush. (2014). Casual sexual relationships and mental health in adolescence and emerging adulthood. *Journal of Sex Research, 51:* 121–130.

Satinsky, S., & K. N. Jozkowski. (2015). Female sexual subjectivity and verbal consent to receiving oral sex. *The Journal of Sex & Marital Therapy, 41:* 413–426.

Scimeca, G., A. Bruno, G. Pandolfo, U. Mico, V. M. Romeo, E. Abenavoli, A. Schjimmenti, R. Zoccali, & M. R. A. Muscatello. (2013). Alexithymia, negative emotions, and sexual behavior in heterosexual university students from Italy. *Archives of Sexual Behavior, 42:*117–127.

Simms, D., & Byers, E. (2013). Heterosexual daters' sexual initiation behaviors: Use of the theory of planned behavior. *Archives of Sexual Behavior, 42:* 105–116.

Sohn, K. (2016). Men's revealed preferences regarding women's promiscuity. *Personality and Individual Differences, 95:* 140–146.

Sprecher, S. (2014, March 10). Evidence of change in men's versus women's emotional reactions to first sexual intercourse: A 23-year study in a human sexuality course at a midwestern university. *The Journal of Sex Research,* online.

Sprecher, S., & Treger, S. (2015). Virgin college students' reasons for and reactions to their abstinence from sex: Results from a 23-year study at a midwestern U.S. university. *Journal of Sex Research, 52:* 936–948.

Starr, P. (Spring 2016). Polyamory. Presentation, Sociology of Human Sexuality, Department of Sociology, East Carolina University.

Stephenson, K. R., A. H. Rellini, & C. M. Meston. (2013). Relationship satisfaction as a predictor of treatment response during cognitive behavioral sex therapy. *Archives of Sexual Behavior, 42:* 143–152.

Symons, K., H. Vermeersch, & M. Van Houtte. (2014). The emotional experiences of early first intercourse: A multi-method study. *Journal of Adolescent Research, 29:* 533–560.

Trinh, S. L. (2016). Enjoy your sexuality, but do it in secret. *Psychology of Women Quarterly, 40:* 96–107.

True Love Waits. (2016). Retrieved from http://www.lifeway.com/n/Product-Family/True-Love-Waits.

Van de Bongardt, D., E. Reitz, & M. Dekovic. (2016). Indirect over-time relations between parenting and adolescents' sexual behaviors and emotions through global self esteem. *The Journal of Sex Research, 53:* 273–285.

Van den Brink, F., M. A. M. Smeets, D. J. Hessen, J. G. Talens, & L. Woertman. (2013). Body satisfaction and sexual health in Dutch female university students. *Journal of Sex Research, 50:* 786–794.

Vannier, S. A., & L. F. O'Sullivan. (2010). Sex without desire: Characteristics of occasions of sexual compliance in young adults' committed relationships. *Journal of Sex Research, 47:* 429–439.

Vasilenko, S. A., E. S. Lefkowitz, & J. L. Maggs. (2012). Short-term positive and negative consequences of sex based on daily reports among college students. *Journal of Sex Research, 49:* 558–569.

Vazonyi, A. I., & D. D. Jenkins. (2010). Religiosity, self-control, and virginity status in college students from the "Bible belt": A research note. *Journal for the Scientific Study of Sex, 49:* 561–568.

Walsh, S. (2013). Match's 2012 singles in America survey. Retrieved from http://www.hookingupsmart.com/2013/02/07/hookinguprealities/matchs-2012-singles-in-america-survey/

Wester, K. A., & A. E Phoenix. (April 8–12, 2013). Are there really rules and expectations in talking relationships? Gender differences in relationship formation among young adults. Research and Creative Week, East Carolina University.

Wetherill, R. R., D. J. Neal, & K. Fromme. (2010). Parents, peers, and sexual values influence sexual behavior during the transition to college. *Journal Archives of Sexual Behavior, 39:* 682–694.

Woertman, L., & F. Van den Brink. (2012). Body image and female sexual functioning and behavior: A review. *Journal of Sex Research, 49:* 184–211.

Wood, J. R., A. McKay, T. Komarnicky, & R. R. Milhausen. (2016). Was it good for you too? An analysis of gender differences in oral sex practices and pleasure ratings among heterosexual Canadian university students. *Canadian Journal of Human Sexuality, 25:* 21–29.

Wright, P. J., A. K. Randall, & J. G. Hayes. (2012). Predicting the condom assertiveness of collegiate females in the United States from the expanded health belief model. *International Journal of Sexual Health, 24:* 137–153.

Chapter 7

Adolfsen, A., J. Iedema, & S. Keuzenkamp. (2010). Multiple dimensions of attitudes about homosexuality: Development of a multifaceted scale measuring attitudes toward homosexuality. *Journal of Homosexuality, 57:* 1237–1257.

Averett, K. H. (2016). The gender buffet. *Gender & Society, 30:* 189–212.

Baiocco, R., L. Fontanesi, F. Santamaria, S. Loverno, B. Marasco, E. Baumgartner, B. Willoughby, & F. Laghi. (2015). Negative parental responses to coming out and family functioning in a sample of lesbian and gay young adults. *Journal of Child and Family Studies, 24:* 1490–1500.

Becker, A. B., & M. E. Todd. (2013). A new American Family? Public opinion toward family studies and perceptions of the challenges faced by children of same-sex parents. *Journal of GLBT Family Studies, 9:* 425–448.

Biblarz, T. J., & E. Savci. (2010). Lesbian, gay, bisexual, and transgender families. *Journal of Marriage and Family, 72:* 480–497.

Blosnich, J. R., M. C. Marsiglio, S. Gao, A. J. Gordon, J. C. Shipherd, M. Kauth, G. R. Brown, & M. J. Fine. (2016). Mental health of transgender veterans in US states with and without discrimination and hate crime protection. *American Journal of Public Health, 106:* 534–540.

Chase, L. M. (2011). Wives' tales: The experience of trans partners. *Journal of Gay & Lesbian Social Services, 23:* 429–451.

Clarke, V., & M. Smith. (2015). "Not hiding, not shouting, just me": Gay men negotiate their visual identities. *Journal of Homosexuality, 62:* 4–32.

Daboin, I., J. L. Peterson, & D. J. Parrott. (2015). Racial differences in sexual prejudice and its correlates among heterosexual men. *Cultural Diversity and Ethnic Minority Psychology, 21:* 258–267.

D'Amico, E., & D. Julien. (2012). Disclosure of sexual orientation and gay, lesbian, and bisexual youth's adjustment: Associations with past and current parental acceptance and rejection. *Journal of GLBT Family Studies, 8:* 215–242.

Davis-Delano, L. R. (June 2, 2014). Characteristics of activities that affect the development of women's same-sex relationships. *Journal of Homosexuality,* online.

Duncan, D., G. Prestage, & J. Grierson. (2015). Trust, commitment, love and sex: HIV, monogamy, and gay men. *Journal of Sex & Marital Therapy, 41:* 345–360.

Finneran, C., & R. Stephenson. (2014). Intimate partner violence, minority stress, and sexual risk-taking among U.S. men who have sex with men. *Journal of Homosexuality, 61:* 288–306.

Fredriksen-Goldsen, K., H. J. Kim, C. Shiu, J. Goldsen, & C. A. Emlet. (2015). Successful aging among LGBT older adults: Physical and mental health–related quality of life by age group. *Gerontologist, 55:* 154–168.

Gates, G. (2015, Winter). Family formation and raising children among same sex couples. *Family Focus, 60*(4): F26–F27. Published by the National Council on Family Relations.

Gates, G. J. (2011). How many people are lesbian, gay, bisexual and transgender? The Williams Institute. UCLA School of Law. Retrieved from http://williamsinstitute.law.ucla.edu/wp-content/uploads/Gates-How-Many-People-LGBT-Apr-2011.pdf

Gato, J., & A. M. Fontaine. (2016). Attitudes toward adoption by same-sex couples: Effects of gender of the participant, sexual orientation of the couple, and gender of the child. *Journal of GLBT Family Studies, 12:* 46–67.

Glass, V. Q. (2014). "We are with family": Black lesbian couples negotiate rituals with extended families. *Journal of GLBT Family Studies, 10:* 79–100.

Goldberg, A. E., & K. R. Allen. (2013). Same-sex relationship dissolution and LGB stepfamily formation: Perspectives of young adults with LGB parents. *Family Relations, 62:* 529–544.

Gonzales, G. (2014). Same-sex marriage: A prescription for better health. *New England Journal of Medicine, 370:* 1373–1376.

Gotta, G., R. J. Green, E. Rothblum, S. Solomon, K. Balsam, & P. Schwartz. (2011). Heterosexual, lesbian, and gay male relationships: A comparison of couples in 1975 and 2000. *Family Process, 50:* 353–376.

Green, M., & A. M. Humble. (November 13, 2015). Being queer in long term care. Poster, Annual Conference of the National Council on Family Relations, Vancouver, Canada.

Hall, S., & D. Knox. (2016). Relationship and sexual behaviors of a sample of 9,410 university students. Unpublished data collected for this text. Department of Family and Consumer Sciences, Ball State University and Department of Sociology, East Carolina University.

Hanssen, J. K. (2015). The donor figuration: A progenitor, father or friend? How young people in planned lesbian families negotiate with their donor. *Sexualities, 18:* 276–296.

Hille, J. (November 9, 2014). Asexuals and masturbation: Pleasure beyond sexuality. Presentation, Annual Meeting of the Society for the Scientific Study of Sex, Omaha, NE.

Hu, J., J. Hu, G. Huang, & X. Zheng. (2016). Life satisfaction, self-esteem, and loneliness among LGB adults and heterosexual adults in China. *Journal of Homosexuality, 63:* 72–86.

Humble, A. M. (November 5–9, 2013). Same-sex weddings in Canada: An ecological analysis of support. Poster, Annual Meeting of the National Council on Family Relations, San Antonio, TX.

Iantiffi, A., & W. O. Bockting. (2011). View from both sides of the bridge? Gender, sexual legitimacy and transgender people's experiences of relationships. *Culture, Health & Sexuality, 13:* 355–370.

Johnson, C. W., A. A. Singh, & M. Gonzalez. (2014). "It's complicated": Collective memories of transgender, queer, and questioning youth in high school. *Journal of Homosexuality, 61:* 419–434.

Kelly, M., & E. Hauck. (2015). Doing housework, redoing gender: Queer couples negotiate the household division of labor. *Journal of GLBT Family Studies, 11:* 438–464.

Kinsey, A. C., W. B. Pomeroy, & C. E. Martin. (1948). *Sexual behavior in the human male.* Philadelphia: Saunders.

Kinsey, A. C., W. B. Pomeroy, C. E. Martin, & P. H. Gebhard. (1953). *Sexual behavior in the human female.* Philadelphia: Saunders.

Kirby, B. J., & C. Michaelson (2015). Comparative morality judgments about lesbians and gay men teaching and adopting children. *Journal of Homosexuality, 62:* 33–50.

Kuper, L. E., R. Nussbaum, & B. Mustanski. (2012). Exploring the diversity of gender and sexual orientation identities in an online sample of transgender individuals. *Journal of Sex Research, 49:* 244–254.

Kurdek, L. A. (1994). Conflict resolution styles in gay, lesbian, heterosexual nonparent, and heterosexual parent couples. *Journal of Marriage and Family, 56:* 705–722.

_____. (2008). Change in relationship quality for partners from lesbian, gay male, and heterosexual couples. *Journal of Family Psychology, 22:* 701–711.

Lalicha, J., & K. McLaren. (2010). Inside and outcast: Multifaceted stigma and redemption in the lives of gay and lesbian Jehovah's Witnesses. *Journal of Homosexuality, 57:* 1303–1333.

Leddy, A., N. Gartrell, & H. Bos. (2012). Growing up in a lesbian family: The life experience of adult daughters and sons of lesbian mothers. *Journal of GLBT Family Studies, 8:* 243–257.

Lee, T., & G. R. Hicks. (2011). An analysis of factors affecting attitudes toward same-sex marriage: Do the media matter? *Journal of Homosexuality, 58:* 1391–1408.

Lyons, M., A. Lynch, G. Brewer, & D. Bruno. (2014). Detection of sexual orientation ("gaydar") by homosexual and heterosexual women. *Archives of Sexual Behavior, 43:* 345–352.

Macapagal, K., G. J. Greene, Z. Rivera, & B. Mustanski. (2015). "The Best Is Always Yet to Come": Relationship stages and processes among young LGBT couples. *Journal of Family Psychology, 29:* 309–320.

Mahaffey, A. L., & A. D. Bryan. (2016). Changing attitudes through social influence: Does social distance matter? *Journal of Homosexuality, 63*: 28–51.

Manning, J. (2015). Positive and negative communicative behaviors in coming-out conversations. *Journal of Homosexuality, 62*: 67–97.

McIntyre, S. L., E. A. Antonucci, & S. C. Haden. (2014). Being white helps: Intersections of self-concealment, stigmatization, identity formation, and psychological distress in racial and sexual minority women. *Journal of Lesbian Studies, 18*: 158–173.

McLean, K. (2004). Negotiating (non)monogamy: Bisexuality and intimate relationships. In R. C. Fox (Ed.), *Current research on bisexuality* (pp. 82–97). New York: Harrington Park Press.

Mena, J. A., & A. Vaccaro. (2013). Tell me you love me no matter what: Relationships and self-esteem among GLBQ young adults. *Journal of GLBT Family Studies, 9*: 3–23.

Mock, S. E., & R. P. Eibach. (2012). Stability and change in sexual orientation identity over a ten-year period in adulthood. *Archives of Sexual Behavior, 41*: 641–648.

Moser, C. (2016). Defining sexual orientation. *Archives of Sexual Behavior, 45*: 505–508.

National Coalition of Anti-Violence Programs. (2015). *2014 National hate crimes report: Anti-lesbian, gay, bisexual and transgender violence in 2014.* New York: National Coalition of Anti-Violence Programs. Retrieved from http://www.avp.org/storage/documents/Reports/2014_HV_Report-Final.pdf

Newcomb, M. E., M. Birkett, H. L. Corliss, & B. Mustanski. (2014). Sexual orientation, gender, and racial differences in illicit drug use in a sample of US high school students. *American Journal of Public Health, 104*: 304–310.

Overby, L. M. (2014). Etiology and attitudes: Beliefs about the origins of homosexuality and their implications for public policy. *Journal of Homosexuality, 61*: 568–587.

Padovano-Janik, A. K., V. M. Brabender, & P. A. Rutter. (2015). Young adult daughters of lesbian mothers speak: A qualitative study on identify formation. *Journal of GLBT Family Studies, 11*: 465–492.

Panozzo, D. (2015). Child care responsibility in gay male parented families: Predictive and correlative factors. *Journal of GLBT Family Studies, 11*: 248–277.

Parsons, J., T. Starks, S. DuBois, C. Grov, & S. Golub. (2013). Alternatives to monogamy among gay male couples in community survey: Implications for mental health and sexual risk. *Archives of Sexual Behavior, 42*: 303–312.

Persson, T. J., & J. G. Pfaus. (2015). Bisexuality and mental health: Future research directions. *Journal of Bisexuality, 15*: 82–98.

Peter, T., & C. Taylor. (2014). Buried above ground: A university based study of risk/protective factors for suicidality among sexual minority youth in Canada. *Journal of LGBT Youth, 11*: 125–149.

Pizer, J. C., B. Sears, C. Mallory, & N. D. Hunter. (2012). Evidence of persistent and pervasive workplace discrimination against GLBT people: The need for Federal legislation prohibiting discrimination and providing for equal employment benefits. *Loyola of Los Angeles Law Review, 45*: 715–779.

Power, J. J., A. Perlesz, R. Brown, M. J. Schofield, M. K. Pitts, R. McNair, & A. Bickerdike.

(2013). Bisexual parents and family diversity: Findings from the work, love, play study. *Journal of Bisexuality, 12*: 519–538.

Pynes, J. E. (2016). The Boy Scouts of America: Slowly changing. *Journal of Homosexuality, 63*: 52–71.

Reinhardt, R. U. (2011). Bisexual women in hetero-sexual relationships: A study of psychological and sociological patterns: A reflective paper. *Journal of Bisexuality, 11*: 439–447.

Resource Guide to Coming Out for African Americans. (2011).

Roberts, A. L., M. M. Glymour, & K. C. Koenen. (2013). Does maltreatment in childhood affect sexual orientation in adulthood? *Archives of Sexual Behavior, 42*: 161–171.

Rosenberger, J., D. Herbenick, D. Novak, & M. Reece. (2014). What's love got to do with it? Examinations perception and sexual behaviors among gay and bisexual men in the United States. *Archives of Sexual Behavior, 43*: 119–128.

Rothman, E. F., M. Sullivan, S. Keyes, & U. Boehmer. (2012). Parents' supportive reactions to sexual orientation disclosure associated with better health: Results from a population-based survey of LGB adults in Massachusetts. *Journal of Homosexuality, 59*: 186–200.

Russell, S. T., C. Ryan, R. B. Toomey, R. M. Diaz, & J. Sanchez. (2011). Lesbian, gay, bisexual and transgender adolescent school victimization: Implications for young adult health and adjustment. *Journal of School Health, 81*: 223–230.

Sasnett, S. (2015). Are the kids all right? A qualitative study of adults with gay and lesbian parents. *Journal of Contemporary Ethnography, 44*: 196–222.

Scherrer, K. S. (2016). Gay, lesbian, bisexual, and queer grandchildren's disclosure process with grandparents. *Journal of Family Issues, 37*: 739–764.

Schoephoerster, E., & C. Aamlid. (2016). College students' attitude toward same sex parenting. *College Student Journal, 50*: 102–106.

Scrimshaw, E. W., M. J. Downing, Jr., & K. Siegel. (2013). Sexual venue selection and strategies for concealment of same-sex behavior among non-disclosing men who have sex with men and women. *Journal of Homosexuality, 60*: 120–145.

Sevecke, J. R., K. N. Rhymer, E. P. Almazan, & S. Jacob. (2015). Effects of interaction experiences and undergraduate coursework on attitudes toward gay and lesbian issues. *Journal of Homosexuality, 62*: 821–840.

Sharpe, A. (2012). Transgender marriage and the legal obligations to disclose gender history. *Modern Law Review, 75*: 33–53.

SIECUS (Sexuality Information and Education Council of the United States). (2016). Retrieved January 2016 from http://www.siecus.org/index.cfm?fuseaction=Page.viewPage&pageId=591&parentID=477

Suen, Y. T. (2015). To date or not to date, that is the question: Older single gay men's concerns about dating. *Sexual and Relationship Therapy, 30*: 143–155.

Svab, A., & R. Kuhar. (2014). The transparent and family closets: Gay men and lesbians and their families of origin. *Journal of GLBT Family Studies, 10*: 15–35.

Umberson, D., M. B. Thomeer, & A. C. Lodge. (2015). Intimacy and emotion work in lesbian, gay, and heterosexual relationships. *Journal of Marriage and Family, 77*: 542–556.

Van Eeden-Moorefield, B., K. Malloy, & K. Benson. (November 13, 2015). Gay men's (Non)monogamy ideals and lived experiences. Poster, Annual Meeting of the National Council on Family Relations, Vancouver, Canada.

Van Houdenhove, E., L. Gijs, G. T'Sjoen, & P. Enzlin. (2015). Stories about asexuality: A qualitative study on asexual women. *Journal of Sex & Marital Therapy, 41*: 262–281.

Van Willigen (April 15, 2015). Panel member. Continuing debates around federal, state and individual rights: The case of marriage in the United States. East Carolina University.

Vinjamuri, M. (2015). Reminders of heteronormativity: Gay adoptive fathers navigating uninvited social interactions. *Family Relations, 64*: 263–277.

Woodford, M. R., J. M. Chonody, A. Kulick, D. J. Brennan, & K. Renn. (2015). The LGBQ Microaggressions on Campus Scaake: A scale development and validation study. *Journal of Homosexuality, 62*: 1660–1687.

Wright, P. J., & S. Bae. (2013). Pornography consumption and attitudes toward homosexuality: A national longitudinal study. *Human Communication Research, 39*: 492–513.

Yarhouse, M. A., A. Atkinson, H. Doolin, & J. S. Ripley. (2015). A longitudinal study of forgiveness and post-disclosure experience in mixed-orientation couples. *American Journal of Family Therapy, 43*: 138–150.

Yost, M., & G. Thomas. (2012). Gender and binegativity: Men's and women's attitudes toward male and female bisexuals. *Archives of Sexual Behavior, 41*: 691–702.

Zammitt, K. A., J. Pepperell, & M. Coe. (2015). Implementing an ally development model to promote safer schools for LGB youth: A transdisciplinary approach. *Journal of Homosexuality, 62*: 687–700.

Chapter 8

Aalgaard, R. A., R. M. Bolen, & W. R. Nugent. (2016). A literature review of forgiveness as a beneficial intervention to increase relationship satisfaction in couples therapy. *Journal of Human Behavior in the Social Environment, 26*: 46–55.

Alanen, J. (2016). Custom or crime? (Part I of IV): Catalysts and consequences of forced marriage. *American Journal of Family Law, 29*: 227–242.

Amato, P. R. (2015a). Marriage, cohabitation and mental health. *Family Matters. 96*: 5-13.

———. (November 12–14, 2015b). Revisiting the intergenerational transmission of divorce (ITD). Annual Meeting of the National Council on Family Relations, Vancouver, Canada.

Amato, P. R., A. Booth, D. R. Johnson, & S. F. Rogers. (2007). *Alone together: How marriage in America is changing.* Cambridge, MA: Harvard University Press.

Anderson, J. R., M. J. Van Ryzin, & W. J. Doherty. (2010). Developmental trajectories of marital happiness in continuously married individuals: A group-based modeling approach. *Journal of Family Psychology, 24*: 587–596.

Ashwin, S., & O. Isupova. (2014). "Behind every great man. . . .": The male marriage wage premium examined qualitatively. *Journal of Marriage and Family, 76*: 37–55.

Averett, S. L., L. M. Argys, & J. Sorkin. (2013). In sickness and in health: An examination of relationship status and health using data from the

Canadian National Public Health Survey. *Review of Economics of the Household, 2:* 599–633.

Ballard, S. M., & A. C. Taylor. (2012). *Family life education with diverse populations.* Thousand Oaks, CA: Sage.

Barzoki, M. H., N. Seyedroghani, & T. Azadarmaki. (July 2012). Sexual dissatisfaction in a sample of married Iranian women. *Sexuality and Culture,* online.

Bough, E. J., & D. R. Coughlin. (2012). Family life education with Black families. In S. M. Ballard & A. C. Taylor (Eds.), *Family life education with diverse populations* (pp. 235–254). Thousand Oaks, CA: Sage.

Buri, J. R., C. E. Cromett, S. J. Pappas, H. L. Lucas, & N. T. Arola. (August 2014). Soul mates, love, and prospects for marital success. Poster, Annual Meeting of the American Psychological Association, Washington, DC.

Burton-Chellew, M. N., & R. I. M. Dunbar. (2015). Romance and reproduction are socially costly. *Evolutionary Behavioral Sciences, 9:* 229–241.

Campbell, K., L. C. Silva, & D. W. Wright. (2011). Rituals in unmarried couple relationships: An exploratory study. *Family and Consumer Sciences Research Journal, 40:* 45–57.

Carroll, J. S., L. R. Dean, L. L. Call, & D. M. Busby. (2011). Materialism and marriage: Couple profiles of congruent and incongruent spouses. *Journal of Couple & Relationship Therapy, 10:* 287–308.

Casad, B. J., M. M. Salazar, & V. Macina. (2015). The real versus the ideal: Predicting relationship satisfaction and well-being from endorsement of marriage myths and benevolent sexism. *Psychology of Women Quarterly, 39:* 119–129.

Chapman, B., & C. Guven. (2016). Revisiting the relationship between marriage and wellbeing: Does marriage quality matter? *Journal of Happiness Studies, 17:* 533–551.

Chen, E. Y. J., R. D. Enright, & E. Y. L. Tung. (2016). The influence of family unions and parenthood transitions on self-development. *Journal of Family Psychology, 30:* 341–352.

Choi, H., & N. F. Marks. (2013). Marital quality, socioeconomic status, and physical health. *Journal of Marriage and Family, 75:* 903–919.

Coontz, S. (2016). *The way we never were: American families and the nostalgia trap.* New York: Basic Books.

Cottle, N. R., R. Hammond, K. Yorgason, K. Stookey, & B. Mallet. (November 5–9, 2013). Marital quality among current and former college students. Poster, Annual Meeting of the National Council on Family Relations, San Antonio, TX.

Dollahite, D. C., & L. D. Marks. (2012). The Mormon American family. In R. Wright, C. H. Mindel, T. Van Tran, & R. W. Habenstein (Eds.), *Ethnic families in America: Patterns and variations* (5th ed., pp. 461–486). Boston: Pearson.

Finkel, E. J. (August 22, 2015). Panel on modern romance: Dating, mating, and more. Presentation, Annual Meeting of the American Sociological Association, Chicago.

Fisher, H. (August 22, 2015). Panel on modern romance: Dating, mating, and more. Presentation, Annual Meeting of the American Sociological Association, Chicago.

Flood, S. M., & K. R. Genadek. (2016). Time for each other: Work and family constraints among couples. *Journal of Marriage and Family, 78:* 142–164.

Foran, H. M., K. M. Wright, & M. D. Wood. (2013). Do combat exposure and post-deployment mental health influence intent to divorce? *Journal of Social and Clinical Psychology, 32:* 917–938.

Gibson, V. (2002). *Cougar: A guide for older women dating younger men.* Boston: Firefly Books.

Gorman, L., A. Blow, R. Bowles, A. Farero, & M. Kees. (November 13, 2015). Soldier and spouse mental well-being and family health. Poster, Annual Meeting of the National Council on Family Relations, Vancouver, Canada.

Gottman, J., & S. Carrere. (September/October 2000). Welcome to the love lab. *Psychology Today,* p. 42.

Hall, S. S., & R. Adams. (2011). Newlyweds' unexpected adjustments to marriage. *Family and Consumer Sciences Research Journal, 39:* 375–387.

Hall, S., & D. Knox. (2016). Relationship and sexual behaviors of a sample of 9,978 university students. Unpublished data collected for this text. Department of Family and Consumer Sciences, Ball State University and Department of Sociology, East Carolina University.

Harris, V., K. Bedard, D. Moen, & P. Alvarez-Perez. (2016). The role of friendship, trust, and love in happy German marriages. *Marriage & Family Review, 52:* 262–304.

Huyck, M. H., & D. L. Gutmann. (1992). Thirty something years of marriage: Understanding experiences of women and men in enduring family relationships. *Family Perspective, 26:* 249–265.

Jackson, J. B., R. B. Miller, M. Oka, & R. G. Henry. (2014). Gender differences in marital satisfaction. *Journal of Marriage and Family, 76:* 105–129.

James, S. L. (2015). Variation in trajectories of women's marital quality. *Social Science Research, 49:* 16–30.

Kilmann, P. R., H. Finch, M. M. Parnell, & J. T. Downer. (2013). Partner attachment and interpersonal characteristics. *Journal of Sex and Marital Therapy, 39:* 144–159.

Langley, C. (2016). Father knows best: Paternal presence and sexual debut in African-American adolescents living in poverty. *Family Process, 55:* 155–170.

Lucier-Greer, M., & J. Mancini. (November 19, 2014). Military-related stressors & psychological vulnerability: The role of marital warmth. Paper, Annual Meeting of the National Council on Family Relations, Baltimore, MD.

Luu, S. (November 2014). Reciprocal relationships between attitudes, time together, and satisfaction. Poster, Annual Meeting of the National Council on Family Relations, Baltimore, MD.

McDonald, J., J. Olson, A. Lanning, W. Goddard, & J. Marshall. (November 12–14, 2015). Protective effect of spousal empathy on marital satisfaction and adjustment. Annual Meeting of the National Council on Family Relations, Vancouver, Canada.

Miller, R., J. Canlas, & J. Jackson. (November 2014). Marital quality and physical health. Paper, Annual Meeting of the National Council on Family Relations, Baltimore, MD.

Mitchell, B. A. (2010). Midlife marital happiness and ethnic culture: A life course perspective. *Journal of Comparative Family Studies, 41:* 167–183.

Murdock, G. P. (1949). *Social structure.* New York: Free Press.

Murray, C. I., J. G. Villalobos, L. Perez, & K. L. Camelo. (November 13, 2015). Immigrant families: Trading one stress and conflict situation for another. Poster, Annual Meeting of the National Council on Family Relations, Vancouver, Canada.

Niehuis, S., A. Reifman, & K. H. Lee. (2015). Disillusionment in cohabiting and married couples: A national study. *Journal of Family Issues, 36:* 951–973.

Olson, J., J. Marshall, W. Goddard, & D. Schramm. (November 2014). Shared religious beliefs, prayer, and forgiveness as predictors of marital satisfaction. Paper, Annual Meeting of the National Council on Family Relations, Baltimore, MD.

O'Neal, C. W., J. A. Mancini, M. Lusier-Greer, & A. L. Arnold. (November 12–14, 2015). Vulnerability and resilience in military families: Impacts on family functioning. Annual Meeting of the National Council on Family Relations, Vancouver, Canada.

Pellebon, D. A. (2012). The African American family. In R. Wright, Jr., C. H. Mindel, T. Van Tran, & R. W. Habenstein (Eds.), *Ethnic families in America: Patterns and variations* (5th ed., pp. 326–360). Boston: Pearson.

Pew Research: Pew Forum on Religion and Public Life. (2008). The U.S. religious landscape survey. Retrieved from http://pewresearch.org /pubs/743/united-states-religion

Prabu, D., & L. Stafford. (2015). A relational approach to religion and spirituality in marriage: The role of couples' religious communication in marital satisfaction. *Journal of Family Issues, 36:* 232–249.

Proquest Statistical Abstract of the United States, 2016, online ed. Washington, DC: U.S. Bureau of the Census.

Sheff, E. (2014). *The polyamorists next door.* Lanham, MD: Rowman & Littlefield.

Sherman, M. D., K. R. Hawkey, & L. M. Borden. (2015). The experience of reintegration for military families. *National Council on Family Relations Report,* Fall/60.3: 21–22.

Simons, L. G., K. A. S. Wickrama, T. K. Lee, M. Landers-Potts, C. Cutrona, & R. D. Conger. (2016). Testing family stress and family investment explanations for conduct problems among African American Adolescents. *Journal of Marriage and Family, 78:* 498–515.

Spencer, J., & P. Amato. (November 2011). Marital quality across the life course: Evidence from latent growth curves. Presentation, Annual Meeting of the National Council on Family Relations, Orlando, FL.

Spierling, T. (November 12–14, 2015). Promoting resilience in military families faced with deployment. Annual Meeting of the National Council on Family Relations, Vancouver, Canada.

Stafford, L. (2016). Marital sanctity, relationship maintenance, and marital quality. *Journal of Family Issues, 37:* 119–131.

Teachman, J. (2016). Body weight, marital status, and changes in marital status. *Journal of Family Issues, 37:* 74–96.

Tili, T. R., & G. G. Barker. (2015). Communication in intercultural marriages: Managing cultural differences and conflicts. *Southern Communication Journal, 80:* 189–210.

Tyndall, B. D., & C. A. Christie-Mizell. (2016). Mastery, homeownership, and adult roles during the transition to adulthood. *Sociological Inquiry, 86:* 5–28.

Wheeler, B., S. Bertagnolli, & J. Yorgason. (November 2012). Marriage: Exploring predictors of marital quality in husband-older, wife-older, and same-age marriage. Poster, Annual Meeting of the National Council on Family Relations, Phoenix, AZ.

Wick, S., & B. S. Nelson Goff. (2014). A qualitative analysis of military couples with high and low trauma symptoms and relationship distress levels. *Relationship Therapy: Innovations in Clinical and Educational Interventions, 13:* 63–88.

Williams, N. D., A. Foye, & F. Lewis. (2016). Applying structural family therapy in the changing context of the modern African American single mother. *Journal of Feminist Family Therapy, 28:* 30–47.

Woldarsky, M., & L. S. Greenberg. (2014). Interpersonal forgiveness in emotion-focused couples' therapy: Relating process to outcome. *Journal of Marital and Family Therapy, 40:* 49–67.

Woszidlo, A., & C. Segrin. (2013). Negative affectivity and educational attainment as predictors of newlyweds' problem solving and marital quality. *Journal of Psychology, 147:* 49–73.

Wright, R., C. H. Mindel, T. Van Tran, and R. W. Habenstein. (2012). *Ethnic families in America: Patterns and variations,* 5th ed. Boston: Pearson.

Chapter 9

Bean, H., K. M. Eberle, & J. A. Paul. (2016). Can we talk about stay at home moms? Empirical findings and implications for counseling. *Family Journal, 24:* 23–30.

Carey, A. R., & P. Trapp. (October 20 , 2013). Companies' workplace policies. *USA Today,* p. A1.

Carlson, M., & J. Hans. (November 12–14 , 2015). Finding an efficient division of household labor: A grounded theory inquiry. Annual Meeting of the National Council on Family Relations, Vancouver, Canada.

Cohn, D., G. Livingston, & W. Wang. (April 8, 2014). After decades of decline, a rise in stay-at-home mothers. Pew Research Center. Retrieved from http://www.pewresearch.org/fact-tank/2014 /04/08/7-key-findings-about-stay-at-home -moms/

Coontz, S. (2016). *The way we never were: American families and the nostalgia trap,* 2nd ed. New York: Basic Books.

Etzioni, A. (2011). The new normal. *Sociological Forum, 26:* 779–789.

Fales, M. R., D. A. Frederick, J. R. Garcia, K. A. Gildersleeve, M. G. Haselton, & H. E. Fisher. (2016). Mating markets and bargaining hands: Mate preferences for attractiveness and resources in two national U.S. studies. *Personality and Individual Differences, 88:* 78–87.

Fiona, C. S., A. W. Chau, & K. Y. Chan. (2012). Financial knowledge and aptitudes: Impacts on college students' financial well-being. *College Student Journal, 46:* 114–132.

Flood, S. M., & K. R. Genadek (2016). Time for each other: Work and family constraints among couples. *Journal of Marriage and Family, 78:* 142–164.

Gartzia, L., & J. Fetterolf. (2016). What division of labor do university students expect in their future lives? Divergences and communalities of female and male students. *Sex Roles, 74:* 121–135.

Gentile, B., & J. D. Pierce. (August 2014). Positive effects of daycare on adult cognitive flexibility and overall interpersonal communication. Annual Meeting of the American Psychological Association, Washington, DC.

Helms, H. M., J. K. Walls, A. C. Crouter, & S. M. McHale. (2010). Provider role attitudes, marital satisfaction, role overload, and housework: A dyadic approach. *Journal of Family Psychology, 24:* 568–577.

Hochschild, A. R. (1989). *The second shift.* New York: Viking.

_____. (1997). *The time bind.* New York: Metropolitan Books.

Hoffnung, M., & M. Williams. (2013). Balancing act: Career and family during college-educated women's 30s. *Sex Roles, 68:* 321–334.

Hoser, N. (2012). Making it a dual-career family in Germany: Exploring what couples think and do in everyday life. *Marriage and Family Review, 48:* 643–666.

Johnson, M. D., N. L. Galambos, & J. R. Anderson. (2016). Skip the dishes? Not so fast! Sex and housework revisited. *Journal of Family Psychology, 30:* 203–213.

Kahn, J. R., J. Garcia-Manglano, & S. M. Bianchi. (2014). The motherhood penalty at midlife: Long-term effects of children on women's careers. *Journal of Marriage and Family, 76:* 56–72.

Karaffa, K., L. Openshaw, J. Koch, H. Clark, C. Harr, & C. Stewart. (2015). Perceived impact of police work on marital relationships. *Family Journal, 23:* 120–131.

Kornrich, S., J. Brines, & K. Leupp. (2013). Egalitarianism, housework, and sexual frequency in marriage. *American Sociological Review, 78:* 26–50.

Lewchuk, W., A. Tambureno, M. Lafleche, S. Procyk, C. Cook, D. Dyson, L. Goldring, K. Lior, A. Meisner, J. Shields, & P. Viducis. (2016). The Precarity Penalty: How insecure employment disadvantages workers and their families. *Alternative Routes, 27:* 87–108.

Liu, M. (2015). An ecological review of literature on factors influencing working mothers' child care arrangements. *Journal of Child & Family Studies, 24:*161–171.

Määttä, K., & S. Uusiautti. (2012). Seven rules on having a happy marriage along with work. *The Family Journal, 20:* 267–271.

Marie Dow, D. (2016) Integrated motherhood: Beyond hegemonic ideologies of motherhood. *Journal of Marriage and Family, 78:* 180–196.

Maroto, M. L. (2015). Pathways to bankruptcy: Accumulating disadvantage and the consequences of adverse life events. *Sociological Inquiry, 85:* 183–216.

McBridge, M. C., & K. M. Bergen. (2014). Voices of women in commuter marriages: A site of discursive struggle. *Journal of Social and Personal Relationships, 31:* 554–557.

Merrill, J., & D. Knox. (2010). *Finding love from 9 to 5.* New York: Praeger.

Meteyer, K., & Maureen Perry-Jenkins. (2012). Father involvement among working-class, dual-earner couples. *Fathering: A Journal of Theory, Research, & Practice about Men as Fathers, 8:* 379–403.

Milkie, M. A., K. M. Nomaguchi, & K. E. Denny. (2015). Does the amount of time mothers spend with children or adolescents matter? *Journal of Marriage and Family, 77:* 355–372.

Minnotte, K. L., M. C. Minnotte, & D. E. Pedersen. (2013). Marital satisfaction among dual-earner couples: Gender ideologies and family-to-work conflict. *Family Relations, 62:* 686–698.

Minnottea, K. L., D. E. Pedersena, S. E. Mannonb, & G. Kiger. (2010). Tending to the emotions of children: Predicting parental performance of emotion work with children. *Marriage & Family Review, 46:* 224–241.

Opree, S. J., & M. Kalmijn. (2012). Exploring causal effects of combining work and inter-generational support on depressive symptoms among middle-aged women. *Ageing & Society, 32:* 130–146.

Parker, K., & W. Wang. (March 14 , 2013). Modern parenthood: Roles of moms and dads converge as they balance work and family. *Pew Research: Social & Demographic Trends.* Retrieved from http://www.pewsocialtrends.org/2013/03/14 /modern-parenthood-roles-of-moms-and-dads -converge-as-they-balance-work-and-family/

Pew Research Center. (November 4, 2015). Raising kids and running a household: How working parents share the load. Retrieved from http:// www.pewsocialtrends.org/2015/11/04/raising -kids-and-running-a-household-how-working -parents-share-the-load/

Proquest Statistical Abstract of the United States, 2016, online ed. Washington, DC: U.S. Bureau of the Census.

Ruberton, P. M., J. Gladstone, & S. Syubomirsky. (April 1–6, 2016). How your bank balance buys happiness: The importance of "cash on hand" to life satisfaction. *Emotion.*

Schoen, R., N. M. Astone, K. Rothert, N. J. Standish, & Y. J. Kim. (2002). Women's employment, marital happiness, and divorce. *Social Forces, 81:* 643–662.

Sefton, B. W. (1998). The market value of the stay-at-home mother. *Mothering, 86:* 26–29.

Sohn, K. (2016). The role of spousal income in the wife's happiness. *Social Indicators Research, 126:* 1007–1024.

Stanfield, J. B. (1998). Couples coping with dual careers: A description of flexible and rigid coping styles. *Social Science Journal, 35:* 53–62.

Stykes, J. B. (2015). What matters most? Money, relationships, and visions of masculinity as key correlates of father involvement. *Fathering: A Journal of Theory, Research & Practice about Men as Fathers, 13:* 60–79.

Treas, J., T. Van der Lippe, & T. C. Tai. (2011). The happy homemaker? Married women's well-being in cross-national perspective. *Social Forces, 90:* 111–132.

Vanderkam, L. (2010). *168 hours: You have more time than you think to achieve your dreams.* Portfolio Press (online).

Vault Office Romance Survey. (2016). Retrieved April 22 from http://www.vault.com/blog /general-articles/romance-is-in-the-air-the -2016-office-romance-survey-results-are-here/

Walls, J. K., H. M. Helms, & J. G. Grzywacz. (2016). Intensive-mothering beliefs among full time employed mothers of infants. *Journal of Family Issues, 37:* 245–269.

Wang, W., K. Parker, & P. Taylor. (May 29, 2013). Breadwinner moms: Mothers as the sole or primary provider in four-in-ten households with children. *Pew Social & Demographic Trends.* Retrieved fromhttp://www.pewsocialtrends .org/2013/05/29/breadwinner-moms/

Westrupp, E. M., L. Strazdins, A. Martin, A. Cooklin, S. R. Zubrick, & J. M. Nicholson. (2016). Maternal work–family conflict and psychological distress: Reciprocal relationships over 8 years. *Journal of Marriage and Family*, 78: 107–126.

Wheeler, B., & J. Kerpelman. (November 5–9, 2013). Change in frequency of disagreements about money: A "gateway" to poorer marital outcomes among newlywed couples over the first five years of marriage. Poster, Annual Meeting of the National Council on Family Relations, San Antonio, TX.

Wheeler, B., J. Kerpelman, & J. Yorgason. (November 12–14, 2013). Economic hardship and financial distress: A contextual examination. Annual Meeting of the National Council on Family Relations, Vancouver, Canada.

Williams, A. V., E. W. Dunn, G. M. Sandstrom, S. S. Dickerson, & K. M. Madden. (February 11, 2016). Is spending money on others good for your heart? *Health Psychology.*

Williams, D. T., J. E. Cheadle, & B. Goosby. (2015). Hard times and heart break: Linking economic hardship and relationship distress. *Journal of Family Issues, 36:* 924–950.

Yang, J., & A. Gonzalez. (2013, February 25, 2013). Virtual versus office work. *USA Today,* Sec. B.

Yang, J., & P. Trap. (January 25, 2016). Non-monetary perk at work. *USA Today,* p. A1.

Chapter 10

Adams, H. L., & L. R. Williams. (January 2014). "It's not just you two": A grounded theory of peer-influenced jealousy as a pathway to dating violence among acculturating Mexican American adolescents. *Psychology of Violence,* online.

al-Khateeb, H. M., & G. Epiphaniou. (January 14–18, 2016). How technology can mitigate and counteract cyber-stalking and online grooming. *Computer Fraud and Security,* ISSN 1361-3723. Retrieved from http://dx.doi.org/10.1016/S1361-3723(16)30008-2

Bennett, S., V. L. Banyard, & L. Garnhart. (2014). To act or not to act, that is the question? Barriers and facilitators of bystander intervention. *Journal of Interpersonal Violence, 29:* 3, 476–496.

Bouman, A. (2013). 5 personal safety apps that watch your back. *PC World.* Retrieved March 29, 2016, from http://www.pcworld.com/article/2057930/5-personal-safety-apps-that-watch-your-back.html

Brownridge, D. A. (2010). Does the situational couple violence-intimate terrorism typology explain cohabitors' high risk of intimate partner violence? *Journal of Interpersonal Violence, 25:* 1264–1283.

Buvik, K., & B. Baklien. (2016). "Girls will be served until you have to carry them out": Gendered serving practices in Oslo. *Addiction Research & Theory, 24:* 17–24.

Carroll, M. H., J. E. Rosenstein, J. D. Foubert, M. D. Clark, & L. M. Korenman. (April 11, 2016). Rape myth acceptance: A comparison of military service academy and civilian fraternity and sorority students. *Military Psychology,* online.

Cascardi, M. (2016). From violence in the home to physical dating violence victimization: The mediating role of psychological distress in a prospective study of female adolescents. *Journal of Youth & Adolescence, 45:* 777–792.

Centers for Disease Control and Prevention. (2016). The National Intimate Partner and Sexual Violence Survey. Retrieved May 10, 2016, from http://www.cdc.gov/violenceprevention/nisvs/index.html

Cho, H., & L. Huang. (May 2016). Aspects of help seeking among collegiate victims of dating violence. *Journal of Family Violence,* online.

Cohn, A., H. M. Zinzow, H. S. Resnick, & D. G. Kilpatrick. (2013). Correlates of reasons for not reporting rape to police: Results from a national telephone household probability sample of women with forcible or drug-or-alcohol facilitated/incapacitated rape. *Journal of Interpersonal Violence, 28:* 455–473.

Cravens, J. D., J. B. Whiting, & R. O. Aamar. (November 13, 2015). Why I stayed/left: An analysis of voices of intimate partner violence on social media. Annual Meeting of the National Council on Family Relations, Vancouver, Canada.

Cunha, O. S., & R. A. Goncalves. (2016). Severe and less severe intimate partner violence: From characterization to prediction. *Violence and Victims, 31:* 235–250.

DeSmet, O., K. Uzieblo, T. Loeys, A. Buysse, & T. Onraedt. (2015). Unwanted pursuit behavior after breakup: Occurrence, risk factors, and gender differences. *Journal of Family Violence, 30:* 753–767.

Dominguez, M. M., J. High, E. Smith, B.Cafferky, P. Dharnidharka, & S. Smith. (November 5–9, 2013). The intergenerational transmission of family violence: A meta-analytic review. Poster, Annual Meeting of the National Council on Family Relations, San Antonio, TX.

Eggett, K. N., & M. Irvin. (April 16, 2016). Sexual violence prevention programs: A meta-analysis. Poster, Annual Meeting of the Southern Sociological Society, Atlanta, GA.

Eke, A., N. Hilton, G. Harris, M. Rice, & R. Houghton. (2011). Intimate partner homicide: Risk assessment and prospects for prediction. *Journal of Family Violence, 26:* 211–216.

Elmquist, J., C. Wolford-Clevenger, H. Zapor, J. Febres, R. C. Shorey, J. Hamel, & G. L. Stuart. (2016). A gender comparison of motivations for physical dating violence among college students. *Journal of Interpersonal Violence, 31:* 186–203.

Fellmeth, G., C. Heffernan, J. Nurse, S. Habibula, & D. Sethi. (2015). Educational and skills based interventions to prevent relationship violence in young people. *Research on Social Work Practice, 25:* 90–102.

Foshee, V. A., N. C. Gottfredson, H. L. M. Reyes, M. S. Chen, C. David-Ferdon, N. E. Latzman, A. T. Tharp, & S. T. Ennett. (April 2016). Developmental outcomes of using physical violence against dates and peers. *Journal of Adolescent Health,* online.

Gershoff, G. T., & A. Grogan-Kaylor. (2016). Spanking and child outcomes: Old controversies and new meta-analyses. *Journal of Family Psychology,* online. doi:10.1037/fam0000191

Glass, N., A. Clough, J. Amber, G. Hanson, J. Barnes-Hoyt, A. Waterbury, J. Alhusen, M. Ehrensaft, K. T. Grace, & N. Perrin. (2015). A safety app to respond to dating violence for college women and their friends: The MyPlan study randomized controlled trial protocol. *BMC Public Health, 15:* 1–13.

Graham, A. M., H. K. Kim, & P. A. Fisher. (2012). Partner aggression in high-risk families from birth to age 3 years: Associations with harsh parenting and child maladjustment. *Journal of Family Psychology, 26:* 105–114.

Hall, S., & D. Knox. (2012). Double victims: Sexual coercion by a dating partner and a stranger. *Journal of Aggression, Maltreatment & Trauma, 22:* 145–158.

_____. (2016). Relationship and sexual behaviors of a sample of 9,948 university students. Unpublished data collected for this text. Department of Family and Consumer Sciences, Ball State University and Department of Sociology, East Carolina University.

Halligan, C., D. Knox, & J. Brinkley. (2013). Trapped: Technology as a barrier to leaving an abusive relationship. *College Student Journal, 47:* 644–648.

Halpern-Meekin, S., W. D. Manning, P. C. Giordano, & M. A. Longmore. (2013). Relationship churning, physical violence, and verbal abuse in young adult relationships. *Journal of Marriage and Family, 75:* 2–12.

Hayes, B., J. Freilich, & S. Chermak. (2016). An exploratory study of honor crimes in the United States. *Journal of Family Violence, 31:* 303–314.

Heath, N. M., S. M. Lynch, A. M. Fritch, & M. M Wong. (2013). Rape myth acceptance impacts the reporting of rape to the police: A study of incarcerated women. *Violence Against Women, 19:* 1065–1078.

Henning, K., & J. Connor-Smith. (2011). Why doesn't he leave? Relationship continuity and satisfaction among male domestic violence offenders. *Journal of Interpersonal Violence, 26:* 1366–1387.

Hines, D. A., & K. M. Palm Reed. (2015). An experimental evaluation of peer versus professional educators of a bystander program for the prevention of sexual and dating violence among college students. *Journal of Aggression, Maltreatment & Trauma, 24:* 279–298.

Holland, K. J., V. C. Rabelo, & L. M. Cortina. (2016). Collateral damage: Military sexual trauma and help-seeking barriers. *Psychology of Violence, 6:* 253–261.

Kaiser Permanente Family Violence Prevention Program. (2016). Mobile app serves as safety decision aid for women facing violence in their intimate relationship. Retrieved March 22, 2016, from https://xnet.kp.org/domesticviolence/news/myplan_app.html

Katz, J., & H. Rich. (2015). Partner covictimization and post-breakup stalking, pursuit, and violence: A retrospective study of college women. *Journal of Family Violence, 30:* 189–199.

Kennedy, T., & R. Ceballo. (2016). Emotionally numb: Desensitization to community violence exposure among urban youth. *Developmental Psychology, 52:* 778–789.

Klipfel, K. M., S. E. Claxton, & M. H. M. Van Dulmen. (2014). Interpersonal aggression victimization within casual sexual relationships and experiences. *Journal of Interpersonal Violence, 29:* 557–569.

Kothari, C. L., K. V. Rhodes, J. A. Wiley, J. Fink, S. Overholt, M. E. Dichter, S. C. Marcus, & C. Cerulli. (2012). Protection orders protect against assault and injury: A longitudinal study of police-involved women victims of intimate partner violence. *Journal of Interpersonal Violence, 27:* 2845–2868.

Langston, L., & S. Sinozich. (2014). Rape and sexual assault among college age females, 1995–2013. Bureau of Justice Statistics. Retrieved from http://www.bjs.gov/index.cfm?ty=pbdetail&iid=5176

Lee, B. (2011). The role of mobile apps in the fight against intimate partner violence. Huff Post Impact. Retrieved March 20, 2016, from http://www.huffingtonpost.com/becky-lee/the-role-of-mobile-apps-i_b_934857.html

Lee, M. S., S. Begun, A. P. DePrince, & A. T. Chu. (April 11, 2016). Acceptability of dating violence and expectations of relationship harm among adolescent girls exposed to intimate partner violence. *Psychological Trauma: Theory, Research, Practice, and Policy*, online.

Lippy, C. & S. DeGue. (2016). Exploring alcohol policy approaches to prevent sexual violence perpetration. *Trauma, Violence, & Abuse*, 17: 26–42.

Liu, S., M. M. Dore, & I. Amrani-Cohen. (2013). Treating the effects of interpersonal violence: A comparison of two group models. *Social Work with Groups*, 36: 59–72.

Lyndon, A. E. H., C. Sinclair, J. MacArthur, B. Fay, E. Ratajack, & K. E. Collier. (2012). An introduction to issues of gender in stalking research. *Sex Roles*, 66: 299–310.

Ma, J., Y. Han, A. Grogan-Kaylor, J. Delva, & M. Castillo. (2012). Corporal punishment and youth externalizing behavior in Santiago, Chile. *Child Abuse & Neglect*, 36: 481–490.

Maharaj, N. (April 23, 2016). Perspectives on treating couples impacted by intimate partner violence. *Journal of Family Violence*, online.

Marcus, R. E. (2012). Patterns of intimate partner violence in young adult couples: Nonviolent, unilaterally violent, and mutually violent couples. *Violence & Victims*, 27: 299–314.

Mathes, E. W. (2013). Why is there a strong positive correlation between perpetration and being a victim of sexual coercion? An exploratory study. *Journal of Family Violence*, 28: 783–796.

McCleary-Sills, J., S. Namy, J. Nyoni, D. Rweyemamu, A. Salvatory, & E. Steven. (2016). Stigma, shame and women's limited agency in help-seeking for intimate partner violence. *Global Public Health*, 11: 224–235.

Miller, J. D., A. Zeichner, & L. F. Wilson. (2012). Personality correlates of aggression: Evidence from measures of the five-factor model, UPPS model of impulsivity, and BIS/BAS. *Journal of Interpersonal Violence*, 27: 2903–2919.

Murray, C. E., K. King, & A. Crowe. (2016). Understanding and addressing teen dating violence. *Family Journal*, 24: 52–59.

Mustapha, A., & C. Muehlenhard. (November 8, 2014). Women's and men's reactions to being sexually coerced: A quantitative and qualitative analysis. Presentation, Annual Meeting of the Society for the Scientific Study of Sex, Omaha, NE.

NNEDV. (2009). Technology safety quick tips. National Network to End Domestic Violence, Safety Net Project. Retrieved from http://nnedv .org/downloads/SafetyNet/OVW/NNEDV _TechSafetyQuickTipsChart_2011.pdf

Nybergh, L., V. Nander, & G. Krantz. (2016). Theoretical considerations on men's experiences of intimate partner violence: An interview based study. *Journal of Family Violence*, 31: 191–202.

O'Brien, C., J. Keith, & L. Shoemaker. (2016). Don't tell: Military culture and male rape. *Psychological Services*, 12: 357–365.

O'Leary, D. K., H. Foran, & S. Cohen. (2013). Validation of fear of partner scale. *Journal of Marital and Family Therapy*, 39: 502–514.

Palmer, J. E. (2016). Recognizing the continuum of opportunities for third parties to prevent and respond to sexual and dating violence on a college campus. *Crime Prevention and Community Safety*, 18: 1–18.

Pendry, P., F. Henderson, J. Antles, & E. Conlin. (November 18, 2011). Parents' use of everyday conflict tactics in the presence of children:

Predictors and implications for child behavior. Poster, Annual Meeting of the National Council on Family Relations, Orlando, FL.

Powers, R. A., & S. S. Simpson. (2012). Self-protective behaviors and injury in domestic violence situations: Does it hurt to fight back? *Journal of Interpersonal Violence*, 27: 3345–3365.

Raghavan, C., S. C Tamborra, & T. Tamborra. (2015). Development and preliminary validation of the multidimensional sexual coercion questionnaire (MSCQ). *Journal of Sexual Aggression: An International Interdisciplinary Forum for Research, Theory and Practice*, 21: 271–289.

Rodgers, K. B., S. T. J. Hust, & J. Liu. (November 13, 2015). Rape myth acceptance, self-efficacy, and perceived norms: Factors associated with the intentions to seek help and report sexual assault. Annual Meeting of the National Council on Family Relations, Vancouver, Canada.

Romero-Martinez, A., M. Lila, & L. Moya-Albiol. (2016). Empathy impairments in intimate partner violence perpetrators with antisocial and borderline traits: A key factor in the risk of recidivism. *Violence & Victims*, 31: 347–360.

Rothman, E. F., D. Exner, & A. L. Baughman. (2011). The prevalence of sexual assault against people who identify as gay, lesbian, or bisexual in the United States: A systematic review. *Violence & Abuse*, 12: 55–66.

Shorey, R. C., J. Febres, H. Brasfield, & G. L. Stuart. (August 12, 2012). The prevalence of mental health problems in men arrested for domestic violence. *Journal of Family Violence*, online. Retrieved from http://www.springerlink.com .jproxy.lib.ecu.edu/content/0g67243666512182 /fulltext.pdf

Shorey, R. C., J. K. McNulty, T. M. Moore, & G. L. Stuart. (2016). Being the victim of violence during a date predicts next-day cannabis use among female college students. *Addiction*, 111: 492–498.

Sidebotham, P. (2013). Rethinking filicide. *Child Abuse Review*, 22: 305–310.

Smeaton, G., & P. Anderson. (November 7, 2014). Gender majority status and tactics used to gain sex from a reluctant partner. Presentation, Annual Meeting of the Society for the Scientific Study of Sex, Omaha, NE.

Southworth, C., J. Finn, S. Dawson, C. Fraser, & S. Tucker. (2007). Intimate partner violence, technology and stalking. *Violence Against Women*, 13: 842–856. doi:10.1177/1077801207302045

Stith, S. M. (November 12–14, 2015). Assessing risk for intimate partner violence in the military. Annual Meeting of the National Council on Family Relations, Vancouver, Canada.

Stoleru, M., & E. Costescu. (2014). (Re)Producing violence against women in online spaces. *Philobiblon*, 19: 95–114.

Temple, J., H. Choi, M. Brem, C. Wolford-Clevenger, G. Stuart, M. Peskin, & J. Elmquist. (2016). The temporal association between traditional and cyber dating abuse among adolescents. *Journal of Youth & Adolescence*, 45: 340–349.

Ward, C. L., C. Gould, J. Kelly, & K. Mauff. (2015). Assessing the impact of parenting on child behaviour and mental health. *SA Crime Quarterly*, 51: 9–22.

Ward, J. T., M. D. Krohn, & C. L. Gibson. (2014). The effects of police on trajectories of violence: A group-based, propensity score matching analysis. *Journal of Interpersonal Violence*, 29: 440–475.

Whitaker, M. P. (2014). Motivational attributions about intimate partner violence among male and female perpetrators. *Journal of Interpersonal Violence*, 29: 517–535.

Wright, P. J., & R. S. Tokunaga. (2016). Men's objectifying media consumption, objectification of women and attitudes supportive of violence against women. *Archives of Sexual Behavior*, 45: 955–964.

Yazedjian, A., and M. Toews. (November 12–14, 2015). Initiating a hookup: Implications for sexual assault prevention. Annual Meeting of the National Council on Family Relations, Vancouver, Canada.

Chapter 11

Adoption USA: National Survey of Adoptive Parents. (2015). U.S. Department of Health and Human Services. Retrieved from http://www .statisticbrain.com/adoption-statistics/

Ames, C. M., & W. V. Norman. (2012). Preventing repeat abortion in Canada: Is the immediate insertion of intrauterine devices postabortion a cost-effective option associated with fewer repeat abortions? *Contraception*, 85: 51–55.

Baden, A. L. (2016). "Do you know your real parents?" and other adoption microaggressions. *Adoption Quarterly*, 19: 1–25.

Baumle, A. K. (2013). The cost of parenthood: Unraveling the effects of sexual orientation and gender on income. *Social Science Quarterly*, 90: 983–1002.

Black, C. A., A. M. Moyer, & A. E. Goldberg. (November 2014). Adoptive families contact with birth families: The role of social media and technology. Poster, National Council on Family Relations, Baltimore, MD.

Bongaarts, J., & C. Z. Guilmoto. (2015). How many more missing women? Excess female mortality and prenatal sex selection, 1970–2015. *Population and Development Review*, 41: 241–269.

Brandes, M., C. Hamilton, J. van der Steen, J. de Bruin, R. Bots, W. Nelen, & J. Kremer. (2011). Unexplained infertility: Overall ongoing pregnancy rate and mode of conception. *Human Reproduction*, 26: 360–368.

Burge, P., E. Meiklejohn, D. Groll, & N. Burke. (2016). Making choices: Adoption seekers' preferences and available children with special needs. *Journal of Public Child Welfare*, 10: 1–20.

Byrne, T., & V. Bravo. (February 15, 2016). Zika and family planning. [Based on Treato consumer survey.] *USA Today*.

Canario, C., B. Figueiredo, & M. Ricou. (2013). Women and men's psychological adjustment after abortion: A six-months' perspective pilot study. *Journal of Reproductive and Infant Psychology*, 29: 262–275.

Caspi, J., D. Lardier, & V. Barrios. (November 2014). Siblings and adolescent substance abuse: A family treatment double-bind. Poster, Annual Meeting of the National Council on Family Relations, Baltimore, MD.

Colen, C. G., D. M. Ramey, & C. R. Browning. (February 29, 2016). Declines in crime and teen childbearing: Identifying potential explanations for contemporaneous trends. *Journal of Quantitative Criminology*, online.

Curtin, S. C., J. C. Abma, & S. J. Ventura. (December 2013). Pregnancy rates for U.S. women continue to drop. U.S. Department of Health and Human Services. NCHS Data # 136.

Dervin, D. (2016). Where have all the children gone? *The Journal of Psychohistory, 43:* 262–276.

Dougall, K. M., Y. Beyene, & R. D. Nachtigall. (2013). Age shock: Misperceptions of the impact of age on fertility before and after IVF in women who conceived after age 40. *Human Reproduction, 28:* 350–356.

Elaut, E., A. Buysse, P. De Sutter, J. Gerris, G. De Cuypere, & G. T'Sjoen. (2016). Cycle-related changes in mood, sexual desire and sexual activity in oral contraception-using and nonhormonal-contraception-using couples. *Journal of Sex Research, 53:* 125–136.

Falcon, M., F. Valero, M. Pellegrini, M. Rotolo, G. Scaravelli, J. Joya, O. Vall, et al. (2010). Exposure to psychoactive substances in women who request voluntary termination of pregnancy assessed by serum and hair testing. *Forensic Science International, 196:* 22–26.

Finer, L. B., L. F. Frohwirth, L. A. Dauphinne, S. Singh, & A. M. Moore. (2005). Reasons U.S. women have abortions: Quantitative and qualitative reasons. *Perspectives on Sexual and Reproductive Health, 37:* 110–118.

Fingerman, K. L., K. Kim, K. S. Birditt, & S. H. Zarit. (2016). The ties that bind: Midlife parents' daily experiences with grown children. *Journal of Marriage and Family, 78:* 431–450.

Foster, D. G., K. Kimport, H. Gould, S. C. M. Roberts, & T. A. Weitz. (2013). Effect of abortion protesters on women's emotional response to abortion. *Contraception, 87:* 81–87.

Frisco, M. L., & M. Weden. (2013). Early adult obesity and U.S. women's lifetime childbearing experiences. *Journal of Marriage and Family, 75:* 920–932.

Garrett, T. M., H. W. Baillie, & R. M. Garrett. (2001). *Health care ethics,* 4th ed. Upper Saddle River, NJ: Prentice Hall.

Geller, P., C. Psaros, & S. L. Kornfield. (2010). Satisfaction with pregnancy loss aftercare: Are women getting what they want? *Archives of Women's Mental Health, 13:* 111–124.

Goldberg, A. E., L. A. Kinkler, H. B. Richardson, & J. B. Downing. (2011). Lesbian, gay, and heterosexual couples in open adoption arrangements: A qualitative study. *Journal of Marriage and Family, 73:* 502–518.

Greil, A. L., K. S. Slauson-Blevins, S. Tiemeyer, J. McQuillan, & K. M. Shreffler. (2016). A new way to estimate the potential need for infertility services among women in the United States. *Journal of Women's Health, 25:* 133–138.

Grindlay, K., & D. Grossman. (2016). Prescription birth control access among U.S. women at risk of unintended pregnancy. *Journal of Women's Health, 25:* 249–254.

Gunther, I., K. Harttgen, & I. Gunther. (2016). Desired fertility and number of children born across time and space. *Demography, 53:* 55–83.

Guttmacher Institute. (2016). Abortion facts. Retrieved May 20 from https://www.guttmacher.org/fact-sheet/induced-abortion-united-states?gclid=CNm0sLWb6MwCFYsCaQodTWINIw

Hall, S., & D. Knox. (2016). Relationship and sexual behaviors of a sample of 9,711 university students. Unpublished data collected for this text. Department of Family and Consumer Sciences, Ball State University and Department of Sociology, East Carolina University.

Healy, M. (December 17, 2013). The web has transformed adoption, for good and bad. *USA Today,* p. 3D.

Hoffnung, M., & M. Williams. (2013). Balancing act: Career and family during college-educated women's 30s. *Sex Roles, 68:* 321–334.

Jones, C. (2016). Openness in adoption: Challenging the narrative of historical progress. *Child & Family Social Work, 21:* 85–93.

Juffer, F., M. van Ijzendoorn, & J. Palacios. (2011). Children's recovery after adoption. *Infancia y Aprendizaje, 34:* 3–18.

Katz, P., J. Showstack, J. F. Smith, R. D. Nachtigall, S. G. Millstein, H. Wing, M. L. Eisenberg, L. A. Pasch, M. S. Croughan, & N. Adler. (2011). Costs of infertility treatment: Results from an 18-month prospective cohort study. *Fertility and Sterility, 95:* 915–921.

Kleinert, E., O. Martin, E. Brahler, & Y. Stobel-Richter. (2015). Motives and decisions for and against having children among nonheterosexuals and the impact of experiences of discrimination, internalized stigma, and social acceptance. *Journal of Sex Research, 52:* 174–185.

Kondapalli, L. A., & A. Perales-Puchalt. (2013). Low birth weight: Is it related to assisted reproductive technology or underlying infertility? *Fertility and Sterility, 99:* 303–310.

Kucur Suna, K., G. Ilay, A. Aysenur, K. Han, U. Eda Ulku, U. Pasa, & C. Fatma. (2016). Effects of infertility etiology and depression on female sexual dysfunction. *Journal of Sex & Marital Therapy, 42:* 27–35.

Lee, D. (2006). Device brings hope for fertility clinics. Retrieved August 20, 2015, from http://www.indystar.com/apps/pbcs.dll/article?AID=/20060221/BUSINESS/602210365/1003

Lee, K., & A. M. Zvonkovic. (2014). Journeys to remain childless: A grounded theory examination of decision-making processes among voluntarily childless couples. *Journal of Social and Personal Relationships, 31:* 535–553.

Luk, B. H., & A. Y. Loke. (2015). Relationships, and quality of life of couples: A systematic review. *Journal of Sex & Marital Therapy, 41:* 610–625.

Major, B., M. Appelbaum, & C. West. (August 13, 2008). Report of the APA task force on mental health and abortion.

Marcell, A. V., S. E. Gibbs, I. Choiriyyah, F. L. Sonenstein, N. M. Astone, J. H. Pleck, & J. K. Dariotis. (2016). National needs of family planning among US men aged 15 to 44 years. *American Journal of Public Health, 106:* 733–739.

McQuillan, J., A. L. Greil, K. M. Shreffler, P. A. Wonch-Hill, K. C. Gentzler, & J. D. Hathcoat. (2012). Does the reason matter? Variations in childlessness concerns among U.S. women. *Journal of Marriage and Family, 74:* 1166–1181.

Mendoza, N., E. Soto, & R. Sanchez-Borrego. (2016). What are the risks of hormonal contraceptive use in middle-age women? *Maturitas, 84:* 100.

Morita, M., H. Ohtsuki, & M. Hiraiwa-Hasegawa. (March 30, 2016). Does sexual conflict between mother and father lead to fertility decline? A questionnaire survey in a modern developed society. *Human Nature,* online.

Pollmann-Schult, M. (2014). Parenthood and life satisfaction: Why don't children make people happy. *Journal of Marriage and Family, 76:* 310–336.

Proquest Statistical Abstract of the United States, 2016, online ed. Washington, DC: U.S. Bureau of the Census.

Puri, S., & R. D. Nachtigall. (2010). The ethics of sex selection: A comparison of the attitudes and experiences of primary care physicians and physician providers of clinical sex selection services. *Fertility and Sterility, 93:* 2107–2114.

Richards, M. J., M. Peters, J. Sheeder, & P. Kaul. (January 2, 2016). Contraception and adolescent males: An opportunity for providers. *Journal of Adolescent Health,* online.

Rowe, H., S. Holton, M. Kirkman, C. Bayly, L. Jordan, K. McNamee, J. McBain, V. Sinnott, & J. Fisher. (2016). Prevalence and distribution of unintended pregnancy: The understanding fertility management in Australia and National Survey. *Australian & New Zealand Journal of Public Health, 40:* 104–109.

Sandler, L. (July 19, 2010). One and done. *Time,* pp. 34–41.

Sandlow, J. I. (2013). Size does matter: Higher body mass index may mean lower pregnancy rates for microscopic testicular sperm extraction. *Fertility and Sterility, 99:* 347.

Schmidt, L., T. Sobotka, J. G. Bentzen, & A. Nyboe Andersen. (2012). Demographic and medical consequences of the postponement of parenthood. *Human Reproduction Update, 18:* 29–43.

Scott, L. S. (2009). *Two is enough.* Berkeley, CA: Seal Press.

Seccombe, K. (2015, Winter). China's one child policy: Impressions of a Fullbrighter. *Family Focus, 60*(4): 31F–32F. Published by the National Council on Family Relations.

Shapiro, C. H. (November 2012). Decade of change: New interdisciplinary needs of people with infertility. Paper, National Council on Family Relations, Phoenix, AZ.

Singer, E. (2010). The "W.I.S.E. Up!" tool: Empowering adopted children to cope with questions and comments about adoption. *Pediatric Nursing, 36:* 209–212.

Steinberg, J. R., J. M. Tschann, D. Furgerson, & C. C. Harper. (2016). Prosocial factors and pre-abortion psychological health: The significance of stigma. *Social Science & Medicine, 150:* 67–75.

Sugiura-Ogasawara, M., S. Suzuki, Y. Ozaki, K. Katano, N. Suzumori, & T. Kitaori. (2013). Frequency of recurrent spontaneous abortion and its influence on further marital relationship and illness: The Okazaki cohort study in Japan. *Journal of Obstetrics and Gynaecology Research, 39:* 126–131.

Tal, G., J. Lafortune, & C. Low. (2014). What happens the morning after? The costs and benefits of expanding access to emergency contraception. *Journal of Policy Analysis and Management, 33:* 70–93.

Tanaka, K., & N. E. Johnson. (2016). Childlessness and mental well-being in a global context. *Journal of Family Issues, 37:* 1027–1045.

U.S. Department of Commerce. (2016). Cost of rearing a child born in 2013 to age 18. Retrieved from http://www.usda.gov/wps/portal/usda/usdahome?contentidonly=true&contentid=2014/08/0179.xml

Van Geloven, N., F. Van der Veen, P. M. M. Bossuyt, P. G. Hompes, A. H. Zwinderman, & B. W. Mol. (2013). Can we distinguish between infertility and subfertility when predicting natural conception in couples with an unfulfilled child wish? *Human Reproduction, 28:* 658–665.

Weitz, T. A., D. Taylor, S. Desai, U. D. Upadhyay, J. Waldman, M. F. Battistelli, & E. A. Drey. (2013). Safety of aspiration abortion performed by nurse practitioners, certified nurse midwives, and physician assistants under a California legal waiver. *American Journal of Public Health, 103:* 454–461.

Chapter 12

Adler, M., & K. Lenz. (November 19, 2014). Father involvement with young children in the U.S. and Germany. Paper, Annual Meeting of the National Council on Family Relations, Baltimore, MD.

Andersson, M. A. (2016). The long arm of warm parenting. *Journal of Family Issues, 37:* 879–901.

Armstrong, A. B., & E. F. Clinton. (2012). Altering positive/negative interaction ratios of mothers and young children. *Child Behavior and Family Therapy, 34:* 231–242.

Baumrind, D. (1966). Effects of authoritative parental control on child behavior. *Child Development, 37:* 887–907.

Beato, A., A. Pereira, L. Barros, & P. Muris. (2016). The relationship between different parenting typologies in fathers and mothers and children's anxiety. *Journal of Child & Family, 25:* 1691–1701.

Berryhill, M. B., K. L. Soloski, J. A. Durtschi, & R. R. Adams. (2016). Family process: Early child emotionality, parenting stress, and couple relationship quality. *Personal Relationships, 23:* 23–41.

Borba, M. (2016). *Unselfie: Why empathic kids succeed in our all-about-me world.* New York: Touchstone Books.

Brown, G. L., S. M. Kogan, J. Kim, & J. Cho. (2015, November 13). Fatherhood, impulsivity, and health in low SES, African American men. Poster, Annual Meeting of the National Council on Family Relations, Vancouver, Canada.

Brummelte, S., & L. A. M. Galea. (2016). Postpartum depression: Etiology, treatment and consequences for maternal care. *Hormones and Behavior, 77:* 153–166.

Byrd-Craven, J., B. J. Auer, D. A. Granger, & A. R. Massey. (2012). The father-daughter dance: The relationship between father-daughter relationship quality and daughters' stress response. *Journal of Family Psychology, 26:* 87–94.

Carr, K., & T. R. Wang. (2012). "Forgiveness isn't a simple process: It's a vast undertaking": Negotiating and communicating forgiveness in nonvoluntary family relationships. *Journal of Family Communication, 12:* 40–56.

Coles, R. L. (2015). Single father families: A review of the literature. *Journal of Family Theory and Review, 7:* 144–166.

Copeland, L. (October 23, 2012). Tech keeps tabs on teen drivers. *USA Today,* p. A3.

Corthorn, C., & N. Milicic. (2016). Mindfulness and parenting: A correlational study of non-meditating mothers of preschool children. *Journal of Child & Family Studies, 25:* 1672–1683.

Craig, L., A. Powell, & J. Brown. (2015). Co-resident parents and young people aged 15–34: Who does what housework? *Social Indicators Research, 121:* 569–588.

Crutzen, R., E. Nijhuis, & S. Mujakovic. (2012). Negative associations between primary school children's perception of being allowed to drink at home and alcohol use. *Mental Health and Substance Use, 5:* 64–69.

Daryanani, I., J. L. Hamilton, L. Y. Abramson, & L. B. Alloy. (January 15, 2016). Single mother parenting and adolescent psychopathology. *Journal of Abnormal Child Psychology,* online.

Davis, J. L., & B. Manago. (2016). Motherhood and associative moral stigma: The moral double bind. *Stigma and Health, 1:* 72–86.

Dearden, K., B. Crookston, H. Madanat, J. West, M. Penny, & S. Cueto. (2013). What difference can fathers make? Early paternal absence compromises Peruvian children's growth. *Maternal & Child Nutrition, 9:* 143–154.

Dervin, D. (2016). Where have all the children gone? *The Journal of Psychohistory, 43:* 262–276.

Dill, J. (2015). The parent trap: The challenge of socializing for autonomy and independence. *Society, 52:* 150–154.

Doty, J. (November 12–14, 2015). Trajectories of perceived closeness with fathers and mothers from adolescence to adulthood. Annual Meeting of the National Council on Family Relations, Vancouver, Canada.

Durtschi, J. A., & K. L. Soloski. (November 2012). The dyadic effects of coparenting and parental stress on relationship quality. Presentation, National Council on Family Relations, Phoenix, AZ.

Edwards, R. T., C. Jones, V. Berry, J. Charles, P. Linck, T. Bywater, & J. Hutchings. (2016). Incredible Years Parenting programme: Cost-effectiveness and implementation. *Journal of Children's Services, 11:* 54–72.

Flood, S. M., & K. R. Genadek. (2016). Time for each other: Work and family constraints among couples. *Journal of Marriage and Family, 78:* 142–164.

Fry, R. (2016, May 24). For first time in modern era, living with parents edges out other living arrangements for 18 to 34 year olds. *Pew Research Center.* Retrieved from http://www.pewsocialtrends.org/2016/05/24/for-first-time-in-modern-era-living-with-parents-edges-out-other-living-arrangements-for-18-to-34-year-olds/

Gelabert, E., S. Subirà, L.García-Esteve, P. Navarro, A. Plaza, E. Cuyàs, et al. (2012). Perfectionism dimensions in major postpartum depression. *Journal of Affective Disorders, 136:* 17–25.

Golombok, S., S. Zadeh, S. Imrie, V. Smith, & T. Freeman. (February 11, 2016). Single mothers by choice: Mother-child relationship's psychological adjustment. *Journal of Family Psychology,* online.

Gordon, M., & J. Hull. (2014, November 19). Father involvement and adolescent's achievement: A mediational analysis. Paper, Annual Meeting of the National Council on Family Relations, Baltimore, MD.

Gray, P. B., J. R. Garcia, B. S. Crosier, & H. E. Fisher. (2015). Dating and sexual behavior among single parents of young children in the United States. *Journal of Sex Research, 52:* 121–128.

Gray, S. A. O., K. K. Sweeney, R. Randazzo, & H. M. Levitt. (2016). "Am I Doing the Right Thing?": Pathways to parenting a gender variant child. *Family Process, 55:* 123–138.

Haag, P. (2011). *Marriage confidential.* New York: Harper Collins.

Harpel, T., & K. Gentry. (2014, November 19). "I felt like a dad": Expectant fathers and ultrasounds. Paper, Annual Meeting of the National Council on Family Relations, Baltimore, MD.

Henchoz, Y., A. A. N'Goran, S. Deline, J. Studer, S. Baggio, & G. Gmel. (2016). Associations of age at cannabis first use and later substance abuse with mental health and depression in young men. *Journal of Substance Use, 21:* 85–91.

Henderson, A., S. Harmon, & H. Newman. (2016). The price mothers pay, even when they are not buying it: Mental health consequences of idealized motherhood. *Sex Roles, 74:* 512–526.

Hipwell, A. E., S. D. Stepp, E. L. Moses-Kolko, S. Xiong, E. Paul, N. Merrick, S. McClellan, D. Verble, & K. Keenan. (March 12, 2016). Predicting adolescent postpartum caregiving from trajectories of depression and anxiety prior to childbirth: A 5-year prospective study. *Archives of Women's Mental Health,* online.

Holmes, E. K., T. Sasaki, & N. L. Hazen. (2013). Smooth versus rocky transitions to parenthood: Family systems in developmental context. *Family Relations, 62:* 824–837.

Hong, R., & A. Welch. (2013). The lived experiences of single Taiwanese mothers being resilient after divorce. *Journal of Transcultural Nursing, 24:* 51–59.

Hyde, A., J. Drennan, M. Butler, E. Howlett, M. Carney, & M. Lohan. (2013). Parents' constructions of communication with their children about safer sex. *Journal of Clinical Nursing, 22:* 3438–3446.

Irving, C. M., & R. A. Richardson. (November 19, 2014). Parent-child connectedness and positive youth development: Longitudinal links. Paper, Annual Meeting of the National Council on Family Relations, Baltimore, MD.

Jang, J. B., & S. E. Mernitz. (November 12–14, 2015). Geographic distance to parents in the transition to adulthood in the United States. Annual Meeting of the National Council on Family Relations, Vancouver, Canada.

Janssen, H. J., V. Eishelsheim, M. Dekovic, & G. J. N. Bruinsma. (2016). How is parenting related to adolescent delinquency? A between- and within-person analysis of the mediating role of self-control, delinquent attitudes, peer delinquency, and time spent in criminogenic settings. *European Journal of Criminology, 13:* 169–194.

Keim, B., & A. L. Jacobson. (2011). *Wisdom for parents: Key ideas from parent educators.* Toronto: de Sitter Publications of Canada.

Killewald, A. (2013). A reconsideration of the fatherhood premium: Marriage, coresidence, biology, and fathers' wages. *American Sociological Review, 78:* 96–116.

King, K. A., R. A. Vidourek, & A. L. Merianos. (2016). Authoritarian parenting and youth depression: Results from a national study. *Journal of Prevention & Intervention in the Community, 44:* 130–139.

Kings, C. A., T. Knight, D. Ryan and J. A. Macdonald. (April 28, 2016). The 'Sensory Deprivation Tank': Phenomenological analysis of men's expectations of first-time fatherhood. *Psychology of Men & Masculinity,* online.

Knox, D., & S. Milstein. (2017). *Human sexuality: Making informed choices,* 5th ed. Reddington, CA.: Best Value Publishers.

Kuo, P., & B. Volling. (November 2014). Coparenting perceptions across the transition to second-time parenthood. Paper, Annual Meeting of the National Council on Family Relations, Baltimore, MD.

Leavitt, C. E., B. T. McDaniel, M. K. Maas, & M. E. Feinberg. (November 12–14, 2015). Parenting stress and sexual satisfaction: A dyadic approach. Annual Meeting of the National Council on Family Relations, Vancouver, Canada.

Lehr, M., B. Wecksell, L. Nahum, D. Neuhaus, K. Teel, L. Linares, & A. Diaz. (2016). Parenting stress, child characteristics, and developmental delay from birth to age five in teen mother-child dyads. *Journal of Child & Family Studies, 25:* 1035–1043.

Levtov, R, N. van der Gaag, M. Greene, M. Kaufman, & G. Barker. (2015). *State of the World's Fathers: A MenCare Advocacy Publication.* Retrieved from http://sowf.s3.amazonaws.com/wp-content/uploads/2015/06/08181421/State-of-the-Worlds-Fathers_23June2015.pdf

Lowe, K., A. M., Dotterer, & J. Francisco. (2015, March 15). "If I pay, I have a say!" Parental payment of college education and its association with helicopter parenting. *Emerging Adulthood,* online.

Luthar, S. S., & L. Ciciolla. (2016). What it feels like to be a mother: Variations by children's developmental stages. *Developmental Psychology, 52:* 143–154.

Maier, C., & C. R. McGeorge. (2013). Positive perceptions of single mothers and fathers: Implications for therapy. Annual Meeting of the National Council on Family Relations, San Antonio, TX.

Mashoa, S. W., D. Chapmana, & M. Ashbya. (2010). The impact of paternity and marital status on low birth weight and preterm births. *Marriage & Family Review, 46:* 243–256.

McKinney, C., & K. Renk. (2008). Differential parenting between mothers and fathers: Implications for late adolescents. *Journal of Family Issues, 29:* 806–827.

Metler, D., & S. Small. (November 12–14, 2015). Wise parenting: An empirical study. Paper, Annual Meeting of the National Council on Family Relations, Vancouver, Canada.

Milkie, M. A., K. M. Nomaguchi, & K. E. Denny. (2015). Does the amount of time mothers spend with children or adolescents matter? *Journal of Marriage and Family, 77:* 355–372.

Moroney, S. (2016). Master bedrooms and master suites. *Journal of Family History, 41:* 81–94.

Nelson, L. J., L. M. Padilla-Walker, & M. G. Nielson. (2015). Is hovering smothering or loving? An examination of parental warmth as a moderator of relations between helicopter parenting and emerging adults' indices of adjustment. *Emerging Adulthood,* online. doi:10.1177/2167696815576458

Newman, K. (Winter 2015). The accordion family. *Family Focus, 60*(4): F29–F30. Published by the National Council on Family Relations.

Oppenheimer, J. (2002). *Seinfeld: The making of an American icon.* New York: HarperCollins.

Otters, R. V., & J. F. Hollander. (2015). Leaving home and boomerang decisions: A family simulation protocol. *Marriage & Family Review, 51:* 39–58.

Ozyurt, G., O. Gencer, Y. Ozturk, & A. Ozbek. (2016). Is triple P positive parenting program effective on anxious children and their parents? 4th month follow up results. *Journal of Child and Family Studies, 25:* 1646–1655.

Padilla-Walker, L. M., L. J. Nelson, & J. S. Carroll. (2012). Affording emerging adulthood: Parental financial assistance of their college-aged children. *Journal of Adult Development, 12:* 50–58.

Panetta, S. M., C. L. Somers, A. R. Ceresnie, S. B. Hillman, & R. T. Partridge. (2014). Maternal and paternal parenting style patterns and adolescent emotional and behavioral outcomes. *Marriage & Family Review, 50:* 342–359.

Park, H., & A. S. Lau. (2016). Socioeconomic status and parenting priorities: Child independence and obedience around the world. *Journal of Marriage and Family, 78:* 43–59.

Payne, K., & P. Trapp. (April 30, 2013). What makes parenting tougher today? *USA Today* (survey by Survey.com), p. D1.

Petrovic, M., V. Vasic, O. Petrovic, & M. Santric-Milicevic. (May 4, 2016). Positive parenting attitudes and practices in three transnational eastern European countries: Bosnia and Herzegovina, Macedonia and Serbia. *International Journal of Public Health,* online.

ProQuest Statistical Abstract of the United States, 2016, online ed. Washington, DC: U.S. Bureau of the Census.

Puhlman, D., & K. Pasley. (November 12–14, 2015). Types of maternal gatekeeping and father involvement: Fathers' perspective. Annual Meeting of the National Council on Family Relations, Vancouver, Canada.

Riina, E. M., & S. M. McHale. (2015). African American couples' coparenting satisfaction and marital characteristics in the first two decades of marriage. *Journal of Family Issues, 36:* 902–923.

Roubinov, D. S., L. J. Luecken, N. A. Gonzales, & K. A. Crnic. (2016). Father involvement in Mexican-origin families: Preliminary development of a culturally informed measure. *Cultural Diversity and Ethnic Minority Psychology, 22:* 277–287.

Sandberg-Thoma, S. E., A. R. Snyder, & B. J. Jang. (2015). Exiting and returning to the parental home for boomerang kids. *Journal of Marriage and Family, 77:* 806–818.

Senior, J. (2014). *All joy and no fun: The paradox of modern parenthood.* New York: HarperCollins.

Slinger, M. R., & D. J. Bredehoft. (November 3–5, 2010). Relationships between childhood overindulgence and adult attitudes and behavior. Poster, Annual Meeting of the National Council on Family Relations, Minneapolis, MN.

Steinmetz, K. (October 26, 2015). Help! My parents are millennials. *Time,* pp. 36–43.

Stykes, J. B. (2015). What matters most? Money, relationships, and visions of masculinity as key correlates of father involvement. *Fathering: A Journal of Theory, Research & Practice about Men as Fathers, 13:* 60–79.

Su, J. H. (2012), Pregnancy intentions and parents' psychological well-being. *Journal of Marriage and Family, 74:* 1182–1196.

Surjadi, F. F., F. O. Lorenz, R. D. Conger, & K. A. S. Wickrama. (2013). Harsh, inconsistent parental discipline and romantic relationships: Mediating processes of behavioral problems and ambivalence. *Journal of Family Psychology, 27:* 762–772.

Sweeney, K., A. E. Goldberg, & R. L. Garcia. (November 12–14, 2015). Gatekeeping around childcare among, gay, lesbian, and heterosexual parents. Annual Meeting of the National Council on Family Relations, Vancouver, Canada.

Theobald, D., D. P. Farrington, & A. R. Piquero. (2015). Does the birth of a first child reduce the father's offending? *Australian & New Zealand Journal of Criminology, 48:* 3–23.

Thompson, M., & J. J. Beckmeyer. (November 13, 2015). Teen mothers' relations with their child's father: Implications for FLE. Poster, Annual Meeting of the National Council on Family Relations, Vancouver, Canada.

Tully, L., & C. Hunt. (2016). Brief parenting interventions for children at risk of externalizing behavior problems: A systematic review. *Journal of Child & Family Studies, 25:* 705–719.

Uji, M., A. Sakamoto, K. Adachi, & T. L. Kitamura. (2014). The impact of authoritative, authoritarian and permissive parenting styles on children's later mental health in Japan: Focusing on parent and child gender. *Journal of Child & Family Studies, 23:* 293–302.

Valtchanov, B. L., D. C. Parry, T. D. Glover, & C. M. Mulcahy. (2015). "A whole new world": Mothers' technologically mediated leisure. *Leisure Sciences, 38:* 50–67.

Walcheski, M. J., & D. J. Bredehoft. (November 3–5, 2010). Exploring the relationship between overindulgence and parenting styles. Poster, Annual Meeting of the National Council on Family Relations, Minneapolis, MN.

Walls, J. K., H. M. Helms, & J. G. Grzywacz. (2016). Intensive-mothering beliefs among full time employed mothers of infants. *Journal of Family Issues, 37:* 245–269.

Wightman, P., R. Schoeni, & K. Robinson. (May 3, 2012). Familial financial assistance to young adults. Paper, Annual Meeting of the Population Association of America, New Orleans, LA.

Williams, L., & E. Anthony. (2015). A model of positive family and peer relationships on adolescent functioning. *Journal of Child & Family Studies, 24:* 658–667.

Willoughby, B. J., J. N. Hersh, L. M. Padilla-Walker, & L. J. Nelson. (2015). "Back-Off" helicopter parenting and a retreat from marriage among emerging adults. *Journal of Family Issues, 36:* 669–692.

Wilson, K. R., S. S. Havighurst, & A. E. Harley. (2012). Tuning in to kids: An effectiveness trial of a parenting program targeting emotion socialization of preschoolers. *Journal of Family Psychology, 26:* 56–65.

Wiseman, R. (2013). *Masterminds and wingmen.* New York: Harmony Books.

Yavorsky, J. E., C. M. Kamp-Dush, & S. J. Schoppe-Sullivan. (2015). The production of inequality: The gender division of labor across the transition to parenthood. *Journal of Marriage and Family, 77:* 662–679.

Yoon, Y., K. Newkirk, & M. Perry-Jenkins. (2015). Parenting stress, dinnertime rituals, and child well-being in working class families. *Family Relations, 64:* 93–107.

Yu, J., M. Roberts, Y. Shen, & M. Wong. (2015). Behavioral family therapy for Chinese preschoolers with disruptive behavior: A pilot study. *Journal of Child & Family Studies, 24:* 1192–1202.

Zeiders, K. H., K. A. Updegraff, A. J. Umaña-Taylor, S. M. McHale, & J. Padilla. (2016). Familism values, family time, and Mexican-origin young adults' depressive symptoms. *Journal of Marriage and Family, 78:* 91–106.

Chapter 13

Aalgaard, R. A., R. M. Bolen, & W. R. Nugent. (2016). A literature review of forgiveness as a beneficial intervention to increase relationship satisfaction in couples therapy. *Journal of Human Behavior in the Social Environment, 26:* 46–55.

Aboujaoude, E., W. Salame, & L. Naim. (2015). Telemental health: A status update. *World Psychiatry, 13:* 223–230.

Abrahamson, I., H. Rafat, K. Adeel, & M. J. Scho-field. (2012). What helps couples rebuild their relationship after infidelity. *Journal of Family Issues, 33*: 1494–1519.

Albuquerque, S., M. Pereira, & I. Narciso. (2016). Couple's relationship after the death of a child: A systematic review. *Journal of Child and Family Studies, 25*: 30–53.

Baer, R. A., J. Carmody, & M. Hunsinger. (2012). Weekly change in mindfulness and perceived stress reduction program. *Journal of Clinical Psychology, 68*: 755–765.

Berk, R. A. (2015). The greatest veneration: Humor as a coping strategy for the challenges of aging. *Social Work in Mental Health, 13*: 30–47.

Bermant, G. (1976). Sexual behavior: Hard times with the Coolidge Effect. In M. H. Siegel & H. P. Zeigler (Eds.), *Psychological research: The inside story.* New York: Harper and Row.

Boss, P. (2013). Myth of closure: What is normal grief after loss, clear or ambiguous? Annual Meeting of the National Council on Family Relations, San Antonio, TX.

Boterhoven de Haan, K. L., J. Hafekost, D. Lawrence, M. G. Sawyer, & S. R. Zubrick. (2015). Reliability and validity of a short version of the general functioning subscale of the McMaster Family Assessment Device. *Family Process, 54*: 116–123.

Brand, J. E. (2015). The far-reading impact of job loss and unemployment. *Annual Review of Sociology, 41*: 359–375.

Burke, M. L., G. G. Eakes, & M. A. Hainsworth. (1999). Milestones of chronic sorrow: Perspectives of chronically ill and bereaved persons and family caregivers. *Journal of Family Nursing, 5*: 387–484.

Burr, W. R., & S. R. Klein. (1994). *Reexamining family stress: New theory and research.* Thousand Oaks, CA: Sage.

Carter, Z. A. (2016). Married and previously married men and women's perceptions of communication on Facebook with the opposite sex: How communicating through Facebook can be damaging to marriages. *Journal of Divorce and Remarriage, 57*: 36–55.

Cox, R. B., J. S. Ketner, & A. J. Blow. (2013). Working with couples and substance abuse: Recommendations for clinical practice. *The American Journal of Family Therapy, 41*: 160–172.

Derby, K., D. Knox, & B. Easterling. (2012). Snooping in romantic relationships. *College Student Journal, 46*: 333–343.

Doria, M. V., H. Kennedy, C. Strathie, & S. Strathie. (2014). Explanations for the success of video interaction guidance (VIG): An emerging method in family psychotherapy. *The Family Journal, 22*: 78–87.

Doss, B. D., L. N. Cicila, E. J. Georgia, M. K. Roddy, K. M. Nowlan, L. A. Benson, & A. Christensen. (2016) A randomized controlled trial of the web-based OurRelationship program: Effects on relationship and individual functioning. *Journal of Consulting and Clinical Psychology, 84*: 285–296.

Ellison, C. G., A. K. Henderson, N. D. Glenn, & K. E. Harkrider (2011). Sanctification, stress, and marital quality. *Family Relations, 60*: 404–420.

Falconier, M. K., F. Nussbeck, G. Bodenmann, H. Schneider, & T. Bradbury. (2015). Stress from daily hassles in couples: Its effects on intradyadic stress, relationship satisfaction, and physical and psychological well being. *Journal of Marital and Family Therapy, 41*: 221–235.

Finan, L. J., J. Schultz, M. S. Gordon, & C. M. Ohannessian. (November, 2014). Parental problem drinking, family functioning, and adolescent outcomes. Presentation, Annual Meeting of the National Council on Family Relations, Baltimore, MD.

Frisby, B. N., S. M. Horan, & M. Booth-Butterfield. (2016). The role of humor styles and shared laughter in the postdivorce recovery process. *Journal of Divorce & Remarriage, 57*: 56–75.

Grases, G., C. Sanchez-Curto, E. Rigo, & D. Androver-Roig. (2012). Relationship between positive humor and state and trait anxiety. *Ansiedad y Estrés, 18*: 79–93.

Hall, S., & D. Knox. (2016). Relationship and sexual behaviors of a sample of 9,684 university students. Unpublished data collected for this text. Department of Family and Consumer Sciences, Ball State University and Department of Sociology, East Carolina University.

Hall, W. (2015). What has research over the past two decades revealed about the adverse health effects of recreational cannabis use? *Addiction, 110*: 19–35.

Hertlein, K. M., M. L. Blumer, & J. H. Mihaliokos. (2015). Marriage and family counselors perceived ethical issues related to online therapy. *Family Journal, 23*: 5–12.

Hill, E. W. (2010). Discovering forgiveness through empathy: Implications for couple and family therapy. *Journal of Family Therapy, 32*: 169–185.

Hottes, T. S., L. Bogaert, A. E. Rhodes, D. J. Brenan, & D. Gesink. (2016). Lifetime prevalence of suicide attempts among sexual minority adults by study sampling strategies: A systematic review and meta-analysis. *American Journal of Public Health, 106*: 1–12.

Hudson, C. G. (2012). Declines in mental illness over the adult years: An enduring finding or methodological artifact? *Aging & Mental Health, 16*: 735–752.

Jackman, M. (2015). Understanding the cheating heart: What determines infidelity intentions? *Sexuality and Culture, 19*: 72–84.

Jeanfreau, M. M., A. P. Jurich, & M. D. Mong. (2013). An examination of potential attractions of women's marital infidelity. *American Journal of Family Therapy, 42*: 14–28.

Johnson, M. D., & T. N. Bradbury. (2015). Contributions of social learning theory to the promotion of healthy relationships: Asset or liability? *Journal of Family Theory & Review, 7*: 13–27.

Kanat-Maymon, Y., A. Antebi, & S. Zilcha-Mano. (2016). Basic psychological need fulfillment in human-pet relationship and well being. *Personality and Individual Differences, 92*: 69–73.

Kanewisher, E. J. W., & S. M. Harris. (2015). Deciding not to undo the "I Do": Therapy experiences of women who consider divorce but decide to remain married. *Journal of Marital and Family Therapy, 41*: 367–380.

Kim, H. W., C. A. Pepping, & J. Petch. (2016). The gap between couple therapy research efficacy and practice effectiveness. *Journal of Marital and Family Therapy, 42*: 32–44.

Kincaid, E. (2015, August 9). Online therapy is growing incredibly fast: Here's why that matters. *Inside Tech.* Retrieved from http://news360.com/article/306350835#

Klein, M. (August 20, 2015). Ashley Madison: Play around, or just play? Sexual intelligence. Retrieved from https://sexualintelligence.wordpress.com/2015/08/30/ashley-madison-playing-around-or-just-playing/

Lammers, J., & J. Maner. (2016). Power and attraction to the counternormative aspects of infidelity. *Journal of Sex Research, 53*: 54–63.

Lane, C. D., P. S. Meszaros, & T. Savla. (November 2012). Developing the family resilience measure. Paper, Annual Meeting of the National Council on Family Relations, Phoenix, AZ.

Lee, Y., S. L. Hofferth, S. M. Flood, & K. Fisher. (2016). Reliability, validity, and variability of the subjective well-being questions in the 2010 American Time Use Survey. *Social Indicators Research, 126*: 1355–1373.

Lotspeich-Younkin, F., & S. Bartle-Haring. (November 2012). Differentiation and relationship satisfaction: Mediating effects of emotional intimacy and alcohol/substance use. Paper, Annual Meeting of the National Council on Family Relations, Phoenix, AZ.

MaddoxShaw, A. M., G. K. Rhoades, E. S. Allen, S. M. Stanley, & H. J. Markman. (2013). Predictors of extradyadic sexual involvement in unmarried opposite-sex relationships. *Journal of Sex Research, 50*: 598–610.

Magaziner, J. (September/October 2012). The new technologies of change. *Psychology Networker,* pp. 42–47.

Maple, M., H. E. Edwards, V. Minichiello, & D. Plummer. (2013). Still part of the family: The importance of physical, emotional and spiritual memorial places and spaces for parents bereaved through the suicide death of their son or daughter. *Mortality, 18*: 54–71.

McCarthy, M. J., & E. Bauer. (2015). In sickness and in health: Couples coping with stroke across the life span. *Health and Social Work, 40*: 92–100.

Morell, V. (1998). A new look at monogamy. *Science, 281*: 1982.

Mrug, S., A. Tyson, B. Turan, & D. A. Granger. (2016) Sleep problems predict cortisol reactivity to stress in urban adolescents. *Physiology & Behavior, 155*: 95–101.

Negash, S., M. Cui, F. D. Fincham, & K. Pasley. (2014). Extradyadic involvement and relationship dissolution in heterosexual women university students. *Archives of Sexual Behavior, 43*: 531–539.

Omarzu, J., A. N. Miller, C. Shultz, & A. Timmerman. (June 2012). Motivations and emotional consequences related to engaging in extramarital relationships. *International Journal of Sexual Health, 24*, online.

Picci, R., F. Oliva, F. Trivelli, C. Carezana, M. Zuffanieri, L. Ostacoli, P. Furlan, & R. Lala. (2015). Emotional burden and coping strategies of parents of children with rare diseases. *Journal of Child and Family Studies, 24*: 514–522.

Power, J., M. Goodyear, D. Mayberry, A. Reupert, B. O'Hanlon, R. Cuff, & A. Perlesz. (2016). Family resilience in families where a parent has a mental illness. *Journal of Social Work, 16*: 66–82.

Preyde, M., C. VanDonge, J. Carter, K. Lazure-Valconi, S. White, G. Ashbourne, R. Penney, K. Frensch, & G. Cameron. (2015). Parents of youth in intensive mental health treatment: Associations between emotional and behavioral disorders and parental sense of competence. *Child and Adolescent Social Work Journal, 32*: 317–327.

Reed, K., A. J. Ferraro, M. Lucier-Greer, & C. Barber. (November 2014). Adverse family influences and depression: Identifying points of intervention. Presentation, Annual Meeting of the National Council on Family Relations, Baltimore, MD.

Reiser, J. E., S. L. Murphy, & C. J. McCarthy. (2016). Stress prevention and mindfulness: A psychoeducational and support group for teachers. *Journal for Specialists in Group Work, 41:* 117–139.

Rodriguez-Rey, R., J. Alonso-Tapia, & H. Hernansaiz-Garrido. (2016). Reliability and validity of the Brief Relience Scale (BRS) Spanish version. *Psychological Assessment, 28:* e101–e110.

Russell, V. M, L. R. Baker, & J. K. Mcnulty. (2013). Attachment insecurity and infidelity in marriage: Do studies of dating relationships really inform us about marriage? *Journal of Family Psychology, 27:* 241–251.

Salvador, A., C. Crespo, A. Martins, S. Santos, & M. Canavarro. (2015). Parents' perceptions about their child's illness in pediatric cancer: Links with caregiving burden and quality of life. *Journal of Child and Family Studies, 24:* 1129–1140.

Scuka, R. F. (2015). A clinician's guide to helping couples heal from the trauma of infidelity. *Journal of Couple & Relationship Therapy: Innovations in Clinical and Educational Interventions, 14:* 141–168.

Sitnick, S. L., K. Masyn, L. L. Ontai, & K. J. Conger. (2016). Mothers' physical illness in one and two parent families. *Journal of Family Issues, 37:* 902–920.

Swan, D. J., & S. C. Thompson. (2016). Monogamy, the protective fallacy: Sexual versus emotional exclusivity and the implication for sexual health risk. *Journal of Sex Research, 53:* 64–73.

Thomas, R., & J. Matusitz. (2016). Pet therapy in correctional institutions: A perspective from relational-cultural theory. *Journal of Evidence-Informed Social Work, 13:* 228–235.

Thomeer, M. B. (2016). Multiple chronic conditions, spouse's depressive symptoms, and gender within marriage. *Journal of Health & Social Behavior, 57:* 59–76.

Vladimirov, D., S. Niemela, J. Auvinen, M. Timonen, & S. Keinanen-Kiukaaniemi. (2016). Changes in alcohol use in relation to sociodemographic factors in early midlife. *Scandinavian Journal of Public Health, 44:* 249–257.

Walker, A. C., J. D. Hathcoat, & S. A. Harnas. (November 12–14, 2015). Violent loss and religious coping: A multi group path analysis. Annual Meeting of the National Council on Family Relations, Vancouver, Canada.

Walters, A. S., & B. D. Burger. (2013). "I love you, and I cheat": Investigating disclosures of infidelity to primary romantic partners. *Sexuality & Culture, 17:* 20–49.

Chapter 14

Al-Gharaibeh, F. M. (2015). The effects of divorce on children: Mothers' perspectives in UAE. *Journal of Divorce & Remarriage, 56:* 347–368.

Allen, E. S., & D. C. Atkins. (2012). The association of divorce and extramarital sex in a representative U.S. sample. *Journal of Family Issues, 33:* 1477–1493.

Amato, P. R. (November 12–14, 2015). Revisiting the intergenerational transmission of divorce (ITD). Annual Meeting of the National Council on Family Relations.

Anderson, L. R. (2016). Lowest divorce rate in 35 years. National Center for Family & Marriage Research. Bowling Green State University. http://www.bgsu.edu/ncfmr/resources/data

/family-profiles/anderson-divorce-rate-us-geo-2015-fp-16-21.html

Baglivio, M. T., & N. Epps. (2016). The interrelatedness of adverse childhood experiences among high-risk juvenile offenders. *Youth Violence & Juvenile Justice, 14:* 179–198.

Bourassa, K. J., D. A. Sbarra, & M. A. Whisman. (2015). Women in very low quality marriages gain life satisfaction following divorce. *Journal of Family Psychology, 29:* 490–499.

Brenner, R., & D. Knox. (2016). Recovery from breakup of a romantic relationship. Unpublished data.

Brenner, R. E., & D. G. Vogal. (August 7, 2014). Positive thought content valence after a breakup: Development of the positive and negative ex-relationship thoughts scale. Poster, Annual Meeting of the American Psychological Association, Washington, DC.

Bromfield, N. F., S. Ashour, & K. Rider. (2016). Divorce from arranged marriages: An exploration of lived experiences. *Journal of Divorce & Remarriage, 57:* 280–297.

Brown, S. M., & J. Porter. (2013). The effects of religion on remarriage among American women: Evidence from the National Survey of Family Growth. *Journal of Divorce & Remarriage, 54:* 142–162.

Clarke, S. C., & B. F. Wilson. (1994). The relative stability of remarriages: A cohort approach using vital statistics. *Family Relations, 43:* 305–310.

Coontz, S. (2016). *The way we never were: American families and the nostalgia trap*, 2nd ed. New York: Basic Books.

DeGreeff, B. L., & C. A. Platt. (2016). Green-eyed (step) monsters: Parental figures' perceptions of jealousy in the stepfamily. *Journal of Divorce & Remarriage, 57:* 112–132.

Djamba, Y. K., L. C. Mullins, K. P. Brackett, & N. J. McKenzie. (2012). Household size as a correlate of divorce rate: A county-level analysis. *Sociological Spectrum, 32:* 436–448.

Doherty, W. J., S. M. Harris, & K. W. Didericksen. (2016). A typology of attitudes toward proceeding with divorce among parents in the divorce process. *Journal of Divorce & Remarriage, 57:* 1–11.

Faircloth, M., D. Knox, & J. Brinkley. (March 21–24, 2012). The good, the bad and technology mediated communication in romantic relationships. Paper, Southern Sociological Society, New Orleans, LA.

Fisher, H., & J. R. Garcia. (2016). Singles in America. Retrieved from http://www.singlesinamerica.com/

Fonseca, G., D. Cunha, C. Crespo, & A. P. Relvas. (2016). Families in the context of macroeconomic crises: A systematic review. *Journal of Family Psychology, 30:* 687–697.

Gager, C. T., S. T. Yabiku, & M. R. Linver. (2016). Conflict or divorce? Does parental conflict and/or divorce increase the likelihood of adult children's cohabiting and marital dissolution? *Marriage & Family Review, 52:* 243–261.

Ganong, L. H., & M. Coleman. (1999). *Changing families, changing responsibilities: Family obligations following divorce and remarriage*. New York: Lawrence Erlbaum.

Garneau, C. L., F. Adler-Baeder, & B. Higginbotham. (2016). Validating the Remarriage Belief Inventory as a dyadic measure for stepcouples. *Journal of Family Issues, 37:* 132–150.

Gatins, D., C. R. Kinlaw, & L. Dunlap. (2015). Do the kids think they're okay? Views on the impact of marriage and divorce. *Journal of Divorce & Remarriage, 54:* 313–328.

Goetting, A. (1982). The six stations of remarriage: The developmental tasks of remarriage after divorce. *The Family Coordinator, 31:* 213–222.

Graham, J. L., E. Keneski, & T. J. Loving. (Winter 2014s). Mental and physical health correlates of nonmarital relationship dissolution. *NCFR Report, Family Focus.* Minneapolis, MN: National Council on Family Relations.

Hall, S., & D. Knox. (2016). Relationship and sexual behaviors of a sample of 9,650 university students. Unpublished data collected for this text. Department of Family and Consumer Sciences, Ball State University and Department of Sociology, East Carolina University.

Halligan, C., J. Chang, & D. Knox. (2014). Positive effects of parental divorce on undergraduates. *Journal of Divorce & Remarriage, 55:* 557–567.

Hansson, M., & T. Ahborg. (2016). Factors contributing to separation/divorce in parents of small children in Sweden. *Nordic Psychology, 68:* 40–57.

Hawkins, A. J., B. J. Willoughby, & W. J. Doherty. (2012). Reasons for divorce and openness to marital reconciliation. *Journal of Divorce & Remarriage, 53:* 453–463.

Herman, G. (2016). Same sex divorce. *American Journal of Family Law, 29:* 198–199.

James, S. L. (2015). Variation in marital quality in a national sample of divorced women. *Journal of Family Psychology, 29:* 479–489.

Jensen, T., S. Guo, K. Shafer, & J. Larson. (November 2014). Marriage order and relationship stability: A propensity score analysis. Paper, Annual Meeting of the National Council on Family Relations, Baltimore, MD.

Jensen, T. M., & G. L. Bowen. (2015). Mid and late-life divorce and parents' perceptions of emerging adult children's emotional reactions. *Journal of Divorce & Remarriage, 56:* 409–427.

Jensen, T. M., B. M. Lombardi, & J. H. Larson. (2014). Adult attachment and step parenting issues: Couple quality as a mediating factor. *Journal of Divorce & Remarriage, 56:* 80–94.

Kanewisher, E. J. W., & S. M. Harris. (2015). Deciding not to undo the "I Do": Therapy experiences of women who consider divorce but decide to remain married. *Journal of Marital and Family Therapy, 41:* 367–380.

Karraker, A., & K. Latham. (2015). In sickness and in health? Physical illness as a risk factor for marital dissolution in later life. *Journal of Health and Social Behavior, 56:* 59–73.

Killewald, A. (2016). Money, work, and marital stability: Assessing change in the gendered determinants of divorce. *American Sociological Review, 81:* 696–719.

Kim, H. (2011). Exploratory study on the factors affecting marital satisfaction among remarried Korean couples. *Families in Society, 91:* 193–200.

Knopfli, B., S. Cullati, D. S. Courvoisier, C. Burton-Jeangros, & P. Perrig-Chiello. (January 5, 2016). Marital breakup in later adulthood and self-rated health: A cross-sectional survey in Switzerland. *International Journal of Public Health*, online.

Konstam, V., S. Karwin, T. Curran, M. Lyons, & S. Celen-Demirtas. (2016). Stigma and divorce: A relevant lens for emerging and young adult women? *Journal of Divorce & Remarriage, 57:* 173–194.

Kulu, H. (2015). Marriage duration and divorce: The seven-year itch or a lifelong itch? *Demography, 51:* 881–893.

Lawick, J., & M. Visser. (2015). No kids in the middle: Dialogical and creative work with parents and children in the context of high conflict divorces. *Australian & New Zealand Journal of Family Therapy, 36:* 33–50.

Lawson, E. J., & F. Satti. (2016). The aftermath of divorce: Postdivorce adjustment strategies of South Asian, Black, and White women in the United States. *Journal of Divorce & Remarriage, 57:* 411–431.

Lucier-Greer, M., F. Adler-Baeder, S. A. Ketring, K. T. Harcourt, & T. Smith. (2012). Comparing the experiences of couples in first marriages and remarriages in couple and relationship education. *Journal of Divorce & Remarriage, 53:* 55–75.

Martin-Uzzi, M., & D. Duval-Tsioles. (2013). The experience of remarried couples in blended families. *Journal of Divorce & Remarriage, 54:* 43–57.

Masheter, C. (1999). Examples of commitment in post divorce relationships between spouses. In J. M. Adams & W. H. Jones (Eds.), *Handbook of interpersonal commitment and relationship stability* (pp. 293–306). New York: Academic/Plenum Publishers.

Mason, A. E., R.W. Law, A. E. Bryan, R. M. Portley, & D. A. Sbarra. (2012). Facing a breakup: Electromyographic responses moderate self-concept recovery following a romantic separation. *Personal Relationships, 19:* 551–568.

McCann, E., J. Dworkin, & J. McGuire. (November 12–14, 2015). Digital divorce: Co-parenting in the era of technology. Annual Meeting of the National Council on Family Relations, Vancouver, Canada.

McIntosh, J. E., Y. D. Wells, B. M. Smyth, & C. M. Long. (2008). Child-focused and child-inclusive divorce mediation: Comparative outcomes from a prospective study of post separation adjustment. *Family Court Review, 46:* 105–115.

McNamee, C. B., P. Amato, & V. King. (2014). Nonresident father involvement with children and divorced women's likelihood of remarriage. *Journal of Marriage and Family, 76:* 862–874.

Mirecki, R. M., J. L. Chou, M. Elliott, & C. M. Schneider. (2013). What factors influence marital satisfaction? Differences between first and second marriages. *Journal of Divorce & Remarriage, 54:* 78–93.

Mogilski, J. K., & L. L. M. Welling. (April 8, 2016). Staying friends with an ex: Sex and dark personality traits predict motivations for post relationship friendship. *Personality and Individual Differences,* online.

Morgan, E. S. (1944). *The Puritan family.* Boston: Public Library.

Northrup, J. C., & S. Shumway. (2014). Gamer widow: A phenomenological study of spouses of online video game addicts. *The American Journal of Family Therapy, 42:* 269–281.

Nuru, A. K., & T. R. Wang. (2014). "She was stomping on everything that we used to think of as family": Communication and turning points in cohabiting (step) families. *Journal of Divorce & Remarriage, 55:* 145–163.

Oppenheimer, J. (2002). *Seinfeld: The making of an American icon.* New York: HarperCollins.

Park, H., & J. M. Raymo. (2013). Divorce in Korea: Trends and educational differentials. *Journal of Marriage and Family, 75:* 110–126.

Perrig-Chiello, P., S. Hutchinson, & D. Morselli. (2015). Patterns of psychological adaptation to divorce after a long term marriage. *Journal of Social & Personal Relationships, 32:* 386–405.

Plauche, H. P., L. D. Marks, & A. J. Hawkins. (June 27, 2016). Why we choose to stay together: Qualitative interviews with separated couples who chose to reconcile. *Journal of Divorce & Remarriage, 57:* 317–337, online. Retrieved from http://dx.doi.org/10.1080/10502556.2016.1185089

Scarf, M. (2013). *The remarriage blueprint: How remarried couples and their families succeed or fail.* New York: Scribner.

Schrobsdorff, S. (August 3, 2015). The rise of the "good divorce." *Time,* pp. 27–38.

Simon, C. (2015). *Boys in the trees.* New York: Flatiron.

Soares, A. L. G., L. D. Howe, A. Matijasevich, F. C. Wehrmeister, A. M. B. Menezes, & H. Goncalves. (2016). Adverse childhood experiences: Prevalence and related factors in adolescents of a Brazilian birth cohort. *Child Abuse & Neglect, 51:* 21–30.

South, A. L. (2013). Perceptions of romantic relationships in adult children of divorce. *Journal of Divorce & Remarriage, 54:* 126–141.

Sprecher, S., C. Zimmerman, & B. Fehr. (2014). The influence of compassionate love on strategies used to end a relationship. *Journal of Social and Personal Relationships, 31:* 697–705.

Stack, S., & J. Scourfield. (2015). Recency of divorce, depression and suicide risk. *Journal of Family Issues, 36:* 695–715.

Steiner, L. M., S. Durand, D. Groves, & C. Rozzell. (2015). Effect of infidelity, initiator status, and spiritual well being on men's divorce adjustment. *Journal of Divorce & Remarriage, 56:* 95–108.

Sullivan, M. E. (2016). Family law mediation: The master checklist. *American Journal of Family Law, 30:* 58–63.

Tach, L., & A. Eads. (2015). Trends in the economic consequences of marital and cohabitation dissolution in the United States. *Demography, 52:* 401–432.

Tan, K., C. R. Agnew, L. E. VanderDrift, & S. M. Harvey. (2015). Committed to us: Predicting relationship closeness following nonmarital romantic relationship breakup. *Journal of Social and Personal Relationships, 32:* 456–471.

Tavares, L P., & A. Aassve. (2013). Psychological distress of marital and cohabitation breakups. *Social Science Research, 42:* 1599–1611.

Thomas, K. W. (2015). *Conscious uncoupling: Five steps to living happily even after.* New York: Harmony Books of Crown Publishing.

Tong, S. T. (2013). Facebook use during relationship termination: Uncertainty reduction and surveillance. *Cyberpsychology, Behavior, and Social Networking, 16:* 788–793.

Tumin, D., S. Han, & Z. Qian. (2015). Estimates and meanings of marital separation. *Journal of Marriage and Family, 77:* 312–322.

Van Tilburg, T. G., M. J. Aartsen, & S. Van der Pas. (2015). Loneliness after divorce: A cohort comparison among Dutch young old adults. *European Sociological Review, 31:* 243–252.

Var, M. A., A. C. McCullars, C. N. Selwyn, J. Langhinrichsen-Rohling, & L. Turner. (August 2014). Motivations for initiating contact with ex-partners (MICE) scale: Analysis and factor structure. Poster, Annual Meeting of the American Psychological Association, Washington, DC.

Warrener, C., J. M. Koivunen, & J. L. Postmus. (2013) Economic self-sufficiency among divorced women: Impact of depression, abuse, and efficacy. *Journal of Divorce & Remarriage, 54:* 163–175.

Weaver, J. M., & T. J. Schofield. (2015). Mediation and moderation of divorce effects on children's behavior problems. *Journal of Family Psychology, 29:* 39–48.

Zeleznikow, L., & J. Zeleznikow. (2015). Supporting blended families to remain intact: A case study. *Journal of Divorce & Remarriage, 56:* 317–335.

Chapter 15

Ahmed, A. A., G. A. H. Van den Elsen, M. A. Van der Marck, & M. G. M. Olde Rickkert. (2014). Medicinal use of cannabis and cannabinoids in older adults: Where is the evidence? *American Journal of the American Geriatrics Society, 62:* 410–411.

Alterovitz, S. R., & G. A. Mendelsohn. (2013). Relationship goals of middle-aged, young-old, and old-old Internet daters: An analysis of online person ads. *Journal of Aging Studies, 27:* 159–165.

Bamonti, P., S. Lombardi, P. R. Duberstein, D. A. King, & K. A. Van Orden. (2016). Spirituality attenuates the association between depression symptom severity and meaning in life. *Aging & Mental Health, 20:* 494–499.

Barovick, H. (March 22, 2012). Niche aging. *Time,* pp. 84–87.

Bauman, A., D. Merom, F. C. Bull, D. M. Buchner, & M. A. F. Singh. (2016). Updating the evidence for physical activity: Summative reviews of the epidemiological evidence, prevalence, and interventions to promote "active aging." *Gerontologist, 56:* 268–280.

Bedor, E. (2016). It's not you, it's your (old) vagina: Osphena's articulation of sexual dysfunction. *Sexuality & Culture, 20:* 38–55.

Benson, J. J., & M. Coleman. (2016). Older adults developing a preference for living apart together. *Journal of Marriage and Family, 78:* 797–812.

Ben-Zur, H. (2012). Loneliness, optimism, and well-being among married, divorced, and widowed individuals. *Journal of Psychology, 146:* 23–36.

Blackburn, J., J. L. Locher, & M. L. Kilgore. (2016). Comparison of long-term care in nursing homes versus home health: Costs and outcomes in Alabama. *Gerontologist, 56:* 215–221.

Bodkin, H. (June 9, 2016). Sex robots to storm into the British bedroom within ten years. *The Telegraph News.* Retrieved from http://www.telegraph.co.uk/news/2016/06/09/sex-robots-to-storm-into-the-british-bedroom-within-ten-years/

Brown, S. L., & I. F. Lin. (March 2012). The Gray Divorce Revolution: Rising divorce among middle aged and older adults, 1990–2009. National Center for Marriage and Family Research. Bowling Green State University. Working Paper Series. WP-12- 04.

Brown, S. L., & S. K. Shinohara. (2013). Dating relationships in older adulthood: A national portrait. *Journal of Marriage and Family, 75:* 1194–1202.

Chao, S.-F. (2016). Changes in leisure activities and dimensions of depressive symptoms in later life: A 12-year follow-up. *Gerontologist, 56:* 397–407.

Cheng, J. O., R. S. K. Lo, & J. Woo. (2013). Anticipatory grief therapy for older persons nearing the end of life. *Aging Health, 9.1:* 103 et passim.

Chonody, J. M., & B. Teater. (2016). Why do I dread looking old? A test of social identity theory, terror management theory, and the double standard of aging. *Journal of Women & Aging, 28:* 112–126.

Crespo, M., & V. Fernandez-Lansac. (2014). Factors associated with anger and anger expression in caregivers of elderly relatives. *Aging & Mental Health, 18:* 454–462.

Denmark, F. L., & T. Zarbiv. (2016). Living life to the fullest: A perspective on positive aging. *Women & Therapy, 39:* 315–321.

Ford, P. (2011). *Glenn Ford: A life.* Madison, WI: University of Wisconsin.

Fuller-Iglesias, H., & T. Antonucci. (2016). Familism, social network characteristics, and well-being among older adults in Mexico. *Journal of Cross-Cultural Gerontology, 31:* 1–17.

Hensley, B., P. Martin, J. A. Margrett, M. MacDonald, I. C. Siegler, & L. W. Poon. (2012). Life events and personality predicting loneliness among centenarians: Findings from the Georgia Centenarian Study. *Journal of Psychology, 146:* 173–188.

Hogsnes, L., C. Melin-Johansson, K. Gustaf Norbergh, & E. Danielson. (2014). The existential life situations of spouses of persons with dementia before and after relocating to a nursing home. *Aging & Mental Health, 18:* 152–160.

Iveniuk, J., L. J. Waite, E. Laumann, M. K. McClintock, & A. D. Tiedt. (2014). Marital conflict in older couples: Positivity, personality, and health. *Journal of Marriage and Family, 76:* 130–144.

Johnson, C. L., & B. M. Barer. (1997). *Life beyond 85 years: The aura of survivorship.* New York: Springer Publishing.

Johnson, J. D., C. J. Whitlatch, & H. L. Menne. (2014). Activity and well-being of older adults: Does cognitive impairment play a role? *Research on Aging, 36:* 147–160.

Karraker, A., & J. DeLamater. (2013). Past year inactivity among older married persons and their partners. *Journal of Marriage and Family, 75:* 142–163.

Koren, C., S. Simhi, S. Lipman-Schiby, & S. Fogel. (May 10, 2016). The partner in late-life repartnering: Caregiving expectations from an intergenerational perspective. *International Psychogeriatrics,* online.

Lee, Y., & I. Chi. (2016). Do cognitive leisure activities really matter in the relationship between education and cognition? Evidence from the aging, demographics, and memory study (ADAMS). *Aging & Mental Health, 20:* 252–261.

Leopold, T., & C. M. Lechner. (2015). Parents' death and adult well being: Gender, age, and adaptation to filial bereavement. *Journal of Marriage and Family, 77:* 747–760.

Leopold, T., M. Raab, & H. Engelhardt. (2014). The transition to parent care: Costs, commitments, and caregiver selection among children. *Journal of Marriage and Family, 76:* 300–318.

Lumsdaine, R., & S. Vermeer. (2015). Retirement timing of women and the role of care responsibilities for grandchildren. *Demography, 52:* 433–454.

Manning, W. D., & S. L. Brown. (2015). Aging cohabitation couples and family policy: Different sex and same-sex couples. *Public Policy Aging Report, 25:* 94–97.

Margolis, R. (2016). The changing demography of grandparenthood. *Journal of Marriage and Family, 78:* 610–622.

McGowan, C. M. (2011). Legal aspects of end of life care. *Critical Care Nurse, 31:* 64–69.

Murphy, J. S., D. P. Nailbone, J. L. Wetchler, & A. B. Edwards. (2015a). Caring for aging parents: The influence of family coping, spirituality/religiosity, and hope on the marital satisfaction of family caregivers. *American Journal of Family Therapy, 43:* 238–250.

Murphy, S. L., K. D. Kochanek, J. Q. Xu, & E. Arias. (2015b). NCHS data brief, no. 229. Based on 2014 data. Hyattsville, MD: National Center for Health Statistics.

Nguyen, A., L. Chatters, R. Taylor, & D. Mouzon. (2016). Social support from family and friends and subjective well-being of older African Americans. *Journal of Happiness Studies, 17:* 959–979.

Ory, B., & T. Huijts. (2015). Widowhood and well-being in Europe: The role of national and regional context. *Journal of Marriage and Family, 77:* 730–746.

Parlevliet, J. L., J. MacNeil-Vroomen, B. M. Buurman, S. E. Rooij, & J. E. Bosmans. (2016). Health-related quality of life at admission is associated with postdischarge mortality, functional decline, and institutionalization in acutely hospitalized older medical patients. *American Geriatrics Society, 64:* 761–776.

Pilkauskas, N. V., & R. E. Dunifon. (2016). Understanding grandfamilies: Characteristics of grandparents, nonresident parents, and children. *Journal of Marriage and Family, 78:* 623–633.

Price, C. A., & O. Nesteruk. (November 5–9, 2013). Being married in retirement: Can it be a double-edged sword? Annual Meeting of the National Council on Family Relations, San Antonio, TX.

Proquest Statistical Abstract of the United States, 2016, online ed. Washington, DC: U.S. Bureau of the Census.

Rauer, A. (February 22, 2013). From golden bands to the golden years: The critical role of marriage in older adulthood. Annual Meeting of the Southeastern Council on Family Relations, Birmingham, AL.

Read, S., E. Grundy, & E. Foverskov. (2016). Socio-economic position and subjective health and well-being among older people in Europe: A systematic narrative review. *Aging & Mental Health, 20:* 529–542.

Ribenstein, C. L., J. Duff, I. Prilleltensky, Y. Jin, S. Dietz, N. D. Myers, & O. Prilleltensky. (2016). Demographic group differences in domain-specific well-being. *Journal of Community Psychology, 44:* 419–515.

Sadana, R., E. Blas, S. Budhwani, T. Koller, & G. Paraje. (2016). Healthy aging: Raising awareness of inequalities, determinants, and what could be done to improve health equity. *Gerontologist, 56:* 178–193.

Scheetz, L. T., P. Martin, & L. W. Poon. (2012). Do centenarians have higher levels of depression? Findings from the Georgia Centenarian Study. *Journal of the American Geriatrics Society, 60:* 238–242.

Stahl, L. (May 4, 2014). Living to 90 and beyond. *60 Minutes.* CBS. *The State of Grandfamilies in America, 2015.* Annual report. Retrieved from http://www.gu.org/LinkClick.aspx?fileticket=nv03BXVlGAI%3d&tabid=157&mid=606

Syme, M. L., & T. J. Cohn. (2016). Examining aging sexual stigma attitudes among adults by gender, age, and generational status. *Aging & Mental Health, 20:* 36–45.

Wang, M., K. Henkens, & H. Solinge. (2011). Retirement adjustment: A review of theoretical and empirical advancements. *American Psychologist, 66:* 204–213.

Wiemers, E. E., & S. M. Bianchi. (2015). Competing demands from aging parents and adult children in two cohorts of American women. *Population & Development Review, 41:* 127–146.

Yelland, E. (March 12, 2016). Over the hill and between the sheets: Exploring sex in later life. Annual Meeting of the Southeastern Council on Family Relations, Orlando, FL.

NAME INDEX

Brown, G. L., 232
Brown, G. R., 138
Brown, J., 241
Brown, L. L., 74
Brown, R., 147
Brown, S. L., 39, 40, 299, 302, 303
Brown, S. M., 285
Browning, C. R., 214
Brownridge, D. A., 191
Brown-Waite, Ginny, 298
Bruinsma, G. J. N., 242
Brummelte, S., 231
Bruno, A., 127
Bruno, D., 135
Bryan, A. D., 148
Bryan, A. E., 278
Buchner, D. M., 307
Buckwalter, J. Galen, 80
Budgeon, S., 31
Budhwani, S., 302
Bulanda, J. R., 57
Bull, F. C., 307
Burge, P., 218
Burger, B. D., 257
Buri, J. R., 169, 171
Burke, M. L., 263
Burke, N., 218
Burke-Winkelman, S., 100
Burr, B. K., 7, 82
Burr, W. R., 253
Burton-Chellew, M. N., 157
Burton-Jeangros, C., 285
Busby, D., 22, 97
Busby, D. M., 39, 126, 169
Buscaglia, Leo, 153
Buss, D. M., 86
Butler, Judith, 51
Butler, M., 241
Buunk, A. P., 86
Buurman, B. M., 298
Buvik, K., 199
Buysse, A., 194, 215
Byers, E., 128
Byers, E. S., 117
Byrd-Craven, J., 233
Byrne, T., 6, 211
Byron, Lord, 155
Bywater, T., 245

C

Cafferky, B., 197
Call, L. L., 169
Camelo, K. L., 166
Cameron, G., 254
Campbell, A. C., 83
Campbell, J. A., 207
Campbell, K., 66, 170
Campbell, L., 65
Canario, C., 222
Canavarro, M., 253
Canlas, J., 171
Cannon, D., 96
Cannon, Nick, 166
Carey, A. R., 181
Carey, K. B., 120
Carey, M. P., 120
Carey, Mariah, 166
Carezana, C., 252
Carlson, M., 187
Carmody, J., 251
Carney, M., 241
Carr, K., 241
Carrere, S., 169
Carroll, J. S., 39, 126, 169, 229
Carroll, M. H., 199
Carter, C. S., 72, 73

Carter, G. L., 83
Carter, J., 254
Carter, M., 96
Carter, S., 80
Carter, Z. A., 255
Carvalho, M. R., 97
Casad, B. J., 158
Cascardi, M., 197
Caspi, J., 213
Castillo, M., 195
Caughlin, J. P., 86, 106
Ceballo, R., 195
Celen-Demirtas, S., 273
Centers for Disease Control and
     Prevention (CDC), 191, 251
Ceresnie, A. R., 237
Cerulli, C., 204
Chan, K. Y., 188
Chaney, C., 84
Chang, I. J., 35, 120
Chang, J., 34, 120, 280
Chang, M., 108
Chang, S., 111
Chao, S. F., 298
Chaplin, Charles, 166
Chaplin, Oona, 166
Chapman, B., 154, 169
Chapman, Gary, 70
Chapmana, D., 244
Charles, J., 245
Chase, L. M., 145
Chatters, L., 299
Chau, A. W., 188
Chaucer, Geoffrey, 73
Cheadle, J. E., 177
Chemtob, Nancy, 273
Chen, E. Y. J., 157
Chen, M., 119
Chen, M. S., 197
Cheng, J. O., 306
Chermak, S., 196
Chi, I., 298
Chiou, W., 36
Chiu, Y. P., 36
Cho, H., 193
Cho, J., 232
Cho, Margaret, 146
Choi, H., 170, 171, 193
Choiriyyah, I., 209
Chonody, J. M., 136, 294
Chou, J. L., 286
Christensen, A., 110, 265
Christensen, U., 109
Christie-Mizell, C. A., 157
Chu, A. T., 197
Chuong, K., 111
Cicila, L. N., 265
Ciciolla, L., 231
Clara Li, P. C., 75
Clark, H., 178
Clark, M. D., 199
Clarke, S. C., 287
Clarke, V., 139
Claxton, S. E., 199
Clemans, K. H., 48
Clinton, E. F., 244
Clough, A., 198
Cody, M. J., 36
Coe, M., 138
Cohen, J. A., 40
Cohen, M., 4, 38, 104
Cohen, S., 204
Cohn, A., 192
Cohn, D., 4, 188
Cohn, T. J., 302
Colbert, Stephen, 48
Coleman, M., 40, 96, 286, 307
Colen, C. G., 214

Coles, R. L., 243
Collier, K. E., 194
Conger, K. J., 253
Conger, R. D., 160, 236
Conlin, E., 197
Conner, B., 130
Connor-Smith, J., 200
Cook, C., 177
Cook, J., 35
Cook, R. E., 60
Cooke-Jackson, A., 122
Cooklin, A., 182
Coontz, S., 11, 12, 28, 40, 153, 184,
     269
Coontz, Stephanie, 29, 177, 270
Cooper, A., 120
Cooper, C. A., 53
Cooper, M. L., 87
Copeland, L., 242
Córdova, J. V., 58
Corliss, H. L., 139
Corthorn, C., 237
Cortina, L. M., 195
Coskunpinar, A., 100
Costescu, E., 198
Costerana, J. D., 16, 203, 204
Cottle, N. R., 7, 168
Coughlin, D. R., 159, 160
Courvoisier, D. S., 285
Couter, A. C., 65
Cox, R. B., 260
Coyne, S., 97
Coyne, S. M., 97
Craig, L., 58, 241
Cravens, J. D., 16, 203, 204
Crawford, Michael, 284
Crespo, C., 253, 272
Crespo, M., 296
Crnic, K. A., 232
Cromett, C. E., 169, 171
Crookston, B., 233
Crosier, B. S., 243
Crosnoe, R., 58
Croughan, M. S., 217
Crouter, A. C., 184
Crowe, A., 191, 204
Crutzen, R., 238
Cueto, S., 233
Cuff, R., 252
Cui, M., 258
Cullati, S., 285
Cunha, D., 272
Curran, M. A., 27
Curran, T., 273
Curtin, S. C., 223
Cutrona, C., 160
Cuyàs, E., 231
Cyders, M. A., 100

D

Daboin, I., 137
Dalai Lama, 305
D'Amico, E., 142
Danielson, E., 299
Dargie, E., 38
Dariotis, J. K., 209
Darnton, K., 22
Daryanani, I., 243
Dauphinne, L. A., 221
David-Ferdon, C., 197
Davila, J., 75
Davis, J. L., 233
Davis, K., 82
Davis-Delano, L. R., 135
Dawson, S., 198
Dawson, Shawn, 139
Day, Nicholas, 229

de Bruin, J., 217
De Cuypere, G., 215
de Sade, Marquis, 103
De Sutter, P., 215
Dean, L. R., 169
Dearden, K., 233
Dee, Kiki, 211
DeGeneres, Ellen, 166
DeGreeff, B. L., 288
DeGue, S., 205
Dekovic, M., 116, 242
DeLamater, J., 123, 301
Deline, S., 238
Delva, J., 195
DeMaris, A., 57
Denmark, F. L., 307
Denney, J. T., 32
Denny, K. E., 179, 242
Dent, D. V., 33
DePrince, A. P., 197
Derby, K., 258
Dervin, D., 223, 228
Desai, S., 222
DeSmet, O., 194
Dharnidharka, P., 197
Dial, B., 82
Diamond, L. M., 71
Diaz, A., 244
Diaz, R. M., 142
Dichter, M. E., 204
Dick, D. M., 23
Dickerson, S. S., 177
Diedericksen, K. W., 270
Dietz, S., 302
Dignam, P., 21
Dignan, P., 34
Dijkstra, P., 79
Dill, J., 235
Dion, Celine, 166
Dir, A. L., 100
Dirac, Paul A.M., 21
Djamba, Y. K., 276
Dodge, B., 130
Dodge, B. S., 130
Doherty, W. J., 171, 270, 274
Dollahite, D. C., 161
Dominguez, M. M., 197
Doolin, H., 144
Dore, M. M., 191
Doria, M. V., 265
Dosch, A., 119
Doss, B. D., 110, 265
Dotson-Blake, K. P., 116
Dotterer, A. M., 233
Doty, J., 242
Dougall, K. M., 217
Douglas, Michael, 166
Douglas, William O., 171
Downer, J. T., 169
Downing, J. B., 219
Downing, M. J., 145
Doyle, M., 32
Dragojlovic, A., 8
Draper, Don, 97
Drennan, J., 241
Drescher, Fran, 145
Drey, E. A., 222
Driessnack, M., 100
Du Bois, S. N., 38
Dubbs, S. L., 86
Duberstein, P. R., 299
DuBois, S., 143
Duff, J., 302
Duggan, M., 36
Dunbar, R. I. M., 157
Duncan, D., 144
Dunifon, R. E., 304
Dunlap, L., 281

Merom, D., 307
Merrick, N., 231
Merrill, J., 180, 181
Meston, C. M., 127
Meszaros, P. S., 250
Meteyer, K., 184
Metler, D., 242
Michael, R. T., 125
Michaelson, C., 148
Michelmore, K., 39
Michniewicz, K.S., 59
Mico, U., 127
Middelstadt, S. E., 130
Mihaloliakos, J. H., 265
Milhausen, R. R., 124
Milicic, N., 237
Milkie, M. A., 179, 242
Miller, A. J., 39
Miller, A. N., 256
Miller, J. D., 197
Miller, M. Ramsay, 75
Miller, R., 171
Miller, R. B., 169
Miller, S., 121
Milligan, Spike, 177
Millstein, S. G., 217
Milne, C., 70, 78
Milstein, S., 239
Mindel, C. H., 159
Minichiello, V., 263
Minnotte, K. L., 184
Minnotte, M. C., 184, 186
Minnottea, K. L., 58
Mintz, L., 130
Mirecki, R. M., 286
Miss Your Mate, 37
Mitchell, B. A., 170
Mock, S. E., 133, 136
Moen, D., 74, 169, 170
Mogilski, J. K., 279
Mol, B. W., 217
Molinares, C., 120
Mong, M. D., 256
Mongeau, P. A., 117, 118, 119
Monk, J. K., 4
Monro, S., 61
Montesi, J., 130
Moore, A. M., 221
Moore, Julianne, 299
Moore, T. M., 199
Morell, V., 256
Morgan, E. S., 271
Morita, M., 213
Moroney, S., 233
Morris, H., 120
Morselli, D., 278
Moser, C., 133
Moses-Kolko, E. L., 231
Mouzon, D., 299
Moya-Albiol, L., 197
Moyer, A., 40
Moyer, A. M., 219
Mrug, S., 252
Muehlenhard, C., 198
Mueller, M. P., 119
Muise, A., 126
Mujakovic, S., 238
Mulcahy, C. M., 231
Mullan, K., 58
Mullins, L. C., 276
Muncer, S., 83
Muraco, J. A., 27
Murdock, G. P., 154
Muris, P., 65, 237
Murnen, S. K., 55
Murphy, J. S., 297
Murphy, S. L., 251, 295, 305
Murray, C., 29

Murray, C. E., 191, 204
Murray, C. I., 166
Muscatello, M. R. A., 127
Musses, Anthony, 95
Mustafa, Junaid E., 263
Mustanski, B., 133, 134, 139, 143
Mustapha, A., 198
Myers, J., 50
Myers, N. D., 302

N

Nachtigall, R. D., 216, 217
Nagao, K., 129
Nahum, L., 244
Nailbone, D. P., 297
Naim, L., 265
Nakajima, K., 129
Namy, S., 198
Nander, V., 193
Narciso, I., 263
Nardi, A. E., 97
National Association for the
    Research and Therapy of
    Homosexuality (NARTH),
    136
National Association of School
    Psychologists, 136
National Association of Social Work-
    ers, 136
National Coalition of Anti-Violence
    Programs, 138
The National Coalition of Anti-
    Violence Programs, 138
Natkin, R., 23
Nautal, A. P., 79
Navarro, P., 231
Neal, D. J., 121
Negash, S., 77, 258
Nelemans, S. A., 82
Nelen, W., 217
Nelms, B. J., 58
Nelson, L. J., 229, 234
Nesteruk, O., 300
Neto, F., 67
Neuhaus, D., 244
Newcomb, M. E., 139
Newkirk, K., 240
Newman, H., 230
Newman, K., 241
N'Goran, A. A., 238
Nguyen, A., 299
Nicholson, J. M., 182
Niehuis, S., 158
Nielson, M. G., 234
Niemela, S., 261
Nietzsche, Friedrich, 157
Nijhuis, E., 238
Nilsson, C. J., 109
NNEDV, 198
Nomaguchi, K. M., 179, 242
Norman, W. V., 220
Northrup, J., 70
Northrup, J. C., 274
Norton, A. M., 97
Novak, D., 144
Noval, G., 82
Nowlan, K. M., 265
Nugent, W. R., 170, 258
Nurse, J., 205
Nuru, A. K., 287
Nussbaum, R., 133, 134
Nussbeck, F., 249
Nussbeck, F. W., 66, 67
Nybergh, L., 193
Nyoni, J., 198

O

Oakley, Tyler, 204
Oberbeek, G., 82
O'Brien, C., 200
O'Brien, L., 57
O'Connor-Petruso, S. A., 99
Ogolsky, B. G., 4
O'Hanlon, B., 252
Ohannessian, C. M., 260
Ohtsuki, H., 213
Oka, M., 169
Okumu, E., 119
Olde Rickkert, M. G. M., 299
O'Leary, D. K., 204
O'Leary, K. D., 40
Oliva, F., 252
Oliver, Mary, 71
Oliver, Vicki, 236
Olmstead, S. B., 77
Olson, J., 169, 170, 171
Omarzu, J., 256
O'Neal, C. W., 163
Onraedt, T., 194
Ontai, L. L., 253
Openshaw, L., 178
Oppenheimer, J., 30, 233, 270
Opree, S. J., 186
Orbe, M. P., 122
Ory, B., 305
Ostacoli, L., 252
O'Sullivan, L. F., 117, 129
Ota, R., 79
Otters, R. V., 241
Overall, N. C., 105
Overby, L. M., 135
Overholt, S., 204
Ozaki, Y., 129, 220
Ozay, B., 79
Ozbek, A., 243
Ozturk, Y., 243
Ozyurt, G., 243

P

Padgett, D., 34
Padilla, J., 242
Padilla-Walker, L. M., 229, 234
Padovano-Janik, A. K., 147
Paige, Satchel, 302
Paik, A., 116
Palacios, J., 218
Palm-Reed, K. M., 205
Paltrow, Gwyneth, 289
Pande, R., 78
Pandolfo, G., 127
Panetta, S. M., 237
Panozzo, D., 147
Pappas, S. J., 169, 171
Paraje, G., 302
Park, H., 227, 276
Park, N., 36
Parker, K., 178, 179
Parlevliet, J. L., 298
Parnell, M. M., 169
Parrott, D. J., 137
Parry, D. C., 231
Parsons, J., 143
Partridge, R. T., 237
Pasa, U., 217
Pasch, L. A., 217
Pasley, K., 232, 258
Patel, Sunita, 150
Paul, E., 231
Paul, J. A., 179
Payne, K., 239

Payne, K. K., 40
Payne, P. B., 7
Pedersen, D. E., 184
Pedersena, D. E., 58, 186
Pellebon, D. A., 159, 160
Pellegrini, M., 221
Pendry, P., 197
Penhollow, T. M., 123
Penney, R., 254
Penny, M., 233
Pepe, N. A., 53
Pepperell, J., 138
Pepping, C. A., 263
Perales-Puchalt, A., 218
Pereira, A., 237
Pereira, M., 263
Perez, L., 166
Perilloux, C., 86
Perlesz, A., 147, 252
Perrig-Chiello, P., 278, 285
Perrin, N., 198
Perry-Jenkins, M., 240
Perry-Jenkins, Maureen, 184
Persson, T. J., 138
Peskin, M., 193
Petch, J., 263
Peter, T., 139
Peters, K., 57
Peters, M., 216
Peterson, J. L., 137
Petrovic, M., 237
Petrovic, O., 237
Pettigrew, J., 97
Pew Research Center (2012), 56
Pew Research Center (2015), 54,
    78, 182
Pew Research: Pew Forum on
    Religion and Public Life,
    165
Pfaus, J. C., 138
Phillips, Emo, 301
Phoenix, A. E., 119
Picci, R., 252
Pierce, J. D., 185
Pilkauskas, N. V., 304
Piquero, A. R., 232
Pitt, Brad, 10
Pittman, J., 7
Pitts, M. K., 147
Pizer, J. C., 142
Platt, C. A., 288
Plauche, H. P., 272
Plaza, A., 231
Pleck, J. H., 209
Plummer, D., 263
Pollard, M. S., 74
Pollmann-Schult, Matthias, 211
Pomeroy, W. B., 135
Poon, L. W., 299, 305
Pope, J. C., 6
Porges, S. W., 72, 73
Porter, J., 285
Porter, Nora, 120
Portley, R. M., 278
Postmus, J. L., 279
Powell, A., 241
Power, J., 252
Power, J. J., 147
Powers, R. A., 204
Prabu, D., 170
Prestage, G., 144
Preyde, M., 254
Price, C. A., 300
Prickett, K., 58
Prilleltensky, I., 302
Prilleltensky, O., 302
Procsa, A., 59
Procyk, S., 177

Wilson, B. F., 287
Wilson, Gretchen, 285
Wilson, K. R., 241
Wilson, L. F., 197
Wimberly, Teresa Carol, 201
Winfrey, Oprah, 31, 107, 218
Wing, H., 217
Wiseman, R., 235
Woertman, L., 127, 129
Woldarsky, M., 170
Wolford-Clevenger, C., 193, 196
Wonch-Hill, P. A., 212
Wong, M., 240
Wong, M. M., 192
Woo, J., 306
Wood, J. R., 124
Wood, M. D., 163
Woodford, M. R., 136
Woods, Crystal, 156
Woods, Tiger, 164, 255, 256
Woody, E. Z., 126
Wooldridge, K., 66

Woszidlo, A., 101, 170
Wright, D. W., 170
Wright, K. M., 163
Wright, P. J., 128, 137, 194
Wright, R., 159
Wu, E., 108
Wu, H., 40
Wu, P., 36
Wunsch, S., 124

X

Xiong, S., 231
Xu, J. Q., 295, 305
Xu, X., 66, 75

Y

Yabiku, S. T., 281
Yang, J., 186, 188

Yang, X., 18
Yarhouse, M. A., 144
Yavorsky, J. E., 233
Yazedjian, A., 7, 199
Yelland, E., 301
Yodanis, C., 79
Yoneda, A., 75
Yoo, H. C., 79
Yoon, Y., 240
Yorgason, J., 166, 177
Yorgason, K., 168
Yoshida, K., 22
Yost, M., 138
Young, M., 123
Yu, J., 240

Z

Zabriskie, R. B., 174
Zadeh, S., 243
Zammitt, K. A., 138

Zapor, H., 196
Zarbiv, T., 307
Zarit, S. H., 210
Zavattini, G. C., 101
Zeichner, A., 197
Zeiders, K. H., 242
Zeleznikow, J., 287
Zeleznikow, L., 287
Zemanek, L. J., 9
Zeta-Jones, Catherine, 166
Zhang, S., 110
Zheng, X., 137
Zickuhr, K., 98
Zilcha-Mano, S., 9, 252
Zimmerman, C., 271
Zinzow, H. M., 192
Zoccali, R., 127
Zubrick, S. R., 182, 252
Zuffanieri, M., 252
Zusman, M., 116
Zvonkovic, A. M., 211
Zwinderman, A. H., 217

1-1 **Explain the concept of marriage and the different types of marriage.** Marriage is a legal relationship that binds a couple together to create and care for children. Alternatives to this traditional definition of marriage include common-law marriage and polygamy. A common-law marriage involves a heterosexual couple presenting themselves as married, despite the lack of a formal legal contract.

marriage a legal relationship that binds a couple together for the reproduction, physical care, and socialization of children. (1-1)

common-law marriage a heterosexual cohabiting couple presenting themselves as married. (1-1)

marriage benefit when compared to being single, married persons are healthier, happier, live longer, have less drug use, etc. (1-1b)

polygamy a generic term for marriage involving more than two spouses. (1-1c)

polygyny type of marriage involving one husband and two or more wives. (1-1c)

polyandry type of marriage in which one wife has two or more husbands. (1-1c)

pantagamy a group marriage in which each member of the group is "married" to the others. (1-1c)

1-2 **Explain the differences between different types of families.** A family refers to a group of two or more people related by blood, marriage, or adoption. An individual is born into their family of orientation. Once an individual marries, he or she begins to create his or her family of procreation. Depending on who lives in the household, families can be categorized as nuclear, binuclear, extended, transnational, or blended. Depending on the working status of parents in the home, families can be categorized as traditional, modern, or postmodern.

family a group of two or more people related by blood, marriage, or adoption. (1-2a)

transnational family family in which the mother and child live in another country from the father. (1-2a)

civil union a pair-bonded relationship given legal significance in terms of rights and privileges. (1-2a)

domestic partnerships relationships in which cohabiting individuals are given some kind of official recognition by a city or corporation so as to receive partner benefits (e.g., health insurance). (1-2a)

family of orientation also known as the family of origin, the family into which a person is born. (1-2b)

family of procreation the family a person begins typically by getting married and having children. (1-2b)

nuclear family consists of you, your parents, and your siblings or you, your spouse, and your children. (1-2b)

traditional family the two-parent nuclear family, with the husband as bread-winner and the wife as homemaker. (1-2b)

modern family the dual-earner family, in which both spouses work outside the home. (1-2b)

postmodern family lesbian or gay couples and mothers who are single by choice, which emphasizes that a healthy family need not be the traditional heterosexual, two-parent family. (1-2b)

binuclear family a family in which the members live in two households. (1-2b)

blended family a family created when two individuals marry and at least one of them brings a child or children from a previous relationship or marriage. Also referred to as a stepfamily. (1-2b)

extended family the nuclear family or parts of it plus other relatives such as grandparents, aunts, uncles, and cousins. (1-2b)

1-3 **Outline the differences between marriage and family.** Marriage can be thought of as a social relationship that sometimes leads to the establishment of a family (e.g., children). Indeed, every society or culture has mechanisms (from "free" dating to arranged marriages) for guiding their youth into permanent emotional, legal, or social relationships (marriage) that are designed to have and rear offspring. Although the concepts of marriage and the family are sometimes used synonymously, they are distinct. For example, marriage is usually initiated by a formal ceremony, whereas none is required for the creation of a family. Ages of the individuals involved in marriage tends to be similar, whereas families represent more than one generation. Although individuals in marriage usually choose each other, members of a family are born or adopted into the family. Spouses can voluntarily withdraw from marriage, but parents are unable to divorce themselves from obligations to children. These differences and more are described in Table 1.2.

1-4 **Paraphrase in your own words the changes that have occurred in marriage and the family.** The advent of industrialization, urbanization, and mobility is associated with the demise of familism (e.g., focus on what is important for the family) and the rise of individualism (focus on what is important for the individual). When family members functioned together as an economic unit, they were dependent on one another for survival and were concerned about what was good for the family. This familistic focus on the needs of the family has since shifted to a focus on self-fulfillment, known as individualism. Individualism and the quest for personal fulfillment are thought to have contributed to high divorce rates, absent fathers, and parents spending less time with their children. Additionally, since 1950 many changes have occurred in family relationship values, gender roles, sexual values, homogamous mating, cultural discussion of intimate relationships, divorce, homosexuality, scientific scrutiny, family housing, and communication technology.

familism philosophy in which decisions are made in reference to what is best for the family as a collective unit. (1-4a)

individualism philosophy in which decisions are made on the basis of what is best for the individual. (1-4a)

1-5 Outline the different frameworks for viewing marriage and the family. The different theoretical frameworks for viewing marriage and the family include the social exchange, family life course development, family life cycle, structure-function, conflict, symbolic interaction, family systems, human ecology, and feminist. The social exchange framework operates from a premise of utilitarianism—the theory that individuals rationally weigh the rewards and costs associated with behavioral choices. The family life course development framework emphasizes the important role transitions of individuals that occur in different periods of life and in different social contexts. The family life cycle framework emphasizes the various developmental tasks family members face across time (e.g., marriage, childbearing, preschool, school-age children, teenagers). If developmental tasks at one stage are not accomplished, functioning in subsequent stages will be impaired. Structure-functionalists view the family as an institution with values, norms, and activities meant to provide stability for the larger society. Such stability depends on families performing various functions for society. Conflict framework views individuals in relationships as competing for valuable resources (time, money, power). Conflict theorists recognize that family members have different goals and values that produce conflict. The symbolic interaction framework views marriages and families as symbolic worlds in which the various members give meaning to one another's behavior. The term *symbolic interaction* refers to the process of interpersonal interaction and involves the concepts of the definition of the situation, the looking-glass self, and the self-fulfilling prophecy. The family systems framework views each member of the family as part of a system and the family as a unit that develops norms of interacting, which may be explicit or implicit. The human ecology framework looks at family as an ecosystem that interacts with the environment. A feminist framework views marriage and family as contexts of inequality and oppression for women.

theoretical frameworks a set of interrelated principles designed to explain a particular phenomenon. (1-5)

social exchange framework views interaction and choices in terms of cost and profit. (1-5a)

utilitarianism individuals rationally weigh the rewards and costs associated with behavioral choices. (1-5a)

family life course development the stages and process of how families change over time. (1-5b)

family life cycle stages that identify the various developmental tasks family members face across time. (1-5b)

structure-function framework emphasizes how marriage and family contribute to society. (1-5c)

conflict framework the view that individuals in relationships compete for valuable resources. (1-5d)

symbolic interaction framework views marriages and families as symbolic worlds in which the various members give meaning to each other's behavior. (1-5e)

family systems framework views each member of the family as part of a system and the family as a unit that develops norms of interaction. (1-5f)

human ecology framework views the family and the environment as an ecosystem. (1-5g)

feminist framework views marriage and family as contexts of inequality and oppression for women. (1-5h)

1-6 Choices in relationships—view of the text. The central theme of this text is choices in relationships. Although we will make many choices, among the most important are whether to marry, whom to marry, when to marry, whether to have children, whether to remain emotionally/sexually faithful to one's partner, and whether to protect oneself from sexually transmitted infections and unwanted pregnancy. Though structural and cultural influences are operative, a choices framework emphasizes that individuals have some control over their relationship destiny by making deliberate choices to initiate, nurture, or terminate intimate relationships.

1-7 Explain why researching marriage and family is important, and describe the standard sequence and caveats of conducting a research project. Research is important because it helps to provide evidence for or against a hypothesis. When conducting a research project, researchers follow a standard sequence that includes seven steps: identifying the topic of research, reviewing the literature, developing hypotheses, deciding on the type of study and method of data collection, getting IRB approval, collecting and analyzing data, and writing and publishing results. When conducting or analyzing research, it is important to note how the participants were sampled, whether there was a control group, age differences between respondents, clarity of terminology, the existence of researcher bias, the time lag between when the research was published and when it is consumed, distortion of data, and the use of deception.

hypothesis a suggested explanation for a phenomenon. (1-7a)

cross-sectional research studying the whole population at one time (e.g., finding out from all persons now living together at your university about their experience). (1-7a)

longitudinal research studying the same subjects across time (e.g., collecting data from the same couple during each of their four years of living together during college). (1-7a)

1-8 Explain emerging trends in marriage and the family. Marriage will continue to be the dominant (over 60% report the desire to marry) lifestyle choice of adults in the United States. However, an increasing percentage will not just put off marriage, but do so for good, making older never-married individuals a growing segment of the U.S. population. Diversity in marriage and family life will also continue as evidenced by same-sex marriages/families, single-parent families, childfree families, and poly families. The latter reflects several adults pair bonding with each other and deciding to live together with their children.

2-1 Outline the various aspects of singlehood. Singlehood refers to the state of being unmarried. There are many benefits of singlehood, including freedom to do as one wishes, a variety of lovers and spontaneous lifestyle, the ability to have friends of both sexes, responsible only for oneself and one's finances, avoiding control of movement and behavior, and avoiding the emotional/ financial stress of divorce. However, there are also many limitations, such as increased extended-family responsibilities, increased job expectations, isolation, decreased privacy and safety, feeling different, and lower income. Over time, the legal division between the married and unmarried has blurred. Unmarried partnerships are often legally recognized as civil unions and domestic partnerships.

singlehood state of being unmarried. (2-1e)

2-2 Explain the various mechanisms of finding a partner. College students often meet potential partners through hanging out, wherein individuals go out in groups where the agenda is just to meet other people and have fun. Hanging out sometimes leads to hooking up, which is defined as a sexual encounter that occurs between individuals who have no relationship commitment. Other avenues for meeting potential partners include meeting on the Internet, speed dating, and international dating services.

hanging out going out in groups where the agenda is to meet others and have fun. (2-2a)

hooking up having a one-time sexual encounter in which there are generally no expectations of seeing one another again. (2-2b)

2-3 Define the advantages and disadvantages of long-distance relationships. Advantages of long-distance relationships include positive labeling, keeping the relationship "high," increased time to devote to school or one's career, and an abundance of personal time and space. Disadvantages of long-distance relationships include frustration over not being with one's partner, increased loneliness, and greater relationship stress. Additionally, individuals in long-distance relationships may miss out on other activities and relationships, have less physical intimacy, spend a great deal of money on phone calls and travel, and have issues discussing relationship problems. To maintain long-distance relationships, consider engaging in the following activities: maintain daily contact via text messaging or Skype, stay busy when apart, avoid arguing during conversations, stay monogamous, and be creative with each other.

long-distance dating relationship (LDDR) lovers are separated by a distance, usually 500 miles, which prevents weekly face-to-face contact. (2-3)

2-4 Define cohabitation and the different types of cohabitation relationships. There are nine types of cohabitation relationships. The here and now cohabiters are not focused on the future of the relationship, but cohabit because it works for them currently. Testers, on the other hand, are cohabiting in order to assess whether the relationship will have a future. Engaged cohabiters are planning to marry. Money savers are not so much focused on the future of their relationship, but recognize that cohabitation is economically convenient. Pension partners are older, previously married individuals who cohabit and sustain their living situation through collecting pension. Alimony maintenance refers to women who cohabit but do not marry in order to continue receiving alimony payments. Security blanket cohabiters are not necessarily evaluating the potential for a future with their partner, but would rather be with anyone than be alone. Rebellious cohabiters are those individuals who are making a statement to their parents through cohabitation, to show their parents that they are independent and can make their own choices. Lastly, marriage never cohabiters reject the institution of marriage in general, and never intend to marry.

cohabitation (living together) two unrelated adults (by blood or by law) involved in an emotional and sexual relationship who sleep in the same residence at least four nights a week for three months. (2-4)

domestic partnership a relationship in which individuals who live together are emotionally and financially interdependent and are given some kind of official recognition by a city or corporation so as to receive partner benefits. (2-4a)

2-5 Define living apart together (LAT) relationships, and explain the advantages and disadvantages of doing so. LAT relationships permit increased space and privacy, an abundance of career or work space, and permittance for variable sleep needs, allergies, social needs, and blended family needs. Additionally, LAT keeps the relationship exciting, and allows for maintenance of self-expression and comfort, cleanliness, and residence maintenance. However, there is a stigma associated with LAT. It is more expensive to maintain two residences, prevents couples from establishing a shared history, and provides no legal protection.

living apart together (LAT) a long-term committed couple who does not live in the same dwelling. (2-5)

satiation a stimulus loses its value with repeated exposure or people get tired of each other if they spend relentless amounts of time with each other. (2-5b)

2-6

Discuss current trends in singlehood. Singlehood will (in the cultural spirit of diversity) lose some of its stigma; more young adults will choose this option; and those who remain single will, increasingly, find satisfaction in this lifestyle. Individuals will continue to be in no hurry to get married. Completing their education, becoming established in their career, and enjoying hanging out and hooking up will continue to delay serious consideration of marriage. The median age for women getting married is 27; for men, 29. This trend will continue as individuals keep their options open in America's individualistic society. Cohabitation will become the typical first union for young adults. The percent of cohabitants will increase not just for those who live together before marriage (now about two-thirds) but also in the prevalence of serial cohabitation. Previously, only those rebelling against the institution of marriage lived together. Today, cohabitation has become normative, and fewer will transition to marriage, even among the engaged. Living apart together will also increase, particularly among middle and older adults who have less to gain from cohabitation or marriage.

3-1 **Define and discuss terminology of gender roles.** Whereas sex refers to the biological distinction between males and females, gender refers to the behaviors associated with being female or male. In other words, biology determines sex, and behavior determines gender. Gender identities are formed through socialization, wherein one learns the attitudes, values, beliefs, and behaviors appropriate to various social positions. Through socialization, individuals also learn gender roles. Biology defines sex roles, or those behaviors defined by biological constraints. In some instances, individuals can develop gender dysphoria, where their gender identity does not match the sex assigned at birth. This dysphoria may lead to individuals identifying as transgender or transsexual.

sex the biological distinction between being female and being male. (3-1a)

intersexed individuals people with mixed or ambiguous genitals. (3-1a)

intersex development refers to congenital variations in the reproductive system, sometimes resulting in ambiguous genitals. (3-1a)

gender the social and psychological behaviors associated with being female or male. (3-1b)

socialization the process through which we learn attitudes, values, beliefs, and behaviors appropriate to the social positions we occupy. (3-1b)

gender identity the psychological state of viewing oneself as a girl or a boy and, later, as a woman or a man. (3-1c)

gender dysphoria the condition in which one's gender identity does not match one's biological sex. (3-1c)

transgender a generic term for a person of one biological sex who displays characteristics of the opposite sex. (3-1c)

cross-dresser a generic term for individuals who may dress or present themselves in the gender of the opposite sex. (3-1c)

transsexual an individual who has the anatomical and genetic characteristics of one sex but the self-concept of the other. (3-1c)

gender roles behaviors assigned to women and men in a society. (3-1d)

sex roles behaviors defined by biological constraints. (3-1d)

gender role ideology the proper role relationships between women and men in a society. (3-1e)

3-2 **Explain the various theories of gender role development.** Sociobiological theory emphasizes the interaction of one's biological or genetic inheritance with one's social environment to explain and predict human behavior. The bioecological model, on the other hand, emphasizes that the relationship between genetics and one's social environment goes both ways. The cognitive-developmental theory of gender role development suggests that a child's cognitive development influences the ways that children respond to gender cues in the environment. Social learning theory and identification theory focus less on the role of biology in gender role development. Social learning theory suggests that individuals internalize gender definitions through reward and punishment for certain behaviors. Identification theory draws on Freudian ideology, and suggests that children acquire the characteristics and behaviors of their same-sex parent through a process of identification.

biosocial theory (sociobiology) emphasizes the interaction of one's biological or genetic inheritance with one's social environment to explain and predict human behavior. (3-2a)

parental investment any investment by a parent that increases the chance that the offspring will survive and thrive. (3-2a)

sociobiology emphasizes the interaction of one's biological or genetic inheritance with one's social environment to explain and predict human behavior. (3-2a)

3-3 **Discuss the agents of socialization that help define gender roles.** There are six primary agents of socialization involved in defining gender roles. First, individuals learn gender roles through their family. From birth, females and males are given pink or blue onesies, dolls, or footballs, etc. Peers also influence gender roles. Many religions provide rules and suggestions for how women and men should behave. Similarly, educational institutions often reward individuals for adhering to traditional gender performance. The economy influences how individuals define gender roles, as evidenced by occupational sex segregation, wherein there is a concentration of women and men in different occupations. Lastly, mass media supplies countless examples of gender performance that influence how individuals define gender roles.

Fa'afafine in Samoan society, these are effeminate males socialized and reared as females due to the lack of women to perform domestic chores. (3-3c)

3-4 Explain the consequences of traditional gender role socialization for girls and boys, women and men. There are positive and negative consequences of traditional gender role socialization for girls and boys, women and men. Negative consequences of traditional female role socialization include lower income, the feminization of poverty, a higher risk for sexually transmitted infections, a negative body image, experiencing various types of sexism, and lower marital satisfaction. Positive consequences of traditional female role socialization include a longer life expectancy, a strong focus on one's relationships, a greater initiative to keep relationships on track in terms of initiating a relationship and moving a relationship forward, or toward help if necessary. Another positive consequence is a strong bond with children. For traditionally socialized males, negative consequences include an identity that is directly tied to his occupation, pressure to avoid emotional expression, a fear of intimacy, disadvantage in custody cases, and a shorter life expectancy. Traditionally socialized males experience the benefit of freedom of movement, a greater pool of potential partners, and the norm of initiating a relationship.

occupational sex segregation the concentration of women in certain occupations and men in other occupations. (3-3e)

feminization of poverty the idea that women disproportionately experience poverty. (3-4a)

sexism an attitude, action, or institutional structure that subordinates or discriminates against an individual or group because of their sex. (3-4a)

benevolent sexism the belief that women are innocent creatures who should be protected and supported. (3-4a)

3-5 Discuss how gender roles have changed and continue to change. Androgyny, gender role transcendence, and gender postmodernism emphasize that gender roles are changing. Androgyny manifests physiologically, through intersexed individuals. Androgyny may also manifest behaviorally, through the blending or reversal of traditional male and female behaviors. Androgyny may also imply flexibility of traits. Beyond the concept of androgyny is that of gender role transcendence, which refers to abandoning gender frameworks and looking at phenomena independent of traditional gender categories. Gender postmodernism abandons the notion of gender as natural and emphasizes that gender is socially constructed.

androgyny a blend of traits that are stereotypically associated with masculinity and femininity. (3-5a)

gender role transcendence abandoning gender frameworks and looking at phenomena independent of traditional gender categories. (3-5b)

3-6 Explore trends in gender roles. Imagine a society in which women and men each develop characteristics, lifestyles, and values that are independent of gender role stereotypes. Characteristics such as strength, independence, logical thinking, and aggressiveness are no longer associated with maleness, just as passivity, dependence, emotions, intuitiveness, and nurturance are no longer associated with femaleness. Both sexes are considered equal, and women and men may pursue the same occupational, political, and domestic roles. These changes are occurring . . . slowly. Another change in gender roles is the independence and ascendency of women. Women will less often require marriage for fulfillment, will increasingly take care of themselves economically, and will opt for having children via adoption or donor sperm rather than foregoing motherhood. That women are slowly outstretching men in terms of education will provide the impetus for these changes.

4-1 Discuss the different ways of viewing love. Love is characterized in many ways. While some view love as romantic (an intense love whereby the lover believes in love at first sight, only one true love, and love conquers all), others view love through a "realistic" lens, whereby love is conjugal (the love between married people characterized by companionship, calmness, comfort, and security). Some scholars explore the various love styles, including ludic, pragma, eros, mania, storge, agape, and compassionate. In 1986, Sternberg posited the triangular view of love, which defines love by measuring the degrees of intimacy, passion, and commitment involved in the relationship. This triangulation results in many categories of relationships, including nonlove, liking, infatuation, romantic love, conjugal love, fatuous love, empty love, and consummate love. Other scholars view love through the five love languages, which refer to the manners through which individuals express their love. Some demonstrate their love through gifts, while others show their love through quality time, works of affirmation, acts of service, or physical touch.

lust sexual desire. (4-1)

infatuation emotional feelings based on little actual exposure to the love object. (4-1)

romantic love an intense love whereby the lover believes in love at first sight, only one true love, and love conquers all. (4-1a)

conjugal (married) love the love between married people characterized by companionship, calmness, comfort, and security. (4-1a)

ludic love style love style that views love as a game in which the love interest is one of several partners, is never seen too often, and is kept at an emotional distance. (4-1b)

pragma love style love style that is logical and rational; the love partner is evaluated in terms of assets and liabilities. (4-1b)

eros love style love style characterized by passion and romance. (4-1b)

mania love style an out-of-control love whereby the person "must have" the love object; obsessive jealousy and controlling behavior are symptoms of manic love. (4-1b)

storge love style a love consisting of friendship that is calm and nonsexual. (4-1b)

agape love style love style characterized by a focus on the well-being of the love object, with little regard for reciprocation; the love of parents for their children is agape love. (4-1b)

compassionate love emotional feelings toward another that generate behaviors to promote the partner's well-being. (4-1b)

five love languages identified by Gary Chapman and now part of American love culture, these are gifts, quality time, words of affirmation, acts of service, and physical touch. (4-1d)

polyamory open emotional and sexual involvement with three or more people. (4-1e)

swinging persons who exchange partners for the purpose of sex. (4-1e)

4-2 Explore the idea of social control of love. Social control of love refers to the degree to which society creates rules for whom an individual is allowed to select a mate. The ultimate social control of love is demonstrated through arranged marriage, wherein mate selection occurs when parents select an "appropriate" spouse for their offspring.

arranged marriage mate selection pattern whereby parents select the spouse of their offspring. (4-2)

4-3 Explain the six different theories on the origins of love. The six different theories on the origins of love include evolutionary, learning, sociological, psychosexual, biochemical, and attachment. Evolutionary theory explains that individuals are motivated to emotionally bond with a partner to ensure a stable relationship for producing and rearing children. Learning theory emphasizes that love feelings develop in response to certain behaviors engaged in by the partner; love develops when there is a high frequency of positive behavior and a low frequency of negative behavior. Sociological theory posits four stages of love development, including rapport, self-revelation, mutual dependency, and fulfillment of personality needs. Psychosexual theory suggests that love results from blocked biological sexual desires. Biochemical theory focuses on the transmission of oxytocin and vasopressin hormones in the development and maintenance of social bonding. Lastly, attachment theory emphasizes that a primary motivation in life is to be emotionally connected with other people.

evolutionary theory of love theory that individuals are motivated to emotionally bond with a partner to ensure a stable relationship for producing and rearing children. (4-3a)

oxytocin a hormone released from the pituitary gland during the expulsive stage of labor that has been associated with the onset of maternal behavior in lower animals. (4-3e)

4-4 Discuss how love is a context for problems. Love relationships can become a context for problems when love is unrequited. In some cases, love leads to an increase in risky and dangerous choices, like an individual who begins to smoke because his or her partner does so. When parents disapprove of one's partner choice, the relationship with the individual's parents can end. Love relationships become contexts for problems when partners carry on simultaneous relationships outside of a polyamorous agreement. Some relationships are abusive, which has many consequences for victims. Many also experience depression when love relationships end.

unrequited love a one-sided love where one's love is not returned. (4-4a)

4-5 Explore the different factors related to how love develops in new relationships. The mass media provides countless examples of love relationships that shape how individuals define love. Culture also provides various rules and strategies for developing love in new relationships. Love development in new relationship is also dependent on psychological conditions, including whether individuals perceive reciprocal liking, whether they are drawn to a potential mate's personality qualities, an individual's self-esteem, and the extent to which individuals are able and willing to disclose information about themselves. This new love is more likely to last when both partners' needs are met, when there are few options for other love relationships, and when both partners make an investment in the relationship.

alexithymia a personality trait which describes a person with little affect. (4-5b)

4-6 Discuss cultural factors in relationship development.

Individuals are not free to become involved with/marry whomever they want. Rather, their culture and society radically restrict and influence their choice. The best example of mate choice being culturally and socially controlled is the fact that less than 1% of the over 63 million marriages in the United States consist of a Black spouse and a White spouse. Endogamy and exogamy are also two forms of cultural pressure operative in mate selection.

endogamy the cultural expectation to select a marriage partner within one's social group. (4-6a)

exogamy the cultural expectation that one will marry outside the family group. (4-6b)

pool of eligibles the population from which a person selects an appropriate mate. (4-6b)

4-7 Consider the sociological factors involved in relationship development.

Numerous sociological factors are at work in bringing two people together who eventually marry. In general, individuals tend to select a mate with similar characteristics to themselves (homogamy). When selecting a mate, individuals consider race, age, intelligence, education, open-mindedness, social class, appearance, career, marital status, religion, politics, etc. Individuals are likely to select a mate that is similar to them on many of these factors.

homogamy tendency to select someone with similar characteristics. (4-7a)

marriage squeeze the imbalance of the ratio of marriageable-age men to marriageable-age women. (4-7a)

open-minded being open to understanding alternative points of view, values, and behaviors. (4-7a)

mating gradient the tendency for husbands to be more advanced than their wives with regard to age, education, and occupational success. (4-7a)

circadian preference refers to an individual's preference for morningness–eveningness in regard to intellectual and physical activities. (4-7a)

spatial homogamy the tendency for individuals to marry who grew up in close physical proximity. (4-7a)

4-8 Consider the psychological factors involved in relationship development.

Psychologists have focused on complementary needs, exchanges, parental characteristics, and personality types with regard to mate selection. Complementary-needs theory refers to the tendency to select mates whose needs are opposite and complementary to one's own needs. Exchange theory is focused on finding the partner who offers the greatest rewards at the lowest costs (rewards, costs, profit, loss, alternative). Role theory emphasizes that a son or daughter models after the parent of the same sex by selecting a partner similar to the one the parent selected as a mate. Attachment theory emphasizes the drive toward psychological intimacy and a social and emotional connection. In regards to personality types and mate selection, psychologists have identified several undesirable personality characteristics of a potential mate: being controlling, narcissistic, exhibiting poor impulse control, being hypersensitive, having an inflated ego, being a perfectionist, insecure, being controlled, suffering from substance abuse, and being unhappy.

complementary-needs theory tendency to select mates whose needs are opposite and complementary to one's own needs. (4-8a)

exchange theory theory that emphasizes that relations are formed and maintained between individuals offering the greatest rewards and least costs to each other. (4-8b)

role theory of mate selection emphasizes that a son or daughter models after the parent of the same sex by selecting a partner similar to the one the parent selected as a mate. (4-8c)

attachment theory of mate selection emphasizes the drive toward psychological intimacy and a social and emotional connection. (4-8d)

dark triad personality term identifying traits of "bad boys" including narcissistic, deceptive, and no empathy. (4-8f)

4-9 Define the engagement period.

Engagement refers to the period of time during which committed, monogamous partners focus on wedding preparations and systematically examine their relationship. Before the wedding, engaged partners should attend premarital counseling to make sure both partners are prepared for marriage. Additionally, the engaged couple should visit each partner's parents.

engagement period of time during which committed, monogamous partners focus on wedding preparations and systematically examine their relationship. (4-9)

4-10 Discuss factors that may cause couples to delay or call off their wedding.

Several factors are related to low marital success. If one of the partners in an engagement is younger than 18, partners should consider calling off or delaying the wedding. Additionally, if they have known their partner for less than two years, are in an abusive relationship, or if the relationship has a high frequency of negative comments and a low frequency of positive comments, they should consider calling off or postponing the wedding. When partners exhibit numerous significant differences, have been "on-and-off," experience dramatic parental disapproval, and/or experience low sexual satisfaction, the partners likely should not marry at this time. Partners who have limited relationship knowledge, are considering marriage for the wrong reasons, or want to marry to let love die, should delay or call off the wedding ceremony.

cyclical relationships when couples break up and get back together several times. (4-10f)

4-11 Explain current trends in love relationships.

Love will continue to be one of the most treasured experiences in life. Love will be sought, treasured, and, when lost or ended, will be met with despair and sadness. After a period of recovery, a new search will begin. As our society becomes more diverse, the range of potential love partners will widen to include those with demographic characteristics different from our own. Romantic love will continue and love will maintain its innocence as those getting remarried love just as deeply and invest in the power of love all over again. The development of a new love relationship will involve the same cultural constraints and sociological and psychological factors identified in the chapter. Individuals are not "free" to select their partner but do so from the menu presented by their culture. Once at the relationship buffet, factors of homogamy and exchange come into play. These variables will continue to be operative. Becoming involved with a partner with similar characteristics as one's own will continue to be associated with a happy and durable relationship.

5-1 **Outline the relationship between verbal and nonverbal communication.** Communication is both verbal and nonverbal. Although most communication is focused on verbal content, most interpersonal communication is nonverbal. Flirting is a good example of both nonverbal and verbal behavior. For example, if the male holds the hand of the female, she must squeeze his hand before he can entwine their fingers. Females generally serve as sexual gatekeepers and control the speed of the interaction toward sex. Additionally, a great deal of social discourse depends on saying things that sound good but that have no meaning in terms of behavioral impact.

communication the process of exchanging information and feelings between two or more people. (5-1)

nonverbal communication the "message about the message," using gestures, eye contact, body posture, tone, volume, and rapidity of speech. (5-1)

flirting playful banter with the goal of eliciting the other person's response or interest. (5-1)

5-2 **Discuss the role of technology and communication in romantic relationships.** Technology has an enormous effect on romantic relationships. The youth of today are being socialized in a hyper-digital age where traditional modes of communication will be replaced by gadgets and texting will become the primary mode of communication. This shift to greater use of technology affects relationships in both positive and negative ways. On the positive side, it allows for instant and unabated connection. However, technology can become a relationship problem when texting becomes the primary method of communication, or with overuse of social media sites. Another way in which technology affects communication, particularly in romantic relationships, is sexting. Sexting is a highly pervasive behavior, despite consequences that may result. Communication via computer between separated lovers, spouses, and family members is becoming more common. Video-mediated communication (VMC) facilitates this communication.

nomophobia the individual is dependent on virtual environments to the point of having a social phobia. (5-2a)

texting text messaging (short typewritten messages—maximum of 160 characters sent via cell phone). (5-2a)

tech etiquette social norms for cell phone use in public. (5-2c)

sexting sending erotic text and photo images via a cell phone. (5-2d)

video-mediated communication (VMC) communication via computer between separated lovers, spouses, and family members. (5-2e)

5-3 **Explain a few strategies for communicating effectively in relationships.** To effectively communicate, couples should prioritize communication, avoid negative and make positive statements to their partner, establish and maintain eye contact, establish empathy, ask open-ended questions, use reflective listening, use "I" statements, touch frequently, identify specific new behavior they want, stay focused on the issue and avoid branching, make specific resolutions to disagreements, give congruent messages, share power, keep the process of communication going, and prepare conversation content on first dates.

empathy the ability to emotionally experience and cognitively understand another person and his or her experiences. (5-3)

open-ended questions questions that encourage answers that contain a great deal of information. (5-3)

closed-ended questions questions that allow for a one-word answer and do not elicit much information. (5-3)

reflective listening paraphrasing or restating what a person has said to indicate that the listener understands. (5-3)

"I" statements statements that focus on the feelings and thoughts of the communicator without making a judgment on others. (5-3)

authentic speaking and acting in a manner according to what one feels. (5-3)

"you" statements statements that blame or criticize the listener and often result in increasing negative feelings and behavior in the relationship. (5-3)

branching in communication, going out on different limbs of an issue rather than staying focused on the issue. (5-3)

congruent message one in which verbal and nonverbal behaviors match. (5-3)

power the ability to impose one's will on one's partner and to avoid being influenced by the partner. (5-3)

principle of least interest principle stating that the person who has the least interest in a relationship controls the relationship. (5-3)

5-4 **Discuss the relationship between gender and communication.** Women and men differ in their approach to and patterns of communication. Women tend to be more communicative about relationship issues, view a situation emotionally, and initiate discussions about relationship problems. On the other hand, men tend to lack emotionality.

5-5 **Explore the trends of self-disclosure and secrets in relationships.** Withholding information and being dishonest may affect the way one feels about oneself and relationships with others. One aspect of intimacy in relationships is self-disclosure, which involves revealing personal information and feelings about oneself to another person. Increased self-disclosure in intimate relationships is related to increased relationship stability. In romantic relationships, most couples keep secrets. Women and spouses tend to keep more secrets than single men. Keeping secrets is also more common among Black and homosexual couples. Secrets are also highly common in families.

5-6 Define lying and explain its prevalence in American relationships. Relationships are compromised by dishonesty, lying, and cheating. Dishonesty and deception take various forms. A direct lie is when an individual says something that is not true. Not correcting an assumption is another form of dishonesty. Lying is highly pervasive in American society, and high profile instances of lying are easy to recall from popular culture. Lying is also present in catfishing, whereby a person completely makes up an online identity to trick a person into getting involved in a romantic relationship with him or her. Lying is epidemic in college student romantic relationships. Cheating may be defined as having sex with someone else while involved in a relationship with a romantic partner; this is also highly pervasive in undergraduate relationships.

catfishing process whereby a person makes up an online identity and an entire social facade to trick a person into becoming involved in an emotional relationship. (5-6b)

5-7 Outline the differences between the two theories of relationship communication. Symbolic interactionism and social exchange are theories that help explain the communication process. Interactionists examine the process of communication between two actors in terms of the meanings each attaches to the actions of the other. Definition of the situation, the looking-glass self, and taking the role of the other are all relevant to understanding how partners communicate. Exchange theorists suggest that the partners' communication can be described as a ratio of rewards to costs. Rewards are positive exchanges, such as compliments, compromises, and agreements. Costs refer to negative exchanges, such as critical remarks, complaints, and attacks. When the rewards are high and the costs are low, the outcome is likely to be positive for both partners (profit). When the costs are high and the rewards low, neither may be satisfied with the outcome (loss).

5-8 Outline the steps in conflict resolution. To resolve conflicts, partners should first address recurring, disturbing issues, identify new desired behaviors, and identify perceptions to change. Next, they should summarize their partner's perspectives and work together to create alternative win–win solutions. After generating solutions, partners should focus on forgiving one another. To make this process successful, partners should avoid employing defense mechanisms like escapism, rationalization, projection, and displacement.

brainstorming suggesting as many alternatives as possible without evaluating them. (5-8e)

amae expecting a close other's indulgence when one behaves inappropriately. (5-8f)

defense mechanisms unconscious techniques that function to protect individuals from anxiety and minimize emotional hurt. (5-8g)

escapism the simultaneous denial of and withdrawal from a problem. (5-8g)

rationalization the cognitive justification for one's own behavior that unconsciously conceals one's true motives. (5-8g)

projection attributing one's own feelings, attitudes, or desires to one's partner while avoiding recognition that these are one's own thoughts, feelings, and desires. (5-8g)

displacement shifting one's feelings, thoughts, or behaviors from the person who evokes them onto someone else. (5-8g)

5-9 Explain current trends in communication and technology. The future of communication will increasingly involve technology in the form of texting, smartphones, Facebook, etc. Such technology will be used to initiate, enhance, and maintain relationships. Indeed, intimates today may text each other 60 times a day. Over 2,000 messages a month are not unusual. Social networking sites such as Facebook are particularly valuable for international students in helping them to maintain a strong sense of connectivity and bonding while they are temporarily out of their home country.

6-1 **Define alternative sexual values.** At least three sexual values guide choices in sexual behavior: absolutism, relativism, and hedonism. Absolutism is a sexual value system that is based on unconditional allegiance to the authority of religion, law, or tradition. One example of absolutism is asceticism, or the belief that giving in to carnal lusts is wrong and that one must rise above the pursuit of sensual pleasure to a life of self-discipline and self-denial. Relativism is when sexual decisions are made in reference to the emotional, security, and commitment aspects of the relationship. Friends with benefits and consensually nonmonogamous relationships are examples of this sexual value. Hedonism is the belief that the ultimate value and motivation for human actions lie in the pursuit of pleasure and the avoidance of pain.

sexual values moral guidelines for sexual behavior in relationships. (6-1)

absolutism belief system based on unconditional allegiance to the authority of religion, law, or tradition. (6-1a)

asceticism the belief that giving in to carnal lusts is wrong and that one must rise above the pursuit of sensual pleasure to a life of self-discipline and self-denial. (6-1a)

relativism sexual decisions are made in reference to the emotional, security, and commitment aspects of the relationship. (6-1b)

friends with benefits relationship a relationship between nonromantic friends who also have a sexual relationship. (6-1b)

concurrent sexual partnerships those in which the partners have sex with several individuals concurrently. (6-1b)

swinging relationships involve married/pair-bonded individuals agreeing that they may have sexual encounters with others. (6-1b)

hedonism belief that the ultimate value and motivation for human actions lie in the pursuit of pleasure and the avoidance of pain. (6-1c)

sexual double standard the view that encourages and accepts sexual expression of men more than women. (6-1c)

6-2 **Outline the sources of sexual values.** The sources of one's sexual values are numerous and include one's education, religion, and family, as well as technology, television, social movements, and the Internet.

6-3 **Discuss sexual behaviors.** Definitions of "sex" vary, but undergraduates generally agree that vaginal and anal sex are "definitely" sex, while kissing is "definitely not" sex. Some individuals are asexual and thus present an absence of interest in having sex with someone else. Despite varying definitions of sex, sexual behavior is dictated by social scripts. Social scripts are defined as the identification of the roles in a social situation, the nature of the relationship between the roles, and the expected behaviors of those roles. For example, in regard to kissing, two individuals kiss because they are in a relationship where the expectation is such that they are expected to kiss. Sexual behaviors include sex, masturbation, oral sex, intercourse, and cybersex.

asexual an absence of sexual behavior with a partner and oneself. (6-3a)

social scripts the identification of the roles in a social situation, the nature of the relationship between the roles, and the expected behaviors of those roles. (6-3a)

masturbation stimulating one's own body with the goal of experiencing pleasurable sexual sensations. (6-3b)

coitus sexual union of a man and woman by insertion of the penis into the vagina. (6-3d)

sexual readiness determining when one is ready for first intercourse in reference to contraception, autonomy of decision, consensuality, and absence of regret. (6-3e)

cybersex any consensual sexual experience mediated by a computer that involves at least two people. (6-3f)

kink typically refers to BDSM (bondage and discipline/dominance and submission/sadism and masochism). (6-3g)

6-4 **Explain sexuality in relationships.** Sexuality occurs in a social context that influences its frequency and perceived quality. Never-married individuals report the lowest level of sexual satisfaction. In contrast, 85% of the married and pair-bonded individuals reported emotional satisfaction in their sexual relationships. Hence, although never-married individuals have more sexual partners, they are less emotionally satisfied. Marital sex is distinctive for its social legitimacy, declining frequency, and satisfaction (both physical and emotional). The meanings of intercourse for separated or divorced individuals vary. For many, intercourse is a way to reestablish their crippled self-esteem. The most common sexual difficulties for men include impairment in function, hyperactive desire, premature ejaculation, and erectile difficulty, and the most common sexual difficulties for women include absent or delayed orgasm, hyperactive desire, and lack of responsive desire. Pornography can become a context for conflict due to the discrepancy in use between men and women.

satiation the state in which a stimulus loses its value with repeated exposure. (6-4b)

new relationship energy (NRE) refers to the euphoria of a new emotional/sexual relationship that dissipates over time. (6-4b)

CHAPTER REVIEW LEARNING OBJECTIVES / KEY TERMS

CHAPTER 6

6-5 **Discuss the prerequisites for sexual fulfillment in a relationship.** In order to achieve sexual fulfillment in a relationship, individuals must have knowledge about themselves and their bodies. Sexual fulfillment also implies having a positive body image. Effective sexual functioning also requires good physical and mental health. Relationship satisfaction is associated with sexual satisfaction; committed, loving relationships report greater sexual satisfaction. Researchers have emphasized that traditional gender roles inhibit sexual fulfillment in a relationship, because they dictate restrictive rules for women's sexual behavior. Through adoption of an egalitarian perspective, a couple can achieve greater sexual fulfillment. Compared with less condom-assertive females, more condom-assertive females have more faith in the effectiveness of condoms, believe more in their own condom communication skills, perceive that they are more susceptible to STIs, believe there are more relational benefits to being condom assertive, believe their peers are more condom assertive, and intend to be more condom assertive. Sexually fulfilled partners are comfortable expressing what they enjoy and do not enjoy in the sexual experience. Researchers found that both men and women who reported initiating sex more frequently and who perceived their partner as initiating more frequently reported greater sexual satisfaction. Additionally, expectations must be realistic to achieve sexual fulfillment. Partners may differ in sexual interest and desire. This sometimes results in sexual compliance, wherein an individual willingly agrees to participate in sexual behavior without having the desire to do so. To achieve sexual fulfillment, couples should avoid spectatoring.

condom assertiveness the unambiguous messaging that sex without a condom is unacceptable. (6-5d)

STI sexually transmitted infection. (6-5d)

sexual compliance an individual willingly agrees to participate in sexual behavior without having the desire to do so. (6-5h)

spectatoring mentally observing one's own and one's partner's sexual performance. (6-5i)

6-6 **Explain current trends in sexuality and relationships.** The future of sexual relationships will involve continued individualism as the driving force in sexual relationships. Numerous casual partners (hooking up) will continue to characterize about 75% of individuals in late adolescence and early twenties. As these persons reach their late twenties, the goal of sexuality begins to transition to seeking a partner—not just to hook up and have fun with but to settle down with. This new goal is accompanied by new sexual behaviors such as delayed first intercourse in the new relationship, exclusivity, and movement toward marriage. The monogamous move toward the marriage context creates a transitioning of sexual values from hedonism to relativism to absolutism, where strict morality rules become operative in the relationship (expected fidelity). Sexual robots will also become more visible and their use will continue. Artificial intelligence expert Noel Sharkey reported that teenagers risk losing their virginity to sophisticated humanoid robots (Roxxxy or Rocky True Companion).

7-1 Define terminology related to GLBTQIA relationships. Sexual orientation (also known as sexual identity) is a classification of individuals as heterosexual, bisexual, or gay, based on their emotional, cognitive, and sexual attractions and self-identity. Heterosexuality refers to the predominance of cognitive, emotional, and sexual attraction to individuals of the other sex. Homosexuality refers to the predominance of cognitive, emotional, and sexual attraction to individuals of the same sex, and bisexuality is cognitive, emotional, and sexual attraction to members of both sexes. The term *lesbian* refers to homosexual women, while the term *gay* refers to both homosexual men and women. The word *transgender* is a generic term for a person of one biological sex who displays characteristics of the other sex. Transsexuals are individuals with the biological and anatomical sex of one gender (e.g., male) but the self-concept of the other sex (e.g., female). Cross-dressing is a broad term for individuals who may dress or present themselves in the gender of the other sex. The term *queer* is a self-identifier to indicate that the person has a sexual orientation other than heterosexual. *Genderqueer* means that the person does not identify as either male or female since the person does not feel sufficiently like one or the other.

LGBTQIA a term that has emerged to refer collectively to **l**esbians, **g**ays, **b**isexuals, **t**ransgender **i**ndividuals, those **q**uestioning their sexual orientation/sexual identity (the term may also refer to queer), those who are **i**ntersexed, and **a**sexual (some also refer to the A as ally/friend of the cause and asexual). (7-1)

asexual means that there is an absence of sexual attraction/arousal to a partner. (7-1)

sexual orientation (sexual identity) a classification of individuals as heterosexual, bisexual, or homosexual, based on their emotional, cognitive, and sexual attractions and self-identity. (7-1)

heterosexuality the predominance of emotional and sexual attraction to individuals of the other sex. (7-1)

homosexuality predominance of emotional and sexual attraction to individuals of the same sex. (7-1)

bisexuality emotional and sexual attraction to members of both sexes. (7-1)

lesbian homosexual woman. (7-1)

gay homosexual women or men. (7-1)

transgender individuals who express their masculinity and femininity in nontraditional ways consistent with their biological sex. (7-1)

transsexual individual with the biological and anatomical sex of one gender but the self-concept of the other sex. (7-1)

cross-dresser broad term for individuals who may dress or present themselves in the gender of the other sex. (7-1)

queer a self-identifier to indicate that the person has a sexual orientation other than heterosexual. (7-1)

genderqueer the person does not identify as either male or female since he or she does not feel sufficiently like one or the other. (7-1)

7-2 Discuss the various beliefs about causes and malleability of sexual orientation. Many people believe that biology is at least one cause of homosexuality. Those that believe biology is responsible for homosexuality tend to refer to one's pattern in mate selection as sexual orientation. Those who believe that homosexuality is caused by one's environment or choice tend to refer to this pattern as sexual preference. The term *sexual identity* is increasingly being used, because it connotes more about the person than does sexuality. Individuals who believe that homosexual people choose their sexual orientation tend to think that homosexuals can and should change their sexual orientation through conversion therapy. However, data confirm that conversion therapy is ineffective and misguided.

conversion therapy (reparative therapy) therapy designed to change a person's homosexual orientation to a heterosexual orientation. (7-2b)

7-3 Explore attitudes toward homosexuality and their effects. The United States, along with many other countries throughout the world, is predominantly heterosexist. Heterosexism refers to the denigration and stigmatization of any behavior, person, or relationship that is not heterosexual. Heterosexism results in prejudice and discrimination against homosexual and bisexual people. There are five dimensions of attitudes toward homosexuality. First, one's general attitude toward homosexuality is important: does the individual believe that homosexuality is normal or abnormal? Second, should homosexuals be granted the same rights as heterosexuals in regard to marriage and adoption? Third, an individual's feelings in regard to having a gay neighbor or colleague and public displays of homosexual affection tell much about his or her attitudes toward homosexuality. Lastly, whether an individual feels that homosexuality is accepted in society already is indicative of homonegativity. While homonegativity attaches negative connotations to being gay, homophobia refers to overt negative attitudes and emotions toward homosexuality. Homonegativity, homophobia, biphobia, and transphobia can result in hate crimes and internalized homophobia. There are various effects of antigay and trans bias and discrimination on heterosexuals.

heterosexism the denigration and stigmatization of any behavior, person, or relationship that is not heterosexual. (7-3)

homophobia negative (almost phobic) attitudes toward homosexuality. (7-3a)

homonegativity a construct that refers to antigay responses such as negative feelings (fear, disgust, anger), thoughts ("homosexuals are HIV carriers"), and behavior ("homosexuals deserve a beating"). (7-3a)

hate crime instances of violence against homosexuals. (7-3a)

internalized homophobia a sense of personal failure and self-hatred among lesbians and gay men resulting from the acceptance of negative social attitudes and feelings toward homosexuals. (7-3a)

ally development model professionals provide consistent exposure to the discriminatory patterns against GLBT individuals. (7-3b)

biphobia (binegativity) refers to a parallel set of negative attitudes toward bisexuality and those identified as bisexual. (7-3b)

transphobia negative attitudes toward transsexuality or those who self-identify as transsexual. (7-3b)

CHAPTER REVIEW

CHAPTER 7 LEARNING OBJECTIVES / KEY TERMS

7-4 Discuss the risks and benefits of coming out. Coming out refers to the process of being open and honest about one's sexual orientation and identity. There are several risks of coming out. Individuals worry about the reactions of their parents and families, and the consequences these reactions may have. There is also potential for harassment and discrimination at school and/or the workplace, and an increased risk of hate crime victimization. On the other hand, there are several benefits of coming out. Those who have come out report higher levels of acceptance from parents, lower levels of alcohol and drug use, and fewer identity and adjustment problems.

coming out being open and honest about one's sexual orientation and identity. (7-4a)

7-5 Explore GLBT relationships. GLBT individuals and couples noted more stress in reference to coming out as individuals and as a couple (if and when), and greater hesitancy to commit and less family/institutional support for their relationship. Otherwise, gay and heterosexual couples are amazingly similar in regard to having equal power and control, being emotionally expressive, perceiving many attractions and few alternatives to the relationship, placing a high value on attachment, and sharing decision making. Like many heterosexual women, most gay women value stable, monogamous relationships that are emotionally as well as sexually satisfying. Gay men are often stereotyped as preferring sexual relationships with many partners, but most prefer monogamy. However, men express greater acceptance of casual sex than women. In GLBT relationships, roles in reference to housework, emotion work, and child care tend to be shaped by time availability and personal preferences as well as labor force participation and citizenship. While a great deal is known about transgender individuals, little is known about transgender relationships.

down low nongay-identifying men who have sex with men and women meet their partners out of town, not in predictable contexts, or on the Internet. (7-5f)

7-6 Outline the legal history of same-sex marriage. In June 2015 the Supreme Court ruled that same sex marriage was legal in all 50 states. The decision was 5–4. Justice Anthony Kennedy, the pivotal swing vote, wrote the majority opinion. Earlier, also by a 5–4 decision, the Supreme Court declared DOMA (the Defense of Marriage Act) unconstitutional on equal protection grounds, thus giving same-sex married couples federal recognition and benefits, including the right to inherit from a spouse who dies without a will, the benefit of not paying inheritance taxes upon the death of a spouse, the right to make crucial medical decisions for a spouse under the Family Medical Leave Act (FMLA), the right to collect Social Security survivor benefits, and the right to receive health insurance coverage under a spouse's plan.

Defense of Marriage Act (DOMA) legislation passed by Congress denying federal recognition of homosexual marriage and allowing states to ignore same-sex marriages licensed by other states. (7-6)

7-7 Discuss some GLBT parenting issues. Children with mixed-orientation parents may be raised by a gay or lesbian parent, a gay or lesbian stepparent, a heterosexual parent, and a heterosexual stepparent. A gay or lesbian individual or couple may have children through the use of assisted reproductive technology, including in vitro fertilization, surrogate mothers, and donor insemination. Some issues arise in GLBT parenting. First, gay male parents are often regarded as suspect. Gay men suffer from heteronormativity, wherein their ability to function as parents is under scrutiny because of their place in the heterosexual order. Interviews with women raised by lesbian mothers revealed that these women felt an openness to differences in others, felt like a strong people, and identified as advocates. LGBTQ parents tend to be less strict in gender socialization than heterosexual parents. While heterosexual parents believe that children are or should be heterosexual and encourage traditional gender socialization (e.g., ribbon in hair for female babies), LGBTQ parents provide their children with a variety of gendered options for clothing, toys, and activities (e.g., the gender buffet). While critics suggest that children reared by same-sex parents are disadvantaged, there are no data to support this fear. Little research has been done on the development and well-being of children in transgender families. Although several respected national organizations have gone on record in support of treating gays and lesbians without prejudice in parenting and adoption decisions, lesbian and gay parents are often discriminated against in child custody, visitation, adoption, and foster care.

7-8 Explain current trends in GLBTQIA relationships. While heterosexism, homonegativity, biphobia, and transphobia have historically been entrenched in American society, moral acceptance and social tolerance/acceptance of gays, lesbians, bisexuals, and transsexuals as individuals, couples, and parents will increase. Indeed, Mahaffey and Bryan (2016) confirmed that GLBT attitudes are responsive to social influence. As a result of a more accepting culture, more GLBTQIA individuals will come out, their presence will become more evident, and tolerance, acceptance, and support will increase. A change in policy by the Boy Scouts allowing gays and lesbians to be members is another example of change/increased acceptance (Pynes, 2016).

8-1 Discuss motivations and functions of marriage and the transition to egalitarian marriage. Some individuals get married because they view marriage as the ultimate expression of their love for each other. Individuals also anticipate a sense of personal fulfillment through marriage. Although marriage does not ensure it, companionship is the greatest expected benefit of marriage in the United States. Some individuals marry because they want to have children, and prefer to do so in a marital context. Others marry for the economic security of marriage. Being married is associated with positive mental health. There are several societal functions of marriage. Bonding a male and female together for reproduction functions to create an environment where offspring will be produced, and parents will be obligated to provide physical care and socialization to their young. Additionally, marriage gives the state legal leverage to force parents to be responsible for child rearing. Marriage also serves to regulate sexual behaviors and stabilize adult personalities. The very nature of the marriage relationship has also changed from being very traditional or male-dominated to being very modern or egalitarian.

forced marriages those in which the parents force the child to marry a person of the parents choosing. (8-1d)

8-2 Outline the personal and social functions of weddings and honeymoons. The wedding itself is a rite of passage, both civil and religious, that marks the transition from fiancée and fiancé to spouse. Wedding ceremonies still reflect traditional cultural definitions of women as property. For example, the father of the bride usually walks the bride down the aisle and "gives her away" to her husband. In some cultures, the bride is not even present at the time of the actual marriage. The wedding is a time for the respective families to learn how to cooperate with each other for the benefit of the couple. Honeymoons also have personal and social functions. They provide the couple with a period of recuperation from the usually exhausting demands of preparing for and being involved in a wedding ceremony and reception. Honeymoons also provide a time for the couple to be alone to solidify their new identity from that of an unmarried to a married couple.

rite of passage an event that marks the transition from one social status to another. (8-2)

artifact concrete symbol that reflects the existence of a cultural belief or activity. (8-2a)

honeymoon the time following the wedding whereby the couple becomes isolated to recover from the wedding and to solidify their new status change from lovers to spouses. (8-2b)

8-3 Explore legal and social changes that occur after marriage. After the wedding and honeymoon, the new spouses begin to experience changes in their legal, personal, and marital relationship. Unless the partners have signed a prenuptial agreement specifying that their earnings and property will remain separate, the wedding ceremony makes each spouse part owner of what the other earns in income and accumulates in property. New spouses experience an array of personal changes in their lives. One consequence of getting married is an enhanced sense of self-esteem and sense of mastery and that marriage is good for one's mental health. Marriage affects relationships with others. A couple in love withdraws from other relationships (both related and nonrelated). Abandoning one's friends after marriage may be problematic because one's spouse cannot be expected to satisfy all of one's social needs. One effect of getting married is disenchantment. It may not happen in the first few weeks or months of marriage, but it is almost inevitable. Marriage affects relationships with parents. Time spent with parents and extended kin radically increases when a couple has children. Marriage involves the need for spouses to discuss and negotiate how they are going to get and spend money in their relationship.

disenchantment (disillusionment) the transition from a state of newness and high expectation to a state of mundaneness tempered by reality. (8-3d)

satiation a stimulus loses its value with repeated exposure. (8-3d)

8-4 **Discuss diversity in marriage relationships.** Researchers have emphasized the various racial, ethnic, structural, geographic location, and contextual differences in marriage and family relationships. Although higher rates of Black female single-parent families (compared to White female single-parent families) exist, this does not reflect a disregard for marriage, but is a response to the economic reality of Black men. Hispanics tend to have higher rates of marriage, early marriage, higher fertility, nonmarital child rearing, and prevalence of female householder. They also have two micro family factors: male power and strong familistic values. Hispanic and non-Hispanic are the most frequent interracial/interethnic unions. Black–White marriages are the most infrequent. There are three main types of military marriages. In one type of military marriage, an individual falls in love, gets married, and subsequently joins the military. A second type of military marriage is one in which one or both of the partners is already a member of the military before getting married. The final and least common type is known as a military contract marriage, in which a military person will marry a civilian to get more money and benefits from the government. Although religion may be a central focus of some individuals and their marriage, Americans in general have become more secular, and as a result religion has become less influential as a criterion for selecting a partner. With increased globalization, international matchmaking Internet opportunities, and travel abroad programs, there is greater opportunity to meet/marry someone from another country.

polyamory refers to multiple intimate sexual and/or loving relationships with the knowledge and consent of all partners involved. (8-4d)

poly families multi-partner relationships that raise children and function as families. (8-4d)

military contract marriage a military person will marry a civilian to get more money and benefits from the government. (8-4e)

May–December marriage age-dissimilar marriage (ADM) in which the woman is typically in the spring of her life (May) and her husband is in the later years (December). (8-4j)

cougar a woman, usually in her thirties or forties, who is financially stable and mentally independent and looking for a younger man with whom to have fun. (8-4j)

8-5 **Explore the definition of and factors related to marriage success.** Marital success refers to the quality of the marriage relationship measured in terms of stability and happiness. There are various factors related to happy marriages, including time spent together, the ability of the couple to share communication and humor, and many more. Researchers of marital success emphasize different factors related to marital success. Symbolic interactionists emphasize the subjective nature of marital happiness and point out that the definition of the situation is critical. On the other hand, family developmental theorists emphasize developmental tasks that must be accomplished to enable a couple to have a happy marriage. Exchange theorists focus on the exchange of behavior of a kind and at a rate that is mutually satisfactory to both spouses. Structural functionalists regard marital happiness as contributing to marital stability, which is functional for society. There are five patterns of marital happiness across time, derived from axes of stability and happiness.

marital success the quality of the marriage relationship measured in terms of stability and happiness. (8-5a)

marriage rituals deliberate repeated social interactions that reflect emotional meaning to the couple. (8-5a)

connection rituals habits which occur daily in which the couple share time and attention. (8-5a)

8-6 **Explain current trends in marriage relationships.** Diversity will continue to characterize marriage relationships of the future. The traditional model of the husband provider, stay-at-home mom, and two children will continue to transition to other forms, including more women in the workforce, single-parent families, and smaller families. What will remain is the intimacy/companionship focus that spouses expect from their marriages. Openness to interracial, interreligious, cross-national, and age-discrepant relationships will increase. The driving force behind this change will be the U.S. value of individualism that minimizes parental disapproval. An increased global awareness, international students, and study abroad programs will facilitate increased opportunities and a mindset of openness to diversity in terms of one's selection of a partner.

9-1 Outline the connection between money and relationships. Money is major for both individuals and couples. Money is related to life satisfaction. Researchers have identified gender differences in what women and men want in regard to money in the partners they marry. In addition, money affects relationship formation and security—poverty related to delayed relationship formation, lower marriage rates under 35, and fewer households with children. Poverty is related to less time spent together and having disagreements about sex. It is also related to lower physical, psychological, and marital health. However, poverty can have positive effects through removing couples from consumerism. Money tends to equate to power in relationships and is directly related to marital happiness.

Consumerism to buy everything and to have everything now. (9-1)

9-2 Explore the relationship between work and marriage. To manage work life and marriage, couples should try to turn negatives into positives, be creative, tolerate dissimilarity, and be committed to the relationship. Some professions are more stressful on couples than others, such as police work. Women and mothers also participate in the labor force. Sixty-eight percent of wives with children are in the workforce. Traditional conceptions of motherhood suggest mothers should work part-time and be child-centered and pair-bonded with someone with high income. African American mothers expect to work full-time and depend on extended family and community for child care. Many couples today are involved in dual-career marriages, wherein both spouses pursue careers and may or may not include dependents.

mommy track stopping paid employment to be at home with young children. (9-2b)

dual-career marriage one in which both spouses pursue careers. (9-2d)

HIS/HER career marriage a husband's and wife's careers are given equal precedence. (9-2d)

commuter marriages a type of long-distance marriage where spouses live in different locations during the workweek (and sometimes for longer periods of time) to accommodate the careers of the respective spouses. (9-2d)

HER/HIS career marriage a wife's career is given precedence over her husband's career. (9-2d)

THEIR career marriage a career shared by a couple who travel and work together (e.g., journalists). (9-2d)

9-3 Discuss the effects of a wife's employment on the spouse and the marriage overall. A major challenge is for women to combine a career and motherhood. While some new mothers enjoy their work role and return to work soon after their children are born, others anguish over leaving their baby to return to the workforce. Managing the spheres of work and family may result in role overload. Because women have traditionally been responsible for most of the housework and child care, employed women come home from work to the second shift, or housework and child care that have to be done after work. Another stressful aspect of employment for employed mothers in dual-earner marriages is role conflict. When an individual feels anxiety over not being able to fulfill all of her role obligations, role strain occurs. Husbands report benefits from their wives' employment, including relief from sole financial responsibility and greater freedom to change their profession. Additionally, dual-earner marriages report the highest marital satisfaction.

role overload not having the time or energy to meet the demands of their responsibilities in the roles of wife, parent, and worker. (9-3)

role conflict being confronted with incompatible role obligations. (9-3)

second shift housework and child care that are done when the parents return home after work. (9-3)

role strain the anxiety that results from being able to fulfill only a limited number of role obligations. (9-3)

9-4 Explain the effects of parents' work on children. Abundant research confirms that maternal employment has no significant negative effects on young children. Mothers' employment is at conflict with intensive mothering ideals of unemployed mothers. Indeed, mothers with young children are least likely to be in the workforce. Mothers tend to return to the workforce when children are teens. Dual-income parents struggle with not getting enough quality time with children. Dual-income parents also face child care challenges. Day care options include a center, a home-based day care, or care by a relative. While most mothers prefer relatives (spouse or partner or another relative) for the day-care arrangement for their children, 23% of 1- to 2-year-old children and 18% of children 3 to 4 are in center-based day care programs.

9-5 **Discuss some ways that families balance work and family life.** Work is definitely stressful on individuals, spouses, and relationships. Economic challenges in general have been linked to relationship distress, depression, partner's discord, parenting stress, and coparenting dysfunction. In some cases, spillover occurs, wherein work spreads into family life in the form of the worker/parent doing overtime, taking work home, attending seminars organized by the company, being on call during the weekend/vacation, and always being on the computer. To avoid spillover, many employees employ the superperson strategy. They work as hard and efficiently as possible to meet the demands of work and family separately, in order to get the most out of both spheres of life. Individuals engage in the first shift at their place of employment, mothers then complete the second shift, and increasingly the third shift. Ways of dealing with the various stresses and difficulties involved in balancing work and family life include cognitive restructuring, delegating responsibilities, limiting commitments, time management strategies, and role compartmentalization. Finding a balance between work and leisure is challenging.

spillover thesis work spreads into family life in the form of the worker/parent doing overtime, taking work home, attending seminars organized by the company, being "on call" on the weekend/during vacation, and always being on the computer in reference to work. (9-5)

superperson strategy involves working as hard and as efficiently as possible to meet the demands of work and family. (9-5a)

superwoman (supermom) a cultural label that allows a mother who is experiencing role overload to regard herself as particularly efficient, energetic, and confident. (9-5a)

third shift the emotional energy expended by a spouse or parent in dealing with various family issues. (9-5a)

cognitive restructuring viewing a situation in positive terms. (9-5b)

shift work having one parent work during the day and the other parent work at night so that one parent can always be with the children. (9-5d)

role compartmentalization separating the roles of work and home so that an individual does not dwell on the problems of one role while physically being at the place of the other role. (9-5e)

9-6 **Explain current trends in money, work, and family life.** Families will continue to be stressed by work. Employers will, increasingly, ask employees to work longer and do more without the commensurate increases in salary or benefits. Businesses are struggling to stay solvent and workers will take the brunt of the instability. The number of wives who work outside the home will increase—the economic needs of the family will demand that they do so. Husbands will adapt, most willingly, some reluctantly. Children will become aware that budgets are tight, tempers are strained, and leisure with the family in the summer may not be as expansive as previously. As children go to college they can benefit from exposure to financial management information—being careful about credit card debt and how they spend money (Fiona et al., 2012). While the percent of wives in the workforce may increase, the percent of mothers who do not work outside the home is increasing. The percent in 2012 was 29%, up from 23% in 1999 (Cohn et al., 2014). Difficulty finding employment and concerns about the employment effects on children are explanations.

Define types of relationship abuse

CHAPTER 10 LEARNING OBJECTIVES / KEY TERMS

CHAPTER REVIEW

10-1 **Define the different types of relationship abuse.** There are several types of abuse in relationships. Examples of physical violence include pushing, throwing something at the partner, slapping, hitting, and forcing the partner to have sex. There are two types of intimate partner violence. One type is situational couple violence (SCV) where conflict escalates over an issue (e.g., money, sex) and one or both partners lose control. A second type of violence, referred to as intimate terrorism (IT), is designed to control the partner. Some examples of emotionally abusive behaviors of one's partner include refusal to talk to the partner as a way of punishing the partner, making personal decisions for the partner (e.g., what to wear, what to eat, whether to smoke), throwing a temper tantrum and breaking things to frighten the partner, criticizing/belittling the partner to make him or her feel bad, and acting jealous when the partner is observed talking or texting a potential romantic partner. Abuse may take the form of stalking. To react to a stalker, individuals might make a direct statement to the person, seek formal protection, avoid the perpetrator when possible, and use informal coping methods.

violence physical aggression with the purpose to control, intimidate, and subjugate another human being. (10-1a)

intimate partner violence an all-inclusive term that refers to crimes committed against current or former spouses, boyfriends, or girlfriends. (10-1a)

situational couple violence conflict escalates over an issue and one or both partners lose control. (10-1a)

intimate terrorism behavior designed to control the partner. (10-1a)

battered woman syndrome (battered woman defense) legal term used in court that the person accused of murder was suffering from to justify their behavior. Therapists define battering as physical aggression that results in injury and accompanied by fear and terror. (10-1a)

uxoricide the murder of a woman by a romantic partner. (10-1a)

intimate partner homicide murder of a spouse. (10-1a)

filicide murder of an offspring by a parent. (10-1a)

parricide murder of a parent by an offspring. (10-1a)

siblicide murder of a sibling. (10-1a)

emotional abuse nonphysical behavior designed to denigrate the partner, reduce the partner's status, and make the partner feel vulnerable to being controlled by the partner. (10-1b)

revenge porn posting nude photos of ex; a form of emotional and sexual abuse; some states considering legislation against this behavior. (10-1b)

stalking (unwanted pursuit behavior) unwanted following or harassment of a person that induces fear in the victim. (10-1e)

obsessive relational intrusion the relentless pursuit of intimacy with someone who does not want it. (10-1e)

cyber victimization harassing behavior which includes being sent threatening email, unsolicited obscene email, computer viruses, or junk mail (spamming); can also include flaming (online verbal abuse) and leaving improper messages on message boards. (10-1e)

cyber control use of communication technology, such as cell phones, email, and social networking sites, to monitor or control partners in intimate relationships. (10-1e)

10-2 **Discuss some reasons for violence and abuse in relationships.** Research suggests that numerous factors contribute to violence and abuse in intimate relationships. These factors operate at the cultural, community, individual, and family levels. Violence and abuse in the family may be linked to such cultural factors as violence in the media, acceptance of corporal punishment, gender inequality, and the view of women and children as property. Community violence itself presents in the form of robberies, stabbings, and shootings. Factors that contribute to violence and abuse in the family include social isolation, poverty, and inaccessible or unaffordable health care, day care, elder care, and respite care services and facilities. Various individual motivations for violence and abuse include dependency, jealousy, need to control, unhappiness and dissatisfaction, history of aggressiveness, quick involvement, blaming others for problems, and more. Individuals in "churner" relationships report higher rates of domestic violence. Family factors associated with domestic violence and abuse include being abused as a child, having parents who abused each other, and not having a father in the home.

corporal punishment the use of physical force with the intention of causing a child to experience pain, but not injury, for the purpose of correction or control of the child's behavior. (10-2a)

honor crime (honor killing) refers to unmarried women who are killed because they bring shame on their parents and siblings; occurs in Middle Eastern countries such as Jordan. (10-2b)

10-3 Discuss patterns of sexual abuse in undergraduate relationships. Based on data from the National Crime Victimization Survey (NCVS) of rape and sexual assault victimization against females aged 18 to 24 who are enrolled and not enrolled in college, rape and sexual assault was 1.2 times higher for nonstudents than for students, but the rate of not reporting sexual victimization to police was higher among students than nonstudents. About 85% of rapes are perpetrated by someone the woman knows. Rape also occurs in same-sex relationships. Gay, lesbian, and bisexual individuals are not immune to experiencing sexual abuse in their relationships. Alcohol is the most common rape drug, but rophypnol is also a common date-rape drug. A person under the influence cannot give consent. Hence, a person who has sex with someone who is impaired is engaging in rape. Rape is usually discussed as a female issue, but men experience rape as well. Men are traumatized by the experience and have limited healing venues.

double victims individuals who report being a victim of forced sex by both a stranger and by a date or acquaintance. (10-3a)

acquaintance rape nonconsensual sex between adults (of same or other sex) who know each other. (10-3a)

female rape myths beliefs that deny victim injury or cast blame on the woman for her own rape. (10-3a)

male rape myths beliefs that deny victim injury or make assumptions about his sexual orientation. (10-3a)

date rape one type of acquaintance rape which refers to nonconsensual sex between people who are dating or are on a date. (10-3a)

Rophypnol causes profound, prolonged sedation and short-term memory loss; also known as the date rape drug, roofies, Mexican Valium, or the "forget (me) pill." (10-3d)

10-4 Outline abuse patterns in marriage relationships. The chance of abuse in a relationship increases with marriage. The longer individuals know each other and the more intimate their relationship, the greater the abuse. Abuse in marriage may differ from unmarried abuse in that the husband may feel ownership of the wife and feel the need to control her. Marital rape, now recognized in all states as a crime, is forcible rape by one's spouse. Some states (Washington) recognize a marital defense exception for third-degree rape in which force is not used even though there is no consent. Over 30 countries have no laws against marital rape.

marital rape forcible rape by one's spouse—a crime in all states. (10-4c)

10-5 Discuss the effects of abuse. Abuse has devastating effects on the physical and psychological well-being of victims. Abuse between parents also affects the children. Abuse has devastating consequences. Being a victim of intimate partner violence is associated with symptoms of depression, anxiety, fear, feeling detached from others, inability to sleep, and irritability. The most dramatic effects of abuse occur on pregnant women, which include increased risk of miscarriage, birth defects, low birth weight, preterm delivery, and neonatal death. Negative effects may also accrue to children who witness domestic abuse (e.g., depression).

10-6 Define the cycle of abuse. The cycle of abuse begins when a person is abused and the perpetrator feels regret, asks for forgiveness, and engages in positive behavior (gives flowers). The victim, who perceives few options and feels anxious terminating the relationship with the abusive partner, feels hope for the relationship at the contriteness of the abuser and does not call the police or file charges. After the forgiveness, couples usually experience a period of making up or honeymooning, during which the victim feels good again about the partner and is hopeful for a nonabusive future. However, stress, anxiety, and tension mount again in the relationship, which the abuser relieves by violence toward the victim. Such violence is followed by the familiar sense of regret and pleadings for forgiveness, accompanied by a new round of positive behavior.

periodic reinforcement reinforcement that occurs every now and then (unpredictable). The abused victim never knows when the abuser will be polite and kind again (e.g., flowers and candy). (10-6a)

10-7 Explain current trends in abuse in relationships. Fellmeth et al. (2015) assessed the efficacy of educational and skills-based interventions to prevent relationship and dating violence in adolescents and young adults across a broad spectrum of research and found no evidence of effectiveness of interventions on episodes of violence, attitudes, or behaviors. However, progress toward reducing sexual assaults on college and university campuses is under way. Title IX is designed to empower students to combat campus violence/rape. The law requires colleges and universities receiving federal funding to take seriously a complaint of violence/rape either by filing a federal complaint or a civil lawsuit. The reality of universities taking rape on campus seriously is slow to take hold. Brock Turner, a Stanford undergraduate, served three months in jail for raping an unconscious female on campus—a slap on the risk for a heinous crime. Reducing family violence through education involves altering aspects of American culture that contribute to such violence. Researchers have recently emphasized the need for bystander intervention programs that sensitize individuals to be aware of abuse and to intervene. Such bystander programs led by peer educators are more effective in altering attitudes.

11-1 **Examine the social influences that motivate individuals to have children, the lifestyle changes that result from such a choice, and the costs of rearing children.** Society tends to be pronatalist, encouraging childbearing. Our family, friends, religion, and government encourage positive attitudes toward parenthood. While social influences are important, so are individual motivations to have children. These motivations include the desire to love and be loved by a child, companionship, personal fulfillment, and to recapture one's own childhood. After having a child, daily routines become focused around the needs of the children, and living arrangements change to provide space for the new addition. Some parents must change their work schedules. Another major lifestyle change is the loss of freedom of activity and flexibility in one's personal schedule. Having children is expensive—costs begin with prenatal care and continue at childbirth. The positives and negatives of having children continue throughout one's life.

pronatalism cultural attitude which encourages having children. (11-1a)

11-2 **Discuss the factors related to deciding the number of desired children.** More women are deciding not to have children or to have fewer children. The driving force behind decisions to remain childfree is the importance the spouses gave to their relationship and the strength of their conviction. There are three phases of the decision-making process: agreement, acceptance, and closing the door. Most research on deciding for or against having children has been conducted on heterosexuals. Existing research on homosexual desires for parenthood demonstrate that homosexual preferences for parenthood are similar to heterosexual preferences. Some couples decide to have one child because more children will interfere with their lifestyles and careers, or simply do not want to experience pregnancy again. The most preferred family size for non-Hispanic White women is the two-child family. Couples are more likely to have a third child if they already have two girls rather than two boys. More than three children are often born to parents who are immersed in a religion that encourages procreation. Contraception and emergency contraception are used to preserve the preferred family size.

procreative liberty the freedom to decide to have children or not. (11-2)

childlessness concerns the idea that holidays and family gatherings may be difficult because of not having children or feeling left out or sad that others have children. (11-2a)

antinatalism opposition to children. (11-2a)

competitive birthing having the same number (or more) of children in reference to one's peers. (11-2f)

emergency contraception (postcoital contraception) refers to various types of morning-after pills. (11-2h)

11-3 **Outline the differences between types and causes of infertility, and the success using assisted reproductive technologies.** Six percent of adult women in the United States meet the criteria for infertility. There are several different types of infertility, including primary infertility, secondary infertility, and pregnancy wastage. Infertility in the woman is related to her age, not having been pregnant before, blocked fallopian tubes, endocrine imbalance that prevents ovulation, dysfunctional ovaries, chemically hostile cervical mucus that may kill sperm, and effects of STIs. Obesity also affects women's fertility. Some common causes of infertility of men include low sperm production, poor semen motility, effects of STIs, and interference with passage of sperm through the genital ducts due to an enlarged prostate. Assisted reproductive technology is very costly, but only somewhat effective.

infertility the inability to achieve a pregnancy after at least one year of regular sexual relations without birth control, or the inability to carry a pregnancy to a live birth. (11-3)

conception refers to the fusion of the egg and sperm. Also known as fertilization. (11-3b)

pregnancy when the fertilized egg is implanted (typically in the uterine wall). (11-3b)

11-4 **Explore factors related to adoption.** There are various routes to adoption, including public, through a private agency, independent adoption, kinship, and as a stepparent. Motives for adopting a child include an inability to have a biological child, a desire to give a child a permanent loving home, or desire to avoid contributing to overpopulation by having more biological children. Children who are adopted have an enormous advantage over those who are not adopted. Adopted children tend to have greater physical growth, attachment, cognitive development, school achievement, etc. outcomes than their nonadopted peers. The cost of an adoption varies by the type of adoption. The least expensive adoption is adoption via being a foster parent, while the most expensive adoptions are international. Another controversy is whether adopted children should be allowed to obtain information about their biological parents.

11-5 **Define and discuss foster parenting.** Some individuals seek the role of parent via foster parenting. Foster care may be temporary or long term. A foster parent has made a contract with the state for the service, has judicial status, and is reimbursed by the state. Foster parents are screened for previous arrest records and child abuse and neglect. They are licensed by the state, and some states require a foster parent orientation program.

foster parent neither a biological nor an adoptive parent but a person who takes care of and fosters a child taken into custody. (11-5)

11-6 **Discuss the history and issues surrounding abortion.** Abortion remains a controversial issue in the United States. When this country was founded, abortion was legal and accepted until the time of "quickening." Opposition to abortion grew in the 1870s, led by a fierce campaign aimed at making abortion illegal unless performed by a licensed physician. The procedure was made illegal in the 1880s. Although illegal, abortions continued at great risk through the 1950s. In 1973, *Roe v. Wade* guaranteed the right of a woman to have a legal abortion. The most frequently cited reasons for having an abortion today are that having a child would interfere with a woman's education, work, or ability to care for dependents, followed by an inability to afford the costs of a baby. Individuals adopt a political stance toward abortion that is either pro-life or pro-choice. The debate over abortion often involves the presumed physical and psychological effects of the procedure. Vacuum aspiration, a frequently used method in early pregnancy, does not increase risks to future childbearing, but late-term abortions increase the risks of subsequent miscarriages, premature deliveries, and babies with low birth weight. Among women who have a single, legal, first trimester abortion, mental health risks are equivalent to women who deliver an unplanned pregnancy.

induced abortion the deliberate termination of a pregnancy through chemical or surgical means. (11-6)

spontaneous abortion (miscarriage) the unintended termination of a pregnancy. (11-6)

abortion rate the number of abortions per thousand women aged 15 to 44. (11-6a)

abortion ratio refers to the number of abortions per 1,000 live births. Abortion is affected by the need for parental consent and parental notification. (11-6a)

parental consent a woman needs permission from a parent to get an abortion if under a certain age, usually 18. (11-6a)

parental notification a woman has to tell a parent she is getting an abortion if she is under a certain age, usually 18, but she does not need parental permission. (11-6a)

therapeutic abortions abortions performed to protect the life or health of the woman. (11-6b)

11-7 **Explain current trends in deciding about children.** As birthrates in the United States and Western Europe continue to fall, being childfree will lose some of its stigma. Indeed, the pregnancy rate for women aged 15–29 has dropped steadily since 1990. Individualism and economics are the primary factors responsible for reducing the obsession to have children. Once the personal, social, and economic consequences of having children come under close scrutiny, the automatic response to have children will be tempered.

12-1 Review the nature of parenting choices and identify some of the basic choices parents make. Parents endeavor to make the best decisions in rearing their children. Their choices have a profound impact on their children. When making parental decisions, parents must consider that not making a decision is to make a decision, all parental choices involve trade-offs, to reframe "regretful" parental decisions, and that parental choices are influenced by society and culture. There are seven basic parental choices, which include deciding: (1) whether or not to have a child, (2) the number of children to have, (3) the interval between children, (4) the method of discipline, (5) the degree to which they will invest time with their children, (6) whether or not to coparent (the parents cooperate in the development of the lives of their children), and (7) how much technological exposure they will allow their children at what age.

12-2 Outline the roles of parents. Although finding one definition of parenting is difficult, there is general agreement about the various roles parents play in the lives of their children. New parents assume at least seven roles. A major role of parents is the physical care of their children. Beyond providing physical care, parents are sensitive to the emotional needs of children in terms of their need to belong, to be loved, and to develop positive self-concepts. All parents think they have a philosophy of life or set of principles their children will benefit from. Parents fulfill their role as a teacher by sharing this philosophy or principles with their children. New parents are also acutely aware of the costs for medical care, food, and clothes for infants, and seek ways to ensure that such resources are available to their children. Parents also feel the need to protect their children from harm. The family is a major agent for health promotion—not only in promoting healthy food choices, responsible use of alcohol, nonuse of drugs, and safe driving skills, but also in ending smoking behavior. To build a sense of family cohesiveness, parents often foster rituals to bind members together in emotion and in memory.

parenting defined in terms of roles including caregiver, emotional resource, teacher, and economic resource. (12-2)

boomerang generation adult children who return to live with their parents. (12-2d)

12-3 Discuss the effects of transitioning to parenthood. The mother, father, and two of them as a couple undergo changes and adaptations during the transition to parenthood. Being a mother, particularly a biological or adoptive mother (in contrast to a stepmother), is a major social event for a woman. Most new mothers become emotionally bonded with their babies and resist separation, but not all mothers feel joyous after childbirth, and some experience postpartum depression or postpartum psychosis. Men receive limited socialization for the role of father. Nevertheless, there has been a major cultural shift in how fatherhood is conceptualized. While economic provider remains an important factor in how men view their role as fathers, increasingly, men are becoming more active in the physical care of and emotional engagement with their children. Some fathers experience postpartum depression following the birth of a baby. Children impact a couple's marriage by reducing the amount of time the spouses spend together, creating financial worries, and adding stress to relationships. Regardless of how children affect relationship satisfaction, spouses report more commitment to their relationship once they have children.

transition to parenthood period from the beginning of pregnancy through the first few months after the birth of a baby during which the mother and father undergo changes. (12-3)

oxytocin hormone from the pituitary gland during the expulsive stage of labor that has been associated with the onset of maternal behavior in lower animals. (12-3a)

baby blues transitory symptoms of depression in a mother 24 to 48 hours after her baby is born. (12-3a)

postpartum depression a more severe reaction following the birth of a baby which occurs in reference to a complicated delivery as well as numerous physiological and psychological changes occurring during pregnancy, labor, and delivery; usually in the first month after birth but can be experienced after a couple of years have passed. (12-3a)

postpartum psychosis a reaction in which a woman wants to harm her baby. (12-3a)

safe haven (Baby Moses law) place where mother of infant can take her baby and leave it without fear of prosecution. (12-3a)

gatekeeper role term used to refer to the influence of the mother on the father's involvement with his children. (12-3b)

12-4 Review facts about parenthood. Parenting involves responding to the varying needs of children as they grow up, and parents require help from family and friends in rearing their children. Views of children have changed over time. In fact, the very concept of childhood is relatively new. Concepts of childhood and parenting continue to change. Now, as millennials are having children, they have reacted to their own overscheduled childhoods; these millennials take a less directorial approach and want their children to try new things. Although parents often take the credit and the blame for the way their children turn out, they are only one among many influences on child development. Peer influence, siblings, teachers, media, and the Internet influence the development of children. Parents also feel pressure to teach children to think for themselves, develop their children's gender identity, and select the best parenting style.

helicopter parents parents who seek to manage the lives of their children long beyond childhood/early adolescence. (12-4a)

responsiveness refers to the extent to which parents respond to and meet the needs of their children. (12-4f)

demandingness the manner in which parents place demands on children in regard to expectations and discipline. (12-4f)

12-5 **Define and discuss principles of effective parenting.** Numerous principles are involved in being effective parents. First and most importantly, parents should provide time, love, praise, encouragement, and acceptance. Second, parents should avoid overindulgence in not only gifts, but in overnurturing without structure. Parents who monitor their children and teens and know where their children are, who they are with, and what they are doing are less likely to report that their adolescents receive low grades, or are engaged in early sexual activity, delinquent behavior, and alcohol or drug use. Parents should monitor their children's pornography exposure to avoid the development of sexist and/or unhealthy notions of sex and relationships. "Technological advances" was identified by 2,000 parents as the top issue (violence was second) that makes parenting children today tougher than in previous years. Monitoring children's technology exposure may protect children from harm. Parents should also set limits, and discipline children for inappropriate behavior. Having family meals together can assist parents in remaining emotionally connected with their children. Parents should encourage responsibility, establish a norm of forgiveness, teach empathy, and provide sex education. Parents should express confidence in their children, and respond creatively to teen years.

reactive attachment disorder common among children who were taught as infants that no one cared about them; these children have no capacity to bond emotionally with others since they have no learning history of the experience and do not trust adults, caretakers, or parents. (12-5a)

overindulgence defined as more than just giving children too much; includes overnurturing and providing too little structure. (12-5b)

time-out a noncorporal form of punishment that involves removing the child from a context of reinforcement to a place of isolation. (12-5f)

emotional competence teaching the child to experience emotion, express emotion, and regulate emotion. (12-5k)

12-6 **Outline the issues that single parents face.** Single parents enter their role through divorce or separation, widowhood, adoption, or deliberate choice to rear a child or children alone. Single parents face many challenges. They must respond to the demands of parenting with limited help. Some single parents regard their parental role as interfering with their sexual relationships. Single-parent families, particularly those headed by women, report that money is always lacking. Moreover, if the other parent is completely out of the child's life, the single parent needs to appoint a guardian to take care of the child in the event of the parent's death or disability. Single women who decide to have a child have poorer pregnancy outcomes than married women. Another consequence for children of single-parent mothers is that they often do not have the opportunity to develop an emotionally supportive relationship with their father. Growing up in a single-family home increases the likelihood that the adult child will have a first child while unmarried and in a cohabitation relationship, thus perpetuating the single-family structure.

single-parent family family in which there is only one parent and the other parent is completely out of the child's life through death, sperm donation, or abandonment, and no contact is made with the other parent. (12-6)

single-parent household one parent has primary custody of the child/children with the other parent living outside of the house but still being a part of the child's family; also called binuclear family. (12-6)

12-7 **Discuss current trends in parenting.** For the first time in more than 130 years, adults aged 18 to 34 were more likely to be living in their parents' home (32.1%) than they were to be living with a spouse or partner in their own household (31.6%) (Fry, 2016). As parents face increasing difficulty with rearing their children who are growing up amid massive exposure via the Internet/social media to an ever-changing society, they may reach out for help with parenting. Incredible Years is an example of an effective parenting program. A final trend in parenting is increased time fathers spend with their children, particularly young children.

13-1 Define stress and crisis and their sources. Stress is a reaction of the body to substantial or unusual demands (physical, environmental, or interpersonal). Stress is often accompanied by irritability, high blood pressure, and depression. A crisis is a situation that requires changes in normal patterns of response behavior. A family crisis is a situation that upsets the normal functioning of the family and requires a new set of responses to the stressor. Sources of stress and crises can be external, such as the hurricanes that annually hit our coasts or devastating tornadoes in the spring.

Other examples of an external crisis are economic recession, downsizing, or military deployment. Both stress and crisis events are normal aspects of family life and sometimes reflect a developmental sequence. Crisis events may have a cumulative effect: the greater the number in rapid succession, the greater the stress. The ABCX model of family stress was developed by Reuben Hill in the 1950s to explain how individuals and families experience and respond to stressors.

stress reaction of the body to substantial or unusual demands (physical, environmental, or interpersonal). (13-1)

crisis a crucial situation that requires change in one's normal pattern of behavior. (13-1)

resiliency a family's strength and ability to respond to a crisis in a positive way. (13-1a)

family resiliency the successful coping of family members under adversity that

enables them to flourish with warmth, support, and cohesion. (13-1a)

13-2 Discuss some helpful stress-management strategies. When possible, choose a positive view of the crisis situation. For example, survivors of hurricanes, tornados, and earthquakes routinely focus on the fact that they and their loved ones are alive rather than the loss of their home or material possessions. A betrayal can be seen as an opportunity for forgiveness, unemployment as a stage to spend time with one's family, and ill health as a chance to appreciate one's inner life. Exercising allows individuals to manage stress more effectively. Being immersed in a context

of relationships with one's parents/siblings, friends, and extended family is associated with positive adjustment to a crisis event. A love relationship also helps individuals cope with stress. A strong religious belief is also associated with coping with stress and loss. A sense of humor is related to lower anxiety, and is used to cope with aging, divorce, and caring for the mentally ill. Adequate sleep is necessary for optimum health and for dealing with stress. The presence of a dog or cat is associated with psychological well-being.

sanctification viewing the marriage as having divine character or significance. (13-2e)

13-3 Discuss some harmful stress-management strategies. Some coping strategies not only are ineffective for resolving family problems but also add to the family's stress by making the problems worse. Harmful stress-management strategies include keeping feelings inside, taking out frustrations on or blaming others, and denying or avoiding the problem. Women are more

likely than men to view as helpful such strategies as sharing concerns with relatives and friends, becoming more involved in religion, and expressing emotions. Men are more likely than women to use potentially harmful strategies such as using alcohol, keeping feelings inside, or keeping others from knowing how bad the situation is.

13-4 Discuss some common crisis events that families face. Some of the more common crisis events that spouses and families

face include physical illness, mental illness, an extramarital affair, unemployment, substance abuse, and death.

palliative care health care for the individual who has a life-threatening illness which focuses on relief of pain/suffering and support for the individual. (13-4a)

extramarital affair refers to a spouse's sexual involvement with someone outside the marriage. (13-4c)

extradyadic involvement refers to sexual involvement of a pair-bonded individual with someone other than the partner; also called extrarelational involvement. (13-4c)

Coolidge effect term used to describe waning of sexual excitement and the effect of novelty and variety on increasing sexual arousal. (13-4c)

down low term refers to African American married men who have sex with men and hide this from their spouse. (13-4c)

snooping investigating (without the partner's knowledge or permission) a romantic partner's private communication (e.g., text messages, email, and cell phone

use) motivated by concern that the partner may be hiding something. (13-4c)

alienation of affection law which gives a spouse the right to sue a third party for taking the affections of a spouse away. (13-4c)

chronic sorrow grief-related feelings that occur periodically throughout the lives of those left behind. (13-4f)

13-5 **Define and discuss relationship/marriage therapy.** All couples might consider consulting a relationship/marriage therapist about their relationship rather than remaining in an unhappy relationship or ending a relationship that can be improved. Signs to look for in your own relationship that suggest you might consider seeing a therapist include chronic arguing, feeling distant/avoiding each other, being unable or unwilling to address issues that create tension/dissatisfaction, feeling depressed, drifting into a relationship with someone else, increased drinking, and privately contemplating separation or breaking up. Effective marriage therapy usually involves seeing the spouses together (conjoint therapy). The problem of the couple, their age, the number of years they have been in a relationship, their motivation, and the skill/personality of the therapist are all involved in whether a couple report improvement from therapy. Most therapists report use of a behavioral or cognitive-behavioral therapeutic approach. An alternative to face-to-face therapy is telerelationship therapy, which uses the Internet.

behavioral couple therapy therapeutic focus on behaviors the respective spouses want increased or decreased, initiated or terminated. (13-5c)

telerelationship therapy therapy sessions conducted online, often through Skype, where both therapist and couple can see and hear each other. (13-5d)

13-6 **Explain current trends regarding stress and crisis in relationships.** Stress and crisis will continue to be a part of relationships. No spouse, partner, marriage, family, or relationship is immune. A major source of stress will be economic—the difficulty in securing and maintaining employment and sufficient income to take care of the needs of the family. Relationship partners will be challenged by whatever crisis events occur. The greater the number of crisis events, the shorter the time between the events and the severity of the events, the more difficult the adjustment.

CHAPTER 14 LEARNING OBJECTIVES / KEY TERMS

14-1 **Discuss the factors and process of ending a relationship/getting a divorce.** Several factors are predictive of maintaining a relationship or letting it go. In addition, there is a process in terms of what should be considered before deciding to end a relationship/divorce. Women have identified deal-breakers as dating someone who was secretive with their texts, lazy, shorter than them, or a virgin. Deal-breakers for men were dating someone who was disheveled/unclean, lazy, or had no career path. All relationships have difficulties, and all necessitate careful consideration of various issues before making a decision to end the relationship or to get a divorce. Couples should consider improving the relationship rather than ending it, acknowledge that terminating a relationship will be painful, select a proper medium of breaking up, blame themselves when talking with their partner, cut off the relationship completely, learn from the relationship, and clean their Facebook page. Not all separations lead to divorce.

divorce the legal ending of a valid marriage contract. (14-1)

14-2 **Discuss the macro factors that contribute to divorce.** Sociologists emphasize that social context creates outcome. Whereas women were historically dependent on their husbands to provide for them, women have gained much economic independence. Women now have greater freedom to exit unhappy or abusive marriages due to economic independence. Many of the protective, religious, educational, and recreational functions of the family have been largely taken over by outside agencies. Family members may now look to these agencies rather than to each other within the family for fulfilling these needs. Although meeting emotional needs remains an important and primary function of the family, fewer reasons exist to keep a family together. Increased social acceptability and legal ease of divorce may affect the frequency of divorce. Religious institutions have also become more accepting of divorced individuals. Because most individuals know someone who is divorced, the practice has become normalized.

no-fault divorce neither party is identified as the guilty party or the cause of the divorce. (14-2e)

14-3 **Discuss the micro factors that contribute to divorce.** Macro factors are not sufficient to cause a divorce. Micro factors are the reasons spouses end relationships. The most common reasons couples seek divorce are because they grow apart and no longer have anything in common. Couples also report falling out of love, and some spouses do not make time to be together and nurture their relationship. Just as love feelings are based on partners making the choice to engage in a high frequency of positive behavior toward each other, negative feelings result when these positive behaviors stop and negative behaviors begin. Thoughts of divorce may then begin. Affairs may also lead to divorce. Couples may grow apart due to changing values or satiation. There are 20 common reasons that couples seek divorce.

satiation a stimulus loses its value with repeated exposure; also called habituation. (14-3h)

14-4 **Outline the consequences of divorce for spouses and parents.** There are many positive and negative consequences of divorce. Many individuals report increased mental and spiritual wellness. Sometimes it is difficult to get over a partner. Recovery from a terminated romantic relationship is related to being selective about one's thoughts—not dwelling on positive memories of the former relationship and focusing on negative aspects of the relationship. Both women and men experience a drop in income following divorce, but women may suffer more. How money is divided at divorce depends on whether the couple had a prenuptial agreement or a postnuptial agreement. Researchers have concluded that maintaining a connection with one's ex provides an opportunity for ex-partners to exchange desirable resources after romantic relationship dissolution.

postnuptial agreement an agreement about how money is to be divided should a couple later divorce, which is made after the couple marry. (14-4b)

14-5 **Explore the consequences of divorce for children.** The act of separation/divorce is a major adverse childhood experience. But there are both negative and positive outcomes of experiencing divorce of one's parents. Negative outcomes include economic hardship, lack of concentration in school, sleeping disorders, and an increase in challenging the parent/being stubborn. Children of divorce may choose to notice the positive aspects of divorce rather than buy into the cultural script that "divorce is terrible and my life will be ruined because of my parent's divorce." Some children of divorced parents are very deliberate in trying not to repeat the mistakes of their parents. Overall, the negative outcomes of divorce for children are balanced by positives.

divorce mediation meeting with a neutral professional who negotiates child custody, division of property, child support, and alimony directly with the divorcing spouses. (14-5)

collaborative practice (collaborative divorce) a process that brings a team of professionals (lawyer, psychologist, mediator, social worker, financial counselor) together to help a couple separate and divorce in a humane and cost-effective way. (14-5)

negotiation identifying both sides of an issue and finding a resolution that is acceptable to both parties. (14-5)

arbitration third party listens to both spouses and makes a decision about custody, division of property, child support, and alimony. (14-5)

litigation a judge hears arguments from lawyers representing the respective spouses and decides issues of custody, child support, division of property, etc. (14-5)

14-6 **Outline the prerequisites for having a "successful" divorce.** Some of the behaviors spouses can engage in to achieve a "successful" divorce include mediating rather than litigating the divorce, coparenting with the ex-spouse, taking some responsibility for the divorce, avoiding drug use, engaging in aerobic exercise, continuing interpersonal connections, letting go of anger, and allowing time to heal. Engaging in these behaviors will allow divorcing partners to minimize the negative consequences of divorce for their children.

14-7 **Define and discuss remarriage.** Divorced spouses are not sour on marriage. Although they may want to escape from the current spouse, they are open to having a new spouse. Most of the divorced remarry and do so for many of the same reasons as those in their first marriage—love, companionship, emotional security, and a regular sex partner. Other reasons are unique to remarriage and include financial security (particularly for a woman with children), help in rearing one's children, the desire to provide a "social" father or mother for one's children, escape from the stigma associated with the label "divorced person," and legal threats regarding the custody of one's children. Individuals who remarry face several challenges, including boundary maintenance, and reconciling remarriage with their emotions, psyche, community, parents, and finances.

negative commitment spouses who continue to be emotionally attached to and have difficulty breaking away from ex-spouses. (14-7a)

14-8 **Define stepfamilies and outline the developmental tasks stepfamilies must complete.** Stepfamilies, also known as blended, binuclear, remarried, or reconstituted families, represent the fastest growing type of family in the United States. Stepfamilies must complete several developmental tasks to achieve success and happiness. The newly married couple must nurture their new marriage relationship and be patient for relationships to form with children of their spouse. Stepfamilies should have realistic expectations. Stepparents must accept their stepchildren as they are, but partners must give each other parental authority. Stepfamilies should work together to create new family rituals and should be supportive of the children's relationship with the absent parent. Similarly, stepfamilies should cooperate with the child's biological parent and consider living apart together to reduce the stain of stepfamily living.

blended family family wherein spouses in a remarriage bring their children to live with the new partner and at least one other child. (14-8)

binuclear family family that lives in two households as when parents live in separate households following a divorce. (14-8)

stepfamily family in which spouses in a new marriage bring children from previous relationships into the new home. (14-8)

stepism the assumption that stepfamilies are inferior to biological families. (14-8)

developmental task a skill that, if mastered, allows a family to grow as a cohesive unit. (14-8a)

14-9 **Discuss current trends in divorce and remarriage.** As divorce continues to be stigmatized in our society, a number of attempts will continue to be made to reduce the sting of divorce. Conscious uncoupling will not be easy as new partners, division of property, and scheduling time with the children test the new plan with the reality of divorce. But the conscious attempt to make divorce easier for children is clearly evident. And divorce may be becoming easier for adults. Compared to earlier decades, the divorced of today are less lonely. Other attempts to mitigate the negatives of divorce are workshops/education programs focused on communication, conflict resolution, and parenting skills for the divorced.

divorcism the belief that divorce is a disaster. (14-9)

15-1 Define age and ageism. All societies have a way to categorize their members by age. And all societies provide social definitions for particular ages. A person's age may be defined chronologically, physiologically, psychologically, sociologically, and culturally. Every society has some form of ageism. Ageism is reflected in negative stereotypes of the elderly—forgetful, lonely, impoverished. Ageism also occurs when older individuals are treated differently because of their age, such as when they are spoken to loudly in simple language, when it is assumed they cannot understand normal speech, or when they are denied employment due to their age. Ageism is also expressed by invisibility.

age term which may be defined chronologically (number of years), physiologically (physical decline), psychologically (self-concept), sociologically (roles for the elderly/retired), and culturally (meaning age in one's society). (15-1a)

ageism the systematic persecution and degradation of people because they are old. (15-1b)

ageism by invisibility when older adults are not included in advertising and educational materials. (15-1b)

gerontophobia fear or dread of the elderly, which may create a self-fulfilling prophecy. (15-1b)

gerontology the study of aging. (15-1c)

15-2 Explore factors related to caregiving for the frail elderly. Thirty percent of adults in the United States provide care for a loved one, often the frail elderly. Most children choose to take care of their elderly parents. These women provide family caregiving and are known as the sandwich generation because they take care of their parents and their children simultaneously. The number of individuals in the sandwich generation will increase for many reasons, including increased longevity, chronic diseases rather than immediate death, having fewer siblings to help with elder care, a commitment to caring for one's parents, and a lack of support for the caregiver.

frail term used to define elderly people if they have difficulty with at least one personal care activity (feeding, bathing, toileting). (15-2)

family caregiving adult children providing care for their elderly parents. (15-2)

sandwich generation generation of adults who are "sandwiched" between caring for their elderly parents and their own children. (15-2)

15-3 Discuss some issues in confronting the elderly. Numerous issues become concerns as people age. In middle age, the issues are early retirement (sometimes forced), job layoffs (recession-related cutbacks), age discrimination (older people are often not hired and younger workers are hired to take their place), separation or divorce from a spouse, and adjustment to children leaving home. For some in middle age, grandparenting is an issue if they become the primary caregiver for their grandchildren. As couples move from the middle to the later years, the issues become more focused on income, health, retirement, and sexuality.

age discrimination a situation where older people are often not hired and younger workers are hired to take their place. (15-3)

dementia loss of brain function that occurs with certain diseases. It affects memory, thinking, language, judgment, and behavior. (15-3c)

blurred retirement an individual working part-time before completely retiring or taking a "bridge job" that provides a transition between a lifelong career and full retirement. (15-3e)

phased retirement an employee agreeing to a reduced work load in exchange for reduced income. (15-3e)

15-4 Define successful aging. Healthy aging has been defined by the World Health Organization as developing and maintaining functional ability in the later years including physical, mental, and psychosocial. It is recognized that these abilities interact in environments (physical, social, and policy) that facilitate these abilities. Paramount in the definition of successful aging is health. Having interpersonal, community, physical, and psychological well-being are associated with individuals who have a high income, are married, are a white-collar professional, and own their own home.

15-5 Explore dating and family relationships among the elderly. Relationships in the later years vary. Some elderly men and women are single and date. Dating is more common among men than women and declines with age. Compared to nondaters, daters are more socially advantaged, college educated, and have more assets, better health, and more social connectedness. Marital satisfaction in elderly marriages is related to a high frequency of expressing love feelings to one's partner. Another significant role for the elderly is that of grandparent. Grandparents see themselves as caretakers, emotional and/or economic resources, teachers, and historical connections on the family tree. Grandchildren report enormous benefits from having a close relationship with grandparents, including development of a sense of family ideals, moral beliefs, and a work ethic. Feeling loved is also a major benefit.

grandfamilies families in which children reside with and are being raised by grandparents. (15-5d)

15-6 **Explain the effects of the death of an elderly person on families, spouses, and the dying individual.** While the death of one's parents is often one's first encounter with death, the death of one's spouse happens later in life and is one of the most stressful adult life events a person experiences. Compared to both the married and the divorced, the widowed are the most lonely and have the lowest life satisfaction. Just as technology has changed the way relationships begin (e.g., text messaging), its use in memorializing the deceased is increasing. Some individuals prepare for the end of their own life through anticipatory grief therapy. Those who died within one year of this therapy reported understanding the end of their lives without remorse or anxiety. The major fear expressed by respondents was of the dying process, not death itself.

thanatology the examination of the social dimensions of death, dying, and bereavement. (15-6)

15-7 **Discuss current trends among the elderly in the United States.** As the aging population increases in size, greater acceptance of aging will occur. There will also be a new emphasis on physical exercise as the pathway to physical, psychological, and social health in the later years. This will include a focus on the freedom of the elderly to pursue areas of interest, staying busy, and enjoying recreational activities. Living apart together will increasingly become a lifestyle option for the elderly who are single, widowed, or divorced. Finally, robotic companions for the elderly are being used in Asian countries such as Japan. They will soon make their way to America.

M&F
ONLINE
STUDY YOUR WAY
WITH STUDYBITS!

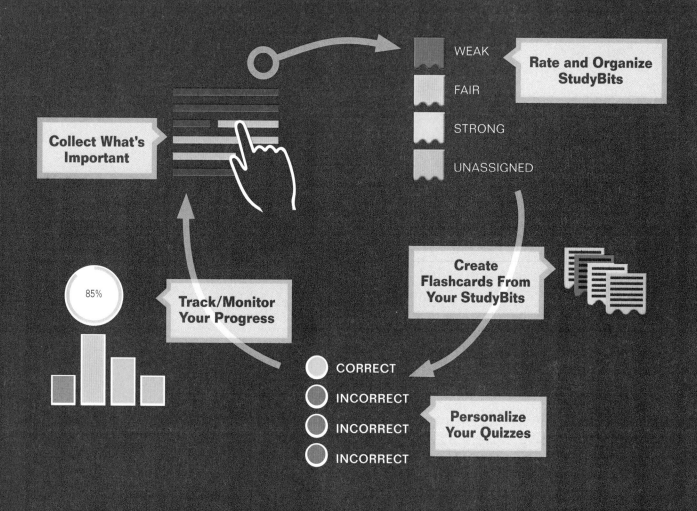

WEAK

FAIR

STRONG

UNASSIGNED

Rate and Organize StudyBits

Collect What's Important

Create Flashcards From Your StudyBits

85%

Track/Monitor Your Progress

CORRECT

INCORRECT

INCORRECT

INCORRECT

Personalize Your Quizzes

4LTR PRESS

M&F
ONLINE

PREPARE FOR TESTS ON
THE STUDYBOARD!

⬤ CORRECT

◯ INCORRECT

◯ INCORRECT

◯ INCORRECT

**Personalize Quizzes
from Your StudyBits**

**Take Practice
Quizzes by Chapter**

CHAPTER QUIZZES

▶ Chapter 1

Chapter 2

Chapter 3

Chapter 4

4LTR
PRESS

Access M&F ONLINE at www.cengagebrain.com